Lecture Notes in Computer Science 548

Edited by G. Goos and J. Hartmanis

Advisory Board: W. Brauer D. Grie

T0230103

R. Kruse   P. Siegel (Eds.)

Symbolic and Quantitative Approaches to Uncertainty

European Conference ECSQAU
Marseille, France, October 15-17, 1991
Proceedings

Springer-Verlag

Berlin Heidelberg New York
London Paris Tokyo
Hong Kong Barcelona
Budapest

Series Editors

Gerhard Goos
GMD Forschungsstelle
Universität Karlsruhe
Vincenz-Priessnitz-Straße 1
W-7500 Karlsruhe, FRG

Juris Hartmanis
Department of Computer Science
Cornell University
Upson Hall
Ithaca, NY 14853, USA

Volume Editors

Rudolf Kruse
Computer Science Department, Technical University of Braunschweig
Bultenweg 74/75, W-3300 Braunschweig, FRG

Pierre Siegel
EIRP-Université de Provence - case H
3 place Victor Hugo, F-13331 Marseille Cedex 3, France

CR Subject Classification (1991): I.2.3

ISBN 3-540-54659-6 Springer-Verlag Berlin Heidelberg New York
ISBN 0-387-54659-6 Springer-Verlag New York Berlin Heidelberg

Typesetting: Camera ready by author
Printing and binding: Druckhaus Beltz, Hemsbach/Bergstr.
45/3140-543210 - Printed on acid-free paper

Preface

In recent years a variety of formalisms have been developed which address such aspects of handling imperfect knowledge as uncertainty, vagueness, imprecision, incompleteness, and partial inconsistency. Some of the most familiar approaches in this research field are nonmonotonic logics, modal logics, probability theory (Bayesian and non-Bayesian), belief function theory, and fuzzy sets and possibility theory.

The ESPRIT Basic Research Action 3085, entitled Defeasible Reasoning and Uncertainty Management Systems (DRUMS), aims to contribute to the elucidation of similarities and differences between the formalisms mentioned above. It consists of 11 active European research groups working on this topic. Their activities have already been coordinated, but there is a need for a larger forum where researchers working on imperfect knowledge in Europe can meet and discuss their scientific results. The European Conference on Symbolic and Quantitative Approaches to Uncertainty (ECSQAU), sponsored by ESPRIT Basic Research Action 3085, serves this need.

This volume contains the papers accepted for the ECSQAU, several articles presenting the activities of the DRUMS groups, two manuscripts by invited speakers. Unfortunately, due to lack of time, the third invited speaker, L. Zadeh, could not provide a paper.

The Executive Scientific Committee for the conference consisted of: Philippe Besnard (Rennes), John Bigham (London), Michael Clarke (London), Didier Dubois (Paris), Rudolf Kruse (chair, Braunschweig).

Our particular thanks go to the many referees who have been part of the reviewing process for this conference. We gratefully acknowledge the work of the reviewers who were also members of the scientific committee: B. Bouchon-Meunier, M. Delgado, D. Driankov, L. Farinas del Cerro, J. Fox, Ch. Froidevaux, D.M. Gabbay, R. Lopez de Mantaras, A. Mamdani, O. Paillet, H. Prade, M. Reinfrank, E. Sanchez, P. Smets, D.J. Spiegelhalter, K. Sundermeyer, D. Vermeir, C. Whitney, H.-J. Zimmermann, as well as the other reviewers: J. Gebhardt, J. Heinsohn, F. Klawonn, B. Nebel, U.G. Oppel, G. Paaß.

We would like to thank the universities in Braunschweig and Marseille for the support they gave the organizers, and we extend our gratitude to Detlef Nauck for his efficient and knowledgeable support. Pierre Siegel was responsible for the local organization in Marseille.

We hope that this conference will lead to future joint research and successful collaboration in Europe.

August 1991   Rudolf Kruse, Pierre Siegel

Table of Contents

Invited Lectures

Abduction in Labelled Deductive Systems - A Conceptual Abstract 3
  D.M. Gabbay

Nonmonotonic Inference, Expectations, and Neural Networks 12
  P. Gärdenfors

DRUMS Presentations

Introduction 31

Imprecise Quantifiers and Conditional Probabilities 33
  S. Amarger, D. Dubois, and H. Prade

Default Logics 38
  P. Besnard

Propagation of Uncertainty in Dependence Graphs 42
  J. Cano, M. Delgado, and S. Moral

Efficient Algorithms for Belief Functions Based on the Relationship
Between Belief and Probability 48
  M. Clarke and N. Wilson

A Brief Overview of Possibilistic Logic 53
  D. Dubois, J. Lang, and H. Prade

A Modal Analysis of Possibility Theory 58
  L. Fariñas del Cerro and A. Herzig

An Extended Logic Language for Representing Belief 63
  J. Fox, P. Krause, and M. Dohnal

Graded Default Logics 70
  Ch. Froidevaux, P. Chatalic, and J. Mengin

Linguistically Expressed Uncertainty: Its Elicitation and Use
in Modular Expert Systems 76
  L. Godo and R. Lopez de Mantaras

Reasoning with Mass Distributions and the Context Model 81
  R. Kruse, J. Gebhardt, and F. Klawonn

Advance Prototyping 86
  S. Parsons

The Transferable Belief Model 91
  P. Smets, Y-T Hsia, A. Saffiotti, R. Kennes, H. Xu, and E. Umkehrer

Contributed Papers

Learning with CASTLE 99
  S. Acid, L.M. de Campos, A. González, and R. Molina

A New Approach to Inference Under Uncertainty for
Knowledge Based Systems 107
  J.F. Baldwin

Learning of Uncertain Classification Rules in Medical Diagnosis 115
  E. Binaghi

Assertional Default Theories 120
  G. Brewka

The Reliability of Reasoning with Unreliable Rules and Propositions 125
  L. Cardona, J. Kohlas, and P.A. Monney

Uncertainty in the Valuation of Risky Assets 130
  A. Chateauneuf, R. Kast, and A. Lapied

Assessment of Qualitative Judgements for Conditional Events in
Expert Systems 135
  G. Coletti, A. Gilio, and R. Scozzafava

Automated Reasoning About an Uncertain Domain 141
F.S. Corrêa da Silva, D. Robertson, and P. Chung

Using Defeasible Logic for a Window on a Probabilistic
Database: Some Preliminary Notes 146
J. Cussens and A. Hunter

From Data Analysis to Uncertainty Knowledge Analysis 153
E. Diday

Difference Fuzzy Relation Equations: Studies in Dynamical Systems 161
A. Di Nola, W. Pedrycz, and S. Sessa

Towards a Logic for a Fuzzy Logic Controller 166
D. Driankov and H. Hellendoorn

Handling Active Databases with Partial Inconsistencies 171
O. Etzion

An Extension of the Possibility Theory in View
of the Formalization of Approximate Reasoning 176
L. Gâcogne

Probabilistic Regions of Persistence 182
S.D. Goodwin, E. Neufeld, and A. Trudel

Formalizing Pertinence Links in Inheritance Reasoning:
Preliminary Report 190
E. Grégoire

A Hybrid Approach for Modeling Uncertainty in Terminological Logics 198
J. Heinsohn

Fuzzy Control Research at Siemens Corporate R&D 206
H. Hellendoorn and M. Reinfrank

Handling Partially Ordered Defaults in TMS 211
U. Junker and G. Brewka

Computing Extensions of Default Theories 219
  F. Lévy

An Evidential Reasoning Approach to the Classification of
Satellite Images 227
  G. Lohmann

PRESS - A Probabilistic Reasoning Expert System Shell 232
  Z. Luo and A. Gammermann

Induction of Uncertain Rules and the Sociopathicity Property
in Dempster-Shafer Theory 238
  Y. Ma and D.C. Wilkins

Hierarchical Default Logic 246
  C. MacNish

A Logic of Imprecise Monadic Predicates and its Relation
to the S5-Modal Fuzzy Logic 254
  A. Nakamura

Every Complex System can be Determined by a Causal Probabilistic Network
Without Cycles and Every Such Network Determines a Markov Field 262
  U.G. Oppel

Probabilistic Default Reasoning Involving Continuous Variables 267
  G. Paass

Revision in Propositional Calculus 272
  O. Papini

A Constraint-based Approach to Uncertain and Imprecise Reasoning.
Application to Expert Systems 277
  T. Pontet

Random Closed Sets: A Unified Approach to the Representation
of Imprecision and Uncertainty 282
  P. Quinio and T. Matsuyama

Knowledge Extraction in Trivalued Propositional Logic 287
  A. Rauzy

Using Maximum Entropy to Identify Unsafe Assumptions in
Probabilistic Expert Systems 292
  P.C. Rhodes and G.R. Garside

On Truth and Utility 297
  E.H. Ruspini

On Commitment and Cumulativity in Default Logics 305
  T. Schaub

A Tableau-Based Characterisation for Default Logic 310
  C.B. Schwind and V. Risch

Restraining the Proliferation of Worlds in Probabilistic
Logic Entailments 318
  P. Snow

Managing Uncertainty in Environmental Analysis:
An Application to Measurement Data Interpretation 323
  M. Spies

Handling Uncertainty in Knowledge-Based Computer Vision 328
  L.E. Sucar, D.F. Gillies

Probabilistic Reasoning with Facts and Rules in Deductive Databases 333
  H. Thöne, U. Güntzer, and W. Kießling

An Entity-Relationship Approach to the Modelling of
Vagueness in Databases 338
  R.M. Vandenberghe and R.M. de Caluwe

A Preferential Model Semantics for Default Logic 344
  F. Voorbraak

Elementary Hyperentailment - Nonmonotonic Reasoning About Defaults 352
  E. Weydert

Author Index 361

INVITED LECTURES

Abduction in Labelled Deductive Systems
A Conceptual Abstract

D M Gabbay[*]
Department of Computing, Imperial College
180 Queen's Gate, London SW7 2BZ

Abstract

A Theory of Abduction and Induction is outlined within the framework of *Labelled Deductive Systems* (*LDS*). It is argued that abductive principles are dependent on the computation procedures and are to be considered as items of data in the database.

1 Intuitive Theory of Labelled Abduction

This section will introduce our intuitive theory of abduction within the framework of *Labelled Deductive Systems*. We shall answer the following questions:

- what is a database
- what is a query system
- what is abduction

and give some simple examples.

The new ideas we shall put forward are:

- abduction depends on proof procedures
- abductive principles can be part of the data. In other words, a declarative item of data can be either a formula or a principle of abduction

The more precise machinery for these concepts will be developed in later sections. This section will discuss the intuitive ideas.

The basic situation we are dealing with can be presented as

$$\Delta \quad \vdash ?!Q$$
$$\text{data} \quad \text{?query or ! input}$$

Figure 1

It is a relationship between a database and a formula. The relationship is either declarative (ie $?Q$, Q a query) or imperative ($!Q$, Q is an input or a demand to perform abduction or a demand for explanation etc). In the imperative case there is an interaction between Δ and Q and a new database Δ' emerges.

We have argued elsewhere [1, 2] that the most general and useful database is the one where the data is structured and the proof procedures use the structure.

In this set up, the abduction rules are extra moves that help answer the query or help change the database as a result of the query or input.

Thus to do abduction we need more precise proof procedures or update procedures for structured databases and then on top of that we can define the extra abductive rules.

The exact proof procedures can be conviently formalised in the framework of *LDS* see [1, 2] described intuitively in the next section. Meanwhile let us illustrate our ideas through a series of examples.

---

[*]Research Supported by SERC grant GR/G29861, Rule Based Systems. I am grateful to M D'Agustino for critically reading the manuscript.

Example 1.1 The database below is a Horn clause database. It is labelled in the sense that each clause is named. The query is D. The query does not follow from the database as it is. We are going to use it to illustrate principles of abduction.

	Data	Query
a_1	$I \wedge T \to D$	$? D$
a_2	$L \to I$	
a_3	$L \wedge S \to T$	
a_4	$O \wedge P \to T$	
a_5	L	

The database literals have no meaning. Let us give them a meaning. In the Stanford University English Department, there are two main ways of getting a PhD title. One can either put forward a thesis, stay in the department for 4-5 years acquiring and displaying an immense breadth of knowledge and pass an interview, or one can write a very good publication and get a job offer from another university in the top ten in the country. The database then becomes:

Data

a_1 Interview $\wedge$ Thesis $\to$ Degree

a_2 Lecture $\to$ Interview

a_3 Lecture $\wedge$ Scholarly Survey $\to$ Thesis

a_4 (Job) Offer $\wedge$ Publications $\to$ Thesis

a_5 Lecture

Query

? Degree

Another interpretation for the same database is a component interpretation. To do the laundry (D) one needs a washing machine (T) and washing powder (I). For washing powder one can use dishwashing soap (L). For a washing machine one may use a dishwasher (S) and dishwashing soap or one may handwash (P) but then one at least needs a spinner (O).

We thus get in this case

Data

a_1 Washing Powder $\wedge$ Washing Machine $\to$ Laundry

a_2 Dishwashing Soap $\to$ Washing Powder

a_3 Diswashing Soap $\wedge$ Dishwasher $\to$ Washing Machine

a_4 Spinner $\wedge$ Handwash $\to$ Washing Machine

a_5 Diswashing Soap.

Query

? Laundry

We now list several possible abductive principles for the query $?D$. The principles depend on the computation, so let us suppose that we compute the query prolog like, where the pointer always starts at the top clause (assume $a_1 > a_2 > a_3 > a_4 > a_5$.)

We note that in logic programming [4] abduction for Horn clause programs is done via a system of the form (Δ, I, A), where Δ is the program, I is a set of integrity constraints and A is a set of literals which are *abducible*. Whenever an abducible literal is encountered in the computation (eg $?D$) it is immediately added to the database provided it does not violate the integrity constraints.

Let us now examine our options:

Example 1.2 [Possible principles of Abduction]

1. The first option is to abduce on anything as soon as needed. This corresponds in our case, to no integrity constraints and every literal is abducible.
   In this case we add D to the database, ie the Abduction principle yields D. In the component example such abduction makes no sense. I want to know which parts are missing so that we can get them and wash our clothes.

2. The second option is to abduce on literals which are not heads of clauses. In this case, we add S. This is because S is the first literal encountered in the top down order of execution. Note that we do not use here a set of abducibles. The structure of the database determines what we add.

3. If our underlying logic is not classical logic but some other resource logic, we will not succeed by adding S to the database because that would require the "use" of L twice. Once to make I succeed in clause a_2 and once to make T succeed in clause a_3. In the component example we need more dishwashing soap if we use a dishwasher, and we have only one lot of it (ie a_5).
   Note that the database is structured and thus we can add

   a_6 L

   and $\{a_1, \ldots, a_5\}$ is *not* the same database as $\{a_1, \ldots, a_6\}$.

Anyway, if the underlying logic is a resource logic, the result of our abduction will be $O \wedge P$, unless we are prepared to add another copy of L.

4. If we require the weakest logical assumption (in classical logic) which makes the goal succeed then we must add $S \vee (O \wedge P)$. This abduction principle is independent of the computation.

5. In co-operative answering, the abduction principle takes the top level clause. In this case the answer is T. To the query "$?D$" we answer "yes if T". Think of the thesis example. If an ordinary student wants to know what is missing to get a PhD, the obvious answer is "a thesis" and not "a paper and a job offer from Harvard".

6. The power of our labelling mechanism can be easily illustrated by a more refined use of the labels. If atoms are labelled, for example, by cost (laundry example) the abduction principle can aim for minimal cost. One can also "cost" the computation itself and aim to abduce on formulas giving maximal provability with a least number of modus ponens instances.

Example 1.3 To show that the abduction depends on the computation let us change the computation to forward chaining or Gentzen like rules. From

$$\text{Data} \vdash ?D$$

we get

$$I \wedge T \to D, I, S \to T, O \wedge P \to T \quad \vdash ?D$$

which reduces to

$$T \to D, S \to T, O \wedge P \to T, \quad \vdash ?D$$

which reduces to the following by chaining:

$$S \to D, O \wedge P \to D, \quad \vdash ?D$$

As we see, not many abduction possibilities are left!

So far we have discussed the possibilities of abduction principles being added to proof rules. We now come to our second new idea, namely:

- Abduction principles are data!

Example 1.4 Consider the following database and query:

a_1 A

a_2 $A \to (B \to S)$

a_3 B

. . . .

a_4 X, abduce on structrure to find X.

a_5 $B \to D$
   The goal is $?S + D$.

By writing $S + D$ for the goal we are saying we want to partition the database, which is a list of assumptions, into two parts, the first part must prove S and the second part must prove D. This is done in resource logics, where one pays attention to the question of which part of the database proves what.
   Such considerations arise in many areas for example in what is known as *parsing as logic*.
   Consider the text:
Mary hit John. He cried.
   The way this can be analysed is by assuming that each word is assigned a wff of some resource logic (actually concatenation logic, see [3]) with a label. This assignement is done at the lexical level. Thus a noun n is assigned $n' : NP$. An intranstive verb v_1 is assigned $v_1' : NP \to S$. A transitive verb v_2 is assigned $v_2' : NP \to (NP \to S)$. The pronoun 'he' is assigned an abduction principle. Our problem becomes:
Data

1. Mary$'$: NP

2. hit$'$: $NP \to (NP \to S)$

3. John$'$: NP

4. he: Abduce on structure. Take the first literal up the list.

5. cried$'$: $NP \to S$.

Query

Prove $?S$ or $S + S$ or $?S + S + S\dots$ etc, in order to show we have a text of sentences.

We are thus saying that Anaphora resolution makes use of structural abduction.

The reader should note that anaphora resolution is a complex area and we are not making any linguistic claims here beyond the intuitive example that abduction principles can be treated as data. We do admit however that logical principles underlying database management do seem to be operative in natural language understanding and we are working full steam ahead in making our case.

Coming back to our view of abduction as data, we are really saying:

- A database can either display data items or give us pointers to where to get them.

Thus a labelled database can look as in Figure 2.

$$
\begin{array}{l}
n_1\text{: data } m \\
\vdots \quad \vdots \\
n_k\text{: get datum from }\dots \\
\vdots \quad \vdots
\end{array}
$$

Abductive Labelled Database

Figure 2

I would like to give next a combined example of planning and parsing, based on ideas of [3].

Example 1.5 [Planning] Consider the situation described by figure 3.

There are three languages involved

1. The database language containing the predicates $On(x, y)$ and $Free(x)$

2. The imperative (Input) command language with the predicates $Move(x, y)$.

3. The mixed metalanguage with the connectives "$\wedge$" for "and" and "$\Rightarrow$" for "precondition and action imply postcondition".

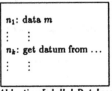

$$
\begin{array}{lll}
a & t_1\text{: } On(a, b) & \\
b \quad c & t_1\text{: } On(b, tab) & \leftarrow Move(a, c) \\
& t_1\text{: } On(c, tab) & \\
\hline
\quad a & t_2\text{: } On(a, c) & \leftarrow Move(a, tab) \\
b \quad c & & \\
\hline
b \quad c \quad a & t_3\text{: } On\,(a, tab). &
\end{array}
$$

$$On(x, y)\wedge\ Free(x)\wedge\ Free(z)\wedge Move(x, z) \Rightarrow On(x, z)\wedge Free(y)\wedge\ Free(x)$$

Figure 3

The diagram describes the initial layout of the blocks ready to respond to command. t_1 labels all data true at the initial situation and t_2 and t_3 the additional data after each of the actions. We have

$$t_1 < t_2 < t_3.$$

If we query the system with

$$?\ On(a, x)$$

we get three answers, with different labels, indicating where the answer was obtained in the database, namely:

$$
\begin{array}{l}
\vdash t_1 :\ On(a, b) \\
\vdash t_2 :\ On(a, c) \\
\vdash t_3 :\ On(a, tab)
\end{array}
$$

The reply to the user is determined by the system as the answer proved with the stronger label, namely:

$$On(a, tab)$$

Call the deductive system governing the planning consideration LDS_1[1]. This system involves proving where the blocks are after which action. This system accepts commands in logical form $Move(x, y)$. It does not accept commands in English. If the command comes in English, which we can represent as *move x onto y*, it needs to be parsed into the LDS_1 language. This is done in a parsing logic LDS_0. The following diagram explains the scheme:

---

[1]We remark in passing that this approach offers a *conceptual* (not computational) solution to the frame problem. Conceputally, given an initial labelled database and a sequence of actions to be performed, we model the sequence by another labelled database; the database obtained by adding the results of the actions to the initial database. We label the additions appropriately. This idea will be pursued elsewhere. There are several such "non-monotonic" solutions in the literature. This is probably the most general

English Input:
move *a* onto *c*. move it onto table

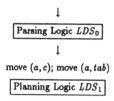

Figure 4

The following diagram describes the database-query problem of LDS_0:

move': $NP \to (NP \to S)$ $?S + S$
   a': NP
   c': NP
move': $NP \to (NP \to S)$
   it: use abduction. First use structural abduction to
          get the first NP higher in the list, then use
          inferential abduction to try and get maximal
          inferential effects in LDS_1.
   tab': NP

Notice that the abduction principle in LDS_0 also uses inferential effect in LDS_1. Intuitively we are trying to abduce on who "it" refers to. If we choose "it" to be a block which is already on the table, it makes no sense to move it onto the table. Thus the command when applied to the database will produce no change. The abduction principle gives preference to abduced formulas which give some effect.

From the logical point of view we are using the following principle, (see also Example 1.9):

- Abduction principles can serve as items of data in one database Δ_0, being a pointer to another database Δ_1 where some computation is carried out jointly involving both databases and the result is the abduced data item in Δ_0.

Example 1.6 [Logic Programming Abduction] The abductive system in logic programming can be schematically put into our form by making use of the way the Prolog pointer scans the database. An abductive system has the form (Δ, I, A), where $\Delta = (C_1, \ldots, C_n)$ is a sequence of clauses and literals, where I are the integrity constraints and where A is the set of abducible atoms. This system can be translated into the following Horn clause database:

(0) $C_0 =$ Abduce on the goal by checking whether the goal is in A and whether when added it satisfies the integrity constraints.

(1) C_1

    $\vdots$ $\vdots$

(n) C_n

We are now ready for our next conceptual step. If an abductive principle is to be considered as a declarative item of data, say Q_{Abduce}, then what would be the meaning of

$$\Delta \;?! \; Q_{Abduce}$$

For the imperative interaction $!Q_{Abduce}$, the meaning is obvious, we simply apply the abductive principle to the database and get a new database. However the query meaning of the abductive principle is a bit more difficult to explain in general, and we may need to provide an explanation for each specific case. For example, if the abduction prinicple abduces a formula B, then $\Delta ? Q_{Abduce}$ would mean $\Delta ? B$. This seems all right at first sight, however, the problem here can be that the abduction process by its nature tries to find B's which are not available in the database and so the answer to the query $\Delta ? Q_{Abduce}$ will always be no. This is clearly unacceptable. We must seek another meaning for the query.

Let us for the time being, accept only the imperative reading of $\Delta ! Q_{Abduce}$. We can immediately allow ourselves to write databases with clauses containing Q_{Abduce} in them. Let us see through a few examples what this means.

Example 1.7 Let $\Delta = \{Q_{Abduce} \land B \to D\}$. Think of the above as a database, and assume the computation procedure to be Prolog like. We consider the following query

$$\Delta ? D$$

which reduces to

$$\Delta?(Q_{Abduce}, B)$$

which reduces to

$$\Delta, B?B$$

which succeeds.

Here we assumed that Q_{Abduce} yields B. Our database is similar, in this case, to the Prolog database:

$$Assert\ (B) \wedge B \to D$$

Indeed, asserting is a form of unconditional abduction.

Example 1.8 [Abduction and Negation by Failure] From our point of view, negation by failure is abduction. This point has also been made in [4]. However, we want to make our position crystal clear to avoid confusion. We believe that abduction is a principle of reasoning of equal standing to deduction and that every logical system is comprised of both proof rules and abductive rules. This view has developed through our interaction with the logics of common sense reasoning and our work in natural language understanding [3], and it is put forward in [1, 2]. Negation by failure is not central to our scheme, though it is an interesting example from our point of view.

We begin with a precisely specified proof system. The query $\Delta?Q$ can be algorithmically checked. If the algorithm succeeds, the answer is yes. The algorithm may loop or it may fail. We may be able to prove that for the particular $\Delta?Q$, the algorithm must fail (eg in a case where none of the rules can even be applied). In this case we can say $\Delta?Q$ *finitely fails* (relative to the algorithm). Thus the notion of *finite failure* can be defined for any proof theoretic system.

Given a system, we can consider the following abduction principles which we call $Fail(Q, B)$:

$$\text{If } \Delta?Q \text{ finitely fails then abduce (or assert) } B.$$

To make our example specific, let us choose a language and computation procedures. By an atomic literal let us understand either an atom $\{p, q, r, \ldots\}$ or an abduction principle $Fail(a, b)$, where a, b are atoms. By clauses let us understand Horn clauses of literals. Goals are conjunctions of literals. Thus we can write the following clauses:

1. $q \wedge Fail(a, b) \wedge c \to p$
2. $Fail(q, r)$
3. $a \to Fail(b, b)$.

To explain the computational meaning, we will translate into Prolog. Ordinary Prolog is not expressive enough for our purpose, so we use N-Prolog [5-7] with negation by failure, mainly because it allows hypothetical reasoning, ie embedded implications.

We translate:

$$Fail(a, b) \mapsto (\neg a \to b).$$

After translation, the database becomes:

1. $q \wedge (\neg a \to b) \wedge c \to p$
2. $\neg q \to r$
3. $a \wedge \neg b \to b$

which is meaningful computationally in N-Prolog.

A Horn clause with negation by failure of the form:

$$a \wedge \neg b \to c$$

can be translated back into our abductive language as

$$a \to Fail(b, c)$$

A Prolog goal of the form $\neg a$ an be translated as $Fail(a, \emptyset)$, $\emptyset$ is truth.

N-Prolog is not as expressive as our abductive language. In our abductive language we also have the imperative meaning of

$$\Delta?\ Fail(a, b)$$

which means *apply* the abduction to Δ.

This would correspond to

$$Assert\ (\neg a \to b)$$

in N-Prolog. N-Prolog does not allow for that. The syntax is defined in such a way that we do not get goals of the form $\Delta?(\neg a \to b)$. The N-Prolog computation rule would require in this case to add $\neg a$ to Δ, which is not meaningful.

The connection between abduction and negation by failure was observed in [4]. Since their abductive systems have the restricted form (Δ, I, A) as described in Example 1.6, they need to rewrite the Horn clause program into a more convenient form, translating the Prolog $\neg a$ as a^* and adding the integrity constraint:

$$a \wedge a^* \to .$$

Example 1.9 [A Conversation between two Intelligent Databases] We have the logical means to allow for two *LDS* databases to negotiate and reach an understanding. Imagine two databases S and H exchanging formulas continuously. At time n, the databases have evolved through the sequences

$$\Delta_1^S, \ldots, \Delta_n^S$$

and

$$\Delta_1^H, \ldots, \Delta_n^H.$$

At time n, database S sends a logical input I_n^S to database H and conversely, database H sends an input I_n^H to database S. The two databases use abduction to update themselves. Thus

$$\Delta_{n+1}^H = Abduce(\Delta_n^H, I_n^S)$$

and

$$\Delta_{n+1}^S = Abduce(\Delta_n^S, I_n^H).$$

To continue and communicate we need action principles for sending the next input. This is also part of our abduction scheme as hinted at in Example 1.5

2   The *LDS* Framework

The *LDS* logical framework involves a departure from, and a generalisation of, the traditional concepts of logic. The basic declarative unit in traditional logic is that of a formula A. Logical deduction or other logical manipulations are performed on sets or lists of formulas. In *LDS* the basic notion of a declarative unit is that of a labelled formula, of the form $t : A$, where A is a formula and t is a label.

Consider the question "what is a database and what is a query?". The traditional answer is:

$$\Delta \vdash ?! \ Q$$
$$\Delta \text{ is a set of wffs.} \qquad Q \text{ is a wff.}$$

In *LDS* we have that Δ is a set of labelled wffs $t_i : A_i$ and Q is a labelled wff of the form $s : B$.

The database gets structured from the structure of the labels. The proof theory manipulates the wff and the labels.

The role of the label is to provide additional information about the formula which is not of the same declarative nature as that of the formula itself. The label t in $t : A$ can represent the degree of reliability of the item of data A, or can be a λ-term representing a proof of A, or as in the case of many valued logics, t can indicate the range of truth values of A. Thus, depending on the logical system involved, the intuitive meaning of the labels vary. In querying databases, we may be interested in labelling the assumptions so that when we get an answer to a query we can indicate, via its label, from which part of the database the answer was obtained. Another area where labelling is used is temporal logic. We can time stamp assumptions as to when they are true and, given those assumptions, query whether a certain conclusion will be true at a certain time.

The consequence notion for labelled deduction is essentially the same as that of any logic: given the assumptions, does a conclusion follow?

When introducing an *LDS*, we need to introduce not only the notion of a wff, as we traditionally do, but also the notion of a label. We thus need an algebra or a logic for the labels. Then the declarative units of our *LDS* system can be defined as pairs $t : A$.

Note that the process can be reapplied recursively and it makes sense to label labelled formulas, since these are now the new declarative units. Thus we may have $\alpha : t : A$, where α and t come from different sets of labels. We may use wffs from another logical system for the α's.

The following summarises the situation:

Wheras in the traditional logical system the consequence is defined using proof rules on the formulas, in the *LDS* mehtodology [1,2] the consequence is defined by using rules on both formulas and their labels. Formal rules are then established for manipulating labels and this allows for more scope in decomposing the various features of the consequence relation. The meta-level features can be reflected in the labels and logical features can be reflected in the rules operating on the formulas.

The manipulation of the labels is not arbitrary, rather it follows rigorous disciplines inherent to the logics being dealt with. For example, for the case of implication '$\rightarrow$', the following equation must be satisfied:

$$t \text{ labels } A \rightarrow B \text{ iff } \forall x \in L[\text{If } x \text{ labels } A \text{ then } t + x \text{ labels } B].$$

L is a set of labels and '+' is a binary associative operation. Different logics have the freedom of choice of **L** and '+' can be numerical addition (for Lukasiewicz' logics), λ-functional application (for intuitionistic logic and the Curry-Howard interpretation) or multiset union (for Girard's linear implication). For non-monotonic reasoning systems, the labels could be formulas of some underlying monotonic system and '+' could represent some logical operations in the underlying system.

For example modus ponens will propagate the labels as follows:

$$\alpha : A$$
$$\underline{\beta : A \rightarrow B}$$
$$\beta + \alpha : B$$

and the $\rightarrow$ introduction rule will be

show $t : A \rightarrow B$

$x : A$	assume
$\vdots$	
$\vdots$	
$t + x : B$	show

exit $t : A \rightarrow B$

The *LDS* basic proof theoretic framework involves the interaction between two structures of declarative units which can be formulas with various labels, denoted by Δ and Γ. Δ is the *data* structure and Γ is the *goal* structure.

The interaction is symbolically written as

$$\Delta \; ?! \; \Gamma$$

For example we may have Δ as a set of formulas $\{A_1, \ldots, A_n\}$ and Γ as sequence of goals $(G_1, \ldots, G_n)$ (here we use no labels) and the interaction can be a Prolog like computation for the goals from the data.

Another example is the same structure as above with $n = 1$ and with the interaction being abduction, the simplest addition B to the data that will force

$$A_1, \ldots, A_n, B \vdash G_1$$

in some logic.

A third possible interaction can be some consistent database $\Delta' \supseteq \{A_1, \ldots, A_n, G_1\}$.

A fourth interaction can be generating a model for Δ in which G_1 does not hold.

The *LDS* framework is a discipline involving notions of data and goal structures in terms of labelling algebras and precise procedures for each pure type of interaction (proof, abduction, induction, updates, explanation, analogy) and ways of mixing these procedures.

We can also develop fibred semantics for the above notions and study their connections.

3 Labelled Abductive Mechanisms

The basic *deductive* apparatus of *LDS* is a precise system of rules allowing one to show (or fail to show) whether $\Delta \vdash \Gamma$, for Δ a data structure and Γ a goal structure. Most be useful among the goal structures is the unit structure of the form $t : G$. Thus for the purpose of explaining what abduction is going to be in our framework, we assume that the notion of

$$\Delta \vdash t : G$$

is precisely algorithmically defined, thus yielding a particular *LDS* system **L**. We now schematically explain how abduction principles fit into this framework. Consider a database Δ, containing $\alpha : X$ inside it, which we write as $\Delta[\alpha : X]$ schematically with $t : X$. Somewhere in the structure Δ, α is a label and X is a propositional variable standing for a wff. For any particular choice of X, say $X = A$, $\Delta[\alpha : A]$ is a proper database.

Suppose we want to prove a goal $t : G$. Then for some (maybe none) wffs A_i we may have

$$\Delta[\alpha : A_i] \vdash t : G$$

A principle of abduction

$$Abduce(\alpha : X)$$

is a computation (algorithm) that can choose one or more of the A_i above.

Of course for different $\alpha, t,$ and G we get different A_i.

Example 3.1 1. $A \rightarrow (A \rightarrow B)$

2. Abduce last element

3. A

In linear logic, we need two copies of A to get B. (2) abduced the last element in the data, giving us another copy of A. However if the database is enriched, the last element may be different.

Here the abduction principle is structural and is not dependent on the goal.

The importance of the above point of view is:

1. Databases can take abductive principles as part of their data

2. The abductive principle is relative to the computation procedure and the rest of the database. Thus when new data is put in, the abudctive principle changes. We get a strong learning component in the database.

An inductive principle is a special case of abductive principle which learns a rule $A \rightarrow B$ as opposed to a fact. (atom q). Mathematically there is no difference.

References

1. D M Gabbay, Labelled Deductive Systems, manuscript 1989, to appear as a book with OUP. Part 1 published as CIS Report, Munich 1990.

2. D M Gabbay, Labelled Deductive Systems, A Position Paper, in Proceedings Logic Colloquium 90, Springer Verlag 1991.

3. D M Gabbay, R Kempson, Labelled Abduction and Relevance, unpublished draft.

4. K Eshghi, R A Kowalski, Abduction Compared with Negation by Failure, Proc 6th ICLP 89, MIT Press 1989.

5. N Oliveti, L Terracini, N-Prolog and Equivalence of Logic programs Part 1, Manuscript, University of Torino, 1991.

6. D M Gabbay, U Reyle, N-Prolog, An Extension of Prolog with Hypothetical Implication, Journal of Logic Programming, 4, 319-355, 1984.

7. D M Gabbay, N-Prolog Part II, Journal of Logic Programming 5, 251-283, 1985.

Nonmonotonic inference, expectations, and neural networks[1]

Peter Gärdenfors

Cognitive Science

Department of Philosophy

University of Lund

S-223 50 Lund, Sweden

E-mail: Peter.Gardenfors@fil.lu.se

1. Introduction

In some recent articles David Makinson and I have argued that the areas of nonmonotonic logic and belief revision are very closely related (see Makinson and Gärdenfors 1990, Gärdenfors 1990, 1991, and Gärdenfors and Makinson 1991). In particular, we show in Gärdenfors (1991), and Gärdenfors and Makinson (1991) how various forms of nonmonotonic inferences can be given a unified treatment in terms of how *expectations* are used in reasoning.

The guiding idea is that when we try to find out whether β follows from α, the background information that we use for the inference does not only contain what we firmly believe, but also information about what we *expect* in the given situation. For instance, if we know that someone is a Spanish woman, we anticipate her to be dark and temperamental. Such expectations can be expressed in different ways: by default assumptions, statements about what is normal or typical, etc. These expectations are not full beliefs but *defeasible* in the sense that if the premise α is in conflict with some of the expectations, we don't use them when determining whether β follows from α.

I want to show that expectations are the same kind of information as 'full' beliefs; the difference is that they are more defeasible than those beliefs. Consequently, the expectations used in nonmonotonic inferences need no special notation, but they can be expressed in the same language as regular beliefs. This is one side of the unified treatment of nonmonotonic reasoning. For simplicity I shall work with a standard propositional language L which will be assumed to be closed under applications of the *boolean connectives* ¬ (negation), ∧ (conjunction), ∨ (disjunction), and → (implication). We will use α, β, γ, etc. as variables over sentences in L. It is also convenient to introduce the symbols T and ⊥ for the two

---

[1]The material in this paper draws heavily on Gärdenfors (1991), Gärdenfors and Makinson (1991) and Balkenius and Gärdenfors (1991).

sentential constants "truth" and "falsity". We will assume that the underlying logic includes *classical propositional logic* and that it is compact.

All the different expectations will be formulated in L. In contrast to many other theories of nonmonotonic reasoning there are thus no default rules or other additions to the basic language, such as modal operators, that will be used to express the defeasible forms of information.

The key idea can be put informally as follows:

α nonmonotonically entails β iff β follows logically from α together with 'as many as possible' of the set of our expectations as are compatible with α.

In order to makes this more precise, we must, of course, specify what is meant by 'as many as possible'.[1] But before turning to technicalities, let me illustrate the gist of the analysis by a couple of examples. 'α nonmonotonically entails β' will be denoted $\alpha \vdash \beta$ as usual.

Example 1: Let the language L contain the following predicates:

> Sx: x is a Swedish citizen
> Ix: x has Italian parents
> Px: x is a protestant

Assume that the set of expectations contains $Sb \rightarrow Pb$ and $Sb \wedge Ib \rightarrow \neg Pb$, for all individuals b. Assuming that the set of expectations is closed under logical consequences it also contains $Sb \rightarrow \neg Ib$ and, of course, the logical truth $Sb \wedge Ib \rightarrow Sb$. If we now learn that b is a Swedish citizen, that is Sb, this piece of information is consistent with the expectations and thus we can conclude that $Sb \vdash Pb$ according to the recipe above.

On the other hand, if we learn both that b is a Swedish citizen and has Italian parents, that is $Sb \wedge Ib$, then this information is *inconsistent* with the set of expectations and so we cannot use all expectations when determining which inferences can be drawn from $Sb \wedge Ib$. The most natural expedient is to give up the expectation $Sb \rightarrow Pb$ and the consequence $Sb \rightarrow \neg Ib$. The contracted set of expectations which contains $Sb \wedge Ib \rightarrow \neg Pb$ and its logical consequences, in a sense (to be made precise below), contains 'as many as possible' of the sentences in the set of expectations that are compatible with $Sb \wedge Ib$. So, by the general rule above, we have $Sb \wedge Ib \vdash \neg Pb$. This shows that $\vdash$ is indeed a nonmonotonic inference operation.

Example 2: Let us suppose that L contains the following predicates:

---

[1]This idea is related to the idea of 'minimal change' within the theory of belief revision (see Gärdenfors (1988), pp. 66-68).

Sx: x is Sicilian

Bx: x is blond

Hx: x is hot-tempered

Assume that the set of expectations contains the expectations Sx → Hx and Bx → ¬Hx and, consequently ¬(Sx & Bx).[1] From this we conclude that if all we know about Luigi is that he is a Sicilian, then we expect him to be hot-tempered (and not blond); and if all we know about Felicia is that she is blond, then we expect her to be cool (and not a Sicilian). Now, suppose that, contrary to our expectations, Amadeo is a blond Sicilian, that is Sa & Ba. What can one conclude concerning his temper?

According to the recipe above, since this information is *inconsistent* with the expectations, we should look for a subset of these that contains as many elements of as possible and which is consistent with Sa & Ba. There are three possible choices. (1) Retain Sx → Hx and give up Bx → ¬Hx. In this case we have Sa & Ba ⊢ Ha. (2) Give up Sx → Hx and keep Bx → ¬Hx. In this case we have Sa & Ba ⊢ ¬Ha. (3) Give up *both* Sx → Hx and Bx → ¬Hx. In this situation we can't conclude anything non-trivial about Amadeo's temper.

In this example there is no unique solution but we are faced with a *choice* which cannot be decided by logical considerations alone. If one believes that the expectation that blonds are cool override the expectation that Sicilians are hot-tempered (because, for example, the former is biologically grounded, while the latter is merely a matter of cultural factors), then one would go for the second solution. But if one has no reason to favor one generalization over the other, then one may remain agnostic, that is, go for the third solution.

These simple examples are presented just to give an indication of how a set of expectations can be utilized in determining a nonmonotonic inference relation. The main technical problem to be solved is to present a more rigorous formulation of the general criterion above. In this paper I outline how this has been handled in Gärdenfors and Makinson (1991) and how the concept of expectation is interpreted in Balkenius and Gärdenfors (1991) in terms of reasoning in neural networks.

The fact that α nonmonotonically entails β will be denoted α ⊢ β. The inference relation ⊢ will sometimes be written with a subscript to mark that it belongs to a particular family of inference relations. We will also introduce the notation $C(\alpha)$ for the set of all nonmonotonic conclusions that can be drawn from α, that is, β ∈ $C(\alpha)$ iff α ⊢ β

---

[1]This example is a variation of the so called Nixon diamond.

The set of 'expectations', which are all sentences in L, will be denoted Δ. In the main part of the paper it will be assumed that Δ is consistent and *closed under logical consequences*, i.e. $\Delta = Cn(\Delta)$. The problem in focus is how to define which elements of the set Δ to give up when adding a new piece of information α that is inconsistent with Δ.

2. Postulates for nonmonotonic inference operations

In this section I shall present some axioms for nonmonotonic inference operations which will be used for a representation theorem in the following section. Most of the axioms will be familiar from earlier studies in this area. It was Gabbay (1985) who suggested to focus the study of nonmonotonic logics in terms of the consequence relations they generate. Later investigations along the axiomatic lines include Kraus, Lehmann and Magidor (1990), Makinson (1991), and Makinson and Gärdenfors (1990), Lindström (1991). One restriction of my presentation is that I shall only be working with *finite* sets of premises in my formulation of the axioms. Many of the earlier works have also investigated the more general infinite versions of the postulates.

Following Lindström (1991) we say that a relation $\vdash\!\!\!\sim$ between propositions is an *inference relation* iff it satisfies the four conditions:

If $\alpha \vdash \gamma$, then $\alpha \vdash\!\!\!\sim \gamma$	*(Supraclassicality)*
If $\vdash \alpha \leftrightarrow \beta$ and $\alpha \vdash\!\!\!\sim \gamma$, then $\beta \vdash\!\!\!\sim \gamma$	*(Left Logical Equivalence)*
If $\vdash \beta \rightarrow \gamma$ and $\alpha \vdash\!\!\!\sim \beta$, then $\alpha \vdash\!\!\!\sim \gamma$	*(Right Weakening)*
If $\alpha \vdash\!\!\!\sim \beta$ and $\alpha \vdash\!\!\!\sim \gamma$, then $\alpha \vdash\!\!\!\sim \beta \wedge \gamma$	*(And)*

Clearly, Supraclassicality implies:

$\alpha \vdash\!\!\!\sim \alpha$	*(Reflexivity)*

and Right Weakening and And together imply:

If $\alpha \vdash\!\!\!\sim \beta_i$ for all $\beta_i \in B$ and $B \vdash \gamma$, then $\alpha \vdash\!\!\!\sim \gamma$	*(Closure)*

By the *basic postulates* for nonmonotonic inference we mean the above four for the concept of an inference relation plus the following, where $\vdash\!\!\!\sim \alpha \rightarrow \beta$ is an abbreviation for $\top \vdash\!\!\!\sim \alpha \rightarrow \beta$:

If $\alpha \vdash\!\!\!\sim \beta$, then $\vdash\!\!\!\sim \alpha \rightarrow \beta$	*(Weak Conditionalization)*

$$\text{If } \not\hspace{-2pt}\vdash \neg\alpha \text{ and } \vdash \alpha \to \beta, \text{ then } \alpha \vdash \beta \qquad\qquad \textit{(Weak Rational Monotony)}$$

$$\text{If } \alpha \vdash \bot, \text{ then } \alpha \vdash \bot \qquad\qquad\qquad\qquad \textit{(Consistency Preservation)}$$

These basic postulates correspond, under the translation of Makinson and Gärdenfors (1990), to the 'basic postulates' of the logic of belief revision. The key idea of that translation is that a statement of the form $\beta \in K^*_\alpha$, where K^*_α is the revision of a belief state K by a sentence α, is seen as a nonmonotonic inference from α to β given the set K of sentences as *background* expectations. So the statement $\beta \in K^*_\alpha$ for belief revision is translated into the statement $\alpha \vdash \beta$ for nonmonotonic logic (or into $\alpha \vdash_K \beta$, if one wants to emphasize the role of the background beliefs). It turns out, as shown there, that the translations of the postulates (K*1) - (K*6) from Gärdenfors (1988) correspond respectively precisely to Closure, Reflexivity, Weak Conditionalization, Weak Rational Monotony, Consistency Preservation, and Left Logical Equivalence.

By the *extended* set of postulates for nonmonotonic inference we mean the basic postulates plus the following three:

$$\text{If } \alpha \vdash \beta \text{ and } \beta \vdash \alpha, \text{ then } \alpha \vdash \gamma \text{ iff } \beta \vdash \gamma \qquad \textit{(Cumulativity)}$$

$$\text{If } \alpha \vdash \gamma \text{ and } \beta \vdash \gamma, \text{ then } \alpha \vee \beta \vdash \gamma \qquad \textit{(Or)}$$

$$\text{If } \alpha \not\hspace{-2pt}\vdash \neg\beta \text{ and } \alpha \vdash \gamma \text{ then } \alpha \wedge \beta \vdash \gamma \qquad \textit{(Rational Monotony)}$$

The postulate Or is equivalent to the following, given the postulates for inference relations:

$$\text{If } \alpha \wedge \beta \vdash \gamma, \text{ then } \alpha \vdash \beta \to \gamma \qquad \textit{(Conditionalization)}$$

Conditionalization is the translation in Makinson and Gärdenfors (1990) of the postulate (K*7) for belief revision. Weak Conditionalization is the special case when $\alpha = \top$. Similarly, for Rational Monotony and its weak version. Rational Monotony is equivalent to the translation in Makinson and Gärdenfors (1990) of the postulate (K*8) for belief revision.

3. Expectation orderings

From an epistemological perspective it seems intuitively plausible that our expectations about the world do not all have the same strength. For example, we consider some rules to be almost universally valid, so that an exception to the rule would be extremely unexpected; while other rules are better described as rules of thumb that we use for want of more precise information. In brief, our expectations are all defeasible (unless logically valid), but they exhibit varying *degrees of defeasibility*.

In order to make these ideas more precise, we shall now assume that there is an ordering $\leq$ of the sentences in L. '$\alpha \leq \beta$' should be interpreted as 'β is at least as expected as α' or 'α is at least as surprising as β. '$\alpha < \beta$' will be written as an abbreviation for 'not $\beta \leq \alpha$' and '$\alpha \approx \beta$' is an abbreviation for '$\alpha \leq \beta$ and $\beta \leq \alpha$'. The relation $\leq$ will be assumed to satisfy the following postulates:

(E1) If $\alpha \leq \beta$ and $\beta \leq \gamma$, then $\alpha \leq \gamma$ *(Transitivity)*

(E2) If $\alpha \vdash \beta$, then $\alpha \leq \beta$ *(Dominance)*

(E3) For any α and β, $\alpha \leq \alpha \wedge \beta$ or $\beta \leq \alpha \wedge \beta$ *(Conjunctiveness)*

The first postulate on the expectation ordering is very natural for an ordering relation. The second postulate says that a logically stronger sentence is always less expected. From this it follows that the relation $\leq$ is reflexive. The third constraint is crucial for the results to come, but presumably the one that is most open to criticism. It concerns the relation between the degrees of expectation of a conjunction $\alpha \wedge \beta$ and the corresponding degrees of α and β respectively.

From (E2) it follows immediately that $\alpha \wedge \beta \leq \alpha$ and $\alpha \wedge \beta \leq \beta$, so (E3) entails that $\alpha \wedge \beta \approx \alpha$ or $\alpha \wedge \beta \approx \beta$. Clearly we cannot interpret the degrees of expectation in terms of their *probabilities*, since (E3) is violated by any probability measure.

Note that the three conditions imply *connectivity*: either $\alpha \leq \beta$ or $\beta \leq \alpha$. For by (E3) and (E2) either $\alpha \leq \alpha \wedge \beta \leq \beta$ or $\beta \leq \alpha \wedge \beta \leq \alpha$ and we conclude by (E1). The dominance condition also immediately implies that $\alpha \wedge \neg\alpha \leq \beta$, and thus the three conditions together imply that for all $\alpha \in$ L, either $\alpha \leq \beta$ for all $\beta \in$ L or $\neg\alpha \leq \beta$ for all $\beta \in$ L. By way of comparison, (E1) to (E3) are three of the five conditions used in Gärdenfors (1988) and Gärdenfors and Makinson (1988) to define a notion of "epistemic entrenchment" for the logic of theory change.

Let me return to how the ordering $\leq$ can be used to determine when α nonmonotonically imples β. One way of interpreting the key idea in the introduction $\alpha \vdash \beta$ is to say that β follows from α together with all the propositions that are 'sufficiently well' expected in the light of α. How well is 'sufficiently well'? A natural idea is to require that the added sentences be strictly more expected than $\neg\alpha$ in the ordering. This motivates the following:

Definition: $\vdash$ is a *comparative expectation* inference relation iff there is an ordering $\leq$ satisfying (E1) - (E3) such that the following condition holds:

(C$\vdash$) $\alpha \vdash \gamma$ iff $\gamma \in Cn(\{\alpha\} \cup \{\beta: \neg\alpha < \beta\})$

This definition can now be used together with the postulates of the previous section to present a representation thereom (proved in Gärdenfors and Makinson (1991)).

Theorem 1. Let ≤ be an expectation ordering over L. Then the inference relation $\vdash_\leq$ that it determines by (C⊦) satisfies the extended set of postulates of Section 2.

Theorem 2. Let ⊦ be any inference relation on L that satisfies the extended set of postulates. Then ⊦ is a comparative expectation inference relation, i.e., there is an expectation ordering ≤ over L such that ⊦ = $\vdash_\leq$.

The proof is based on the following definition of the expectation ordering: $\alpha \leq \beta$ iff either $\alpha \wedge \beta \in Cn(\emptyset)$ or $\neg(\alpha \wedge \beta) \not\vdash \alpha$. This definition, and the verification that it yields the desired properties, parallel those used in Gärdenfors and Makinson (1988) to represent revision operations in terms of epistemic entrenchment relations.

4. Expectations generated by neural networks

I have now outlined how nonmonotonic inferences may be interpreted in terms of underlying *expectations*. These are propositions, just as are our 'ordinary' beliefs, and they include the latter among them. On this approach, there is no need for a special formalism to express default beliefs. In Makinson and Gärdenfors (1990), Gärdenfors (1990), and Gärdenfors and Makinson (1991) it has also been argued that by using the notion of expectation, one can give a unified treatment of the theory of *belief revision* and that of nonmonotonic inference relations. This is accomplished by viewing the relation of 'epistemic entrenchment' used in Gärdenfors (1988) and Gärdenfors and Makinson (1988) as a kind of expectation ordering (as in the proof of Theorem 2). Belief revision and nonmonotonic reasoning can be viewed as basically *the same process*, albeit used for two different purposes.

Expectations have, so far, been treated as primitive notions. But where do they come from? One answer is to define an expectation ordering by using a nonmonotonic inference operation as in the proof of Theorem 2. However, in our opinion, this is like putting the cart in front of the horse, since the nonmonotonic inferences are what is to be *explained* with the aid of expectations.

A better answer is to view expectations as emerging from *learning processes*. Expectations can be regarded as a way of summarising previous experience in a cognitively economical way. This will be the topic of the final two sections, where the learning and reasoning process will be modelled by *neural networks*.[1]

---

[1]These two sections are, to a large extent, borrowed from Balkenius and Gärdenfors (1991).

First of all we need a general description of neural networks. We can define a neural network N as a 4-tuple $\langle S,F,C,G\rangle$. Here S is the space of all possible *states* of the neural network. The dimensionality of S corresponds to the number of parameters used to describe a state of the system. Usually $S=[a,b]^n$, where $[a,b]$ is the working range of each neuron and n is the number of neurons in the system. We will assume that each neuron can take excitatory levels between 0 and 1. This means that a state in S can be described as a vector $x = \langle x_1,...,x_n\rangle$ where $0 \leq x_i \leq 1$, for all $1 \leq i \leq n$. The network N is said to be binary if $x_i = 0$ or $x_i = 1$ for all i, that is if each neuron can only be in two excitatory levels.

C is the set of possible *configurations* of the network. A configuration $c \in C$ describes for each pair i and j of neurons the connection c_{ij} between i and j. The value of c_{ij} can be positive or negative. When it is positive the connection is *excitatory* and when it is negative it is *inhibitory*. A configuration c is said to be *symmetric* if $c_{ij} = c_{ji}$ for all i and j.

F is a set of *state transition functions* or *activation functions*. For a given configuration $c \in C$, a function $f_c \in F$ describes how the neuron activities spread through that network.

G is a set of *learning functions* which describe how the configurations develop as a results of various inputs to the network. In the sequel the learning functions will play no significant role.

The two spaces S and C interact by means of the difference equations

$$x(t+1) = f_{c(t)}(x(t))$$

$$c(t+1) = g_{x(t)}(c(t))$$

where $s \in S$, $f \in F$, $c \in C$ and $g \in G$.

This gives us two interacting subsystems in a neural network. First, we have the system $\langle S,F\rangle$ that governs the *fast* changes in the network, i.e. the transient neural activity. Then, we have the system $\langle C,G\rangle$, that controls the *slower* changes that correspond to all learning in the system. By changing the behaviour of the functions in the two sets F and G, it is possible to describe a large set of different neural mechanisms. Generally the state transition functions in F have much faster dynamics than the learning functions in G. We will assume that the state in C is fixed while studying the state transitions in S.

We want to argue that there is a very simple way of defining the notion of a *schema* within the theory of neural networks that can be seen as a generalization of the notion of a proposition. The definition we propose is that a schema α corresponds to a vector $\langle \alpha_1,...,\alpha_n\rangle$ in the state space S. That a schema α is currently *represented* in a neural network with an activity vector $x = \langle x_1,...,x_n\rangle$ means that $x_i \geq \alpha_i$, for all $1 \leq i \leq n$. There is a natural way of defining a partial order of 'greater informational content' among schemata by putting $\alpha \geq \beta$ iff $\alpha_i \geq \beta_i$ for all $1 \leq i \leq n$. There is a minimal schema in this ordering, namely $0 = <0,...,0>$ and a maximal element $1 = <1,...,1>$.

In the light of this definition, let us consider some general desiderata for schemata. Firstly, it is clear that depending on what the activity patterns in a neural network correspond to, schemata as defined here can be used for representing objects, situations, and actions.

Secondly, if $\alpha \geq \beta$, then β can be considered to be a more *general* schema than α and α can thus be seen as an *instantiation* of the schema β. The part of α not in β, is a *variable* instantiation of the schema β. This implies that all schemata with more information than β can be considered to be an instantiation of β with different variable instantiations. Thus, schemata can have variables even though they do not have any *explicit* representation of variables. Only the *value* of the variable is represented and not the variable as such. The index of the instantiation is identified with the added activity vector α-β.

Thirdly, it will soon be shown that schemata support default assumptions about the environment. The neural network is thus capable of filling in missing information.

There are some elementary operations on schemata that will be of interest when we consider nonmonotonic inferences in a neural network. The first operator is the *conjunction* $\alpha \cdot \beta$ of two schemata $\alpha = <\alpha_1,...,\alpha_n>$ and $\beta = <\beta_1,...,\beta_n>$ which is defined as $<\gamma_1,...,\gamma_n>$, where
$\gamma_i = \max(\alpha_i,\beta_i)$ for all i. In terms of cones, $\alpha \cdot \beta$ is just the intersection of the cones representing α and β. If we consider schemata as corresponding to observations in an environment we can interpret $\alpha \cdot \beta$ as the *coincidence* of two schemata, i. e. the simultaneous observation of two schemata.

Secondly, the *complement* α^* of a schema $\alpha = <\alpha_1,...\alpha_n>$ is defined as $<1-\alpha_1,...,1-\alpha_n>$ (recall that 1 is assumed to be the maximum activation level of the neurons, and 0 the minimum). In general, the complementation operation does not behave like negation since, for example, if $\alpha = <0.5,...,0.5>$, then $\alpha^* = \alpha$. However, if the neural network is assumed to be binary, that is if neurons only take activity values 1 or 0, then * will indeed behave as a classical negation on the class of binary-valued schemas.

Furthermore, the interpretation of the complement is different from the classical negation since the activities of the neurons only represent *positive* information about certain features of the environment. The complement α^* reflects a lack of positive information about α. It can be interpreted as a schema corresponding to the observation of everything but α. As a consequence of this distinction it is pointless to define implication from conjunction and complement. The intuitive reason is that it is impossible to observe an implication directly. A consequnce is that the ordering $\geq$ only reflects greater *positive* informational content.

However, something similar to classical negation can be constructed in a number of ways. We can let the schema <0.5,...,0.5> represent total lack of information. A greater activity will correspond to positive information and a smaller to negative information. The ordering $\geq$ can be changed to reflect this interpretation if we let $\alpha \geq \beta$ iff $|\alpha_i-0.5| \geq |\beta_i-0.5|$ and α_i and β_i both lie on the same side of 0.5, for all i. In this ordering <0.5,...,0.5> is the minimal schema and 1 and 0 are both maximal.

Finally, the *disjunction* $\alpha \oplus \beta$ of two schemata $\alpha = <\alpha_1,...,\alpha_n>$ and $\beta = <\beta_1,...,\beta_n>$ is defined as $<\gamma_1,...,\gamma_n>$, where $\gamma_i = \min(\alpha_i,\beta_i)$ for all i. The term 'disjunction' is appropriate of this operation only if we consider schemata to represent propositional information. Another interpretation that is more congenial to the standard way of looking at neural networks is to see α and β as two instances of a *variable*. $\alpha \oplus \beta$ can then be interpreted as the *generalization* from these two instances to an underlying variable.

It is trivial to verify that the De Morgan laws $\alpha \oplus \beta = (\alpha^* \cdot \beta^*)^*$ and $\alpha \cdot \beta = (\alpha^* \oplus \beta^*)^*$ hold for these operations. The set of all schemata forms a distributive lattice with zero and unit, as is easily shown. It is a boolean algebra if the underlying neural network is binary. In this way we have alrady identified something that looks like a *propositional* structure on the set of *vectors* representing schemata.

A desirable property of a network that can be seen as performing *inferences* of some kind is that it, when given a certain input, stabilizes in a state containing the results of the inference. In the theory of neural network such states are called resonant states. In order to give a precise definition of this notion, consider a neural network N = <S,F,C,G>. Let us assume that the configuration c is fixed (or changes very slowly) so that we only have to consider one state transition function f_c. For a fixed c in C, let $f_c^0(x) = f_c(x)$ and $f_c^{n+1}(x) = f_c \circ f_c^n(x)$. Then a state y in S is called *resonant* if it has the following properties

(i) $f_c(y) = y$ (equilibrium)

(ii) If for any $x \in S$ and each $\varepsilon > 0$ there exists a $\delta > 0$
      such that $|x-y| < \delta$, then $|f_c^n(x)-y| < \varepsilon$ when $n \geq 0$ (stability)

(iii) There exists a δ such that if $|x-y| < \delta$, then
      $\lim_{n \to \infty} f_c^n(x) = y$ (asymptotic stability).

Here $|.|$ denotes the standard euclidean metric on the state space S. A neural system N is called *resonant* if for each fixed c in C and each x in S there exists a n > 0, that depends only on c and x, such that $f_c^n(x)$ is a resonant state.

If $\lim_{n \to \infty} f_c^n(x)$ exists, it is denoted by $[x]_c$ and $[.]_c$ is called the *resonance function* for c. It follows from the definitions above that all resonant systems have a resonance function. For a resonant system we can then define *resonance equivalence* as $x \sim y$ iff $[x]=[y]$. It follows that ~ is an equivalence relation on S that partitions S into a set of equivalence classes.

It can be shown (Cohen and Grossberg 1983) that a large class of neural networks have resonance functions. A common feature of these types of neural networks is that they are based on *symmetrical* configuration functions C, that is, the connections between two neurons are equal in both directions.

The function $[.]_c$ can be interpreted as filling in *default* assumptions about the environment, so that the schema represented by $[\alpha]_c$ contains information about what the network *expects* to hold when given α as input. Even if α only gives a partial description of, for example, an object, the neural network is capable of supplying the missing information in attaining the resonant state $[\alpha]_c$. The expectations are determined by the configuration function c, and thus the expectations are more 'global' than the 'local' input α. They will change according to the equation $c(t+1) = g_{x(t)}(c(t))$ given above, where $g_{x(t)}$ is the learning function for the network. Thus the network will adapt its expectations, albeit slowly sometimes, if the network encounters evidence that conflicts with the current expectations.

5. Nonmonotonic inferences in a neural network

We now turn to the problem of giving an *interpretation* of the activities of a neural network which will show it to perform nonmonotonic inferences. A first idea for describing the nonmonotonic inferences performed by a neural network N is to say that $[\alpha]_c$ contains the nonmonotonic conclusions to be drawn from α. However, in general we can not expect the schema α to be included in $[\alpha]_c$, that is, $[\alpha]_c \geq \alpha$ does not always hold. Sometimes a neural network *rejects* parts of the input information – in pictorial terms it does not always believe what it sees.

So if we want α to be included in the resulting resonant state we have to modify the definition. The most natural solution is to 'clamp' α in the network, that is to add the *constraint* that the activity levels of all neurons is above α_i, for all i. Formally, we obtain this by first defining a function f_α via the equation $f_\alpha(x) = f(x) \cdot \alpha$ for all $x \in S$. We can then, for any resonant system, introduce the function $[.]_c{}^\alpha$ for a configuration $c \in C$ as follows:

$$[x]_c{}^\alpha = \lim_{n \to \infty} f_\alpha{}^n(x)$$

This function will result in resonant states for the same neural networks as for the function $[.]_c$. (Since we work with a fixed configuration c for a given network, the subscript c will be suppressed in the sequel.)

The key idea of this sectio is then to define a nonmonotonic inference relation $\vdash$ between schemata in the following way:

$\alpha \hspace{1mm}\vdash\hspace{-2mm}\sim \beta$ iff $[\alpha]^\alpha \geq \beta$

This definition fits very well with the interpretation that nonmonotonic inference are based on *expectations* as developed in Section 3. Note that α and β in the definition are officially not *propositions* but schemas which are defined in terms of *neural* activity vectors in a neural network. However, in the definition of $\vdash\hspace{-2mm}\sim$ they are *treated as* propositions. Thus, in the terminology of Smolensky (1988), we make the transition from the subsymbolic level to the symbolic simply by giving a different *interpretation* of the structure of a neural network. We do this without assuming two different systems as Smolensky does, but the symbolic level *emerges* from the subsymbolic in one and the same system. This kind of double interpretation of an information processing system is also discussed in Gärdenfors (1984).

Before turning to an investigation of the general properties of $\vdash\hspace{-2mm}\sim$ generated by the definition we want to illustrate it by showing how it operates for a simple neural network.

Example: The network consists of four neurons with activities $x_1,...,x_4$. Neurons that interact are connected by lines. Arrows at the ends of the lines indicate that the neurons excite each other; dots indicate that they inhibit each other. If we consider only schemata corresponding to binary activity vectors, it is possible to identify schemata with *sets* of active neurons. Let three schemata α,β,γ correspond to the following activity vectors $\alpha=<1\ 1\ 0\ 0>$, $\beta=<0\ 0\ 0\ 1>$, $\gamma=<0\ 1\ 1\ 0>$. Assume that x_4 inhibits x_3 more than x_2 excites x_3. Given α as input the network will activate γ, thus $\alpha \vdash\hspace{-2mm}\sim \gamma$. Extending the input to $\alpha\cdot\beta$ causes the network to withdraw γ since the activity x_4 inhibits x_3. In formal terms $\alpha\cdot\beta \not\vdash\hspace{-2mm}\sim \gamma$.

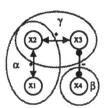

One way of characterizing the nonmonotonic inferences generated by a neural network is to study them in terms of the general postulates for nonmonotonic logics were presented in Section 2. It follows immediately from the definition of $[.]^\alpha$ that $\vdash\hspace{-2mm}\sim$ satisfies the property of *Reflexivity*: If we say that a schema β follows logically from α, in symbols $\alpha \vdash \beta$, just when $\alpha \geq \beta$, then it is also trival to verify that $\vdash\hspace{-2mm}\sim$ satisfies *Supraclassicality*:

If we turn to the operations on schemata, the And postulate is also trivial:

If $\alpha \vdash\hspace{-2mm}\sim \beta$ and $\alpha \vdash\hspace{-2mm}\sim \gamma$, then $\alpha \vdash\hspace{-2mm}\sim \beta \cdot \gamma$ *(And)*

More interesting is the following property:

If $\alpha \vdash\hspace{-2mm}\sim \beta$ and $\beta \vdash \alpha$, then $\alpha \vdash\hspace{-2mm}\sim \gamma$ iff $\beta \vdash\hspace{-2mm}\sim \gamma$ *(Cumulativity)*

Cumulativity has become an important touchstone for nonmonotonic systems (Gabbay 1985, Makinson 1989, 1991). Given the basic postulates, it is equivalent to:

If $\alpha \vdash \beta$ and $\beta \vdash \alpha$, then $\alpha \vdash \gamma$ iff $\beta \vdash \gamma$ *(Reciprocity)*

It is therefore interesting to see that the inference operation defined here seems to satisfy Cumulativity (and thus Reciprocity) for almost all neural networks where it is defined. However, it is possible to find cases where it is not satisfied:

Counterexample to Reciprocity: The network illustrated below is a simple example of a network that does not satisfy Reciprocity (or Cumulativity). If we assume that there is a strong excitatory connection between α and β it follows that $\alpha \vdash \beta$ and $\beta \vdash \alpha$ since α and β does not receive any inhibitory inputs. Suppose that $\alpha=<1\ 0\ 0\ 0>$ is given as input. Since we have assumed that the inputs to x3 interact additively it follows that γ receives a larger input than δ, because of the time delay before δ gets activated. If the inhibitory connection between γ and δ is large, the excitatory input from β can never effect the activity of x3. We then have $\alpha \vdash \gamma$ and $\alpha \nvdash \delta$. If instead $\beta=<0\ 1\ 0\ 0>$ is given as input, the situation is the opposite, and so δ get excited but not γ, and consequently $\alpha \nvdash \gamma$ and $\alpha \vdash \delta$ Thus, the network does not satisfy Reciprocity.

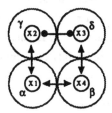

A critical factor here seems to be the *linear* summation of inputs that locks x2 and x3 to inputs from the outside because the inhibitory connection between them is large.

Extensive computer simulations have been performed of networks wich obey 'shunting' rather than linear summation of excitatory and inhibitory inputs. They suggest that reciprocity is satisfied in all networks that obeys shunting interaction of the inputs.

For the disjunction operation it does not seem possible to show that any genuinely new postulates are fulfilled. The following special form of transitivity is a consequence of Cumulativity (cf. Kraus, Lehmann, and Magidor (1990), p. 179):

If $\alpha \oplus \beta \vdash \alpha$ and $\alpha \vdash \gamma$, then $\alpha \oplus \beta \vdash \gamma$

This principle is thus satisfied whenever Cumulativity is.

The general form of Transitivity, i.e. if $\alpha \vdash \beta$ and $\beta \vdash \gamma$, then $\alpha \vdash \gamma$, is not valid for all α, β, and γ, as can be shown by the first example above. Nor is *Or* generally valid:

If $\alpha \sim \gamma$ and $\beta \sim \gamma$, then $\alpha \oplus \beta \sim \gamma$ *(Or)*

Counterexample to Or: The following network is a simple counterexample: x_1 excites x_4 more than x_2 inhibits x_4. The same is true for x_3 and x_2. Giving $\alpha = <1\ 1\ 0\ 0>$ or $\beta = <0\ 1\ 1\ 0>$ as input activates x_4, thus $\alpha \sim \gamma$ and $\beta \sim \gamma$. The neuron x_2 which represents schema $\alpha \oplus \beta$ on the other hand has only inhibitory connections to x_4. As a consequence $\alpha \oplus \beta \not\sim \gamma$.

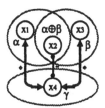

In summary, following Balkenius and Gärdenfors (1991), it has been shown that by introducing an appropriate schema concept and exploiting the higher-level features of a resonance function in a neural network it is possible to define a form of nonmonotonic inference relation. It has also been established that this inference relation satisfies some of the most fundamental postulates for nonmonotonic logics. The construction presented in this section is an example of how symbolic features can emerge from the subsymbolic level of a neural network.

It remains an open question whether there is any interesting class of neural networks for which an expectation ordering can be defined. Such networks would, according to Theorems 1 and 2, satisfy the extended set of postulates for nonmonotonic inference.

6. Conclusion

The aim of this article is a twofold reduction: Firstly, it is argued that nonmonotonic inferences can be reduced to the notion of expectation. Secondly, it is proposed that expectations can be modelled in a fruitful way in neural networks.

However, neural networks is only *one* way of modelling expectations. And apart from what has been discussed here, it seems to me that the notion of expectation is central for many cognitive processes apart from nonmonotonic reasoning. Hence it is a great interest for cognitive science in general to investigate different models of expectations. However, with the exception of 'expected utility', the concept does not seem to be much studied within cognitive psychology.[1] One further exception is Dubois and Prade's (1991) work on the connections between epistemic entrenchment and *possibility logic*, which points to a different direction. In conclusion, I would like to recommend that the notion of expectation

---

[1] And expected utility has to do with expectations of *values*, not expectations about *knowledge* as is the contents of the expectations studied in this paper.

be studied from a variety of approaches. There are numerous potential applications of such studies.

Acknowledgements

Research for this article has been supported by the Swedish Council for Research in the Humanities and Social Sciences. I want to thank the participants of the Cognitive Science seminar in Lund for helpful comments.

References

Balkenius, C. and Gärdenfors P. (1990), "Nonmonotonic inferences in neural networks", pp. 32-39 in *Principles of Knowledge Representation and Reasoning: Proceedings of the Second International Conference*, J.A. Allen, R. Fikes, and E, Sandewall, eds. (San Mateo, CA: Morgan Kaufmann).

Cohen, M.A. and S. Grossberg (1983), "Absolute stability of global pattern formation and parallel memory storage by competitive neural networks," *IEEE Trans-actions on Systems, Man, and Cybernetics*, SMC-13, 815-826.

Dubois, D. and H. Prade (1991), "Epistemic entrenchment and possibility logic", to appear in *Artificial Intelligence*.

Gabbay, D. (1985), "Theoretical foundations for nonmonotonic reasoning in expert systems", in *Logic and Models of Concurrent Systems*, K. Apt, ed. (Berlin: Springer-Verlag).

Gärdenfors, P. (1984), "The dynamics of belief as a basis for logic," *British Journal for the Philosophy of Science 35*, 1-10.

Gärdenfors, P. (1988), *Knowledge in Flux: Modeling the Dynamics of Epistemic States* (Cambridge, MA: The MIT Press, Bradford Books).

Gärdenfors, P. (1990), "Belief revision and nonmonotonic logic: Two sides of the same coin?", in *ECAI 90: Proceedings of the 9th European Conference on Artificial Intelligence*, L. Carlucci Aiello, ed. (London: Pitman Publishing), 768-773.

Gärdenfors, P. (1991), pp. 585-590 in *Principles of Knowledge Representation and Reasoning: Proceedings of the Second International Conference*, J.A. Allen, R. Fikes, and E, Sandewall, eds. (San Mateo, CA: Morgan Kaufmann).

Gärdenfors, P. and D. Makinson. (1988), "Revisions of knowledge systems using epistemic entrenchment", in *Proceedings of the Second Conference on Theoretical Aspects of Reasoning about Knowledge,* M. Vardi, ed. (Los Altos, CA: Morgan Kaufmann), 83-95.

Gärdenfors, P. and D. Makinson. (1991), "Nonmonotonic inferences based on expectations", manuscript.

Kraus, S., D. Lehmann, and M. Magidor, (1990), "Nonmonotonic reasoning, preferential models and cumulative logics", *Artificial Intelligence 44*, 167-207.

Lindström, S. (1991), "A semantic approach to nonmonotonic reasoning: Inference operations and choice", manuscript, Department of Philosophy, Uppsala University.

Makinson, D. (1989), "General theory of cumulative inference", in M. Reinfrank, J. de Kleer, M. L. Ginsberg, and E. Sandewall, eds., *Non-Monotonic Reasoning* (Berlin: Springer Verlag, Lecture Notes on Artificial Intelligence no 346).

Makinson, D. (1991), "General patterns in nonmonotonic reasoning", to appear as Chapter 2 of *Handbook of Logic in Artificial Intelligence and Logic Programming, Volume II: Non-Monotonic and Uncertain Reasoning.* (Oxford: Oxford University Press).

Makinson, D. and P. Gärdenfors (1990), "Relations between the logic of theory change and nonmonotonic logic", in G.Brewka & H.Freitag eds, *Arbeitspapiere der GMD nº 443: Proceedings of the Workshop on Nonmonotonic Reasoning*, 7-27. Also in A. Fuhrmann and M. Morreau (eds.) *The Logic of Theory Change*, (Berlin: Springer Verlag, Lecture Notes in Artificial Intelligence nº 465), 185-205.

Smolensky, P. (1988), "On the proper treatment of connectionism," *Behavioral and Brain Sciences 11*, 1-23.

DRUMS PRESENTATIONS

ESPRIT II   Basic Research Action 3085.

D R U M S

DEFEASIBLE REASONING AND
UNCERTAINTY MANAGEMENT SYSTEMS

GENERAL INTRODUCTION.

This presentation reports the on-going activities of the Basic Research Action DRUMS.
This 2.5-year large scale European research project studies several aspects of Uncertainty
in Artificial Intelligence. It is supported by a Grant from the Commission of the European
Communities, ESPRIT II program. It involves 8 university laboratories, 3 research
institutions and 3 industrial research centres.

The aim of this fundamental research project is to study the use and integration of several
forms of non-standard logics that could be applied to problems of defeasible reasoning
and uncertainty management. This explains the collaboration of partners from different
but complementary disciplines.

The final aim of DRUMS is to attempt the integration of the various logics into a general
model able to cope with the various forms of ignorance, and its implementation in
inference engines.

The strength of the project resides in its interdisciplinarity and collaborative approach,
combining symbolic, qualitative and quantitative methods. Each method has a role in the
realization of an expressive uncertainty management system, but none alone covers the
whole domain. Integrating these different methods could lead to a system more powerful
than that which could be obtained by juxtaposing them.

DRUMS PARTICIPANTS.

DRUMS project is organized in four research programmes (RP 1 to RP 4) and regroups the following partners.

RP 1: Logical Models for Defeasible Reasoning

Philippe Besnard, IRISA., Rennes, France

Christine Froidevaux, Laboratoire de Recherche en Informatique, Université Paris Sud, Orsay, France

Pierre Siegel, LIUP, Université de Provence, Marseille, France

RP 2: Possibilistic Models of Reasoning under Uncertainty and Vagueness

Henri Prade, IRIT, Université Paul Sabatier, Toulouse, France

Didier Dubois, IRIT, Université Paul Sabatier, Toulouse, France

Ramon Lopez de Mantaras, Artificial Intelligence Group, C.E.A.B., Blanes, Spain

RP 3: Models of Belief for Approximate Reasoning

Philippe Smets, IRIDIA, Université Libre de Bruxelles, Belgium.

Michael Clarke, Dept of Computer Sciences and Statistics, Queen Mary and Westfield, London, UK

Miguel Delgado, Department of Computer Science and AI, Universidad de Granada, Granada, Spain

RP 4: Combined Modes of Reasoning with Uncertainty

John Fox, Imperial Cancer Research Funds, London , United Kingdom

Abe Mamdani, Dept of Electrical Engineering, Queen Mary and Weastfield, London, UK

Three scientific advisers have joined the project.

Luis Farinas del Cerro, IRIT, Université Paul Sabatier, Toulouse, France

John Bigham, Dept of Electrical Engineering, Queen Mary and Weastfield, London, UK

Rudolph Kruse, Inst. Betriebssysteme u. Rechnerverbund, Technische Univ. Braunschweig, Germany

In order to give some feedback from the industrial needs to the partners of DRUMS, three industrial partners have been invited to join the project:

Kurt Sundermeyer, Research Institute Berlin, Daimler Benz A.G., Berlin, Germany.

Chris Whitney, British Telecom, Ipswich, UK

Olivier Paillet, CGE Alcatel, Laboratoire de Marcoussis, Marcoussis, France

IMPRECISE QUANTIFIERS AND CONDITIONAL PROBABILITIES[1]

Stéphane Amarger – Didier Dubois – Henri Prade
Institut de Recherche en Informatique de Toulouse
Université Paul Sabatier – C.N.R.S.
118 route de Narbonne, 31062 Toulouse Cedex, France

Expert rules used in knowledge-based systems are often pervaded with uncertainty and subject to exceptions. Numerical quantifiers are a natural way of expressing the proportion of exceptions or the probability of encountering them. The *available* knowledge about the proportion of A's being B's, or more generally the probability P(B|A) for an A to be a B, may be pervaded with interval-like imprecision or vagueness. For instance we know that P(B|A) $\in$ [0.7,0.8], or that "most A's are B", where the linguistic quantifier "most" is modelled by a fuzzy set restricting the possible values of the value of the proportion |A $\cap$ B| / |A| (where | | denotes the cardinality).

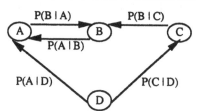

Figure 1 : An example of network

Then, given a collection of pieces of information of this kind which gives birth to a network as the one of Fig. 1, we are interested in computing the tightest bounds on the value of a proportion (or of a conditional probability) we want to estimate, without using systematic independence assumptions as in Bayesian approach (Pearl, 1988). A missing arrow in such a network corresponds to a quantifier or a conditional probability which is completely unknown (then represented by the interval [0,1]). All probabilities that we handle are (bounds of) conditional probabilities in a network where cycles are allowed, and no prior probability information is required in order to start the inference process in the approach reported here (contrary to Quinlan (1983)'s INFERNO system or Baldwin (1990)'s support logic programming). Our view of a knowledge base in this

---
[1] This research is supported by the European Esprit-II Basic Research Action n° 3085 entitled "Defeasible Reasoning and Uncertainty Management Systems (DRUMS).

paper is thus a collection of general statements regarding a population X of objects ; these statements express in imprecise terms the proportions of objects in various subclasses of X, that belong to other subclasses. This knowledge base allows for answering queries about a given object, given a subclass to which it belongs (also called its "reference class" by Kyburg (1974)). To do so we just apply to this object the properties of this subclass, implicitly assuming that it is a typical element of this class. If more information becomes available for this object, we just change its reference class accordingly.

Our approach is in complete contrast with Bayesian networks. In the latter the network is the result of a data compression procedure that accounts for conditional independence properties existing in a joint probability distribution. In our approach the data consists of incomplete statistics under the form of interval-valued conditional probabilities, and a network is only a display of the raw data expressing local constraints on an unknown joint probability distribution. Our approach leaves room for inconsistent specification (which can be detected by constraint propagation), while a Bayesian network is always consistent.

The intended purpose of the research is to discuss local vs. global strategies for computing what can be deduced about the value of proportions (or more generally, conditional probabilities) representing numerical quantifiers from pieces of knowledge pertaining to other numerical quantifiers. More particularly we have i) developed a global strategy algorithm for doing that, and ii) found out optimal local patterns for implementing a local computation approach. The advantages of local methods are twofold : making the computation simpler and preserving explanation capabilities for the inference system.

In that respect, a basic pattern for local inference is the following so-called quantified syllogism :

A's are B's with $P(B|A) \in [P_*(B|A), P^*(B|A)]$; B's are A's with $P(A|B) \in [P_*(A|B), P^*(A|B)]$
B's are C's with $P(C|B) \in [P_*(C|B), P^*(C|B)]$; C's are B's with $P(B|C) \in [P_*(B|C), P^*(B|C)]$

A's are C's with $P(C|A)$ C's are A's with $P(A|C)$

where P_* and P^* respectively denote lower and upper bounds, and where we are interested in computing the tightest bounds which can be deduced on $P(C|A)$ and $P(A|C)$.

The following bounds can be shown to be the tightest ones :

lower bound :

$$P_*(C|A) = P_*(B|A) \max\left(0, \; 1 - \frac{1 - P_*(C|B)}{P_*(A|B)}\right)$$

upper bound :

$$P*(C|A) = \min\left(1, 1 - P*(B|A) + \frac{P*(B|A) \cdot P*(C|B)}{P*(A|B)},\right.$$
$$\left.\frac{P*(B|A)P*(C|B)}{P*(A|B)P*(B|C)}, \frac{P*(B|A)P*(C|B)}{P*(A|B)P*(B|C)}[1 - P*(B|C)] + P*(B|A)\right)$$

Other patterns of reasoning involving conjunctions or disjunctions in the expressions of the conditional probabilities to derive, have been obtained. Moreover we have established the local optimality of the bounds computed in these local inference patterns (i.e. proof that the tightest bounds are obtained for each of the patterns); see (Dubois et al., 1990), (Amarger et al., 1991a).

The local inference approach also takes advantage of an extended form of Bayes rule expressed in terms of conditional probabilities only (Amarger et al., 1991a, b) namely

$$\forall A_1, ..., A_k, P(A_1|A_k) = P(A_k|A_1) \prod_{i=1}^{k-1} \frac{P(A_i|A_{i+1})}{P(A_{i+1}|A_i)}$$

(with all involved quantities positive), from which useful inequalities are obtained in case only lower and upper bounds are available. See (Amarger et al., 1991a,b) for details and for a procedure exploiting this rule in a network.

Then the constraint propagation method we use and that exploits local inference rules is the following : recursively apply the quantified syllogism to generate the missing arcs. This step is performed until the probability intervals can no more be improved. Then recursively apply the extended Bayes rule to improve the arcs previously generated, and continue the whole procedure until no improvement takes place.

Using results established in (Dubois et al., 1990 ; Amarger et al., 1991a) we can also handle queries about bounds of probabilities like $P(A \cup B|C)$, $P(A \cap B|C)$, $P(C|A \cap B)$ or $P(C|A \cup B)$. This can be also achieved by adding nodes corresponding to $A \cap B$ or $A \cup B$ in the network with the corresponding arrows ; see (Amarger et al., 1991b). Although our approach does not require independence assumptions, it is possible to use them if they hold, in order to improve bounds ; see (Amarger et al., 1991b) for preliminary results.

A global optimization approach, where in the most general case we are faced to a linear programming problem with a fractional linear objective function, has been also developed ; see Paass (1988), van der Gaag (1990) for related works. The interest of the optimization approach is mainly to have a tool which gives the optimal results in order to compare them to what is obtained with local propagation methods. A procedure, based on a transformation of a knowledge base with quantifiers (or conditional probabilities) into a set of linear constraints has been devised for automated reasoning ; it makes use of the simplex method (the fractional linear programming problem can indeed be reduced to standard linear programming; see (Amarger et al., 1990, 1991a). A preliminary comparison of the local computation method with the results obtained by the global approach are very encouraging for the local approach ; see Amarger et al. (1991a, b).

The main motivation in Zadeh (1985)'s approach to syllogistic reasoning is to cope with *linguistic* quantifiers, where the possible values of the corresponding proportions (or conditional probabilities) are restricted by means of fuzzy sets of the real interval [0,1]. The above quantified syllogism has been extended to fuzzy intervals, i.e. fuzzy sets with a unimodal membership function as in Fig. 2 (Dubois and Prade, 1988). We thus obtain fuzzy intervals containing the possible values of probabilities of interest.

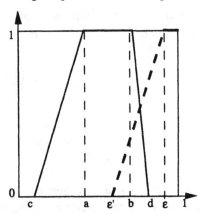

Figure 2 : <u>Examples of fuzzy intervals</u>

More recently, using an interval semantics for relative order of magnitude (Dubois and Prade, 1991a), counterparts of well-known inference rules which are known to hold for probabilities *infinitely* closed to 1 (e.g., see Pearl (1988)), have been established with a finistic semantics, namely

$$P(b|a) \ Vo(\varepsilon) \ 1, \ P(c|a) \ Vo(\varepsilon') \ 1 \Rightarrow P(c|a \wedge b) \ Vo(\varepsilon'/(1-\varepsilon)) \ 1$$
$$P(b|a) \ Vo(\varepsilon) \ 1, \ P(c|a \wedge b) \ Vo(\varepsilon') \ 1 \Rightarrow P(c|a) \ Vo(\varepsilon+\varepsilon'-\varepsilon\varepsilon') \ 1$$
$$P(c|a) \ Vo(\varepsilon) \ 1, \ P(c|b) \ Vo(\varepsilon') \ 1 \Rightarrow P(c|a \vee b) \ Vo(2(\varepsilon+\varepsilon')) \ 1$$

where x $Vo(\varepsilon)$ y $\Leftrightarrow$ 1 $- \varepsilon \leq$ min(x/y, y/x) $\leq$ 1. Thus P(b|a) $Vo(\varepsilon)$ 1 means "P(b|a) is close to 1". Again it can be generalized to fuzzy intervals ending at 1, as the one pictured in Fig. 2. It points out that it might be interesting to consider the above approach when conditional probabilities are either close to 1, close to 0 or unknown, i.e. to develop a qualitative probability version of the handling of imprecise conditional probabilities.

Among other related points which are currently investigated, let us mention the study of the relationship between conditional objects (a symbolic counterpart of conditional probability such that the conditional probability Prob(A|B) can be considered as the probability of the conditional object "A|B") and non-monotonic logic (Dubois and Prade, 1991b). See Léa Sombé (1990) for a comparison of the imprecise quantifier approach with other methods for reasoning under incomplete information.

References

Amarger S., Dubois D., Prade H. (1991a) Handling imprecisely-known conditional probabilities in conjunctive and disjunctive patterns. Proc.UNICOM "AI and Computer Power : The Impact of Statistics" Seminar, London, 13-14 March.

Amarger S., Dubois D., Prade H. (1991b) Constraint propagation with imprecise conditional probabilities. Proc. of the 7th Conf. on Uncertainty in Artificial Intelligence, UCLA, Los Angeles, July 13-18, Morgan & Kaufmann, Palo Alto, Ca., 26-34.

Amarger S., Epenoy R., Grihon S. (1990) Reasoning with conditional probabilities – A linear programming based method. Proc. of the DRUMS Esprit Project, RP2 Workshop, Albi, France, April 1990, (published by IRIT, Univ. P. Sabatier, Toulouse, France), 154-167.

Baldwin J. (1990) Computational models of uncertainty reasoning in expert systems. Computers and Math. with Appl., 19, 105-119.

Dubois D., Prade H. (1988) On fuzzy syllogisms. Computational Intelligence (Canada), 4, 171-179.

Dubois D., Prade H. (1991a) Semantic considerations on order of magnitude reasoning. Preprints of IMACS Workshop on Decision Support Systems and Qualitative Reasoning, Toulouse, France, March 13-15, 299-302. Proceedings (M. Singh, L. Travé-Massuyèes, eds.), Elsevier, Amsterdam, to appear.

Dubois D., Prade H. (1991b) Conditional objects and non-monotonic reasoning. Proc. 2nd Inter. Conf. on Principles of Knowledge Representation and Reasoning (KR'91), Cambridge, MA, April 22-25, 1991, 175-185.

Dubois D., Prade H., Toucas J.M. (1990) Inference with imprecise numerical quantifiers. In : Intelligent Systems : State of the Art and Future Directions (Z. Ras, M. Zemankova, eds.), Ellis Horwood Ltd., Chichester, 52-72.

Léa Sombé (Besnard P., Cordier M.O., Dubois D., Fariñas del Cerro L., Froidevaux C., Moinard Y., Prade H., Schwind C., Siegel P.) (1990) Reasoning Under Incomplete Information in Artificial Intelligence : A Comparison of Formalisms Using a Single Example. Wiley, New York.

Kyburg H. (1974) The Logical Foundation of Statistical Inference. D. Reidel, Dordrecht.

Paass G. (1988) Probabilistic logic. In : Non-Standard Logics for Automated Reasoning (D. Dubois, P. Smets, A. Mamdani, H. Prade, eds.), Academic Press, London, Ch. 8, 213-251.

Pearl J. (1988) Probabilistic Reasoning in Intelligent Systems: Networks of Plausible Inference. Morgan and Kaufmann, San Mateo, Ca.

Quinlan J.R. (1983) INFERNO : a cautious approach to uncertain inference. The Comp. Res., 12, 255-269.

van der Gaag L.C. (1990) Computing probability intervals under independency constraints. Proc. of the 6th Conf. on Uncertainty in Artificial Intelligence, Cambridge, Mass., July 27-29, 491-495.

Zadeh L.A. (1985) Syllogistic reasoning in fuzzy logic and its application to usuality and reasoning with dispositions. IEEE Trans. on Systems, Man and Cybernetics, 15(6), 745-763.

Default Logics

Philippe Besnard, I.R.I.S.A.
Domaine Universitaire, Campus Beaulieu
F-35000 Rennes, France

Formalization of deductive reasoning fits into a standard, canonical form corresponding to closure operators, as Tarski first showed. Certainly, it is so because deductive reasoning develops a single line of argument, there cannot be concurrent and exclusive arguments. In contrast, *defeasible reasoning deals with incompatible lines of reasoning*. More precisely, defeasible reasoning supports alternative and mutually exclusive conclusions drawn from incomplete information. Hence, any formalization for defeasible reasoning has to reflect that. Indeed, default logics, that model a certain kind of defeasible reasoning, admit multiple sets of conclusions. These are conflicting with each other. In some cases, they are all legitimate and no conclusion should impose over others. However, there are cases where a particular conclusion clearly vanishes in light of others. In fact, default logics lack some device causing the more appropriate conclusions, if any, to overrule the opposing ones. The underlying notion is that of preference, by which some of the conclusions are retained whereas others are discarded. The reader is urged to observe how natural all this reveals in the context of defeasible reasoning, as it simply extends the basic paradigm (where some conclusion formerly drawn is thrown away on the arrival of new information yielding the opposite conclusion).

An obvious kind of preference arises from specificity, that takes place when defeasible reasoning develops upon rules with exceptions. The idea is that one tends to give priority to the most specific information. For instance, knowing that "birds can fly" and "vertebrates cannot fly", even in the presence of the rule "all birds are vertebrates", one is expected to conclude that a given bird can fly (it is supposed that nothing else is known about that bird). The rule concerning only birds is given priority over the rule concerning vertebrates. Since all birds are vertebrates, the rule "birds can fly" is more specific than the rule "vertebrates cannot fly": it applies to a smaller number of cases. Intuitively, it is especially motivated by those cases. Accordingly, preference by specificity is very natural. As far as default logics are concerned, the question is then to identify some notion of specificity, and to model it in the setting of rules with exceptions.

The example given above is uncontroversially the paradigm for preference by specificity, as evidenced by the literature on the subject (see for instance [Touretzky 1984] [Poole 1985] [Loui 1987] [Geffner 1988] [Horty, Thomason & Touretzky 1990]). For more elaborated cases however, there is no such an agreement. In particular, the effect of preference by specificity largely differs from one author to another. It seems to us that it is worth examining what generalizing principles are admissible, from which the basic case can be extended: thus, the overall *coherence* of the resulting notion of preference by specificity would at least be guaranteed (contrasting the current trends seeking for *completeness*: as many cases as possible are made to fall under the developed notion of preference by specificity).

Accordingly, the basis for our notion is simply the basic case of preference by specificity, and *no other case is to be taken as primitive*. The basic case is depicted below:

$$A \quad \rightarrow \quad C$$
$$\Downarrow \qquad\qquad\qquad \text{\underline{Prefer C}}$$
$$B \quad \rightarrow \quad \neg C$$

The conventions are as follows:
- Rules without exceptions are indicated by a double arrow $\Rightarrow$
- Rules with exceptions are indicated by a simple arrow $\rightarrow$
- The notation $\neg C$ indicates a conclusion C^* that yields a contradiction from C

An important remark is in order: as opposed to some rival proposals, the notion of preference by specificity developed here requires that *the overruling and overruled conclusions are logically incompatible* from the theory under consideration. Otherwise, no general property would be inherited! In the above example for instance, birds would inherit no property from vertebrates if the basic case were defined by an arbitrary C' instead of $\neg C$.

The first coherence principle that we propose deals with enforcing specificity, it roughly states that introducing a more specific link in a chain of arguments cannot make the end conclusion to be preferred if it were not:

	A ▸┼......▸┼ C				A ▸┼......▸┼ C	
From	⬥		to	$\Downarrow$		
	▸┼......▸┼ $\neg C$			B ▸┼......▸┼ $\neg C$		

<u>Prefer C</u>	implies	<u>Prefer C</u>
<u>Make no choice</u>	implies	<u>Do not prefer $\neg C$</u>

Notation: ▸┼ and ⬥ stand for any rule, whether with exceptions or not.

That is, the basic schema extends to all cases obtained by adding a rule without exceptions as the first link in a chain of arguments.

Our second coherence principle guarantees that consequences of preferred conclusions must be preferred as well:

	A ⤃ ...... ⤃ C		A ⤃ ...... ⤃ C ⤃ B
From	↖	to	↖
	⤃ ...... ⤃ ¬C		⤃ ...... ⤃ ¬C ⤃ B′
	<u>Prefer C</u>	implies	<u>Prefer B</u>

Our third coherence principle states that the basic schema applies at *any* stage in a chain of arguments:

	A ⤃ ...... ⤃ C		D ⤃ A ⤃ ...... ⤃ C
From	↖	to	↖ ↖
	B ⤃ ... ⤃ ¬C		E ⤃ B ⤃ ... ⤃ ¬C
	<u>Prefer C</u>	implies	<u>Prefer C</u>

The fact that the path from D to C can be longer than the path from D to ¬C is not enough to make it ¬C to be chosen: preference by specificity *differs* from the "shortest path" approach to inheritance reasoning [Touretzky 1986].

Our fourth, and last, coherence principle, turns out to be the most fruitful in addition to being especially simple:

	A ⤃ ... → ... ⤃ C		A ⤃ ... ⇒ ... ⤃ C
From	↖	to	↖
	⤃ ...... ⤃ ¬C		⤃ ...... ⤃ ¬C
	<u>Prefer C</u>	implies	<u>Prefer C</u>
	<u>Make no choice</u>	implies	<u>Do not prefer ¬C</u>

Intuitively, preferring C means that the arguments developed in the reasoning from A to C are strong. Now, replacing the argument "an A′ is a C′ apart from some exceptions" used in the course of the reasoning from A to C by the argument that in fact "each A′ is a C′ with no exceptions" can only strengthen the reasoning from A to C.

The resulting notion of specificity covers a rather large spectrum and provides some indications about the utility of a given notion of preference by specificity. For instance, if the basic schema is enlarged to a greater number of rules then the notion of preference by specificity covers more cases, most of them are controversial: intuition is lost while the overall benefit is far from obvious. More details about this particular point and also about other properties can be found in [Moinard 1990].

References

[Geffner H. 1988]
On the Logic of Defaults, *Proc. AAAI*-88, St-Paul (Mn), pp. 449-454.

[Horty J. F., Thomason R. H. & Touretzky D. S. 1990]
A Skeptical Theory of Inheritance in Nonmonotonic Semantic Networks, *Artificial Intelligence* 42, pp. 311-348.

[Loui R. P. 1987]
Defeat among Arguments: A System of Defeasible Inference, *Computational Intelligence* 3, pp. 100-106.

[Moinard Y. 1990]
Preference by Specificity in Default Logic, submitted.

[Poole D. 1985]
On the Comparison of Theories: Preferring the Most Specific Explanation, *Proc. IJCAI*-85, Los Angeles (Ca), pp. 144-147.

[Touretzky D. S. 1984]
Implicit Ordering of Defaults in Inheritance Systems, *Proc. AAAI*-84, Austin (Tx), pp. 322-325.

[Touretzky D. S. 1986]
The Mathematics of Inheritance, Morgan Kaufmann, Los Altos (Ca).

Propagation of Uncertainty in Dependence Graphs *

José Cano, Miguel Delgado, Serafín Moral,
Departamento de Ciencias de la Computación e I.A.
Universidad de Granada. 18071 Granada, Spain.

Abstract

In this paper the main results of DRUMS RP3.3 Task 'Propagation of Uncertainty in Dependence Graphs' are presented. It is divided in two parts. In the first one, it is considered a new calculus with imprecise probabilities, which is not as uninformative as classical one, [6, 7, 9]. In the second one, the axiomatic squeme given in [11] has been adapted to Pearl's causal networks, [10], by introducing three new axioms. Then, this axiomatic framework is particularized to the new calculus of upper and lower probabilities. It is shown that upper and lower probabilities may be propagated on causal networks on an analogous way to probabilities.

1   Introduction

Assume a variable X taking values on a finite set U. Any probability distribution about it, $p : U \to [0, 1]$, induces a probability measure, P, that is a mapping, $P : \mathcal{P}(U) \to [0, 1]$, given by $P(A) = \sum_{u \in A} p(a)$. This probability measure expresses the relative frequencies (objective interpretation) or the degrees of belief (subjective interpretation) about events in U.

Probability Theory needs an exact value of uncertainty for every subset A from U. However, there are situations in which our 'a priori' knowledge or past experience is so weak for a given variable that may be difficult to express them in this precise way. It may be more convenient and closer to reality to allow a more flexible way of representing our state of knowledge, for example, by means of probability intervals.

In this paper it is studied a very general framework: convex sets of probability distributions with a finite set of extreme points, $H = \text{CH}\{p_1, \ldots, p_n\}$, where CH stands for convex hull. This representation was considered by Dempster, [6], and recently by Walley, [12], from a subjective point of view. In [3] we have considered an objective perspective.

A convex set, H, may determine a family of probability intervals (P_*, P^*), given by,

$$P_*(A) = Inf\{P(A) \mid p \in H\} \qquad P^*(A) = Sup\{P(A) \mid p \in H\}$$

---

*This work has been supported by the Commission of the European Communities under ESPRIT BRA 3085: DRUMS.

For each $A \subseteq U$, we have the interval $[P_*(A), P^*(A)]$ of possible probability values. However this transformation is not biunivoque: different convex sets may define the same system of intervals. It is possible to associate with a family of intervals a convex set H' of probability distributions, the one given by, $H' = \{p \mid P_*(A) \leq P(A) \leq P^*(A), \forall A \subseteq U\}$. It can be easily shown that $H \subseteq H'$. In this sense, we may say that if we transform a convex set on a family of intervals then we lose information: we are adding more probabilities to the set H, that is, increasing the indetermination.

In the second section of this paper we summarize the calculus for convex sets of probabilities developed in [9, 3]. The main contribution is in the introduction of a new conditioning procedure that is not as uninformative as the one previously used, [6, 1, 7].

On the other hand, we have considered also the problem of distributed calculus with convex sets of probabilities. The problem is as follows. If X is an n-dimensional variable $(X_1, \ldots, X_n)$, each one of the X_i taking values on finite set, U_i, with cardinal k_i, then to represent a simple probability distribution we need $\prod_{i=1}^{n} k_i$ values, which is impracticable in most of real situations. Systems of distributed calculus for probabilities ([10, 8]) take advantage of the 'a priori' knowledge about independence relationships among variables to express a probability distribution as combination of several pieces of probabilistic information given in smaller frames, and to calculate conditional probabilities by means of them. Shenoy, Shafer, [11], have shown that this system of distributed calculus may be applied to any uncertainty formalism in which there are two operations defined, marginalization and combination, verifying a system of three axioms. However, Shenoy and Shafer's work is only focussed on calculus and the decomposition of initial knowledge is given by hypothesis, no relating it with independence relationships among variables. In section three of this paper it is considered a richer axiomatic framework in which this aspect is covered. Furthermore, it is shown that Pearl's propagation formulas for causal directed networks, [10], may be also generalized.

Finally, it is shown that the calculus previously developed for convex sets of probabilities verifies the axiomatic system and then can be propagated on causal directed networks.

Given the space requeriments of this paper, only the main points of this paper will be considered, referring to the full papers for a deeper and more detailed presentation.

2 Calculus with Convex Sets of Probabilities

In [9, 3] we have developed a calculus with convex sets of probabilities. The main results are summarized in this section. If X is a variable taking values on U, then an imprecise probabilistic piece of information about X, will be a convex set, H, of probability distributions with a finite set of extreme points $H = \text{CH}\{p_1, \ldots, p_n\}$.

If Y is a variable taking values on V, then a imprecise conditional probabilistic information of Y given X is a convex set, T, of possible conditional probability distributions, with a finite set of extreme points: $T = \text{CH}\{t_1, \ldots, t_m\}$. Each one of the t_j is a mapping

$$t_j : U \times V \to [0,1]$$

such that $\forall u \in U, t_j(u,.)$ is a probability distribution on V, that is $\sum_{v \in V} t_j(u,v) = 1$.

Example 2.1 *Assume that $U = \{u_1, u_2, u_3\}$ and $V = \{v_1, v_2\}$. Let us consider that as 'a priori' information on U we have the convex set H with extreme points*

	u_1	u_2	u_3
p_1	0.8	0.1	0.1
p_2	0.0	1.0	0.0
p_3	0.2	0.0	0.8

As conditional information of Y given X, we have the following points,

	(u_1, v_1)	(u_1, v_2)	(u_2, v_1)	(u_2, v_2)	(u_3, v_1)	(u_3, v_2)
t_1	0.8	0.2	0.9	0.1	0.0	1.0
t_2	0.0	1.0	0.5	0.5	0.9	0.1

If $H = \mathrm{CH}\{p_1, \ldots, p_n\}$ is an 'a priori' information about X and $T = \mathrm{CH}\{t_1, \ldots, t_m\}$ is a conditional information of Y given X, then a global information is defined as the convex set, $H \otimes T$, of probability distributions on $U \times V$ generated by points,

$$\{p_1.t_1, \ldots, p_1.t_m, p_2.t_1, \ldots, p_2.t_m, \ldots, p_n.t_1, \ldots, p_n.t_m\}$$

where $p_i.t_j(u, v) = p_i(u).t_j(u, v)$.

Example 2.2 *In former example the global information $H \otimes T$ defined on $U \times V$ is the convex set generated by points,*

	(u_1, v_1)	(u_1, v_2)	(u_2, v_1)	(u_2, v_2)	(u_3, v_1)	(u_3, v_2)
$p_1.t_1$	0.64	0.16	0.09	0.01	0.00	0.10
$p_2.t_1$	0.00	0.00	0.90	0.10	0.00	0.00
$p_3.t_1$	0.16	0.04	0.00	0.00	0.00	0.80
$p_1.t_2$	0.00	0.80	0.05	0.05	0.09	0.01
$p_2.t_2$	0.00	0.00	0.50	0.50	0.00	0.00
$p_3.t_2$	0.00	0.20	0.00	0.00	0.72	0.08

If we have a convex set of probability distributions, $H = \mathrm{CH}\{p_1, \ldots, p_n\}$, on $U \times V$ for variable (X, Y) then the marginal information induced on sets U and V, is given by the convex sets, $H^{\downarrow U}$ and $H^{\downarrow V}$ generated by points $\{p_1^{\downarrow U}, \ldots, p_n^{\downarrow U}\}$ and $\{p_1^{\downarrow V}, \ldots, p_n^{\downarrow V}\}$, respectively. Where $p_i^{\downarrow U}$ is a probability distribution on U given by $p_i^{\downarrow U}(u) = \sum_{v \in V} p_i(u, v)$. Analogously $p_i^{\downarrow V}(v) = \sum_{u \in U} p_i(u, v)$.

If we start with a convex set H of probabilities on U and a convex set, T, of conditional probabilities of Y given X, and then we calculate $(H \otimes T)^{\downarrow V}$ we get the generalization of *Total Probability Theorem*.

Example 2.3 *In our example $(H \otimes T)^{\downarrow V}$ is given by the convex set with extreme points (non extreme points have been removed):*

	v_1	v_2
q_1	0.9	0.1
q_2	0.14	0.86

Finally, in this section, we consider the problem of conditioning. Assume that $H = \mathrm{CH}\{p_1, \ldots, p_n\}$ is a convex set for variable X and that we have observed 'X belongs to A', then the result of conditioning is the convex set, $H|A$, generated by points $\{p_1.l_A, \ldots, p_n.l_A\}$ where l_A is the likelihood associated with set A ($l_A(u) = 1$, if $u \in A$; $l_A(u) = 0$, otherwise).

It is important to remark that $H|A$ is a convex set of differently normalized functions. If we call $r_i = \sum_{u \in U} p_i(u).l_A(u) = P_i(A)$, then by calculating $(p_i.l_A)/r_i$ we get the conditional probability distribution $p_i(.|A)$. The set $H' = \{p(.|A) \mid p \in H\}$ was propossed by Dempster, [6], as the set of conditioning, and has been widely used. However, this set produces very large intervals, the reason being that, by normalizing each probability, we loose the information provided by values r_i.

To associate probability intervals with $H|A$ we have proposed, [9], the following procedure:

- Consider the extreme points of $H|A$: $\{p_1.l_A, \ldots, p_n.l_A\}$

- Normalize each extreme point, calculating $p_i(.|A)$, and assigning it, at the same time, a possibility value, $\pi(p_i(.|A))$, equal to $r_i/(\text{Max } r_k)$.

- If Π is the possibility measure defined by above possibility values and N its dual necessity measure, then lower and upper intervals are calculated as,

$$P_*(B|A) = \text{I}(P_i(B|A) \mid N) \quad P^*(B|A) = \text{I}(P_i(B|A) \mid \Pi)$$

and I stands by the Choquet's integral, [5].

Example 2.4 *If* $U = \{u_1, u_2, u_3\}$ *and* $H = \text{CH}\{p_1, p_2\}$ *where*

	u_1	u_2	u_3
p_1	0.5	0.5	0.0
p_2	0.1	0.0	0.9

If $A = \{u_1, u_2\}$ *then* $H|A$ *has as extreme points,*

	u_1	u_2	u_3		u_1	u_2	u_3	π
$p_1.l_A$	0.5	0.5	0.0	$p_1(.|A)$	0.5	0.5	0.0	1.0
$p_2.l_A$	0.1	0.0	0.0	$p_2(.|A)$	1.0	0.0	0.0	0.1

The intervals without taking into account the possibilities are,

$$u_1 \to [0.5, 1] \qquad u_2 \to [0, 0.5] \qquad u_3 \to [0.0, 0.0]$$

and by using Choquet's integral, we obtain,

$$u_1 \to [0.5, 0.55] \qquad u_2 \to [0.45, 0.5] \qquad u_3 \to [0.0, 0.0]$$

3 Propagation of Convex Sets of Probabilities

In this section we summarize the results of [2, 4] for propagation of uncertainty in directed acyclic graphs (DAG).

If we have an n-dimensional variable $(X_1, \ldots, X_n)$ taking values on $U_1 \times \ldots \times U_n$, then a DAG is a means of expressing dependence relationships among variables X_i (see D-separation criterium in [10]).

For example, in above figure X_1 is a direct cause of X_3 and this variable is a direct cause of X_5. Then X_1 and X_5 are dependent, but they become indepndent if we know the value of X_3.

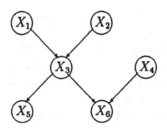

In [2] we show that this structure may be used to calculate with different uncertainty representations, generalizing Pearl's propagation algorithms, [10]. We follow Shenoy, Shafer, [11], axiomatic approach. On it it is considered that pieces of information on a given theory are represented by valuations. The set of possible valuations defined on frame $\prod_{i \in I} U_i$, where $I \subseteq \{1, \ldots, n\}$, is denoted by $\mathcal{V}_I$. Two basic operations have to be defined on the set of all the valuations,

- *Marginalization.-* If $J \subseteq I$ and $V_1 \in \mathcal{V}_I$ then the marginalization of V_1 to J is a valuation $V_1^{\downarrow J}$ defined on $\mathcal{V}_J$.

- *Combination.-* If $V_1 \in \mathcal{V}_I$ and $V_2 \in \mathcal{V}_J$, then its combination is a valuation $V_1 \otimes V_2$ defined on $\mathcal{V}_{I \cup J}$

In [11] it is considered that valuations verify the following three first axioms. We have added Axioms 3-6.

1. $V_1 \otimes V_2 = V_2 \otimes V_1, \quad (V_1 \otimes V_2) \otimes V_3 = V_1 \otimes (V_2 \otimes V_3)$.

2. If $I \subseteq J \subseteq K$, and $V \in \mathcal{V}_J$ then $(V^{\downarrow J})^{\downarrow I} = V^{\downarrow I}$.

3. If $V_1 \in \mathcal{V}_I$, $V_2 \in \mathcal{V}_J$, then $(V_1 \otimes V_2)^{\downarrow I} = V_1 \otimes V_2^{\downarrow (J \cap I)}$.

4. *Neutral Element.-* There exits one and only one valuation V_0 defined on $U_1 \times \ldots \times U_n$ such that $\forall V \in \mathcal{V}^I, \forall J \subseteq I$, we have $V_0^{\downarrow J} \otimes V = V$.

5. *Contradiction.-* There exits one and only one valuation, V_c, defined on $U_1 \times \ldots \times U_n$, such that $\forall V, V_c \otimes V = V_c$.

6. $\forall V \in \mathcal{V}_\emptyset$, if $V \neq V_c^{\downarrow \emptyset}$, then $V = V_0^{\downarrow \emptyset}$.

Example 3.1 *Valuations for imprecise probabilities are convex sets of non-necessarily normalized functions. The operations of combination and marginalization are based on the ones defined on former section. The neutral element is the convex set with only one element, the function h_0, where $h_0(u) = 1, \forall u \in U_1 \times \ldots \times U_n$. The contradiction has an only point: the null function, $h_c(u) = 0, \ \forall u \in U_1 \times \ldots \times U_n$. In [4] we show that these valuations verify Axioms 1-6.*

With these six axioms, we can define conditional valuations and show the following representation theorem, [2], which is not considered in [11].

Theorem 3.1 *If we have a DAG associated with $(X_1, \ldots, X_n)$ and we have a valuation for each variable X_i conditioned to its parents, then there exists one and only one global valuation, V, valid for $(X_1, \ldots, X_n)$.*

Finally in [2], it is shown that if we want to calculate the conditioning of the global valuation V to some observations $\{O_i\}_{i \in I}$, and later to marginalize it to every subset, U_j, then it is not necessary to use valuation V directly. It is enough to use the initial pieces of information (conditional valuation for each variable given its parents) and the observations, O_i, organizing the calculus as a system of messages passing on the associated DAG. Pearl's propagation formulas, [10], are expressed in terms of operations with valuations and shown to ve verified if Axioms 1-6 are fulfilled.

References

[1] Campos L.M. de, M.T. Lamata, S. Moral (1990) The concept of conditional fuzzy measure. International Journal of Intelligent Systems 5, 237-246.

[2] Cano J.E., M. Delgado, S. Moral (1991) An axiomatic for the propagation of uncertainty in directed acyclic networks. Submitted to the International Journal of Approximate Reasoning.

[3] Cano J.E., S. Moral, J.F. Verdegay-López (1991) Combination of Upper and Lower Probabilities. In: Proceedings of the 7th Conference on Uncertainty in A.I. (D'Ambrosio, Smets, Bonissone, eds.) 61-68.

[4] Cano J.E., S. Moral, J.F. Verdegay-López (1991) Propagation of convex sets of probabilities in directed acyclic graphs. Tech. Report DECSAI N. 91-2-3.

[5] Choquet G. (1953/54) Theorie of capacities. Ann. Inst. Fourier 5, 131-292.

[6] Dempster A.P. (1967) Upper and lower probabilities induced by a multivalued mapping. Ann. Math. Statis. 38, 325-339.

[7] Fagin R., J.Y. Halpern (1990) A new approach to updating beliefs. Research Report RJ 7222. IBM Almaden Research Center.

[8] Lauritzen S.L., D.J. Spiegelharter (1988) Local computation with probabilities on graphical structures and their application to expert systems. J. of the Royal Statistical Society, B 50, 157-224.

[9] Moral S., L.M. de Campos (1990) Updating uncertain information. Proceedings 3rd. IPMU Conference, Paris 1990, 452-454.

[10] Pearl J. (1989) Probabilistic Reasoning with Intelligent Systems. Morgan & Kaufman, San Mateo.

[11] Shenoy P.P., G. Shafer (1990) Axioms for probability and belief-function propagation. In: Uncertainty in Artificial Intelligence, 4 (Shachter, Levitt, Kanal, Lemmer, eds.) 169-198.

[12] Walley P. (1991) Statistical Reasoning with Imprecise Probabilities. Chapman and Hall, London.

EFFICIENT ALGORITHMS FOR BELIEF FUNCTIONS BASED ON THE RELATIONSHIP BETWEEN BELIEF AND PROBABILITY

Mike Clarke and Nic Wilson
Department of Computer Science
Queen Mary and Westfield College
University of London

Introduction

One of the major perceived problems with practical applications of Dempster-Shafer theory is that, as usually implemented, it involves repeated application of Dempster's Rule of Combination to explicitly stored mass functions, so that the combination of m simple support functions may, in the worst case, involve computing and storing 2^q real numbers, where q is the smaller of the number of functions to be combined and the size of the underlying frame.

Some previous approaches to this problem have focussed on showing that special cases can be dealt with efficiently. For example Gordon and Shortliffe (1985) and later Shafer and Logan (1987) showed that efficient algorithms could be found for the hierarchical case. Shafer and Shenoy (1988) generalised this to propagation of belief functions in Markov Trees, but again there are restrictions on the structure of the network if efficiency is to be achieved. Another approach is to use the fast Möbius transform (Kennes and Smets, 1990) but, although this is an improvement over the naive algorithm, the complexity is still exponential.

For practical applications it seems likely that one will not want to calculate the belief precisely for all subsets but only to reasonable accuracy for a few significant subsets. We give below a method of doing this using a Monte-Carlo algorithm. The use of Monte-Carlo methods has also been suggested by Pearl (1988), Kampke (1988) and Kreinovich and Borrett (1990), however our formulation is based on a theoretical model that also leads to a new exact algorithm and it can be naturally generalised to wider logical frameworks than the usual Dempster-Shafer theory.

This work is supported by ESPRIT Basic Research Action No. 3085.
Defeasible Reasoning and Uncertainty Management Systems (DRUMS)

The sources of evidence model

To form the basis of the implementation an alternative theoretical formulation of belief functions has been developed in terms of *sources of evidence* and their probability of being reliable. The theory is described in detail in Wilson (1989); briefly it is as follows.

Let Θ be the frame of discernment, the elements of which can be thought of as the mutually exclusive and exhaustive potential outcomes of some investigation. In a medical application Θ might be the set of possible diseases about which evidence is being obtained. In the simplest model we are trying to deduce the identity of a single element x of Θ. We have a number of *sources* S_i, i=1...m, each of which provides *evidence* A_i in some logical language. In the classical Dempster-Shafer formulation A_i will be a subset of Θ and the evidence that S_i gives will be to the effect that $x \in A_i$, but it is important to note for future developments that, in general, the evidence A_i can be in any logical language.

Each source S_i on a given occasion on which it gives evidence may be either *reliable*, with probability p_i, or *unreliable*. If S_i is reliable we know for certain that x is in A_i, if S_i is unreliable then it gives us no information at all. Given this framework, it can be shown (Wilson, 1989) that, under compelling assumptions, the Dempster-Shafer belief, Bel(X), in a subset X of the frame Θ is just the probability that, under this model, we can deduce from the evidence that the true outcome x is in X (or more generally that the evidence logically entails X).

The correspondence between this model and the standard formulation is that each source, and the evidence that it gives, corresponds to a simple support function in which p_i is the mass allocated to subset A_i with $1-p_i$ being allocated to Θ and zero to all other subsets.

This representation in terms of probability not only enables belief functions to be evaluated by Monte Carlo methods but also leads to exact algorithms that are radically different from those previously proposed. More detail about the algorithms is given below, but to give a general view of what has been achieved we first give the results of some timing experiments carried out on a practical implementation (Sun 3/60, Modula2).

In the table that follows m is the number of evidences that are being combined (sources) and n is the size of the frame, i.e. $|\Theta|$. The time shown for "mass-based" methods is in fact the time to carry out $2^{\min(m,n)}$ real multiplications, which is the smallest possible worst-case complexity of any method that explicitly computes the combined mass function.

m	n	Monte-Carlo	Exact	Mass-based
15	15	7 secs	9 secs	3 secs
20	20	11 secs	13 secs	1 min
25	25	13 secs	46 secs	1 hour
30	30	15 secs	3 mins	1 day
35	35	17 secs	8 mins	1 month
50	50	25 secs	2 hours	3000 years

The Monte-Carlo algorithm

The sources-of-evidence model for simple support functions described above is essentially a concrete specialisation of the original model of Dempster (1967) in which, if Bel_1 ,..., Bel_m are belief functions on a finite frame Θ, each Bel_i can be expressed as the extension of a probability function P_i on a finite set Ω_i via a compatibility function $\Gamma_i : \Omega_i \rightarrow 2^\Theta$ where the "meaning" of Γ_i is: for every $\varepsilon_i \in \Omega_i$, if ε_i holds then so does $\Gamma_i(\varepsilon_i)$.

The mass function m_i is given, for $\varepsilon_i \in \Omega_i$, by $m_i(\Gamma_i(\varepsilon_i)) = P_i(\varepsilon_i)$ and, for $\Theta \supseteq X$,

$$Bel_i(X) = \sum_{\varepsilon_i : X \supseteq \Gamma_i(\varepsilon_i)} P_i(\varepsilon_i)$$

Now let $Bel = Bel_1 \oplus ... \oplus Bel_m$ be the combination of the Bel_i using Dempster's Rule and let $\Omega = \Omega_1 x ... x \Omega_m$. For $\varepsilon = (\varepsilon_1,...,\varepsilon_m)$ define $\Gamma(\varepsilon) = \cap_i \Gamma_i(\varepsilon_i)$ and define the "independent probability function" P' on Ω by $P'((\varepsilon_1,...,\varepsilon_m)) = \prod_i P_i(\varepsilon_i)$. Following Dempster (1967)

$$Bel(X) = P'(X \supseteq \Gamma(\varepsilon) \mid \Gamma(\varepsilon) \neq \phi) \quad \text{where} \quad P'(\Gamma(\varepsilon) \neq \phi) = \sum_{\varepsilon : \Gamma(\varepsilon) \neq \phi} P'(\varepsilon)$$

The Monte-Carlo algorithm uses this equation to estimate $Bel(X)$. Each trial is of the form

Step1: Randomly choose an ε for which $\Gamma(\varepsilon)$ is not null by:
    1.1) for $i = 1,...,m$ randomly choose ε_i with probability P_i
    1.2) compute $\Gamma(\varepsilon)$
    1.3) if $\Gamma(\varepsilon) = \phi$ then repeat Step 1
                    else   do Step 2

Step 2: If $\Gamma(\varepsilon)$ is a subset of X then the trial succeeds otherwise it fails.

The proportion of trials out of N that succeed can easily be shown to have expectation $Bel(X)$ with standard error bounded above by $1/(2\sqrt{N})$. Furthermore, for the simple support function case, the time for each trial can be shown to be linear in m and n. The expected number of times that step 1 is executed is proportional to $(1-P'(\Gamma(\varepsilon)=\phi))^{-1}$ so if there is a high degree of inconsistency a considerable number of random number generations will be wasted, and this seems to be the only disadvantage of the method. However it could be argued that Dempster's rule is of doubtful validity anyway in such cases.

The table of timings given above was computed for a probability of inconsistency of 0.5 and 1000 trials, for which three standard errors is about 0.05, sufficient accuracy for most applications. In making comparisons with the mass-based algorithms it should be emphasised that these timings for the Monte-Carlo and exact algorithms are for computing the belief of one subset only. If the complete belief function is required over the whole of 2^Θ then of course the Monte-Carlo computation would be exponential in $n=|\Theta|$. In practice interest will be centred on small subsets of high belief for which Step 2 of the algorithm can be adapted. Furthermore it is straightforward to extend the method to non-simple support functions (by using each random number in step (1) to choose one of several subsets) and to calculate belief in many X's at once by extending step 2 in the obvious (and linear) way.

Exact algorithm

The same theoretical formulation also leads to an exact algorithm that can be used in cases where the Monte-Carlo algorithm is unsuitable. Full details are in Wilson (1989), but briefly the idea is to express the event $X \supseteq \Gamma(\varepsilon)$ as a conjunction of disjunctions over the ε_i and their complements. By using identities of Boolean algebra, together with some heuristics for efficiency, the probability of $X \supseteq \Gamma(\varepsilon)$ can be evaluated in terms of the elementary $P_i(\varepsilon_i)$. Full details are again in Wilson (1989). Approximate theoretical analysis of the average-time complexity of the exact algorithm shows it be of the form $n^{\log(m)}$, worse than polynomial but better than exponential.

Updating Belief Functions

The same framework can be used to effect an integration of Dempster-Shafer and Bayesian theory. The combined belief function Bel can be seen as the result of extending a probability function, P^{DS} on Ω say, using the compatibility relation above, where $P^{DS}(\varepsilon)=0$ if $\Gamma(\varepsilon)= \phi$ and $K.P'(\varepsilon)$ otherwise for some normalising constant K. A probability function P on Θ should now satisfy the constraints induced by P^{DS}, i.e. for all $\Theta \supseteq X$,

$$P(X) \geq \sum_{\varepsilon:\, \Gamma(\varepsilon) \neq \phi} P^{DS}(\varepsilon)$$

Now let e be the body of evidence on which Bel is based. If a new piece of evidence e' is now received then, given that we can come up with likelihoods $l(x)=Pr(e'|x,e)$ for all $x \in \Theta$, all such compatible probability functions P can be updated and it is natural to consider the infimum $P_*(X|e',e)$ for $\Theta \supseteq X$. Wilson (1991b) shows, as previously did Wasserman (1990), that

$$P_*(X|e',e) = \frac{\displaystyle\sum_{B:X \supseteq B} m(B)l_*(B)}{\displaystyle\sum_{B:X \supseteq B} m(B)l_*(B) \; + \; \sum_{B:X \supseteq B} m(B)l^*(B \backslash X)}$$

where $l_*(X)=\min_{x \in X} l(x)$ and $l^*(X)=\max_{x \in X} l(x)$.

If Bel is the combination by Dempster's Rule of a number of belief functions then $P_*(X|e',e)$ can be calculated using a modified version of the Monte-Carlo algorithm in which step 1 is the same as above while Step 2 is replaced by

Step 2': If $X \supseteq \Gamma(\varepsilon)$ then $U:=U+l_*(\Gamma(\varepsilon))$ else $V:=V+l^*(\Gamma(\varepsilon) \backslash X)$

in which case $\frac{U}{U+V}$ converges to $P_*(X|e',e)$, U and V having been initialised to zero.

References

Dempster, A.P. (1967) Upper and Lower Probabilities Induced by a Multi-valued Mapping. *Ann. Math, Statist.* 38, 325-339.

Gordon, J. and Shortliffe, E.H. (1985) A Method of Managing Evidential Reasoning in a Hierarchical Hypothesis Space, *Artificial Intelligence,* 26, 323-357.

Kampke (1988) About Assessing and Evaluating Uncertain Inferences Within the Theory of Evidence. *Decision Support Systems* 4, 433-439.

Kreinovich, V. and Borrett, W. (1990) Monte-Carlo Methods Allow to Avoid Exponential Time in Dempster-Shafer Formalism. Tech.Report UTEP-CS-90-5, Computer Science Dept. University of Texas at El Paso.

Kyburg, H.E., Jr. (1987) Bayesian and Non-Bayesian Evidential Updating. *Artificial Intelligence* 31, 271-293.

Pearl, J. (1988) *Probabilistic Reasoning in Intelligent Systems: Networks of Plausible Inference.* Morgan Kaufmann.

Shafer, G. and Logan, R. (1987) Implementing Dempster's Rule for Hierarchical Evidence. *Artificial Intelligence,* 33, 271-298.

Shafer and Shenoy, P.P. (1988) Local Computation in Hypertrees, Working Paper No. 201, School of Business, University of Kansas.

Kennes, R. and Smets, P. (1990) Computational Aspects of the Mobius Transform. *Proc. 6th Conference on Uncertainty in Artificial Intelligence,* Cambridge, Mass.

Wasserman, L.A. (1990) Prior Envelopes Based on Belief Functions. *Annals of Statistics,* 18, 1, 454-464.

Wilson, P.N. (1989) Justification, Computational Efficiency and Generalisation of the Dempster-Shafer Theory. Research Report No.15, Dept. of Computing and Math. Sciences, Oxford Polytechnic. Also to appear in *Artificial Intelligence.*

Wilson, P.N. (1991a) A Monte-Carlo Algorithm for Dempster-Shafer Belief, Research Report, Dept. of Computer Science, Queen Mary and Westfield College. Also to appear in *Proceedings of 7th Conference on Uncertainty in Artificial Intelligence.*

Wilson, P.N. (1991b) Likelihood Updating of a Belief Function, Research Report, Dept. of Computer Science, Queen Mary and Westfield College, University of London.

A BRIEF OVERVIEW OF POSSIBILISTIC LOGIC

Didier Dubois – Jérôme Lang – Henri Prade
Institut de Recherche en Informatique de Toulouse
Université Paul Sabatier – C.N.R.S.
118 route de Narbonne, 31062 Toulouse Cedex, France

The intended purpose of this research[1] is i) to show the specificity of possibilistic logic with respect to other logics with weighted statements, in particular its ability to deal both with uncertainty and vagueness, ii) to develop proof methods for possibilistic logic, and iii) to relate its ability to cope with partial inconsistency to belief revision and non-monotonic reasoning issues. See Léa Sombé (1990) for an introduction to possibilistic logic among other non-classical logics.

Several approaches have been proposed for dealing with uncertainty and/or vagueness in theorem proving ; see Dubois et al. (1991a) for an overview. However a large part of them are based on *fuzzy* logic, which completely departs from *possibilistic* logic. Fuzzy logic deals with propositions involving vague predicates (or properties whose satisfaction can be a matter of degree) and manipulates truth degrees which are truth-functional with respect to each connective, whereas possibilistic logic involves certainty and possibility degrees which are not compositional for all connectives and which are attached to classical formulae, i.e. containing only non-vague propositions or predicates (in the simplest case). The lack of complete certainty about the truth of a considered formula is to be understood as a consequence of a lack of complete information.

A possibilistic logic formula is a first order logic formula with a numerical weight between 0 and 1 which is a lower bound on a possibility measure Π or on a necessity measure N. Thus this lower bound should obey the characteristic axioms governing these measures, i.e. $\forall p, \forall q, N(p \wedge q) = \min(N(p),N(q))$ and $\Pi(p \vee q) = \max(\Pi(p),\Pi(q))$ respectively for necessity and possibility measures (Zadeh, 1978 ; Dubois and Prade, 1988), with the duality relation $N(p) = 1 - \Pi(\neg p)$. However we only have $N(p \vee q) \geq \max(N(p),N(q))$ and $\Pi(p \wedge q) \leq \min(\Pi(p),\Pi(q))$. Moreover we have the usual limit conditions $\Pi(\perp) = N(\perp) = 0$, $\Pi(T) = N(T) = 1$, where $\perp$ and T stand for the

---

[1] Supported by the European Esprit-II Basic Research Action number 3085 entitled "Defeasible Reasoning and Uncertainty Management Systems" (DRUMS).

contradiction and the tautology respectively. The weight attached to a formula represents to what extent it is possible or it is certain that the formula holds for true given the available information. A semantics has been proposed first when only lower bounds on a necessity measure are used (Dubois et al., 1989) and then extended to the general case where lower bounds of both possibility and necessity are allowed (Lang et al., 1991). For the sake of brevity let us only indicate the semantics attached to a set $\mathcal{K}$ of (classical) formulas p_i, $i = 1,n$ weighted by lower bounds α_i of the necessity type, i.e. $\forall i$, $N(p_i) \geq \alpha_i$. The fuzzy set $M(p_i,\alpha_i)$ of interpretations of (p_i,α_i) is defined by the characteristic function

$$\forall \omega, \mu_{M(p_i,\alpha_i)}(\omega) = \max(\mu_{M(p_i)}(\omega), 1 - \alpha_i)$$

where $\mu_{M(p_i)}(\omega) = 1$ if ω is a model of p_i and $\mu_{M(p_i)}(\omega) = 0$ if ω is not a model of p_i. The lack of certainty in p_i, estimated by $1 - \alpha_i$, is committed to the interpretations which are not models of p_i. By performing the conjunction of the $M(p_i,\alpha_i)$'s, we associate each interpretation ω with a weight equal to $\pi(\omega) = \min_{i=1,n} \mu_{M(p_i,\alpha_i)}(\omega)$. Thus the weights attached to formulas in the knowledge base $\mathcal{K} = \{(p_i,\alpha_i)\}$ induce an ordering among the interpretations (according to their level of possibility $\pi(\omega)$). It is very similar to Shoham (1988)'s preferential model semantics ; see (Dubois and Prade, 1991b) on this point. It can be checked that $\forall i$, $N(p_i) = 1 - \prod(\neg p_i) \geq \alpha_i$, with $\prod(p_i) = \sup\{\pi(\omega), \omega \in M(p_i)\}$, which is the definition (Zadeh, 1978) of a possibility measure $\prod$ from a possibility distribution π, in this setting.

The following deduction rules (Dubois and Prade, 1987, 1990a) have been proved sound and complete for the above-mentioned semantics, see (Dubois et al., 1989, Lang et al., 1991)

$$\frac{N(p) \geq \alpha \, , \, N(q) \geq \beta}{N(\text{Res}(p,q)) \geq \min(\alpha,\beta)} \qquad \frac{N(p) \geq \alpha \, , \, \prod(q) \geq \beta}{\prod(\text{Res}(p,q)) \geq \begin{cases} \beta \text{ if } \alpha + \beta > 1 \\ 0 \text{ otherwise.} \end{cases}}$$

where $\text{Res}(p,q)$ is the resolvent of p and q. If we want to compute the certainty degree which can be attached to a formula, we add to the knowledge base the negation of the formula to evaluate with a necessity degree equal to 1. Then it can be shown that any lower bound obtained on $\perp$, by resolution, is a lower bound of the necessity of the formula to evaluate. First order logic automatic deduction methods can be extended to possibilistic logic. Various strategies for applying the above extended resolution principles, which make use of ordered search methods (Dubois et al., 1987), as well as, the generalization of semantic evaluation techniques like the Davis and Putnam' procedure (Lang, 1990) have been carried out. Also preliminary results on possibilistic logic programming have been obtained (Dubois et al., 1991b).

The introduced semantics enables us to define the degree *of partial inconsistency* of a knowledge base $\mathcal{K}$ which is equal, in the case of necessity-weighted formulas, to $\text{Inc}(\mathcal{K}) = 1 - \sup_\omega \min_{i=1,n} \mu_{M(p_i,\alpha_i)}(\omega)$. Then it can be shown that this degree estimates to what extent the lower bounds in the knowledge base violate the characteristic axiom of necessity measures and to what extent the fuzzy set of models of the knowledge base is empty. It has been also shown that is it possible to reason with such partially inconsistent knowledge bases, still preserving the above-mentioned soundness and completeness results (Lang et al., 1991). An important point when reasoning with a partially inconsistent possibilistic knowledge base is that the conclusions which can be deduced with a degree strictly greater than the degree of inconsistency are still valid.

Possibilistic logic implements a non-monotonic reasoning in case of partial inconsistency. Indeed, it has been shown (Dubois and Prade, 1991b) that the preferential entailment (in the sense of Shoham (1988)) $\models_\pi$, defined by

$$p \models_\pi q \Leftrightarrow N(q \mid p) > 0$$

$$\text{with } N(q \mid p) = 1 - \Pi(\neg q \mid p) \text{ and } \Pi(q \mid p) = \begin{cases} 1 \text{ if } \Pi(p) = \Pi(p \wedge q) \\ \Pi(p \wedge q) \text{ if } \Pi(p) > \Pi(p \wedge q) \end{cases}$$

(where π is the possibility distribution, associated with the semantics of the knowledge base $\mathcal{K}$, underlying Π), is in complete agreement with non-monotonic consequence relations obeying the axiomatics of system P proposed by Kraus et al. (1990). See also Gärdenfors (1991) on the link between non-monotonicity issues and necessity-like measures called "expectations".

Moreover it has been established in (Dubois and Prade, 1991b) that we have $N(q \mid p) > 0$ if and only if it is possible to deduce (q,β) from $\mathcal{K} \cup \{(p,1)\}$ with $\beta > \text{Inc}(\mathcal{K} \cup \{(p,1)\})$, where N is the necessity measure defined from π associated with $\mathcal{K}$. Since $N(q \mid p) > 0$ behaves like a non-monotonic consequence relation $p \vdash q$, it illustrates the close relation that there exists between non-monotonic reasoning and belief revision (Makinson and Gärdenfors, 1991), in the possibilistic framework. The links between possibility theory and the theory of revision of symbolic knowledge bases developed by Gärdenfors indicate that there is a deep coherence between the reasoning methods in possibilistic logic and recent developments in purely symbolic approaches to reasoning with incomplete or contradictory knowledge. More specifically it has been shown that Gärdenfors (1988)' epistemic entrenchment relations are equivalent to the qualitative counterpart of necessity measures (Dubois and Prade, 1990b). This explains that the ability of possibilistic logic to deal with partial inconsistency is related to a belief revision mechanism in agreement with Gärdenfors' epistemic entrenchment relation. Moreover the lack of known updating rules in possibility theory has led us to investigate counterparts of updating rules existing in probability theory ; a possibilistic Jeffrey-like rule for updating a possibility distribution on the basis of another possibility distribution has been proposed (Dubois and Prade, 1990d). The reader is referred to (Dubois and Prade, 1991c) for a detailed analysis of belief revision in possibility theory. Besides, the problem of recovering consistency in a partially inconsistent knowledge base $\mathcal{K}$ by building maximal consistent sub-bases (obtained by deleting suitable pieces of knowledge in $\mathcal{K}$) is discussed in (Dubois et al., 1991c). The problem of reasoning with paraconsistent pieces of knowledge which violate the requirement $\min(N(p),N(\neg p)) = 0$ (a consequence of the axiomatics of necessity measures) has been recently discussed (Dubois et al., 1991e).

As pointed out in (Dubois et al., 1989), the weighted clause $(\neg p \lor q, \alpha)$, understood as $N(\neg p \lor q) \geq \alpha$ is semantically equivalent to the weighted clause $(q, \min(\alpha, v(p)))$ where $v(p)$ is the truth value of p, i.e. $v(p) = 1$ if p is true and $v(p) = 0$ if p is false. This remark is very useful for hypothetical reasoning, since by "transferring" a sub-formula from a clause to the weight part of the formula we are introducing explicit assumptions. Indeed changing $(\neg p \lor q, \alpha)$ into $(q, \min(v(p), \alpha))$ leads to state the piece of knowledge under the form "q is certain at the degree α, *provided that* p is true". More generally, the weight or label can be a function of logical (universally quantified) variables involved in the clause. The weight is no more just a degree but in fact a label which expresses the context in which the piece of knowledge is more or less certain. This is to be related to "possibilistic Assumption-based Truth Maintenance Systems" (with weighted justifications and/or hypotheses, which have been defined (Dubois et al., 1990, 1991d) and exemplified on a diagnosis problem. The approach contrasts with other uncertainty handling ATMS in the sense that the symbolic processing and the calculus of uncertainty are no longer separated here. Besides, applications to discrete optimization and to the handling of prioritized constraints are presented in (Lang, 1991).

Moreover the presence of logical variables in the weight also enables the expression of some graduality attached to *vague predicates* (as in the rule "the younger the person, the more certain he/she is single", where "young" is a vague predicate) in a simple way, as $N(single(x)) \geq \mu_{young}(age(x))$ in our example. It would then allow for a flexible interface between the symbolic knowledge base and numerical inputs. Vague predicates can thus be handled by introducing their characteristic functions in the weights. This remark together with theoretical results (Dubois and Prade, 1990a) on the extension of the resolution rules in possibilistic logic in presence of vague predicates enables us to accommodate vague predicates ; see also (Dubois et al., 1991e).

Lastly, deduction in possibilistic logic has been shown in perfect agreement (see Dubois et al., 1991a, e) with Zadeh (1979)'s approach to approximate reasoning which is based on the combination and the projection of possibility distributions. Paralleling existing results about network inference techniques for reasoning with probability measures or belief functions, some preliminary work (Dubois and Prade, 1990c) has been done indicating that the framework of possibility theory is also liable of inference methods based on hypergraphs (Shafer and Shenoy, 1990).

References

Dubois D., Lang J., Prade H. (1987) Theorem-proving under uncertainty – A possibilistic theory-based approach. Proc. 10th Inter. Joint Conf. on Artificial Intelligence, Milano, Italy, 984-986.

Dubois D., Lang J., Prade H. (1989) Automated reasoning using possibilistic logic : semantics, belief revision, variable certainty weights. Proc. 5th Workshop on Uncertainty in A.I., Windsor, Ont., 81-87.

Dubois D., Lang J., Prade H. (1990) Handling uncertain knowledge in an ATMS using possibilistic logic. In : Methodologies for Intelligent Systems 5 (Z.W. Ras, M. Zemankova, M.L. Emrich, eds.), North-Holland, Amsterdam, 252-259.

Dubois D., Lang J., Prade H. (1991a) Fuzzy sets in approximate reasoning – Part 2 : Logical approaches. Fuzzy Sets and Systems, 25th Anniversary Memorial Volume, 40, 203-244.

Dubois D., Lang J., Prade H. (1991b) Towards possibilistic logic programming. Proc. 8th Inter. Conf. on Logic Programming (ICLP'91), Paris, June 25-28, (K. Furukawa, ed.), The MIT Press, Cambridge, Mass., 581-595.

Dubois D., Lang J., Prade H. (1991c) Inconsistency in possibilistic knowledge bases – To live or not live with it. In: Fuzzy Logic for the Management of Uncertainty (L.A. Zadeh, J. Kacprzyk, eds.), Wiley, to appear.

Dubois D., Lang J., Prade H. (1991d) A possibilistic assumption-based truth maintenance system with uncertain justifications, and its application to belief revision. Proc. ECAI Workshop on Truth-Maintenance Systems, Stockholm, Aug. 6, 1990, Lecture Notes in Computer Sciences, Springer Verlag (J.P. Martins, M. Reinfrank, eds.), to appear.

Dubois D., Lang J., Prade H. (1991e) Handling uncertainty, context, vague predicates, and partial inconsistency in possibilistic logic. Proc. "Fuzzy Logic in Artificial Intelligence" : a Workshop to be held in conjunction with the 12th Inter. Joint Conf. on Artificial Intelligence (IJCAI-91), Sydney, Australia, Aug. 25.

Dubois D., Prade H. (1987) Necessity measures and the resolution principle. IEEE Trans. on Systems, Man and Cybernetics, 17, 474-478.

Dubois D., Prade H. (1988) (with the collab. of H. Farreny, R. Martin-Clouaire, C. Testemale) Possibility Theory – An Approach to Computerized Processing of Uncertainty. Plenum Press, New York.

Dubois D., Prade H. (1990a) Resolution principles in possibilistic logic. Int. J. of Approx. Reas., 4, 1-21.

Dubois D., Prade H. (1990b) Epistemic entrenchment and possibilistic logic. In : Tech. Report IRIT/90-2/R, IRIT, Univ. P. Sabatier, Toulouse, France. Artificial Intelligence, to appear.

Dubois D., Prade H. (1990c) Inference in possibilistic hypergraphs. Abridged version in Proc. 3rd Inter. Conf. on Information Processing and Management of Uncertainty in Knowledge-Based Systems, Paris, France, July 2-6, 1990, 228-230. Full version to appear in (B. Bouchon-Meunier, R.R. Yager, L.A. Zadeh, eds.), Lecture Notes in Computer Science Series n° 521, Springer Verlag, 1991.

Dubois D., Prade H. (1990d) Updating with belief functions, ordinal conditional functions and possibility measures. Preprints 6th Conf. on Uncertainty in A.I., Cambridge, Mass., July 27-29, 307-315. To appear in : Uncertainty in Artificial Intelligence 6 (P.P. Bonissone, M. Henrion, L.N. Kanal, J.F. Lemmer, eds.), North-Holland, Amsterdam.

Dubois D., Prade H. (1991a) Fuzzy sets in approximate reasoning – Part 1 : Inference with possibility distributions. Fuzzy Sets and Systems, 25th Anniversary Memorial Volume, 40, 143-202.

Dubois D., Prade H. (1991b) Possibilistic logic, preference models, non-monotonicity and related issues. Proc. 12th Inter. Joint Conf. on Artificial Intelligence, Sydney, Australia, Aug. 24-30.

Dubois D., Prade H. (1991c) Belief change and possibility theory. In : Belief Revision (P. Gärdenfors, ed.), Cambridge University Press, to appear.

Gärdenfors P. (1988) Knowledge in Flux – Modeling the Dynamics of Epistemic States. MIT Press, Cambridge.

Gärdenfors P. (1991) Nonmonotonic inferences based on expectations : a preliminary report. Proc. 2nd Inter. Conf. on Principle of Knowledge Representation and Reasoning, Cambridge, Mass. (J. Allen et al., eds.), Morgan & Kaufmann, 585-590.

Kraus S., Lehmann D., Magidor M. (1990) Nonmonotonic reasoning, preferential models and cumulative logics. Artificial Intelligence, 44, 134-207.

Lang J. (1990) Semantic evaluation in possibilistic logic. Abridged version in Proc. 3rd Inter. Conf. on Information Processing and Management of Uncertainty in Knowledge-Based Systems (IPMU), Paris, France, July 2-6, 1990, 51-55. Full version to appear in (B. Bouchon-Meunier, R.R. Yager, L.A. Zadeh, eds.), Lecture Notes in Computer Science Series n° 521, Springer Verlag, 1991.

Lang J. (1991) Possibilistic logic as a logical framework for min-max discrete optimisation problems and prioritized constraints. Proc. Inter. Workshop on Fundamentals of Artificial Intelligence Research (FAIR'91), Smolenice Castle, Czechoslovakia, Sept. 8-12, 1991, Springer Verlag, to appear.

Lang J., Dubois D., Prade H. (1991) A logic of graded possibility and certainty coping with partial inconsistency. Proc. 7th Conf. on Uncertainty in A.I., UCLA, Los Angeles, July 13-15, Morgan Kaufmann, 188-196.

Léa Sombé (Besnard P., Cordier M.O., Dubois D., Fariñas del Cerro L., Froidevaux C., Moinard Y., Prade H., Schwind C., Siegel P.) (1990) Reasoning Under Incomplete Information in Artificial Intelligence : A Comparison of Formalisms Using a Single Example. Wiley, New York.

Makinson D., Gärdenfors P. (1991) Relation between the logic of theory change and nonmonotonic logic. In : The Logic of Theory Change (A. Fuhrmann, M. Morreau, eds.), Lecture Notes in Computer Sciences, n° 465, Springer Verlag, Berlin.

Shafer G., Shenoy P.P. (1990) An axiomatic framework for Bayesian and belief-function propagation. In : Uncertainty in Artificial Intelligence 4 (R.D. Shachter et al., eds.), North-Holland, Amsterdam, 119-198.

Shoham Y. (1988) Reasoning About Change – Time and Causation from the Standpoint of Artificial Intelligence. The MIT Press, Cambridge, Mass.

Zadeh L.A. (1978) Fuzzy sets as a basis for a theory of possibility. Fuzzy Sets and Systems, 1, 3-28.

Zadeh L.A. (1979) A theory of approximate reasoning. In : Machine Intelligence 9 (J.E. Hayes, D. Michie, L.I. Mikulich, eds.), Elsevier, New York, 149-194.

A MODAL ANALYSIS OF POSSIBILITY THEORY

Luis Fariñas del Cerro, Andreas Herzig

IRIT
Université Paul Sabatier
118 Route de Narbonne, F-31062 Toulouse Cédex, France
email: {farinas,herzig}@irit.fr, fax: (33) 61 55 62 58

Abstract
In this paper we study possibility theory from the point of view of modal logic. Our first and main result is that the logic of qualitative possibility is nothing else than Lewis's conditional logic VN. Second, we propose a multi-modal logic able to support possibility theory. Some connexions between these formalisms are stressed.

1. Introduction

To find models able to support reasoning under uncertainty is an important problem for Artificial Intelligence as well as Logic and Formal Philosophy. Several models have been proposed, like probability theory, belief structures, decomposable confidence measures, qualitative neccessity or possibility theory. This last theory (and dually necessity theory) has been introduced by D. Dubois and H. Prade in 1986 [Dubois & Prade 88] and seems to be a "nice" point of view from which several other models can be observed. Given a set of events this theory allows to associate an uncertainty degree to each event, thanks to a function P mapping events (being sets of elementary events) into the real interval [0,1] which satisfies the following axioms:

P1. $\qquad$ $P(\text{True}) = 1$

P2. $\qquad$ $P(\text{False}) = 0$

P3. $\qquad$ $P(A \cup B) = \max(P(A), P(B))$

The function P is called a *possibility measure*. It induces a relation "$\geq$" between events defined by $A \geq B$ if and only if $P(A) \geq P(B)$. We call $\geq$ a relation *agreeing strictly* with P. $A \geq B$ means that A is at least possible as B. This relation is called *qualitative possibility relation* and satisfies the following conditions:

QP1. (tautology) $\qquad$ True $\geq$ F

QP2. (compatibility) $\qquad$ $A \geq B$ or $B \geq A$

QP3. (transitivity) $\qquad$ if $A \geq B$ and $B \geq C$ then $A \geq C$

QP4. (non triviality) $\qquad$ True > False

QP5. (disjunctive stability) $\qquad$ if $B \geq C$ then for each A, $A \cup B \geq A \cup C$

where A, B and C represent sets of events, False stands for the empty set and True for the total set of events.

Just as Kraft, Pratt, and Seidenberg did for probabilities [Scott 64], D. Dubois [Dubois 86] established the formal relation between possibility theory and qualitative possibility relations.

In a recent work P. Gärdenfors and D. Makinson have established a similar relation between quantitative and qualitatives plausibility measures. Such measures allow them to characterize an interesting class of nonmonotonic reasoning [Gärdenfors, Makinson 91].

2. From Qualitative Possibility to Lewis's System VN

In this section we present a conditional logic obtained from qualitative possibility relations, and we prove that it is exactly Lewis's VN logic. Thus we proceed in the same manner as Segerberg did for probability measures [Segerberg 71].

2.1 Qualitative Possibility Logic (QPL)

Considering that events are represented not by sets of elementary events, but by propositional formulas, we can represent the qualitative possibility relation as a particular dyadic connective. Formally we define a propositional language with the classical connectives : $\wedge$, $\vee$, $\neg$, etc. plus $\geq$. Formulas of QPL (called qualitative formulas) are defined as usual, in particular $F \geq G$ is a qualitative formula if F and G are qualitative formulas. The axiomatics of QPL is the following:

QPL0.	Classical axioms
QPL1.	$(F \geq G \wedge G \geq H) \rightarrow F \geq H$
QPL2.	$F \geq G \vee G \geq F$
QPL3.	$\neg(\text{False} \geq \text{True})$
QPL4.	$\text{True} \geq F$
QPL5.	$F \geq G \rightarrow F{\vee}H \geq G{\vee}H$

with the inference rules

QPL6.	modus ponens
QPL7.	If $F \leftrightarrow G$ then $F \geq G$

Since the axioms of this conditional logic and the axioms of qualitative possibility are exactly the same we can assume that this logic is the logic of qualitative possibility. We stress that the axioms Q1,..., Q5 for qualitative possibility relations correspond to formulas without nested $\geq$-operators. On the contrary in logic QPL, nested $\geq$-operators are allowed.

QPL can be considered a conditional logic: As indicated above, the formula $F \geq G$ expresses that the possibility degree of G is less or equal than the possibility degree of F. In other words, it is at least as possible that F as it is that G.

2.2 Lewis's System VN

D. K. Lewis [Lewis 73] defined a conditional logic called VN. Its language is that of classical logic augmented by a conditional dyadic connective. Let us to denote this conditional connective by $\geq$ as previously. Hence the language of VN is the same language of qualitative formulas as for QPL. One reading Lewis gives for a formula of the form $F \geq G$ is that "it is at least as possible that F as it is that G". This gives already a hint about the proximity of VN and QPL. The axioms of VN are

VN0.	Classical axioms
VN1.	$(F \geq G \wedge G \geq H) \rightarrow F \geq H$
VN2.	$F \geq G \vee G \geq F$
VN3.	$\neg(\text{True} \geq \text{False})$

and the inference rules are

VN4.	modus ponens
VN5.	If $F \rightarrow (G_1 \vee ... \vee G_n)$ then $(G_1 \geq F) \vee ... \vee (G_n \geq F)$

2.3 The Equivalence Theorem

Theorem (Equivalence of QPL and VN). QPL0, ..., QPL7 is an alternative axiomatization of the conditional logic VN.

3. Possibility logic (PL)

Originally, possibility theory has been introduced in terms of a measure on events, and in the literature one can find many applications of possibility theory where these measures are manipulated directly. That motivates search of logics which model such numerical representations explicitly in the language. In this section we present a tentative of such a formalization by introducing a multi-modal logic which also axiomatizes the multi-relational models of the previous section.

Up to now we have used the concept of possibility instead of the dual notion of necessity. As the latter concept is traditionally used as a primitive in modal logics, we have preferred to state our multi-modal logic in terms of necessity[1].

---

[1] We can switch easily from one concept to the other thanks to their duality: To every possibility measure P there is associated a function N mapping events into [0,1] by $N(A) = 1 - P(-A)$. N is called a *necessity measure*, and it satisfies

N1.	$N(\text{True}) = 1$
N2.	$N(\text{False}) = 0$
N3.	$N(A \cap B) = \min(N(A), N(B))$

As before, we can associate to N a relation "$\geq$" between events defined by $A \geq B$ if and only if $N(A) \geq N(B)$ such that the necessity counterpart of Dubois's theorem holds. This relation is called *qualitative necessity relation*. (We use the same symbol for the relation than before.) Dually to the axiomatization of qualitative possibility logic QPL in section 2, we can define qualitative necessity logic (QNL) by axioms QNL0, ..., QNL7, all of which coincide with that of QPL except QPL5 which is replaced by

QNL5. $F \geq G \rightarrow F \wedge H \geq G \wedge H$

3.1 Axiomatics

The language of a possibility logic PL$_P$ is a multi-modal extension of the classical propositional language with a parameter set P. To each parameter p $\in$ P we associate a modal operator [p]. Formulas of PL$_P$ (called quantitative formulas) are defined as usual, in particular [p] F is a formula if F is a formula. We may read [p] F as "the necessity of F is at least p". As usual, <p> F is an abreviation for $\neg$ [p] $\neg$F.

The axiomatics of possibility logic PL$_P$ is an extension of classical logic:

PL0.   Classical axioms
PL1.   [p] True
PL2. $\neg$ [1] False
PL3.   ([p] F $\wedge$ [p] G) $\leftrightarrow$ [p] (F $\wedge$ G)
PL4.   ([p] F $\rightarrow$ [p] G) $\vee$ ([q]G$\rightarrow$ [q]F)

with the inference rules

PL5.   modus ponens
PL6.   If F $\leftrightarrow$ G then [p] F $\leftrightarrow$ [p] G

Thus, PL$_P$ is a multi-modal logic where the operator [1] is axiomatized as in modal logic KD, and every other operator [p] as in modal logic K. Moreover, PL$_P$ states a particular interaction between modal operators.

3.2 From Qualitative Possibility Logic to Possibility Logic

We define a translation mapping qualitative formulas of QPL into formulas of the possibility logic PL$_P$ indexed by a *finite* parameter set P = {p_1,... ,p_n}. This will allow to embed qualitative possibility logic QPL into possibility logic.

Definition. Let P a parameter set. The translation T$_P$ from the language of QPL into that of PL$_P$ is such that

- T$_P$(F) = F if F is an atomic formula
- T$_P$(F $\geq$ G) = (<p_1>T$_P$(G) $\rightarrow$ <p_1>T$_P$(F)) $\wedge$ ... $\wedge$ (<p_n>T$_P$(G) $\rightarrow$ <p_n>T$_P$(F))
- and homomorphic elsewhere

By this translation we get that every expression of possibility theory representable by a qualitative possibility formula is captured exactly by a quantitative possibility formula.

4. Acknowledgements

We are indebted to our neighbours and friends D. Dubois and H. Prade for useful suggestions concerning possibility theory, and to D. Makinson for his comments on a first version of this note.

5. References

D. Dubois (1986), Belief Structures, Possibility Theory, Decomposables Confidence Measures on finite sets. Computer and Arti. Intell. vol 5, N° 5 pp 403-417.

D. Dubois, H. Prade (1988), Possibility Theory: An Approach to Computerized Processing of Uncertainty. Plenum Press, New York.

P. Gärdenfors, D. Makinson (1991), Nonmonotonic Inference based on Expectation Ordering. Manuscript.

D. Makinson (1991), letter, march 1991.

G. E. Hughes , M. J. Cresswell (1968), An Introduction to Modal Logic. Methuen & Co.

D. K. Lewis (1973), Counterfactuals. Harvard University Press.

D. Scott (1964), Measurement structures and linear inequalities. Jounal of Mathematical Psychology, Vol. 1, 233-247.

K.Segerberg (1971), Qualitative probability in a modal setting. In: Proc. of the Second Scandinavian Logic Symposium (ed. J. E. Fenstad), North Holland.

An Extended Logic Language For Representing Belief

John Fox, Paul Krause and Mirko Dohnal

Imperial Cancer Research Fund Laboratories
Lincoln's Inn Fields, London, United Kingdom

Abstract

The DRUMS project is addressing a variety of symbolic and numerical techniques for reasoning under uncertainty and with incomplete information. This paper discusses work which is directed towards identifying a unifying framework which will enable a variety of uncertainty handling techniques to be integrated in a single programming environment.

1. Goals Of Research

The main aim of our activity within the DRUMS research programme is to develop a logic programming language extended to include a principled framework for reasoning about belief in sentences. The main goal is a general framework for integrating quantitative and qualitative uncertainty calculi, but a range of specific numerical, symbolic and mixed methods will be implemented. Our project is committed to three deliverables: (1) a kernel inference language incorporating extensions for reactive update of the belief database (a prototype for which is discussed in [6]); (2) demonstration of a framework for loose coupling of multiple calculi (an initial implementation has been developed); (3) a framework for tightly coupling calculi within the language.

2. Background

A central requirement of our contribution to the DRUMS project is an understanding of the common structure, if any, of the many proposals for quantitative and qualitative management of uncertainty.

Even if for no other reason than it being the best understood, probability theory still remains the dominant theory, or gold standard, for all the proposed calculi for reasoning with uncertain or incomplete information. An important distinction between probability theory (and indeed all the other numerical calculi proposed in DRUMS) and classical logic, is that whereas in logic we are only interested in whether the proof of a proposition's truth or falsity exists (with no guidance as to how to behave when both can be proven simultaneously), in probability theory we may take into account all possible proofs of a proposition to enable finer distinctions in degrees of belief to be made (and the choice of weightings of the proofs so constrained as to allow the coherent aggregation of conflicting evidences).

The advantage of a rigorous implementation of a fully intentional system such as bayesian probability is that all possible interactions between rules and evidences are taken into account on each data update. There are, however, two serious disadvantages. The first is that in the most general case, probabilistic belief update is far too computationally intensive to be implemented in a realistic application. The second is the familiar old chestnut of the difficulty of actually eliciting all of the required numerical values. However, that the general solution to a problem is NP-hard does not imply that it may not be possible to make simplifying assumptions which enable an efficient algorithm to be implemented in a specific instance. The work of Pearl [10], Shafer & Shenoy [11] and Lauritzen & Spiegelhalter [8], for example, has identified classes of topologies of the underlying graphical representation for which numerical belief update may be implemented using efficient message passing algorithms. This technique may be extended to most of the current uncertainty representations. This has led to a great deal of work towards the development of graphical structures in which the dependencies and influences between knowledge items are explicitly represented. It is perhaps becoming clear that the correct structuring of the knowledge that is relevant in a given decision making context is as important, if not more important, than the numerical values that are propagated through the graph.

However, the difficulty of *reliably* eliciting large sets of numerical data (whether conditional probabilities, belief masses or whatever) still remains. This is the main practical motivation for investigating non-numerical techniques for uncertainty management. One simple solution is to label the edges in the graph with a '+' or a '-', indicating that the evidence nodes, respectively, support or oppose the dependant hypothesis, without providing precise numerical weightings. A measure of the degree of belief in a proposition is then obtained by simply adding up the number of supporting arguments, and subtracting the number of opposing arguments. This approach has been extensively used in applications developed by members of this group, and has proven to be very effective. Indeed the work of Dawes [1] confirms that in the absence of reliable weightings this use of an "improper linear model with uniform weightings" is the best approach to take. This may be seen as a simple qualitative model for belief update. The work of Wellman [12] provides for a more comprehensive qualitative model of probabilistic belief maintenance.

Rather different qualitative approaches have emerged in the development of non-standard logics. Here beliefs are modelled as defeasible rather than revisable (e.g. default and other non-monotonic logics). Again, as with classical logics, these logics would normally only require the existence of a consistent proof of a proposition to determine its truth value. The difference with classical logic is that the discovery of additional information may lead to the retraction of a previously believed hypothesis. And these logics are often applied to problems where there may be an interaction between (for example) defaults which enables conflicting conclusions to be drawn. However, the existence of conflicting proofs of both the truth and the falsity of a proposition must be resolved by introducing some notion which enables one proof to be preferred over another. The logics remain two valued logics of truth and falsity, although there is work under way which is directed at enriching the logic with a lattice structure enabling at least a partial order to be imposed on the degree of belief in the hypotheses of interest (as reflected in a number of contributions to this conference).

The approach we are taking towards developing an extended framework which may be used to represent all of the various symbolic and numeric aspects of belief and uncertainty is to consider a logic of argumentation. Classical logic provides a formal basis for the identification of valid arguments. We extend classical logic so that not just one argument, but all arguments supporting or opposing a hypothesis are considered in a given decision making context. That is, the logic is used to structure the problem. We hold this to be the key component of a practical decision making system. As arguments are identified, the support they confer on a hypothesis or its negation is aggregated to provide a measure of the degree of belief in the hypotheses of interest. The aggregation operation will depend on the calculus used to represent the uncertainty or vagueness associated with the arguments. The choice of calculus will in turn depend on the representation requirements and the information which is available in a given task.

3. Resume Of First Year's Work

We can define logical criteria which enable the degree of belief in a hypothesis to be established using a logical theorem prover, such as prolog [3]. However, it is difficult to model those aspects of a practical reasoning machine which involve "side-effects" using pure logic. Practical reasoning about beliefs however requires, for example, frequent database update. Essential attributes of an extended logic language suitable for implementing practical reasoning machines are that it allow a clean separation to be made of proof from side effects, such as data update and propagation, and that it facilitates a declarative representation of belief update calculi. The extended logic language should contain a pure theorem proving component and a cleanly separable facility for opportunistic database update according to "reactive" or data-driven rules.

A language that embodies the reactive approach, "Sceptic", has been designed, implemented and documented as a DRUMS deliverable [6]. Sceptic is a state- or event-driven production rule interpreter written in standard Edinburgh Prolog. Sceptic rules are fired by passing "triggers" to the Sceptic interpreter and evaluating the conditions of triggered productions. Rule conditions can be arbitrary predicates (e.g. calling belief calculi) and rule actions can have any desired side-effect (e.g. to update the belief set).

This evaluate/update modularisation facilitates combination of a number of uncertainty calculi. Probabilistic, possibilistic and simple unweighted evidence combination procedures which compute degrees of belief in propositions are implemented in pure Prolog without side-effects. Invocation of calculi is controlled by a reactive harness written in Sceptic, which updates and provides belief maintenance over the central belief database. Several prototype programs have been written by our group using this approach. However, although these programs demonstrate that distinct calculi can be easily coupled, they are unsatisfactory in that they fail to provide an integrated framework for multiple calculi. Current work is directed at correcting this.

4. Current Work

A number of separate pieces of work are being carried out to explore distinct aspects of using and combining numerical and non-numerical uncertainty calculi. These work packages are intended to inform the design of the final language.

4.1 Metrics for uncertainty under total ignorance.

This work assumes that we can construct the dependency graph by standard deductive methods but that we may have no source of information about weights on the edges. The question is addressed as to whether it is possible to compute a measure of relative uncertainty of the terminal nodes based solely on the topological properties of the graph. (For example it has often been suggested that the longer a line of reasoning, such as the path between an evidence node and a conclusion node, the less reliable the conclusion.) Dohnal [2] shows how the necessary minimum conditions for forming a metric may be met on such graphs and, with additional assumptions on how uncertainty should "distribute" over the graph, numerical values for the uncertainty of beliefs (nodes) can be obtained. The additional assumptions, however, are application-specific and the technique can provide no guidance as to what may be the appropriate assumptions for any given application.

4.2 Semiqualitative arithmetic.

This work addresses the situation where weights are available for some edges in the belief network but not for others. If evidences are presented that only connect to conclusions through fully weighted paths then standard propagation techniques can be used. If, however, unweighted edges are encountered the appropriate computations are undefined. We have therefore investigated an idea from qualitative reasoning that the standard arithmetic operators can be redefined to accept qualitative values (e.g. +, -), but extending the idea by allowing the operators to accept real numbers (e.g. probabilities) as well so that in the mixed case propagation can continue. However if we assume that the qualitative +/- represent numbers whose sign we know but not their magnitude (cf. Wellman's qualitative probability) we lose all the information (precision) provided by those weights which are available, and in certain conditions the revised operators still have undefined results[4]. However it appears that if we interpret +/- as intervals these difficulties can be overcome [9].

4.3   Argumentation as a unifying inference mechanism.

The aim of this work package is to provide a single computational schema capable of accommodating monotonic and non-monotonic deduction, and qualitative and quantitative weights on inference steps. As mentioned in the section 2., we are developing a logic of argumentation (LA) which is used to identify the appropriate structuring of a problem in a specific context. In classical logic we have a simple notion of syntactic entailment. If a proposition P is deducible from a knowledge-base KB, we write:

$$KB \vdash P$$

One valid proof suffices to establish this entailment. In LA, a proposition P is derived with associated qualifier S_p, and grounds G_p:

$$KB \vdash (P, S_p, G_p)$$

The qualifier S_p may be taken from a symbolic or a numerical dictionary, and represents the force and sign of the associated argument concerning P. The grounds G_p are represented by a label summarising the proof that has been used to establish P. Different proofs and/or different qualifiers represent different arguments concerning P, and in general each proposition P will have a set of proofs, represented by triples (P, S_{pi}, G_{pi}), associated with it. The union of grounds over all arguments corresponds to the standard dependency network.

In order for some comparison of the degrees of belief in competing hypotheses to be made, the qualifiers associated with each hypothesis must be aggregated over all arguments. [7] contains some discussion of the desirable properties of a suitable aggregation operator. Its exact form will, of course, depend on the uncertainty calculus (or calculi) represented by the qualifiers and the complexity of the interactions between proofs. For example, in the simple improper linear model with uniform weighting, aggregation is a straightforward counting up of arguments. If the qualifiers are probabilities, on the other hand, aggregation may involve a calculation over the entire dependency network.

It is intended that the "qualifiers" of arguments can be qualitative, quantitative or mixed; current work is intended to establish whether this can in fact be the case. However, based on our practical experience in developing systems, our interests lean towards developing symbolic techniques of "argumentation". A nice property of the formalisation is that conclusions are theory-relative so that contradictions (which can arise if, say, knowledge base theories are inconsistent) are also theory-relative, with the result that at the meta-level there are no contradictions. This permits explicit detection of, and reasoning about, contradiction at the meta-level.

4.4 Qualitative equivalence of quantitative calculi.

The work in section 4.2 has led to the conjecture that quantitative belief representations and their associated calculi have the same formal qualitative structure - i.e. at the qualitative level they will produce identical qualitative results notwithstanding differences in the formal semantics. If this proves to be correct it would provide a basis for combining uncertainty values for dependency networks where edges in the graph have weights of different types. This possibility is currently being investigated.

5. A Logic Language Incorporating Multiple Belief Representations.

It is currently anticipated that the extended logic language will be based on a refined version of Sceptic. This language, "Stoic", will have no built in facilities for uncertainty management but is intended to provide a well-defined interface for incorporating alternative inference methods based on the framework of argumentation which was discussed in the previous section. The following is a simplified outline of the basic functionality of the language "Stoic".

Terms can be processed in imperative ("tell") mode or interrogative ("ask") mode:

tell(Term) If Term is not currently in the database add it and propagate all its logical implications. Propagation rules are written as productions.

ask(Term, Result) Generate the set of provable instances of Term given the current database state and return them as Result. Proofs are executed in Prolog.

User queries and production conditions are evaluated by the ask/2 proof procedure. By default this is Prolog, but this can be changed to a user-defined proof procedure. As mentioned, a procedure which carries out argumentation rather than proof will be available in the final version. As with the language Sceptic there is a clean separation between proof and action. Actions are handled using an extended production rule component of Stoic:

procedure stoic(Sentence)

1 Initialise the list variable Trigs to the empty list and term variable Term to Sentence.
2 Append Term to Trigs.
3 Set the term variable Current_term equal to the head of Trigs.
4 If Current_term is neither a primitive nor a production trigger then assert Current_term in the Stoic database.
5 If Current_term is a primitive (built-in) function then call the function.
6 If Current_term unifies with the trigger of a Stoic rule then:
   a. attempt to prove the conjunction of the rule conditions on the current database, using the predicate ask/2.
   b. for each successful instance of the conjunction unify all bound variables of the condition with matching free variables in the rule actions.
   c. for each instantiated action term append it to Trigs.
7 Set Trigs to the tail of Trigs.
8 If Trigs is the empty list then halt, otherwise go to 3.

6. Modifying Stoic To Accommodate Multiple Uncertainty Calculations

Stoic's default operation is to test database conditions using the prolog theorem prover, but its functionality can be changed by redefining ask/2. In the proposed language this will be modified to execute a two-phase argumentation procedure as follows:

(i) arguments for/against a goal proposition are constructed using the application-specific knowledge base.

(ii) belief in the goal proposition is evaluated by aggregating the arguments for the proposition and their associated qualifiers.

Appropriate database update and belief maintenance rules are assumed in the definition of tell/ 1. The operation of these procedures can be changed by redefining the rules. At least two update procedures will be supplied as library procedures.

A number of quantitative and qualitative types (e.g. point/interval probabilities, possibilities and the symbolic +/- type) and the appropriate belief evaluation procedure will be supplied in a library. These are defined using a generic protocol; if additional uncertainty types are required then a set of type descriptions and a suitable revision procedure must be defined.

To cope with the possibility of mixed uncertainty types in an application, a built in mechanism for semiqualitative combination of uncertainty values will be provided. The generality of this mechanism will depend upon whether our conjecture of section 4.4 that different uncertainty mechanisms have identical properties at the qualitative level proves to be correct.

7. Summary

We have discussed a variety of work packages which are directed towards enabling a variety of symbolic and numerical techniques to be integrated in a practical reasoning environment. The approach we have taken in this work has very much been driven by our past experience at developing complete systems. Our hope is that by taking this approach, we may both inform and exploit the more theoretical work which is in progress within the DRUMS programme.

References:

[1] Dawes R M, 1979, "The robust beauty of improper linear models in decision making", *American Psychologist* 34 pp 571-582.

[2] Dohnal M, Krause P and Parsons S, 1991, *Using symbolic distances among heterogeneous hypotheses as a relative measure of their uncertainty* Technical Report, Advanced Computation Laboratory, Imperial Cancer Research Fund.

[3] Fox J, 1986, "Three Arguments for Extending the Framework of Probability" in Kanal L N and Lenner J F (eds), *Uncertainty and Artificial Intelligence,* Elsevier Science Publishers.

[4] Fox J and Krause P J, 1990, "Combining symbolic and numerical methods for defeasible reasoning" *Proceedings of Colloquium on Uncertainty Management*, Institute of Electrical Engineers, London.

[5] Fox J and Krause P J, 1991, "Symbolic Decision Theory and Autonomous Systems" in D'Ambrosio B D, Smets P and Bonissone P P (eds), *Uncertainty in Artificial Intelligence: Proceedings of the Seventh Conference*, San Mateo, Calif.: Morgan Kaufmann.

[6] Hajnal S, Fox J and Krause P, 1990, *Sceptic User Manual* Technical Report, Advanced Computation Laboratory, Imperial Cancer Research Fund.

[7] Krause P J and Fox J, 1991 "Combining symbolic and numerical methods for reasoning un-

der uncertainty" in *AI and Computer Power: The Impact on Statistics*, Unicom Seminars Ltd.

[8] Lauritzen S L and Spiegelhalter D, 1988, "Local computations with probabilities on graphical structures and their application to expert systems" *J Roy. Statist. Soc.* **B 50** (2) pp 157-224.

[9] Parsons S and Fox J, 1991, "Qualitative and interval algebras for robust decision making under uncertainty" in *Proceedings of IMACS Workshop on Qualitative Reasoning and Decision Support Systems*, Toulouse, France.

[10] Pearl J, 1988, *Probabilistic Reasoning in Intelligent Systems: Networks of Plausible Inference*, San Mateo, Calif.: Morgan Kaufmann.

[11] Shafer G, Shenoy P and Mellouli, 1987, "Propagating Belief Functions in Qualitative Markov Trees", *International Journal of Approximate Reasoning* **1** pp 349-400.

[12] Wellman M P, 1990, "Fundamental Concepts of Qualitative Probabilistic Networks", *Artificial Intelligence* **44** pp 257-303.

Graded Default Logics

Christine Froidevaux, Philippe Chatalic, Jérôme Mengin

LRI - URA 410 CNRS

Université Paris 11

F-91405 ORSAY

email: chris@lri.lri.fr

1. Motivation

When dealing with incomplete information, one can have many kinds of reasoning. Thus there exists several logics for representing them. The Research Program 1.2 intends to use the technique of modelling a logic by means of another in order to investigate their similarities and differences.

Especially, this Research Program was devoted to the study of two particular logics:
- default logic, (which is a symbolic logic that aims at modelling defeasible reasoning), and
- possibilistic logic, (a numerical logic which allows to represent different levels of certainty of the pieces of knowledge, by means of numbers),
and to the definition of graded default logic.

2. Defeasible and uncertain reasoning

There are many situations in which intelligent agents have to reason with incomplete information. Thus the information about the world is better described as beliefs than as knowledge. We are here interested in two aspects of beliefs. On the one hand, beliefs may have strengths, in the sense that some beliefs may appear more certain than others. These different degrees of certainty can be revealed by expressions in natural language such as :
> May be it will rain tomorrow.
> It is highly probable that he will come.
> Certainly he will send a letter next week.

On the other hand, beliefs may be defeasible, in the sense that they may be retracted if they are found to be false. Let us take the famous example about birds.
> Tweety is a bird
> Penguins do not fly
> Birds fly (normally).

We would like to conclude that Tweety flies.
Now, if we later discover that Tweety is a penguin, we no longer want to infer that Tweety flies. In this case, new beliefs can invalidate previously deduced beliefs. This property is called nonmonotonicity and arises in any kind of default reasoning.
These two aspects of beliefs can be combined as shown in the following example [7], where defaults are more or less certain.
> Generally when Bob attends a meeting then Mary does not
> Generally when Albert comes, the meeting is not quiet
> The fact that Mary and Bob do not attend the same meeting is less certain than the
fact that Albert's presence makes the meeting not quiet.

3. Graded logic

Our approach is in accordance with the principles of possibilistic logic [6, 7], which are based on the evaluation of a preorder.

When uncertain beliefs are used in some reasoning, the deduced beliefs should not be more certain that each of the beliefs used in this deduction (*principle 1*). Similarly, if a belief can be obtained in several ways, with different grades, then its degree of certainty is greater than or equal to each of these grades (*principle 2*). With partially ordered values, this leads us naturally to consider greatest lower bounds and least upper bounds of grades. As a consequence, the set of all possible grades will be considered as a lattice [3]. It is worth noticing that formulas known with full certainty also can be considered as graded formulas having a particular grade T, which is greater than any other mentioned grade. Thus, we use the lattice generated by T and the grades appearing in the knowledge base.

Graded logic [5] deals with graded formulas. A *graded formula* consists in a pair $(f\ \alpha)$, where f is a classical formula called *support* and α is a *grade*, which reflects a minimum confidence we have in the support. The grade represents a *lower bound of the degree of certainty* of this formula. Note that a lower bound merely states some constraint on the degree of certainty but is not the degree itself. This agrees with the fact that it represents only a *minimal* confidence. Thus, in our framework, it is possible to have various graded formulas with the same support but with different grades.

We restrict ourselves to the case of propositional formulas. Extension of the following notions to the case of first order graded calculus is discussed at the end of [5].

Definition 1 : Let *Prop* be a set of propositional variables and let P be the propositional language over *Prop*. Let Γ_0 be a finite set of partially ordered grades and $(\Gamma, \wedge, \vee, \leq)$ the free distributive lattice generated by $\Gamma_0 \cup \{T\}$, such that T is the greatest element of Γ. The **language** of graded formulas induced by P and Γ is the set $L_{P,\Gamma} = \{(f\ \alpha)\ /\ f \in P, \alpha \in \Gamma\}$.
Let $S \subseteq L_{P,\Gamma}$, the support of S is defined as the set $\overline{S} = \{f\ /\ \exists \alpha \in \Gamma, (f\ \alpha) \in S\}$.

The symbol $\leq$ is used to represent the partial order defined on the set of grades Γ. Symbols $\wedge$ and $\vee$ denote respectively the *meet* and *join* operations defined on Γ. Then, $\alpha \wedge \beta$ represents the greatest lower bound (*glb*) of α and β, and $\alpha \vee \beta$ represents their least upper bound (*lub*).

A natural way to extend a classical formal system is to keep the same axiom schemes (graded by $\sqrt{}$) and to specify for each inference rule, how the grade of the conclusion is obtained.

In the following we propose a natural extension Σ_Γ of the well-known Hilbert system :

GA1) $(p \rightarrow (q \rightarrow p)\quad T)$

GA2) $((p \rightarrow (q \rightarrow r)) \rightarrow ((p \rightarrow q) \rightarrow (p \rightarrow r))\ T)$

GA3) $((p \rightarrow q) \rightarrow (\neg q \rightarrow \neg p)\ T)$

$$\frac{\begin{array}{ll}(p & \alpha\ ) \\ (p \rightarrow q & \beta\ )\end{array}}{(q \qquad \alpha \wedge \beta\ )} \quad (R1)$$

Rule R1 extends the classical modus ponens and is called the **graded modus ponens** inference rule. This rule specifies that the grade of the conclusion cannot be greater than any of the grades used in the premises, that it must be comparable to each of them and that we choose the best one satisfying these constraints. This is in accordance with principle 1.

We propose two additional inference rules:

$$\frac{(p\quad \alpha\ )}{(p\quad \beta\ )\ \forall\ \beta \leq \alpha} \quad (R2) \qquad\qquad \frac{\begin{array}{ll}(p & \alpha\ ) \\ (p & \beta\ )\end{array}}{(p \quad \alpha \vee \beta\ )} \quad (R3)$$

Both of these rules are intuitively satisfactory. The **weakening rule R2** merely says that if α is a lower bound of the degree of certainty of p, any $\beta \leq \alpha$ will also be such a lower bound. Similarly, the **strengthening rule R3** says that if both α and β are lower bounds of the degree of certainty of p, their least upper bound $\alpha \vee \beta$ must also be a lower bound of the certainty degree of p, which agrees with principle 2.

The distributivity property allows one to perform inferences rules in any order.

The notion of derivablity is defined in a classical way. The set of theorems of a graded theory S over Γ will be denoted by $Th_\Gamma(S)$.

Example : Let $S = \{ (p \quad \alpha), (r \quad \gamma), (p \rightarrow q \quad \beta), (r \rightarrow s \quad \delta) \}$. Assume we know that $\gamma \leq \alpha$ and $\delta \leq \beta$ and nothing else. Two deductions may be performed using the graded modus ponens rule:

Using R_1, from $(p \quad \alpha)$ and $(p \rightarrow q \quad \beta)$ we deduce $(q \quad \alpha \wedge \beta)$ and from $(r \quad \gamma)$ and $(r \rightarrow s \quad \delta)$ we deduce $(s \quad \delta \wedge \gamma)$.

Notice that although the degrees of certainty of p and $p \rightarrow q$ (respectively r and $r \rightarrow s$) are not comparable, we obtain that we have more confidence into q than into s since $\delta \wedge \gamma \leq \alpha \wedge \beta$.

4. Graded default logic

We have seen how the introduction of degrees of certainty into classical logic by means of elements of a lattice leads to a new uncertainty logic. This formalism is essentially based on the graded modus ponens rule. An interesting feature of this approach is that its principles can be preserved under nonmonotonic inference. In order to formalize human reasoning with uncertain and defeasible beliefs, we could reasonably attempt to associate with nonmonotonic inference rules degrees of certainty. In fact, this is straightforward for default rules of Reiter's formalism [13, 1]. A first version of graded default logic has been introduced by Froidevaux & Grossetête [9, 10], and a generalization of this concept is proposed in [5].

The set of beliefs will be translated into a graded default theory. Let us recall that a default d is a specific nonmonotonic inference rule of the form (u : v / w), where u, v and w are elements of *P*; u is called the *prerequisite* of d, v its *justification* and w its *consequent*. A default without prerequisite is considered as being of the form (true : v / w). A *graded default* over a lattice Γ is an inference rule of the form (u : v / w $\quad \alpha$), with α in Γ.

Definition 2 : A graded default theory Δ is defined as the union of a set of graded formulas W and of a set of graded defaults D.

As a default can be considered as a specific (nonmonotonic) inference rule, we can apply principle 1 to it. More precisely, if a graded default d = (u : v / w $\quad \beta$) can be activated, that is, if its prerequisite u is known with some grade α and nothing contradicts v, then we infer w with the grade $\alpha \wedge \beta$, according to principle 1. Note that the activation of d is blocked if v is inconsistent, whatever the degree of certainty of $\neg v$ may be.

Now we combine specific graded inference rules and fixpoint characterization in order to define sets of graded nonmonotonic theorems.

Definition 3 : Let $\Delta = D \cup W$ be a graded default theory and E be a set of graded formulas. The sequence $(E_i)_{i \geq 0}$ is defined as follows :

$E_0 = W$ and for $i \geq 0$,

$E_{i+1} = Th_\Gamma (E_i \cup \{ (w \quad \alpha \wedge \beta) / (u : v / w \quad \beta) \in D, (u \quad \alpha) \in E_i \text{ and } \neg v \notin \overline{E} \})$.

E is a **graded extension** for Δ iff $E = \cup_{i \geq 0} E_i$.

Graded default theories are obviously connected to default theories as defined by Reiter. More precisely graded extensions are closely linked to classical extensions.

Theorem [10] : Let $\Delta = D \cup W$ be a graded default theory, F a set of formulas and E a set of graded formulas. If E is a graded extension for Δ then $\overline{E}$ is an extension of $(\overline{D}, \overline{W})$.

Conversely, if F is an extension for (D , W) there is some graded extension for (D , W) such that $F = \overline{E}$.

From this, it results that a graded default theory may have one extension, more than one extension or no extension at all. Moreover an extension of D ∪ W is Γ-consistent iff W is Γ-consistent. Also, graded default logic satisfies the nonmonotonicity property.

5. Links with possibilistic logic

Our treatment of uncertainty is closely related to *possibilistic logic*, a formalism introduced by Dubois and al. [7] as a numerical logic of uncertainty. Possibilistic logic handles uncertainty by means of two dual measures, a necessity measure and a possibility measure, both mapping the set of sentences into the interval [0,1]. The semantics of possibilistic logic is defined by using fuzzy sets of classical interpretations.
Our approach adopts and generalizes the principles that govern necessity measures, by considering that the grades are not necessarily numerical values and do not constitute any more a totally ordered set. It is worth noticing that graded logic corresponds to a possibilistic logic handling merely necessity measures.
A possibilistic theory where only necessity degrees are used is a set S of pairs (f α), where f is a closed well formed formula of propositional calculus, and $\alpha \in [0, 1]$ a lower bound of its necessity. It is possible to translate such a theory into a graded default theory (D, W) , graded on a totally ordered lattice. Then W contains all the elements of S of the form (a,1), and where an element (f α) of S with α<1 is translated into the free default (: f / f), to which is attached the coefficient α.
 Graded extensions have been proved to correspond to maximally consistent subbases of possibilistic theories. In fact, multiple sets of beliefs are not allowed in possibilistic logic. Conflicting beliefs do not yield alternative sets of beliefs but give an α-consistent base. Assume that C is such an α-consistent set of clauses. Then Dubois and Prade consider as valid all the formulas obtained by resolution from C with a grade strictly greater than α [7] .
In order to get a closer connection between graded theorems and possibilistic theorems, we have to modify slightly our definition of graded extension.

We successively activate the defaults in a decreasing order, level by level. If we discover at some level two contradictory defaults, then the process is stopped, and only the formulas obtained in the preceding levels are kept. Since the defaults are considered level by level, in a decreasing order, as soon as we obtain a formula f with a grade α, we are sure that no best lower bound can be later discovered. Thus we defined *linear extensions* [10].

Our formalism is more expressive than possibilistic logic in the sense that it enables us to express uncertain beliefs in a distinct way depending on whether they are defeasible or not.

6. A theorem prover for free graded default theories

A default is said to be free when it has the form (: f / f). In this case it is possible to give a proof theoretic definition of a nonmonotonic theorem of free graded default theory. [2] presented a theorem prover based on this definition of a nonmonotonic theorem; this theorem prover uses a resolution strategy which was introduced by Bossu and Siegel [4]. In order to adapt it to free graded default theory, this resolution strategy is extended to the graded logic underlying the coefficient propagation used in graded default logic. Then the theorem prover [11] is extended to add this coefficient propagation. Notice that this theorem prover is incremental, in the sense that adding a new free graded default, or asking a new question, does not imply that the theorem prover restarts its computation from the beginning, but just computes a further step. The general case of free graded default theories lacks the proof theoretic definition of a nonmonotonic graded theorem (as we have to look for the "best coefficient" that we can find for a formula, there cannot be any "local proof"). But in the case where the order among the defaults is total, a proof procedure which directly goes to the maximal coefficient we can find for a formula, is described. Then the introduction of the coefficients does not increase the complexity of the theorem prover.

7. Future work and conclusion

In this paper we have proposed a framework to handle uncertainty in a logical setting. The graded logic has been defined and we have applied its basic principles to the case of default logic. These principles could also be applied to other nonmonotonic logics. We are now investigating this point in the research program RP 1.1. Recently Philippe Besnard and Wilmer Pereira have proposed to introduce grades into another nonmonotonic formalism, namely Siegel's supposition logic [14] (research program RP 1.3).

Our presentation of graded logic is restricted to the propositional case. We are now formalizing graded first-order theories

Several attempts have been done to translate the two dual measures of possibilistic logic into modal logic. Recent work by Farinas [8] uses a multimodal logic. We are now studying a multimodal approach for graded logic, with a Kripke's semantics. In order to do this, we extend the language of graded formulas, allowing for formulas of the form :

$$(r\ \alpha) \to (s\ \beta).$$

A search for efficient proof procedures in graded logic also would be in order. A theorem prover for only a subclass of graded default theories has been provided in [11].
New strategies involving a calculus over the lattice could be investigated. Some work along this direction has been done for the special case of possibilistic logic [6].

The existence of a link beetween possibilistic logic and our framework is due to the fact that both approaches satisfy the two basic principles we stated earlier. This is not the case for other numerical formalisms such as probabilistic settings [12] that use the principle of additivity.

This work shows how a symbolic logic can capture some features of a numerical logic, and thus allows us to handle aspects of both nonmonotonic and uncertain reasoning. This work is a first step towards the integration of possibilistic logic and default logic and has given rise to graded supposition logic.

References

[1] Besnard P. (1989), *An introduction to default logic*, Springer Verlag, Heidelberg.
[2] Besnard P. Quiniou R, & Quinton P., (1983), A theorem prover for a decidable subset of first order logic, Proc. of AAAI-83, Washington D.C., 27-30.
[3] Birkhoff G. (1973), *Lattice Theory*, American Mathematical Society Colloquium Publications, vol. XXV.
[4] Bossu G. and Siegel P., (1985), Saturation, nonmonotonic reasoning and the closed-world assumption, Artificial Intelligence 25, 13-63.
[5] Chatalic P. and Froidevaux C. (1991), *Graded logics: A framework for uncertain and defeasible knowledge*, Proc. of the Int. Symp. on Methodologies and Intelligent Systems, ISMIS-91, Charlotte.
[6] Dubois D. Lang J. and Prade H., (1987), *Theorem proving under uncertainty - A possibilistic theory-based approach*, Proc. of the 10th IJCAI, Milan, 984-986.
[7] Dubois D. and Prade H. (with the collaboration of Farreny H., Martin-Clouaire R., Testemale C.) (1988), *Possibility Theory: An approach to computerized processing of uncertainty*. Plenum Press, New-York.
[8] Farinas del Cerro L., Herzig A. (1991), *A modal analysis of possibility theory*, Proc. of Fundamentals of Artificial Intelligence Research (FAIR' 91) Smolenice, Czechoslovakia, sept. 8-12, 1991. Springer Verlag.
[9] Froidevaux C. and Grossetête C. (1989), *Graded default theories* , Proc. of the Workshop on Nonmonotonic Reasoning, GMD, Sankt-Augustin, December 13-15, 1989, 179-187.
[10] Froidevaux C. and Grossetête C. (1990), *Graded default theories for uncertainty*, Proc. of the 9th ECAI, Stockholm, 283-288. Also in Proc. of DRUMS Workshop, Marseille, February 24-27, 1990.

[11] Mengin J. (1991), *A theorem prover for free default graded theories*, Technical report LRI n° 637, University Paris 11. Also in Proc. of DRUMS Workshop, Albi, 1990.
[12] Nilsson N.J. (1986) *Probabilistic logic*, Artificial Intelligence 28, 71-87.
[13] Reiter R. (1980) *A logic for default reasoning*, Artificial Intelligence 13, 81-132.
[14] Siegel P. and Schwind C., Hypothesis theory for nonmonotonic reasoning, submitted.

Linguistically expressed uncertainty: its elicitation and use in modular expert systems

L. Godo, R. Lopez de Mantaras

Institut d'Investigació en Intel.ligència Artificial
Centre d'Estudis Avançats de Blanes, CSIC
Camí Sta. Barbara, s/n,
17300 Blanes,

Abstract

This paper describes the work performed in the ESPRIT Basic Research Action DRUMS, on the elicitation and use of finite sets of linguistic espressions of uncertainty within modular expert systems. Such finite sets of linguistic terms, together with their connective operators define multiple-valued local logics associated to different modules implementing different subtasks of the expert system. Taking this into account, our aim was twofold: first, to provide a general logical framework in order to be able to work simultaneously with several local multiple-valued logics, and second, to develop a software tool to help in the process of the elicitation of the linguistic expressions and of the connective operators within these local logics.

1. A General Logical Framework

Many of the uncertainty management methods used in expert systems can be considered as the set of mechanisms that a certain underlying multiple-valued local logic supplies: certainty values (either numerical or linguistic) would be truth-values of that logic, the rules in a knowledge base would be a set of axioms and, finally, the mechanisms of uncertainty combination and propagation would be the set of inference rules. Then, inference engines are nothing more than implementations of proof calculi of these multiple-valued logical systems. As it is known, every logical system should have both a syntactical and semantical formalizations. The obtention of a *general logical framework* has been made by modelling multiple-valued logics as Institutions and as Entailment Systems. The theories of "institutions" (Goguen and Burstall, 1983) and Entailment Systems (Meseguer, 1989) formalize the intuitive notion of a logical system from the model and proof theoretic point of view respectively. The concept of "General Logic" given by Meseguer in (Meseguer, 1989) takes into account both approaches, besides introducing the notion of "proof calculus". In such framework, any commitment to particular logical systems is avoided by defining general logical structures once and for all at the more general level of instituions or entailment systems (Harper, Sannella and Tarlecki, 1989).

Along this line, we have shown that multiple-valued logics can be structured as families of institutions, parametrized by a class of truth-values algebras (Agustí-Cullell, Esteva, Garcia and Godo, 1990). A class of truth-values algebra is specified by a set of axioms, usually equations, that the operations of these algebras (i.e., the logical connective operators) must fulfil. Then, for each particular algebra an institution is defined by: 1) a category of signatures, giving vocabularies for the language and, for each signature; 2) the set of sentences of the language (usual sentences together with a subset of truth-values); 3) the class of models, which give meaning to the sentences by interpreting the relation symbols as "fuzzy relations" whose membership functions take values in the truth-values algebra; 4) a satisfaction relation between models and sentences, invariant under signature morphisms. On the other hand, given a category of signatures and the sentences of the language, an associated Entailment System can be defined by an entailment relation between sentences generated from a set of sound inference rules and a set of logical axioms.

The possibility of relating several local logics to allow communication between modules within a modular expert system with uncertainty management capabilities is then based on the notion of institution morphism and/or mapping of entailment systems. It has been shown that each morphism of truth-values algebras generates a corresponding institution morphism. This is a very general result that must be particularized to the entailment systems approach since the most interesting mappings relating different local logics in modular expert systems are those that preserve inference.

2. Mappings of Entailment Systems.

For our purposes of analyzing inference preserving mappings between local logics defined by entailment systems, it is enough to consider such Entailment Systems as pairs $(L, |\text{-})$, where L is a language (a set of sentences), and $|\text{-}$ is an entailment relation defined on $2^L x L$.

Let M and M' be two modules of a modular expert system, and $(L, |\text{-})$ and $(L', |\text{-}')$ their corresponding logics. To establish a correspondence from module M to module M', a mapping $H: L \dashrightarrow L'$ relating their languages, is needed. In (Agustí et al., 91) we have analyzed three natural requirements for the mapping H with respect to the entailment systems $|\text{-}$ and $|\text{-}'$. These requirements are the following ones:

RQ-1.   *If $\Gamma |\text{-} e$, then $H(\Gamma) |\text{-}' H(e)$*

where Γ and e respectively denote a set of formulas and a formula of L. This requirement corresponds to the definition proposed by J. Meseguer in (Meseguer, 89) for mappings of entailment systems. With this requirement we assure that for every formula deducible from a set of formulas Γ in M, its correspondent formula in M' by the mapping, H(e), will also be deducible in M' from the correspondent formulas of H(Γ). In other words, there is no inferential power lost when translating from M to M' through a mapping H satisfying RQ-1. Nevertheless the main drawback of requirement RQ-1 is that it does not forbid to deduce from H(Γ), in M', formulas that are not translations of any formula deducible from Γ in M. The property means that, in the case of modules representing different experts, an expert E' related to M', using knowledge coming from an expert E related to M, will be able to deduce the same facts than E, but not only those facts.

RQ-2.   *If H(Γ) |-' H(e), then Γ|- e*

This is the inverse requirement of RQ-1. So, in this case all deductions in M' involving only translated formulas from M are translations of deductions in M, or equivalently if a fact is not deducible in M, then its correspondent fact in M' will neither be deducible from the translated knowledge

RQ-3.   *If H(Γ) |-' e', then there exists e such that Γ|- e and H(e) |-' e'.*

This requirement assures that every formula deducible from H(Γ) in M' must be in agreement with what can be deduced from Γ in M. This requirement is slightly different from RQ-2, in the sense that it not necessary that *e'* be exactly a translation of a deducible formula *e* from Γ, but only something deducible from such a translation. In the framework of logics for uncertainty management, *e'* can be interpreted as a "weaker" form of *e*, i.e. a formula expressing more uncertainty than *e*.

Let us consider the particular case of local multiple-valued logics in MILORD (Agustí et al., 91) defined on finite truth-values algebras $A = \langle A_n, 0, 1, N, T, I \rangle$, where A_n is an ordered set of linguistic truth-values with 0 and 1 as the minimum and maximum elements respectively, N a negation operator, T a conjunction operator and I an implication operator. For each algebra A, the corresponding entailment system $(L_A, |\text{-}_A)$, relevant to MILORD, is given by the following set of axioms

(A-1) $((p_1 \& p_2) \& p_3 \dashrightarrow p_1 \& (p_2 \& p_3), 1)$
(A-2) $(p_1 \& (p_2 \& p_3) \dashrightarrow (p_1 \& p_2) \& p_3, 1)$
(A-3) $(p_1 \& p_2 \dashrightarrow p_2 \& p_1, 1)$
(A-4) $(\neg\neg p \dashrightarrow p, 1)$

and the following inference rules

(RI-1) WEAKENING: Γ, (p, V) |- (p, V'), where $V \subseteq V' \subseteq A_n$ and Γ is a set of sentences,

(RI-2) NOT-introduction: (p, V) |- ($\neg$p, N(V)),

(RI-3) AND-introduction: $(p_1, V_1), (p_2, V_2)$ |- $(p_1 \& p_2, T(V_1, V_2))$,

(RI-4) MODUS PONENS : $(p_1, V_1), (p_1 \text{-->} q_1, V_2)$ |- $(q_2, T(V_1, V_2))$.

In this case, given two algebras A and A' and an order preserving mapping h: A --> A', the next theorems give conditions for a mapping H: L_A --> $L_{A'}$ defined by H[(e,V)] = (e, h(V)) to satisfy requirements RQ-1, RQ-2 and RQ-3.

Theorem 1: The mapping H satisfies the requirement RQ-1 if, and only if, the mapping h fulfils the following conditions:

1. $h(T(V_1, V_2)) \supseteq T'(h(V_1), h(V_2))$
2. $h(N(V)) = N'(h(V))$

Theorem 2: The mapping H satisfies the requirement RQ-2 provided that the mapping h fulfils the following conditions:

1. if $h(V_1) \subseteq h(V_2)$ then $V_1 \subseteq V_2$
2. $h(T(V_1, V_2)) \subseteq T'(h(V_1), h(V_2))$
3. $h(N(V)) = N'(h(V))$

Theorem 3: The mapping H satisfies the requirement RQ-3 provided that the mapping h fulfils the following conditions:

1. $h(T(V_1, V_2)) \subseteq T'(h(V_1), h(V_2))$
2. $h(N(V)) = N'(h(V))$

From these results it is clear that if the mapping h is a morphism from A to A' then requirements RQ-1 and RQ-3 are satisfied, and if h is a monomorphism then the requirement RQ-2 is also satisfied.

3. Elicitation of connective operators

The connective operators associated to each local logic are matrices on the set of terms used by the expert to express uncertainty within each module of the expert system. These operators should reflect as closely as possible the way in which th expert combines and propagates uncertainty within each module. There is overwhelming evidence based on psychological studies (Kuipers, Moskowitz and Kassirer, 1988) about the disadvantages of having a numerical representation for the set of terms expressing uncertainty. Therefore, the central idea of our work has been the consideration of the linguistic terms as a list of ordered labels assuming no underlying numerical representation and then eliciting logical operators directly from the expert. For each logical connective, a set of desirable properties is defined and these properties act as constraints on the set of possible solutions. In this way all the operators fulfilling the set of constraints are generated and the expert may select one of them. We have shown that this elicitation process can be implemented by formulating it as a constraint satisfaction problem (Lopez de Mantaras, Godo and Sanguesa, 1990). More specifically, we have worked on two implementations, a general one for any kind of operator, and an "and" connective-oriented implementation which takes advantage of some particular constraints (associativity, commutativity, neutral element, absorbent element, and monotonicity), that are always present in the specification of these operators, to improve the efficiency of the process. Both implementations are based on an efficient forward checking algorithm.

Once the set of possible solutions is built, an heuristic is used to guide the expert in the final selection process. Futher work will include the elicitaion of the linguistic expressions of uncertainty and the generation of connective operators for partially ordered sets of linguistic terms

References

Agustí-Cullell J., Esteva F., Garcia P., Godo L. (1990) "Formalizing Multiple-valued Logics as Institutions", Abridged version in the *Proc. of the 3rd IPMU Conference*, Paris, France, July 2-6, 1990, pp. 355-357. Full version to appear in (B. Bouchon-Meunier, R.R. Yager, L.A. Zadeh, eds.), Lecture Notes in Computer Science, Springer Verlag.

Agustí-Cullell, Esteva F., Garcia P., Godo L., López de Mántaras R., Murgui L., Puyol J., Sierra C. (1991) "Structured Local Fuzzy Logics in Milord", Research Report IIIA 91/3. Artificial Intelligence Research Institute, Centre d'Estudis Avaçats de Blanes.

Goguen J., Burstall R.M. (1983) "Introducing Institutions", *Proc. Workshop on Logics of Programs*, Carnegie-Mellon University, Lectures Notes in Computer Science, Springer Verlag.

Harper R., Sannella D., Tarlecki A. (1989) "Structure and Representation in LF", *Proc. 4th IEEE Symposium on Logic of Computer Science*.

Kuipers B., Moskowitz A.J., Kassirer J.P. (1988) "Critical Decisions under Uncertainty: Representation and Structure, *Cognitive Science* 12, pp. 177-210.

López de Mántaras R., Godo L., Sanguesa R. (1990) "Connective operators Elicitation for Linguistic Term Sets", *Proc. Intl. Conference on Fuzzy Logic and Neural Networks*, Iizuka, Japan, July 20-24, 1990, pp. 729-733.

Meseguer J. (1989) "General Logics". In H.D. Ebbinghaus et al. (eds.), *Proc. Logic Colloqium'87*. North-Holland.

Reasoning with Mass Distributions and the Context Model

R. Kruse, J. Gebhardt, and F. Klawonn
Department of Computer Science
Technical University of Braunschweig
Germany

The research group *Uncertainty and Vagueness in Knowledge Based Systems* concentrates its interest mainly on numerical methods for the treatment of uncertainty and vagueness, emphasizing the importance of the use of clear semantics in the development of models. Uncertain knowledge can be represented in the framework of mass distributions (basic probability assignments), if an appropriate interpretation is chosen. Within this model the possible operations on the vague data investigated and methods for reasoning with mass distributions are derived. From a more general point of view this model can be seen as a special case of the context model, which integrates various approaches to uncertainty and vagueness like Bayes Theory, Dempster-Shafer Theory, the Transferable Belief Model, and Possibility Theory with its references to the epistemic interpretation of fuzzy sets.

Reasoning with Mass Distributions

The variety of models for the representation of knowledge with aspects of vagueness or uncertainty ranges from purely probabilistic (Bayesian) models, quantitative approaches based on measure theory to logical calculi. The different approaches aim to model several aspects of vagueness and uncertainty. But in order to decide, which model is appropriate for a certain 'real world application', it is necessary to have well-defined semantics as a basis for the model. Also the admissible operations applicable to the vague data are determined by the semantics.

One of the reasons for criticism on Dempster-Shafer Theory, especially the application of Dempster's rule of combination, which can be justified under certain assumptions (Kruse and Schwecke, 1990b), is the use of this theory without careful consideration of adequate semantics. The interpretation of belief functions as upper probabilities or as mappings induced by random sets leads to semantics in a strictly probabilistic framework, which is not always appropriate. Describing a non-probabilistic interpreation of mass distributions (basic probability assignments) leads to a model in which the concepts of Dempster-Shafer theory obtain a well-defined meaning, that determines their use or non-applicability in special situations.

In order to motivate the non-probabilistic interpretation of mass distributions, the following scenario is considered. A set of sensors (subexperts or contexts) specifies imprecise information about the domain (or universe of discourse) in the form of subsets of the domain, which contain the 'true' element. The set of sensors is assumed to be weighted with respect to their importance or reliability. Therefore, the specified subsets of the sensors together with the weights of the sensors induce a weighting of the subsets of the universe of discourse, that corresponds to a mass distribution, representing the 'measure of belief' committed to the subsets.

We always presuppose the closed world assumption for our universe of discourse. This does not impose any restrictions on our model, since in the case of the open world assumption for the sample space, we can consider an extended universe of discourse with an additional element which represents the unknown, but possible elements not contained in Ω and therefore, the closed world assumption holds for the extended universe of discourse.

According to the closed world assumption each sensor should be able to specify a *nonempty* subset of possible elements. However, some of the sensors might be faulty or unable to specify a certain set. These sensors have to be neglected and their weights have to be redistributed among the remaining sensors.

Different updating schemes like Dempster's rule of combination and strong conditioning can be distinguished in this model by the treatment of sensors that specified (partially) contradicting information (Kruse, Nauck, and Klawonn, 1991).

The universe of discourse, that is considered, is sometimes only a coarse representation of an inaccessible refined space, where sets of indistinguishable elements correspond to a single element in the coarser space. In this case we can only see the projection of the mass distribution on the refined space to the coarser space. A new evidence in the (refined) space would lead to an updated mass distribution in the coarser space, carrying more information. Using this notion we can compare mass distributions, where those mass distributions that are updatings of others, represent more specific information, and are therefore called specializations (Kruse and Schwecke, 1990a). It turns out that the idea of specialization can also be interpreted as a flow of evidence masses, floating from supersets to subsets.

Specialization is a very general concept, in whose terms updating schemes but also propagation of knowledge can be described. This property is exploited in a tool for data fusion applications (Kruse, Schwecke, and Klawonn, 1991), where the universe of discourse is a product space composed of various sample spaces, each representing a characteristic of the domain. The qualitative dependencies of the characteristics are encoded in a hypertree, in which the cyclic dependencies are eliminated (Kruse and Schwecke, 1989), whereas mass distributions and specialization matrices are used for the qualitative knowledge. The propagation algorithm is based on the assumption that the computation can be carried out in (small) subspaces of the product space involving only a few characteristics with direct dependencies. This leads to an efficient algorithm, which is suitable for utilization of parallel computer architectures.

The concept of specialization and the propagation algorithm are not restricted to belief functions but can also be applied within other frameworks for the representation of vague or uncertain knowledge such as probability theory or fuzzy sets (Kruse and Schwecke, 1990c, Kruse, Schwecke, and Heinsohn, 1991).

The Context Model

One of the most important problems in the area of vagueness and uncertainty modelling is the fact that the foundations of some popular models have not been clarified for a long time. As a consequence many a criticism on these models (f.e.: application of belief functions and fuzzy sets) is still pending.

There is no doubt about the need for a clear semantics of data and operations on them in an environment of partial ignorance. Otherwise the dangerous situation may occur that the incautious use of ad-hoc models gives arise for inconsistencies and paradoxial behaviour as known from applications of the Certainty Factor Model in expert systems.

For this reason Gebhardt and Kruse (1991) have developed the Context Model which provides a formal framework for the handling of vagueness and uncertainty and supports a better understanding and comparison of existing models like given by Bayes Theory, Dempster-Shafer Theory, Transferable Belief Theory, and Possibility Theory with its references to the epistemic interpretation of fuzzy sets.

The Context Model is based on the idea of generalizing crisp characterizations of objects (i.e.: tuples of attribute values that belong to domains of appropriate data types) to an environment of vagueness and uncertainty.

In our approach vagueness is related to the specification of so-called vague characteristics that formalize imprecise, perhaps contradicting and partly incorrect representations of the corresponding object's characterization within a finite number of consideration contexts.

Uncertainty, on the other hand, is connected with the additional valuation of vague characteristics, since a decision maker should be enabled to quantify his or her degree of belief in the chosen specification. So the theory of measurement appears to be the adequate tool for the representation of uncertainty aspects, whereas vague characteristics are defined to be mappings from an appropriate set of contexts into the set of all subsets of a given domain.

Valuated vague characteristics are either interpreted as objects (physical point of view) or as specifications of vague observations of inaccessible crisp characteristics (epistemic point of view). In both cases reasonable operations on vague characteristics have to be defined. So we have considered specialization (f.e.: context conditioning, data revision), combination, connection, refinement, coarsening and other operations that are necessary in the field of data fusion.

It turns out that the Bayesian approach and the Dempster-Shafer-Smets approach to the modelling of vagueness and uncertainty coincide with special types of valuated vague characteristics and the mentioned operations on them.

Related to a given decision problem the typical structuring used in Bayes Theory is conform to so-called fuzzy-precise valuated characteristics due to sets of exhaustively separated contexts, whereas the typical Dempster-Shafer-Smets structuring tends to coincide with the application of valuated vague characteristics with respect to simplified consideration contexts. Context coarsening and the resulting loss of information emphasizes the approximative properties of the Dempster-Shafer-Smets Model, which, of course, reduces the complexity of inference and decision making processes in practice. A further loss of information has to be accepted, whenever Possibility Theory is chosen to be applied.

References

Gebhardt J., Kruse R. (1991) The Context Model - A Uniform Approach to Vagueness and Uncertainty. In R. Lowen and M. Roubens (Eds.): Proceedings of the 4th IFSA Congress: Computer, Management & System Science, IFSA, Brussels, 82-85

Kruse R., Nauck D., Klawonn F. (1991) Reasoning with Mass Distributions. In: B.D. D'Ambrosio, P. Smets, P.P. Bonissone (eds.). Uncertainty in Artificial Intelligence: Proceedings of the Seventh Conference. San Mateo, Calif., Morgan Kaufmann, 182-187

Kruse R., Schwecke E. (1989) On the Treatment of Cyclic Dependencies in Causal Networks. Proc. 3rd IFSA Congress, Seattle, 416-419

Kruse R., Schwecke E. (1990a) Specialisation - A New Concept for Uncertainty Handling with Belief Functions. International Journal of General Systems 18, 49-60

Kruse R., Schwecke E. (1990b) On the Combination of Information Sources. Proc. 3rd IPMU Conference, Paris, 440-442

Kruse R., Schwecke E. (1990c) Fuzzy Reasoning in a Multidimensional Space of Hypotheses. Int. J. Approximate Reasoning 4, 47-68

Kruse R., Schwecke E., Heinsohn J. (1991) Uncertainty Handling in Knowledge Based Systems: Numerical Methods. Series Artificial Intelligence, Springer, Berlin

Kruse R., Schwecke E., Klawonn F. (1991) On a Tool for Reasoning with Mass Distributions. Proc. 12th International Joint Conference on Artificial Intelligence, Sidney, Morgan Kaufmann (to appear)

Advance Prototyping

Simon Parsons

Department of Electronic Engineering, Queen Mary and Westfield College
Mile End Road, London E1 4NS, UK.

1. Introduction

The goal of this research is the construction of a prototype reasoning system that deals with uncertainty by using more than one uncertainty handling formalism. This activity is motivated by our belief that no single formalism is adequate for describing real world problems exactly, so that the use of several formalisms in combination will always produce better results than a single formalism. As a result we are interested both in ways of combining information expressed in different formalisms, and in ways of using several formalisms in combination to solve reasoning problems. We have approached this task from the application point of view, selecting a reasoning task that involves dealing with a real world problem in which the uncertainty cannot be easily "shoehorned" into a single uncertainty handling formalism. The chosen problem, that of assessing the validity of predictions of protein topology, is discussed in Section 2. In the absence of strong theoretical results on how information expressed in different formalisms might be combined, we have looked for practical, yet sound, methods of combination that do not require such deep theoretical foundations. The more promising of the approaches we have investigated are discussed in Section 3, and Section 4 describes how they may be used to integrate different forms of knowledge in our prototype system.

2. Problem description

The problem chosen as the basis of the prototype reasoning system was that of guiding the constraint based search for predictions of protein topology, by providing certainty values for classes of predictions based upon the relative strengths of the constraints that the predictions conform with.

2.1 Protein topology prediction

Proteins are complex biological macromolecules that form the main components of living organisms and control most biological processes. The three dimensional structure of proteins is closely linked to their function, and this makes knowledge of their structure highly important. Unfortunately, whilst it is relatively easy to determine the low level structure of a given protein in terms of the amino acids which constitute it, it is difficult and time consuming to accurately determine the full three dimensional structure by biochemical means. This has lead to an interest in computer based methods for structure prediction.

Clark *et al* [1991] describe a system for the prediction of the topological structure of proteins using constraint based search. It has been suggested in the literature that a number of rules concerning the arrangement of secondary structures are true for most proteins, and these are used as constraints. As each possible structure for a particular protein is generated it is tested against a set of constraints chosen from those in the literature. If any constraints are violated, the structure is rejected. Unfortunately the constraints, whilst generally true in the sense that they hold more often than they don't hold, are all violated by some known protein. This has lead to the proposal that the applicability of the constraints be modelled by attaching some form of certainty value to them. This would allow the relative likelihood of a structure to be assessed by the combined certainty values of the constraints that it conforms to.

2.2 Sources of uncertainty

The problem with using a single uncertainty handling formalism to model the certainty of applicability of the constraints is that the data does not fit any single existing formalism. The data is broadly probabilistic, being based on a survey of proteins of known structure. However, given that the largest number of proteins surveyed is 33, the data can hardly be regarded as reliable. We also have two sets of probability values. The first set is derived from a set of 33 proteins [Clark *et al* 1990] each of which was tested against five of the six constraints in which we are interested. These figures may be regarded as a lower bound since the class of proteins tested is somewhat more general than the class for which the constraints were devised. A set of upper bounds were obtained by testing all six constraints against eight proteins of the type for which the constraints are expected to apply. The situation is complicated by the fact that all but one of the proteins have no uniquely determined structure, so that some constraints hold for some possible structures of some proteins and don't hold for other possible structures of the same protein. In other words, for these particular proteins, it is not possible to determine whether some constraints hold. So, whilst an interval probability formalism seems appropriate for modelling some of the constraints, others would seem to require a method such as evidence theory that is capable of explicitly modelling ambiguity. Finally, for the one constraint that is not analysed by Clark *et al* [1990] we have no data on the lower probability limit. What we do have, however, is a heuristic ranking of the constraints, in order of applicability, by two knowledgeable biochemists [Taylor and Green 1989]. We would like to incorporate this information in our system to model the final constraint.

3. Techniques for combined modes of reasoning

As argued above, we have uncertainty data that is best modelled by more than one formalism. Given the lack of precise formal methods for combining information expressed in these formalisms, we have investigated a number of hybrid methods which are capable of a degree of integration of different types of information.

3.1 Semiqualitative algebras

Recognising that the mechanism of probability theory is fragile when confronted with imprecise and incomplete information, we have investigated ways of increasing its ability to cope with degraded information. We defined two robust algebras, Q2 and Q3, [Parsons 1990a], [Parsons and Fox 1991] for uncertain inference. Q2 is an extension of normal arithmetic to handle the qualitative values (-, 0, +), and is most suitable for handling largely symbolic data, though it is clearly capable of handling numerical values. Q3 is based on interval data, and is particularly appropriate for handing imprecise numerical values, though it can deal with symbolic values as well. These two systems define the limits of a family of qualitative algebras of varying precision, between which we can switch as required [Travé-Massuyès and Piera 1989], and which are closely related to systems for order of magnitude reasoning [Parsons 1991a]. Although the investigations were carried out in the framework of probability theory, there is no reason to doubt the applicability of the algebras to other formalisms.

3.2 Integration by degradation

It has been proposed [Dohnal et al 1991] [Parsons 1991b] that when viewed at an abstract level, all values in all uncertainty handling formalisms have the same qualitative meaning. Both a probability $p(a) = 0.6$, and a possibility $\pi(a) = 0.8$ are reasons for believing that a is true. It is further suggested that if all formalisms have a similar qualitative behaviour, then it is possible to freely integrate values from all the formalisms at the qualitative level. To validate this approach it is necessary to perform a detailed qualitative analysis of all the formalisms in which we are interested. We have already [Parsons 1991] tackled probabilistic propagation in belief networks using techniques from qualitative reasoning [Bobrow 1984], and have results echoing those of Wellman [1990]. $p(a)$ increases and decreases with $p(b)$ if $p(a|b) > p(a|\neg b)$, and the joint influence of $p(b)$ and $p(c)$ on $p(d)$ exceeds their combined individual influences if $p(d|b,c) + p(d|\neg b,\neg c) > p(d|\neg b,c) + p(d|\neg b,\neg c)$. Work is in progress to apply similar methods to propagation based on possibility and evidence theories, and a further robust algebra, Q4, has been defined to extend Q2 and Q3 to describe the propagation of changes in belief. This approach is closely related to that of argumentation [Fox and Krause 1991], and if our analysis bears out our intuition, it will demonstrate the validity of the argumentation procedure.

3.3 Handling symbolic values

Partially ordered sets of symbolic values may be combined using intuitively plausible "and" and "or" combinators in such a way that combinations behave monotonically and it is possible to establish a partial order between them [Parsons 1990b]. Thus given a partially ordered set of values $h > m > 1$, we can reason that $h \vee' 1 > m$ and $h \wedge' m > h \wedge' 1$ where $\vee'$ and $\wedge'$ correspond to "or" and "and" respectively. This interpretation of the "and" combinator is equivalent to an intuitive averaging of values. An alternative is to consider the "and" combinator as a simple aggregation so that $h \vee' 1 > 1$, and this too has been explored.

4. How integration is achieved

The methods discussed in the previous section permit the integration of values from different uncertainty handling formalisms in a number of ways. Firstly, the use of robust algebras enables us to import numerical and symbolic data from any formalism into a given formalism. This is achieved by degradation. Given that we wish to import, say, the value $\pi(a) = 0.8$ into a probabilistic system, we degrade it, considering it simply as a reason for believing in a. This reason may be expressed as a probability whose value is unknown, and we can thus take $p(a) = [0, 1]$, a value that may be handled by our robust methods. The same mechanism can be used to import symbolic data. If a is known to be true by default, then we can take $p(a) = [0, 1]$ since there is a reason to believe in a, and we may do the same if a is derived with some arbitrary symbolic value somewhere between true and false.

There is further scope for integration when we consider how belief values change when evidence is taken into account. Consider a hypothesis a whose possibility $\pi(a)$ is known to increase with a given piece of evidence e. Our robust algebras allow us to consider this increase, when degraded, to be an increase in another uncertainty measure, say probability. Thus we know that $p(a)$ increases with e. This change may then be propagated through a probabilistic database, using the semiqualitative algebras to determine the direction of changes in belief in other hypotheses given the change in a. So we can, for example, deduce that $p(d)$, where d is a successor of a, will increase with e, an event which is only described in terms of possibilities. The approach thus allows us to integrate information about change in belief derived in any formalism with uncertain information in a given formalism to determine changes of belief in terms of that formalism.

The ability to reason about ordered values extends this approach by helping to combat the effects of degradation. Integration by degradation tends to lose information. Given that we know $\pi(a) = 0.6$ and $\pi(b) = 0.8$, it is clear that b is more possible than a. If we translate these values into probabilities, we have $p(a) = p(b) = [0, 1]$ although intuitively we might feel that $p(a) < p(b)$. This is the price that we pay for the integration of data from different formalisms. Reasoning about ordered values allows us to preserve information such as $p(a) < p(b)$ and permits deductions such as the following. $\pi(a)$ and $\pi(b)$ both increase with evidence e, a increases more than b. Thus both $p(a)$ and $p(b)$ increase with e, $p(a)$ increasing more than $p(b)$. Now, $p(c)$ increases with $p(a)$ as quickly as $p(d)$ increases with $p(b)$, so $p(c)$ increases more than $p(d)$ when e is known.

References

Clark, D, A., Shirazi, J. and Rawlings, C. J. (1990): Constraint based search in the prediction of protein topology and the evaluation of topological folding rules, DRUMS RP4 Workshop, Palma de Mallorca.

Clark, D, A., Shirazi, J. and Rawlings, C. J. (1991) Protein topology prediction through constraint based search and the evaluation of topological folding rules, to appear in Protein Engineering.

Dohnal, M., Parsons, S. and Krause, P. (1991): A degrading approach to the evaluation of uncertainty along a heterogeneous reasoning path. DRUMS technical report.

Fox, J. and Krause, P. (1991): Decision making and autonomous systems, 7th Conference on Uncertainty in AI.

Parsons, S. (1990a): On using qualitative algebras in place of metatheories for reasoning under uncertainty, a preliminary report, DRUMS RP4 Workshop, Palma de Mallorca.

Parsons, S. (1990b): Symbolic reasoning under uncertainty, Technical Report, Department of Electronic Engineering, Queen Mary and Westfield College.

Parsons, S. (1991a): Integration, argumentation, and qualitative reasoning, DRUMS Workshop on Integration, Blanes.

Parsons, S. (1991b): Interval algebras and order of magnitude reasoning, 6th International Conference on AI in Engineering.

Parsons, S. and Fox, J. (1991): Qualitative and interval algebras for robust decision making under uncertainty, IMACS Workshop on Qualitative Reasoning and Decision Support Systems.

Taylor, W. R. and Green, N. M. (1989): The predicted secondary structure of the neucleotide binding domain of six cation-transporting ATPases leading to a probable tertiary fold. European J. Biochemistry, 179, 241-248.

Travé-Massuyès, L., and Piera, N. (1989): The orders of magnitude models as qualitative algebras. 11th International. Joint Conference on AI.

Wellman, M. P. Fundamental concepts of qualitative probabilistic networks, Artificial Intelligence, 44, pp 257-303, 1990.

The transferable belief model

Ph. Smets, Y-T Hsia, A. Saffiotti, R. Kennes, H. Xu and E. Umkehrer.
IRIDIA, Université Libre de Bruxelles.

IRIDIA researches focus on the transferable belief model, a model that has been developped to represent some one's degree of beliefs. This model is based on the use of belief functions and is closely related to the model that Shafer has described in his book (Shafer 1976). More recent presentations are given in Smets (1988, 1990f). The generalization of the Bayesian Theorem when all probabilities functions are generalizerd into belief functions had been derived in Smets (1978), (see also Smets 1986, 1991c).

1) *A typology of uncertainty models* is explored in Smets (1990a). A serious danger in computer implementation of approximate reasoning is in the use of inappropriate, unjustified, ad hoc models.

The paper is a plea for the use of correct models. No unique models fits all contexts. An understanding of the forms of ignorance and the nature and the foundations of each model are required. Before using a quantified model, we must

1) provide a meaning for the numbers, i.e. provide canonical examples where the origin of the numbers can be justified
2) understand the fundamental axioms of the model and their consequences. The choice of axioms should be justified by "natural" requirements.
3) study the consequence of the derived models in practical contexts to check their validity and appropriateness

A common error consists in accepting a model because it 'worked' nicely in the past. This property is of course not a proof that the model is correct.

2) *The transferable belief model* (TBM). Smets and Kennes (1990) describes the TBM and compare it with the classical Bayesian model.

The transferable belief model is based on:

1) our degree of belief is quantified by a number between 0 and 1 (not an interval)

2) there exists a two-level structure:
- a credal level where beliefs are entertained and
- a pignistic level where beliefs are used to make decisions

3) beliefs at the credal level are quantified by belief functions.

4) beliefs at the pignistic level are quantified by probability functions.

5) the credal level precedes the pignistic level in that at any time beliefs are entertained (and updated) at the credal level. The pignistic level appears only when a decision needs to be made.

6) when a decision must be made, beliefs at the credal level are transformed into beliefs at the pignistic level, i.e. there exists a transformation from belief functions to probability functions.

Bayesians do not consider an autonomous credal level. The introduction of a two-level model would be useless if decisions were the same as those derived within the Bayesian model. The 'Peter, Paul and Mary' paradigm (Smets and Kennes 1990) shows that it is not the case. The introduction of a credal level therefore is not merely an academic subtlety.

3) Beside the transferable belief model, many *other interpretations* of the use of belief functions have been proposed. In Smets (1990b, 1990c, 1990d), we compare the following interpretations: the upper and lower probabilities, the random sets, the evidentiary value model, the probabilities of modal propositions, etc... These interpretations share the same static representations (how beliefs are allocated) , but differ at the dynamic level (how beliefs are updated).

4) *Decision-making* requires that we derive a probability function that can be used to compute expected utilities of each potential decision. It means that uncertainty at the pignistic level must be quantified by a probability function. But it does not mean that beliefs at the credal level must also be quantified by a probability function. All what is required is that there exists some transformation between the representation at the credal level and the probability function that must exist at the pignisitic level.

We solve that problem by introducing a consistency requirement that corresponds to the following scenario (Smets 1990e, 1991a). Suppose you must receive a friend tonight. It may be either A or B. The one who will come will be selected by a coin: if head, A will show up, if tail, B will show up. But you don't know by now who will show up. You wonder about the drink the visitor will ask for. You can buy only one drink: either beer, or wine or juice. You have your own belief about the fact that A (or B) will ask for beer, wine or juice (they only ask one drink). Given your beliefs about A's preference, you build a probability P_A on the drink space that you would use to buy the drink if you knew that A would show up. Identically with B, you get P_B. These two probability functions are the conditional probability functions given A and B, and the final decision will be based on the probability function obtained by averaging these two conditional probability functions (because of the coin experiment).

But you could also reconsider the problem by building first you belief about the fact that the person who will show up prefers beer, wine, juice (this can be proved to be also the average of the two individual beliefs). Given this joint belief, build then you probability function to be used to decide which drink to buy. The conclusions should be the same (the two probability functions derived by the two approaches should be equal). This consistency requirement is so strong that it permits to derive the unique transformation between any measure of belief and the so called pignistic probability (i.e. the probability function to be used to make decisions).

In Smets (1990e) we show that the whole argument works for any point-wise representation of belief.

5) *Criticisms* have been raised recently against the Dempster-Shafer theory (see Pearls 1990). Most critcisms reflect a misuse of the model. In Smets (1991b) we propose solutions based on the transferable belief model for most of the problems raised against the use of belief functions to quantify someone's beliefs.

6) *Dempster-Shafer theory, nonmonotonicy and surprise.* The Dempster-Shafer (D-S) theory is typically described in a set-theoretic framework. To integrate the D-S theory into a logic-based system such as the ATMS (Laskey and Lehner, 1989), Hsia (1990) formulates it as a logical inference system. Hsia (1991a) suggest that only Dempster's rule of conditioning is the fundamental tool for making inference and Dempster's rule of combination is considered something that has to be explicitly justified using two concepts: the concept of conditioning and the concept of "minimum commitment of belief". Hsia (1991b) suggests that we view belief as potential surprise and use belief functions as a general tool for modeling the notion of surprise. Hsia (1991c) also developed a belief-function based model theory for a proof theory that can be used in performing nonmonotonic reasoning.

7) *The Fast Moebius Transform.* Kennes and Smets (1990a, 1990b) and Kennes (1991) have defined the Fast Moebius Transform, the optimal exact algorithm to transform belief functions, basic belief assigments and commonality functions into each other, and to combine two belief functions by Dempster's rule of combination. Eventhough optimal for the general case, the computation requirements are still heavy.

8) *Integrating Uncertainty Management and Knowledge Representation.* A gap is detected between the fields of Knowledge Representation (KR) and Uncertainty Management (UM). The literature in each field seems to have scarcely taken into account the problems and the results emerged in the other one. On the one hand, most of the insights gained in the last decade of KR research can hardly find a place in the formal machineries developed in the field of UM. On the other hand, attempts at considering uncertainty in KR systems have often turn out to be *ad-hoc* extensions, using UM techniques far removed from the state-of-the-art in UM research. We propose a solution consisting in a formal framework for representing uncertain knowledge in which two components, one dealing with (categorical) knowledge ("KR component") and one dealing with the uncertainty about this knowledge ("UM component"), are singled out. (Saffiotti, 1990a) describes this formal framework in general terms, and gives some examples: in them, first order logic and (a modal extension of) Krypton are used as KR component, while Tarskian truth, Dempster-Shafer theory, possibility theory, and probabilities are used for the UM component. (Saffiotti, 1990b) focuses on applying the general framework to belief functions.

Our framework leads in a natural way to a general AI architecture for integrating a given KR system with an uncertainty calculus. Such "Hybrid Belief Systems" (HBS) may be seen as tools for attaching a (possibly powerful) treatment of uncertainty to a KR system and as a way for extending the applicability of UM calculi to (possibly complex) kinds of knowledge and problems. The current approach to implementing a HBS is based on the idea of dynamically constructing a belief network (in the UM part) which mirrors the inferences performed by the KR system (Saffiotti, 1991). To this purpose, a general system for propagating uncertainty over belief networks has been implemented (Saffiotti and Umkherer, 1991). This system, based on the work of Shenoy and Shafer (1988), may perform propagation according to any of belief function, probability, and possibility theory. A specialized system for propagating belief functions has also been implemented (Xu, 1991), which carefully tackles the issue of efficiency.

9) *Belief functions and default reasoning.* Practical implementation issues of belief functions to solve problems in default reasoning are discussed in Smets and Hsia

(1990). It explains how to propagate beliefs in MacEvidence (Hsia and Shenoy, 1989) with or without modus tollens and how to avoid the 'bad' results described in Pearl (1990)

References

HSIA Y.-T. (1990). The belief calculus and uncertain reasoning. In *Proceedings of the Eighth National Conference on Artificial Intelligence, American Association for Artificial Intelligence*, Boston, Massachusetts, 120-125.

HSIA Y.-T. (1991a). Characterizing belief with minimum commitment. In *Proceedings of the Twelfth International Joint Conference on Artificial Intelligence*, Sydney, Australia (to appear).

HSIA Y.-T. (1991b). Belief and surprise - a belief-function approach. In *Uncertainty in Artificial Intelligence: Proceedings of the Seventh Conference* (B.D. D'Ambrosio, P. Smets, and P.P. Bonissone, eds.), Morgan Kaufman, San Mateo, California (to appear).

HSIA Y.-T. (1991c). A belief-function semantics for cautious nonmonotonicity. Technical Report TR/IRIDIA/91-3, IRIDIA, Université Libre de Bruxelles, Brussels.

HSIA Y.-T. and SHENOY, P.P. (1989). An evidential language for expert systems. In *Proceedings of the Fourth International Symposium on Methodology for Intelligent Systems*, Charlotte, N.C., 9-16.

KENNES R. (1991) Computatioanl aspects of the Moebius transform of a graph. IEEE-SMC, under press.

KENNES R. and SMETS P. (1990a) Computational Aspects of the Möbius Transform. *Uncertainty in Artificial Intelligence Vol. 6* (P.P. Bonissone, M. Henrion, L.N. Kanal, J.F. Lemmer, eds.), North-Holland, Amsterdam, to appear.

KENNES R. and SMETS P. (1990b) Fast algorithms for Dempster-Shafer theory. *Proc. of the 3rd Inter. Conf. on Information Processing and Management of Uncertainty in Knowledge-Based Systems*, Paris, France, July 2-6, 1990, 51-55. To appear in (B. Bouchon-Meunier, R.R. Yager, L.A. Zadeh, eds.), Lecture Notes in Computer Science Series, Springer Verlag.

LASKEY K. B. and LEHNER P. E. (1989). Assumptions, beliefs and probabilities. *Artificial Intelligence*, **41**, 1, 65-77.

PEARL J. (1990) Reasoning with Belief Functions: an Analysis of Compatibility. *Intern. J. Approx. Reasoning*, 4:363-390.

SAFFIOTTI A. (1990a). A Hybrid Framework for Representing Uncertain Knowledge". *Procs. of the Eighth AAAI Conference* (Boston, MA) 653-658.

SAFFIOTTI A. (1990b). "Using Dempster-Shafer Theory in Knowledge Representation". *Procs. of the Sixth Conf. on Uncertainty in AI* (Cambridge, MA) 352-359.

SAFFIOTTI A. (1991). "Inference-Driven Construction of Valuation Systems". IRIDIA Technical Report (In preparation).

SAFFIOTTI A. and UMKEHRER E. (1991) "PULCINELLA: A General Tool for Propagating Uncertainty in Valuation Networks". *Procs. of the 7th Conference on Uncertainty in AI.*

SHAFER G. (1976) A mathematical theory of evidence. Princeton Univ. Press. Princeton, NJ.

SHENOY P.P. and SHAFER G. (1988) "An Axiomatic Framework for Bayesian and Belief-Function Propagation". *Procs. of AAAI Workshop on Uncertainty in AI*: 307-314.

SMETS Ph. (1978) Un modèle mathématico-statistique simulant le processus du diagnostic médical. Doctoral dissertation, Université Libre de Bruxelles, Bruxelles, (Available through University Microfilm International, 30-32 Mortimer Street, London W1N 7RA, thesis 80-70,003)

SMETS Ph. (1986) Bayes' theorem generalized for belief functions. Proc. ECAI-86, vol II., 169-171.ECCAI

SMETS Ph. (1988) Belief functions. in SMETS Ph, MAMDANI A., DUBOIS D. and PRADE H. ed. Non standard logics for automated reasoning. Academic Press, London p 253-286.

SMETS Ph. (1990a) Varieties of ignorance. To appear in *Information Sciences.*

SMETS Ph. (1990b) The transferable belief model and random sets. To appear in *Int. J. Intell. Systems.*

SMETS Ph. (1990c) The Transferable Belief Model and Other Interpretations of Dempster-Shafer's Model. *Uncertainty in Artificial Intelligence Vol. 6* (P.P. Bonissone, M. Henrion, L.N. Kanal, J.F. Lemmer, eds.), North-Holland, Amsterdam, to appear.

SMETS Ph. (1990d) The transferable belief model and possibility theory. *Proc. NAFIPS-90*, pg. 215-218.

SMETS Ph. (1990e) Constructing the pignistic probability function in a context of uncertainty. *Uncertainty in Artificial Intelligence 5*, Henrion M., Shachter R.D., Kanal L.N. and Lemmer J.F. eds, North Holland, Amsterdam, , 29-40.

SMETS Ph. (1990f) The combination of evidence in the transferable belief model. IEEE-Pattern analysis and Machine Intelligence, 12:447-458.

SMETS Ph. (1991a) Belief induced by the knowledge of some probabilities. Technical Report: TR-IRIDIA-91-9

SMETS Ph. (1991b) Resolving misunderstandings about belief functions: A response to the many criticisms raised by J. Pearl. To appear in *Int. J. Approximate Reasoning.*

SMETS Ph. (1991c) Belief functions: the disjunctive rule of combination and the generalized Bayesian theorem. (submitted for publication)

SMETS Ph. and HSIA Y.T. (1990) Default reasoning and the transferable belief model. *Uncertainty in Artificial Intelligence Vol. 6* (P.P. Bonissone, M. Henrion, L.N. Kanal, J.F. Lemmer, eds.), North-Holland, Amsterdam, to appear.

SMETS Ph. and KENNES (1990) The transferable belief model. Technical Report: TR-IRIDIA-90-14.

XU, H. (1991) "An Efficient Implementation of Belief Function Propagation". *Procs. of the 7th Conference on Uncertainty in AI* (to appear).

CONTRIBUTED PAPERS

Learning with CASTLE *

S. Acid   L.M. de Campos   A. González   R. Molina
N. Pérez de la Blanca

Departamento de Ciencias de la Computación e I.A.
Universidad de Granada. 18071 Granada, Spain.

Abstract

We will describe here the learning algorithms we have implemented in CASTLE,
(Causal Structures From Inductive Learning), to learn about causal structures from
examples. A brief introduction to the software ifself and a description of what we
intend to develop and implement in CASTLE are also given. Finally, the use of
CASTLE is illustrated on a simple example.

1   Introduction

The aim of this work is to introduce CASTLE, a tool that can be used so far to learn
causal structures from raw data, propagate knowledge throughout polytrees, simulate and
also edit polytree–dependent distributions.

CASTLE is a C written program following the Open–Look norms using the Sun Mi-
crosystems's XView supplied with OpenWindows 2.0. Given a set of examples stored in
a file, CASTLE, first, estimates the skeleton associated to the joint probability distribution obtained from the data, then gives directions to the branches of the skeleton and
finally estimates the needed probabilities. The result is then a complete singly connected
network (polytree) that can be used later to perform probabilistic inferences within CAS-
TLE either interactively or in batch mode. The reader is referred to ([1]) for details about
how to use CASTLE.

As we have said before, CASTLE also allows the user to edit and simulate polytree-
dependent distributions. These facilities make it possible to test on samples extracted
from polytree-dependent distributions the implemented learning algorithms.

This work is divided in the following sections. Section 2 is a brief description of what
learning is about in the context of causal networks. Section 3 describes the learning
algorithms implemented in CASTLE to learn the skeleton of polytrees. Section 4 is
devoted to the task of recovering the direction of the branches of a polytree-dependent
distribution. Section 5 describes the application of the learning algorithms to a simple
example. Finally, in section 6 we will describe our future lines of research.

---

*This work has been supported by the Commission of the European Communities under ESPRIT
project no 5170: Comparative Testing of Statistical and Logical Learning, Statlog.

2 Causal Networks and Learning

As defined by Pearl, ([4]): Causal networks are directed acyclic graphs (DAGs) in which the nodes represent propositions (or variables), the arcs signify the existence of direct causal dependencies between the linked propositions, and the strengths of these dependencies are quantified by conditional probabilities. In consequence, causal networks are tools capable of organising the knowledge to represent and manipulate relationships of relevance. Moreover, once the knowledge has been codified in a network, it facilitates a rapid response to inference tasks using a minimal amount of memory.

Once the network is constructed it constitutes an efficient device to perform probabilistic inferences. The problem of building such a network remains. The structure and conditional probabilities necessary for characterising the network could be provided either externally by experts or from direct empirical observations.

Under the Bayesian approach, the learning task in causal networks separates into two highly related subtasks, *structure learning*, that is to identify the topology of the network, and *parameter learning*, the numerical parameters (conditional probabilities) for a given network topology.

CASTLE so far is focused on learning structure rather than parameters, although obviously it also need to do some parameters estimation in order to produce a complete causal network.

Since a model with too many links is computationally useless, as it requires too much storage and lengthy procedures to produce predictions or explanations, it is essential that we give the learning process a built-in preference toward simple structures, those that have the fewest possible parameters and embody the fewest possible dependencies.

CASTLE focus on a particular kind of causal structures: polytrees (singly connected networks), networks where no more than one path exists between any two nodes. As a consequence, a polytree with n nodes has no more than $n - 1$ links. It is in polytrees (and specially in trees) where the ability of networks to decompose and modularise the knowledge attains its ultimate realisation. Polytrees does not contain loops, that is, undirected cycles in the underlying network (the network without the arrows or skeleton) and this fact allows a local extremely efficient propagation procedure (see [4]).

3 Learning Polytree's Skeleton

In this section we will describe how CASTLE learns about the skeleton (the **graph** stripped of the arrows) of a nondegenerate distribution $P(x)$ (i.e., a distribution for which there exists a connected directed acyclic graph (DAG) that displays all the dependencies and independencies embedded in $P(x)$) that can be represented by a polytree.

The following theorem can be proven,([4]), :

Theorem 1 *If a nondegenarate distribution $P(x)$ is representable by a polytree F_0, then any Maximum Weight Spanning Tree (MWST) where the weight of the branch connecting X_i and X_j is defined by*

$$I(X,Y) = \sum_{x,y} P(x,y) \log \frac{P(x,y)}{P(x)P(y)} \tag{1}$$

will unambiguously recover the skeleton of F_0.

Examining the proof of the above theorem it can be seen that we can use any *Dep* function satisfying

$$\min(Dep(X,Y), Dep(Y,Z)) > Dep(X,Z) \tag{2}$$

for $X \rightarrow Y \rightarrow Z$, $X \leftarrow Y \leftarrow Z$, $X \leftarrow Y \rightarrow Z$ and $X \rightarrow Y \leftarrow Z$ and not only the Kullback–Leibler measure defined in (1).

In CASTLE we have implemented the following *Dep* functions:

$$Dep(X,Y) = \sum_{x,y} P(x,y) \log \frac{P(x,y)}{P(x)P(y)} \tag{3}$$

$$Dep(X,Y) = -\frac{\sum_{x,y} P(x,y) \log \frac{P(x,y)}{P(x)P(y)}}{\sum_{x,y} P(x,y) \log P(x,y)} \tag{4}$$

$$Dep(X,Y) = \sum_x \sum_y |P(x,y) - P(x)P(y)| \tag{5}$$

$$Dep(X,Y) = \sum_x \sum_y P(x,y)|P(x,y) - P(x)P(y)| \tag{6}$$

$$Dep(X,Y) = \sum_x \sum_y (P(x,y) - P(x)P(y))^2 \tag{7}$$

$$Dep(X,Y) = \sum_x \sum_y P(x,y)(P(x,y) - P(x)P(y))^2 \tag{8}$$

$$Dep(X,Y) = \max_x \max_y |P(x,y) - P(x)P(y)| \tag{9}$$

Some of the *Dep* functions listed above satisfy (2) (details will be given elsewhere).

Although some of the functions listed above verifying (2) are faster to compute than the measure of Kullback–Leibler (3) that is not the reason to offer the user of CASTLE more than one function.

In our software we will never have $Dep(X,Y)$ but an estimation $\widehat{Dep}(X,Y)$ obtained from a file of examples. So we would like to use a function $Dep(X,Y)$ such that the properties of $Dep(X,Y)$ relatives to (2) are kept by $\widehat{Dep}(X,Y)$. Research is currently being carried out to establish how robust our *Dep* functions are.

Let us now describe how to use CASTLE to learn the skeleton of a polytree. After reading a file containing examples, CASTLE displays a node for each variable involved in the examples (see [1] for details). We can now decide to set some constrains on the skeleton we intend to recover, these constrains take the form of forcing the skeleton to include some branches. We now go to the option **Skeleton** in the **Learning** menu and choose a function *Dep* among the possibilities listed above. CASTLE then produces the skeleton of a polytree. If the distribution $P(x)$ we intend to recover can be represented by a polytree, we have chosen a *Dep* function satisfying (2) and the properties of *Dep* are kept by $\widehat{Dep}$ then the skeleton recovered by CASTLE 1.0 is the skeleton of the polytree representing $P(x)$.

The method used to find the MWST is just Kruskal's algorithm, ([2]). Its performance is at most $O(n^2 \log(n))$ where n is the number of nodes. We could have used faster algorithms but the constrains are very easy to deal with when using Kruskal's algorithm.

4 Orientating the Skeleton of a Polytree

Having found the polytree's skeleton we move on to find the directionality of the branches. To recover the directions of the branches we use the following facts: nondegeneracy implies that for any pairs of variables (X_i, X_j) that do not have a common descendent we have

$$I(X_i, X_j) > 0 \tag{10}$$

Furthermore, for the pattern

$$X_i \to X_k \leftarrow X_j \tag{11}$$

we have

$$I(X_i, X_j) = 0 \quad and \quad I(X_i, X_j | X_k) > 0 \tag{12}$$

where

$$I(X_i, X_j | X_k) = \sum_{x_i, x_j, x_k} P(x_i, x_j, x_k) \log \frac{P(x_i, x_j | x_k)}{P(x_i | x_k) P(x_j | x_k)} \tag{13}$$

and for any of the patterns

$$X_i \leftarrow X_k \leftarrow X_j, \quad X_i \leftarrow X_k \to X_j \ and \ X_i \to X_k \to X_j \tag{14}$$

we have

$$I(X_i, X_j) > 0 \quad and \quad I(X_i, X_j | X_k) = 0 \tag{15}$$

Taking all these facts into account we can recover the head–to–head patterns, (11), which are the really important ones. The rest of the branches can be assigned any directions as long as we do not produce more head–to–head patterns.

So far so good but, what happens when we do not have the real distribution to calculate the Kullback–Leibler information but a sample from it. We already have made some hypothesis concerning $\hat{I}$ to recover the skeleton of the polytree, however, now comes a greater problem. Conditions like

$$\hat{I}(X_i, X_j) = 0 \ when X_i \ and \ X_j \ are \ marginally \ independent \tag{16}$$

or

$$\hat{I}(X_i, X_j | X_k) = 0 \ when X_i \ and \ X_j \ are \ conditionally \ independent \ given \ X_k \tag{17}$$

are hardly satisfied. There may even be room for inconsistencies: we may have for the skeleton shown in figure 1 the following inequalities

$$\hat{I}(X_1, X_2) < \hat{I}(X_5, X_6) < \hat{I}(X_1, X_4) < \hat{I}(X_3, X_5) < c < \hat{I}(X_2, X_4) < \hat{I}(X_3, X_6) \tag{18}$$

where c is a threshold used to detect independencies.

In the example displayed in figure 1 we can see that since X_1 and X_2 are independent then the arrows $X_1 \to X_3$ and $X_2 \to X_3$ should be in the polytree; as X_1 and X_4 are also independent, the arrow $X_3 \to X_4$ should also be in the polytree. But X_2 and X_4 are dependent; once the branch X_2–X_3 points at X_3, the branch X_3–X_4 should point at X_4 instead of pointing at X_3: there is then an inconsistency. The same thing happens

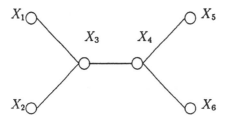

Figure 1:

with the branches X_4–X_5, X_4–X_6 and X_3–X_4. From these two examples, it is obvious that some of the dependencies and—or independencies provided by the data should not be taken into account in order to obtain a polytree structure.

CASTLE in its current state implements two approaches to recover the directions of the branches.

The first one works as follows on the recovered skeleton ([4]):

1. Search the internal nodes of the skeleton, beginning with the one having more neighbours left, until a multi–parent node Y is found using one of the tests in (19) to find any possible structure of the form $X \rightarrow Y \leftarrow Z$ where X and Z denote adjacent nodes to Y in the skeleton.

2. Being Y multi–parent, the nodes which are not parents of Y in the polytree become descendents of Y.

3. For each node C having one incoming arrow from Y, resolve the directionality of all of its remaining adjacent W branches using one of the test in (19) to find the structures of the form $Y \rightarrow C \leftarrow W$

4. Repeat steps 1 through 3 until no further directionality can be discovered.

To find the causal structures having the form $X \rightarrow Y \leftarrow Z$, we can use

$$\hat{I}(X,Z) < c \quad or \, \hat{I}(X,Z) < \hat{I}(X,Z|Y) \quad or \; a \; \chi^2 - test \; of \; independence \qquad (19)$$

We will now describe the second approach to the problem of recovering the direction of the branches.

In the previous method for orientating the skeleton, there is no criterion to decide the (in)dependencies that should be preserved, and it does the selection blindly, depending on the order in which the nodes are examined.

This second method to orientate the skeleton is based on the same criteria to distinguish head-to-head arrows, except the χ^2- test of independence, but providing some guidance to decide which (in)dependencies should be preserved in the case of conflict. The basic ideas are the following:

- If $I(a,b) < I(e,d) < c$,(a and b, e and d are independent), then the independence between a and b has more priority and must be preserved first.

- *If $c < I(a,b) < I(e,d)$,(a and b, e and d are dependent), then the dependence between e and d has more priority and must be preserved first.*

Moreover, the user may decide whether he/she prefers to preserve dependencies first or independencies first, using always the above rules between dependencies or between independencies. This corresponds with a orientation method based on a search with priorities.

If we used the independence first criterion for the example shown in (18) for figure 1, we would loose the dependence between X_2 and X_4, and the independence of X_3 and X_5. Using the dependence first criterion, we would loose the independencies of X_1 and X_4 and of X_5 and X_6. The results are shown in figure 2

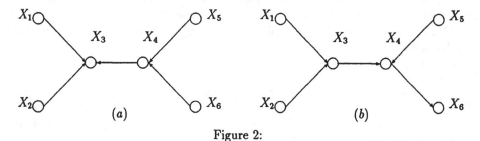

Figure 2:
(a) polytree obtained with independency first. (b) polytree obtained with dependency first.

In any case, we are loosing the weaker (in)dependencies compatible with the selected criterion.

We can use another selection criterion. To transform the range of variation of both independencies, $[0, c]$, and dependencies, $[c, maximum\ value\ of\ I()]$, into a common range in which we can compare the strengths of them, thus preserving first the strongest (in)dependencies.

Any of the methods the user can choose to find the direction of the branches may leave some of them undirected. CASTLE **completes** the network assigning direction to the undirected branches, constrained to not producing more head–to–head patterns.

5 Test Example

We will now test CASTLE on a simple example. The goal is to find relationships of (in)dependency between classes of animals and attributes that can be measured to the animals and between the attributes themselves. Although the network of inference we are about to find can be used for classification purposes, we believe its strength lays on the relations it portraits since very often the human performance to obtain such relations is very poor.

In our simplified problem we have the following seven variables, the possible values of each one are given in brackets. The variables are *class* (mammal, fish, reptile, bird), *milk* (yes, no), *homeothermic* (hot, cold), *habitat* (land, sea, air), *reproduction* (oviparous,

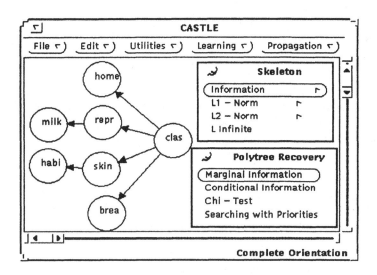

Figure 3: *Running* CASTLE

viviparous), *breathing* (lungs, gills) and *skin-covering* (none, hair, feathers, scales). The learning sample contains only the following animals: bat, dolphin, dog, horse, eagle, cock, sparrow, tuna, shark, anchovy, snake, lizard and sea turtle.

When CASTLE is run on this problem it produces basically three different polytrees depending on the dependency measure used to find the skeleton and to orientate it. Although any of the three shows interesting properties of (in)dependency we will comment only the polytree obtained when using the Kullback-Leibler information measure. The obtained polytree is shown in figure 3.

The most interesting properties of the obtained polytree are: the variables directly influencing the class of each animal are *reproduction, homeothermic, skin-covering* and *breathing*. Furthermore, all these variables are conditionally independent given the class under study. Moreover, the variables *milk* and *habitat* influence on the kind of animal only if we do not know the value of the variables *reproduction* and *sking-covering* respectively.

To end this section let us note on an obvious but interesting point. It is clear that increasing the size of the sample the network would be much more reliable. However, it can also be seen that even for a very small number of samples the obtained net does not produce unrealistic (in)dependence relationships. What seems clear is that these simple polytrees could be refined and also used to extract and improve the expert's knowledge on a problem.

6   Future Research

Although as it is at the moment CASTLE is a limited tool for learning structure from raw data, we intend to research on and include the following possibilities in the software:

- The use of more complex searching techniques to minimise the cost, measured as a function of the inconsistencies, of the recovered polytree and

- Study how close the recovered polytree–dependent distribution is to the real distribution when this cannot be represented by a polytree.

- Amplify the **set contraints** option to allow the user to include other kind of restrictions like: keeping some variables independent, forcing some variables to be independent when others appear dependent and so on.

These are the first steps we intend to take to improve CASTLE. We would also like to deal with the following problems in the future. Learning more complex causal structures ([5],[11]) and estimation of the parameters needed in the network ([8],[9]), to carry out this second task we could benefit from the Bayesian approach to Image Analysis ([7],[3]). We would also like to introduce the use of upper and lower probabilities in the learning process.

Acknowledgement
CASTLE's graphical edition facilities are inspired on those developed in ENTORNO, a software written by the team of the ESPRIT project DRUMS at the DECSAI. The propagation software has also been borrowed from ENTORNO.

References

[1] Acid, S., Campos,L.M.de, González, A., Molina, R. and Pérez de la Blanca, N. (1991) CASTLE: Causal Structures from Inductive Learning. Release 1.0. *Technical Report no 91-4-1*. Dept of Computer Science and A.I. (DECSAI). University of Granada.

[2] Aho, A.V., Hopcroft, J.E. and Ullman, J.E. (1987) *Data Structures and Algorithms*. Addison–Wesley.

[3] Molina, R. and Ripley, B.D. (1989). Using spatial models as priors in image analysis. *J. Appl. Statist*, **16**, 193–206.

[4] Pearl, J. (1988) *Probabilistic Reasoning in Intelligent Systems: Networks of Plausible Inference*. Morgan and Kaufmann.

[5] Pearl, J. and Verma, T.S. (1990) A Formal Theory of Inductive Causation. *Technical Report R-155* Department of Computer Science. University of California.

[6] Rajski, C. (1964) On the normed information rate of discrete random variables. Trasl of the *Third Praga Congress*, 583–585.

[7] Ripley, B.D. (1988) *Statistical Inference for Spatial Processes*. Cambridge Univ. Press.

[8] Spiegelhalter, D. J. (1986) Probabilistic reasoning in predictive expert systems. In *Uncertainty in Artificial Intelligence* (eds L.K. Kanal and J. Lemmer) 48-68. Amsterdam: North-Holland

[9] Spiegelhalter, D. J. and Lauritzen, S.L. (1990) Sequential Updating of Conditional Probabilities on Directed Graphical Structures. *Networks*, **20**, 579–605.

[10] Statlog (1990). Technical Annex of ESPRIT project :*Comparative Testing of Statistical and Logical Learning, Statlog*.

[11] Verma, T.S. and Pearl, J. (1990) Equivalence and Synthesis of Causal Models In *Proc, Sixth Conference on Uncertainty in Artificial Intelligence*. Cambridge Mass, 220–227.

A NEW APPROACH TO INFERENCE UNDER UNCERTAINTY FOR KNOWLEDGE BASED SYSTEMS

J. F. Baldwin[*]
University of Bristol

1. INTRODUCTION

Uncertainties

Expert systems for diagnosis, decision support systems, robot and real time control, engineering design etc. must necessarily use incomplete, contaminated and imprecise knowledge. A database of diseases with associated symptoms may not register presence or absence of a given symptom for a given disease. We can say that the symptom may or may not be present. We may be able to express this incompleteness in terms of probabilities. This is a form of incomplete information and is common in real application areas. Incompleteness can arise because of complete absence of knowledge or through only knowing approximately the answer. In the latter case this might be expressed in words with imprecise meaning such as "tall", "strong", "probable" etc. This imprecision can be taken into account by expressing it by means of fuzzy sets, ZADEH 1965, 75, 83. These fuzzy sets impose a possibility distribution over the set of possible values a variable can take, ZADEH 1978. This in turn imposes a family of possible probability distributions for the value of the variable. Contaminated knowledge arises from noise present in the system, perhaps through the unreliability of a communication channel or the unreliability of a measuring device etc. This form of uncertainty can be represented in probabilistic terms, perhaps as a family of conditional probability distributions, but may also require the use of fuzzy sets to express imprecision once again. Imprecise knowledge is fuzzy. Most everyday concepts cannot be precisely defined by means of necessary and sufficient conditions. The meaning of concepts which are acquired through examples of their usage and their applicability to new situations which do not perfectly match with those used previously cannot be deduced with certainty.

The numbers required to express these uncertainties will not themselves be known with certainty. It might be felt that in the face of uncertain uncertainties one should abandon an attempt at direct numeracy and express the uncertainty relationships linguistically and provide a calculus which will cope with these directly. We prefer to work with mass assignments which can express families of distributions to take account of this imprecision and fuzzy set theory to translate linguistically expressed uncertain statements into numerical form. A mass assignment is equivalent to a basic probability assignment in Shafer's theory of evidence, SHAFER 1976, SHENOY 1989, SHENOY AND SHAFER 1990, SMETS 1988, 1990, ZADEH 1986. A voting model will be introduced to interpret fuzzy sets, BALDWIN 1990a, BALDWIN and PILSWORTH 1990 and this further used to derive mass assignments given possibility distributions via fuzzy set descriptions. For a discussion of various approaches to the management of uncertainty see DUBOIS and PRADE 1990a, 90b, KLIR and FOLGER 1988, LOPEZ DE MANTARAS 1990.

2. MASS ASSIGNMENTS AND MEASURES

MASS ASSIGNMENTS

A mass assignment over a finite frame of discernment F is a function m

$m : P(F) \rightarrow [0. 1]$ where $P(F)$ is the power set of F, such that

---

[*] Professor Baldwin is SERC senior research fellow

$$\sum_{A \in P(F)} m(A) = 1 \; ; \; m(\emptyset) = 0$$

This axiom is relaxed in **BALDWIN 1991** to obtain a pseudo Boolean mass assignment algebra

$m(A)$ for any $A \subseteq F$ represents a probability mass allocated to exactly the subset A of F and to no subset of A. This corresponds to the basic probability assignment function of the Dempster / Shafer theory of evidence.

A family of mass assignments can be denoted by $m(. \mid z1, ..., zn)$ where zi are parametrs defining the family and satisfy constraints $\alpha_i \leq C_i(z1, ..., zn) \leq \beta_i \; ; \; 0 \leq \alpha_i, \beta_i \leq 1, \; \alpha_i \leq \beta_i$ where C_i are linear. We will see below that family of mass assignments result from combining mass assignments.

SUPPORT MEASURES

A **necessary support measure** is a function
$Sn : P(F) \rightarrow [0, 1]$
satisfying the following axioms
$Sn(\emptyset) = 0$ and $Sn(F) = 1$

$$Sn(\bigcup_i Ai) \geq \sum_i Sn(Ai) - \sum_{i<j} Sn(Ai \cap Aj) + ... + (-1)^{n+1} Sn(\bigcap_i Ai)$$

where $Ak \subseteq F$, all k
Thus

$$Sn(A) = \sum_{B \subseteq A} m(B) \; ; \text{ for any } A \subseteq F$$

is such a measure which we call the necessary support measure for the mass assignment m.

A **possible support measure**, Sp is dual to the necessary support measure. It satisfies
$Sp(A) = 1 - Sn(\overline{A}) \; ;$ for any $A \subseteq F$, where $\overline{A}$ is the complement of A

$$Sp(A) = \sum_{A \cap B \neq \emptyset} m(B) \; ; \text{ for any } A \subseteq F$$

is such a measure which we call the possible support measure for the mass assignment m.

It should be noted that
$Sn(A) = 1 - Sp(\overline{A}) \; ;$ for any $A \subseteq F$

A **support pair** for any $A \subseteq F$ resulting from the family of mass assignments $m(. \mid z1, ..., zn)$ is given by
$$\left[\min_{zi} Sn(A), \max_{zi} Sp(A) \right]$$
This defines an interval containing $Pr(A)$.

FOCAL ELEMENTS

Every subset, A, of F for which $m(A) \geq 0$ is called a focal element. If M is the set of focal elements from F for m then the mass assignment can be represented by $\{L_i : m_i\}$ where

$L_i \in M$ and $m(L_i) = m_i$.
This can also be written as $m = L_i : m_i$.

We can also denote this mass assignment by (m, F).

Total ignorance is then represented by the mass assignment F : 1. In this case the only focal element is F so that m(F) = 1 and m(A) = 0 for all subsets, A, of F other than F.

3. COMBINING MASS ASSIGNMENTS

If we are given two mass assignments (m1, M1) and (m2, M2) how can we combine them to give a mass assignment (m M)? Two questions can be asked. What do we mean by the concept "combining" and for any definition of such a concept is the result a unique mass assignment or a family of mass assignments. We will define two concepts of combining.

GENERAL ASSIGNMENT METHOD

Consider the two mass assignments (m1, M1) and (m2, M2) where M1 = {L1k} for k = 1, 2, ..., n1 and M2 = { L2k} for k = 1, 2, ..., n2 where each Lij are subsets of F for which m1(L1k) ≠ 0; k = 1, ..., n1, m2(L2k) ≠ 0 ; k = 1, ..., n2.

Let * be some binary set theoretic operation such as intersection or union. Let (m, M) be the result of combining (m1, M1) and (m2, M2) with respect to * and we will denote this by
(m(. | P), M) = (m1, M1) +∗ (m2, M2)
where m represents a unique assignment or family of mass assignments. If a unique assignment results then m(. | { }) = m.

The combination operation * is defined by the general assignment algorithm now stated. This is consistent with treating the mass assignments as families of probability distributions and combining these families of probability distributions.

Let M = {Lmij} for which Lmij = L1i * L2j for all i, j such that L1i * L2j ≠ Ø
and

$$m(Y) = \sum_{i,j : L1i * L2j = Y} m'(L1i * L2j) ; \quad \text{for any } Y \subseteq M$$

where m'(L1i * L2j), for i = 1, ..., n1 and j = 1, ..., n2 satisfies

$$\sum_j m'(L1i * L2j) = m1(L1i) \text{ for i = 1, ..., n1}$$

$$\sum_i m'(L1i * L2j) = m2(L2j) \text{ for j = 1, ..., n2}$$

and
m'(L1i * L2j) = 0 if L1i * L2j = Ø , for i = 1, ..., n1 and j = 1, ..., n2

Consider a matrix of cells Cij where i = 1, ..., n1 and j = 1, ..., n2. Let cell Cij contain label L1i * L2j with associated mass m'ij = m'(L1i * L2j). Then the ith row masses of the cell tableau must add up to m1(L1i) for all i and the jth column masses mist add up to m2(L2j) for all j. Cells with null set entries are allocated the mass 0. This will not in general give a unique solution. For the non unique case, any allocation can be modified by alternatively adding and subtracting a quantity at vertices around a loop made up of alternative horizontal and vertical jumps. The quantity must be such that no cell mass entries go negative. This is simply the assignment algorithm from the field of operations research.
If a unique solution is not obtained, the family of solutions can be parametrised.

Example
F = {a, b, c, d, e}
(m1, M1) = a : 0.2, {b, c} : 0.3, {c, d, e} : 0.5
(m2, M2) = {a, b} : 0.3, b : 0.1, {c, d, e} : 0.6

Combining with respect to intersection gives

$(m, M) = (m1, M1) +_\cap (m2, M2) = a : 0.2, b : 0.2, c : 0.1, \{c, d, e\} : 0.5$ since

	0.3 {a, b}	0.1 b	0.6 {c, d, e}
0.2 a	a 0.2	Ø 0	Ø 0
0.3 {b, c}	b 0.1	b 0.1	c 0.1
0.5 {c, d, e}	Ø 0	Ø 0	{c, d, e} 0.5

so that for this example a unique solution is obtained.

Example

$F = \{a, b, c, d, e\}$

$(m1, M1) = a : 0.2, \{b, c\} : 0.3, \{c, d, e\} : 0.5$

$(m2, M2) = \{a, b\} : 0.3, \{b, c\} : 0.1, \{c, d, e\} : 0.6$

Combining with respect to intersection gives

$(m, M) = (m1, M1) +_\cap (m2, M2)$

$$= a : 0.2, b : 0.1, c : 0.1 + 2x, \{b, c\} : 0.1 - x, \{c, d, e\} : 0.5 - x$$

where $0 \le x \le 0.1$, since

	0.3 {a, b}	0.1 {b, c}	0.6 {c, d, e}	
0.2 a	a 0.2	Ø 0	Ø 0	
0.3 {b, c}	b 0.1	{b, c} 0.1-x	c 0.1+x	$0 \le x \le 0.1$
0.5 {c, d, e}	Ø 0	c 0+x	{c, d, e} 0.5-x	

This family of mass assignments corresponds to the following family of probability distributions

$a : 0.2, b : 0.2 - x - y1, c : 0.6 + x + y1 - y2 - y3, d : y2, e : y3$

where $0 \le y1 \le 0.1 - x$, $0 \le y2 + y3 \le 0.5 - x$, $yi \ge 0$ all i.

COMPLEMENTATION AND RESTRICTIONS

The complement of a mass assignment (m, M), denoted by $\overline{(m, M)}$, is (m', F') where the set of focal elements $F' = \{L'i\}$ where $L'i$ is the complement of Li with respect to F and the mass associated with $L'i$ is $m(L'i) = m(Li)$.

If $m = \{Li : mi\}$ and, for some k, $L'1$ and $L'2$ are chosen such that $L'1 \cup L'2 = Lk$ and $m(L'1), m(L'2)$ are chosen such that $0 < m(L'1) + m(L'2) \le mk$ then

$$m' = \begin{cases} \{Li : mi \mid i \ne k\} \cup \{L'1 : m(L'1)\} \cup \{L'2 : m(L'2)\} \\ \qquad \text{if } m(L'1) + m(L'2) < mk \\ \{Li : mi \mid i \ne k\} \cup \{L'1 : m(L'1)\} \cup \{L'2 : m(L'2)\} \cup \{Lk : mk - m(L'1) - m(L'2)\} \\ \qquad \text{if } m(L'1) + M(L'2) = mk \end{cases}$$

is a <u>restriction of m</u> and is denoted by $m' < m$.

4. FUZZY SETS AND MASS ASSIGNMENTS

Let f be a normalised fuzzy set, $f \subseteq F$, such that

$$f = \sum_{x_i \in F} x_i / \chi_f(x_i) \quad ; \quad \chi_f(x_1) = 1, \chi_f(x_k) \leq \chi_f(x_j) \text{ for } k > j$$

where $\chi_f(x)$ is the membership level, $x \varepsilon [0, 1]$, of x in f

The mass assignment associated with f is

$x_1 : 1 - \chi_f(x_2), \{x_1, ..., x_i\} : \chi_f(x_i) - \chi_f(x_{i+1}) \text{ for } i = 2, ... ; \text{ with } \chi_f(x_k) = 0 \text{ for } x_k \notin F$

This defines a family of probability distributions over F for the instantiation of variable X, given the statement
X is f
This definition is consistent with the voting model with the constant threshold model described above.

5. ITERATIVE ASSIGNMENT METHOD

This is discussed in BALDWIN (1990 b, c, d, e). We summarise the method here and discuss further how the method handles incomplete information.
Suppose an apriori mass assignment m_a is given over the focal set A whose elements are subsets of the power set $P(X)$ where X is a set of labels. This assignment represents general tendencies and is derived from statistical considerations of some sample space or general rules applicable to such a space.

Suppose we also have a set of specific evidences $\{E1, E2, ..., En\}$ where for each i, Ei is (mi, Fi) where Fi is the set of focal elements of $P(X)$ for Ei and mi is the mass assignment for these focal elements. These evidences are assumed to be relevant to some object and derived by consideration of this object alone and not influenced by the sample space of objects from which the object came from.

We wish to update the apriori assignment m_a with $\{E1, ..., En\}$ to give the updated mass assignment m such that the minimum information principle concerned with the relative information of m given m_a is satisfied.

The iterative assignment method updates m_a first with E1 to give $m^{(1)}$. This is updated with E2 to give $m^{(2)}$ and so on until $m^{(n)}$ is reached. $m^{(i)}$ satisfies Ei but not necessarily E1, ..., E(i-1). m_a is then replaced with $m^{(n)}$ and the whole process repeated. This is repeated until the process converges in which case
$m^{(1)} = m^{(2)} = ... = m^{(n)} = m'$ say. This process can be depicted as

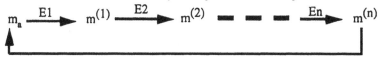

The one step algorithm is as follows:
Consider that we wish to update the mass assignment m with E to give the mass assignment m' where

$m = (t, T)$ where $t = \{t1, ..., tm\}$, $T = \{T1, ..., Tm\}$, Ti is a subset of $P(X)$. i.e.
$m = T1 : t1, ..., Tm : tm$

and $E = (t^E, T^E)$ where $t = \{t^E1, ..., t^Es\}$, $T^E = \{T^E1, ..., T^Es\}$, T^Ei is a subset of $P(X)$.
$E = T^E1 : t^E1, ... , T^Es : t^Es$
$m' = (t', T')$ where $t' = \{t'1, ..., t'r\}$ and $T' = \{T'1, ..., T'r\}$
$T' = Set\{Bag\{Ti \cap T^Ej \mid Ti \cap T^Ej \neq \emptyset\}\}$

$$t'k = \sum_{i,j : Ti \cap T^Ej = T'k} K_j \; ti \; t'j \qquad \text{for } k = 1, ..., r$$

where

$$K_j = \frac{1}{1 - \sum_{q : Tq \cap T^Ej = \emptyset} tq} \qquad \text{for } j = 1, ..., s$$

It should be noted that the label set can change from stage to stage of the complete process

6. A NONMONOTONIC LOGIC EXAMPLE

All Jacob's hire cars are non-automatic   i.e $Pr(\neg a \mid h) = 1$
60% of non-automatic cars have 5 forward gears   i.e $Pr(g \mid \neg a) = 0.6$
No Jacob's hire cars has 5 forward gears   i.e. $Pr(g \mid h) = 0$
Only 5% of automatic cars have 5 forward gears   i.e. $Pr(g \mid a) = 0.05$
70% of cars are nonautomatic   i.e $Pr(a) = 0.7$

Query:
Given that a particular car is believed with degree 0.9 to be non-automatic and with degree 0.7 to be a Jacob's hire car, what is the probability that the car has 5 gears?
ie given $Pr'(\neg a) = 0.9$, $Pr'(h) = 0.7$ determine $Pr'(g)$

The general information about cars provides the following
$Pr(g \neg a) = 0.63$, $Pr(ga) = 0.015$, $Pr(\neg g \neg a) = 0.07$, $Pr(\neg ga) = 0.285$
so that the apriori distribution over instantiations of AHG where A is a or $\neg a$, H is h or $\neg h$ and G is g or $\neg g$ is
$\{\neg ah \neg g, \neg a \neg h \neg g\} : 0.07$, $\neg a \neg hg : 0.63$, $a \neg hg : 0.015$, $a \neg h \neg g : 0.285$
The first and third general statements are logic rules and eliminates $\{\neg ahg, ahg, ah \neg g\}$
From this apriori we can determine
$Pr(g \mid \neg ah) = 0$, $Pr(g \mid \neg a \neg h) = 0.63 / (0/63 + z) = [0.9, 1]$ where $0 \leq z \leq 0.07$, and
$Pr(g \mid a \neg h) = 0.015 / 0.3 = 0.05$

The specific evidences can be combined using the general assignment method to give
$Pr'(\neg ah) = 0.7$, $Pr'(\neg a \neg h) = 0.2$, $Pr'(a \neg h) = 0.1$, $Pr'(ah) = 0$
since

	$h : 0.7$	$\neg h : 0.3$
0.9 $\neg a$	$\neg ah$ 0.7	$\neg a \neg h$ 0.2
0.1 a	Not Allowed $\emptyset$ 0	$a \neg h$ 0.1

The general assignment method uses the general logic statements to disallow label "ah"
The apriori distribution can be updated using this specific combined information using o Jeffrey's rule

Pr'(g) =
    Pr(g | ah)Pr'(ah) + Pr(g | a¬h)Pr'(a¬h) + Pr(g | ¬ah)Pr'(¬ah) + Pr(g | ¬a¬h)Pr'(¬a¬h)
        = 0.2[0.9, 1] + 0.1 0.05 = [0.185, 0.205]

If we use the iteration update algorithm to update the apriori with the combined specific evidence for particular car we obtain
Pr'(g) = 0.205

We can obtain the same results if we update the apriori first with respect to the first evidence and then with the second evidence using the iterative updating assignment algorithm.

7. FUZZY APPLICATIONS

The methods described in this paper can be used for approximate reasoning and fuzzy control. Advantages in using these methods is that both fuzzy and probabilistic evidences are allowed. An initial design of an assignment machine which exploits inherent parallelism has been explored.

8. REFERENCES

Baldwin J.F, (1986), "Support Logic Programming", in: A.I.Jones et al,. Eds., Fuzzy Sets Theory and Applications, (Reidel, Dordrecht-Boston).

Baldwin J.F, (1987), "Evidential Support Logic Programming", Fuzzy Sets and Systems, **24**, pp 1-26.

Baldwin J.F. , Pilsworth B.W, Martin T, (1987), "FRIL Manual", Fril Systems Ltd, St Anne's House, St Anne's Rd, Bristol BS4 4A, UK

Baldwin J.F., (1989), "A New Approach to Combining Evidences for Evidential Reasoning",ITRC Univ. of Bristol Report

Baldwin J.F., (1990a), "Computational Models of Uncertainty Reasoning in Expert Systems", Computers Math. Applic., Vol. 19, No 11, pp 105-119.

Baldwin J.F., (1990b), "Combining Evidences for Evidential Reasoning", Int. J. of Intelligent Systems, To Appear.

Baldwin J.F., (1990c), "Towards a general theory of intelligent reasoning", 3rd Int. Conf IPMU, Paris, July 1990

Baldwin J. F., (1991) Algebra of Mass Assignments ITRC Report, Univ. of Bristol

Baldwin J.F, Pilsworth B.W (1990), "Semantic Unification of Fuzzy Concepts in FRIL", Proceedings of the 3rd International IMPU Conference, Paris.

Baldwin J, F, (1990d), Evidential Reasoning under Probabilistic and Fuzzy Uncertainties, in "An introduction to Fuzzy Logic Applications in Intelligent Systems Ed. R. R. Yager and L. A. Zadeh, Kluwer Academic Publishers, To Appear

Baldwin J, F. , (1990 e), Inference under uncertainty for Expert System Rules, ITRC 152 Univ. of Bristol Report, To Appear

Baldwin J.F. (1990f), Inference for Information Systems containing Probabilistic and Fuzzy Uncertainties, in Fuzzy Logic for the Management of Uncertainty, Ed. Lotfi L. Zadeh and Janusz Kacpzyk, Wiley & Sons, To Appear

Baldwin J.F. (1990g), The management of fuzzy and probabilistic uncertainties for knowledge based systems, ITRC Univ of Bristol Report No. 154, To appear in AI Encyclopaedia

Dubois D., Prade H., (1990a), "Fuzzy sets in approximate reasoning, Part 1 Inference and possibility distributions", To Appear in Fuzzy Sets and Systems.

Dubois D., Prade H., (1990b), "Fuzzy sets in approximate reasoning, Part 2 Logical Approaches", To Appear in Fuzzy Sets and Systems.

Jeffrey R., (1965) "The Logic of Decision", McGraw-Hill, New York

Klir G.J., Folger T.A., (1988), Fuzzy Sets, Uncertainty, and Information, Prentice-Hall

Lauritzen S.L, Spiegelhalter D.J., (1988), "Local computations with probabilities on graphical structures and their application to expert systems", J. Roy. Stat. Soc. Ser. B 50(2), 157-224

Lopez de Mantaras R., (1990), Approximate Reasoning models, Ellis Horwood Ltd

Martin T.P. , Baldwin J.F. (1990), "An Abstract Mechanism for Handling Uncertainty", Proceedings of the 3rd International IMPU Conference, Paris.

Pearl J., (1988), "Probabilistic reasoning in Intelligent Systems", Morgan Kaufmann Pub. Co.

Pearl J., (1990), "Reasoning with Belief functions : An analysis of compatibility", Int. J. of Approx Reasoning, vol 4, n0. 5/6. pp 363-389.

Shafer G., (1976), "A mathematical theory of evidence" , Princeton Univ. Press

Shenoy P.P., (1989), "A Valuation - Based Language for Expert Systems, Int. J. of Approx. Reasoning, V0l 3, No. 5.

Shenoy P.P, Shafer G., (1990), "Axioms for probability and belief-function propagation, in Uncertainty in Artificial Intelligence 4, Eds Shachter et al, North Holland

Smets P., (1988), Belief Functions, in Non-Standard Logics for Automated Reasoning, Eds Smets et al, Academic Press, pp 253-286

Smets P., (1990), The combination of Evidences in the Transferable Belief Model, IEEE Trans. PAMI 12, 442-258

Zadeh L, (1965), "Fuzzy sets", Information and Control, **8,** pp 338-353.

Zadeh L,. (1975), Fuzzy logic and Approximate Reasoning, Synthese, 30, pp407-428

Zadeh L, (1978), "Fuzzy Sets as a basis for a theory of Possibility", Fuzzy Sets and Systems **1,** 3-28

Zadeh L., (1983), "The role of fuzzy logic in the management of uncertainty in expert systems, Fuzzy Sets and Systems, 11, pp199-227

Zadeh L., (1986), "A simple view of the Dempster-Shafer theory of evidence and its implications for the role of combination, AI Mag. 7(2), 85-90.

LEARNING OF UNCERTAIN CLASSIFICATION RULES
IN MEDICAL DIAGNOSIS

Elisabetta Binaghi

Istituto di Fisica Cosmica e Tecnologie Relative - C.N.R.

Via Ampere 56, 20133 Milano

Abstract

In the paper a fuzzy learning algorithm is presented and its application to a real medical problem is detailed.

Keywords

Learning, Classification, Osteoporosis

1.Introduction

In the paper an intuitive learning by example algorithm is presented which adopts a direct method based on fuzzy reasoning operators to automatically infer the strenght of implication of medical diagnostic classification rules (Binaghi E, 1990), (Binaghi E, et al 1991) given a training set of clinical cases.

The classification rules involved in medical diagnostic processes may be modelled in terms of fuzzy production rules, R_i: $A_i \rightarrow^{wt} D_k$ (Zadeh L A, 1981a): where

- A_i is a fuzzy compound declarative proposition of the form

$S_1 is A_{1,J1} And \ldots And S_n is A_{n,Jn}$, and the term $S_h is A_{h,Jh}$ represents the linguistic description of a medical sign concerned;

- $A_{h,Jh}$ is a term belonging to the predefined term set of the linguistic variable S_h It denotes a fuzzy set in a given universe of discourse U_h characterized by a membership function $\mu_{A_{J,jh}}(u_h), u_h \in U_h$. Applying the rule pertaining to composition (Zadeh L A, 1981a) , the membership function of the global fuzzy set associated with the antecedent A_i of the rule R_i is obtained.

- $D_k, 1 \leq k \leq K$ belongs to a predefined set of diagnostic classes

- w_i^k is a term expressing the strength of implication in the fuzzy production rule, i.e. the degree of satisfaction or certainty with which a conclusion may be inferred. It belongs to the term set of a linguistic variable W the values of which are the possible linguistic expression of the strength of implication for a given application and is therefore a fuzzy set defined in the interval [0,1].

The possibility value $\Pi(D_k)$ of assigning the diagnostic class D_k to a given image structure is computed according to Zadeh's possibility theory (Zadeh L A, 1981b).

2.Learning of Fuzzy Production Rules

Various methods have been proposed as ways of learning in fuzzy environment. How to obtain the relations between the variables from a collection of statistical data has been studied by Pedrycz (1984,1985), using the method of fuzzy relational equations. A stastistical method of learning the membership of fuzzy naming relations from imprecise descriptions of the input patterns has been reported by De Mori and Saitta (1980) and applied in the medical diagnosis field (Lesmo L, 1982). J. Aguilar Martin and R. Lopez de Mantaras (1982) present a system capable of learning the meaning of linguistic descritors of concepts basing on Augmented Transition Networks and Semantic Networks.

In this work the problem of learning fuzzy classification rules is formulated in terms of how to automatically induce, from a training set of example T^* , the strengths of implication w_i^k for each rule R_i and for a given diagnostic class D_k. These examples are diagnosed clinical cases, each of which may be formalized in the following form:

$$t^k = [u_t ; jd_t^k], \quad t^k \in T^k$$

where u_t is the vector of measurements obtained in correspondence with the selected set of signs, jd_t^k is the expert's judgement expressing the strength or degree of satisfaction with which the given patient having signs u_t may be assigned to the diagnostic class D_k. We assume that experts must use predefined linguistic labels to express their mental judgement.

Given the diagnostic class D_k, let: l ,the cardinality of the set of all the possible antecedent $\{A_i\}$, m , the cardinality of the training set T^k, and p, the cardinality of the term set W containing the terms with which the strength of the implication may be expressed.

Matrices M_1^k and M_2^k are then defined:

$$M_1^k = \begin{matrix} \mu_{A_1}(u_1) \dots \cdots \mu_{A_1}(u_p) \\ \dots \\ \mu_{A_l}(u_1) \dots \cdots \mu_{A_l}(u_p) \end{matrix} \qquad M_2^k = \begin{matrix} \mu_{w_1}(jd_1^k) \dots \mu_{w_k}(jd_1^k) \\ \dots \\ \mu_{w_1}(jd_p^k) \dots \cdots \mu_{w_k}(jd_p^k) \end{matrix}$$

By performing the matrix product $G = M_1^k o M_2^k$ using max-min operators, matrix G with dimension $l \times m$ is obtained. The element g_{ij} expresses the induced degree of certainty with which the rule $A_i \rightarrow^{w_j} D_k$ may be generated.

A decision-making activity is performed to select the best strength value w_j^k which may be assigned to each $A_{i,} D_k$ pair. The rule $A_i \rightarrow w_j^k D_k$ is created if: $g_{ij} = \max_h(g_{hj})$ $1 \le h \le m$

In conjunction with the above condition we have: $g_{ij} > ts$ being ts the threshold value.

3.The Learning of Classification Rules in the Diagnosis of Osteoporosis

Osteoporosis is defined as an "an absolute decrease in the amount of bone to a level below that required for mechanical support" (Wyngaarden & Smith 1985).

Pathogenetic mechanisms and risk factors are cumulative and may be multiple in any given patient. These considerations suggested the design of a knowledge-based system that could function as an active support in the diagnosis of involutional osteoporosis. In this context medical knowledge can be formalized and stored in terms of a set of fuzzy conditional statements.

The symptoms considered are 29, including: Hematic and Chemical Parameters, Mineralometric Parameters, Generic Risk Factors, Specific Risk Factors. Each symptom is considered a linguistic variable and linguistic description of corresponding symptoms are represented in terms of fuzzy propositions of the form X is A. Membership functions have been elicited with a traditional interview, by evaluating "degrees of certainty" in the answer of several medical experts and by setting suitable parameters for standard piecewise quadratic functions defined by Zadeh (1981a). Three diagnostic classes expressing the degree of severity of the disease are introduced for each disease category: Definite, Possible, Excluded. Each class is treated as a linguistic variable with term sets that can cover all the linguistic expressions used by the physicians in discribing the diagnostic situation. the term set is: $T = \{very\ low, low, medium, high, very\ high\}$

Reasonable numerical representatives for linguistic fuzzy values have been selected to facilitate fuzzy inference. Following the method presented in Adlassnig annd Kolarz (1982), the computed numerical values are: $very\ low = 0.1$ $low = 0.25$, $medium = 0.5$, $high = 0.75$, $high = 0.75$, $very\ high = 0.9$.

The examples considered were clinical cases of female subjects diagnosed as postmenopausal and senile osteoporosis. Background knowledge, in the form of rules, has been used to prune the antecedent explosion for each diagnostic subclass considered.

Results obtained for each diagnostic subclass are the following:

- Conclamata Osteoporosis
  - N. of Examples = 9   Thresh. = 0.5 N. of Rules = 54
- Osteoporosis in Progress
  - N. of Examples = 53   Thresh. = 0.5 N. of Rules = 98
- Pre-Osteoporosis
  - N. of Examples = 100   Thresh. = 0.5 N. of Rules = 228

The implemented fuzzy logic inference mechanism used the generated rules to deduce diagnostic conclusions. Clinical cases used as examples have been diagnosed correctly. Automated results have been compared with the clinical diagnosis for 50 cases. The results coincided with the 89% of cases.

Plans to extend the set of test cases have been made. The accuracy of the generated rules will be evaluated by using the extended test sets and will be compared with the accuracy resulting form of rules elicited with the direct interviews.

References

Aguilar Martin J., R. Lopez de Mantara. The process of classification and learning the meaning of linguistic descriptors of concepts, In: Approximate Reasoning in Decision Analysis. Gupta M M and Sanchez E (eds), pp.165-175.

Binaghi E (1990). A Fuzzy Logic Inference Model for a Rule-Based System in Medical Diagnosis, Expert Systems, 7(3): 134-141.

Binaghi E, Della Ventura A, Rampini A, Schettini R (1991). A Fuzzy Knowledge-Based System for Biomedical Image Interpretation, Lecture Notes in Computer Science, R. Yager and B. Bouchon eds., Springer Verlag, June 1991 (in press).

De Mori R and Saitta L (1980). Automatic learning of fuzzy naming relations over finite languages. Information Sciences. 21: 93-139.

Lesmo L, Saitta L, Torasso P (1982). Learning of Fuzzy Production Rules for Medical Diagnosis. In: Approximate Reasoning in Decision Analysis. Gupta M M and Sanchez E (eds), pp.249-260.

Pedrycz W(1984). An identification algorothm in fuzzy relational systems. Fuzzy Sets and System. 13:153-167.

Pedrycz W (1985). Applications of Fuzzy Relational Equations for methods of reasoning in presence of Fuzzy Data. Fuzzy Sets and Systems. 16: 163-175.

Wyngaarden and Smith eds. (1990), Cecil Textbook of Medicine" Saunders.

Zadeh L A (1981). PRUF - a meaning representation language for natural languages. In: Fuzzy Reasoning and its Applications, Mamdani E H and Gaines B R. (eds) Academic Press, London, pp. 1-58

Zadeh L A (1981). Fuzzy Sets as a Basis for a Theory of Possibility. Fuzzy Sets and Systems, 5: 3-28.

Assertional Default Theories

Gerhard Brewka
GMD, Postfach 12 40,
D-5205 Sankt Augustin, Germany

1. Background

This paper presents some modifications of Reiter's Default Logic DL (Reiter 80), one of the most expressive and most widely used nonmonotonic formalisms. Two problems with this logic have been discussed in an earlier paper (Brewka 91):

1) The consistency conditions (justifications) of defaults applied within one extension are not jointly consistent with the generated extension. Reiter's fixed point definition only guarantees that each consistency condition in isolation is consistent with the extension. This leads to counterintuitive results as discussed in (Poole 89).

2) DL is not cumulative (Makinson 89), that is the addition of formulas contained in all extensions of a default theory (D,W) to W may change the set of generated extensions and hence the skeptically derivable formulas. This makes it questionable whether the skeptical derivability relation of DL can be characterized as an inference relation at all. What we usually expect from an inference relation is that it makes knowledge which is implicit in the premises explicit, but adding implicit knowledge in an explicit form to the premises should not change the inferences.

The solution to both problems developed in (Brewka 91), the logic CDL, is based on a shift from simple propositions to more complicated structures called assertions. Basically, an assertion (a,X) consists of a first-order formula a and a (finite) set of formulas X, the support of a. The intuitive meaning of the assertion is: a is believed since X is consistent with what is believed and the consistency conditions of other believed fomulas. Given an assertional default theory (D,W), where D is a set of Reiter defaults and W a set of assertions, extensions can be defined in the following way:

Definition 1: *An extension of an assertional default theory (D,W) is a fixed point of the operator Γ which, given a set of assertions S, produces the smallest set of assertions S´ such that*

1) $W \subseteq S´,$

2) $Th_S(S´) = S´,$

3)   *if $(A{:}B/C) \in D$, $(A,\{J_1,....J_k\}) \in S´$, and*

   $\{B, C\} \cup Form(S) \cup Supp(S)$ *is consistent,*

   then $(C,\{J_1,....J_k,B,C\}) \in S´$.

Here Form(S) = {p | (p,X) ∈ S} andSupp(S) = {r_i | (p,{r_1,...,r_n}) ∈ S, 1≤i≤n}. Th_S(A) is the smallest set such that A ⊆ Th_S(A) and if (p_1,J_1),...,(p_k,J_k) ∈ Th_S(A) and p_1, ..., p_k |- q, then (q,J_1 ∪ ... ∪ J_k) ∈ Th_S(A).[1]

In (Brewka 91) CDL is shown to satisfy existence of extensions, semi-monotony, and cumulativity. An Etherington-style semantics for CDL has been presented in (Schaub 91).

2. The floating conclusions problem

Unfortunately CDL's solution to the two problems mentioned in Section 1 introduces a new problem (Brewka et al 91): the floating conclusions problem. Floating conclusions are conclusions that appear in every extension, but with different supports. Consider the following assertional default theory:

Example 1)   :¬A/B, :¬B/A, (A -> C,{}), (B -> C,{})

CDL generates two extensions, one containing (C, {¬A,B}), the other one (C, {¬B,A}), but there is no assertion with supported formula C in all extensions. This is unfortunate since intuitively C should be contained in the skeptical beliefs, even if there are different supports for it. The question we want to address in this paper is: can the floating conclusions problem of CDL be solved in a way such that the nice properties of the logic, e.g. cumulativity, existence of extensions, are not destroyed.

The answer will be yes. Our solution is based on the following basic ideas:

- We extend assertions and admit multiple supports, i.e. assertions of the form (a, X_1,..., X_n).

- Instead of generating multiple extensions, we generate a single set of credulous beliefs containing all the former extensions. This is possible, since the assertions carry support information with them, i.e. (a,X) is not necessarily inconsistent with (¬a,Y). It is necessary since each of the former extensions could only "see" itself, but we have to look at various (old) extensions if there are different reasons for believing a proposition.

- We have to define skeptical belief in a new way.

It turns out that a notion of extension can be introduced without reference to a fixed point construction.

3. CDL* - Basic Definitions

We now define the nonmonotonic logic CDL*.

Definition 2: *An assertion is of the form (a, X_1,..., X_n) where a, the asserted formula, is a proposition and X_i, the supports of the assertion, are (finite) sets of propositions.*

If n=1 then the assertion is called *basic*. A support is called *tautological* if the conjunction of its elements is a tautology. Equivalence transformations on the supports are possible. We will assume that tautological supports are always represented as the empty set.

---

[1] "|-" stands for classical provability.

Definition 2 is the straightforward extension of CDL assertions to the case where one proposition may have different supports. However, the intended meaning of the supports has changed slightly. In CDL (a, X) means: a is believed <u>since</u> $\neg X$ is disbelieved[2]. Here (a, X1,...,Xn) means: a is believed <u>if</u> $\neg X1$ is not believed, or ... or $\neg Xn$ is disbelieved <u>and it is possible (given the available information), to disbelieve</u> $\neg Xi$. Possible here means there is an extension (in the former, multiple extension sense) with which X is consistent. Thus the strength of the meaning of an assertion lies between CDL assertions and a default of the form :X/a which says: a is believed <u>if</u> $\neg X$ is not believed.

Definition 3: *Let S be a set of assertions, $J = \{j_1,...,j_n\}$ a set of propositions. We say J is consistent with respect to S (S-consistent) iff J is consistent with $S' = \{p \mid (p, X1, ..., \varnothing, ... ,Xn) \in S\}$.*

Intuitively: J is not S-consistent if S contains "strict" information that it is impossible to jointly believe all elements of J. This definition will be used to check whether the supports of different assertions fit together. A simple example: assume (a,{c,d}) and (b,{e}) are given. We want to know whether we can derive (a & b, {c,d,e}) from this. If S is empty then, obviously, {c,d,e} is S-consistent and we want to include the assertion for a & b in our belief set. If, however, S contains ($\neg c \vee \neg e$, $\varnothing$) then this shows that {c,d,e} cannot be jointly consistent and we do not want to include the assertion for a & b.

We next define the (monotonic) theorems for a set of assertions in the following way:

Definition 4: *Let S and W be sets of assertions. $Th_W(S)$ is the smallest set such that*

1) $S \subseteq Th_W(S)$,

2)   if $(a_1,X_1),...,(a_n,X_n) \in Th_W(S)$, $a_1,...,a_n \mid - b$, and $X_1 \cup...\cup X_n$ is W-consistent,

        then $(b, X_1 \cup...\cup X_n) \in Th_W(S)$.

3) $(a, X_1, ..., X_n) \in Th_W(S)$ iff $(a, X_i) \in Th_W(S)$ for $1 \leq i \leq n$.

Note that according to this definition it makes no difference whether, for instance (a, X_1, X_2) is contained in a set of premises or both (a, X_1) and (a, X_2).

Definition 5: *Let $T = (D, W)$ be an assertional default theory. The credulous belief set E of T is defined inductively as the union of all E_i ($i \geq 0$), where*

        $E_0 = W$, and

        $E_{i+1} = Th_W(E_i) \cup \{(c, X \cup \{b,c\}) \mid a: b \mid c \in D, (a, X) \in S, X \cup \{b,c\}$ is W-consistent$\}$.

Note that this definition is purely inductive. As we produce one set of beliefs instead of multiple fixed points the definition of skeptically derivable assertions is more involved. We first reintroduce the notion of an extension:

Definition 6: *Let E be the credulous belief set of an assertional default theory (D,W). S is an extension of E iff it is a maximal subset of the basic assertions of E such that $Form(S) \cup Supp(S)$ is W-consistent.*

We now can define the skeptical conclusions. Intuitively, an assertion is skeptically derivable if it has support in every extension:

---

[2]We use $\neg X$ to denote the negation of the conjunction of the elements of X.

Definition 7: *Let E be the credulous belief set of an assertional default theory (D,W). An assertion $(q,X_1,..., X_n) \in E$ is skeptically derivable iff for every extension S of E there is $X_i (1 \leq i \leq n)$ such that $(q, X_i) \in S$.*

The floating conclusions problem is solved in CDL*. Let us reconsider Example 1):

:¬A/B, :¬B/A, (A -> C,{ }), (B -> C,{ })

The credulous belief set contains among other assertions:

1)   (A, {¬B, A})   2)   (B, {¬A, B})   3)   (C, {¬B, A})

4)   (C, {¬A, B})   5)   (C, {¬A, B},{¬B, A})

There are two extensions, generated by 1) and 3), respectively 2) and 4). The first, obviously, contains 3), the second 4). For that reason (C, {¬A, B},{¬B, A}) is skeptically derivable. 1) - 4) are not skeptically derivable.

4. Properties of CDL*

We first explore the relationship between CDL and the new logic CDL*. We first show that CDL extensions are contained in the CDL* credulous belief set..

Proposition 1: *If T = (D,W) is a well-based CDL theory (i.e. Form(W) $\cup$ Supp(W) is consistent) then every CDL-extension of T is a CDL*- extension of T.*

In the fixed point definition of CDL there is a condition that defaults can only be applied if justification and consequent are consistent with Form(S) $\cup$ Supp(S). The applicability condition for defaults implicit in our definition of the extension had to be much weaker, of course, as there may be mutually incompatible supports for propositions. This leads to the inclusion of more than the CDL-extensions in the CDL* extension. Consider the following example:

Example 2)   D = {:b/b}, W = {(a,{¬b})}

In CDL we obtain the single extension Th$_S$(W). The default is not applied as ¬b is in the support of W. In the new definition, however, the credulous belief set contains (b,{b}). This shows that more than the CDL extensions are considered. This is a consequence of the changed meaning of supports. The supports of W play more a conditional role than in CDL: *if my beliefs are consistent with ¬b (and it is possible that they are), then I believe a* instead of *I believe a since my beliefs are consistent with ¬b.*

A consequence of this behaviour is that not all assertions in W are skeptically derivable. Here (a, {¬b}) is not, as there is an assertion (b,{b}) in the credulous belief set. Given the new meaning of assertions this behaviour is entirely reasonable.

Example 2 shows that due to the changed meaning of assertions the converse of Proposition 1 does not hold in the general case, i.e. there may be CDL*-extensions which are not CDL-extensions. There is a special case, however, where the converse holds:

Proposition 2: *Let T = (D,W) be a CDL theory such that Supp(W) is empty. Every CDL*-extension of T is a CDL- extension of T.*

We next prove semi-monotonicity and cumulativity. (The existence of extensions is obvious from the inductive definition of the credulous belief set.) We have even a stronger form of semi-monotonicity: not only the addition of defaults lets the credulous belief set and hence the extensions grow monotonically, but also the addition of assertions with non-empty supports. This does, obviously, not imply that skeptical derivability is monotonic in these cases.

Proposition 3: *Let T = (D,W) and T' = (D ∪ D', W ∪ W') default theories, E, respectively E' their credulous belief sets. If W' does not contain an assertion with empty reason then E ⊆ E'.*

Also cumulativity is satisfied:

Proposition 4: *Let T = (D,W) and T' = (D, W ∪ {(p, X1, ..., Xn)}) be default theories, E, respectively E' their credulous belief sets. If (p, X1, ..., Xn) ∈ E then E = E'.*

5. Conclusion

The research reported in this paper was originally motivated by some defects in Reiter's DL. A first solution, CDL, solved the problems but introduced a new one, the floating conclusions problem. We therefore developed a new default logic, CDL*, which is distinct from CDL in the following respects:

- assertions with multiple supports are admitted
- one single set of credulous beliefs containing all CDL-extensions is defined inductively
- skeptical derivability is defined in a new way.

The logic is cumulative and semi-monotonic. Due to the inductive definition of the credulous belief set we expect simpler implementations than for, e.g., DL. Among other things the logic can serve as the theoretical basis of Dressler's NMATMS. It gives intuitively expected results and is more expressive than comparable systems, e.g. Poole's approach (Poole 88).

References

(Brewka 91) Brewka, Gerhard, Cumulative Default Logic: In Defense of Nonmonotonic Inference Rules, *Artificial Intelligence* 51, to appear, 1991

(Dressler 89) Dressler, Oskar, An Extended Basic ATMS, *Proceedings 2nd International Workshop on Non-Monotonic Reasoning*, Grassau, Germany, Springer, LNAI 346 (1989) 143-163.

(Makinson 89) Makinson, David, General Theory of Cumulative Inference, *Proceedings 2nd International Workshop on Non-Monotonic Reasoning*, Grassau, Germany, Springer, LNAI 346 (1989) 1-18.

(Brewka et al 91) Brewka, Gerhard, Makinson, David, Schlechta, Karl, Cumulative Inference Relations for JTMS and Logic Programming, Proc. First International Workshop on Logic Programming and Non-Monotonic Reasoning, Washington, 1991, extended version to appear in Proc. NIL-90, Workshop on Nonmonotonic and Inductive Logics, Karlsruhe 1990, 1991

(Poole 88) Poole, David, A Logical Framework for Default Reasoning, *Artificial Intelligence* 36 (1988) 27-47.

(Poole 89) Poole, David, What the Lottery Paradox Tells Us About Default Reasoning, *Proceedings First International Conference on Principles of Knowledge Representation and Reasoning*, Toronto (1989) 333-340.

(Reiter 80) Reiter, Raymond, A Logic for Default Reasoning, *Artificial Intelligence* 13 (1980) 81-132.

(Schaub 91) Schaub, Torsten, Assertional Default Theories: A Semantical View, *Proc. Second International Conference on Principles of Knowledge Representation and Reasoning* (KR-2), 1991

THE RELIABILITY OF REASONING WITH UNRELIABLE RULES AND PROPOSITIONS

L. Cardona, J. Kohlas, P.A. Monney

Institute for Automation and Operations Research
University of Fribourg
CH-1700 Fribourg (Switzerland)
E-mail Kohlas@cfruni51

Abstract

In this paper, the well known mathematical theory of evidence (Shafer, 1976) will be considered from a point of view which is different from usual. Simple belief functions (hints) will be regarded as arguments which are not fully reliable (Kohlas, 1989). This implies that the construction of argumentation chains for a particular hypothesis will have limited reliability. Since there are usually many different ways to argue in favour of a hypothesis, the problem to be addressed is to determine the overall reliability of the arguments.

The point of view adopted here places the model of reasoning with unreliable arguments into the framework of combinatorial reliability theory as developed for the study of technical systems composed of unreliable components (see also Provan, 1990). Most approaches proposed so far for the combination of evidence could be qualified as "forward chaining" methods because all available information is combined to obtain an overall result. In contrast, the method favored in this paper is "backward chaining". In fact, starting with a hypothesis, arguments for it are looked for, searching for sub-hypotheses or subgoals, for which in turn further arguments may be developed. This permits to obtain sequentially refined bounds on the credibility of the hypothesis. In this way, in many cases it becomes possible to avoid the tedious task to combine all hints, even those which do not contribute much to the judgment of the hypothesis.

As an example of an idea inherited from reliability theory, the so-called factorization method can be mentionned. It can be regarded as a mechanism for reasoning with assumptions and represents an alternative procedure to the well known Markov tree approach (Shafer et al., 1986) for the elimination of disturbing dependencies between evidences.

126

1. Introduction.

Consider a set $\{p_1, \ldots, p_n\}$ of atomic propositions which can be true or false. These propositions are related through a certain number of rules $\{R_1, \ldots, R_k\}$ of the form *if $p_i \wedge \ldots \wedge p_j$ then p_k*. Uncertainty is introduced in this framework because it is not possible to decide whether a proposition is true or not. We only dispose of a hint which can be reliable or not. The notion of a hint is extensively discussed in the paper of Kohlas et al. (1990). If the hint is reliable (with probability m_i), then proposition p_i must be true. So one might think of m_i as the degree of credibility of p_i induced by the hint. In contrast, if the hint is not trustworthy (with probability $1 - m_i$), then nothing can be inferred and both p_i and $\neg p_i$ might be true. Note that $1 - m_i$ is **not** the credibility that p_i is false. This allows to speak of m_i as the reliability of p_i. In the same way, the rules too are not fully reliable and r_k represents the credibility that rule R_k is valid or the reliability of the rule.

These elements can be visualized in a bipartite oriented graph as pictured in figure 1, where the rectangles represent rules and circles represent propositions.

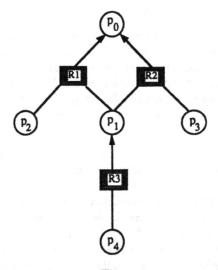

Figure 1

It is supposed that the graph contains no circuit (oriented cycles). This type of model is called an **inference network**. Now consider the hypothesis that a given proposition p_h is true. The problem to be addressed is then how to construct arguments for this hypothesis from the given unreliable information about propositions and rules.

2. Inference trees.

To start with, consider the case where the graph is a tree, as for example in figure 2, and suppose that we are interested in the hypothesis that proposition p_1 is true. Each node of the tree, which represents either a proposition or a rule, is called an **argument**. A set of arguments whose validity permits to logically deduce p_1 is called a **proof**. More precisely, a proof is a set of arguments A such that it is possible to prove p_1 assuming that all arguments in A are true and all arguments outside A are false. For example, $A_1 = \{p_2, p_3, R_1\}$ is a proof, but $A_2 = \{p_2, p_4, R_1\}$ is not. The link with reliability theory is established if we regard the arguments as the individual components of a technical system and the proofs as the links of the system, a component being called functioning iff its corresponding argument is true. In the example from figure 2, the system can be decomposed into three parallel **modules**. In fact, the system is in good state (p_1 can be proved) if and only if at least one of the subsystems S_1, S_2 or S_3 is in good state, where S_1 is the subtree $\{p_2, p_3, R_1\}$, S_2 the subtree $\{p_4, p_5, p_6, p_7, p_8, R_2, R_3\}$ and $S_3 = \{p_1\}$. The notion of module is well known in reliability theory and can be properly defined in terms of boolean functions (Kohlas, 1987).

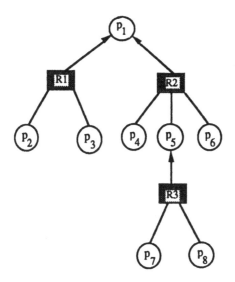

Figure 2

The link with reliability theory is exposed in details in the paper of Kohlas (1989). The idea to use network reliability methods in the context of modelling reasoning under uncertainty has also been put forward in a recent paper by Provan (1990) where connections between logics and evidence theory are examined. In consequence, if $cr(p_i)$ denotes the overall credibility of p_i, then

$$cr(p_7) = m_7, cr(p_8) = m_8 \tag{1}$$

$$cr(p_5) = 1 - (1 - m_5)(1 - r_3 cr(p_7) cr(p_8)) \tag{2}$$

$$cr(p_1) = 1 - [(1 - m_1)(1 - r_1 cr(p_2) cr(p_3))(1 - r_2 cr(p_4) cr(p_5) cr(p_6))] \tag{3}$$

$$cr(p_2) = m_2, cr(p_3) = m_3, cr(p_4) = m_4, cr(p_6) = m_6. \tag{4}$$

This corresponds to a **forward chaining** approach because we start computing credibility from the leaves in direction of the goal proposition p_1. But one might think also of a **backward chaining** procedure. In this case, the chaining develops as follows. At first, only rules having the goal proposition as conclusion are considered (in figure 2, only rules R_1 and R_2). Together with the propositions involved in these rules, this defines a subtree T_1 of the original tree T. Since the true credibility in each leaf proposition p_i of T_1 is at least m_i, a lower bound for the overall credibility in the goal proposition is obtained by setting $cr(p_i) = m_i$ for each leaf proposition. Similarly, an upper bound is obtained when $cr(p_i)$ is set to 1 for those propositions which are leaves in T_1 but not in the original tree T. If these bounds are judged not sufficiently close, then a further step is performed by considering a new rule whose conclusion is in T_1, thereby augmenting the partial tree T_1 to a new tree T_2. The bounds obtained from T_2 will of course be tighter than those obtained with T_1. Partial trees are developped in this way until either the bounds are judged to be tight enough, or the original tree is considered, in which case the two bounds coincide. An important question in this approach is how to select further rules (arguments) to improve the credibility bounds.

3. General inference networks.

How can inference networks which are not trees be handled? Consider the graph given in figure 1. It is easily seen that proposition p_1 introduces a disturbing dependency. However, if p_1 is considered to be true, then the credibility in p_0 is

$$p^+ = 1 - (1 - m_0)(1 - m_2 r_1)(1 - m_3 r_2). \tag{5}$$

On the other hand, if p_1 false, then the credibility in p_0 is simply $p^- = m_0$. The credibility in p_1 itself is

$$q_1 = 1 - (1 - m_1)(1 - m_4 r_3) = m_1 + (1 - m_1) m_4 r_3 \tag{6}$$

and therefore the exact overall credibility in p_0 is

$$cr(p_0) = q_1 p^+ + (1 - q_1) p^-. \tag{7}$$

This method to cope with dependencies is called **factorization** or **hypothetical reasoning**. It is a well known technique in reliability theory and can be applied to much more complicated situations with multiple sources of dependencies (Kohlas, 1989). In fact, the reliability of any monotone system can eventually be obtained by repeated factorization. The computational efficiency of the method relies finally on the number of dependencies involved and also on the sequence in which the factorizations are performed. This represents an alternative to the traditional Markov tree approach to cope with dependencies (Shafer et al., 1986). Note that factorization methods are also well known in Bayesian networks (Pearl, 1988). This method can also be incorporated in a backward chaining procedure which is extensively discussed in the paper of Cardona et al. (1991). This paper contains also a complete formal description of the ideas presented in this paper.

4. Outlook.

During the backward chaining process, the selection of further arguments is crucial for obtaining tight credibility bounds as quickly as possible. Therefore, heuristics based on the notion of importance of an argument can be envisaged. This is only one aspect of the more general question of computational efficiency to be addressed. An explication module highlighting the most striking arguments should also be incorporated in the system. Furthermore, the possibility to consider hints for negated propositions and rules involving such propositions should be introduced. This can generate internal contradictions which can be resolved by Dempster's rule. Finally, let's mention the relation of the model discussed in this paper with the assumption-based truth maintenance systems (ATMS) in artificial intelligence (Blackmond Laskey et al., 1989).

5. References

Blackmond Laskey K.; Lehner P.E. (1989): Assumptions, Beliefs and Probabilities. *Artificial Intelligence*, 41, 65–77.

Cardona L.; Kohlas J.; Monney P.A. (1991): Reasoning on Inference Nets with Unreliable Arguments *Institute for Automation and Operations Research, University of Fribourg*, No. 185. (to appear).

Kohlas, J. (1987): *Zuverlässigkeit und Verfügbarkeit*. Teubner, Stuttgart.

Kohlas, J. (1989): The Reliability of Reasoning with Unreliable Arguments. *Institute for Automation and Operations Research, University of Fribourg*, No. 168. To appear in *The Annals of Operations Research*.

Kohlas J.; Monney P.A. (1990): Modeling and Reasoning With Hints. *Institute for Automation and Operations Research, University of Fribourg*, No. 174.

Pearl J. (1988): *Probabilistic Reasoning in Intelligent Systems. Networks of Plausible Inference*. Morgan and Kaufman.

Provan G.M. (1990): A Logic-Based Analysis of Dempster-Shafer Theory. *Int. J. of Approximate Reasoning* 4 451–495.

Shafer G. (1976): *A Mathematical Theory of Evidence*. Princeton University Press.

Shafer, G.; Shenoy, P.P.; Meloulli K. (1986): Propagating Belief Functions in Qualitative Markov Trees. *Intern. J. of Approximate Reasoning*, 1, 349-400.

A. Chateauneuf, R. Kast, A. Lapied[1]

Comunication at ECSQAU, Marseille 15-17 october 91

Uncertainty in the valuation of risky assets

Risky financial assets are defined by their future random payments or their returns, in most modern Finance models. Under the hypothesis that markets do not allow arbitrage opportunities, it has been shown in modern Finance models (Black and Scholes' [1973] famous option valuation formula for instance) that assets are valuated by the expectation of their random payments with respect to a probability distribution. This distribution is called the implicit distribution because it is not the objective distribution that was used to describe uncertainty. Because there are no arbitrages, the value of an asset is a linear function of its random payments, and under some assumptions a Riesz decomposition theorem can be used to express this linear functional as a mathematical expectation.

In the first part of the paper we indicate which No Arbitrage assumptions (we distinguish two) give the linearity and the positivity necessary to use the decomposition theorem when considering a probability space $(S, \mathcal{A}, P)$ where S, the set of states, is not necessarily finite. The precise result we obtain is important because it allows to give an economic foundation to general Finance models under the assumption that uncertainty is described by a probability space. Such an economic foundation had already been given (Arrow [1953]) in a more general setting, since in Arrow's model uncertainty is described merely through a measurable space $(S, \mathcal{A})$ (no probability distribution is given; on the other hand there is some restriction since only a finite S was considered).

We keep this type of generality in the second part of the paper where we define an asset by the list of its future payments. Future payments are contingent to states of nature in a given measurable space $(S, \mathcal{A})$ but we do not assume it is probabilized, nor finite. First we show that translating No Arbitrage assumptions in this non probabilized setting, leads again to a valuation of assets in terms of mathematical expectation. Then we consider an asset valuation founded on the representation of an ordering consistent with market prices. Market prices rank marketed assets; this ranking is extended to the set of all assets under some assumptions related to the way the market works. One assumption can give a mathematical expectation valuation of future payments in the same way the No Arbitrage assumptions did in equilibrium models. However it can be weakened so as to allow some kind of arbitrage opportunities which can be observed in real markets. On the mathematical level this last model is interesting by its representation of an ordering which can be less stringent than the mathematical expectation obtained under no arbitrage. Because arbitrage possibilities leave some indeterminacy in the formation costs of portfolios replicating assets, the valuation of these assets is not expressed by a mathematical expectation but by a Choquet's integral with respect to a capacity (we use Schmeidler's [1986] , [1989] and Yaari's [1987] models). This capacity is implicitly revealed by market prices, prices which, because of arbitrage possibilities, leave some indeterminacy upon assets valuation. The implicit capacity, like the implicit probability in the No Arbitrage theory, is the market appreciation of uncertainty on random payments. When a market is complete, i.e. when there is a sufficient number of marketed assets to replicate any relevant payment scheme by way of a linear combination of marketed assets (portfolio), the implicit distribution is unique and can be calculated using market prices. The determination of a capacity requires many more data than the determination of a probability, this is the price to pay for the indeterminacy arbitrage possibilities leave upon assets valuation.

---

[1]A. Chateauneuf, Université de Paris I, R. Kast, CNRS, Marseille, A. Lapied, Université de Toulon.

1. The case of probabilized uncertainty.

1.1. Arrow's model of assets market with a finite set of states of the world.

Arrow [1953] built up a model in which agents, using assets portfolios, could achieve their optimal consumptions in any uncertain states of the world. Arrow's assets pay one unit of money if a certain state of the world obtains, nothing otherwise. Prices of these assets (one asset for each state of the world) are positive and can be normalized so that they sum to one. Hence they can be interpreted as a probability distribution on the set of states. This distribution is not an objective distribution, even if such an objective distribution exists, nor a subjective distribution agents could assess to the states in order to make their decisions. It is a weighting of the states made by prices which express an aggregation of agents behavior towards uncertainty.

A side result of this model is that assets values are their expected payoffs with respect to the distribution revealed by prices. This is obtained under a "No Arbitrage" asumption (implicit in all equilibrium models): "two assets that are the same can't sell at different prices". This implies that the value of a portfolio is its formation cost, which, in turn implies that the value functional (defined on the set of assets: real valued functions on the set of states) is linear. The functional is positive because of an other "No Arbitrage" assumption: an asset with positive payments must have a non negative value.

1.2. Assets valuation in modern finance models.

Arrow's model and its conclusions can be generalized so as to encompass valuation models in finance, notably the famous one by Black and Scholes. These models assume uncertainty to be described by a probability space $(S, \mathcal{A}, \mu)$ where μ is known.

For instance in the Black and Scholes model, μ is such that the process of future random prices (of the underlying security) is a generalized Wiener process with a constant drift and known instantaneous variance.

The set Y of assets can be taken to be the space $L^2(S, \mathcal{A}, \mu)$ endowed with the L^2 norm topology . Let M ($Y \supseteq M$) denotes the set of marketed assets, and assume the characteristic function 1_S of S, belongs to M (the riskless asset paying one unit of money in all states). Let Θ denote the set of portfolios θ which can be built with marketed assets. By definition a portfolio θ is defined as the list $\theta(y) \in \mathbb{R}$, $y \in M$ of quantities of marketed asset y with which portfolio θ is formed, where only a finite number of $\theta(y)$ is different from zero. Such a portfolio θ uniquely yields an asset, say θ^* the payments of whom

satistfy $\theta^* = \sum_{y \in M} \theta(y) \, y$. Notice that the set $\{\theta^*, \theta \in \Theta\}$ = span(M). Span(M) will be referred to as the set of marketable assets and *we assume that the market is complete*, more precisely we assume that Span(M) = Y. Marketed assets $y \in M$ have prices q(y),

and the formation cost of a portfolio defined by $(\theta(y))_{y \in M}$, is: $K(\theta) = \sum_{y \in M} \theta(y) \, q(y)$.

The No Arbitrage assumptions bear upon portfolios.

No Arbitrage1:
Let θ and θ' be two portfolios such that $\theta^* = \theta'^*$, then $K(\theta) = K(\theta')$.

Thanks to this first condition the value v(y) of a marketable asset y is defined as the (unique) formation cost of any portfolio θ generating it : $\forall\theta\in\Theta$ such that $\theta^* = y$, $v(y) = K(\theta)$. It is easy to check that v is linear on Y.

No Arbitrage 2:
Let θ be a portfolio such that $\theta^*\in Y^+$ (i.e. $\mu[\theta^*\geq 0] = 1$ and $\mu[\theta^*>0] > 0$), then $K(\theta) > 0$.

This second condition says that v is positive.
Hence, through the Riesz representation theorem, one gets:

Theorem 1:

> *Under No Arbitrage conditions 1 and 2 there exists a unique probability measure Π on $(S, \mathcal{S})$ absolutely continuous with μ, and such that the value of any asset is the expectation of its payments: $\forall y\in Y$, $v(y) = E_\Pi(y)$.*
> *Π can be interpreted as a probability distribution revealed by market prices.*

2. Generalisation to the case of non probabilized uncertainty.

The relevance of the a priori distribution μ (on which all agents must agree) can be questionned. It has been introduced in dynamic models to describe the stochastic processes of future prices and to give the set of assets a topological structure. In a static model however, uncertainty may be more correctly described by the space $(S, \mathcal{S})$. In what follows the set Y of assets will be taken to be the space $\mathcal{B}(S, \mathcal{S}, \mathbb{R})$ of bounded $\mathcal{S}$-measurable functions from S to $\mathbb{R}$.

2.1. No Arbitrage assumptions.

Let M denote the set of marketed assets, define portfolios θ as in section 1.2. and assume again that the market is complete $(Y = Span(M))$. With the same notations as above the No Arbitrage assumptions are now:

No Arbitrage1':
Let θ and θ' be two portfolios such that $\theta^* = \theta'^*$, then $K(\theta) = K(\theta')$.
No Arbitrage 2':
Let θ be a portfolio such that $\theta^*\in Y^+$ (i.e. $\forall s\in S$ $\theta^*(s) > 0$), then $K(\theta) > 0$.
In such a case the following theorem can be proved:

Theorem 2:

> *Under No Arbitrage conditions 1' and 2', The formation cost of any asset $y\in Y$ is well defined by $v(y) = K(\theta)$ $\forall\theta\in\Theta$ s.t. $\theta^* = Y$, and there exists a unique probability measure Π on $(S, \mathcal{S})$ such that the value of any asset is the expectation of its payments: $\forall y\in Y$, $v(y) = E_\Pi(y)$.*

Notice that in theorem 2 no normalization is required as we assume as in 1.2. that $1_S \in M$ and $q(1_S) = 1$.

2.2. Prices as a ranking revealed by the market.

Market prices obviously rank marketed assets. If non marketed assets were to have a value, they would be ranked according to this value. Assumptions on the way the market functions, similar to the no arbitrage assumptions in equilibrium theory, impose some properties to this ranking.

Our three first conditions are classical necessary and sufficient conditions to represent a preorder (here the ranking $\geq_\gamma$ on Y by a functional. Here $x \geq_\gamma y$ (resp. $>_\gamma$) means that the value of x is greater (resp. strictly greater) than the value of y, $x \sim_\gamma y$ means x and y have the same value.

Condition 1: The market order $\geq_\gamma$ defines a complete preorder on the set of assets.

Condition 2: The market order respects monotonic uniform convergence.

Condition 3: The market order is monotonic in the sense that if x, $y \in Y$ and $a \in \mathbb{R}_+^*$, then $x \geq y + a1_S$ (in the usual sense for real valued functions) implies that $x \geq_\gamma y$.

It is easy to show that conditions 1, 2 and 3 imply that if $x \geq y$ then $x \geq_\gamma y$ (the market order is monotonic with respect to the natural order on assets).

It is well known from decision theory, that a preorder satisfying the previous three conditions can be represented by a continuous real function, say v, defined up to a monotonic transformation, and such that: $x \geq_\gamma y$ if and only if $v(x) \geq v(y)$.

2.2.1. Linear ranking.

Condition 4: If assets x , y and z are such that $x \sim_\gamma y$, then asset $x + z \sim_\gamma y + z$.

Although this last condition might look quite inocuous at first view, it implies a particular (but nonetheless common to most Finance models) market situation: there cannot be any arbitrage opportunities left, as proved by:

Theorem 3:

> *The ranking on Y is such that there exists a unique probability measure Π on (S,s) such that: $\forall x, y \in Y$, $x \geq_\gamma y \Leftrightarrow E_\Pi(x) \geq E_\Pi(y)$, if and only if conditions 1 to 4 are satisfied.*

2.2.2. CHOQUET ranking.

Here we allow some kind of arbitrage opportunities, weakening condition 4 to condition 4':

Condition 4': If assets x , y and z are such that x $\sim_Y$ y and z is comonotonic with x (i.e. $\forall s,t, \in S$ [z(s) - z(t))][x(s) - x(t)] $\geq$ 0) and comonotonic with y, then asset x + z $\sim_Y$ y + z.

Condition 4' can be justified here by the fact that there is no hedging effect when adding z both to x and y, hence the values of the new assets x + z and y + z should remain the same. Hence we obtain:

<u>Theorem 4</u>:

> *The ranking on Y is such that there exists a unique normalized capacity v on*
> *(S,s) such that: $\forall x,y \in Y$, $x \geq_Y y \Leftrightarrow \int_S x \, dv = \int_S y \, dv$ (*), if and only if*
> *conditions 1 to 4 are satisfied.*
> *(*) Here $\forall z \in Y$, $\int_S z \, dv$ denotes Choquet integral of z with respect to capacity v,*
> *i.e.:*
> $$\int_S z \, dv = \int_{R_-} [v(z \geq t) - 1]dt + \int_{R_+} v(z \geq t)dt \ .$$

References

Arrow, K.J. [1953] "Le rôle des valeurs boursières dans l'allocation optimale des risques" in *Économétrie* 40, pp 41-47, Cahiers du CNRS, Paris.

Black, F, M. Scholes [1973] "The pricing of options and corporate liabilities". *Journal of Political Economy*, 81, pp 637-654.

Schmeidler, D. [1986] " Integral representation without additivity" *Proceedings of the American mathematical society*, vol 97, n° 2.

Schmeidler, D. [1989] "Subjective probability and expected utility without additivity" *Econometrica*, 57, pp. 571-587.

Yaari, M. [1987] " Dual theory of choice under uncertainty" *Econometrica*, 55, pp. 95-115.

ASSESSMENT OF QUALITATIVE JUDGEMENTS FOR CONDITIONAL EVENTS IN EXPERT SYSTEMS

G. Coletti ([*]), A. Gilio ([**]), R. Scozzafava ([**])

([*])   Istituto di Matematica per la Ricerca Operativa,   Univer-
        sita` di Palermo (Italy)
([**]) Dipartimento Metodi e Modelli Matematici, Universita` "La
        Sapienza", Roma (Italy)

1. Introduction

In some previous papers (cfr. [7], [2], [3]) *coherent* probability (numerical or qualitative) has been used as an effective
tool to represent uncertainty in the field of Artificial
Intelligence. Given an expert system, in general it is not
realistic to make probabilistic or even qualitative judgements
for *all* relevant uncertain statements : in fact the   methodology
is based on the *subjective* approach of B. de Finetti (cfr. [4],
[5], [6]), which allows to proceed by a gradual assignment of
probabilities. Uncertain   statements   and   information   are
represented by *conditional events*, and it is initially required
to assess probabilities only for a few ones strictly related to
the problem at hand : then a step by step extension of the
evaluations to further events, constituting a *family without any
particular structure*, is possible.

This procedure has been implemented in [7] and [2] in the case of numerical probability, and in [2] and [3] for qualitative probability : in particular, in the latter paper a necessary and sufficient condition for the representability of a qualitative probability by a numerical one has been expressed by means of a *nonlinear* system (see Sect. 2). In this paper, a significant specific condition on the qualitative probability reduces the problem of checking coherence to the study of a *linear* system.

Other existing theories concerning the management of uncertainty are not related to our approach : for a short discussion and some relevant comments and references, see [3].

2. Coherent qualitative probability

Given a finite family $\mathscr{F}$ of n events, we consider the corresponding $m \leq 2^n$ atoms C_k generated by them and, for every event $A \in \mathscr{F}$, the binary m-vector (for which we shall use the same symbol of the relevant event) $A = (x_1, x_2, \ldots, x_m)$, where $x_k = 1$ when $C_k \subset A$, $x_k = 0$ when $C_k \subset A^c$ (the *contrary* of the event A). For a family of n *conditional* events $E_i | H_i$, we consider, among the atoms generated by the 2n events E_i, H_i, with $i = 1, 2, \ldots, n$, those contained in the union (logical sum) H_o of the H_i's and whose number we denote by r .

The concept of coherence can be based on two well known (and equivalent) criteria. This approach refers to an *arbitrary* set $\mathscr{E}$ of conditional events, *with no underlying structure* (such as Boolean ring, σ-algebra, etc.) and the *coherence* of a function $P : \mathscr{E} \rightarrow [0,1]$ entails that P is a *conditional probability distribution*. The converse in general is not true: sufficient conditions for the coherence of P refer to the structure of $\mathscr{E}$, and so the interest for a direct check of coherence is clear.

A qualitative (or comparative) probability is a binary relation $\cdot\geq$ on $\mathscr{E}$, expressing the intuitive idea of *"not less probable than"* ; we may define also the relations $\cdot=$ and $\cdot>$, whose derivation from $\cdot\geq$ is straightforward.

We require that $\cdot\geq$ satisfies the following properties

(A0) $\cdot\geq$ is a *preorder* (i.e., it is reflexive and transitive, but not necessarily complete);

(A1) If $AH \neq \emptyset$, then $A|H \cdot> \emptyset$ ($\emptyset$ is the impossible event).

(A2) If $AH \cdot\geq BK$ and $K \cdot\geq H$, then $A|H \cdot\geq B|K$.

The qualitative probability $\cdot\geq$ is *coherent* if there exists a coherent conditional probability P on $\mathscr{E}$ such that

$$A|H \cdot\geq B|K \implies P(A|H) \geq P(B|K) ,$$

$$A|H \cdot> B|K \implies P(A|H) > P(B|K) .$$

Coherence conditions for qualitative probability on a family of nonconditional events have been established in [1] by means of suitable linear systems. The case of a family $\mathscr{E}$ of *conditional* events has been dealt with in [3] : it requires the study of a *nonlinear* system $\mathscr{N}$ in the unknown vector $W = (w_1, w_2, \ldots, w_r)$

$$\begin{cases} \left[(A_i \cdot H_i)* W\right]\left[K_i * W\right] - \left[(B_i \cdot K_i)* W\right]\left[H_i * W\right] \geq 0, \text{ if } A_i|H_i \cdot\geq B_i|K_i, \\[2mm] \left[(A_i \cdot H_i)* W\right]\left[K_i * W\right] - \left[(B_i \cdot K_i)* W\right]\left[H_i * W\right] > 0, \text{ if } A_i|H_i \cdot> B_i|K_i, \\[2mm] H_i * W > 0 , \qquad K_i * W > 0, \qquad W \geq 0 , \end{cases}$$

where $\cdot$ and $*$ denote *dot* and *scalar* product, respectively.

There are situations in which the above system takes a simpler form, for example it becomes *linear*. One of these situations has been dealt with in [3], where, for every compared pair $A|H$ and $B|K$ of conditional events, it is required that the corresponding *conditioning* events are *equivalent*, i.e. $H \cdot= K$.

In the next Section we give another significant condition on the ordering which makes $\mathcal{N}$ become a linear system $\mathcal{L}$.

3. Main result

We consider an ordering $\cdot\geq$ such that for every pair of compared conditional events $A|H$, $B|K$, also the corresponding conditioning events H and K are comparable.

Introduce the following system $\mathcal{L}$, with unknowns the real numbers α_j , β_k and the r-vector $W = (w_1, w_2, \ldots, w_r)$:

$$
\begin{cases}
\left[A_i \cdot H_i - B_i \cdot K_i \right] * W \geq 0 , & \text{if } A_i | H_i \cdot\geq B_i | K_i \text{ and } H_i \cdot= K_i , \\[2mm]
\left. \begin{array}{l}
\left[A_j \cdot H_j - B_j \cdot K_j \right] * W > 0 \\[2mm]
\left[A_j \cdot H_j - \alpha_j B_j \cdot K_j \right] * W \geq 0 \\[2mm]
\left[\alpha_j B_j^c \cdot K_j - A_j^c \cdot H_j \right] * W \geq 0
\end{array} \right\} & \text{if } A_j | H_j \cdot\geq B_j | K_j \text{ and } H_j \cdot> K_j , \\[2mm]
\left. \begin{array}{l}
\left[A_k^c \cdot H_k - B_k^c \cdot K_k \right] * W > 0 \\[2mm]
\left[B_k \cdot K_k - \beta_k A_k \cdot H_k \right] * W \geq 0 \\[2mm]
\left[\beta_k A_k^c \cdot H_k - B_k^c \cdot K_k \right] * W \geq 0
\end{array} \right\} & \text{if } B_k | K_k \cdot\geq A_k | H_k \text{ and } H_k \cdot> K_k , \\[2mm]
H_h * W > 0 , \ K_h * W > 0 \ (h = i, j, k), \ W \geq 0 , \ \alpha_j > 1 , \ \beta_k > 1 .
\end{cases}
$$

Recall that among the conditional events $A|H$ and $B|K$ there are also the nonconditional events H and K , since they can be written as $H|\Omega$ and $K|\Omega$. Moreover, if the right inequalities are strict, at least one of the corresponding inequalities on the left must be read in the same way.

Theorem – Let $\cdot\geq$ be a comparative probability on $\mathcal{E}$ which satisfies (A1) and (A2). If, for any comparable pair $A_h | H_h \cdot\geq B_h | K_h$, one has $H_h \cdot\geq K_h$ or $K_h \cdot\geq H_h$, then the following two statements are equivalent

(i) the comparative probability $\cdot\geq$ is *coherent* ;

(ii) there exists a solution of the system $\mathcal{L}$.

Proof : See *Appendix.*

Remark : If both $H_h \cdot\geq K_h$ and $K_h \cdot\geq H_h$ hold, H_h and K_h are equivalent : the theorem reduces to the case considered in [3]. Note that by normalizing W we get a probability on the atoms.

References

[1] Coletti G., *Coherent qualitative probability*, Journal of Mathematical Psychology 34 (1990), 297–310.

[2] G. Coletti, A. Gilio and R. Scozzafava, *Coherent qualitative probability and uncertainty in Artificial Intelligence*, Proc. 8th Intern. Conf. on Cybernetics and Systems (Vol. I, ed. C.N. Manikopoulos), New York (1990), in press.

[3] G. Coletti, A. Gilio and R. Scozzafava, *Conditional events with vague information in expert systems*, Lecture Notes in Computer Science (eds. B. Bouchon-Meunier, R.R. Yager, L.A. Zadeh), Springer (1990), in press.

[4] B. de Finetti, *Problemi determinati e indeterminati nel calcolo delle probabilita`*, Rendic. Acc. Naz. Lincei 12 (1930), 367–373.

[5] B. de Finetti, *Sul significato soggettivo della probabilita`*, Fundam. Mathem. 17 (1931), 298–329.

[6] B. de Finetti, *Teoria delle probabilita`*, Vol. 1 e 2, Torino, Einaudi, 1970.

[7] A. Gilio e R. Scozzafava, *Le probabilita` condizionate coerenti nei sistemi esperti*, Atti delle giornate AIRO su Ricerca Operativa e Intelligenza Artificiale, Pisa, Centro di Ricerca IBM (1988), 317–330.

Appendix

Proof of the theorem - Let $\cdot\geq$ be coherent : we prove only the case $A_j|H_j\cdot> B_j|K_j$ and $H_j\cdot> K_j$, so that $P(H_j) > P(K_j) > 0$, $P(A_jH_j) > P(B_jK_j)$. This implies $P(A_jH_j)P(B_j^cK_j) > P(A_j^cH_j)P(B_jK_j)$. We consider only the nontrivial case that $P(B_j^cK_j)$ and $P(B_jK_j)$ are both positive. Denote by $W = (w_1,w_2,...,w_r)$ a probability extending P on the relevant atoms. Then, from the inequality $P(A_jH_j) > P(B_jK_j)$, we obtain $(A_j\cdot H_j - B_j\cdot K_j)* W > 0$ and, for $1 < \alpha_j \leq P(A_jH_j)/P(B_jK_j)$, it is $(A_j\cdot H_j - \alpha_j B_j\cdot K_j)* W \geq 0$. Moreover, if $P(B_j^cK_j) \geq P(A_j^cH_j)$, then $\alpha_j P(B_j^cK_j) > P(A_j^cH_j)$, i.e. $(\alpha_j B_j^c\cdot K_j - A_j^c\cdot H_j)* W \geq 0$ for every $\alpha_j > 1$.

If instead $P(B_j^cK_j) < P(A_j^cH_j)$, then $\alpha_j P(B_j^cK_j) \geq P(A_j^cH_j)$ for every $\alpha_j \geq P(A_j^cH_j)/P(B_j^cK_j)$. Moreover, from $P(A_jH_j)P(B_j^cK_j) > P(A_j^cH_j)P(B_jK_j)$, i.e. $P(A_jH_j)/P(B_jK_j) > P(A_j^cH_j)/P(B_j^cK_j) > 1$, it follows $P(A_jH_j) > \alpha_j P(B_jK_j)$ for $1 < \alpha_j \leq P(A_jH_j)/ P(B_jK_j)$. So, again $(A_j\cdot H_j - B_j\cdot K_j)* W > 0$, $(A_j\cdot H_j - \alpha_j B_j\cdot K_j)* W \geq 0$ and $(\alpha_j B_j^c\cdot K_j - A_j^c\cdot H_j)* W \geq 0$; i.e. , there exist α_j and W which satisfy the inequalities in $\mathscr{L}$ corresponding to the qualitative judgements $A_j|H_j\cdot> B_j|K_j$ and $H_j\cdot> K_j$.

Analogously, it can be proved that there exist $\beta_k > 1$ such that $W = (w_1,w_2,...,w_r)$ satisfies the inequalities in $\mathscr{L}$ corresponding to the other comparisons.

Viceversa, if $\mathscr{L}$ has a solution, put $P(A|H) = (A\cdot H)* W/ (H* W)$ and so on. Then $P : \mathscr{E} \rightarrow [0,1]$ is a (coherent) conditional probability representing $\cdot\geq$.

Automated Reasoning About an Uncertain Domain

Flávio S. Corrêa da Silva †   Dave Robertson †   Paul Chung ‡

† Dept. of AI, Univ. of Edinburgh   ‡ AIAI
80 South Bridge, Edinburgh, Scotland EH1 1HN
email: fcs@aipna.ed.ac.uk dr@aipna.ed.ac.uk chung@aiai.ed.ac.uk

Abstract

In this paper we introduce a resolution-based logic programming language that handles probabilities and fuzzy events. The language can be viewed as a simple knowledge representation formalism, with the features of being operational and presenting a complete declarative semantics. An extended version of this paper can be found in [3].

1   Introduction

Designing expert systems requires *tools for representing* and *manipulating* statements of uncertainty. *Representation tools* must be *expressive*, with at least the expressive power of first-order logic, and *precise*, that is, they must present a well-specified declarative semantics. Uncertainty, on the other hand, has an ambivalent character: it is at the same time *part* of the represented objects and a *property* of these objects. As a result, a precise representation of uncertainty must include a description of how it is measured and of how it attaches to these objects. The requirement for *manipulation tools* stresses the need for computational tractability: if *automated* reasoning for expert systems is a goal, then tools which cannot be implemented are unsatisfactory.

This paper introduces a language presenting *conjointly* the following features:

- it is an extension of - and therefore at least as expressive as - first-order logic (or at least the part of it that admits being automated);

- it contains a precise specification for the uncertainty measures under consideration and how they attach to other elements in the domain;

- it is computable, and an implementation of it is available.

Uncertainty is a multi-faceted concept. This paper focuses on uncertainty measures attached directly to objects in the domain. Even so, at least two different types of measures can be identified: i) *probability* measures and its extensions; ii) measures of *proximity and similarity*. There is no reason to believe that they are mutually exclusive, so the way they may interact is also identified.

The concern with combined representations of multiple measures of uncertainty stems from the works by Bacchus [1] and Halpern [7]. In contrast with our work, which deals with two different measures on the domain, their works emphasise *probability measures* on the domain and on possible worlds. A similar emphasis for measures of similarity is found in [5].

The concern for automated formal reasoning with a well-defined declarative semantics is also found in [4] and [8]. In [4] the concern is with *possibilistic logic programming*, thus placing the uncertainty measure on possible worlds, whereas the approach presented in [8] is based on the existence of a complete lattice of truth-values, an assumption which may not be necessarily fulfilled *per se*. The approach in this paper contrasts with the latter by avoiding this assumption as a definite one, and by construing uncertainty measures as inherent domain properties, rather than syntactical constructs which find their counterparts in a model.

Section 2 introduces a specification of the uncertainty measures and how they interact with each other. Section 3 presents the representation tool, constructed as a logic programming language. The presentation is incremental. First an "uncertainty-free" language is selected. Then it is extended to encompass measures of similarity. Finally, it is extended to admit probabilities. Some conclusions are drawn in section 4.

2 The Uncertainty Model

Probability measures are assumed to be finite and discrete. A *finite discrete probability space* is a pair $(D, \mathcal{P})$ where D is a finite sample space and $\mathcal{P}$ is a discrete probability measure (that is, $X \subseteq D, \mathcal{P}(X) = \sum_{d \in X} \mathcal{P}(d)$, where $\mathcal{P}(d)$ is known for all $d \in D$. X is called an *event* of D).

A *conditional probability measure* of an event X given an event Y is defined as:

- $\mathcal{P}(X|Y) = \frac{\mathcal{P}(X \cap Y)}{\mathcal{P}(Y)}, \mathcal{P}(Y) > 0,$

- $\mathcal{P}(X|Y) = 0, \mathcal{P}(Y) = 0.$

The restriction on D being finite ensures the computability of probability measures. The restriction on discrete probability measures will be justified after fuzzy events are introduced (see below).

Recalling that an event specifies a class of objects in D, *fuzzy set theory* was developed to treat ill-defined classes by allowing fractional memberships: a fuzzy membership function measures the degree to which an element belongs to a class or, alternatively, the degree of similarity between the class to which the element belongs and a reference class. Formally, a fuzzy subset F of a referential set D is defined by an arbitrary mapping $\mu_F : D \to [0, 1]$. $\mu_F(d) = 1$ corresponds to the intuitive notion that $d \in F$ and $\mu_F(d) = 0$ to the notion that $d \notin F$.

Set-theoretic operations can be extended to fuzzy sets by means of *triangular norms and conorms* [9, 13]. A norm of two membership functions corresponds to the generalised operation of intersection for fuzzy sets, and the conorm to the generalised operation of union.

If these set operations are required to be *distributive* and *idempotent*, in order to be kept as close as possible to standard set operations, then the only possible triangular norm and conorm are, respectively, $T = min$ and $\dot{T} = max$ (see [9] for a proof of this result). On the other hand, the simplest existing complementation function is the function $C(x) = 1 - x$. Henceforth, these functions are adopted as extended set operations.

In [9] the concept of algebra (an algebra χ is a set of subsets of D such that $D \in \chi$ and χ is closed under complementation and union [6, 12]) is extended for fuzzy sets, and in [11, 13, 15] the definition of the probability of a fuzzy event is presented, reputed as originally by Zadeh. Given a probability space $(D, \chi, \mathcal{P})$ and assuming that the fuzzy set F belongs to the algebra χ, the probability of the event F is given by the Lebesgue-Stieltjes integral $\mathcal{P}(F) = \int_D \mu_F(d) d\mathcal{P}$. For a finite discrete probability space $(D, \mathcal{P})$, this integral turns to $\mathcal{P}(F) = \sum_{d \in F} \mu_F(d) \times \mathcal{P}(d)$.

It should be noted that the computability of the probability of fuzzy events requires the probability measure to be both finite and discrete.

3 Reasoning with Probabilities and Fuzzy Events

The class of logic programs supported by the programming language is that of *function-free normal programs* under restrictions of *call-consistency* and *allowedness* [10, 14]. The model theory is based on *Clark's completion*, and the proof theory has *SLDNF* as the inference procedure. The restrictions above are imposed to obtain soundness and completeness of this procedure with respect to the model of the completion.

A fuzzy predicate can be defined by analogy with the concept of fuzzy sets previously presented. The interpretation of predicates can be generalised to a function ranging on $I(p) : D^n \to \{\bot\} \cup (0,1]$, with $\top \equiv 1$. This function can be construed as a fuzzy membership function. Moreover, the logical connectives can be interpreted as fuzzy set operators, $\neg$ corresponding to complementation, $\vee$ corresponding to union, $\wedge$ corresponding to intersection, and $\leftrightarrow$ corresponding to set-equivalence. Intuitively, the semantics of a closed formula becomes a "degree of truth", rather than simply one value out of $\{\top, \bot\}$. The result of a query evaluation is a value in $(0,1]$. Let τ denote this value and $\mathcal{T}(C, \tau)$ state that "the truth-degree of C is τ". This evaluation can be operationalised as an *extended SLDNF* procedure, which is related to an *extended completion model* of the program.

The *probability ϱ of a vector of variables $\vec{x}$ satisfying a goal clause C ($\mathcal{P}_{\vec{x}}(C, \varrho)$) given a program P* can be required, and its evaluation depends on a *probability measure* on the set A_P of constants occurring in P. If this measure is *finite* and *discrete*, it is defined by a set of unit clauses $\mathcal{P}(a_i, \varrho_i)$, for all $a_i \in A_P$, extensible to sets of constants (i.e. $\mathcal{P}((a_1, ..., a_n), \varrho_i)$ is assumed to be defined for any $(a_1, ..., a_n) \subseteq A_P$).

Assuming a program P to contain a set of unit clauses defining a finite discrete probability measure on A_P, the *inference procedure* above can be extended to work with the new expressions. Notice that this assumption implies the definitions of the operations of *addition* ($+$) and *multiplication* ($\times$), of the *relations* $>$ and $=$, and of the properties of *non-negativity* ($\varrho \geq 0 \leftarrow \mathcal{P}((a_1, ..., a_n), \varrho)$, *finite additivity* ($\mathcal{P}((a_1, ..., a_n), \varrho) \leftarrow \mathcal{P}(a_1, \varrho_1), ..., \mathcal{P}(a_n, \varrho_n), \varrho = \varrho_1 + ... + \varrho_n$) and *total probability* ($\mathcal{P}(A_P, 1)$).

Conditional probabilities can be fully defined axiomatically based on probability measures. This corresponds to admitting expressions of the form $\mathcal{P}_{\vec{x}}(C_1|C_2, \varrho)$ in the language, and assuming the following system of clauses to make part of any program:

- $\mathcal{P}_{\vec{x}}(C_1|C_2, \varrho) \leftarrow \mathcal{P}_{\vec{x}}(C_2, \varrho_2), \varrho_2 > 0, \mathcal{P}_{\vec{x}}((C_1, C_2), \varrho_1), \varrho = \varrho_1/\varrho_2.$
- $\mathcal{P}_{\vec{x}}(C_1|C_2, 0) \leftarrow \mathcal{P}_{\vec{x}}(C_2, 0).$

Since probabilities are completely defined by measures on the constants of the language, terms of the forms $\mathcal{P}_{\vec{x}}(C, \varrho)$ and $\mathcal{P}_{\vec{x}}(C_1|C_2, \varrho)$ never occur as heads of programs clauses. Moreover, these terms only admit integer truth-degrees.

The following example illustrates the working of the language. A simple program is presented, with two constants - $\{dave, paul\}$. The truth-degrees $\mathcal{T}$ of the unit clauses are given, as well as the probabilities $\mathcal{P}$ of each constant. Some queries are made, including one about probabilities, and the deduction trees for them are presented.

Example Consider the following program:

$free(x) \leftarrow middleaged(x), \neg fat(x).$	$diet(x) \leftarrow fat(x).$	$care(x) \leftarrow diet(x), \neg free(x).$
$checkup(x) \leftarrow care(x).$	$\mathcal{T}(middleaged(paul), 0.4).$	$\mathcal{T}(fat(paul), 0.2).$
$\mathcal{T}(fat(dave), 0.1).$	$\mathcal{P}(paul, 0.7).$	$\mathcal{P}(dave, 0.3).$

And the queries:

$checkup(paul).\quad checkup(dave).\quad \mathcal{P}_x(checkup(x), \varrho).$

The *SLDNF*-trees for the first two queries are as follows:

For $checkup(paul)$:

$$\frac{\dfrac{\mathcal{T}(fat(paul), 0.2)}{\mathcal{T}(diet(paul), 0.2)} \quad \dfrac{\mathcal{T}(middleaged(paul), 0.4) \quad \mathcal{T}(\neg fat(paul), 0.8)}{\mathcal{T}(\neg free(paul), 0.6)}}{\dfrac{\mathcal{T}(care(paul), 0.2)}{\mathcal{T}(checkup(paul), 0.2)}}$$

For $checkup(dave)$:

$$\frac{\dfrac{\mathcal{T}(fat(dave), 0.1)}{\mathcal{T}(diet(dave), 0.1)} \quad \dfrac{middleaged(dave) \in failure \quad \mathcal{T}(\neg fat(dave), 0.9)}{\mathcal{T}(\neg free(dave), 1)}}{\dfrac{\mathcal{T}(care(dave), 0.1)}{\mathcal{T}(checkup(dave), 0.1)}}$$

This defines the set $A = \{(dave, 0.1), (paul, 0.2)\}$ which, together with the clauses $\mathcal{P}(paul, 0.7)$ and $\mathcal{P}(dave, 0.3)$, gives $\varrho = 0.7 \times 0.2 + 0.3 \times 0.1 = 0.17.$ □

4 Conclusions and Further Work

This paper introduces a knowledge representation formalism based on logic programming, capable of dealing with uncertain information in a relatively flexible and comprehensive way. The main feature of the formalism lies on its declarative semantics, allowing a precise definition of what the uncertainty and its measures mean.

Many extensions and improvements are possible to this language:

1. it would be interesting to make it expressive enough to deal with probabilities on possible worlds, and to extend it to work with probability intervals as well as pointwise evaluations;

2. the algorithmic complexity of resolution for the language as it was presented is clearly high, although a more detailed complexity analysis is still to be done. It could possibly be reduced if taxonomical information was available as a tool for pre-encoding probabilities of general classes, envisaged as sorts in an order-sorted domain;

3. for sake of completeness of presentation, soundness and completeness results for the extended *SLDNF*-resolution with respect to completion models should be developed.

These extensions and improvements have been object of study in the project of which the present paper is part, and are due to be presented in future papers. In fact, the extensions listed in item (1) above have already been incorporated to the language, and are presented in [2].

The actual language is implemented in Edinburgh-PROLOG.

Acknowledgements: The first author is a PhD student at the University of Edinburgh, supported by a scholarship from Conselho Nacional de Desenvolvimento Científico e Tecnológico - CNPq - Brazil, grant nr. 203004-89.2. The many suggestions and references provided by D. Dubois, H. Prade, S. Sandri and M. L. Marques are greatly acknowledged. We also thank V. S. Subrahmanian for several suggestions for improvements on the final quality of the paper.

References

[1] F. BACCHUS. *Representing and Reasoning with Probabilistic Knowledge.* MIT Press, 1990.

[2] F. S. CORREA DA SILVA. Automated reasoning with uncertainties. Technical report, University of Edinburgh, Department of Artificial Intelligence, 1991.

[3] F. S. CORREA DA SILVA, D. S. ROBERTSON, and P. CHUNG. Automated reasoning about an uncertain domain. Technical report, University of Edinburgh, Department of Artificial Intelligence, 1991.

[4] D. DUBOIS, J. LANG, and H. PRADE. Automated reasoning using possibilistic logic: Semantics, belief revision and variable certainty weights. In *Proceedings of the 5th Workshop on Uncertainty in Artificial Intelligence*, 1989.

[5] D. DUBOIS and H. PRADE. An introduction to possibilistic and fuzzy logics. In P. Smets, A. Mamdani, D. Dubois, and H. Prade, editors, *Non-standard Logics for Automated Reasoning*. Academic Press, 1988.

[6] R. M. DUDLEY. *Real Analysis and Probability.* Wadsworth & Brooks/Cole, 1989.

[7] J. Y. HALPERN. An analysis of first-order logics of probability. *Artificial Intelligence*, 46:311–350, 1990.

[8] M. KIFER and V. S. SUBRAHMANIAN. On the expressive power of annotated logic programs. In *NACLP'89 - Proceedings of the 1989 North American Conference on Logic Programming*, 1989.

[9] E. P. KLEMENT. Construction of fuzzy σ-algebras using triangular norms. *Journal of Mathematical Analysis and Applications*, 85:543–565, 1982.

[10] K. KUNEN. Signed data dependencies in logic programs. *Journal of Logic Programming*, 7:231–245, 1989.

[11] K. PIASECKI. Fuzzy p-measures and their application in decision making. In J. Kacprzyk and M. Fedrizzi, editors, *Combining Fuzzy Imprecision with Probabilistic Uncertainty in Decision Making*. Springer Verlag, 1988.

[12] Yu. V. PROHOROV and Yu. A. ROZANOV. *Probability Theory.* Springer Verlag, 1969.

[13] P. SMETS. Probability of a fuzzy event: An axiomatic approach. *Fuzzy Sets and Systems*, 7:153–164, 1982.

[14] D. TURI. Logic programs with negation: Classes, models, interpreters. Technical Report CS-R8943, Centre for Mathematics and Computer Science, 1989.

[15] I. B. TURKSEN. Stochastic fuzzy sets: a survey. In J. Kacprzyk and M. Fedrizzi, editors, *Combining Fuzzy Imprecision with Probabilistic Uncertainty in Decision Making*. Springer Verlag, 1988.

Using defeasible logic for a window on a probabilistic database:
Some preliminary notes

James Cussens[1] and Anthony Hunter[2]
[1]Centre for Logic and Probability in IT, King's College, Manresa Road, London, SW3 6LX
[2]Department of Computing, Imperial College, 180 Queen's Gate, London, SW7 2BZ

Introduction

Traditionally there has been a dichotomy between the probabilistic and logical views on uncertainty reasoning in AI. However, there does seem to be an intuitive overlap of the two views. Furthermore, given the relatively unclear understanding of the logical view, there is an argument for trying to establish the nature of the overlap between the probabilistic and logical views. Indeed there is some interesting relevant work that examines this overlap (including Pearl 1988, Neufeld 1990, Baccus 1989).

There is also a technological motivation for examining the inter-relationship between the probabilistic and logical views on uncertainty reasoning. In particular, in machine learning there seem to be some situations where a probabilistic representation has advantages over the logical one and others where a logical representation is superior (Gabbay 1991).

The particular research question we wish to focus on here is: Can we take a probabilistic database and view useful features of that database in a defeasible logic? In addressing this question, we develop an inference system for a probabilistic database that is based on the 'Principle of Total Evidence' and show how this is equivalent to a defeasible logic inference system with rule selection based on the specificity of the conditions of the rule. We compare the resulting inference systems with the 'extreme' probabilities system (Pearl 1988).

We develop our logics as Labelled Deductive Systems. This is part of a larger framework for logics in nonmonotonic reasoning (Gabbay 1989). An interesting subsidiary question in relating probabilistic and logical inference systems is: Does the relationship we establish provide a justification for defeasible logics with explicit representation of preference?

A brief review of defeasible logics

Within artificial intelligence there is a requirement for a "natural" representation of defeasible knowledge such as [1] and [2].

[1]   "A match lights if struck"
[2]   "A match doesn't light if the match is wet"

Such statements constitute "general" or default knowledge. However representing this kind of knowledge is not straightforward in classical logics. A number of approaches have been proposed (for reviews see Besnard 1989, Etherington 1988, Bell 1990, and Donini 1990). Though inter-relationships have been identified between approaches, there is as yet, no clear consensus. Here we focus on defeasible logics.

A number of formalisms for capturing aspects of defeasible reasoning have been proposed (Nute 1988, Pollock 1987, Hunter 1990, Laenens 1990, Loui 1986, Poole 1988), and are motivated by attempting to develop a lucid representation that does not involve listing all exceptions as conditions to rules, and in particular by supporting reasoning with competing arguments, and reasoning with different perspectives.

However, in developing formalisms for defeasible reasoning, if for example the following assertions, [3] and [4], are represented in the knowledge-base with [1] and [2], we do not want to infer a contradiction.

[3]   "A match is struck"
[4]   "A match is wet"

Some formalizations of defeasible logic, such as LDR (Nute 1988), resolve such a conflict be selecting the clause with the most specific antecedent. Other formalizations, (such as Loui 1986), base the resolution of such arguments on a number of criteria such as a preference for clauses that have more of the antecedent literals satisfied by monotonic reasoning.

Alternatively, there are formalizations with mechanisms that select the most appropriate clause based on a specified explicit ordering, such as KAL (Hunter 1990), and Ordered Logic (Vermier 1989, Laenens 1990). For example, we make non-monotonic inferences from an ordered set of clauses by only using the highest ordered formulae, with different defeasible logics defined to order formulae on different criteria. Such an approach avoids the unnatural representation of listing all exceptions to each clause as extra conditions in the antecedent, and furthermore provides an illuminating view on the structure and dynamics of a defeasible database. Under certain circumstances these approaches seem to be directly related to that of partially-ordered default theories (Brewka 1989).

The formalism LDR also captures the notion of a "defeater", which is a rule such that if the antecedent is satisfied, the rule defeats other rules lower in the ordering, but for which the consequent can not be detached. Defeater rules constitute arguments 'against' an inference. As with defeasible rules in LDR, defeater rules are selected on the basis of specificity.

Principle of Total Evidence

The idea here is that when assessing the probability of a given event α, we should calculate its probability value conditional on all the available evidence. This means selecting the most specific reference class within which to situate the event in question.

Let S = 'Match is struck', L = 'Match lights', and W= 'Match is wet'. Suppose that p(L | S) = 0.8 and p(L | S $\wedge$ W) = 0.1. If we wish to assess the probability that a given match lights and all we know (all the evidence) is that it is struck, then using the principle of total evidence we infer that it has probability 0.8 of lighting. If we now learn that the match is struck and is wet then we employ the more specific conditional probability which will inform us that the match has a very low chance of lighting i.e. 0.1. In both cases, we use all the available evidence.

If we view an inference system as deriving propositions from a database, then by using the Principle of Total Evidence as the basis of an inference system, we can infer propositions from a probabilistic database. This contrasts with the usual view of a probabilistic database where from probability values one may only derive further values (or intervals of values).

It is clear that the probabilty-theoretic Principle of Total Evidence is analogous to the notion of specificity as used in defeasible logic. By using the Principle of Total Evidence in a probabilistic inference system, we hope to clarify this relationship. In the next section we develop an inference system based on the Principle of Total Evidence, and after that develop an equivalent logic-based inference system.

An inference system for a probabilistic database

The folllowing is a definition of a probabilistic database:

1. Let K = { $k_1, \ldots, k_n$ } be a set of **attributes**. We can consider it be the set of all attributes of an event that we wish to consider in our database. If q $\in$ K, then q and $\neg$q are both termed **descriptors**, and term q as the complementary descriptor of $\neg$q, and $\neg$q as the complementary descriptor of q. For any descriptor α, we denote $\alpha^\wedge$ as the complementary descriptor of α.

2. Let e be a **simple event** in the space generated by the set of attributes K, ie e = $q_1 \wedge q_2 \wedge .. \wedge q_n$ where for all i, s.t. $1 \leq i \leq n$, $q_i = k_i$ or $q_i = \neg k_i$. A **total description** of e, denoted [e], is defined as follows: if e = $q_1 \wedge \ldots \wedge q_n$, then [e] = { $q_1, \ldots, q_n$ }.

3. A **scenario** $\sigma(e)$ is a partial description of an event e, in other words $\sigma(e) \subseteq$ [e] holds. If there is a descriptor α s.t. $\alpha \in$ [e] and $\alpha \notin \sigma(e)$, then α is **open** by $\sigma(e)$.

4. A probabilistic **database**, denoted Δ, is **complete** w.r.t. a descriptor α if for any scenario $\sigma(e)$ where α is open by $\sigma(e)$, there is a conditional probability statement of the following form:

$$'p(\ \alpha|\ \textstyle\bigwedge_i\beta_i\ ) = \zeta'\ \in\ \Delta$$

where descriptors($\bigwedge_i\beta_i$) $= \sigma(e)$ and the function 'descriptors' is defined as follows:

descriptors($\delta \wedge \gamma$) $= \{\ \delta\ \} \cup$ descriptors(γ) if δ is atomic
descriptors(δ) $= \{\ \delta\ \}$ if δ is atomic

Restricting our inference systems to using complete databases is, we feel, justified in certain applications. In particular, we are developing formalisms for applications in machine learning where obtaining complete databases is often not a problem.

Given a probabilistic database Δ that is complete w.r.t. α, and a scenario $\sigma(e)$, we wish to ascertain a probability value for α if α is open by $\sigma(e)$. If we use the Principle of Total Evidence, then there is only one conditional probability statement '$p(\ \alpha|\ \bigwedge_i\beta_i\ ) = \zeta'\ \in \Delta$ that can be used.

For reasoning about properties, if we compute probability values using Δ and $\sigma(e)$, we can make inferences about the ground properties: if we use some threshold θ, say $1/2$ or $3/4$, we can infer α from Δ with $\sigma(e)$, if the probability of α is greater than the threshold θ. Note, we must have θ at least $1/2$ for consistency.

Furthermore we can reason with a probabilistic database qualitatively. For this we introduce the following definitions:

[D1] $p(\ x\ |\ y\ )$ is high   IFF   '$p(\ x|y\ )\ = \zeta'\ \in\ \Delta$ and $\zeta > \theta$

[D2] $p(\ x\ |\ y\ )$ is low   IFF   '$p(\ x|y\ )\ = \zeta'\ \in\ \Delta$ and $\zeta < (1-\theta)$

[D3] $p(\ x\ |\ y\ )$ is medium   IFF   '$p(\ x|y\ )\ = \zeta'\ \in\ \Delta$ and $(1-\theta) \leqslant \zeta \leqslant \theta$

Hence we can use the following qualitative relations between our conditional probability values:

[R1] $p(\ x\ |\ y\ )$ is high   IFF $p(\ \neg x\ |\ y\ )$ is low

[R2] $p(\ x\ |\ y\ )$ is medium   IFF $p(\ \neg x\ |\ y\ )$ is medium

We reason with a probabilistic database Δ, and a scenario $\sigma(e)$, as a pair $(\Delta, \sigma(e))$. We formalize an inference from this pair, as follows, where θ is the probabilistic threshold value, and $\models$ is the inference relation:

$(\Delta, \sigma(e)) \models \alpha$ if $\alpha \in \sigma(e)$

$(\Delta, \sigma(e)) \models \alpha$ if '$p(\ \alpha\ |\ \bigwedge_i\beta_i\ ) = \zeta'\ \in \Delta$ and $\zeta > \theta$
                        and $p(\ \alpha\ |\ \bigwedge_i\beta_i\ )$ is the preferred conditional probability for α in Δ w.r.t $\sigma(e)$

The notion of preferred conditional probability for a descriptor α is intended to capture the intuition of the Principle of Total Evidence, and is defined as follows:

$p(\ \alpha\ |\ \bigwedge_i\beta_i\ )$ is the **preferred** **conditional** **probability** for α in Δ w.r.t $\sigma(e)$
    if '$p(\ \alpha\ |\ \bigwedge_i\beta_i\ ) = \zeta'\ \in \Delta$
    and for all i $\beta_i \in \sigma(e)$
    and for all other '$p(\ \delta\ |\ \bigwedge_j\gamma_j\ ) = \psi'\ \in \Delta$ s.t. head(α) = head(δ),
        if for all j $\gamma_j \in \sigma(e)$ then descriptors($\bigwedge_j\gamma_j$) $\subseteq$ descriptors($\bigwedge_i\beta_i$)

where we define the function 'head' as head(α) = α, and head($\neg\alpha$) = α. Using these definitions, we can for example infer E follows from a scenario $\{\ A\ \}$, and a probabilistic database Δ, using the conditional statement '$p(\ E\ |\ A\ ) = \zeta'\ \in \Delta$, where $p(\ E\ |\ A\ )$ is high.

Forming a defeasible logic window

We now consider what a window on a probabilistic database is, and how we can form it. We start by considering the following example. The following conditional probabilities, (1), (2) (3) and (4) are in Δ, where Δ is complete with respect to the descriptor E.

(1) $p(A \mid D) = 1$
(2) $p(E \mid A)$ is high
(3) $p(\neg E \mid A \wedge D)$ is high
(4) $p(\neg E \mid D)$ is high

where if 'A' denotes 'adult', 'D' denotes 'dropout', and 'E' denotes 'employed', then (1) represents 'all dropouts are adults', (2) represents 'most adults are employed', (3) represents 'most dropouts, who are adults, are not employed' and (4) represents 'most dropouts are not employed'.

Since Δ is a complete probabilistic database w.r.t descriptor E, we can consider forming a defeasible logic window on Δ. We consider here a window based on just one descriptor, namely E. However, in general we could form a window based on more than one descriptor. The form of the defeasible rules in the defeasible logic representation is as follows, where a(i) is an ordering label, α is the consequent, β is the antecedent, and $\rightarrow$ is a conditional implication symbol:

a(i) : $\beta \rightarrow \alpha$

The consequent is a descriptor, and the antecedent is a conjunction of descriptors (Our terminology is such that 'descriptor' is equivalent to the logical use of 'literal'). The ordering label represents a notion of preference for the rule over other rules with the same consequent, or its negation. A database of defeasible logic rules, denoted Γ, form a partial order. We define below a proof theory to support such databases, where if $\beta \in \sigma(e)$ then $c{:}\,\beta \in \Gamma$:

[A0] $\Gamma \vdash \alpha$ if a(i): $\beta_1 \wedge .. \wedge \beta_n \rightarrow \alpha \in \Gamma$, and $c{:}\,\beta_1 \in \Gamma, ..$, and $c{:}\,\beta_n \in \Gamma$

[A1]   IF $c{:}\,\alpha \in \Gamma$ THEN $\Gamma \vdash \alpha$

Essentially, by [A0] we allow the inference α from a database Γ, if there is a rule in Γ, s.t. (1) the antecedent is satisfied, and (2) there is no rule in Γ that has the antecedent satisfied and is preferred by the ordering relation. We represent the logical rules formed from (1), (2), (3) and (4), as (1'), (2'), (3') and (4') respectively:

(1') $a(i_1)$: $D \rightarrow A$
(2') $a(i_2)$: $A \rightarrow E$
(3') $a(i_3)$: $A \wedge D \rightarrow \neg E$
(4') $a(i_4)$: $D \rightarrow \neg E$

where the ordering on the rules is $i_3 > i_2$ and $i_3 > i_4$ and $i_2 \parallel i_4$. In forming these rules, we have assumed that the conditional probability 'is high' means that the probability value is greater than our threshold value θ. Using the defeasible logic, we can make inferences from (2'),(3'), and (4'). For example, if we have a scenario where A and D hold, then we can infer $\neg E$ using the proof rules.

Essentially, if we use the 'Principle of Total Evidence' in our probabilisitic reasoning system, in order to make inferences from our probabilistic database, we can mimic the inference procedure in our defeasible logic system. The notion of 'Principle of Total Evidence' which is used to select the most appropriate conditional probability, is reflected in the logical system by selecting the highest rule in the partial order which has the antecdent satisfied.

Suppose we extend our probabilistic database with the following conditionals, where Y denotes 'youth', and then (5) represents 'some youths are employed', (6) represents 'some adult youths are employed', (7) represents 'most dropout youths are not employed, and (8) represents 'most dropout adult youths are not employed':

(5) $p(E \mid Y)$ is medium
(6) $p(E \mid Y \wedge A)$ is medium
(7) $p(\neg E \mid Y \wedge D)$ is high
(8) $p(\neg E \mid Y \wedge A \wedge D)$ is high

We now need to consider how to represent the medium conditional probabilities. Since by [R2] we also have the following:

(5a) $p(\neg E \mid Y)$ is medium
(6a) $p(\neg E \mid Y \wedge A)$ is medium

If we reason with the Principle of Total Evidence together with the threshold value high, then we can infer neither E nor ¬E given a scenario { Y }. However, if we are to form a defeasible logic window, how do we support corresponding reasoning? A solution is to represent defeater rules in our logic window. Such rules, if selected by the specificity ordering would over-ride any defeasible inferences lower in the ordering, but not allow their own consequent to be detached. In other words the defeater rules block inferences from the window, but do not add directly to the inferences. The form of the defeasible rules in the defeasible logic representation is as follows, where b(i) is an ordering label, α is the consequent, β is the antecedent, and $\rightarrow$ is a conditional implication symbol:

$$b(i): \quad \beta \rightarrow \alpha$$

The ordering label represents a notion of preference for the rule over other rules with the same consequent, or its negation. However, we need to amend the proof theory by replacing the rule [A0] with [A2] as presented below:

[A2] $\Gamma \mid\!\!\sim \alpha$ if a(i): $\beta_1 \wedge .. \wedge \beta_n \rightarrow \alpha \in \Gamma$, and c: $\beta_1 \in \Gamma, .. ,$ and c: $\beta_n \in \Gamma$
and NOT(a(j): $\delta_1 \wedge .. \wedge \delta_m \rightarrow \alpha^\wedge \in \Gamma$, and c: $\delta_1 \in \Gamma, .. ,$ and c: $\delta_n \in \Gamma$, and j > i)
and NOT(b(j): $\delta_1 \wedge .. \wedge \delta_m \rightarrow \alpha \in \Gamma$, and c: $\delta_1 \in \Gamma, .. ,$ and c: $\delta_n \in \Gamma$, and j > i)

The definition [A2] extends the definition [A0] by adding the extra condition that for a consequent of a rule to be detached, there is no defeater rule in the database that also has its antecedent satisfied and is also higher in the ordering. In the next section we clarify the relationship between the probabilistic representation, and the defeasible logic window.

Formalizing the relationship between the database and window

Given a complete probabilistic database Δ w.r.t a descriptor α, we denote a window function on Δ, w.r.t. to α, as $w(\Delta, \alpha)$, and define it as follows, where θ is the probabilistic threshold value, and $\mu, \lambda \in \{ a, b \}$:

[F1]   IF '$p(\alpha \mid \delta) = \zeta' \in \Delta$ and $p(\alpha \mid \delta)$ is high
        THEN a(i): $\delta \rightarrow \alpha \in w(\Delta, \alpha)$

[F2]   IF '$p(\alpha \mid \delta) = \zeta' \in \Delta$ and $p(\alpha \mid \delta)$ is medium
        THEN b(i): $\delta \rightarrow \alpha \in w(\Delta, \alpha)$ AND b(i): $\delta \rightarrow \alpha^\wedge \in w(\Delta, \alpha)$

[F3]   IF '$p(\alpha \mid \delta) = \zeta' \in \Delta$ and '$p(\varphi \mid \gamma) = \xi' \in \Delta$
        and head(α) = head(φ) and descriptors(δ) $\subseteq$ descriptors(γ)
        and $\mu(i)$: $\delta \rightarrow \alpha \in w(\Delta, \alpha)$ and $\lambda(j)$: $\gamma \rightarrow \varphi \in w(\Delta, \alpha)$
        THEN (j, i) $\in \ _\alpha$⊳

For a scenario $\sigma(e)$, we define the rewrite of the scenario, denoted $C(\sigma(e))$, as follows:

[F4]   IF $\alpha \in \sigma(e)$ THEN c: $\alpha \in C(\sigma(e))$

From the window function applied to one, or more, predicates, together with rewrite of the scenario, we can form the defeasible logic database as follows:

$$\Gamma = w(\Delta, \alpha_1) \cup \ldots \cup w(\Delta, \alpha_n) \cup C(\sigma(e))$$

where the ordering relation, denoted ⊳, is defined as ⊳ $=_{def} \ _{\alpha_1}$⊳ $\cup \ldots \cup \ _{\alpha n}$⊳.

Essentially [F1] rewrites all the high conditional probabilities as defeasible rules, and [F2] rewrites all the medium conditional probabilities as defeater rules. [F3] rewrites the implicit ordering in the inference system based on the Principle of Total Evidence to an explicit ordering, and [F4] takes the assertions in the scenario and labels all of them with the symbol 'c' within the defeasible logic database. We can show the following equivalence between the probabilistic reasoning system and defeasible logic reasoning system:

[Result] For any descriptor, α s.t. $\alpha \in \{ \alpha_{\nu}, \ldots, \alpha_n \}$, then the following equivalence holds, where $|\sim$ is the defeasible logic consequence relation as defined by [A1] and [A2], and $\models$ is the probabilistic consequence relation, where $\Gamma = w(\Delta, \alpha_1) \cup \ldots \cup w(\Delta, \alpha_n) \cup \Xi(\sigma(e))$:

$$(\Delta, \sigma(e)) \models \alpha \ \text{iff} \ \Gamma |\sim \alpha$$

The ordering relation we have defined for our defeasible relation makes explicit the notion of preference based on specificity. Hence, for any rules on our logic database of the form:

$$a(i): \alpha \rightarrow \beta$$
$$a(j): \gamma \rightarrow \delta$$

if head(β) = head(δ), and $i \geqslant j$, then descriptors(γ) $\subseteq$ descriptors(α).

An Alternative View: Pearl's 'Extreme' Probabilities

Pearl claims that an approach such as ours can only be used if we use extreme probabilities. That is, we only adopt the defeasible rule X -> Y if $P(Y|X) = 1 - \varepsilon$ where ε is infinitesimally small. This contrasts with our approach were a probability has only to be 'high' (i.e. $> \beta$) rather than 'extremely high' for there to be a corresponding rule in the defeasible logic window.

Three axioms, which Pearl takes to be intuitive, are sound in his interpretation. They are

1.	Triangularity	$a \rightarrow b, \ a \rightarrow c$	$\rightarrow$	$(a \wedge b) \rightarrow c$
2.	Bayes	$a \rightarrow b, \ (a \wedge b) \rightarrow c$	$\rightarrow$	$a \rightarrow c$
3.	Disjunction	$a \rightarrow c, \ b \rightarrow c$	$\rightarrow$	$(a \vee b) \rightarrow c$

These are not sound under our approach. To take the first example, suppose $\sigma(e) = \{a, b\}$ and $\Delta = \{'p(c \mid a) > \theta', 'p(b \mid a) > \theta', 'p(\neg c \mid a \wedge b) > \theta'\}$ then we will have $a \rightarrow b$, $a \rightarrow c$ and $(a \wedge b) \rightarrow \neg c \in w(\Delta, c)$, contradicting triangularity. Note that such a Δ is indeed possible in our system, though it would not be if θ were infinitesimally close to one, as used in Pearl's system.

It is clear that Pearl's interpretation allows for nice intuitive axioms and Pearl gives examples of reasoning with it. But there are problems: is this a reasonable interpretation? Do people use extreme probabilities? We feel that the answer to both questions is no.

Pearl argues that any logic based on non-extreme logic will be 'extremely complicated'. He argues that the reasoning behind actual default rules is based on the fairly crude 'almost all' logic rather than what he calls the 'logic of the majority'. However we feel that (1) Pearl's 'infinitesimal' approach is considerably less intuitive than our own and (2) ours is an adequately simple method.

Discussion

Once the Principle of Total Evidence has been used to build an inference system for a probabilistic database, it is straightforward to construct an equivalent defeasible logic system. This highlights the similarity between the Principle of Total Evidence and the use of specificity orderings in defeasible logics.

Advantages that accrue from the equivalence of the two approaches includes a mechanism by which probabilistic data may be to used to derive logical databases. This may be enhanced by the possibility of merging such logical databases with background knowledge that is also in a logical form.

We have made use of labels to establish an equivalence between a probabilistic database and a defeasible logic window onto it. Currently, we are studying probabilisitc databases that include representation of the level of certainty we have in our probability values. We are also examining non-probabilistic belief functions, eg. Dempster-Shafer belief functions (Shafer 1976). In order to represent such features in a logic window we use an augmented labelling system. Recent work on Labelled Deductive Systems (Gabbay 1989) provides a framework for further work in this direction.

For translation from the probabilitic representation, Baccus (1989) adopts an analogous threshold notion (i.e. if $p(a|b) > \theta$ holds in the probabilistic representation, then $a \rightarrow b$ holds in the logic representation). However, our logical system also adopts a notion of defeater rules which enriches our knowledge representation capability. Furthermore, this notion is clearly supported by its probabilistic interpretation.

Interesting results from this work include the failure of the defeasible logic, as defined here, to meet the minimal properties (as presented in Gabbay 1985) expected of a non-monotonic consequence relation. Within the proof-theoretic framework of Labelled Deductive Systems we are considering strengthening the defeasible logic.

Another interesting direction is to consider the axioms such as 1 - 3 above as defeasible meta-level axioms. Then if we use incomplete probabilistic databases, we can use the axioms to non-monotonically complete the database. This direction could form part of a larger initiative to use defeasible meta-rules for making assumptions about the nature and usage of a probabilistic database. For example, in Grosof (Grosof 1988) non-monotonic meta-assumptions, such as independence, are made about the nature of the database.

Acknowledgements

This work is currently being funded by UK SERC grants GR/G 29861 and GR/G 29854 for the Rule-based Systems project. Special thanks are due to Dov Gabbay, Donald Gillies, Ng, and Barry Richards.

References

Baccus F (1989) A modest, but semantically well-founded, inheritance reasoner, IJCAI-89, Morgan Kaufmann

Bell J (1990) Non-monotonic reasoning, non-monotonic logics, and reasoning about change, Artificial Intelligence Review, 4, 79 - 108

Besnard P (1989) An Introduction to Default Logic, Springer

Brewka G (1989) Preferred sub-theories: An extended logical framework for default reasoning, IJCAI-89, Morgan Kaufmann

Donini F (1990) Non-monotonic reasoning, Artificial Intelligence Review, 4, 163 - 210

Etherington D (1988) Reasoning with incomplete information, RNAI, Pitman

Gabbay D (1985) Theoretical foundations for non-monotonic reasoning in expert systems, in Apt K, Proc. NATO Advanced Study Institute on Logics and Models of Concurrent Systems, Springer, 439 - 457

Gabbay D (1989) Labelled Deductive Systems, Technical Report, Department of Computing, Imperial College, London, also to be published by Oxford University Press

Gabbay D, Gillies D, Hunter A, Muggleton S, Ng Y, & Richards B (1991) The rule based systems project: using confirmation theory and non-monotonic logics for incremental learning, Proc. of the First Workshop on Inductive Logic Programming, Academic Press

Grosof B (1988) Non-monotonicity in probabilistic reasoning, Uncertainty in Artificial Intelligence, 3

Hunter A (1990) KAL: A linear ordered logic for non-monotonic reasoning, Draft Paper, Department of Computing, Imperial College, London

Laenens E & Vermier D (1990) A fixpoint semantics for ordered logic, J Logic & Computation, 1,

Loui R (1986) Defeat amongst arguments: a system of defeasible inference, Technical Report No 130, Department of Computer Science, University of Rochester, New York

Neufeld E, Poole D, and Aleliunas R (1990) Uncertainty in Artificial Intelligence, 4, 121 - 132

Nute D (1988) Defeasible reasoning and decision support systems, Decision Support Systems, 4, 97-110

Pearl J (1988) Probabilistic Reasoning in Intelligent Systems, Morgan Kaufmann

Poole D (1988) Logical framework for default reasoning, Artificial Intelligence, 36, 27 - 48

Pollock J (1987) Defeasible reasoning, Cognitive Science, 11, 481 - 518

Shafer G (1976) A Mathematical Theory of Evidence, Princeton University Press

Vermier D, Nute D & Geerts P (1989) A logic for defeasible perspectives, Proc. of the 1988 Tubingen Workshop on Semantic Networks and Non-monotonic Reasoning, vol 1, 1 - 27, SNS-Bericht 89-48

FROM DATA ANALYSIS TO UNCERTAINTY KNOWLEDGE ANALYSIS

E. DIDAY
University Paris Dauphine /INRIA

Abstract

The main aim of the symbolic approach in statistics is to extend problems, methods and algorithms used on classical data to more complex data called "symbolic objects"which are well adapted to representing knowledge and which "unify" unlike usual observations which characterize "individual things". We introduce two kinds of symbolic objects : boolean and possibilist. We briefly present some of their qualities and properties. We give some ideas on how statistics and data analysis may be extended on these objects. Finally four kinds of data analysis problems are presented.

Introduction

In data analysis (multidimensional scaling, clustering, exploratory data analysis etc.) more importance is given to the elementary objects which belong to the sample Ω then in classical statistics where attention is focused on the probability laws of Ω ; however, objects of data analysis are generally identified to point of $\mathbb{R}^p$ and hence are unable to treat complex objects coming for instance from large data bases, and knowledge bases. Our aim is to define complex objects called "symbolic objects" inspired by those of oriented object langages in such a way that data analysis become generalized in knowledge analysis. Objects will be defined by intension by the properties of their extension. More precisely, we distinguish objects which "unify" rather than elementary observed objects which characterize "individual things" (their extension) : for instance "the customers of my shop" instead of "a customer of my shop", "a specie of mushroom" instead "the mushroom that I have in my hand".

The aim of this paper is to reduce the gap between statistics or data analysis (where people are not yet very interested in treating this kind of objects) and artificial intelligence (where people are more interested in knowledge representation, reasoning and learning then in knowledge analysis).

1. Boolean symbolic objects

We consider Ω a set of individual things called "elementary objects" and a set of descriptor functions $y_i : \Omega \rightarrow \dot{O}_i$.

A basic kind of symbolic objects are "*events*". An event denoted $e_i = [y_i = V_i]$ where $V_i \subseteq O_i$ is a function $\Omega \rightarrow \{true, false\}$ such that $e_i (w) = true$ iff $y_i (w) \in V_i$. When $y_i(w)$ has no sense (the kind of computer used by a company without computer) $V_i = \phi$ and when it has a meaning but it is not known $V_i = O_i$. The extension of e_i in Ω denoted by $ext (e_i/\Omega)$ is the set of elements $w \in \Omega$ such that $e_i (w) = true$.

An assertion is a conjunction of events $a = \bigwedge_i [y_i = V_i]$; the extension of a denoted $ext(a/\Omega)$ is the set of elements of Ω such that $\forall i \; y_i (w) \in V_i$.

A "*horde*" is a symbolic object which appears for instance, when we need to express relations between parts of a picture that we wish to describe. More generally a horde is a function h from Ω^p in $\{true, false\}$ such that $h(u) = \bigwedge_i [y_i(u_i) = V_i]$ if $u = (u_1,.....,u_p)$. For example : $h = [y_1(u_1) = 1] \wedge [y_2(u_2) = \{3,5\}] \wedge [y_3(u_1) = [30,35]] \wedge [neighbour (u_1, u_2) = yes]$.

A synthesis object is a conjunction or a semantic link between hordes denoted in case of conjunction by $s = \bigwedge_i h_i$ where each horde may be defined on a different set Ω_i by different descriptors. For instance Ω_1 may be individuals, Ω_2 location, Ω_3 kind of job etc. All these objects are detailed in Diday (1991).

2. Modal objects

Suppose that we wish to use a symbolic object to represent individuals satisfying the following sentence : "It is possible that their weight be between 300 and 500 grammes and their color is often red or seldom white" ; this sentence contains two events $e_1 = [\text{color} = \{\text{red, white}\}]$ which lack the modes *possible* , *often* and *seldom* , a new kind of event, denoted f_1 and f_2, is needed if we wish to introduce them $f_1 = possible$ [height = 300,500]] and $f_2 = [\text{color} = \{\textit{often} \text{ red} , \textit{seldom} \text{ white}\}]$; we can see that f_1 contains an *external* mode *possible* affecting e_1 whereas f_2 contains *internal* modes affecting the values contained in e_2. Hence, it is possible to describe informally the sentence by a modal assertion object denoted $a = f_1 \wedge_x f_2$ where $\wedge_x$ represents a kind of conjunction related to the background knowledge of the domain. The case of modal assertions of the kind $a = \bigwedge_i f_i$ where all the f_i are events with external modes has been studied for instance in Diday (1990). This paper is devoted to the case where all the f_i contain only internal modes.

3. Internal modal objects

3.1. A formal definition of internal modal objects

Let x be the background knowledge and

. M^x a set of modes, for instance $M^x = \{\text{often, sometimes, seldom, never}\}$ or $M^x = [0,1]$.

. $Q_i = \{ q_i^j \}_j$ a set of mappings q_i^j from O_i in M^x, for instance $O_i = \{\text{red, yellow, green}\}$,

$M^x = [0,1]$ and q_i^j (red) = 0.1 ; q_i^j (yellow) = 0.3 ; q_i^j (green) = 1, where the meaning of the values

0.1, 0.3, 1 depends on the background knowledge (for instance q_i^j may express a possibility, see §4.1)

. y_i is a descriptor (the *color* for instance) ; it is a mapping from Ω in Q_i. Notice that in the case of boolean objects y_i was a mapping from Ω in O_i, and not Q_i.

Example : if O_i and M^x are chosen as in the previous example and the color of w is red then $y_i(\omega) = r$ means that $r \in Q_i$ be defined by r (red) = 1, r(yellow) = 0, r (green) = 0.
. $OP_x = \{ \cup_x, \cap_x, c_x \}$ where $\cup_x, \cap_x$ expresses a kind of union and intersection between subsets of Q_i and $c_x (q_i)$ (sometimes denoted $\bar{q}_i$, the complementary of $q_i \in Q_i$).

Example : if $q_i^j \in Q_i$ and $Q_i^j \subseteq Q_i$

$$q_i^1 \cup_x q_i^2 = q_i^1 + q_i^2 - q_i^1 q_i^2$$

$$q_i^1 \cap_x q_i^2 = q_i^1 q_i^2 \text{ where } q_i^1 q_i^2 (v) = q_i^1 (v) q_i^2 (v) ; c_x (q_i) = 1 - q_i$$

$$Q_i^1 *_x Q_i^2 = b(Q_i^1) *_x b(Q_i^2) \text{ where } *_x \in \{ \cup_x, \cap_x \} \text{ and}$$

$b(Q_i^j) = \{ \cup_x q_i / q_i \in Q_i^j \}$ and $c_x (Q_i^j) = 1 - c_x (b(Q_i^j))$.

This choice of OP_x is "archimedian" because it satisfies a family of properties studied by Shweizer and Sklar (1960) and recalled by Dubois et Prate (1988).

$\cdot g_x$ is a "comparison" mapping from $Q_i \times Q_i$ in an ordered space L^x.

Example : $L^x = M^x = [0,1]$ and $g_x (q_i^1 , q_i^2) = <q_i^1 , q_i^2>$ the scalar product

$\cdot f_x$ is an "aggregation" mapping from $P(L^x)$ the power set of L^x in L^x . For instance, $f_x (\{L_1,...,L_n\}) =$ Max L_j.

Let $Y = \{y_i\}$ be a set of descriptors and $V = \{V_i\}$ a set of subsets of Q_i such that $V_i = \{q_i^j\} \subseteq Q$. Now we are able now to give the formal definition of an internal modal assertion (called "im" assertion).

Definition of an im assertion

Given OP_x, g_x and f_x, an im object is a mapping a_{yv} from Ω in an ordered space L^x denoted $a = \wedge_i [y_i = \{q_i^j\}_j]$ such that if $\omega \in \Omega$ is described for any i by $y_i(\omega) = \{r_i^j\}$ then

$$a_{yv}(\omega) = f_x(\{g_x(\curlyvee_x q_i^j, \curlyvee_x r_i^j)\}_i).$$

We denote by a_x the set of im objects associated to a background knowledge x and φ the mapping from Ω in a_x such that $\varphi (\omega) = \omega^s = \wedge_{ix} [y_i = y_i (\omega)]$.

3.2. Extension of im objects

There are at least two ways to define the extension of an im object a. The first consists in considering that each element $\omega \in \Omega$ is more or less in the extension of a according to its weight given by a (ω) ; in that case the extension of a denoted Ext (a/Ω) will be the set of couples $\{(\omega, a(\omega)) / \omega \in \Omega\}$. The second requires a given threshold α and then the extension of a will be Ext $(a/\Omega, \alpha) = \{(\omega, a(\omega)) / \omega \in \Omega, a(\omega) \geq \alpha\}$.

3.3. Semantic of im objects

In addition to the modes several other notions may be expressed by an im object a :

a) Certitude : $a(\omega)$ is not true or false as for boolean objects but it expresses a degree of certitude.

b) Variation : it appears at two levels, in an im object denoted $a = \wedge_{ix} [y_i = \{q_i^j\}_i]$; first in each q_i^j, for instance if y_i is the color and q_i^1 (red) = 0.5, q_i^1 (green) = 0.3 it means that there exists a variation between the individual objects which belong into the extension of a (for instance a specie of mushrooms) where some are red and others are green ; second, for given description y_i between the q_i^j (each q_i^j expresses for instance the variation between different kind of species).

c) Doubt : if we say that the color of mushrooms of a specie is red "or" green, it is an "or" of variation, but if we say that the color of the mushroom which is in my hand is red "or" green, it is an "or" of doubt ; hence, if we describe $\omega \in \Omega$ by $\varphi(\omega) = \omega^S = \bigwedge_i [y_i = y_i(\omega)]$ where

$y_i(\omega) = \{r_i^j\}_j$ we express a doubt in each r_i^j and among the r_i^j provided for instance by several experts.

4. Possibilist objects

4.1. The possibilist approach

Here we follow Dubois and Prade (1984) in giving the main idea of this approach.

Definition of a measure of possibility and of necessity

This is a mapping Π from $P(\Omega)$ the power set of Ω in $[0, 1]$ such that

(1) $\Pi(\Omega) = 1$ $\Pi(\phi) = 0$
(2) $\forall A, B \subsetneq \Omega$ $\Pi(A \cup B) = Max(\Pi(A), \Pi(B))$
A measure of necessity is a mapping from $P(\Omega)$ in $[0, 1]$ such that :

(3) $\forall A \subsetneq \Omega$ $N(A) = 1 - \Pi(\bar{A})$.

The following properties may then be shown :

$N(\phi) = 0$; $N(A \cap B) = Min(N(A), N(B))$; $\Pi(\cup_i A_i) = \underset{i}{Max}(\Pi(A_i))$; $N(\cap_i A_i) = \underset{i}{Min}(N(A_i))$; $\Pi(A) \leq$

$\Pi(B)$ if $A \subseteq B$; $Max(\Pi(A), \Pi(\bar{A})) = 1$; $Min(N(A), N(\bar{A})) = 0$; $\Pi(A) \geq N(A)$; $N(A) > 0$ implies $\Pi(A)$

$= 1$; $\Pi(A) < 1$ implies $N(A) = 0$; $\Pi(A) + \Pi(\bar{A}) \geq 1$ and $N(A) + N(\bar{A}) \leq 1$.

Example

We define $\Pi_E(A)$ (resp. $N_E(A)$) as the possibility (resp. the necessity) to get $\omega \in A$ when $\omega \in E$. We say that $\Pi_E(A) = 1$ if this possibility is true and $\Pi_E(A) = 0$ if no. Hence Π_E and N_E are mapping from $P(\Omega)$ in $\{0, 1\}$. It is easy to show that Π_E and N_E satisfy the three axioms.

The theory of possibility models several kind of semantics, for instance :

i) The physical possibility : this expresses the material difficulty for an action to occur :"I have the possibility of carrying 20kg".

ii) The possibility as a concordance with an actual knowledge "it is possible that it will rain today".

iii) The non-astonishement : for instance, "the typicality" for the color of a flower "to be yellow".

4.2. A formal definition of possibilist objects

Here the background knowledge x is denoted p as possibility.

Definition

A possibilist assertion denoted $a_p = \bigwedge_i [y_i = \{q_i^j\}_j]$ *is an im assertion which takes its values in* $LP = [0, 1]$ *such that*

. $\forall i \; Q_i$ *is a set of measures of possibility.*

. $OP_p : \forall i, q_i^1, q_i^2 \in Q_i \; q_i^1 \cup_p q_i^2 = Max(q_i^1, q_i^2) \; ; q_i^1 \cap_p q_i^2 = Min(q_i^1, q_i^2) \; ;$

$c_p(q) = 1 - q.$

. $g_p : g_p(q_i^1, q_i^2) = sup\{min \; q_i^1(v), q_i^2(v) \; / \; v \in O_i\}$

. $f_p : \forall L \subseteq [0, 1] \; f_p(L) = Min(\ell \; / \; \ell \in L)$

Notice that OP_p is defined as in fuzzy sets and g_p has also been proposed by Zadeh (1971).

It is also possible to define a "necessitist" assertion a_n by setting $\forall \omega \in \Omega \; a_n(\omega) = 1 - a_p(c(\omega))$ where $c(\omega) = \varphi^{-1}(c(\omega^s))$ and $c(\omega^s) = \bigwedge_{ip} [y_i = c(r_i)]$ if $\omega^s = \bigwedge_{ip} [y_i = r_i]$.

This results in $a_n(\omega) = 1 - f(\{g_p(q_i, \bar{r_i})\}_i)$ and then $a_n(\omega) = 1 - \underset{i}{Max} \; g_p(q_i, \bar{r_i})$

$\quad = 1 - max \{sup \{min (q_i(v), \bar{r_i}(v) \; / \; v \in O_i\}\}_i$

$\quad = min \{1 - \{sup \; min (q_i(v), \bar{r_i}(v)) \; / \; v \in O_i\}\}_i$

$\quad = min \{inf \{1 - min (q_i(v), \bar{r_i}(v)) \; / \; v \in O_i\}\}_i$

$\quad = min \; inf \{max (1 - q_i(v), r_i(v)) \; / \; v \in O_i\}$

and then finally $a_n(\omega) = min \; g_n(q_i, r_i)$.

It results that a necessitist object is defined by $OP_n = \{\cup_n, \cap_n, c_n\}$ with $\cup_n = \cup_p, \cap_n = \cap_p, c_n = c_p \; ; g_n$

$(q_i, r_i) = inf\{max (\bar{q_i}(v), r_i(v)) \; / \; v \in O_i\}$ and $f_n = min$.

Example

An expert describes a class of objects by the following possibilist assertion (restricted, to simplify, to a single event) :

e_p = [height = [around [12, 15], about {17}]. An elementary object ω is defined by ω^s = [height = close from 16].

The question is to find the possibility and necessity of ω knowing e_p. In this case e_p and ω^s may be written :

$\quad e_p$ = [height = q_1, q_2] and ω^s = [height = r_1] where q_1, q_2, r_1 are possibilist mappings from $O = [0, 20]$ in $[0, 1]$ defined by the background knowledge on figure 1. This means that an object of height 14 (resp. 6) has a possibility 1 (resp. $\frac{1}{2}$). It is then possible to compute the possibility of ω by :

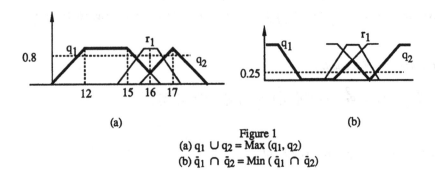

Figure 1
(a) $q_1 \cup q_2 = Max\ (q_1, q_2)$
(b) $\bar{q}_1 \cap \bar{q}_2 = Min\ (\bar{q}_1 \cap \bar{q}_2)$

$$e_p\ (\omega) = g_p\ (q_1 \cup_p q_2, r_1) = \sup\{\min\ (q_1 \cup_p q_2\ (v),\ r_1\ (v))\ /\ v \in \Omega\} = 0.8.$$

The necessity of ω is given by :

$$e_n\ (\omega) = g_n\ (q_1 \cup_p q_2, r_1) = \inf\{\max\ (\overline{q_1 \cup_p q_2}(v),\ r_1\ (v))\ /\ v \in 0\} = 0.25.$$

This example shows that possibilist objects are able to represent not only certitude, variation and doubt but also vagueness (around, about) and inacuracy (close from 16).

5. Some qualities and properties of symbolic objects

5.1. Order, union and intersection between im objects

It is possible to define a partial preorder $\leq_\alpha$ on the im objects by setting that : $a_1 \leq_\alpha a_2$ iff $\forall \omega \in \Omega$ $\alpha \leq a_1\ (\omega) \leq a_2\ (\omega)$.

We deduce from this preorder an equivalence relation R by a_1 R a_2 iff Ext $(a_1 / \Omega, \alpha)$ = Ext $(a_2 / \Omega, \alpha)$ and a partial order denoted $\leq_\alpha$ and called "symbolic order" on the equivalence classes induced from R.

We say that a_1 inherits from a_2 or that a_2 is more general than a_1, at the level α, iff
$a_1 \leq_\alpha a_2$ (which implies $Ext_\alpha\ (a_1 / \Omega, \alpha) \subseteq Ext_\alpha\ (a_2 / \Omega, \alpha)$).
 The symbolic union $a_1 \cup_x a_2$ (resp. intersection $a_1 \cap_x a_2$) at the level α is the conjunction $\wedge_x$ of the im objects b such that Ext $(a_1 / \Omega, \alpha) \cup$ Ext $(a_2 / \Omega, \alpha) \subseteq$ Ext $(b / \Omega, \alpha)$ (resp. Ext $(a_1 / \Omega, \alpha) \cap$ Ext $(a_2 / \Omega, \alpha) \subseteq$ Ext $(b / \Omega, \alpha)$).

5.2. Some qualities of symbolic objects

As in the boolean case, see Brito, Diday (1989), it is possible to define different kinds of qualities of symbolic objects (refinement, simplicity, completeness ...).

For instance, we say that a symbolic object s is complete iff the properties which characterize its extension are exactly those whose conjunction defines the object. More intuitively if I see white dogs in my street and I state "I see dogs", my statement doesn't describe the dogs in a complete way, since I am not saying that they are white.

On the other hand, the simplicity at level α of an im object is the smallest number of elementary events whose extension at level α coincides with the extension of s at the same level.

5.3. Some properties of im objects

It may be shown see Diday (1991) for instance, that given a level α the set of im objects is a lattice for the symbolic order and that the symbolic union and intersection define the supremum and infimum of any couple. It may also be shown that the symbolic union and intersection of complete im objects are complete im objects and hence that the set of complete im objects is also a lattice.

6. An extension of possibility theory on symbolic objects

The notions of σ-algebra, measure and the Kolmogorov axioms may be extended (see Diday 91) in at least two ways

i) the set of samples Ω will be the set of im objects a_x

ii) the usual operators $OP = \{\cup, \cap, c\}$ on classical set theory will be replaced by $OP_x = \{\cup_x, \cap_x, c_x\}$ adapted to the background knowledge. Notice that it may be shown in the case of possibilist objects that OP_x is an idempotent algebra.

Given $A \subseteq a_x$ we denote $a*_\ell$ a "dual" measure of $a_\ell = \hat{\uparrow}_x [y_i = q_i^\ell]$ and Q_i^A the set of q_i^j such that $a = \hat{\uparrow}_x$

$[y_i = q_i^j] \in A$, and we settle

$$a*_\ell (A) = f_x (\{g_x (q_i^\ell, \{\cup_x q_i^j / q_i^j \in Q_i^A\}_i))$$

then it may be shown in the case of possibilist objects that :

i) $a* (a_x) = 1$ and ii) $\forall A_1, A_2 \subseteq a_x$ $a* (A_1 \cup_x A_2) = Max (a* (A_1), a* (A_2))$.

Finally it appears that $a*$ is a kind of possibility of possibility.

7. Statistics and data analysis of symbolic objects

Several works have been recently carried out in this field : for histograms of symbolic objects, see De Carvalho & al (1990) and (1991) ; for generating rules by decision graph on im objects in the case of possibilist objects with typicalities as modes see Lebbe and Vignes (1991) ; for generating overlapping clusters by pyramids on symbolic objects see Brito, Diday (1990).

More generally, four kinds of data analysis may roughly be defined depending on the input and output : a) numerical analysis of classical data tables b) numerical analysis of symbolic objects (for instance by defining distances between objects) c) symbolic analysis of classical data tables, for instance obtaining a factor analysis or a clustering automatically interpreted by symbolic objects d) symbolic analysis of symbolic objects where the input and output of the methods are symbolic objects.

Conclusion

Unlike most work carried out in expert systems, symbolic data analysis constitutes a "critique of pure reasoning" by giving less importance to the inference engine and more importance to the study of the knowledge base, considered as a set of "symbolic objects".
A wide field of research is opened by extending classical statistics to statistics of intensions and more specialy by extending problems, methods and algorithms of data analysis to symbolic objects.

References

. Brito P., Diday E., (1990), *"Pyramidal representation of symbolic objects"*, in NATO ASI Series, Vol. F 61 Knowledge Data and computer-assisted Decisions edited by Schader and W. Gaul. Springer Verlag.

. Dempster A.P., (1990), *"Construction and local computation aspects of network belief functions, in Influence Diagram, Belief Nets, and Decision Analysis"*, Wiley, New York, Chap. 6.

. Diday E., (1990), *"Knowledge representation and symbolic data analysis"*, in NATO ASI Series, Vol. F 61 Knowledge Data and computer-assisted Decisions edited by Schader and W. Gaul. Springer Verlag.

. Diday E., (1991), *"Objets modaux pour l'analyse des connaissances"*, in "Induction symbolique numérique à partir des données" CEPADUES.

. Dubois D., Prade H., (1988), *"Possibility theory"*, Plenum New York.

. Lebbe J., Vignes R., Darmoni S., (1990), *"Symbolic numeric approach for biological knowledge representation : a medical example with creation of identification graphs"*, in : Proc. of Conf. on Data Analysis, Learning Symbolic and Numerical Knowledge, Antibes ed. E. Diday, Nova Science Publishers, Inc., New York.

. Pearl J., (1990), *"Reasoning with belief functions : an analysis of compatibility"*, Int. Journal of approximate reasoning, Vol. 4, N. 5/6, pp. 363.

. Zadeh L.A.(1971), *"Quantitative fuzzy semantics"*, Information Sciences, 159-176.

DIFFERENCE FUZZY RELATION EQUATIONS: STUDIES IN DYNAMICAL SYSTEMS

Antonio Di Nola[+], Witold Pedrycz[++] and Salvatòre Sessa[+]

[+]Università di Napoli, Facoltà di Architettura, Istituto Matematico, Via Monteoliveto 3, 80134 Napoli, Italy

[++]University of Manitoba, Department of Electrical Engineering, Winnipeg, Manitoba, Canada R3T 2N2

Abstract This paper concerns a new type of fuzzy relation equation involving dynamical processes. We introduce a logic-based difference operator forming the left-hand side of the equation. We will analyse properties of this operator, further it will revealed how dynamics, modelled in this format, are related to ambiguity (stated as interval-valued fuzzy sets) of successive states. A comparison with previous types of fuzzy relation equations is pointed out.

Key words and phrases: Dynamical systems, fuzzy relation equation, qualitative modelling, ambiguity propagation, difference operator.

1. Introduction

Dynamical systems can be modelled at different levels of specificity, starting from detailed collection of nonlinear differential equations and arriving to some qualitative statements. The first approach is characteristic for pure numerical analysis, the second one originates from symbolic computation of Artificial Intelligence.

In fuzzy modelling, as highlighted in literature, we take advantage of fuzzy sets as flexible information granulas, thus building an intermediate approach combining advantages of both the approaches above mentioned. In this paper, we will investigate a new type of fuzzy relation equation expressing dynamics of the system in a straightforward way by introducing a difference operator. In its generic form, the equation reads as $\Delta X_k = X_k \text{ o } R$, where the left-hand side of the equation denotes difference (dynamics) in the system and k is an index, $k=1,2,\ldots,N$, for the family of fuzzy sets $\{X_1, X_2, \ldots, X_N\}$. The difference ΔX_k is defined departing from some logic-flavoured constructs such as the equality operator introduced in [4]. Thus our proposed difference calculus differs from the differential and integral calculus for fuzzy sets of D. Dubois and H. Prade [2]. First we will study a difference operator and its properties, further we discuss a so-called inverse problem. In Section 2, we will analyse the basic form of the equation along with its system interpretation including construction aspects (identification). Some numerical studies revealing the performance are also included. Section 3 is devoted to studies on resulting dynamical properties and originating ambiguity. Section 4 contains a numerical example.

2. Difference operator of fuzzy sets

In this Section we define a difference operator between two fuzzy sets. It should be stressed that, since fuzzy sets are considered as well-settled logical constructs, all the operations including difference should be driven by logical-based structures. Bearing this in mind and referring to the definition of equality (equivalence) between fuzzy sets [4], we will introduce difference as a complement of equality. Let A and B be fuzzy sets defined in the same universe of discourse X, card X = n, the degree of equality of A and B at $x_0 \in X$, is expressed as [4] (for concise notation, we put a = $A(x_0)$, b = $B(x_0)$):

$$(a \equiv b) = 1/2 \cdot \{[(a \rightarrow b) \wedge (b \rightarrow a)] + [(\bar{a} \rightarrow \bar{b}) \wedge (\bar{b} \rightarrow \bar{a})]\}, \tag{1}$$

where $\bar{a} = 1 - a$, $\bar{b} = 1 - b$ and "$\rightarrow$" stands for an implication operator induced by a continuous triangular norm [1]. It becomes obvious that the equality occurring between A and B is specified pointwise for each element of X. Therefore (A $\equiv$ B) is seen as a vector of the degrees of equalities,

$$[(A(x_1) \equiv B(x_1)), (A(x_2) \equiv B(x_2)),..., (A(x_n) \equiv B(x_n))].$$

The difference operator is introduced by taking the complement to 1, i.e. (a $\equiv\!|$ b) = 1 - (a $\equiv$ b). In virtue of the discussion on the degree of equality shown in [4], we can deduce the following properties:

(i) (a $\equiv\!|$ b) = 0 iff (a $\equiv$ b) = 1, (a $\equiv\!|$ b) = (b $\equiv\!|$ a),

(ii) if b' < b < a, then (a $\equiv\!|$ b') > (a $\equiv\!|$ b),

(iii) the range of the values achieved by (a $\equiv\!|$ b), for a fixed "a" and a variable "b", is characterized by the interval [0, max{(a $\equiv\!|$ 0), (a $\equiv\!|$ 1)}].

Defining a certain triangular norm and the induced implication, (1) reads as, for the Lukasiewicz implication:

$$(a \equiv b) = \begin{cases} 1 - a + b & \text{if } a > b, \\ 1 & \text{if } a = b, \\ 1 - b + a & \text{if } a < b. \end{cases}$$

Then, obviously the difference operator becomes also a piecewise linear function:

$$(a \equiv\!| b) = \begin{cases} a - b & \text{if } a > b, \\ 0 & \text{if } a = b, \\ b - a & \text{if } a < b. \end{cases}$$

In this case, the values of (a $\equiv\!|$ b), for "a" fixed, are in the interval [0,max{a,1-a}].

It is worthwhile to notice that, in two-valued logic, the difference operator is (a $\oplus$ b) = (a $\wedge \bar{b}$) $\vee$ ($\bar{a} \wedge$ b), a,b $\in$ [0,1]. Note also that (a $\oplus$ b) = 1 if a and b are different and ((a $\oplus$ b) = 0 otherwise. In [4], the inverse problem was also addressed. It is referred for finding solutions to the following inequality,

$$(a \equiv x) \geq c \qquad (2)$$

for a and c given and x being looked for. This inequality has always a nonempty set of solutions. In addition, the set of solutions $\{x \in [0,1] : (a \equiv x) \geq c\}$ reduces to a single element when c = 1. In general, this set is a subinterval of [0,1].

Interpreting (2) as a reconstruction task: determine all the elements x which are known to be similar to "a" to the grade not lower than "c", we can learn that a pointwise reconstruction is possible only in the case when c = 1 (perfect matching). In all remaining cases where c < 1 (partial matching), the variable x can be reconstructed with a certain ambiguity. Bearing in mind that the difference operator produces a complementary result to that given by the equality operator, we formulate the following problem: "determine all x's such that $(a \not\equiv x) \leq c$". Again referring to the previous results, we can observe that a nonempty set of solutions always exists. The reconstruction is ideal (i.e., pointwise) when c = 0. If c' < c, then $\{ x \in [0,1] : (a \not\equiv x) \leq c' \} \subset \{x \in [0,1] : (a \not\equiv x) \leq c\}$. In other words, the reconstruction of "a" returns an interval of values for which the degree of difference is lower than c. If we are looking for x's for which the degree of difference is the lowest one (namely 1), we have only one element x = a.

3. Fuzzy relation equations in modelling dynamical systems

In [1], [3], [5], an exhaustive study on fuzzy models of dynamical systems has been reported. In its basic setting, a first order dynamical system with fuzzy states (fuzzy sets) in discrete universes of discourse is characterized by $X_{k+1} = X_k \circ R$, k = 1,2,...,N, where $X_k : X \rightarrow [0,1]$ and $R : X \times X \rightarrow [0,1]$ is a fuzzy relation expressing all the connections between individual elements of the universe. Consecutive X_k's, e.g. X_1, X_2, result as a series of max-min convolutions of Xo and powers of R.

Another approach is described in Sec. 4: if the state of the system is X_k, we cannot describe explicitly any state in a successive time moment (namely X_{k+1}) but we refer only to dynamics of X_k by specifying ΔX_k. Of course, in this manner we are not committed to point out exactly one X_{k+1}, which might be infeasible, but to all X_k satisfying the constraint imposed by ΔX_k.

3.1. Determination problem

For any model to be introduced and studied, it is of primordial interest to determine all its parameters. In the difference equation, the fuzzy relation R has to be computed. The entire procedure relies on a collection of pairs $(\Delta X_1, X_1)$, $(\Delta X_2, X_2)$,...,$(\Delta X_N, X_N)$. These data form the learning set and we can put them together into a family of equations $\Delta X_k = X_k \circ R$, k = 1,2,...N. Afterwards $\widehat{R}$ is derived in accordance to the following rules:

(i) if the set $\mathcal{R} = \{R : X_k \circ R = \Delta X_k, k = 1,2,...,N\} \neq \phi$, a classic result [1] assures that $\widehat{R} = \max \mathcal{R}$,

$$\widehat{R} = \bigwedge_{k=1}^{N} (X_k \ \alpha \ \Delta X_k)$$

where α is the Gödelian implication,

(ii) in all the remaining situations, i.e. $\mathcal{R} = \phi$, we can utilize optimization procedures yelding an approximate solution to the problem [3],[5].

4. Studies of dynamical properties of a model

In this Section we will study how the fuzzy difference relation equation captures a dynamical behavior of the system described by it. Let us start with the generic form of the equation starting from an initial condition X_0. Then $(X_1 \dashv X_0) = \Delta X_0 = X_0 \circ R$, which, in terms of membership functions, is read as

$$(X_1(Y) \dashv X_0(Y)) = \max_{x \in X} [\min \{X_0(x), R(x,y)\}] = \gamma(y)$$

for $y \in X$. Thus $X_1(y)$ is taken as a straightforward solution to the inverse problem for difference operator. It should be noticed that the uniqueness of the solution is not guaranteed.

To achieve it, we should impose an upper limit of dynamics just setting the inclusion $(X_1 \dashv X_0) \subset X_0 \circ R$ which, in turn, implies that $(X_1(Y) \dashv X_0(Y)) \leq \gamma(y)$ for any $y \in X$. An interesting observation can be derived: the higher the dynamics, the higher ambiguity associated with the successive state of the system, namely $X_1(y)$.

This qualitative (as well as quantitatively expressed) observation states that the dynamics of the system strongly affects prediction of the next state. Usually we obtain an interval of feasible values of the membership functions. This in turn allows us to take another set-theoretic look at dynamical processes as creating uncertainty. In two boundary situations:

(i) if no dynamics, then $\gamma(y) = 0$; of course, $X_1(y)$ is equal identically to $X_0(y)$,

(ii) if there is the highest possible dynamics, then $\gamma(y) = 1$ and $X_1(y)$ covers entirely the unit interval.

In the intermediate situations the value of $X_1(y)$ is localized as any value lying in a certain subinterval of $[0,1]$ induced by $\gamma(y)$. The behavior of a series of states of the model can be projected making use of a sequence of max-min composition operations and solving inverse problems. Hence, if such subinterval is $[X_1^-(y), X_1^+(y)]$, we have $X_1^-(y) \circ R \subset X_1^+(y) \circ R$. Thus one has to solve two inequalities $(X_2 \dashv X_1^-) \subset X_1^- \circ R$, $(X_2 \dashv X_1^+) \subset X_1^+ \circ R$, to determine X_2. Two resulting intervals of possible values of X_2 are then combined either in the most "pessimistic" manner yielding the broadest interval or in the most "optimistic" way producing the most compressed subinterval of $[0,1]$. The process is repeated with X_2^- and X_2^+ such that $(X_3 \dashv X_2^-) \subset X_2^- \circ R$, $(X_3 \dashv X_2^+) \subset X_2^+ \circ R$, and so on. The following numerical example illustrates the above method of computation of successive states. Let R be given by

$$R = \begin{bmatrix} 1.0 & 0.3 & 0.4 \\ 0.2 & 0.5 & 1.0 \\ 0.7 & 1.0 & 0.8 \end{bmatrix}.$$

The starting state $X_0 = [1.0 \ 0.0 \ 0.0]$ gives $X_0 \circ R = [1.0 \ 0.3 \ 0.4]$ and $(X_1 \equiv [1.0 \ 0.0 \ 0.0]) \subset [1.0. \ 0.3 \ 0.4]$, i.e. $(X_1(x_1) \equiv 1.0) \leq 1.0$, $(X_1(x_2) \equiv 0.0) \leq 0.3$, $(X_1(x_3) \equiv 0.0) \leq 0.4$.

Making use of Lukasiewicz-based difference operator, we compute $X_1(x_1) \in [0,1]$, $X_1(x_2) \in [0,0.3]$, $X_1(x_3) \in [0,0.4]$. Next $X_1^- = [0.0 \ 0.0 \ 0.0]$ and $X_1^+ = [1.0 \ 0.3 \ 0.4]$, combined with R, generate two vectors $(X_1^- \circ R) = [0.0 \ 0.0 \ 0.0]$ and $(X_1^+ \circ R) = [1.0 \ 0.4 \ 0.4]$. Furthermore, the inequalities

$$(X_1^- \equiv X_2) \subset [0.0. \ 0.0 \ 0.4],$$
$$(X_1^+ \equiv X_2) \subset [1.0. \ 0.4 \ 0.4],$$

induce the following set of constraints,

$(0 \equiv X_2(x_1)) = 0,$ $\qquad\qquad (1 \equiv X_2(x_1)) \leq 1,$

$(0 \equiv X_2(x_2)) = 0,$ $\qquad\qquad (0.3 \equiv X_2(x_2)) \leq 0,.4$

$(0 \equiv X_2(x_3)) = 0,$ $\qquad\qquad (0.4 \equiv X_2(x_3)) \leq 0.4.$

This, in turn, gives $X_2^{'}(x_i) = 0$ for $i = 1,2,3$ and $X_2^{''}(x_1) \in [0,1]$, $X_2^{''}(x_2) \in [0,0.7]$, $X_2^{''}(x_3) \in [0,0.8]$. For the pessimistic aggregation one obtains,

$$X_2 \in \begin{bmatrix} [0,1] \\ [0,0.7] \\ [0,0.8] \end{bmatrix}.$$

Note that because of high dynamics (several entries of R are equal to 1) only after two successive discrete time moments, X_2 becomes fairly ambiguous (i.e. we have broad intervals of possible values of grades of membership).

REFERENCES

[1] A. Di Nola, W. Pedrycz, E. Sanchez and S. Sessa, Fuzzy Relation Equations and Their Applications to Knowledge Engineering, Kluwer Academic Publishers, Dordrecht (1989).

[2] D. Dubois and H. Prade, Towards fuzzy differential calculus. Part 2: Integration on fuzzy intervals, Fuzzy Sets and Systems 8 (1982), 105-116.

[3] W. Pedrycz, Approximate solutions of fuzzy relational equations, Fuzzy Sets and Systems 2 (1988), 183-202.

[4] W. Pedrycz, Direct and inverse problem in comparison of fuzzy data, Fuzzy Sets and Systems 34 (1990), 223-235.

[5] W. Pedrycz, Neurocomputations in relational systems, IEEE Trans. on Pattern Analysis and Machine Intelligence, to appear.

Towards a *Logic* for a Fuzzy Logic Controller

Dimiter Driankov*   Hans Hellendoorn

Siemens AG
Dept. ZFE IS INF3
Otto-Hahn-Ring 6
8000 Munich 83
Germany

1   Introduction

Fuzzy control is based on fuzzy logic [3], and the core of a fuzzy logic controller (FLC) is a set of fuzzy conditional statements related by the dual notions of fuzzy implication and the so-called compositional rule of inference[2].

However, despite of the use of the logic-related concepts of fuzzy conditional statements, fuzzy implication, and the compositional rule of inference, all of these are used in a mixed declarative/procedural manner. That is, there is no clear distinction between the "declarative" part of a FLC (the fuzzy conditional statements) and the way this declarative knowledge is used in the inference component of a FLC (the compositional rule of inference). To be more specific, the compositional rule of inference is defined directly on the extension (meaning) of a fuzzy conditional statement, rather than on its symbolic counterpart.

Furthermore, the extension of a fuzzy conditional statement is constructed by applying a fuzzy implication operator on the extensions of its antecedent and consequent. Thus, a fuzzy implication is not any longer defined in terms of a function of the truth-values of the symbolic counterparts of the antecedent and the consequent.

In this context, the declarative part of a FLC is nothing else but a collection of "propositions" (fuzzy conditional statements) represented via their extensions and thus yielding a set of equations. Then the inference amounts to "solving" such a system of equations. The clear consequence of all this is the complete lack of any syntactic representation of the declarative part of a FLC and hence, no underlying semantic characterization.

---

*On leave from the University of Linköping, Dept. of Computer Science, Laboratory for Knowledge Representation in Logic, Linköping, Sweden

2   The Basic Idea

The aim of the present work is to provide for a true logic-like description of a FLC by first constructing an appropriate first-order language and then supplying corresponding semantics for the expressions in this language.

Once this is achieved, a FLC can be treated as a set of axioms, each axiom expressing a particular fuzzy conditional statement. Such a fuzzy conditional statement conditions the process control-variables in the consequent on the process state-variables in the antecedent. A model for such a set of axioms will then include the values (variable assignments) of the state-variables and the control-variables which satisfy the axioms.

In this context, the major objective is such a logic which guarantees that the values of the process control-variables determined by the procedural FLC, given certain values for the process state-variables, coincide with the values of these types of variables from the model.

3   The Conventional Representation of a FLC

A fuzzy production rule for a Mamdani-type [1] of a FLC is usually given as:

if e is A and Δe is B then Δu is C

where e is the error-variable defined on the domain E, Δe is the change-of-error variable defined on ΔE, and Δu is the incremental-control variable defined on ΔU and all domains are normalized and discrete. A, B and C are fuzzy sets defined on E, ΔE and ΔU respectively and describing specific fuzzy values of e, Δe and Δu. For example:

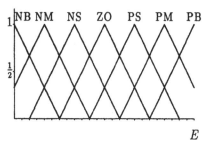

Given specific values A, B and C the rule is represented as a fuzzy relation $\mu_R(e, \Delta e, \Delta u)$ defined as

$$\mu_R(e, \Delta e, \Delta u) = [(\mu_A(e) \wedge \mu_B(\Delta e)) \rightarrow \mu_C(\Delta u)] = \min_{e, \Delta e, \Delta u} (\mu_A(e), \mu_B(\Delta e), \mu_C(\Delta u)) \quad (1)$$

However, the above relation is only one part of the "meaning" of such a production rule representing its declarative semantics.

The other part of the "meaning" of the rule is given by the way in which it is used, i.e. its procedural description. Given crisp values for e and Δe, say e_0 and Δe_0, one proceeds as follows:

- find the degree to which the crisp values e_0 and Δe_0 satisfy the fuzzy values A and B respectively, that is $\mu_A(e_0)$ and $\mu_B(\Delta e_0)$;

- find the minimum of $\mu_A(e_0)$ and $\mu_B(\Delta e_0)$, e.g. $\min(\mu_A(e_0), \mu_B(\Delta e_0)) = \mu_A(e_0)$;

- take all Δu_0 such that

  - if $\mu_C(\Delta u_0) \leq \mu_A(e_0)$ then $\mu_{C^\circ}(\Delta u_0) = \mu_C(\Delta u_0)$,
  - if $\mu_C(\Delta u_0) > \mu_A(e_0)$ then $\mu_{C^\circ}(\Delta u_0) = \mu_A(e_0)$.

Thus at the last step one constructs the fuzzy set C° describing the incremental-output given certain crisp values for e and Δe. C° is called the π-cut of C where π is equal to $\min(\mu_A(e_0, \mu_B(\Delta e_0))$ and

$$\mu_{C^\circ}(\Delta u) = \min(\mu_A(e_0), \mu_B(\Delta e_0)) \circ \mu_R(e, \Delta e, \Delta u). \tag{2}$$

Graphically, the above procedure can be represented as follows:

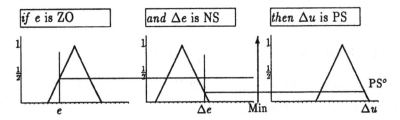

If there are more rules in the rule-base, then the resulting fuzzy sets C_i°, $i = 1, 2, \ldots$, are combined into one fuzzy set $C = \bigcup_i C_i^\circ$. From this fuzzy set, the center of gravity or the middle-of-maxima is taken as the *crisp* output value of the FLC.

4 The Logic-Based Representation of a FLC

The purpose of the logic based representation is to be used as a specification which describes in a declarative way

- the relationship between e, Δe and Δu in terms of their fuzzy values, and

- the expected fuzzy value for the given crisp value for e and Δe.

This logic-based specification represents in a unified way both the declarative meaning of a rule as well as its procedural aspect. The first quesion to answer here is how do we represent symbolically the statement "e is A" where A is a fuzzy set (e.g. NS) with a membership function $\mu_A(u) : E \to [0, 1]$.

linguistic	symbolic	extension of $R_A(e, \mu)$
statement	representation	$r_A = \{(e, \mu) \mid e \in E, \mu \in [0, 1],$
e is A	$\forall e \exists \mu R_A(e, \mu)$	$\mu_A(e) = \mu\}$

Thus given an interpretation $I : R_A \to r_A$ and a variable assignment $VA_e(e) : e \to E$ and $VA_\mu(\mu) : \mu \to [0, 1]$, $\langle I, VA_e, VA_\mu \rangle$ is a model for $\forall e \exists \mu R_A(e, \mu)$ if and only if for each e there exists a μ such that $\langle VA_e, VA_\mu \rangle \in r_A$.

In a similar way we define the semantics for $\forall \Delta e \exists \nu R_B(\Delta e, \nu)$, i.e. Δe is B and $\forall \Delta u \exists \psi R_C(\Delta u, \psi)$, i.e. Δu is C.

On the next step we need to define the π-cut of C representing an arbitrary incremental output C^o. The well-formed formula (wff) expressing this π-cut is given as $\forall \Delta u \forall \psi \exists \pi R_{C^o}(\Delta u, \psi, \pi)$, where the extension of R_{C^o} is defined as:

$$r_{C^o} = \{\langle \Delta u, \psi, \pi \rangle \mid \Delta u \in \Delta U \wedge \psi, \pi \in [0,1] \wedge \psi = \min(\pi, \mu_C(\Delta u))\} \tag{3}$$

This extension describes all possible π-cuts of C, when varying the variable π. A model for R_{C^o} is the pair $\langle I, VA \rangle$ where $I : R_{C^o} \rightarrow r_{C^o}$, $VA : \langle VA_{\Delta u}, VA_\psi, VA_\pi \rangle$, where $VA_{\Delta u} : \Delta u \rightarrow \Delta U$, $VA_\pi : \pi \rightarrow [0,1]$ and $VA_\psi(\psi) = \min(VA_\pi, \mu_C(VA(\Delta u)))$.

Now the symbolic version of a rule is given by the wff

$$\forall e \exists \mu [R_A(e,\mu)] \wedge \forall \Delta e \exists \nu [R_B(\Delta e, \nu)] \wedge \forall \Delta u \exists \psi [R_C(\Delta u, \psi)] \rightarrow \forall \Delta u \forall \pi \exists \psi [R_{C^o}(\Delta u, \psi, \pi)], \tag{4}$$

which encapsulates both the declarative and procedural parts of an conventional fuzzy control rule. That is, given that e is A and Δe is B and Δu is C (see eq. (1)), then the expected incremental output, i.e. C^o is one of the possible π-cuts of C. All π-cuts of C are represented by the set of models for R_{C^o}.

However, given a specific input, i.e. a crisp value for e and Δe, we have to find a specific π-cut for C^o. For this purpose one has the following axioms:

$$\exists e : \quad e_0 = \text{input}(e), \tag{5}$$

$$\exists \Delta e : \quad \Delta e_0 = \text{input}(\Delta e). \tag{6}$$

These two axioms define what the actual values of e and Δe should be equal to some constants e_0 and Δe_0 given in advance.

Once one knows the actual values for e and Δe, then one can define the specific value for π:

$$\exists \pi \forall e \forall \Delta e : (\pi = \min(\mu_A(\text{input}(e)), \mu_B(\text{input}(\Delta e)))) \wedge \forall \Delta u \exists \psi : R_{C^o}(\Delta u, \psi, \pi) \tag{7}$$

There is a unique model for wff's (5), (6) and (7) which is an element of the model-set for wff (4) and this unique model defines the π-cut for C given specific input e_0 and Δe_0.

Since we have more than one rule in the rule-base of a FLC, we will normally get an incremental output which is the union of all the π-cuts for the consequents of the rules, that is $C_1^o \cup C_2^o \cup \ldots \cup C_n^o$. The formula which specifies this union is given as:

$$\forall \Delta u \exists \psi_1, \ldots, \psi_n, \exists \pi_1, \ldots, \pi_n, \exists \omega : R_{C_1^o}(\Delta u, \psi_1, \pi_1) \wedge \ldots \wedge R_{C_n^o}(\Delta u, \psi_n, \pi_n) \rightarrow R^*(\Delta u, \omega)), \tag{8}$$

where the extension of R^* is defined on $C_1^o \cup C_2^o \cup \ldots \cup C_n^o$.

Finally one has to specify the way in which a pointwise control-action is determined given that: $\forall \Delta u \exists \omega : R^*(\Delta u, \omega))$ is the case. This is done by the following two axioms:

$$\forall \Delta u \exists \omega : R^*(\Delta u, \omega) \wedge \neg \exists \omega' : R^*(\Delta u, \omega') \wedge \omega' > \omega \rightarrow \text{MAX}(\omega) \tag{9}$$

The above axiom specifies the maximal membership degree on the extension of R^*.

$$\forall \Delta u_\ell, \Delta u_r \exists \omega, \Delta u :$$
$$\text{MAX}(\omega) \wedge [R^*(\Delta u_\ell, \omega) \wedge \neg \exists \Delta u' \leq \Delta u_\ell : R^*(\Delta u', \omega)] \wedge \tag{10}$$
$$[R^*(\Delta u_r, \omega) \wedge \neg \exists \Delta u' \geq \Delta u_r : R^*(\Delta u', \omega)] \wedge \Delta u = (\Delta u_\ell + \Delta u_r)/2 \rightarrow R^*(\Delta u, \omega)$$

This axiom specifies the middle-of-maxima-value for the pointwise control-action.

5 The Use of a Logic-Based Representation

Having constructed a set of models for the set of axioms defining a FLC, it becomes much easier to formally define and study some of its important properties, namely completeness, consistency, interactivity [2]. Take for example the completeness property, i.e. a fuzzy control algorithm should always be able to infer a "proper" control action for every state of the process. A "proper" control action means that there always should be a fuzzy conditional statement which is satisfied to at least a degree equal or greater than ϵ (usually $\epsilon = 0.5$).

In terms of the axiomatic description of a FLC this property means that there should always be a model for at least one axiom. This in turn implies that the extensions of the predicates expressing the antecedent and consequent of each axiom should be defined in such a way so that each variable assignment should be a model for at least one axiom.

A further advantage of the logic-based FLC is that for example, one can add an additional set of axioms describing explicit steady-state conditions. Then constructing the models for the axioms describing the FLC and the models for the steady-state axioms will help to identify the set of rules which indicate that a corresponding steady-state is to occur. This will be the case if the set of models for the FLC is is a subset of the set of models for the steady-state axioms, i.e. the steady-state is entailed (can be inferred) from the FLC axioms. In the same manner one can axiomatize stability conditions and see whether these are entailed by the axioms of the FLC. The last two applications of the logic-based approach are of uttermost importance, since so far no significant enough results have been produced in the stability analysis of FLCs.

References

[1] Mamdani, E.H., "Advances in the Linguistic Synthesis of Fuzzy-Controllers," *Int. J. Man-Machine Studies*, 8(1976)669–678.

[2] Lee, C.C., "Fuzzy Logic in Control Systems: Fuzzy Logic Controller—Part I," *IEEE Trans. on Systems, Man, and Cybernetics*, 20(2)(1990)404–418.

[3] Zadeh, L.A., "Outline of a New Approach to the Analysis of Complex Systems and Decision Processes," *IEEE Trans. on Systems, Man, and Cybernetics*, 1(1973)28–44.

Handling Active Databases
with Partial Inconsistencies
Opher Etzion

Technion - Israel Institute of Technology
Faculty of Industrial and Management Engineering
Haifa, 32000, Israel

Abstract

Active Database is a database which contains as a part of its schema definitions of derived data stated as computational invariants and constraints stated as logical invariants. The invariants are enforced in an active way.

The information stored in the database might be partially inconsistent with either database definitions or invariants. This paper classifies the inconsistencies types and suggests an appropriate handling mechanism for each type (using either exception-handling mode or modal operators or numeric methods).

1 Types of Inconsistencies in Active Databases

1.1 Database Definition

We are using the PARDES model [ETZION 90] which is an active semantic database model. Definition of the database is done by defining the static schema, computational invariants and logical invariants of the database.

1.1.1 Static Schema

Definition of the structure of data-groups (records, relations, frames in various data models) as well as reference relations among data-elements. *Reference relation* determines that the data-element refers to another object that must exist as long as it is referred.
    Example of a Schema:

Group: Department. Properties: Department-Name, Total-Salaries, Budget.

Group: Employee. Properties: Employee-Name, Department-Affiliation, Manager, Salary.

Reference Relation:

Department-Affiliation <u>refers to</u> Department.

Manager <u>refers to</u> Employee.

Example 1

1.1.2 Computational Invariant

An arithmetic relationship among data-elements in the database that should be maintained at all times. Example:
Total-Salaries := sum(Salary)
is interpreted as:
$\forall$ *x: x is-a Department* $\leadsto$ *Total-Salaries (x)* $= \sum\{$ *Salary(y)* $\mid$ *y is-a Employee and Department-Affiliation(y) = x* $\}$
   This invariant is enforced regardless of the modification that occurs in the database. In this case addition and removal of employees, modification in salaries or re-assignments of employees to department effect the invariant and result in re-calculation of the appropriate instances of Total-Salaries.

1.1.3 Logical Invariant

A logical relationship among data elements that should be maintained at all times. Example:
Total-Salaries $\leq$ *Budget*
which is interpreted as: $\forall$ *x: x is-a Department* $\leadsto$ *Total-Salaries(x)* $\leq$ *Budget(x)*.
This invariant is checked whenever the value of Budget decreases or the value of Total-Salaries increases.

1.2 Inconsistency Types

An inconsistency relative to the database definition may occur in one of the following cases:

1.2.1 Unknown Property-Value

A Data-Group exists in which there is a property with unknown value("null value"). An example is: The property *Spouse-Name* of a person is not given. There are different kinds of unknown values:

Irrelevant Case: It is known that the person is a bachelor, thus the Spouse-name property is not relevant.

Unknown Case: It is known that the person is married, but the spouse-name is not known.

Undetermined Case: The marital-status of the person is not known therefore it is undetermined if the property is unknown or non-relevant.

Typical Case: In case that most of the population have a typical value for a property (example: Almost all the employees are married) and to save space it is not used explicitly.

Current database models do not distinguish among these cases.

1.2.2 Not Unique Property Value

The database receives two or more non-identical values to the same property. Example: For an employee there are two sources about the property *Country-of-Birth* referring to two different countries. We might or might not have information about the reliability of the sources. This type of incompleteness is common in databases that are used in contexts of knowledge acquisition(Expert Database Systems) and support of IS development.

1.2.3 Reference Violation

Reference relation is violated in one of the following cases:

The insert case: A referred object does not exist. Example: An Employee is assigned (using Department-Affiliation) to a Department that currently does not exist.

The delete case: A referred object is removed, without the prior removal of all its references. Example: A Department is removed, but there are employees that are assigned to it.

1.2.4 Constraint Violation

A Constraint is not satisfied in the database. Example: The value of Total-Salaries exceeds the value of Budget for st least one Department.

1.2.5 Computational Invariant Violation

Computational Invariant may be violated in one of two ways:

1. The computation process cannot proceed due to problems of reference. Example: Employee is assigned to a Department that does not exist, thus his salary does not add up to any instance of Total-Salaries. This type of inconsistency is subsumed by the reference violation one.

2. There is a direct update of a data-element that is a calculated value and not a given one. Example: The property Total-Salaries of a given Department is given explicitly, and its value is not identical with the calculated value.

2 Handling the Inconsistency Cases

2.1 Basic Methods

There are several basic methods to handle inconsistent cases in the database area:

Handling Modes: [DATE 81] Mode is a strategy that application developers use to handle inconsistencies. The proposed modes are:

Restrict: Any transaction that creates an inconsistent information to the database is rejected.

Nullify: The inconsistent value is turned into a NULL value. Other values remain in tact.

Cascade: Modifications in the database occur in order to restore consistency.

Forgive: The inconsistent value is marked.

Disconnect: The rule that is contradicted is altered so as not to include the inconsistent instance.

The Employee John Galt is added to Atlas department that does not exist (Reference Violation). Under the different modes:

Restrict: Rollback the transaction.

Nullify: For Employee = John Galt, Department-Affiliation = unknown.

Cascade: Add Department = Atlas.

Forgive: Mark the value Department-Affiliation for John Galt as a reference violation.

disconnect: The property Department-Affiliation of John Galt is not a reference for Department in our enterprise.

Example 2

Modal Approaches: Taken from theoretical studies in *artificial intelligence* using operators such as: Default[REITER 80], Belief[MOORE 85]. In this models we distinguish among information that is *known* to be true and information that is *believed* to be true in a certain context or because it is true in most cases.

Arithmetic Approaches: Taken from models of expert system, using quantitative measurements of *probability, certainty factors, measure of belief* etc, based on evidences [PEARL 88].

2.2 Matching between Inconsistency Cases and Methods

Unknown Property Value: *Default Reasoning.* When a typical value exists or any value that is obtained as a substitute for a known value, we may use modal approach. The approach used is a *Default Reasoning* model following [ETHERINGTON 88].

Not Unique Property Value: Numeric Approach. When a contradictory occurs we use the contradictory input transactions as *evidences*, thus we are using *Evidential Reasoning* [SHAFFER 76] to determine the *measure of belief* in the property value.

Reference Violation: The Modes Approach. If the chosen mode is NULLIFY and there is a default function defined for this value then the modal approach is also used.

Constraint Violation: The Modes Approach. If the chosen mode is NULLIFY and there is a default function defined for this value then the modal approach is also used. If the chosen mode is FORGIVE then it is treated as a contradiction and the numeric approach is also used.

Computational Invariant Violation: The same as the Constraint Violation.

3 Summary

Our model combines three different approaches to the problem of inconsistent information for different cases. We have found *modal* approaches useful for cases where we do not have an explicit knowledge about a value. We have found *numeric* approaches useful for cases where we have contradictory knowledge about a value. We are using the *modes* approaches that has been proposed in database theory in other cases.

4 References

[DATE 81]: C.J. Date -Referential Integrity - *Proc VLDB*, 1981.

[ETHERINGTON 88]: D.W. Etherington - Reasoning with Incomplete Information. *Morgan Kaufman*, 1987.

[ETZION 90]: O. Etzion - PARDES - An Active Semantic Database Model. Technion-Israel Institute of Technology- Technical Report ISE-TR-90-1.

[MOORE 85]: R. C. Moore - Semantical Considerations on Nonmonotonic Logic. *Artificial Intelligence*, 25, pp 75-94, 1985.

[PEARL 88]: J. Pearl - The Probabilistic Reasoning in Intelligent System. *Morgan Kaufman*, 1988.

[REITER 80]: R. Reiter - A Logic for Default Reasoning. *Artificial Intelligence*, 13, pp 81-132, 1980.

[SHAFFER 76]: G. Shaffer - A Mathematical Theory of Evidence. *Princeton University Press*, 1976.

AN EXTENSION OF THE POSSIBILITY THEORY
IN VIEW OF THE FORMALIZATION OF APPROXIMATE
REASONING

L.Gacôgne

Institut d'Informatique d'Entreprise (CNAM) 18 allée J.Rostand 91002 Evry

LAFORIA Université Paris VI   4 place Jussieu 75252 Paris 5

Abstract

Our aim is here to give some indications about the basis of a logic system in order to generalize the possibility theory in the following way :

We want that each sentence receive a couple of confidence values. We call them degrees of obligation and eventuality, in order to translate the notion of truth by the half-sum of these values, and a notion that we can see as the imprecision given to this truth value : the diference eventuality - obligation which we shall call the unknown rather than uncertainty.

In relation to the possibility theory, we whish to leave the general property $\max(ps(P), ps(\neg P)) = 1$ and then leave :

$$nc(P) > 0 \Rightarrow ps(P) = 1 \quad \text{and} \quad ps(P) < 1 \Rightarrow nc(P) = 0$$

The aim of this extension is sitted in the tentation of modelising the degrees of truth and unknown, and their propagation when inferences, in the computing system about approximate reasoning.

We would like that linguistics appreciations with vagueness such "perhaps true", "probably false", "true always three times on four", "often true but very uncertain" etc..., could receive those two degrees in order to determinate an interval whose the widness would be the measure of the imprecision given to the truth degree, and it is this that we call unknown.

Definitions

Let us consider the algebric structure constructed by the set of couples (x,y) in $[0,1]^2$, which satisfy $x \leq y$ (hachured area on the shema), (x will be the degree of obligation and y the degree of eventuality) with the three internal operations :

$$\neg(x,y) = (1-y , 1-x)$$

$(x,y) \wedge (x',y') = (\min(x,x') , \min(y,y'))$ $(x,y) \vee (x',y') = (\max(x,x') , \max(y,y'))$

that we shall call respectively negation, conjonction, disjonction.

Taking the definition $v(x, y) = (x+y)/2$, a truth degree inspired by [Gaines 76], and $i(x,y) = y-x$, we shall note on the other side that four elements have a particular function, we call them :

F = (0, 0) the false, which is the minimal element for the partial ordering $\leq$,

T = (1, 1) the true, which is the maximum,

I = (0, 1) the uncertain, (maximum of the no-obligatory and minimum of the eventual) and at last M = (0.5 0.5) the "certainly half true".

We can then call (really) eventuals couples, those of the segment IT, no-obligatory couples, those of the segment FI.

The first advantage of this axiomatic is to meet again the theory of possibilities on the cut

line [FI] ∪ [IT], which has stability under the three operations ¬, ∧, ∨ above.

We have on the other side, an extension of the Kleene multivalued logic min-max (the certains couples), on the segment [FT], and at last the elementary boolean logic being only constitued by the two points F and T.

The transvers parallels lines with IM are the "equal truth lines".

If P and Q represent two couples of confidence (ob, ev) and (ob', ev'), the shema give a view of ¬P, P ∧ Q, P ∨ Q.

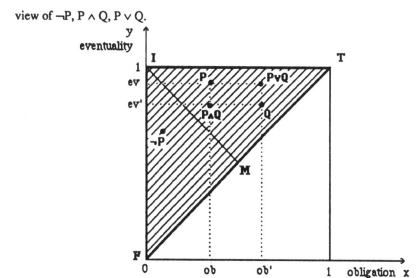

Remark

We could, in the same way, begin from the axiomatic of the couples (v, i) in $[0,1]^2$, such that : $0 \leq v - i/2 \leq v + i/2 \leq 1$ then represented by the figure : (v = truth, i = unknown)

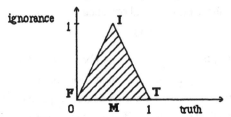

(with the same constants F, T, I, the equal truth lines are here the "verticals lines") the

disadvantage of this second way is not having easy formulas for the definitions of ∧ and ∨, it is the reason why we shall compute rather with the couples (ob, ev).

Properties

The negation is involutive (we check easily that it is a geometric symetrie in relation to IM on the two figures). We shall note that the couples on IM are equal to their negation, it will be called "half true".

The conjonction and the disjonction are idempotentes, commutatives, associatives, mutually distributives because min and max have those properties.

The Morgan properties are satisfied.

We have therefore a distributive lattice, but is not a Boole algebra.

The relation (x,y) ≤ (x',y') defined by (x ≤ x' and y ≤ y') is a dense partial ordering having two extremities F and T.

Implication

We define as in classical logic the operation → by :

$$(x,y) \to (x',y') = \neg(x,y) \vee (x',y') = (\max(1-y, x') , \max(1-x, y'))$$

This definition assuming therefore the contraposition :

$$[\neg(x',y') \to \neg(x,y)] = [(x,y) \to (x',y')]$$

On [F,V], that is to say in the cases of certainty where i = 0, we then have again the

implication of Kleene-Dienes : $p \to q = \max(1-p, q)$

The question of the inference

We could state it in the following algebrics terms : P = (ob, ev) is given and also R =

$P \to Q = (s,t)$, it must resolve Q = (x,y) by the equations

$$s = \max(1-ev, x) \quad \text{and} \quad t = \max(1-ob, y)$$

a) if ¬P ≤ (s,t) is false, there is no solutions, concretely this could say that ¬P is "too strong" that is to say P is not true enough. It must therefore que ¬P ≤ (s,t).

b) if $t = 1-ob$ and $s > 1-ev$, then Q is given with imprecision by $(s,[0,t])$

c) if $s = 1-ev$ and $t > 1-ob$, then Q is given by $([0,s],t)$

d) if $1-ob < t$ and $1-ev < s$, then $Q = (s,t)$

A question is then raised :

Is it possible to admit the solution $Q = (s,t)$ subject to $\neg P \leq (s,t)$? This solution, coming from the logic approach, is not at all acceptable in the view of a system of deduction,

because, if P is known with the low values (0.1 0.2) and if the implication $P \rightarrow Q$ is quite sure with the values (0.8 0.9), then this condition would be satisfied, and we could "deduce" of it Q with those same values (0.8 0.9).

Our problem is not therefore to go on according to the formulas of the implication, but to define and to legitimate formulas about propagation of the ignorance and about the truth when activating rules. (The functional approach with $v(q) \geq v(p \wedge q)$ means that $p \wedge q$ is true as soon as p is true because q is deduced from p [Dubois - Prade 85]).

For the calculus $[P = (ob, ev) , R = P \rightarrow Q = (s,t)] \Rightarrow Q = (x,y)$, we must determine two functions :

$x = f1(ob, ev, s, t)$ and $y = f2(ob, ev, s, t)$ increasing for their 3° and 4° arguments, f1 being increasing face to face to its first argument and f2 to its second.

On the other side intuitively, it will be necessary to have $Q = (ob, ev)$ in the best case that is to say with $s = t = 1$, and $Q = (0, 0)$ in the worst of the case $(s = t = 0)$, and more crudely

P weak $\Rightarrow$ Q weak, P strong $\Rightarrow$ Q strong. It doesnt apply at all to what we have said previously, however, from the functions satisfiying thoses conditions we find thoses of the conjonction, meaning $Q = P \wedge (P \rightarrow Q) = P \wedge (\neg P \vee Q) = P \wedge Q$, the monotonicity $Q \leq P$ is then sure.

We can therefore choose $x = s.ob$ and $y = t.ev$, or also $x = \min(ob, s)$ and $y = \min(ev, t)$, these just mentionned we shall choose because we have defined the conjonction in that way (Mamdani implication).

Fuzzy expert system

Let a set $\{p0, p1, p2, ...\}$ named set of propositionnals variables, we define a "fuzzy expert system" by the datas of a finite number of "facts" or "litterals", that is propositionnals variables allocated with a couple (ob, ev) for each, and a finite number of "rules", that is to say implications of the type $pi_1 \wedge pi_2 \wedge pi_3 \wedge .... \wedge pi_n \rightarrow pj$ affected with a couple (s,t).

Remark : instead of appreciate the couple (s, t) de $P \rightarrow Q$, some systems use the couple formed by $s = nc(P \rightarrow Q)$, $n = nc(Q \rightarrow P)$ [Martin-Clouaire 84].

The theory developed by a such system is by definition the smallest set of facts (propositionnals variables with couples of confidence), contening the initials facts, and closed by deduction. Then the questions raised are : what happens in case of normalization of two couples of confidence infered to a same propositionnal value ? and is finite the theory (stop the inferences ?)

The normalization

Let us take the case of P_0 = (ob, ev) , R = P→Q = (s,t) driving to Q = (min(ob, s), min(ev, t))

next, from Q = (min(ob,s), min(ev,t)) , R' = Q→P = (u,v) which bring on this time :

P_1 = (min(ob,s,u), min(ev,t,v)) with $P_1 \leq P_0$ that is seems absolutely normal, we can advise that there is no inference if the result is less than the one which is already known for a conclusion [Gacôgne 90].

But, more generally if two rules suceed to the same conclusion :

R_1 = P→Q = (s_1,t_1) and R_2 = P→Q = (s_2,t_2) , it is necessary to adopt a principe of normalization for the conclusion, which is not depending of the rule ordering, this one will be realised by taking the max of the confidences brought to the conclusion by the differents rules.

Let us say that in the FRIL system [Baldwin 90], a support (n,p) is affected to each fact, and if a fact is known by several proofs concluing to the supports (n1,p1) and (n2,p2), then it is the operation (max(n1,n2), min(p1,p2)) which is choosed subject to n $\leq$ p.

We shall adopt further the following approach :

If a conclusion Q is infered with the values (obi, evi) directely or by a contraposition.

a) If neither Q nor ¬Q are known that is to say : not in the base of the facts, then (Q obi evi) is of course added in this base.

b) If Q is known with the values (oba, eva), then it is replaced by Q with the new values max(obi, oba), max(evi, eva))

c) If ¬Q is known with the values (obn, evn), then it seems natural to think that the knowledge about ¬Q present more interest than it of its opposite, and in this case it is ¬Q which is replaced by (¬Q, max(obn, 1-evi) max(evn, 1-obi))

In all cases, an already known fact will be therefore modified by an inference only if its confidence grows, that means eventually the confidence in its opposite grows down.

Example

Let us consider the sentences : P = "It rains", M = "I am damped", S = "I go out", A = "I have an umbrella", R = "I take an umbrella".

We give the five rules given with their conclusion and next their premisses (the negations are in parenthesis) :

```
(set 'BR '  ((6 8 (S) P)        ;if it rains, i don't go out
            (6 10 R A)          ;if i have an umbrella, i take it
            (8 10 R S P)        ;if i go out andit rains, i take my umbrella
```

```
(7 10 (M) R)            ;i have an umbrella, then i'm not damped
(9 10 (S) P M)))        ;it rains and i'm damped, i stay in
```

In order to simplify the visualisation, the coefficients are given in tenth, a short Lisp program whose the top function "sef", give its results.

(set 'LF '((P 4 8) (S 7 7))); are the two initials facts given with their two values, the trace of reasonning is the next :

(sef LF BR)

; rule : (6 8 (s) p) with : (4 8)

; opposite of the conclusion modified

; rule : (8 10 r s p) with : (4 7)

; unknown conclusion, therefore accepted

; rule : (0 4 (a) (r)) with : (3 6)

; unknown conclusion, therefore accepted

; rule : (6 10 r a) with : (6 1)

; conclusion modified

; rule : (7 10 (m) r) with : (6 1)

; unknown conclusion, therefore accepted

; rule : (9 10 (s) p m) with : (0 4)

; opposite of the conclusion modified

= ((p 4 8) ((a) 0 4) (r 6 1) ((m) 6 10) (s 7 10))

We can remark, in the final base of facts, that the fact S is stronger in relation to its initials values.

References

D.Dubois H.Prade Théorie des possibilités Masson 1985

L.Gacôgne Contribution à la représentation des connaissances floues et mise en oeuvre d'un système de raisonnement approché. Thèse Paris VII 1990

B.R.Gaines Foundations of fuzzy reasoning. International Journal Man Machine n°8 p.623-668 1976

G.Klir T.Folger Fuzzy sets, uncertainty and applications. Prentice Hall 1988

R.Martin-Clouaire H.Prade On the problems of representation and propagation of uncertainty in expert system. International Journal Man Machine studies 1984

T.Martin J.Baldwin An abstract mechanism for handling uncertainty. Third international conference IPMU Paris 1990.

L.A.Zadeh Fuzzy sets as a basis for a theory of possibility FSS n°1 p.3 1978

PROBABILISTIC REGIONS OF PERSISTENCE

Scott D. Goodwin
Department of
Computer Science
University of Regina
Regina, Saskatchewan
Canada S4S 0A2
goodwin@cs.URegina.ca

Eric Neufeld
Department of
Computational Science
University of Saskatchewan
Saskatoon, Saskatchewan,
Canada, S7N 0W0
eric@USask.ca

André Trudel
Jodrey School of
Computer Science
Acadia University
Wolfville, Nova Scotia,
Canada, B0P 1X0
trudel@AcadiaU.ca

Abstract

Perhaps the most difficult, and certainly the most intensely studied problem in temporal reasoning is the persistence of information—that is, what reasonable inferences can we draw about non-change given partial knowledge of the world and of the changes taking place. Almost all previous work hinges on McCarthy's common sense law of inertia (CSLI): things tend not to change. The obvious consequence of adopting this view is that it becomes reasonable to infer that the duration of non-change is arbitrarily long. For instance, a typical inference in systems that appeal to CSLI is that if a person is alive now, the person will remain alive (arbitrarily long) until something happens that results in the person's death.

We describe a framework that allows a more realistic treatment of persistence by incorporating knowledge about the duration of persistence of information. Inferences, such as a wallet dropped on a busy street tends to remain where it fell for a shorter duration than a wallet lost on a hunting trip, can be drawn in this framework. Unlike the CSLI approach, this inference is possible without knowing what happened to change the wallet's location. We accomplish this by casting the problem of how long information persists as a problem in statistical reasoning.

1. INTRODUCTION

A popular method in AI for representing and reasoning about temporal domains is to define a first order logic that includes some representation for time. For example, the logic may represent time by using a discrete structure such as the integers or a dense structure such as the reals. Since the world is continuous, we are interested in logics that view time as being linear and dense (e.g., the reals).

A logic for reasoning about temporal domains must deal with the persistence problem, that is, what reasonable inferences can we draw about non-change given partial knowledge of the world and of the changes taking place. For instance, if p is true at some point or over some interval, and nothing that affects p is known to occur, is it reasonable to infer that p holds outside the interval in which it is known to hold? More concretely, if "the house is red" is known to be true over the interval $(5,10)$ and we know of nothing that could affect the color of the house, then is it reasonable to assume that "the house is red" persists outside the interval $(5,10)$, say over the interval $(1,20)$?

Almost all previous work on persistence hinges on McCarthy's common sense law of inertia (CSLI): things tend not to change. The obvious consequence of adopting this view is that it becomes reasonable to infer that the duration of non-change is arbitrarily long. For instance, a typical inference in systems that appeal to CSLI is that if a person is alive now, the person will remain alive (arbitrarily long) until something happens that results in the person's death.

Here we describe a framework that allows a more realistic treatment of persistence by incorporating knowledge about the duration of persistence of information. Inferences, such as a wallet dropped on a busy street tends to remain where it fell for a shorter duration than a wallet lost on a hunting trip, can be drawn in this framework—unlike the CSLI approach, this inference is possible without knowing what happened to change the wallet's location. We accomplish this by casting the problem of how long information persists as a problem in statistical reasoning.

2. THE PERSISTENCE PROBLEM

The persistence problem has a long history in AI and has been intensely studied (e.g., [Brown87, Pylyshyn87, Ford91]). It evolved out of the frame problem—how to succinctly state, reliably predict, and efficiently compute non-change in the context of a particular temporal logic: situation calculus [McCarthy69]. In our view, the term "persistence problem" has come to mean "the frame problem in context of any temporal logic" (cf. [Shoham87]), although attention to "efficient computation" seems to have diminished. Here our focus is on the prediction component of the persistence problem: what reasonable inferences can we draw about non-change given partial knowledge of the world and of the changes taking place.

There are at least three aspects to the prediction component of the persistence problem:

1. the *kind* of information that persists,

2. the *direction* of persistence on the time line and

3. the *extent* of persistence.

Let's consider each issue in turn.

The first issue, what kind of information persists, depends on what kind of information there is, i.e., it depends on the ontology. In a "continuous" temporal logic, we are generally interested in two kinds of information: point based and interval based. For example, *"the house is red* is true now" is point based information whereas *"the house is red* was true all day yesterday" is interval based information. Suppose we are interested in whether *"the house is red* will be true in one hour from now." The question then arises about what kind of information persists. Is it reasonable to predict the persistence of the point based information *"the house is red* is true now" and so conclude *"the house is red* will be true in one hour from now?" Would it be reasonable to predict the persistence of the interval based information *"the house is red* was true all day yesterday" and so conclude *"the house is red* will be true in one hour from now?"

The second issue is the direction of persistence: does information persist into the past as well as the future? For example, if we notice a building on the way home from work, then is it not just as reasonable to assume that the building was there the previous day as it is to assume it will be there the following day. Most approaches (e.g., [Kautz86, Shoham86, and Dean90] to name only a few) restrict persistence to the forward direction only.

The third issue involves predicting the duration of persistence. Traditional approaches infer that the duration of non-change is arbitrarily long. For instance, if a person is alive now, the person will remain alive (arbitrarily long) until something happens that results in the person's death.

The first issue was addressed in [Goodwin91]. The approach does not impose a serious restriction. Given something true over an interval, this determines what is true at each point in the interval and this in turn determines what persists. For example, if the "house is red" is true over an interval I, then "house is red" is true at each point in I. "House is red" at the endpoints (open intervals are dealt with in [Goodwin91] by considering a neighbourhood of the endpoints) then persists. See [Trudel90] for an example of a temporal logic that represents interval based information in terms of what is true at the point level. In the remainder of the paper, we focus on the second and third issues.

3. PROBABILISTIC PERSISTENCE

"Arbitrary-duration" persistence is too crude an approximation. Instead, temporal information persists for some finite period of time into the future and/or past. How long does information actually persist? In most cases, we cannot give a definitive answer to this question. For example, if John is currently alive, we cannot determine with certainty the time of his death (assuming we don't murder John). But, from actuarial tables, we can estimate his life expectancy. This is true of most temporal reasoning: although we don't know exactly how long something should persist, we can make reasonable statistical estimates.

We approximate the truth values of a piece of information over time with *regions of persistence*. For example, let running be true at time 100. Assume that a person usually runs for 30 minutes and may sometimes run for up to 50 minutes. We expect running to be true for some 30 minute interval that contains time 100. For simplicity, we assume 100 is located in the center of the interval. We then expect running to persist over the interval (100-15,100+15) and we expect running not to persist outside (100-25,100+25). Over the intervals $(100 - 25, 100 - 15)$ and $(100 + 15, 100 + 25)$ we are unwilling to predict

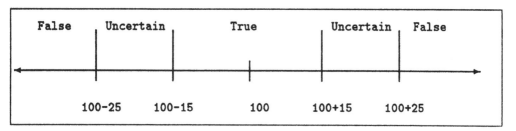

Figure 1: The regions of persistence for running

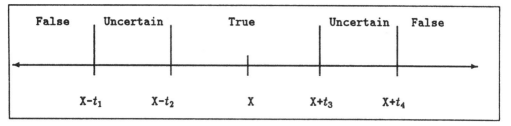

Figure 2: The general regions of persistence

whether running persists. The regions of persistence for running are shown in figure 1.
The regions of persistence *(rop)* are represented by the relation:

$rop(running, -25, -15, 15, 25).$

The general form is:

$rop(\beta, -t_1, -t_2, t_3, t_4)$

where β is a point based item of information. If β is true at time X and nothing is known
to affect β, then β is expected to persist throughout the interval $(X - t_2, X + t_3)$, β may
or may not persist over $(X - t_1, X - t_2)$ and $(X + t_3, X + t_4)$, and β is expected to be false
before $X - t_1$ and after $X + t_4$. So, we predict β is true over $(X - t_2, X + t_3)$, we predict
β is false before $(X - t_1)$ and after $(X + t_4)$ and otherwise we make no prediction. The
general regions of persistence are shown in Figure 2. Note the regions are not necessarily
symmetric around X. It may be that $t_2 \neq t_3$ and/or $t_1 \neq t_4$.

In this instance, we can give the *rop* relation a simple statistical semantics. Assume the
duration of β is normally distributed with typical duration *(mean)* μ and typical variation
(variance) σ^2 about that mean. Suppose we are satisfied to predict β remains true if the
probability of β remaining true is greater than 50% and we wish to predict β is *false* if the
probability is less than 5% (approximately) and otherwise we make no prediction. In this
case, the relation $rop(\beta, -t_1, -t_2, t_3, t_4)$ holds if and only if $t_2 + t_3 = \mu$, $t_1 + t_4 = \mu + 2\sigma$.
This statistical semantics subtly changes the meaning of persistence; rather than stating
that we can be reasonably sure β persists over $(X - t_1, X + t_4)$ it states that we can be
reasonably sure it does not persist *beyond* the interval. This is consistent with the usual
interpretation of a continuous probability distribution function. For example, if *running*
truly has a normal distribution, the duration of a run is less than the mean 50% of the
time. Thus at time X we expect the run to end within t_3 minutes with probability 0.5.

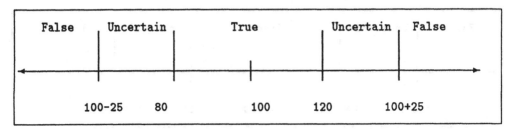

Figure 3: The regions of persistence for running over a longer interval

The semantics of the *rop* relation may vary with the problem domain. For example, if we must be 95% sure that running is true to predict that it is true, we let $t_2 + t_3 = \mu - 2\sigma$ and $t_1 + t_4$ is unchanged.

We conclude this section with examples that use the *rop* relation.

3.1 Running at some point

Suppose we observe John running at time 100 and we believe that, on average, he runs for 30 minutes with a standard deviation of 12.5 minutes. In this case, we assume

$$rop(running, -25, -15, 15, 25)$$

holds. This determines the regions of persistence shown in figure 1. From this we expect running to be true over the interval (85,115) and false before 75 and after 125.

Now instead suppose running is known to be true over the interval (80,120), that is, John has run for 40 minutes, longer than the mean of 30, and we wish to estimate the time at which running will end. We can now use the idea of regions of persistence to reason about the expected endpoint. Suppose, as in the previous instance, we wish to predict running will persist if we are 50% sure it will continue, and we wish to predict it won't if we are 95% sure it won't and we make no prediction otherwise. As before, we assume that the duration of *running* is normally distributed, but we simply consider the expected remaining time for those runs longer than 40 minutes. By conventional methods, we find that about 50% of runs longer than 40 minutes last another 5 minutes and 95% are completed within about 19 minutes.

3.2 Running is known to end

Assume the same parameters for *running*, but we know that John stopped running. We estimate that John began his run after time 70 with probability 0.5. With probability 0.05 (approximately), we expect he did not start the run before time 60. The regions of persistence are shown in figure 4.

Here there are only four regions of persistence since we know running to be false after time 100.

Note in the case where we know that running started at 90 and ended at 100, the *rop* relation is not applicable, since we have complete information about running, there is

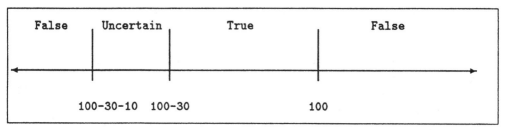

Figure 4: The regions of persistence when running is known to end

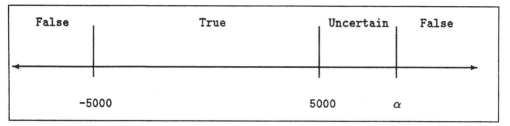

Figure 5: The regions of persistence for the pyramids

nothing to predict.

3.3 Pyramids

Assume the pyramids in Egypt were built in the year 5000 BC, will probably exist for 10,000 years, and will eventually cease to exist (e.g., due to war or pollution). If the time units are years, the pyramids exist over the interval (-5000,1991). The *rop* relation is:

$$rop(pyramids, -5000, -5000, 5000, \alpha) \quad \wedge \quad \alpha > 5000.$$

The regions of persistence for the pyramids are shown in figure 5. There are only four regions of persistence instead of the usual five. This problem is opposite to knowing the end time for running; there is no "likely" region occurring before time 0. We expect the pyramids to exist until the year 5000. They may exist until the year α, where α is a constant which represents some year beyond 5000. We expect the pyramids to not exist after the year α.

4. COMPARISON WITH OTHER WORK

Dean and Kanazawa [Dean88] model persistence with linear or exponential decay functions that assume we know when events started. A truck arrives, for example, and the decay function tells us that the probability it remains decays by 5% every 15 minutes. We have considered somewhat the opposite problem: given an observation of an event in progress, what inferences can we make about its start time and completion time? Given some experience with that particular type of event, we can estimate times beyond which it cannot be reasonably expected to persist and before which it cannot be reasonably expected to have started.

Obviously these are inferences we make given no information to the contrary. No matter how reasonable it is to assume that a runner will continue to run for another 15 minutes, it is perfectly possible for the runner to stop in a second for any reason imaginable. However, the statistical knowledge is still useful: although it is possible the runner may stop running immediately, it isn't reasonable to schedule a meeting with her immediately. Similarly, though the runner may run forever, it seems reasonable to schedule a meeting after 50 minutes.

The approach presented in [Dean88] only works for discrete temporal ontologies and persistence in the forward direction.

5. SUMMARY AND CONCLUSIONS

We have described a probabilistic framework for representing and reasoning about persistence. Where traditional approaches assume temporal information persists forever unless acted upon, we assume temporal informal persists "normally" and may be affected by unspecified actions whose effect is captured by a finite mean and variance. This has some interesting properties, for example, we can easily manage combinations of forward and backward persistence.

To assign different statistical semantics to regions of persistence, we need only change the thresholds of acceptance or rejection. Furthermore, it is trivial to modify the *rop* relation to introduce more regions.

Here we did not consider conflicting regions of persistence. For example, consider the well known "stolen car" problem where a car is parked at time 0 and missing at time 10. We get interesting conflicts between the regions for "car(parked)" persisting beyond 0 and "not car(parked)" persisting before 10.

ACKNOWLEDGEMENTS

The first author acknowledges the support of the Institute for Robotics and Intelligent Systems (IRIS). Research of the second author was supported by IRIS and NSERC grant OGP0099045. Research of the third author was supported by NSERC grant OGP46773.

REFERENCES

[Brown87] Proceedings of the 1987 Workshop: The Frame Problem in Artificial Intelligence, edited by F.M. Brown, Morgan Kaufmann, 1987.

[Dean88] T. Dean, and K. Kanazawa (1988), *Probabilistic Causal Reasoning*. Proceedings of the Seventh Biennial Conference of the Canadian Society for Computational Studies of Intelligence, Edmonton, Canada, 125-132.

[Dean90] T. Dean, and G. Siegle (1990), *An Approach to Reasoning about Continuous Change for Applications in Planning.* Proceedings of the Eighth National Conference on Artificial Intelligence, Boston, USA, 132-137.

[Ford91] Advances in Human and Machine Cognition: The Frame Problem in AI, edited by K. Ford and P. Hayes, Vol. 1, JAI Press Inc, to appear in 1991.

[Goodwin91] S.D. Goodwin, and A. Trudel (1991), *Persistence in continuous first order temporal logics.* To appear in [Ford91].

[Kautz86] H. Kautz (1986), *The logic of persistence.* Proceedings of the Fifth National Conference on Artificial Intelligence, Philadelphia, USA, 401-405.

[McCarthy69] J. McCarthy, and P. Hayes (1969), *Some Philosophical Problems from the Standpoint of Artificial Intelligence.* Machine Intelligence 4, edited by Meltzer and Michie, Edinburgh University Press, 463-502.

[Pylyshyn87] The Robot's Dilemma, edited by Z.W. Pylyshyn, Ablex Publishing, 1987.

[Shoham86] Y. Shoham (1986), *Chronological ignorance: Time, nonmonotonicity, necessity and causal theories.* Proceedings of the Fifth National Conference on Artificial Intelligence, Philadelphia, USA, 389-393.

[Shoham87] Y. Shoham (1987), *What is the frame problem?* Appears in [Brown87].

[Trudel90] A. Trudel (1990), *Temporal integration.* Proceedings of the Eighth Biennial Conference of the Canadian Society for Computational Studies of Intelligence, Ottawa, Canada, 40-45.

FORMALIZING PERTINENCE LINKS IN INHERITANCE REASONING: PRELIMINARY REPORT

E. Grégoire
IRISA
Campus de Beaulieu
F-35042 Rennes Cédex
France

Abstract

Pertinence links in inheritance networks allow one to assert the relevance or the irrelevance of an inheritance link with respect to a given concept. Although pertinence links were included in some of the earliest knowledge-representation formalisms like NETL, they have been omitted in more recent formal accounts of path-based inheritance reasoning. In this paper, we formalize and interpret pertinence links in the context of the important family of upward path-based inheritance reasoners.

1 Introduction

An important form of uncertainty in knowledge-based systems concerns the conflicting information involved in ambiguous inheritance hierarchies. Most recent theoretical studies of nonmonotonic inheritance reasoning focus on restricted formalisms dealing with ordinary inheritance links representing atomic, generic or universally quantified statements like "Tweety is an ostrich", "ostriches are birds", "birds generally fly" or "ostriches generally do not fly". An additional kind of information that one often wishes to represent in an explicit manner within inheritance hierarchies concerns constraints that assert the relevance or the irrelevance of an inheritance link with respect to a given concept. For example, when we know that Tweety is a mechanical ostrich, we might wish to express in an explicit manner that the inheritance link "ostriches are birds" is not relevant as far as Tweety is concerned. The ability to represent such a kind of constraints was already present in some of the earliest knowledge-representation systems like NETL [2], where they were known as *cancellation rules* or *exception rules*. The formalization of these 'pertinence' links has sometimes been completed in the context of very specific interpretations of inheritance, using nonmonotonic logics (e.g. [1], [3]). However, for the sake of simplicity, the concept of pertinence link (in short, *PL*) has not been taken into account in more recent analyses of path-based inheritance, which gave rise to the description of several families of alternative inheritance reasoners (see e.g. [4], [5], [6], [8], [9], [12], [14]).

In this paper, we propose a formal account of PLs in the context of the important class of polynomial-time upward inheritance reasoners [11]. We show that the constraints represented by means of PLs can be enforced along with the upward propagation of information that upward (decoupled) inheritance involves. This also allows us to discover several conflicting intuitions about the interpretation of PLs that enlarge the range of possible path-based inheritance reasoners.

2 Preliminaries

Let us briefly present the framework of path-based inheritance that we shall extend to handle per-tinence links (for more details on this framework, see e.g. [5], [8] or [14]). Path-based inheritance deals with finite acyclic nets whose nodes represent instances and kinds of objects and whose positive and negative arrows, noted $\to$ and $\not\to$, allow one to represent IS-A and IS-NOT-A (ordinary) defea-sible inheritance relationships. Let x and y be two nodes representing kinds of objects, the intuitive meaning of the *(ordinary inheritance) link* $x \to y$ (resp. $x \not\to y$) is "x's are normally y's" (resp. "x's are normally not y's"). Let $\rightsquigarrow$ stand for $\to$ or $\not\to$. We shall say that a link of the form $x \rightsquigarrow y$ *points at* y. A *path* σ in a net Γ is defined as a sequence of joined links in Γ such that only the last link of σ can be negative. Let τ range over sequences of positive links. Paths are defined inductively as follows. Each link is a path, and if $\tau \to p$ is a path, then both $\tau \to p \to q$ and $\tau \to p \not\to q$ are paths. A path of the form $x \rightsquigarrow y$ or $x \to \tau \rightsquigarrow y$ is said to *enable* the assertion $x \rightsquigarrow y$. Path-based inheritance reasoners allow one to obtain zero, one or several *extensions* of Γ, which are subsets of the enabled assertions in Γ. More precisely, an assertion $x \rightsquigarrow y$ belongs to an extension E_i of a net Γ when it is enabled by a path that is *permitted* in E_i, this is noted $\Gamma \triangleright_{E_i} x \rightsquigarrow y$. Many different path-based inheritance reasoners have been proposed in the literature. In this paper, we focus on *upward inheritance reasoners*, which require the permitted paths of the form $x \to \tau \to y \rightsquigarrow z$ to have their longest initial segment $x \to \tau \to y$ permitted. These inheritance reasoners are best interpreted as propagating information upwards, i.e. from more specific to more general classes. Computing an extension of a net is a polynomial-time problem for many upward inheritance reasoners [11].

In the next section, we introduce the concept of pertinence links. We then show how these links can be interpreted in the context of upward inheritance reasoning.

3 Pertinence links

Intuitively, a pertinence link (in short, PL) is a link in an inheritance net whose role consists in asserting the relevance or the irrelevance of another link in the net w.r.t. a given concept. Accord-ingly, this latter concept should be the starting node of the PL, whereas the PL should point at the link whose relevance is addressed. Note that unlike an ordinary inheritance link, which connects two nodes, a PL starts from a node and points at another link. A PL will be called *basic* when it points at an ordinary inheritance link and *meta-level* when it points at another PL. Let us define basic PLs first.

Basic pertinence links

By convention, we shall represent a basic PL together with its target link, i.e. with the link that it points at. Let x, y and z be nodes and $y \rightsquigarrow z$ an ordinary inheritance link.

Definition 1 *A <u>positive basic PL</u> is of the form* $x \to [y \rightsquigarrow z]$ *whereas a <u>negative basic PL</u> is of the form* $x \not\to [y \rightsquigarrow z]$; *their target link is the ordinary inheritance link* $y \rightsquigarrow z$ *and their initial node is* x.

A positive basic PL of the form $x \to [y \to z]$ is represented in the net of Fig. 1.(a). It is intended to assert the relevance w.r.t. the concept x of the information encapsulated within the ordinary link $y \to z$. The negative basic PL of the form $v \not\to [w \to x]$ in the net of Fig. 1.(b) is intended to assert the irrelevance w.r.t. the concept v of the information encapsulated within the ordinary link $w \to x$. The intended intuitive meaning of a negative basic PL $x \not\to [y \rightsquigarrow z]$ is thus "as far as x is concerned, the ordinary inheritance link $y \rightsquigarrow z$ should not be taken into account when activated, i.e. when we can establish that x's are normally y's". The intended intuitive meaning of a positive basic PL

$x \rightarrow [y \leadsto z]$ is "as far as x is concerned, the ordinary inheritance link $y \leadsto z$ should be taken into account when activated, i.e. when we can establish that x's are normally y's".

Note that the presence of a positive basic PL $x \rightarrow [y \rightarrow z]$ is not a sufficient condition to conclude that x's are normally z's in an extension E_i. To obtain that result, we would need to establish (among other things) that x's are y's in E_i. Note that it would be possible to interpret a positive PL of the form $x \rightarrow [y \rightarrow z]$ as a sufficient condition to ensure that x's are z's in E_i. However, such a stronger interpretation is inadequate since it would require the basic PL $x \rightarrow [y \rightarrow z]$ to override any information that indicates that x's are sometimes not y's. For example, in the net of Fig. 1.(a), it is natural to prefer the information encapsulated in the link $w \not\rightarrow y$ over the information encoded within the basic PL because of the greater specificity of the former information.

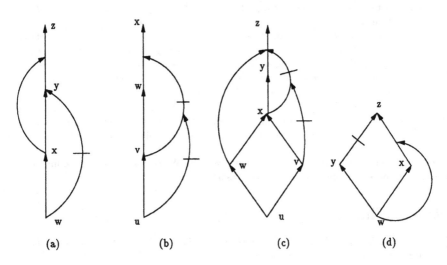

(a)　　　　　　(b)　　　　　　(c)　　　　　　(d)

Figure 1:

Meta-level pertinence links

A *meta-level* PL is a PL whose target link is another PL (i.e. either a basic PL or another meta-level PL). It is *positive* or *negative* depending on whether it is intended to assert the relevance or the irrelevance of its target link.

Definition 2 *A positive (resp. negative) meta-level PL is a positive (resp. negative) link starting from an initial node and pointing at a target link, which is a basic PL or another meta-level PL.*

By convention, a meta-level PL will be represented together with its target link. This latter link can be a basic PL (which is, according to our conventions, represented together with the ordinary inheritance link forming its target link), or recursively, a meta-level PL. The *representation* of a meta-level PL will thus take the form of a 'chain' of meta-level PLs, ended with a unique basic PL, itself ended with an ordinary inheritance link.

For example, in the net of Fig. 1.(b), there is a negative meta-level PL pointing at the pertinence link $v \not\rightarrow [w \rightarrow x]$; it is noted $u \not\rightarrow [v \not\rightarrow [w \rightarrow x]]$. The intended meaning of this meta-level PL is "as far as u is concerned, the PL $v \not\rightarrow [w \rightarrow x]$ that aims at asserting the irrelevance w.r.t. v of the ordinary inheritance link $w \rightarrow x$, is irrelevant".

Chains

Since both meta-level and basic PLs are represented together with their target link, the *representation of a PL* takes the form of a 'chain' of nested PLs ended with an ordinary inheritance link. Actually, such a concept of chain of PLs (in short, *chain*) can be defined directly in the following way. Let t, x, y and z be nodes and $y \rightsquigarrow z$ an ordinary inheritance link.

Definition 3 *An expression of the form* $x \rightsquigarrow [y \rightsquigarrow z]$ *is a* <u>*chain*</u>.
An expression of the form $t \rightsquigarrow [\alpha]$, *where* α *is a chain, is also a* <u>*chain*</u>.

For example, there exist three chains in the net of Fig. 1.(c): $x \not\rightarrow [y \rightarrow z]$, $v \not\rightarrow [x \not\rightarrow [y \rightarrow z]]$ and $w \rightarrow [y \rightarrow z]$. In the following, we shall keep the concepts of chains and of PL distinct, using the former concept when we really want to denote a nested sequence of PLs. By definition, a chain contains zero, one or several meta-level PLs, one basic PL and one ordinary inheritance link. This latter link is called the *last link* of the chain whereas the *initial node* of a chain is defined as being the first node occurring in the chain.

Definition 4 *The* <u>*last link of a chain*</u> *is the unique ordinary inheritance link occurring in the chain. The* <u>*initial node of a chain*</u> *of the form* $x \rightsquigarrow [\alpha]$ *is the node* x.

For example, the last link of each of the three chains occurring in Fig. 1.(c) is $y \rightarrow z$ whereas their initial nodes are x, v and w, respectively. Let us define the sign of a chain as being the sign of its unique basic PL.

Definition 5 *A chain is* <u>*positive (resp. negative)*</u> *iff its unique basic PL is positive (resp. negative).*

The motivation for this definition is the following one. In a chain, the unique basic PL plays an important role. When its sign is positive (resp. negative), the constraint that the chain *might* enforce on its unique ordinary inheritance link is a constraint of relevance (resp. irrelevance). Indeed, the rest of the chain is a nested sequence of applicability conditions on the basic PL. These conditions can block the applicability of the constraint expressed by the basic PL but cannot modify the form (either relevance or irrelevance) of this constraint. For example, the chain $u \rightarrow [v \not\rightarrow [w \rightarrow [x \not\rightarrow y]]]$ is a positive chain because its unique basic PL $w \rightarrow [x \not\rightarrow y]$ is positive. The chain can thus aim at asserting a relevance constraint on the ordinary inheritance link $x \not\rightarrow y$. The first part of the chain (i.e. $u \rightarrow [v \not\rightarrow)$ asserts applicability conditions on the constraint of relevance expressed by the basic PL $w \rightarrow [x \not\rightarrow y]$, but cannot turn this constraint of relevance into a constraint of irrelevance.

Since positive and negative chains represent potential constraints of relevance or irrelevance, chains of opposite signs sharing the same ordinary inheritance link can give rise to "conflicting" arguments about the pertinence of this ordinary inheritance link.

Definition 6 *A positive chain and a negative chain are* <u>*conflicting*</u> *iff they share the same ordinary inheritance link.*

For example, in the net of Fig. 1.(c), the chains $x \not\rightarrow [y \rightarrow z]$ and $v \not\rightarrow [x \not\rightarrow [y \rightarrow z]]$ are conflicting with the chain $w \rightarrow [y \rightarrow z]$.

It is natural to extend the acyclicity condition enforced in the basic formalism to this extended framework that includes PLs. In order to deal with PLs, which involve links that do not exhibit end nodes, we simply define the (virtual) end node of a PL α as being the initial node of the target link of α. Accordingly, let us write $x < y$ when x precedes y according to a given topological sort of the net, taking this additional definition into account.

4 Pertinence links and upward inheritance reasoning

Let us now study which chains can actually influence the pertinence of their last links when upward inheritance reasoning is under consideration. We'll then adapt the concept of permitted path to take the result of this study into account.

Under upward reasoning, a path σ from x to y can be interpreted as a *forward* chain of arguments giving a tentative proof of the assertion between x and y that is enabled by σ. When we test whether σ is permitted or not in an extension E_i, we must evaluate (among other things) the influence of chains whose last links belong to σ. In order for this influence to be effective, for every initial node v of every PL in these chains, there must exist a positive path from x to v that is permitted in E_i. These positive permitted paths assert that x's are v's (in E_i) and, consequently, that the PLs starting from v are relevant from the point of view of x. The notion of *activated* chains formalizes this idea.

Definition 7 *A chain α can be <u>activated</u> (in E_i) w.r.t. a node x in a net Γ iff for every initial node v ($v \neq x$) of every PL in α, we have $\Gamma \rhd_{E_i} x \to v$.*

A chain that cannot be activated w.r.t. x does not enforce any constraint on its ordinary inheritance link, as far as x is concerned. For example, in the net of Fig. 1.(c), the three chains are activated w.r.t. u. If the link between u and v had been negative, then the chain $v \nrightarrow [x \nrightarrow [y \to z]]$ would not have been activated w.r.t. u.

Let us now define an operator, noted $\subset$, that allows us to compare chains with the same last link. Let α_1 and α_2 be two chains in a net Γ.

Definition 8 $\alpha_1 \subset \alpha_2$ *iff* $\exists k_1, ..., \exists k_n (n \geq 1) \in \Gamma$ *s.t.* $\alpha_2 = k_1 \rightsquigarrow [k_2 \rightsquigarrow [...[k_n \rightsquigarrow [\alpha_1]]...]]$.

For example, we have $x \nrightarrow [y \to z] \subset v \nrightarrow [x \nrightarrow [y \to z]]$ in the net of Fig. 1.(c). The operator $\subset$ allows us to formalize the idea that if two chains α_1 and α_2 are activated w.r.t. a common node and if $\alpha_1 \subset \alpha_2$, then we must just take α_2 into account, since α_2 subsumes α_1. These considerations lead us to introduce the following concept of *maximality*.

Definition 9 *A chain α_1 that can be activated (in E_i) w.r.t. a node x is <u>maximal</u> w.r.t. x (in E_i) iff there does not exist another chain α_2 activated (in E_i) w.r.t. x s.t. $\alpha_1 \subset \alpha_2$.*

For example, in the net of Fig. 1.(c), the chains $v \nrightarrow [x \nrightarrow [y \to z]]$ and $w \to [y \to z]$ are maximal w.r.t. u.

As we have explained above, a chain can be interpreted as a basic PL whose influence can be blocked by the meta-level PLs in the chain. Let us explain this feature.
Actually, we can opt between two conflicting interpretations of the role of a meta-level PL in a chain. Under the first interpretation, a meta-level PL is assigned a role of constraint on the (whole) <u>chain</u> that it points at. The second interpretation restricts the scope of this constraint to the PL <u>link</u> that the meta-level PL points at. For example, let us assume that $u \nrightarrow [v \to [w \to [x \to [y \nrightarrow z]]]]$ is a maximal activated chain (in E_i) w.r.t. a node t. This chain is best viewed as a nested sequence of three meta-level PLs, starting from nodes u, v and w, respectively, and influencing the pertinence of the basic PL $x \to [y \nrightarrow z]$. According to the first interpretation, a meta-level PL is given a *global* role in a chain; it asserts the relevance or the irrelevance of the (whole) chain that it points at. Accordingly, each time an activated chain contains a negative meta-level PL, the constraint

represented by the whole chain should not be taken into account. In the example, the negative meta-level PL starting from node u asserts that the whole chain should not be taken into account. This interpretation leads to a first version of the concept of *real* maximal activated chains, which concerns maximal activated chains that are not made void by their meta-level PLs.

Definition 10 *A maximal activated chain is <u>real</u> iff it does not contain any negative meta-level PL.*

According to the second interpretation, a meta-level PL is given a role that is more local in a chain: it influences the pertinence of its target link, only. Accordingly, a negative meta-level PL will assert the irrelevance of its target PL. In the example, the negative meta-level PL starting from u asserts the irrelevance of the meta-level PL starting from node v, but not the irrelevance of the whole remaining chain starting from v. This second interpretation is discussed in the full paper.

The only chains that can actually enforce a constraint on their last links are thus *real maximal activated chains*. There may however exist *conflicting* real maximal activated chains, which assert conflicting constraints of relevance and irrelevance on a same link. To handle some of the resulting conflicts, it seems natural to prefer chains whose initial nodes are *most specific*. A whole range of preference criteria for more specific information can be justified here; they are discussed in the full paper. For example, a very strong criterion requires the initial node of the preferred chain to represent a subclass (or an instance) of the classes represented by the initial node of each preempted chain. In other words, there must exist positive permitted paths between the initial node of the preferred chain and the initial node of each preempted chain. In the following, we shall omit to say that the chains we consider are activated in an extension E_i w.r.t. x.

Definition 11 *A real maximal activated positive (resp. negative) chain whose initial node is x_1 <u>preempts</u> a conflicting real maximal activated negative (resp. positive) chain whose initial node is x_2 iff $\Gamma \rhd_{E_i} x_1 \to x_2$.*

Such a preference criterion does not necessarily allow us to resolve every pair of conflicting real maximal activated chains. We can opt between several basic attitudes when all conflicts cannot be resolved.

- We can decide that the last link of the chains is irrelevant since there exists at least one acceptable constraint asserting that this link is irrelevant. Such an attitude is close to the skeptical attitude of [8] in the sense that it translates a cautious attitude w.r.t. links whose relevance cannot be settled.

- We can decide that the last link of the chains is relevant. This second attitude can be interpreted as a very optimistic one in the sense that it favours relevance constraints over irrelevance ones.

- We can consider both alternatives in parallel.

- Like [6], we can try to express the conflict explicitly and study its effects on other inheritance relationships in the net.

The first three attitudes allow us to decide whether we should take into account an ordinary inheritance link $w \rightsquigarrow y$ belonging to a path σ from x to z when we check whether σ is permitted or not. When we decide that such a link should not be taken into account in this context, we say that this link is *defeated* w.r.t. x. Otherwise, we say that it is *not defeated* w.r.t. x.

Accordingly, the set(s) of permitted paths of a net Γ must be adapted when Γ contains PLs. When upward inheritance reasoning is under consideration, this can be achieved by simply grafting the definition of ordinary links that are not defeated to the basic definition of permitted paths. This can be completed in such a way that we preserve the iterative structure allowing one to check paths for permission according to the increasing order (w.r.t. $<$) of their last nodes. In the full paper, we show that this procedure can be organized in such a way that when a path σ of the form $x \to \tau \to y \leadsto z$ is tested for permission, the permission character of any segment of $x \to \tau \to y$ is already known. Accordingly, the only chains that we must concentrate on at this step are chains whose last links have z as end node.

Note that under our interpretation of chains, a PL allows us to assert the relevance or irrelevance of an ordinary link, not the supremacy of this latter link over conflicting ordinary links. For example in the net of Fig. 1.(d), the PL $w \to [x \to z]$ simply asserts the relevance of the ordinary link $x \to z$ as far as w is concerned, not the supremacy of this latter link over the ordinary link $y \not\to z$. Such a stronger interpretation of chains is not discussed here.

5 An example

As a case study, let us extend the upward inheritance reasoner of [8] to handle PLs. As this reasoner is skeptical, we naturally opt for a skeptical position w.r.t. the conflicting chains that cannot be resolved, i.e. we assume that the last links of these chains are defeated. The new definition of permitted path is as follows. Note that the text in boldface is the only difference from the definition of [8]. This shows that the PLs can be interpreted as constraints whose treatment filters the set of possible permitted paths.

For each node z in Γ (increasingly with $<$),
  <u>do</u>
  For each each node x in Γ s.t. $x < z$, let us consider each path σ from x to z,
  <u>do</u>
  If σ is an ordinary link in Γ then σ is permitted (and thus, $\Gamma \rhd x \leadsto z$).
  If σ is a compound path of the form $x \to \tau \to y \to z$ (resp. $x \to \tau \to y \not\to z$) in Γ, then σ is permitted (which implies $\Gamma \rhd x \to z$ (resp. $\Gamma \rhd x \not\to z$)) iff

  1. $\Gamma \rhd x \to \tau \to y$
  2. $y \to z \in \Gamma$ (resp. $y \not\to z \in \Gamma$) **and is not defeated w.r.t.** x
  3. $x \not\to z \notin \Gamma$ (resp. $x \to z \notin \Gamma$)
  4. $\forall w$ s.t. $\Gamma \rhd x \to \tau_1 \to w$ with $w \not\to z \in \Gamma$ (resp. $w \to z \in \Gamma$) **and not defeated w.r.t.** x, $\exists v \, (v \neq w)$ s.t. $\Gamma \rhd x \to \tau_2 \to v \to \tau_2 \to w$ and $v \to z \in \Gamma$ (resp. $v \not\to z \in \Gamma$) **and is not defeated w.r.t.** x.

  <u>od</u>
<u>od</u>

6 Acknowledgements

Part of this work has been carried out during a stay at UMIACS under a Belgian grant (SPPS/RFO/AI/ 15/2). I gratefully acknowledge Jeff Horty for valuable discussions on this topic.

References

[1] D.W. Etherington, *Reasoning with Incomplete Information*, Research Notes in Artificial Intelligence, Pitman, London, 1988.

[2] S.E. Fahlman, *NETL: a system for representing and using real-world knowledge*, MIT Press, 1979.

[3] C. Froidevaux, Taxonomic default theory, *Proc. ECAI-86*, Pitman, London, pp. 123-129, 1986.

[4] E. Grégoire, Skeptical theories of inheritance and nonmonotonic logics, in: Z.W. Ras (ed.), *Methodologies for Intelligent Systems 4*, North Holland, pp. 430-438, 1989.

[5] E. Grégoire, *Logiques non monotones et intelligence artificielle*, Hermès, Paris, 1990.

[6] E. Grégoire, Skeptical inheritance can be more expressive, in: Aiello L.C. (ed.), *Proc. ECAI-90*, Pitman, London, pp. 326-332, 1990.

[7] E. Grégoire, About the logical interpretation of inheritance hierarchies, *Proc. IPMU-90*, pp. 281-283, 1990.

[8] J.F. Horty, R.H. Thomason and D.S. Touretzky, A skeptical theory of inheritance in nonmonotonic semantic networks, *Artificial Intelligence*, vol. 42, pp. 311-348, 1990.

[9] J.F. Horty and R.H. Thomason, Mixing strict and defeasible inheritance, *Proc. AAAI-88*, pp. 427-432, 1988.

[10] D. Makinson and K. Schlechta, Floating conclusions and zombie paths: two deep difficulties in the directly skeptical approach to defeasible inheritance nets, *Artificial Intelligence*, vol. 48, pp. 199-209, 1991.

[11] B. Selman and H.J. Levesque, The tractability of path-based inheritance, *Proc. IJCAI-89*, pp. 1140-1145, 1989.

[12] L.A. Stein, Skeptical inheritance: computing the intersection of credulous extensions, *Proc. IJCAI-89*, pp. 1153-1158, 1989.

[13] D.S. Touretzky, *The Mathematics of Inheritance Systems*, Morgan Kaufmann, Los Altos, 1986.

[14] D.S. Touretzky, J.F. Horty and R.H. Thomason, A clash of intuitions: the current state of nonmonotonic multiple inheritance systems, *Proc. IJCAI-87*, pp. 476-482, 1987.

A Hybrid Approach for Modeling Uncertainty in Terminological Logics*

Jochen Heinsohn

German Research Center for Artificial Intelligence (DFKI)

Stuhlsatzenhausweg 3

D–6600 Saarbrücken 11, Germany

e-mail: heinsohn@dfki.uni-sb.de

Abstract

This paper proposes a probabilistic extension of terminological logics. The extension maintains the original performance of drawing inferences on a hierarchy of terminological definitions. It enlarges the range of applicability to real world domains determined not only by definitional but also by uncertain knowledge. First, we introduce the propositionally complete terminological language $\mathcal{ALC}$. On the basis of the language construct "probabilistic implication", it is shown how statistical information on concept dependencies can be represented. To guarantee (terminological and probabilistic) consistency, several requirements have to be met. Moreover, these requirements allow to infer implicitly existent probabilistic relationships and their quantitative computation. Consequently, our model applies to domains where both term descriptions and non-categorical relations between term extensions have to be represented.

1 Introduction

Research in knowledge representation led to the development of terminological logics [12], which originated mainly in Brachman's KL-ONE [4]. In such languages, the terminological formalism (*TBox*) is used to represent a hierarchy of terms (*concepts*) that are partially ordered by a subsumption relation: Concept B is *subsumed by* concept A, if, and only if, the set of B's real world objects is necessarily a subset of A's world objects. In this sense, the semantics of such languages can be based on set theory. Two-place relations (*roles*) are used to describe concepts. In the case of *defined* concepts, restrictions on roles represent both necessary and sufficient conditions. For *primitive* concepts, only necessary conditions are specified. The algorithm called *classifier* inserts new generic concepts at the most specific place in the terminological hierarchy according to the subsumption relation. Work on terminological languages led further to *hybrid* representation systems. Systems like BACK, CLASSIC, LOOM, KANDOR, KL-TWO, KRYPTON, MESON, SB-ONE, and YAK (for overview and analyses see [11]) make use of a separation of terminological and assertional knowledge. The

*This work has been carried out in the WIP project which is supported by the German Ministry for Research and Technology BMFT under contract ITW 8901 8. I would like to thank Bernhard Nebel, Bernd Owsnicki-Klewe, and Hans-Jürgen Profitlich for helpful comments on earlier versions of this paper.

assertional formalism (*A Box*) is used to represent assertions about the real world. The mechanism for finding the most specific generic concept an object is an instance of and to maintain consistency between ABox and TBox is called the *realizer*.

Since, on one hand, the idea of terminological representation is essentially based on the possibility of *defining* concepts (or at least specifying necessary conditions), the classifier can be employed to draw correct inferences. On the other hand, characterizing domain concepts only by definitions can lead to problems, especially in domains where certain important properties cannot be used as part of a concept definition. As argued by Brachman [2] this may be the case in "natural" environments (in contrast to "technical/mathematical" environments). The source of the problem is the fact that in natural environments, besides their description, terms can only be characterized as having further *typical* properties or properties that are, for instance, *usually* true. If such properties are interpreted as being categorical, this can lead to problems concerning *multiple inheritance*. However, in the real world such properties often are only *tendencies*, i.e., birds "usually" fly. Tendencies as well as differences in these tendencies cannot be considered in the restrictive framework of term definitions.

We propose an extension of terminological logics that allows one to handle the problems discussed above [7,8]. First, we briefly introduce $\mathcal{ALC}$ [15], a propositionally complete terminological language containing the logical connectives conjunction, disjunction and negation, as well as role quantification. By keeping the TBox semantics, which is based on term descriptions, we are able to use the classifier for extending and reorganizing the terminology. In Section 3 we extend $\mathcal{ALC}$ by defining syntax and semantics of *probabilistic implication*, a construct aimed at considering non-terminological knowledge sources and based on a statistical interpretation. As demonstrated in Section 4, on the basis of the terminological and probabilistic knowledge, certain consistency requirements have to be met. Moreover, these requirements allow one to infer implicitly existent probabilistic relationships and their quantitative computation. The related work is discussed in Section 5. For proofs and details the reader is referred to the full paper [7].

2 The Terminological Language $\mathcal{ALC}$

The basic elements of the terminological language $\mathcal{ALC}$ [15] are concepts and roles (denoting subsets of the domain of interest and binary relations over this domain, respectively). Assume that $\top$ ("top", denoting the entire domain) is a concept symbol, that A denotes a concept symbol, and R denotes a role. Then the concepts (denoted by letters C and D) of the language $\mathcal{ALC}$ are built according to the abstract syntax rule

$$C, D \longrightarrow A \mid \forall R : C \mid \exists R : C \mid C \sqcap D \mid C \sqcup D \mid \neg C$$

To introduce a formal semantics of $\mathcal{ALC}$ we give a translation into set theoretical expressions with $\mathcal{D}$ being the domain of discourse. For that purpose, we define a mapping $\mathcal{E}$ that maps every concept description to a subset of $2^{\mathcal{D}}$ and every role to a subset of $2^{\mathcal{D} \times \mathcal{D}}$ in the following way:

1. $\mathcal{E}[\top] = \mathcal{D}$
2. $\mathcal{E}[\forall R : C] = \{x \in \mathcal{D} | \forall (x, y) \in \mathcal{E}[R] : y \in \mathcal{E}[C]\}$
3. $\mathcal{E}[\exists R : C] = \{x \in \mathcal{D} | \exists (x, y) \in \mathcal{E}[R] : y \in \mathcal{E}[C]\}$
4. $\mathcal{E}[C \sqcap D] = \mathcal{E}[C] \cap \mathcal{E}[D]$
5. $\mathcal{E}[C \sqcup D] = \mathcal{E}[C] \cup \mathcal{E}[D]$
6. $\mathcal{E}[\neg C] = \mathcal{D} - \mathcal{E}[C]$

Concept descriptions are used to state necessary, or necessary and sufficient conditions by means of specializations "$\sqsubseteq$" or definitions "$\doteq$", respectively. Assuming symbol A and concept description C, then "$A \sqsubseteq C$" means the inequality $\mathcal{E}[A] \subseteq \mathcal{E}[C]$, and "$A \doteq C$" means the equation $\mathcal{E}[A] = \mathcal{E}[C]$. A set of well formed concept definitions and specializations forms a *terminology*, if every concept symbol appears at most once on the left hand side and there are no terminological cycles. A concept C_1 is said to be *subsumed by* a concept C_2 in a terminology $\mathcal{T}$, iff for all extension functions satisfying the equations introduced in $\mathcal{T}$, the inequality $\mathcal{E}[C_1] \subseteq \mathcal{E}[C_2]$ holds. Terminological languages as $\mathcal{ALC}$ can be usefully applied to definitional world knowledge. For instance, we may introduce

Example 1

$$
\begin{array}{llll}
animal & \sqsubseteq & \top & \\
antarctic\_animal & \sqsubseteq & animal & \\
antarctic\_bird & \doteq & antarctic\_animal \sqcap bird & \\
\end{array}
\qquad
\begin{array}{lll}
flying & \sqsubseteq & \top \\
bird & \doteq & animal \sqcap (\forall moves\_by : flying) \\
penguin & \sqsubseteq & antarctic\_bird \\
\end{array}
$$

To characterize the expressiveness of terminological languages, we will examine the three different relations imaginable between two concept *extensions*, i.e., (i) inclusion, (ii) disjointness, and (iii) overlapping:

$$\text{(i) } \mathcal{E}[C_1] \subseteq \mathcal{E}[C_2], \quad \text{(ii) } \mathcal{E}[C_1] \cap \mathcal{E}[C_2] = \emptyset, \quad \text{(iii) } \mathcal{E}[C_1] \cap \mathcal{E}[C_2] \neq \emptyset \tag{1}$$

The first case *can* be caused by (terminological) subsumption. To express extensional inclusion (i) *without* a subsumption relation on terms, some hybrid systems introduced non-terminological language constructs such as `implication`. Disjointness (ii) *can* be a terminological property. This is the case if, for instance, the above language construct "concept negation" as contained in the expression $C_1 \sqsubseteq C, C_2 \doteq (C \sqcap \neg C_1)$ is used. To express non-terminological disjointness between concepts, some systems use the language construct `disjoint`. However, the information given in case (iii) cannot be reasonably[1] used in existing terminological logics. It seems to be more suitable to generally consider the "degree of intersection" between the respective concept's extensions and to characterize it using an appropriate technique. The idea behind this generalization is to use a probabilistic semantics for this purpose.

3 The Probabilistic Extension

In the following we consider only one representative for equivalent concept expressions. The algebra based on representatives of equivalence classes and on the logical connectives $\sqcap$, $\sqcup$, and $\neg$ is known as *Lindenbaum algebra* of the set $\mathcal{S}$ of concept symbols. We use the symbols $\mathbf{D}$ for the set of concept descriptions and $\mathbf{D}^-$, $\mathbf{D}^- \subseteq \mathbf{D}$, for the set of *atoms* of the Lindenbaum algebra. For every function $\mathcal{E}$ the set of extensions of the elements in $\mathbf{D}^-$ forms a partition of $\mathcal{D}$. $\mathcal{D}$ is assumed to be finite. As a language construct that takes into account *all* cases (1), we introduce the notion of *probabilistic implication* (p-implication), which is a generalization of the above mentioned implication construct:

Definition 1 *An extension function $\mathcal{E}$ over $\mathbf{D}$ satisfies a p-implication $C_1 \xrightarrow{p} C_2$, written $\models_{\mathcal{E}} C_1 \xrightarrow{p} C_2$, iff $p = |\mathcal{E}[C_1 \sqcap C_2]|/|\mathcal{E}[C_1]|$ holds for concepts $C_1, C_2 \in \mathbf{D}$.*[2]

---

[1]except in stating that concept $C_1 \sqcap C_2$ is not incoherent, i.e., it has a necessarily non-empty extension

[2]The definition can be extended in such a way that a possible uncertainty about the exact probability value can be represented by means of a subrange of $[0,1]$ (see, e.g., [10] for a general examination of numerical models for handling uncertainty).

Theorem 1 *The real-valued set function* $P_{\mathcal{E}} : 2^{\mathbf{D}^-} \to [0,1]$, $P_{\mathcal{E}}(\{C_i\}) = p_i$ *is a probability (function) over* $\mathbf{D}^-$, *iff* $\models_{\mathcal{E}} \top \overset{p_i}{\to} C_i$ *for all* $C_i \in \mathbf{D}^-$. *In particular, the following conditions are satisfied:*

$$P_{\mathcal{E}}(\mathbf{D}^-) = 1$$
$$P_{\mathcal{E}}(D_i) \geq 0 \text{ for all } D_i \subseteq \mathbf{D}^-$$
$$P_{\mathcal{E}}(D_i \cup D_j) = P_{\mathcal{E}}(D_i) + P_{\mathcal{E}}(D_j) \text{ if } D_i \cap D_j = \emptyset$$

For every concept expression $C_i \in \mathbf{D}$ *there exists a subset* $D_i \subseteq \mathbf{D}^-$ *of atoms such that* $C_i = \bigsqcup D_i$. *In this way* $P_{\mathcal{E}}$ *can be extended to concept expressions. In particular,* $P_{\mathcal{E}}(\top) = P_{\mathcal{E}}(\bigsqcup \mathbf{D}^-) = 1$, $P_{\mathcal{E}}(C_i) \geq 0$, *and* $P_{\mathcal{E}}(C_i \sqcup C_j) = P_{\mathcal{E}}(C_i) + P_{\mathcal{E}}(C_j)$ *if* $C_i \sqcap C_j = \bot$ *hold.*

Definition 2 $\{P_{\mathcal{E}} | \models_{\mathcal{E}} \{C_i \overset{p_i}{\to} C_j\}\}$ *is called the set of consistent probability functions.*

From the above explanations it becomes obvious that we use the *relative cardinality* for interpreting the notion of probabilistic implication introduced in Definition 1.

Example 2 *Assume the set* $\{A \sqsubseteq \top, B \sqsubseteq \top, C \doteq A \sqcap B\}$ *of terminological axioms. From the set of symbols* $S = \{\top, A, B\}$ *we obtain* $\mathbf{D}^- = \{\neg A \sqcap \neg B, \neg A \sqcap B, A \sqcap B, A \sqcap \neg B\}$. *Then,* $\mathcal{E}$ *and* $\mathcal{D}$ *with* $|\mathcal{D}| = 100, |\mathcal{E}[A]| = 40, |\mathcal{E}[B]| = 20, |\mathcal{E}[A \sqcap B]| = 10$ *induce a probability function*

$$P_{\mathcal{E}} : \neg A \sqcap \neg B \mapsto 0.5, \quad \neg A \sqcap B \mapsto 0.1, \quad A \sqcap B \mapsto 0.1, \quad A \sqcap \neg B \mapsto 0.3.$$

Example 2 shows that, assuming complete knowledge on domain $\mathcal{D}$ and the cardinalities involved, a probability function $P_{\mathcal{E}}$ over $\mathbf{D}^-$ is induced by extension function $\mathcal{E}$. However, it is generally more realistic to assume less complete knowledge and cardinalities that are rather relative. In the following, we will concentrate on how to extend such knowledge and how to guarantee consistency. For illustrating the meaning of Definition 1, assume that an observer examines the flying ability of a real class of birds. When finishing his study he may have learned that, different from the model of Example 1, relation *moves_by:flying* holds only for a certain percentage p_1 of the birds. The notion of p-implication now allows a representation of universal knowledge·of this kind in a way that maintains the semantics of the roles:

Example 3 *(revises Example 1)*

animal	$\sqsubseteq$	$\top$	*flying*	$\sqsubseteq$	$\top$
antarctic_animal	$\sqsubseteq$	*animal*	*bird*	$\sqsubseteq$	*animal*
antarctic_bird	$\doteq$	*antarctic_animal* $\sqcap$ *bird*	*penguin*	$\sqsubseteq$	*antarctic_bird*
flying_object	$\doteq$	$\forall$*moves_by : flying*	*bird*	$\overset{p_1}{\to}$	*flying_object*

This demonstrates that set theory allows for a consistent semantic basis on which both terminological and probabilistic language constructs can be interpreted. On this basis, the p-implication serves as a generalization of both the "implication" and "disjoint" constructs (now appearing as $A \overset{1}{\to} B$ and $A \overset{0}{\to} B$, respectively) used in many hybrid systems.

Proposition 1 $\forall_{A,B : A \neq \bot, B \neq \bot} :$

$$B \sqsubseteq A \;\Rightarrow\; B \overset{1}{\to} A, \qquad A \overset{0}{\to} B \;\Leftrightarrow\; B \overset{0}{\to} A,$$
$$A \overset{p}{\to} B \text{ and } A \overset{q}{\to} B \;\Rightarrow\; p = q, \qquad A \overset{p}{\to} A \;\Rightarrow\; p = 1.$$

Note that "pointing from exactly one concept to another one" does not mean a restriction concerning the representation of complex "premises and conclusions of rules":[3] in the propositionally complete language $\mathcal{ALC}$ the domain and range concepts of a p-implication may be constructed by means of the operations negation, conjunction, and disjunction.

4 Probabilistic Consistency - Triangular Cases

When representing p-implications, their consistency has to be maintained. The requirements for relative proportions when *three* concepts are involved were examined in [5,9]. The *most specific case*, in which non-trivial assertions can be made, is characterized as follows:

Theorem 2 *Assuming concepts A, B, C, subsumption $B \sqsubseteq A$, p-implications $A \overset{p}{\to} C$, $B \overset{r}{\to} C$, and $A \overset{q}{\to} B$, then this knowledge is (statistically) inconsistent, if the three (equivalent) inequalities are violated:*

- *for known r, q:*

$$q \cdot r \leq \ p \ \leq 1 - q \cdot (1 - r) \tag{2}$$

- *for known p, q:*

$$\begin{cases} \max\{1 - \dfrac{1-p}{q}, 0\} \leq r \leq \min\{\dfrac{p}{q}, 1\} & \text{if } q \neq 0 \\ 0 \leq r \leq 1 & \text{if } q = 0 \end{cases} \tag{3}$$

- *for known p, r:*

$$\begin{cases} 0 \leq q \leq \min\{\dfrac{p}{r}, \dfrac{1-p}{1-r}\} & \text{if } 0 < r < 1 \\ 0 \leq q \leq 1 - p & \text{if } r = 0 \\ 0 \leq q \leq p & \text{if } r = 1 \end{cases} \tag{4}$$

The inequalities specify the range allowed for one probability depending on the other two. To maintain local consistency, the satisfiability of them has to be proved. If exactly two probabilities are given, the inequalities are applied to derive and to keep the information about the range of the other value. In case (3), the condition $q = 0$ implies the range $r \in [0,1]$, but states that B has an empty extension. The following theorem examines a more general case of statistical relationships with three concepts involved. The generality results from a substitution of subsumption $B \sqsubseteq A$ used in Theorem 2 by a less categorical p-implication.

Theorem 3 *Assuming concepts A, B, C, p-implications $A \overset{p}{\to} C$, $A \overset{q}{\to} B$, $q \neq 0$, $B \overset{q'}{\to} A$, and $B \overset{r}{\to} C$, then this knowledge is (statistically) inconsistent, if inequality*

$$\frac{q'}{q} \cdot \max(0, q + p - 1) \ \leq \ r \ \leq \ \min(1, 1 - q' + p \cdot \frac{q'}{q}) \tag{5}$$

is violated.

In analogy to the set of equivalent requirements of Theorem 2 inequality (5) can also be reformulated into equivalent requirements that take into account unknown quantities for p, q, and q'. The whole set $A \overset{p}{\to} C$, $C \overset{p'}{\to} A$, $A \overset{q}{\to} B$, $B \overset{q'}{\to} A$, $B \overset{r}{\to} C$, and $C \overset{r'}{\to} B$ of p-implications is considered in the following theorem. Note that it does not generalize Theorem 3 but serves as an additional consistency requirement. In the case of five consistent p-implications, the (consistent) value of the unknown p-implication is obtained.

---

[3]This was correctly criticized by Yen and Bonissone [17] when discussing our earlier language presented in [9].

Theorem 4 *Assuming concepts A, B, C, p-implications $A \xrightarrow{p} C$, $C \xrightarrow{p'} A$, $A \xrightarrow{q} B$, $B \xrightarrow{q'} A$, $B \xrightarrow{r} C$, and $C \xrightarrow{r'} B$, with $p, p', q, q', r, r' \neq 0$, then this knowledge is (statistically) inconsistent, if equation $r' \cdot p \cdot q' = r \cdot p' \cdot q$ is violated.*

Example 4 *(Dubois and Prade) Assume the notation of Theorem 4, $q' = 0.9$, $q = 0.25$, $p = 0.9$, and $p' = 0.6$. Application of (5) leads to the ranges $[0.54, 1]$ and $[0.1, 0.567]$ for r and r', respectively, which are identical to those derived in [5]. This result however may still lead to inconsistent assumptions for r'. Following Theorem 4 we get ratio $\frac{r}{r'} = 5.4$ and the new consistent range $[0.1, 0.185]$ for r'.*

There are several special cases that are of interest since they present well-known probabilistic requirements. The expressions put in parentheses are optional.

Proposition 2 $\forall_{A,B : A \neq \perp, B \neq \perp}$:

$$(B \sqsubseteq A, C \sqsubseteq A,) A \xrightarrow{q} B, A \xrightarrow{p} C, B \xrightarrow{0} C \Rightarrow p + q \leq 1$$
$$B \sqsubseteq A, C \sqsubseteq B, A \xrightarrow{q} B, A \xrightarrow{p} C, B \xrightarrow{r} C \Rightarrow p = r \cdot q, \ p \leq q, \ p \leq r$$
$$B \xrightarrow{1} C \text{ (given by } B \sqsubseteq C, \text{ e.g.), } A \xrightarrow{q} B, A \xrightarrow{p} C \Rightarrow q \leq p$$
$$B \sqsubseteq C_1, B \sqsubseteq C_2, A \xrightarrow{q} B, A \xrightarrow{p_1} C_1, A \xrightarrow{p_2} C_2 \Rightarrow q \leq \min\{p_1, p_2\}$$
$$B_1 \sqsubseteq C, B_2 \sqsubseteq C, A \xrightarrow{q_1} B_1, A \xrightarrow{q_2} B_2, A \xrightarrow{p} C \Rightarrow p \geq \max\{q_1, q_2\}$$

By explicitly introducing restrictions for the ranges derived by instantiating the consistency requirements, *exceptions* can also be handled. For example, "no penguins fly" is represented by the p-implication *penguin* $\xrightarrow{0}$ *flying_object*. In the categorical cases this corresponds to the overriding of properties in nonmonotonic inheritance networks.

Above, we concentrated on concepts introduced by means of simple terminological axioms involving the specialization operation "$\sqsubseteq$" only. The associated local consistency requirements however have to be strengthened if concept definitions are involved:

Theorem 5 *(Concept Negation and Conjunction)*

$$A \xrightarrow{p} B \Leftrightarrow A \xrightarrow{1-p} \neg B, \qquad A \xrightarrow{p} \neg A \Rightarrow p = 0, \qquad A \xrightarrow{p} C \Leftrightarrow A \xrightarrow{p} A \sqcap C$$

Proposition 3 *The following results are obtained from local (triangular) computations:*

$$A \xrightarrow{p} (A \sqcap B) \Leftrightarrow A \xrightarrow{1-p} (A \sqcap \neg B)$$
$$B \xrightarrow{0} A : (A \sqcup B) \xrightarrow{p} A \Leftrightarrow (A \sqcup B) \xrightarrow{1-p} B$$
$$C \xrightarrow{q_1} A, C \xrightarrow{q_2} B, C \xrightarrow{p} (A \sqcap B) \Rightarrow C \xrightarrow{s} (A \sqcup B) \wedge s = q_1 + q_2 - p$$

The main advantage of examining local *triangular cases* as in Theorems 2 to 5 is that "most" of the inconsistencies are discovered early and can be taken into account just in the *current context* of the three concepts involved. However, testing local consistency requirements *only* for those p-implications that are introduced *explicitly* is no guarantee for *global* probabilistic consistency. In the general case, testing global consistency means to take into account the propositional completeness of the terminological language and leads to a constraint satisfaction problem on a non-discrete domain.

Example 5 *Assume $B_i \sqsubseteq A$, $A \xrightarrow{0.5} B_i$, $i = 1, 2, 3$, $B_1 \xrightarrow{0} B_2$, $B_2 \xrightarrow{0} B_3$, and $B_1 \xrightarrow{0} B_3$. Although global inconsistency is obvious, the three local triangular cases are consistent. Constructing now, e.g., the concept $B_1 \sqcup B_2$ for which $(B_1 \sqcup B_2) \sqsubseteq A$, $A \xrightarrow{1} (B_1 \sqcup B_2)$, and $(B_1 \sqcup B_2) \xrightarrow{0} B_3$ hold, with the help of $A \xrightarrow{0.5} B_3$ we get a new local case that is inconsistent.*

5 Related Work

The importance of providing an integration of both term classification and uncertainty representation[4] was recently emphasized in several publications. However, they differ from each other and from our proposal. Yen and Bonissone [17] consider this integration from a general point of view which, for instance, does not require a concrete uncertainty model. Yen [16] proposes an extension of term subsumption languages to fuzzy logic that aims at representing and handling vague concepts and already differs from our approach in its general objectives. Saffiotti [14] presents a hybrid framework for representing epistemic uncertainty. His extension allows one to model uncertainty about categorical knowledge, e.g., to express one's belief on quantified statements such as "I am fairly (80%) sure that all birds fly". Note the difference from "I am sure that 80% of birds fly", which is modeled in our present paper. The work of Bacchus [1] is important because he not only explores the question of how far one can go using *statistical* knowledge but also presents LP, a logical formalism for representing and reasoning with statistical knowledge. In spite of being closely related to our work, Bacchus does not provide a deep discussion of conditionals and the associated local consistency requirements given by Theorems 2 to 4.

6 Conclusions and Outlook

We have proposed a probabilistic extension of terminological logics that takes into account uncertain knowledge arising when certain properties are, e.g., usually but not categorically true. For this purpose, the notion of *probabilistic implication* based on a statistical interpretation has been introduced. The theoretical approach has several advantages: Probabilistic implication opens the way to an integration of strictly terminological knowledge and the possibility of modeling exceptions, which no longer appear as contradictions [2], but as a set of weaker inequalities that guarantees the consistency of probability assignments. Moreover, being based on conditional probabilities, consistency can be checked in the current context of the three concepts involved. By separating terminological and probabilistic knowledge, processes maintaining the consistency of the terminological part remain operational. In fact, probabilistic consistency depends heavily on correct terminological subsumptions as established by the classifier. Current investigations are related to the further refinement of the rules for testing consistency and to the consideration of assertional (ABox) knowledge. The second aspect however has the consequence that two different semantics of probabilities have to be integrated [6].

References

[1] F. Bacchus. Lp, a logic for representing and reasoning with statistical knowledge. *Computational Intelligence*, 6:209–231, 1990.

[2] R. J. Brachman. 'I lied about the trees' or, defaults and definitions in knowledge representation. *The AI Magazine*, 6(3):80–93, 1985.

[3] R. J. Brachman. The future of knowledge representation. In *Proceedings of the 8th National Conference of the American Association for Artificial Intelligence*, pages 1082–1092, Boston, Mass., 1990.

---

[4]Brachman [3] considers "probability and statistics" as one of the "potential highlights" in knowledge representation. See also the detailed survey given by Pearl [13].

[4] R. J. Brachman and J. G. Schmolze. An overview of the KL-ONE knowledge representation system. *Cognitive Science*, 9(2):171–216, 1985.

[5] D. Dubois and H. Prade. On fuzzy syllogisms. *Computational Intelligence*, 4(2):171–179, May 1988.

[6] J. Y. Halpern. An analysis of first-order logics of probability. In *Proceedings of the 11th International Joint Conference on Artificial Intelligence*, pages 1375–1381, Detroit, Mich., 1989.

[7] J. Heinsohn. A hybrid approach for modeling uncertainty in terminological logics. DFKI Report, German Research Center for Artificial Intelligence, Saarbrücken, Germany, 1991.

[8] J. Heinsohn. A probabilistic extension for term subsumption languages. In *Position Papers 2nd International Workshop on Terminological Logics*, Dagstuhl Castle, Germany, May 6–8 1991. To appear as DFKI/IBM/KIT report.

[9] J. Heinsohn and B. Owsnicki-Klewe. Probabilistic inheritance and reasoning in hybrid knowledge representation systems. In W. Hoeppner, editor, *Proceedings of the 12th German Workshop on Artificial Intelligence (GWAI-88)*, pages 51–60. Springer, Berlin, Germany, 1988.

[10] R. Kruse, E. Schwecke, and J. Heinsohn. *Uncertainty and Vagueness in Knowledge Based Systems: Numerical Methods*. Series Symbolic Computation – Artificial Intelligence. Springer, Berlin, Germany, 1991. In press.

[11] B. Nebel. *Reasoning and Revision in Hybrid Representation Systems*, volume 422 of *Lecture Notes in Computer Science*. Springer, Berlin, Germany, 1990.

[12] P. F. Patel-Schneider, B. Owsnicki-Klewe, A. Kobsa, N. Guarino, R. MacGregor, W. S. Mark, D. McGuinness, B. Nebel, A. Schmiedel, and J. Yen. Term subsumption languages in knowledge representation. *The AI Magazine*, 11(2):16–23, 1990.

[13] J. Pearl. Probabilistic semantics for nonmonotonic reasoning: A survey. In R. J. Brachman, H. J. Levesque, and R. Reiter, editors, *Proceedings of the 1st International Conference on Principles of Knowledge Representation and Reasoning*, pages 505–516, Toronto, Ont., May 1989.

[14] A. Saffiotti. A hybrid framework for representing uncertain knowledge. In *Proceedings of the 8th National Conference of the American Association for Artificial Intelligence*, pages 653–658, Boston, Mass., 1990.

[15] M. Schmidt-Schauß and G. Smolka. Attributive concept descriptions with complements. *Artificial Intelligence*, 48(1), 1991.

[16] J. Yen. Generalizing term subsumption languages to fuzzy logic. In *Proceedings of the 12th International Joint Conference on Artificial Intelligence*, Sydney, Australia, 1991.

[17] J. Yen and P. Bonissone. Extending term subsumption systems for uncertainty management. In *Proceedings of the 6th Conference on Uncertainty in Artificial Intelligence*, Cambridge, Mass., July 1990.

Fuzzy Control Research
at Siemens Corporate R&D

Hans Hellendoorn   Michael Reinfrank

Siemens AG
Dept. ZFE IS INF3
Otto-Hahn-Ring 6
8000 Munich 83
Germany

Abstract

Siemens Corporate R&D has decided to undertake a significant research effort in the field of fuzzy control. Both theoretical and practical aspects of fuzzy control and related areas in fuzzy set theory will be extensively researched in close connection with several universities, research institutes and industrial companies.

Motivation and Introduction

The two main reasons for Siemens's involvement into the area of fuzzy control are:

- The state-of-the-art in fuzzy control reveals clearly that there is a sufficiently wide range of applications where fuzzy control provides results superior to conventional control techniques. Fuzzy control systems are often characterized by their robustness, easy maintainability, and their ability to achieve good controls with comparatively low development and implementation efforts and costs.

- In a wider perspective fuzzy control appears to be very useful when applied to the identification and control of ill-structured systems, where e.g. linearity and time invariance cannot be assumed, the process is characterized by significant transport lags, and is subject to random disturbances. This kind of systems are difficult to model from a conventional point of view.

However the lesson from the state-of-the-art in fuzzy control shows that most of the present applications of fuzzy control systems can be examplified by relatively simple fuzzy control devices embedded in e.g. home appliances, air conditioners, cars, audio and video products, *etc.* We do not believe that fuzzy control when applied to these kinds of problems will completely replace conventional control techniques. Therefore, our strategy is to use it only when it actually has better performance, and provides for an easy integration with conventional approaches.

On the other hand, when looked upon from a wider perspective further research in fuzzy control can provide the formal tools for modelling and using the knowledge of an experienced process operator needed to cope with the control of ill-structured processes. For example, in a lot of cases there is a lack of a well-posed mathematical model. At the same time, the ability of the operator to deal with such a process is recognized and his knowledge of control actions can be described linguistically as a set of rules. Secondly, the human understanding of the process and its conventional mathematical description is alien, and this results in a lack of effective man-machine interface.

Applications of fuzzy logic usually fall into one of the three classes control systems, classification systems, and expert systems.

- Control such as industrial plant control or air conditioning control,

- Classification such as character recognition or situation assessment in environmental protection,

- Expert systems in the classical domains of diagnosis, design and planning.

While in the latter case *fuzzy* expert systems compete with conventional AI-based expert systems and promise only marginal improvements, we expect major advances in the areas of fuzzy control and classification.[1]

Issues in Fuzzy R&D

While for simple applications of fuzzy control the basic technology is available, and the main problems concern efficient design and implementation methods (see below), broadening the scope of the applications to the automation of very complex and ill-understood systems requires more fundamental research and may only be realized in a long term perspective. Some research topics in our current focus of interest are:

- A declarative, logical specification of fuzzy controllers [1] that so far are only described in a procedural way and in particular also formal description methods for the closed system included the fuzzy controller and the process. Our expectation is that, for example, formal stability criteria can be more easily achieved on the basis of such a formalism.

- A systematic combination of conventional and fuzzy control techniques. A first step towards this direction is Palm's fuzzy sliding mode controller [2].

- Results of this work are expected to contribute also to better design methods for fuzzy controllers. Another main area of our interest is self-organizing controllers based on machine learning methods including neural-net based approaches [3].

---

[1]In particular, compared to other uncertainty calculi, fuzzy logic does not offer novel or better solutions to the problems due to long inference chains that usually occur in classical expert systems. On the other hand, in fuzzy control and classification the inference chains are usually short and the main problem often is to evaluate a large number of parameters with informal decision criteria, which is a particular strength of fuzzy set theory.

Besides these research activities, the direct application of some readily available fuzzy control techniques and tools (software and hardware) is of course also of particular interest for a large number of operating groups in Siemens. However, there are a number of difficulties when trying to apply the existing methods and tools for concrete applications, viz.

- The present generation of control engineers are not familiar at all with the theories of fuzzy control, neither have they any practical experience in applying existing techniques and tools.

- There are no courses and text-books available at any level of education (undergraduate, postgraduate and on-site training).

- There is no systematic knowledge of what kind of fuzzy control corresponds to what of kind of control problems.

- There is no general design methodology for the development and implementation of fuzzy controllers.

The last two points show that currently the development of fuzzy control systems is largely a trial and error process. What aggreviates the problem even further is the lack of good software support. These two major problems will be the focus of Siemens R&D in the first phase of the project. Our goal is to come up not with the universal tool for fuzzy control development, but with a set of efficient methods and tools that support the whole life-time of a fuzzy control application including

- Decision criteria: which type of fuzzy control is useful for which type of applications and what are the expected benefits. So far only local experience exists from isolated single applications.

- Design and specification methods.

- Simulation and test environments that are embedded into development packages for conventional control engineering.

- Evaluation criteria for the testing of the performance of fuzzy controllers. Since the philosophy of fuzzy control is often to achieve simple but robust systems with a low effort, evaluation criteria from classical control engineering are often inadequate.

Corporate Strategy and Cooperations

Siemens Corporate R&D has decided to act as both a user and a supplier of the fuzzy technology, and aspires to partial technological leadership in Europe. We think this is a realistic goal, because Siemens has the technological resources needed available in house, plus a significant research potential in the fields of AI, Control theory, and Computer science. So, for example, in the neighborhoud groups there are big projects in the fields of neural nets, qualitative physics, nonmonotonic reasoning and truth-maintainance systems. All these techniques lend themselves to be combined with fuzzy control, e.g. neural nets for self-learning fuzzy controllers, qualitative physics for temporal fuzzy control and truth-maintainance systems for the description of default values and non-monotonicity occuring in fuzzy controllers. Also, there is a wide variety of application areas covered by the Siemens operating groups to test the viability of the fuzzy control related techniques, methodologies, software and hardware products. Examples of these application are projects on home appliances, car electronics, hardware technology, etc., but far more important for Siemens are future works on ill-structured problems, such as in environmental protection areas. At present, the number of researchers directly involved in the fuzzy control project at Siemens R&D itself is about ten, acting as a "Corporate Center of Competence," with sufficient funding for the next five years. In addition to that, there are several smaller, purely application-oriented activities spread over the Siemens operating groups.

In order to catalyse the development efforts, Siemens cooperates closely with Togai InfraLogic, Irvine, a Software House specialized in the field of fuzzy control.

The research activities are embedded into several national and European joint efforts including a German government-funded project on fuzzy logic and its applications to control, classification, and expert systems. The rationale behind these projects is to gather a critical mass of researchers and to bring the substantial research potential available in Europe to bear on practical applications. The European activities are of course complemented by close contacts to American and Japanese institues such as the Berkeley Institute in Soft Computing BISC, and the Yokohama-based LIFE.

Summary

In summary, our goals are:

- To bring the state-of-the-art in fuzzy control into Siemens. Therefore, existing software and hardware tools are tested on a number of pilot applications, in cooperation with operating groups from Siemens, together with external partners.

- Developing a full range of software/hardware products for the development of fuzzy controllers of different types and purposes.

- To study some fundamental issues in fuzzy control so that hard problems in modern control theory can be successfully tackled with fuzzy means.

Finally, we think it is important to provide serious and realistic information to industry and to the public about the principles and the application potential of fuzzy logic, in contrast to the now predominating type of newspaper articles, which use oversimplified presentations and trigger by far exaggerated expectations. Besides intensive discussions with companion disciplines, such as control engineering or artificial intelligence, and, of course, training for engineers and scientists, this kind of "PR-measures" will be crucial if fuzzy control shall be a technique to stay. Its promises for advanced problem solving make it worthwhile trying.

Handling Partially Ordered Defaults in TMS

Ulrich Junker and Gerd Brewka
GMD
P O Box 1240
5205 St. Augustin 1
Fed. Rep. of Germany

1 The Need for Partial Orders

For many applications of default reasoning priorities between defaults play an important role. Generally, the introduction of priorities reduces the number of generated solutions and thus leads to more plausible results[1]. For this reason a number of formalizations, e.g. prioritized circumscription [9, 5], hierarchic autoepistemic logic [8], or preferred subtheories [2] allow for the explicit representation of default priorities. Other approaches, like Geffner's system [4], use the available specificity information to generate priorities automatically.

Our main interest in this paper are computational techniques for partially ordered defaults. Levels of priority which can be expressed for instance in prioritized circumscription or in level default theories [2], are too inflexible for many applications and may force the user to introduce unwanted priorities. We will demonstrate this using two examples, namely inheritance and diagnosis.

Consider for instance an inheritance hierarchy where, according to the general view, defaults about a subclass should override defaults about its superclasses. If multiple inheritance is allowed, that is if a subclass may be linked to multiple superclasses, then the involved priorities cannot adequately be expressed in priority levels.

As an example assume three defaults d_1, d_2, and d_3 are given, where d_i states that instances of class C_i typically have property P_i [2]. Moreover, let the three defaults be pairwise conflicting, that is $i \neq j$ implies $\neg P_i(x) \vee \neg P_j(x)$. Now let C_1 be a subclass of C_2 and assume no other specificity information is given. d_1 obviously has to get higher priority than d_2. But how about d_3? Any assignment to a priority level will introduce a priority between d_3 and either d_1, or d_2, or even both. These priorities, however, are not grounded in the specificity of the involved classes and therefore unwanted.

When partial priority orderings between defaults are allowed this problem disappears. In this case the priority between d_1 and d_2 can be stated without specifying the relation between these defaults and d_3.

Another application that can be used to illustrate the importance of partially ordered defaults is model based diagnosis. It has been shown in [6] how level default theories can be used to express priorities between correctness assumptions. For instance, one

---

[1]This is different to approaches that attach uncertainty degrees to formulas as in [3].

might assume that a certain type T_1 of components is more reliable than another type T_2. If the assumption that a component of type T_1 is correct is given higher priority than the corresponding correctness assumption about a component of type T_2, then diagnoses consisting of the less reliable components are preferred. Also the single fault assumption which prefers diagnoses consisting of exactly one faulty component can easily be expressed within this framework.

Again priority levels turn out to be too inflexible as there may not be enough information to determine the relevant degrees of reliability for all types of components. Partial orders of defaults, that is in this application correctness assumptions, offer the possibility to express what is known about the relative reliabilities and to leave the rest open.

2 Preferred Sets of Defaults

The treatment of partially ordered defaults in this paper is based on [2]. Let $\mathcal{L}$ be a countable first-order language including a constant $\perp$ denoting an inconsistency:

Definition 2.1 *An ordered default theory is a triple* $\Delta = (\mathcal{D}, W, <)$ *where* $W \subseteq \mathcal{L}$, *the facts, is a set of first order formulas,* $\mathcal{D}$, *the defaults, is a set of atomic ground formulas, and* $< \subseteq \mathcal{D} \times \mathcal{D}$ *is a strict partial order s.t.* $\{p \in \mathcal{D} \mid p < d\}$ *is finite for every* $d \in \mathcal{D}$.

More complex defaults must be splitted into an atomic name d that is added to $\mathcal{D}$ and a formula $d \supset \phi$ that is added to W. The partial order restricts the possible solutions of the default theory. It helps to decide which default in a conflict has to be retracted and enforce that dependent defaults are considered after those on which they depend.

However, there are alternative ways for defining solutions of a partially ordered default theory. In [2], a partial order is viewed as an incomplete specification, which can be completed to several total orders:

Definition 2.2 *Let* $\Delta = (\mathcal{D}, W, <)$ *be an ordered default theory. E is a B-preferred subtheory of Δ if there is a sequence* $d_1, d_2, d_3, \ldots$ *of $\mathcal{D}$ such that*

1. $d_i < d_k \Rightarrow i < k$

2. $E = \bigcup_{i=0}^{\infty} E_i$ *where* $E_0 = \emptyset$ *and* $E_{i+1} = $ *if* $E_i \cup W \models \neg d_{i+1}$ *then* E_i *else* $E_i \cup \{d_{i+1}\}$.

Every sequence determines exactly one solution. Different solutions can be obtained by choosing other sequences. The result is a consistent solution if W itself is consistent.

Other approaches separate consistency and ordering completely. For example, Geffner [4] and Grosof [5] first extend the partial order on defaults to a preference relation $\prec$ on sets of defaults, and then pick out consistent sets of defaults such that no other consistent set is preferred to them. Geffner's criterion is:

Definition 2.3 *Let* $\Delta = (\mathcal{D}, W, <)$ *be an ordered default theory. Let* $\prec_g \subseteq 2^{\mathcal{D}} \times 2^{\mathcal{D}}$ *be a preference relation defined as:*

$$D_1 \prec_g D_2 \quad iff \quad D_1 \neq D_2 \text{ and } \forall d \in D_2 - D_1 \exists d' \in D_1 - D_2 : d' < d \tag{1}$$

T is a G-preferred subtheory of Δ iff T is a $\prec_g$-minimal element of $\{D \in 2^{\mathcal{D}} \mid D \cup W \not\models \perp\}$.

Every B-preferred subtheory is a G-preferred subtheory, but not vice versa. A counterexample is given by $a < c$, $b < d$ and $W = \{\neg a \vee \neg b, \neg a \vee \neg d, \neg b \vee \neg c\}$. There are three maximal consistent sets, namely $\{a, c\}$, $\{b, d\}$, and $\{c, d\}$. In Geffner's approach, $\{c, d\}$ is minimal. We cannot obtain it as a B-preferred subtheory because we must start a sequence with a or b.

Moreover, we can show that there is no simple preference relation on sets of defaults for characterizing B-preferred subtheories:

Lemma 2.1 *Let $\mathcal{D} \subseteq \mathcal{L}$ be a set of atomic ground formulas, $< \subseteq \mathcal{D} \times \mathcal{D}$ be a strict partial order s.t. $\{p \in \mathcal{D} \mid p < d\}$ is finite for every $d \in \mathcal{D}$. There is no preference relation $\prec \subseteq 2^{\mathcal{D}} \times 2^{\mathcal{D}}$ such that for all $W \subseteq \mathcal{L}$, T is a B-preferred subtheory of $(\mathcal{D}, W, <)$ iff T is a $\prec$-minimal element of $\{D \in 2^{\mathcal{D}} \mid D \cup W \not\models \bot\}$.*

The following preference relation is a restriction of Geffner's relation and is needed later on. It prefers supersets to subsets and improves a set by replacing several defaults by a *single* default that is smaller:

Definition 2.4 *Let $\Delta = (\mathcal{D}, W, <)$ be an ordered default theory. Let $\prec_l \subseteq 2^{\mathcal{D}} \times 2^{\mathcal{D}}$ be the minimal relation satisfying:*

$$
\begin{array}{lll}
\text{if} \quad D_2 \subset D_1 & \text{then} & D_1 \prec_l D_2 \\
\text{if} \quad \forall d' \in D' : d < d' & \text{then} & (D - D') \cup \{d\} \prec_l (D \cup D') - \{d\}
\end{array}
\tag{2}
$$

T is an L-preferred subtheory of Δ iff T is a $\prec_l$-minimal element of $\{D \in 2^{\mathcal{D}} \mid D \cup W \not\models \bot\}$.

Obviously, if $D_1 \prec_l D_2$ then $D_1 \prec_g D_2$. Hence, every G-preferred subtheory is an L-preferred subtheory. Furthermore, every L-preferred subtheory is a maximal consistent set of defaults. Thus, we have obtained a hierarchy of preferred subtheories of partially ordered defaults. They collapse if the strict partial order $<$ on defaults is modular (i.e. puts the defaults into levels as in [2]).

We will first show that existing approaches for computing preferred subtheories fail for partial orders. Section 3 presents a TMS-based solution for *finite* default theories where violation of the order is checked after the TMS-labeling construction.

3 Interaction of Ordering and Conflicts

Due to the possibility of implicit cycles existing provers for prioritized defaults, e.g. [1], [6] turn out to be too restricted for partial orders. We will illustrate the underlying problem using an example of Baker (personal communication)

Example 3.1 *Let Δ_1 be an ordered default theory $(\mathcal{D}, W_1, <)$ where $\mathcal{D} = \{a, b, c, d\}$, $a < c$, $b < d$ and $W_1 = \{\neg a \vee \neg c, \neg a \vee \neg d, \neg b \vee \neg c, \neg b \vee \neg d\}$.*

Baker/Ginsberg's prover fails for this example since the definitions of rebuttal and refutation underlying their approach are not well-founded for partial orders. Also the approach first developed in [7] and extended to priority levels in [6] fails.

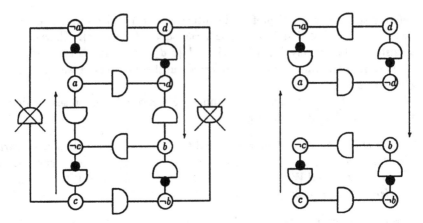

Figure 1: TMS-networks for examples 3.1 (left) and 3.2 (right)

In [7] and [6], default theories are translated to TMS-networks. Basically, defaults become nonmonotonic justifications and the logical dependencies between default conclusions and prerequisites as well as negated consistency conditions are represented in the form of monotonic justifications. In [6], it has been shown that priority levels can easily be encoded by deleting some of the generated justifications, namely those blocking defaults of high priority in case defaults of lower priority are believed.

Figure 1 shows the TMS-network obtained by translating Baker's example. We get two labelings instead of one. The intended labeling makes $a, b, \neg c, \neg d$ IN. The second unwanted labeling makes $\neg a, \neg b, c, d$ IN. It does not correspond to a B-preferred subtheory of the partially ordered default theory since there is no completion of $<$ such that c or d is smaller than a, and c or d is smaller than b.

A deeper analysis shows that the trouble arises from overlapping an order and counterarguments. For this purpose, we reduce Baker's example slightly:

Example 3.2 Let Δ_2 be an ordered default theory $(\mathcal{D}, W_2, <)$ where $\mathcal{D} = \{a, b, c, d\}$, $a < c$, $b < d$ and $W_2 = \{\neg a \lor \neg d, \neg b \lor \neg c\}$.

There are six enumerations respecting $<$ leading to three preferred subtheories:

$$
\begin{array}{lll}
1)\ a,b,c,d\ \{a,b\} & 3)\ b,a,d,c\ \{a,b\} & 5)\ a,c,b,d\ \{a,c\} \\
2)\ a,b,d,c\ \{a,b\} & 4)\ b,a,c,d\ \{a,b\} & 6)\ b,d,a,c\ \{b,d\}
\end{array}
$$

We don't get the labeling $\{c, d, \neg a, \neg b\}$ as a B-preferred subtheory $\{c, d\}$. To block the selection of a we consider its single counterargument, namely $\{d\}$ and put d before a. We denote this by $d <' a$. Similarly, we must put c before b, thus getting a cycle: $a < c$, $c <' b$, $b < d$, $d <' a$.

Hence, a TMS-network is useful for the analysis of the underlying problem, and it hints to a possible solution[2]:

---

[2]These arguments should certainly not prevent someone from trying a simpler implementation. However, the basic problems are the same even if we design an argument system that is directly based on conflicts and orderings as in Geffner [4], and these problems are made explicit in the TMS.

- it shows the explicit dependencies between defaults

- extending it with ordering links shows the cycles that are responsible for the trouble with partially ordered defaults

- partially ordered defaults can be compared with other non-monotonic formalisms (DL, AEL, prioritized defaults) by their TMS-implementations. The TMS points out the technical differences of the logics.

A static solution as for simple priorities is not possible, i.e. we don't find a network whose labelings correspond exactly to the B-preferred subtheories; all justifications contained in a cycle may be needed in some solution, but not in all. We will therefore pursue a dynamic approach: we check violations of the partial order after the TMS labeling is constructed, a process that implicitly completes the partial order.

4 Ordering Check for TMS

First, we construct a TMS-network for an ordered default theory $\Delta = (\mathcal{D}, W, <)^3$. Defaults are applied if we cannot derive their negation. Hence, we obtain simple non-monotonic justifications:

$$NM_{\mathcal{D}} := \{\langle out(\neg d) \to d \rangle \mid d \in \mathcal{D}\} \qquad (3)$$

To handle first-order derivations of negated defaults in TMS we consider conflicts. A *conflict* for $\mathcal{D}, W$ is a subset C of $\mathcal{D}$ that is inconsistent with W (i.e. $C \cup W \models \bot$). A *minimal conflict* for $\mathcal{D}, W$ is a conflict having no proper subset that is also a conflict. Conflicts can be converted into arguments for negated defaults (if $C \cup \{d\}$ is a minimal conflict then $C - \{d\} \cup W \models \neg d$). Therefore, we add a set of monotonic justifications:

$$M_{\mathcal{D},W} := \{\langle in(C - \{d\}) \to \neg d \rangle \mid C \cup \{d\} \text{ is a minimal conflict for } \mathcal{D}, W\} \qquad (4)$$

The resulting TMS-network $J_{\Delta} := M_{\mathcal{D},W} \cup NM_{\mathcal{D}}$ has a regular structure. Especially, it contains no monotonic loops what simplifies the definition of a labeling (or extension). To get it, we consider the following operator:

$$apply_{J,Y}(X) := \{q \mid \exists \langle in(I), out(O) \to q \rangle \in J, I \subseteq X, O \cap Y = \emptyset\} \qquad (5)$$

Then a *labeling T for J* is a fixpoint of this operator , i.e. $T = apply_{J,T}(T)$. Labelings of J_{Δ} correspond to the maximal consistent sets of defaults:

Lemma 4.1 *Let $\Delta = (\mathcal{D}, W, <)$ be an ordered default theory. T is a $\subseteq$-maximal element of $\{D \in 2^{\mathcal{D}} \mid D \cup W \not\models \bot\}$ iff $T \cup \{\neg q \in \mathcal{L} \mid q \in \mathcal{D} - T\}$ is a labeling of J_{Δ}.*

The network J_{Δ} does not take the order on defaults into account. There are maximal consistent sets that are not L-preferred subtheories (e.g. $\{c\}$ in the default theory $(\{a, c\}, \{\neg a \vee \neg c\}, <)$ where $a < c$). In this example, a is retracted by selecting c and applying $\langle in(c) \to \neg a \rangle$ although c has smaller priority than a. In such a case, we can

---

exchange c by a and obtain a consistent theory that is $\prec_l$-smaller. Therefore, we remove justifications leading from a greater node to a smaller one[4]:

$$J_\Delta^< := J_\Delta - \{\langle in(I) \rightarrow \neg q\rangle \in J_\Delta \mid \exists p \in I : q < p\} \tag{6}$$

The remaining justifications may be used for some B-preferred subtheory. This reduced network computes exactly the L-preferred subtheories:

Theorem 4.2 *Let $\Delta = (\mathcal{D}, W, <)$ be an ordered default theory. T is an L-preferred subtheory iff $T \cup \{\neg q \mid q \in \mathcal{D} - T\}$ is a labeling of $J_\Delta^<$.*

Every B-preferred subtheory is also an L-preferred subtheory, but not vice versa as example 3.1 points out. There, $\{c, d\}$ is an L-preferred subtheory since it cannot be improved by exchanging a single default. However, it is no G-preferred subtheory, and no B-preferred subtheory.

If we want to compute only one B/G-preferred subtheory we just compute a fixed enumeration of $\mathcal{D}$ that respects the order $<$ on defaults. According to definition 2.2, it determines a unique B-preferred subtheory, which is also a G-preferred subtheory.

If we are interested in further or all solutions this direct approach is not efficient since different enumerations may yield the same B-preferred subtheory (cf. example 3.2). Alternatively, we can consider L-preferred subtheories and apply a test to them:

1. compute a labeling of the reduced TMS-network (i.e. an L-preferred subtheory T)

2. check whether T is a B- or G-preferred subtheory

If we are interested in G-preferred subtheories we just look whether there is another L-preferred subtheory T' s.t. $T' \prec_g T$. If there is none then T is also a G-preferred subtheory.

For B-preferred subtheories things are more involved because we must find a sequence satisfying definition 2.2. Especially, we must avoid the cycles discussed in section 3. Detecting cycles is difficult. A better solution is to order elements beginning from minimal elements and checking whether all elements can be reached by this process. Hence, we are looking for an enumeration of all defaults. A necessary condition for adding a default at the end of a sequence is that all its $<$-predecessors have already been put into the sequence. If the default is in T no further requirements are needed. If it is not in T then we can add it if we find one of its a counterarguments that is already contained in the partial sequence.

Fortunately, it is not necessary to consider a particular enumeration or all enumerations. Instead we propagate the information that an element has been ordered using special operators. This approach is similar to the groundedness check in [7]. Groundedness errors are also caused by global interactions of defaults and lead to cycles where all nodes are labeled IN.

Now, we formalize the operators needed for our algorithm: We denote the set of $<$-predecessors of q by $pred_{\mathcal{D}, <}(q) := \{p \in \mathcal{D} \mid p < q\}$. Our order-operator $order_{\Delta, T} : 2^{\mathcal{D}} \rightarrow$

---

[4]Constructing such a network requires the computation of (minimal) conflicts as in other approaches, as well as determining $<$-maximal elements of a conflict.

$2^{\mathcal{D}}$ is defined as follows:

$$order_{\Delta,T}(X) := \{q \mid \begin{array}{l} 1) \ pred_{\mathcal{D},<}(q) \subseteq X \text{ and} \\ 2) \ q \in T \text{ or } \neg q \in apply_{J^<_\Delta,T}(T \cap X)\} \end{array} \tag{7}$$

Since this operator is monotonic there exists a unique minimal set Y that is closed w.r.t. $order_{\Delta,T}$ (i.e. $order_{\Delta,T}(Y) \subseteq Y$). We denote it by $order^*_{\Delta,T}(\emptyset)$. This closure abstracts from concrete enumerations. Since every default has only a finite number of predecessors we can show:

Lemma 4.3 Let $\Delta = (\mathcal{D}, W, <)$ be an ordered default theory. Then $d \in order^*_{\Delta,T}(\emptyset)$ iff $\exists d_1, \ldots, d_n : d = d_n$ and $d_i \in order_{\Delta,T}(\{d_1, \ldots, d_{i-1}\})$ for all $i = 1, \ldots, n$.

Now, we are able to show our main result: T is a B-preferred subtheory if and only if it is a labeling and the closure of $order_{\Delta,T}$ contains every default:

Theorem 4.4 *(Main)* Let $\Delta = (\mathcal{D}, W, <)$ be an ordered default theory. T is a B-preferred subtheory of Δ iff $T' := T \cup \{\neg q \mid q \in \mathcal{D} - T\}$ is a labeling of $J^<_\Delta$ and $\mathcal{D} \subseteq order^*_{\Delta,T'}(\emptyset)$.

If T' satisfies the second condition we immediately obtain a sequence $d_1, d_2, d_3, \ldots$ of all defaults by lemma 4.3. Every non-selected default is refuted by some selected defaults that are put before it. If T' is also a labeling then T is consistent, i.e. we cannot refute any selected default.

Vice versa, if T is a B-preferred subtheory then every element d_i in the corresponding sequence $d_1, d_2, d_3, \ldots$ is in $order_{\Delta,T'}(\{d_1, \ldots, d_{i-1}\})$. For every retracted default d, we find an applicable justification for $\neg d$ in $J^<_\Delta$. Since T is also an L-preferred subtheory it is also obtained as a labeling.

To do the check in practice we must extend a network by explicit order links for $<$. However, a minimal set of links is sufficient (i.e. take a relation $\leftarrow \subseteq \mathcal{D} \times \mathcal{D}$ s.t. the transitive closure of $\leftarrow$ yields $<$). This gives rise to an algorithm that propagates information along these links and justifications:

Algorithm 1 Order-check$(\Delta, T) \equiv$

1. $Q := T \cap \{q \in \mathcal{D} \mid \text{there is no } p \text{ s.t. } p < q\}; Y := \emptyset;$

2. **while** $Q \neq \emptyset$ **do** *select a q from Q:*

   (a) **if** $q \notin order_{\Delta,T}(Y)$ **then** $Q := Q - \{q\}$

   (b) **else** $Y := Y \cup \{q\}; Q := Q - \{q\} \cup \{p \in \mathcal{D} \mid q \leftarrow p\}$
   $\cup \{p \in \mathcal{D} \mid \exists (in(X) \rightarrow \neg p) \in J^<_\Delta : q \in X\}$ **end**

3. **if** $\mathcal{D} \subseteq Y$ **then** true **else** false

Now, we apply the algorithm to the troublesome labeling $T' = \{c, d, \neg a, \neg b\}$ of example 3.2. Here, $order_{\Delta,T'}(\emptyset)$ is empty because there is no $<$-minimal default that is in T'. Therefore, Order-check$(\Delta, \{c, d, \neg a, \neg b\})$ returns *false*.

We are currently investigating how to integrate this order check into a TMS-labeling algorithm. The *order*-operator gives some hints how to do this:

1. choose only labels for $<$-minimal elements of the set of unlabeled defaults.

2. if a default is assumed to be retracted by a chosen OUT-label then do not propagate this label because it is not sure whether we can really retract it by smaller defaults.

5 Conclusion

We investigated how to compute preferred sets of defaults that are obtained by partial orders on defaults. Defaults having lower priority must not be used in counterarguments for defaults with higher priority. This yields a first, but weak preference criterion that can easily be handled by compiling the default theory into a Doyle-style TMS-network. A stricter preference criterion requires that defaults used to retract another default are assigned a higher priority. Due to cycles between ordering-links and counterarguments this is not possible for every TMS-labeling. To get rid of those labelings, we extended TMS by an order check. If we are only interested in one preferred solution it can be computed straightforwardly.

Acknowledgements

We would like to thank Kurt Konolige for discussing the topic of this paper and the referees for valuable comments. This work has been supported by the German Ministry for Research and Technology within the joint project TASSO (Grant No. ITW8900A7).

References

[1] A.B. Baker and M.L. Ginsberg. A theorem prover for prioritized circumscription. In *IJCAI-89*, pages 463–467, Detroit, MI, 1989.

[2] G. Brewka. Preferred subtheories: An extended logical framework for default reasoning. In *IJCAI-89*, pages 1043–1048, Detroit, MI, 1989.

[3] C. Froidevaux and C. Grossetête. Graded default theories for uncertainty. In *ECAI-90*, pages 283–288, 1990.

[4] H. Geffner. Conditional entailment: Closing the gap between defaults and conditionals. In *Preprints of Third International Workshop on Nonmonotonic Reasoning*, South Lake Tahoe, CA, 1990.

[5] B. Grosof. Generalizing prioritization. In *KR'91*, pages 289–300, 1991.

[6] U. Junker. Prioritized defaults: Implementation by TMS and application to diagnosis. In *IJCAI-91*, Sydney, Australia, 1991.

[7] U. Junker and K. Konolige. Computing the extensions of autoepistemic and default logics with a truth maintenance system. In *AAAI-90*, pages 278–283, Boston, MA, 1990.

[8] K. Konolige. Hierarchic autoepistemic theories for nonmonotonic reasoning. In *AAAI-88*, pages 439–443, Minneapolis, MN, 1988.

[9] V. Lifschitz. Computing circumscription. In *IJCAI-85*, pages 121–127, 1985.

COMPUTING EXTENSIONS OF DEFAULT THEORIES

F. Lévy
LIPN, University of Paris Nord
Avenue J.B. Clément, 93430 Villetaneuse, France
Phone : (33) (1) 49 40 36 17
E-mail : fl@lipn.univ-paris13.fr

Default logic [Reiter 80] is one of the most popular non monotonic logic, because its formalism is easy to read and works on a set of independant default rules, so describing a system through defaults rules is a modular task. But drawing conclusions from these rules needs the computation of a fix point, and till now, techniques of automatic deduction for default logic are only known for restricted default theories in the propositional case : ordered theories [Etherington 87], Horn theories with some restriction on justifications [Dressler 88] , [Junker 89], [Bonté, Lévy 89]. We present here a correct and complete computational treatment of unrestricted propositional default theories, based on the resolution principle.

The first part recalls the basic features of default theories (1). As the main point of our technique is to consider defaults as assumptions and to determine sets of generating defaults, we give a theoretical global characterisation of these sets (2). Then we define a concept of valid exclusion, which allows the characterisation of sets of generating defaults from the properties of restricted subsets : minimal irregularities (3).

The theoretical results of part (3) allow an encoding of default theories in clausal form with some typed literals and the computation of minimal irregularities (4). The last part provides the techniques to compute sets of generating defaults and extensions (5).

1. Default theories

A **default** has the form $\dfrac{PRE : JUSTIF}{CONS}$, where PRE, JUSTIF and CONS are three well formed formulas. PRE is called the **prerequisite** (or sometimes the premise) of the default, JUSTIF its **justification** and CONS its **consequent**. If the prerequisite, the justification and the consequent of a default are closed formulas, it is said to be a **closed default**. A **default theory** Δ = $(\mathcal{W}, \mathcal{D})$ is a pair consisting of a set $\mathcal{W}$ of first order formulas and a set $\mathcal{D}$ of defaults. Δ is a **closed default theory** if all defaults of $\mathcal{D}$ are closed defaults.

Acceptable sets of belief for closed default theories, called **extensions,** are defined by fixpoints. Precisely, let Γ be the operator from sets of formulas to sets of formulas which, if S is any set of formulas provides the smallest set such that :

1) $\mathcal{W} \subseteq \Gamma(S)$

2) $\Gamma(S) = Th(\Gamma(S))$ (Th(X) is the deductive closure in f. o. l. of the set of formulas X).

3) If $\partial = \dfrac{\text{PRE} : \text{JUSTIF}}{\text{CONS}}$ is any default of D, PRE $\in \Gamma(S)$ and $\neg$JUSTIF $\notin$ S, then CONS $\in \Gamma(S)$.

D e f i n i t i o n : a set E of closed formulas is an extension if and only if $E = \Gamma(E)$.

Any open (i.e.: not closed) default theory can be transformed into a closed default theory, replacing open defaults by all their instances in the language. Extensions of the open default theory are then those of the corresponding closed default theory. In this paper, we consider only closed default theories.

An extension is a set of formulas. But it is interesting to characterize each extension by a set of defaults. Let E be an extension of the (closed) default theory $\Delta = (\mathcal{W}, \mathcal{D})$. Then any default $\partial = \dfrac{\text{PRE} : \text{JUSTIF}}{\text{CONS}}$ of $\mathcal{D}$ such that PRE belongs to E and $\neg$JUSTIF does not belong to E is a **generating default** for E. The extensions of a default theory are in a one to one relation with their sets of generating defaults. One extension E has one set of generating defaults GD(E), and conversely, if GD(E) is known to be a set of generating defaults for an extension, one can easily prove that this extension E is th($\mathcal{W} \cup \{\text{CONS}(\alpha)/ \alpha \in \text{GD}(E)\}$).

2. A characterisation of sets of generating defaults

As a consequence of the definition of extensions, we distinguish the notion of demonstration and that of proof : a demonstration of a formula is a sequence of applications of (standard or default) rules whose last conclusion is the desired formula ; a proof must check the overall consistency, i.e. ensure that an extension involves the desired formula. Our technique to compute extensions determines first the defaults involved in the demonstrations of the prerequisites and the justifications of defaults. From these sets of defaults, we can then deduce which demonstrations are proofs.

2.1 Universes

To use a default in a demonstration, there must exist a demonstration of its prerequisite. We call Universes such sets of grounded defaults . A definition follows.

Let the **context** of a set of defaults S be the deductive closure of its consequents : Context(S) = Th($\mathcal{W} \cup \{\text{CONS}(\alpha) / \alpha \in S\}$).

D e f i n i t i o n : a **Universe** is a set of defaults verifying one of the following conditions :

a) $U = \{ \}$ (where $\{ \}$ denotes the empty set)

b) There is a universe $U_1 \neq U$ and a default α such that PRE(α) belongs to the context of U_1, and $U = U_1 \cup \{\alpha\}$.

c) There is a set U_p ($p \in \Pi$) of universes such that $\forall p \, U_p \neq U$, and $U = \bigcup_{p \in \Pi} U_p$.

This definition admits infinite universes, for it can cope from a theoretical point of view with infinite sets of generating defaults (consider for instance $\mathcal{W} = A(a)$, $\mathcal{D} = \dfrac{A(x) : A(f(x))}{A(f(x))}$).

The **label** of a formula F is the set of minimal universes (for set inclusion) such that F belongs to their context. The label of a default (the assumption representing..) is the label of its prerequisite. Let us note Label(F) the label of the formula or default F. At first, even if we consider infinite infinite universes, they do not appear in labels :

P r o p o s i t i o n 1 : if a formula F is in the context of an universe U, one finite sub-universe of U belongs to the label of F. Consequently, each universe belonging to the label of a formula F is finite

2.2 Regular universe, complete universe.

We say that a universe U is **contradictory** if its context is such that

$$\mathcal{W} \cup \{CONS(\alpha_i) / \alpha_i \in U\} \vdash \bot$$

In the most general case of inconsistency between defaults, we say the universe is irregular.

D e f i n i t i o n : a universe U is **irregular at** (the default) α if α belongs to U and the negation of the justification of α belongs to the context of U :

$$\alpha \in U \quad and \quad \mathcal{W} \cup \{CONS(\alpha_i) / \alpha_i \in U\} \vdash \neg JUSTIF(\alpha).$$

As any formula belongs to the context of a contradictory universe U, contradiction is a special case of irregularity. A universe is **regular** if it is not irregular at any of its defaults.

Another important notion is *completeness*.

D e f i n i t i o n : a universe U is **complete for** $\Delta = (\mathcal{W}, D)$ if for every $\alpha \in D$

if $\left\{ \begin{array}{l} W \cup \{CONS(\alpha_i) / \alpha_i \in U\} \vdash PRE(\alpha) \\ W \cup \{CONS(\alpha_i) / \alpha_i \in U\} \nvdash \neg JUSTIF(\alpha) \end{array} \right\}$ then $\alpha \in U$

These notions allow a correct characterisation of sets of generating defaults :

P r o p o s i t i o n   3 : any extension of a default theory Δ is the context of a complete (for Δ) and regular universe.

The proof is in [Lévy 89]. Just notice that the condition to be *complete and regular* differs from a *maximal regularity* condition : the latter would always yield an extension, whereas with the former, one can have a regular universe which is not complete, while its completed universe is not regular.

3. Valid exclusion

In the method that we propose, an inconsistency can be viewed as an argument to exclude a default. We define here the concept of *valid exclusion,* which is the theoretical translation of the intuitive notion of argument. We give some properties of this notion. The main one, property 6, allows the computation of extensions from labels of inconsistencies. The next parts describe the differents steps of this computation.

3.1 Exclusion basis

D e f i n i t i o n : We say that the default α is **validly excluded from** a universe U if $U \cup \{\alpha\}$ is an irregular universe. U is an **exclusion basis** for α if it is a minimal universe such that α is validly excluded from U. In this case, we say that (α, U) is a minimal irregularity.

Notice that α may or may not be an element of an exclusion basis for itself. The simplest example is $\partial = \frac{: A}{\neg A}$; $\{\partial\}$ is the only exclusion basis for ∂. In this case, we say that U is a **circular exclusion basis**. Of course, a circular exclusion basis is an irregular universe.

L e m m a : every exclusion basis is finite

P r o p o s i t i o n   4 : let Δ a default theory, and U an universe of Δ. A default α is validly excluded from U if and only if α has an exclusion basis included in U. In particular, if U is regular, every default validly excluded from U has a regular exclusion basis included in U.

3.2 A property of valid exclusion

Knowing the whole set of irregularities, all defaults outside a complete and regular universe are not identical to those which are validly excluded from it. Nevertheless, validly excluded defaults characterize complete and regular universes in the following sense :

P r o p o s i t i o n 5 : let Δ a default theory, and U a complete (for Δ) and regular universe. The following property then holds : for any default α which does not belong to U, either (a) α is validly excluded from U, or (b) every universe in the label of α contains at least one default which is validly excluded from U.

An easy consequence of proposition 5 is : given a complete and regular universe, every irregular universe contains a default validly excluded from it . But a set of defaults intersecting all the irregular universes may yield no complete and regular universe, because the remaining defaults do not include an adequate set of valid exclusion basis. We now state the property which allows us to compute complete and regular universes from minimal irregularities.

P r o p o s i t i o n 6 : Every complete and regular universe U is characterized by a set E' of validly excluded defaults verifying :

a) For any minimal irregularity (α, BR), either $\alpha \in E'$, or $BR \cap E' \neq \{ \}$.

b) For any α of E', there is a regular exclusion basis BR for α such that $BR \cap E' = \{ \}$.

E' is linked to U by the relations :

$$E' = \{\alpha \in S - U / \exists V \in label(\alpha), V \subseteq U\}, \quad U = \{\alpha \in S - E' / \exists V \in label(\alpha), V \subseteq S - E'\}$$

4. Determining minimal irregularities of propositional default theories

Our method to compute extensions of propositional default theories is based on proposition 6. We now explain how to compute minimal irregularities using resolution. Next part shows how to apply proposition 6 to the sets of minimal irregularities and compute extensions.

4.1 CAT-correct resolution

To compute minimal irregularities, we use CAT-correct resolution, a form of resolution developed in [Cay & Tay 89]. This strategy is based on the division of data into two groups : typed and non-typed data. Clauses are written in implicative form b d $\rightarrow$ a c, meaning b $\wedge$ d $\Rightarrow$ a $\vee$ c, where a, b, c, d are literals, (b d) is the antecedent and (a c) is the consequent of the clause. Clauses of which each literal in the antecedent is typed are called CAT clauses (CAT : Clause with Typed Antecedent).

The strategy allows the deduction of all CAT clauses. It applies the resolution principle to two clauses if at least one of them is a CAT clause. Furthermore, if only one of the clauses is a CAT, then the literal resolved upon must be :

    - on the consequent side of the CAT,

    - the first non-typed literal on the antecedent of the non-CAT clause (an arbitrary ordering relation for literals is initially determined).

CAT-correct resolution is compatible with the removal of every tautology and every subsumed clause, and deduces then every CAT clause which is neither a tautology nor a subsumed clause.

4.2 Encoding default theories

We want now to encode default rules in such a way that CAT clauses give us every exclusion basis. Each default rule $\delta = \dfrac{A : B}{C}$ is encoded through three formulas :

$$A \wedge \delta \Rightarrow C \qquad (1)$$
$$A \wedge \neg B \Rightarrow \text{Irreg}(\delta) \qquad (2)$$
$$A \Rightarrow \text{Prer}(\delta) \qquad (3)$$

with three typed literals δ, Irreg(δ) and Prer(δ). δ records the use of the default rule to get its conclusion. Since Irreg(δ) appear only in (2), it is equivalent to the irregularity of δ ; likewise, prer(δ) is equivalent to the prerequisite of δ. Different default rules are encoded with different typed literals. Since A, B, C are not necessarily atomic formulas, (1), (2) and (3) have to be put in clausal form.

Clauses minimal for subsumption and involving neither literal Irreg(δ), nor Prer(δ), represent formulas together with one universe of their label. Cat-clauses minimal for subsumption and whose consequent is an Irreg(δ) represent exclusion basis. Cat-clauses minimal for subsumption and whose consequent is an Prer(δ) represent the label of the default δ (the same as its prerequisite's label). We call clauses with Irreg(δ) in their consequent : irregularity clauses, and with Prer(δ) in their consequent : label clauses. The other ones are factual clauses. Note that, as typed literals δ are in the antecedent part of clauses and Irreg(δ) or Prer(δ) are in their consequent part, the literal resolved upon is always a non typed literal, and that we do not need to generate clauses involving more than one literal of the form Irreg(δ) or Prer(δ).

4.3 Example

Let us take first a simple example. For now, we do not generate label clauses. The default theory is :

$$a \; , \; \frac{a : \neg c \wedge b}{b} \; , \; \frac{a : \neg b \wedge c}{c} \; , \; \frac{b : \neg e \wedge d}{d} \; , \; \frac{a : \neg d \wedge e}{e}$$

It is encoded :

$$(1) \rightarrow a$$

(2) a $\delta 1 \rightarrow$ b	(3) a c $\rightarrow$ Irreg($\delta 1$)	(4) a $\rightarrow$ b Irreg($\delta 1$)	(5) a $\rightarrow$ Prer($\delta 1$)

(2) a $\delta 1 \rightarrow$ b (3) a c $\rightarrow$ Irreg($\delta 1$) (4) a $\rightarrow$ b Irreg($\delta 1$) (5) a $\rightarrow$ Prer($\delta 1$)

(6) a $\delta 2 \rightarrow$ c (7) a b $\rightarrow$ Irreg($\delta 2$) (8) a $\rightarrow$ c Irreg($\delta 2$) (9) a $\rightarrow$ Prer($\delta 2$)

(10) b $\delta 3 \rightarrow$ d (11) b e $\rightarrow$ Irreg($\delta 3$) (12) b $\rightarrow$ d Irreg($\delta 3$) (13) b $\rightarrow$ Prer($\delta 3$)

(14) a $\delta 4 \rightarrow$ e (15) a d $\rightarrow$ Irreg($\delta 4$) (16) a $\rightarrow$ e Irreg($\delta 4$) (17) a $\rightarrow$ Prer($\delta 4$)

Factual clauses generated are :

(18) $\delta 1 \rightarrow$ b (19) $\delta 2 \rightarrow$ c (20) $\delta 1 \; \delta 3 \rightarrow$ d (21) $\delta 4 \rightarrow$ e

Irregularity clauses are :

(22) $\delta 2 \rightarrow$ Irreg($\delta 1$) (23) $\delta 1 \rightarrow$ Irreg($\delta 2$) (24) $\delta 1 \; \delta 4 \rightarrow$ Irreg($\delta 3$)

(25) $\delta 1 \; \delta 3 \rightarrow$ Irreg($\delta 4$)

Label clauses are :

(26) $\rightarrow$ Prer($\delta 1$) (27) $\rightarrow$ Prer($\delta 2$) (28) $\delta 1 \rightarrow$ Prer($\delta 3$) (29) $\rightarrow$ Prer($\delta 4$)

Clauses (22) to (25) represent minimal irregularities. The next part gives an algorithm to compute sets of excluded defaults. Knowing a set E' of validly excluded defaults, by proposition

5, a default (a formula) belongs to U (resp : Th(CONS(U))) if and only if at least one universe of its label contains no excluded default.

5 Computation of the validly excluded defaults and extensions

We have now a set of irregularity CAT-clauses : $\delta1 ...\delta n \rightarrow$ Irreg(δ). They represent exclusion basis. We need compute from them sets of validly excluded defaults. Let us first consider some remarks which allow to simplify the problem by deleting clauses or literals.

5.1 A particular case

If we refer to proposition 6, validly excluded defaults must be the distinguished default of some irregularity. So if, for some i, there is no literal Irreg(δi) in the consequent of none of the irregularity clauses, δi is not validly excluded, and deleting it does not modify the solutions of the system. Conversely, if we have a clause $\rightarrow$ Irreg(δi), δi is an excluded default, every exclusion basis involving δi intersects the set of excluded defaults, and the corresponding irregularity clause may be deleted.

The combination of these two remarks works in some simple cases. Consider the example :
Adults (a) typicaly have jobs (j), except for students (st) ; young men (y) typicaly are students, except for professional soldiers (so) ; patriotic and healthy people (p) typicaly are soldiers ; John is young, but adult, patriotic and healthy. The corresponding default theory is :

$$a \, , \, y \, , \, p \, , \quad \frac{a :\neg st \wedge j}{j} \, , \quad \frac{y : \neg so \wedge st}{st} \, , \quad \frac{p : so}{so}$$

which is encoded

(1) $\rightarrow$ a	(2) $\rightarrow$ y	(3) $\rightarrow$ p

(4) a $\delta1 \rightarrow$ j   (5) a st $\rightarrow$ Irreg($\delta1$)   (6) a $\rightarrow$ j Irreg($\delta1$)   (7) a $\rightarrow$ Prer($\delta1$)
(8) y $\delta2 \rightarrow$ st   (9) y so $\rightarrow$ Irreg($\delta2$)   (10) y $\rightarrow$ st Irreg($\delta2$)   (11) y $\rightarrow$ Prer($\delta2$)
(12) p $\delta3 \rightarrow$ so   (13) p $\rightarrow$ so Irreg($\delta3$)   (14) p $\rightarrow$ Prer($\delta3$)

New factual clauses are :
(15) $\delta1 \rightarrow$ j   (16) $\delta2 \rightarrow$ st   (17) $\delta3 \rightarrow$ so
Irregularity CAT-clauses are :
(18) $\delta2 \rightarrow$ Irreg($\delta1$)   (19) $\delta3 \rightarrow$ Irreg($\delta2$)
Label CAT-clauses are :
(20) $\rightarrow$ Prer($\delta1$)   (21) $\rightarrow$ Prer($\delta2$)   (22) $\rightarrow$ Prer($\delta3$)

As Irreg($\delta3$) is not in the consequent of any irregularity clause, $\delta3$ can be deleted. (19) becomes (19') $\rightarrow$ Irreg($\delta2$), so now clause (18) can be deleted. As there remains only the positive clause (19'), the system is solved. Now one knows from factual clauses that the extension is Th({a, y, p, j, so}), and from the label CAT-clauses that the universe is {$\delta1$, $\delta3$}.

5.2 The general case

The method we have exposed in the preceeding paragraph does not work for every default theory. For instance, it does not work in the example of part 4.3. The point is : the default theory must have one single extension, else there is a blocking step in the method where no default and no irregularity clause can be deleted. The technique for multiple extensions is then to explore a tree of choice of deleted defaults. If we consider the oriented graph of dependences between defaults (the irregularity of one depending of the ones in the antecedent part of its irregularity clauses), the choice of paragraph 5.1 is that of a minimal element, and the blocking step corresponds to a circularity in the graph.

The strongly connected components of the graph can be computed and ordered in linear time. Then we choose a default among those in the antecedent of irregularity clauses which are in a minimal strongly connected component. First this default is recorded as hypotheticaly not validly excluded and deleted in the antecedant of clauses, and the method goes on in the same way. The other choice is : the default is recorded as hypotheticaly validly excluded, and clauses involving it in their antecedant part are deleted. At the end, we have a set of validly excluded defaults if and only if the irregularity clauses are consistent with the defaults recorded ; v.i.z. there is an irregularity clause with an empty antecedant for each default recorded as validly excluded, and there is no such clause for any default recorded as not validly excluded.

Let us return to the example of paragraph 4.3. Irregularity clauses are :

(22) $\delta 2 \rightarrow$ Irreg($\delta 1$)　　(23) $\delta 1 \rightarrow$ Irreg($\delta 2$)　　(24) $\delta 1$ $\delta 4 \rightarrow$ Irreg($\delta 3$)

(25) $\delta 1$ $\delta 3 \rightarrow$ Irreg($\delta 4$)

As each default is in the consequent of an irregularity clause, none can be deleted without choice. Minimal clauses for weak subsumption are (22) and (23).

a) If we record $\delta 2$ as not validly excluded and delete it, we have (22') $\rightarrow$ Irreg($\delta 1$), so (23), (24) and (25) are deleted and the set of excluded defaults is the singleton $\{\delta 1\}$, which is consistent with the $\delta 2$ recorded. Since $\delta 1$ appears in (28), the corresponding universe is $\{\delta 2, \delta 4\}$. In the same way, facts are (1) $\rightarrow$ a, (19') $\rightarrow$ c and (21') $\rightarrow$ e.

b) If we record $\delta 2$ as validly excluded and we delete clauses involving it, i.e. (22), $\delta 1$ can then be deleted, so we get :

　　　(23') $\rightarrow$ Irreg($\delta 2$)　　(24') $\delta 4 \rightarrow$ Irreg($\delta 3$)　　(25') $\delta 3 \rightarrow$ Irreg($\delta 4$)

and we need some more choice.

　b.1) We record $\delta 3$ as not validly excluded and delete it. We get (25") $\rightarrow$ Irreg($\delta 4$), and (24') is deleted. (23') and (25") are consistant with the assumptions that we have made. Label clauses yield the set $\{\delta 1, \delta 3\}$ of generating defaults. Facts resulting from clauses (1), (18) and (20) are $\rightarrow$ a, $\rightarrow$ b and $\rightarrow$ d.

　b.2) We record $\delta 3$ as validly excluded and delete (25'). $\delta 4$ can now be deleted. We end with (23') $\rightarrow$ Irreg($\delta 2$) and (25") $\rightarrow$ Irreg($\delta 3$), which is consistant with our assumptions. Label clauses yield (26) $\rightarrow$ Prer($\delta 1$) and (29') $\rightarrow$ Prer($\delta 4$). Facts $\rightarrow$ a, $\rightarrow$ b and $\rightarrow$ e result from clauses (1), (18) and (21).

5.3 Miscellaneous

As is implicit in the last examples, adding irregularity clauses and label clauses does not increase complexity as much as it could seem at a first glance. The best solution is to proceed first factual clauses. Since irregularity clauses and label clauses involve neither untyped literal nor δ literal in their consequent part, they can be resolved only if they are not CAT, and only with a factual CAT clause, all of which have been generated at the previous step. So all the possible resolutions involving one such clause can be performed at the same time. Deduced clauses are of the same type, and, they can only be subsumed by a clause having the same consequent part, which simplifies much the matter.

Resolving irregularity clauses is a problem of finding a kernel in a graph. But the size of this problem is in general smaller than the original one, since it is determined by the number of default rules. A finer use of the structure of strongly connected components than the one we have suggested may still reduce the search space

Compared to [Etherington 87] based on repetitive use of the operator Γ, our algorithm avoids any repeated computation, and terminates in any case. Compared to [Junker 89], the basic complexity is the same, but we avoid the overcost and limitations due to the confusion between contradiction and irregularities.

6. Conclusion

We have presented a theoretical characterisation of sets of defaults generating an extension of a default theory : complete and regular universes. We have then defined the concept of valid exclusion, and have given with the help of that concept another characterisation of complete and regular universes. This last result allows us an encoding of a default theory into a set of clauses involving typed literals. Resolution followed by some deletion algorithms then computes every extension of the default theory. Contrary to previously published papers, this method works for any propositional default theory.

References

[Bonté, Lévy 89] E Bonte, F. Levy : "Une procédure complète de calcul des extensions pour les théories de défauts en réseau"
7ème congrès AFCET-RFIA, Paris, Décembre 1989
[Cay & Tay 89] Michel Cayrol, Pierre Tayrac : "ARC : un ATMS étendu".
L.S.I. Repport n° 323 Nov 1989
[De Kleer 86 a] Johan De Kleer : "An assumption-based TMS" .
Artificial Intelligence vol 28 1986 127-162
[De Kleer 86 b] Johan De Kleer : "Extending the A.T.M.S." .
Artificial Intelligence vol 28 1986 163-196
[Dressler 88] O. Dressler : "Extending the Basic A.T.M.S."
Proceedings Ecai 88, München, Aug. 1988
[Etherington 87] David W. Etherington : "Formalizing Nonmonotonic Reasoning Systems" .
Artificial Intelligence vol 31 1987
[Junker 89] Ulrich Junker : "A Correct Non-Monotonic A.T.M.S."
Proceedings IJCAI 89, Detroit, Aug 1989   1049-1053
[Lévy 89] François Levy "Contribution à la réalisation d'un raisonneur à profondeur variable"
Thése d'université, Université de Paris Nord, Feb. 1989
[Reiter 80] Raymond Reiter : "A logic for default reasoning"
Artificial Intelligence vol 13 april 1980 81-132

An Evidential Reasoning Approach to the Classification of Satellite Images

Gabriele Lohmann
German Aerospace Research Establishment (DLR)
D-8031 Wessling

1 Introduction

In this paper, a new algorithm for classifying satellite images will be presented. The algorithm is based on evidential reasoning and is therefore called EBIS (Evidence-Based Interpretation of Satellite Images). It supports the interpretation of images from remote sensors such as Landsat/Thematic Mapper or Spot/HRV.

The images provided by the sensors are digital, i.e. they are given as an array of picture elements, where each picture element – called "pixel" – is represented by some vector of grey values. A classification is a mapping of the array of pixels into a set of class labels, such that each pixel recieves exactly one label. The labels indicate the class membership of a picture element. Typically, the class labels refer to land cover types such as forest, bodies of water, agriculture, soil types, and the like.

2 Evidence-based Classification

A number of classification algorithms exists and have been used extensively in recent years [4], [6]. However, there are some major deficiencies inherent in these traditional classification schemes, which limit their usefulness considerably. In particular, they require that all object classes can be described by a fixed predetermined probability distribution in the context of a single feature space. Thus, only some special types of images and object classes can be analyzed.

To overcome the limitations inherent in traditional classification methods, the EBIS-scheme was devised. In contrast to traditional methods, several feature spaces and several class descriptors per class based on various statistical models are allowed in EBIS. The methodology underlying the EBIS-algorithm is derived from Shafer's theory of evidence [8]. Feature spaces are viewed as sources of evidence, and belief functions are used to measure the strength of the evidence.

The EBIS-algorithm has two phases. In the first phase, the sources of evidence are identified and object class descriptors are derived. The second phase is the classification phase where the image is classified on the basis of the object class descriptors identified in the first phase. A short overview is presented in figure 1.

training phase

for each class :
    identify sources of evidence
    for each source of evidence :
        derive object class descriptor

classification phase

for each pixel :
    for each class :
        weight ← 0
        for each object class descriptor :
            weight ← weight + weight from current descriptor
    select class that has largest positive weight
    if no class has positive weight, then select NIL-label

Figure 1: the EBIS-algorithm – an overview

In the following, the concept of object class descriptors and of belief functions derived from class descriptors will be explained.

3   Object Class Descriptors

In EBIS, each object class can be represented by any number of descriptors, where each descriptor is based on exactly one feature space. Descriptors are essentially specifications of statistical models, which describe the statistical properties of an object class in some feature space. If the pixel's features match a descriptor well, then this constitutes evidence in favor of the corresponding class hypothesis. If, on the other hand, the feature values do not match the descriptor then the hypothesis is refuted.

For testing purposes, three parametric models have been implemented so far:

1. the Gaussian normal distribution,

2. the multinomial distribution,

3. and the Gibbs random field model [2], [3].

Those models were chosen because they seem to be the most valuable models in the context of satellite image classification. The Gaussian normal distribution is the "classical" model which has found widespread use. The multinomial distribution, on the other hand, has not been used at all so far in this context. However, it seems to be extremely useful, and constitutes a valuable tool for modelling certain types of classes. The Gibbs random field model is used here to model textures.

In EBIS, the object class descriptors are derived from training data. Several methods of parameter estimation have been implemented in EBIS, since each parametric model requires its own parameter estimation procedure. A maximum likelihood estimation is used for Gaussian normal distrubutions, Besag's coding method [2] is used to estimate the parameters of a Gibbs random field, and the parameters of a multinomial distribution can be trivially approximated by histogramming.

4 Weight Functions

The degree to which a pixel's features match a descriptor determines the strength of the evidence for the corresponding class hypothesis. Thus, we need functions that measure the strength of that evidence. In this section, we will claim that weight functions are well suited for this purpose, and a means of deriving weight functions from parametric models will be described.

The main idea advocated here is that instead of defining belief functions – as one would normally expect in an evidential reasoning approach – it is much easier to use the equivalent concept of so-called *weight functions*, and define weight functions instead. The concept of weight functions goes back to Shafer's concept of *weight of evidence* [8].

Weight functions are functionally equivalent to dichotomous belief functions, and the combination of those belief functions by Dempster's rule is equivalent to the addition of the corresponding weight functions. Since the addition of weights is much easier than the application of Dempster's rule, weight functions are used instead of belief functions.

Two alternative approaches to defining weight functions from statistical evidence are proposed. The first approach relates weights of evidence to the information theoretic concept of mutual information, and the second approach is based on a likelihood ratio. In the following, the two approaches will be explained in more detail.

Let $p(\omega|x)$ denote the probability of class ω given the feature vector x, and let $p(\omega)$ denote the prior probability of class ω. If x provides evidence in favor of object class ω, then $p(\omega|x)$ will be greater than $p(\omega)$. On the other hand, if x makes ω less likely, then $p(\omega|x)$ will be smaller than $p(\omega)$. Thus, the term

$$I(x,\omega) = \log \frac{p(\omega|x)}{p(\omega)} = \log \frac{p(x|\omega)}{p(x)}$$

is a measure of the strength of the evidence provided by x. Note that this formula is well known in information theory, where it is generally called *mutual information* (cf. [1], [5]). Some simple computations show that the function $I(\cdot, \omega)$ is additive, and thus can be used as a weight function in the sense explained above.

One of the major problems connected with this function is however, that the term $p(x)$ needs to be evaluated. In some simple cases, this term can be approximated by the image histogram. However, for higher dimensional feature spaces, this term cannot be computed in any reasonable way, and thus an alternative way of defining weight functions is necessary. The following weight function – called *likelihood ratio* – overcomes this problem:

$$LR(x,\omega) = \gamma \, \log \frac{p(x|\omega)}{\tilde{p}}$$

where $|\Delta|$ is some feature space, $\tilde{p} = \frac{1}{|\Delta|}$ and γ is some normalization factor. Note that $LR(x, \omega)$ is positive if $p(x|\omega) > \frac{1}{|\Delta|}$, and negative otherwise. Thus, $LR(x, \omega)$ agrees with our intuitive notion of weights of evidence. Since it is also additive, it can be used as a weight function.

5 Conclusion

A new algorithm – called EBIS – for classifying satellite images was presented. Its main purpose is to overcome the limitations inherent in traditional classification methods, which impose severe constraints on the types of images and object classes that can be analysed. In particular, traditional methods require that all object classes can be identified by just one descriptor of a fixed type in the context of a single feature space.

The EBIS-algorithm does not impose such constraints. Instead, it admits several descriptors of various types for each class, and supports several feature spaces. Thus, it is applicable to a wider range of image data and object classes.

The prime advantage in admitting several descriptors and several feature spaces is that the integration of information from disparate sources becomes much easier. Considering the fact that several new remote sensing satellites will be launched in the near future, and other data sources such as digital elevation models will become available as well, this aspect is of great importance to the analysis of satellite data.

So far, a prototype system of EBIS has been implemented, and preliminary tests have produced encouraging results. Particularly interesting tests have been performed using Landsat/Thematic Mapper data of a test area in the tropical rain forest of Brazil [7]. While traditional classification methods have notoriously failed in these areas due to the complexity of the vegetation classes, EBIS has produced plausible results. Further tests are under way.

6 Acknowledgements

The author would like to thank Prof. Dr. Bernd Radig for his scientific advice. I would also like to thank Mr. Winfried Markwitz, Head of the German Remote Sensing Data Centre (DFD) of the German Aerospace Research Establishment (DLR) for the access to the data and use of DLR facilities. Special thanks to my colleague Helmut Hoensch who performed the first tests of the EBIS system and provided many valuable hints.

References

[1] Norman Abramson. *Information Theory and Coding.* McGraw Hill, 1963

[2] Julian E. Besag. *Spatial Interaction and the Statistical Analysis of Lattice Systems.* Journal of the Royal Statistical Society, Ser.B, Vol.36, 1974, pp.192-236

[3] George R. Cross, Anil K. Jain. *Markov Random Field Texture Models.* IEEE Trans. on Pattern Analysis and Machine Intelligence, Vol. PAMI-5, No.1, January 1983, pp.25-39

[4] R.O.Duda, P.E. Hart. *Pattern Classification and Scene Analysis*. John Wiley & Sons, 1973

[5] Robert G. Gallager. *Information Theory and Reliable Communication*. John Wiley, 1968

[6] H.G. Gierloff-Emden. *Fernerkundungskartographie mit Satellitenaufnahmen*. Verlag Franz Deuticke, Wien, 1989

[7] Helmut Hönsch. *Klassifizierung von Ökosystemen des tropischen Regenwaldes mit Hilfe multitemporaler und multisensoraler Satellitendaten im Staat Acre/Brasilien*. Dissertation in preparation, Universität Trier, Fachbereich Geographie, 1991.

[8] Glenn Shafer. *A Mathematical Theory of Evidence*. Princeton University Press, 1976

PRESS - A PROBABILISTIC REASONING EXPERT SYSTEM SHELL

Zhiyuan Luo and Alex Gammerman

Department of Computer Science, Heriot-Watt University
79 Grassmarket, Edinburgh EH1 2HJ, U.K.

1. INTRODUCTION

Recently much attention and effort have been put on developing and applying causal probabilistic reasoning mechanisms [3, 12, 17, 19]. This is because causal graphs used in these mechanisms are natural and efficient knowledge representation tools for modelling and manipulating some real problems. In general, a causal graph is a directed acyclic graph where a node in the graph represents a variable and a directed edge between two nodes show how the knowledge of one node will affect knowledge on the other. These edges are specified by conditional probabilities attached to each node given all possible states of its parent nodes. There are also prior probabilities, that represent our background knowledge for topmost nodes in the graph.

The graphical structure reflects assumptions of dependencies in the graph [12, 17]. For example, the absence of links between some nodes represents conditional independence assumptions. Efficient storage and propagation require a re-representation of the model as a Markov field on an undirected graph [3, 12]. The graph is then decomposed into a set of cliques. A formation of clique tree allows evidence to be propagated using simple algorithms.

The causal probabilistic reasoning mechanisms can be divided into two groups: exact algorithm (with exact values of belief) [12, 17, 19] and approximate algorithm [10, 16]. The latter uses simulation (or Monte Carlo techniques), and gives approximate values. The accuracy depends on the size of the sample space (number of simulation runs). The computation has polynomial complexity in the size and number of connections in the graph.

In this paper, we attempt to describe a development of a Probabilistic Reasoning Expert System Shell (PRESS). The distinct features of the system are: (1) it offers an interactive graphical tool for constructing and manipulating the knowledge base (a graph and corresponding prior and conditional probabilities); (2) it integrates two different types of causal probabilistic reasoning mechanisms - exact and approximate algorithms - into a common computational framework; (3) it provides control facilities of causal probabilistic reasoning to the user (the most influential evidence on our belief and ordering questions concerning a node of interest); (4) it also allows to form a model in a semi-automated process by extracting the underlying topology directly out of data (structure learning); (5) it deals with imprecise conditional probabilities and revises them as new cases accumulated (parameter learning). These functions have been tested in different applications: medical, forensic science and agricultural forecasting.

2. PROBABILISTIC REASONING SYSTEM

The overall architecture of PRESS is depicted in Fig. 1. The system consists of four main parts: *Model Construction, Preprocessor, Evidence propagation* and *Control facilities.*

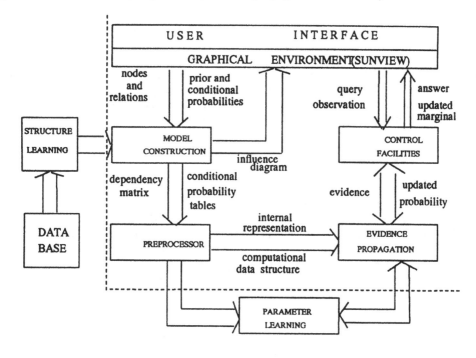

Fig. 1. Architecture of PRESS

In model construction procedure, a graphical tool is used to construct and manipulate causal structures and probability tables. Both continuous and discrete nodes can be assessed. It is assumed that continuous variables have Conditional Gaussian distributions [6, 11]. The preprocessor will deal with the domain knowledge by using different inference techniques for different data representations. The structure and conditional probability tables are processed and transferred into suitable internal representations for evidence propagation. The joint probability distribution is then decomposed into a set of distributions on local groups (cliques). These distributions are initialised from the conditional probability tables and ready to update in the light of evidence. When evidence comes, the evidence propagation procedure allows the user to enter and propagate evidence in the causal structure and update our belief. Both "exact" and "approximate" algorithms for probabilistic reasoning are provided. The "exact" algorithm is developed from CPRS [7, 14] and substantially extended to deal with a mixed combination of discrete and continuous variables based on the latest development [11]. The "approximate" algorithm is derived from STOSS [15], using the stochastic simulation method to perform probabilistic reasoning. The probabilities of a variable are estimated by counting how often the states of the proposition occur in a series of random simulation. The marginal probabilities of discrete variables and means and variances of continuous variables are calculated. The control facilities help the user to control and understand the probabilistic reasoning process. For example, what questions to ask and in what order, or to measure closeness between nodes of interest, etc. All the programs are written in C under UNIX and the graphical interface is programmed in SunView.

3. MACHINE LEARNING PROCEDURES

Learning in PRESS is divided into two groups: structure learning and parameter learning. The aim of structure learning is to identify topology (or structure) given data - nodes, links and directionality of arrows. Parameter learning allows to assess numerical parameters (i.e. the conditional probabilities) for a given network topology from data.

3.1. STRUCTURE LEARNING

Forming a computational model involves two distinct stages. The first is the *construction of model* about some area of knowledge in the form of a causal graph. The second stage involves the development of an *evidence propagation* procedure which will deal with any individual case and will allow to update information on the graph in the light of new evidence. The first stage in its turn also may have two different procedures to form the model. We can construct the model through a *knowledge elicitation* procedure through which an expert or a user may supply information about some area of knowledge in the form of a causal graph and associated conditional probabilities. Alternatively (or in addition) we would like to form the model in a semi-automated process by extracting the underlying topology directly out of data.

The system (PRESS) employs the polytree algorithm developed by J. Pearl [18] in the assumption that underlying distribution can be approximated by a dependency tree. The algorithm consists of two steps: the first is to construct a skeleton tree, and the second is to identify the direction of the branches of the tree by using a series of tests for independence. In the first step, the algorithm allows to find the best approximation of a n-order distribution by a product of (n-1) second order distributions using Chow-Liu algorithm [4]. In the second step, independence test is used to recover as many directions as possible, so that "causal" structure can be imposed on the graph. The polytree algorithm is integrated within PRESS for an alternative way of model construction [8].

3.2. PARAMETER LEARNING

The main idea is to express our doubt on conditional probabilities by adopting Bayesian learning approach [5, 20] and revise the conditional probabilities as new cases accumulate. The algorithm in PRESS represents the imprecision of conditional probabilities explicitly as parameters. These parameters with uncertainty attached to them are defined in the form of probability distributions specified by domain experts or past data. The new case is then to revise the posterior distributions of parameters and cause them to improve accuracy in assessing the conditional probabilities.

According to Spiegelhalter and Lauritzen [20], there are three basic operations involved in sequential updating: dissemination of experience, propagation of evidence and retrieval of new case. Based on local- and global-independence assumptions, these operations can be carried out locally [20]. The former refers to the independence of conditional probability distributions for a node given any particular combinations of parents, and the latter refers to the prior independence of the distributions for each node.

4. APPLICATIONS

Three applications of PRESS are described below. In the first example (medical), PRESS employs both structure learning and parameter learning, and exact propagation algorithm. In the second example, both exact and approximate propagation algorithms are used in evidential assessment. In the last example, both pure and mixed probabilistic models are handled by exact propagation algorithms.

4.1. MEDICAL DATABASE

The medical database we used for extracting a causal tree and sequential updating has 6,387 records on patients suffering from acute abdominal pain. Each record describes 33 symptoms and a diagnostic group. There are 9 possible diagnostic groups and each symptom has a number of values associated with it [9].

The database is randomly divided into two sets: training set and testing set. The training set is used to estimate all parameters of probability distributions needed to specify above graphical representation. The remaining set is used as new cases appeared in the hospital for testing. Now in order to make computer diagnosis we can exploit evidence propagation. We consider each symptom as a variable with a finite values. In the database, each patient has one and only one disease. So these nine diseases are regarded as the different values of a disease variable. Totally, there are 34 variables in our abdominal pain problem. We assume that the probability distributions are Dirichlet. The parameters of the distributions can be estimated from the database.

Having a testing set, it is possible to evaluate the accuracy of computer diagnoses. As a "computer diagnosis" then we take the highest probability and interpret it as a diagnosis for this patient. All the computer diagnoses are compared with their final diagnoses made by the doctors and evaluation matrices are then built. The numbers on the diagonal line indicates the correct cases of computer diagnoses within different diagnostic groups. The overall accuracy can be worked out by the sum of these numbers divided by the total number of patients in the testing set.

A polytree is constructed from training set using structure learning procedure and used to make computer diagnosis [8]. The sequential updating is tested on the same database [13]. It is found that the parameter learning will improve the performance of reasoning system dramatically when the size of training is relatively small.

4.2. FORENSIC SCIENCE

An artificial example in evidential assessment is constructed [1, 2]. Computational procedures based on probabilities for incorporating and assessing evidence obtained in the course of a criminal investigation are described. Both **exact** and **approximate** propagation algorithms can be used in this case [1, 14, 15].

4.3. AGRICULTURAL FORECASTING

This is a part of a project (under DOSES program) to connect casual and forecasting models. In this case PRESS demonstrates how it handles with mixed variables in the sense that some of them are continuous and some are discrete [6]. Evidence is entered into the system concerning those variables and factors which have been observed. The system will then reply with the adjusted probabilities and means and variances of the other variables of the system. Both **pure** and **mixed** probabilistic models can be handled in PRESS.

5. CONCLUSION

A flexible and easy-to-use Probabilistic Reasoning Expert System Shell (PRESS) for presenting graph and performing reasoning has been described. The shell is designed and implemented in an object-oriented programming and interactive graphical way. Control facilities are provided to help the user to understand and control probabilistic reasoning. Furthermore, machine learning procedures can ease knowledge acquisition difficulties and improve the performance of reasoning systems. We believe that this shell system makes construction and manipulation of causal graph easier and provides a new opportunity for the user.

ACKNOWLEDGEMENTS

This research is partially supported by the European Community, DOSES project B6 LIKELY, "Linking Informal Knowledge and Expertise to Forecasting Models".

REFERENCES

1. Aitken, C.G.G. and Gammerman, A.J. (1989) Probabilistic reasoning in evidential assessment, Journal of the Forensic Science Society 29 (1989), 303-316.

2. Aitken, C.G.G. (1988) In discussion of Lauritzen, S.L. and Spiegelhalter, D.J. Local computations with probabilities on graphical structures and their application to expert systems. J.R. Statist. Soc. (Series B) 50 (1988), 200-201.

3. Andreassen, S., Woldbye, M., Falck, B. and Andersen, S.K. (1987) MUNIN - A causal probabilistic network for interpretation of electromyographic findings, Proc. 10th IJCAI 2 (1987), 366-372.

4. Chow, C.K. and Liu, C.N. (1968) Approximating discrete probability distributions with dependence trees, IEEE Trans. on Info. Theory, IT-14 (1968), 462-467.

5. Duda, R.O. and Hart, P.E (1973) Pattern Classification and Scene Analysis, Wiley, New York.

6. Gammerman, A., Aitken, C.G.G., Luo, Z. and Talbot, M. (1991) A computational systems for mixed probabilistic models, submitted to Statistics and Computing.

7. Gammerman, A. (1988) In discussion of Lauritzen, S.L. and Spiegelhalter, D.J. Local computations with probabilities on graphical structures and their application to expert systems, J.R. Statist. Soc. (Series B) 50 (1988), 200.

8. Gammerman, A. and Luo, Z. (1991) Constructing causal trees from a medical database, Technical Report TR91002, Dept. of Computer Science, Heriot-Watt University, Edinburgh, UK.

9. Gammerman, A. and Thatcher, A.R. (1990) Bayesian inference in an expert system without assuming independence, In Advances in Artificial Intelligence (ed. M. Golumbic), 182-219.

10. Henrion, M. (1988) Propagating uncertainty in Bayesian networks by probabilistic logic sampling, In Uncertainty in Artificial Intelligence 2, 149-163.

11. Lauritzen, S.L. (1990) Propagation of probabilities, means and variances in mixed graphical association models, R90-18, Institute for Elektroniske Systemer, Aalborg, Denmark.

12. Lauritzen, S.L. and Spiegelhalter, D.J. (1988) Local computations with probabilities on graphical structures and their application to expert systems (with discussion), J.R. Statist. Soc. (Series B) 50 (1988), 157-224.

13. Luo, Z. and Gammerman, A. (1991) Bayesian learning in a medical database, Technical Report TR91003, Dept. of Computer Science, Heriot-Watt University, Edinburgh, UK.

14. Luo, Z. and Gammerman, A. (1990) A probabilistic reasoning system based on a causal graph approach, IEE Colloquium on Knowledge Engineering, 4/1-4/3, London, UK.

15. Luo, Z. and Gammerman, A. (1990) A stochastic simulation system and its application to causal models, Proc. 3rd International Conference on IPMU in Knowledge-based Systems, 186-189.

16. Pearl, J. (1987) Evidential reasoning using stochastic simulation of causal models, Artificial Intelligence 32 (1987), 245-257.

17. Pearl, J. (1986) Fusion, propagation, and structuring in belief networks, Artificial Intelligence 29 (1986), 241-288.

18. Pearl, J. (1988) Probabilistic Reasoning In Intelligent Systems: Networks Of Plausible Inference, Morgan Kaufmann Publishers, San Mateo, California.

19. Shachter, R.D. (1986) Evaluating influence diagrams, Operations Research 34 (1986), 871-882.

20. Spiegelhalter, D.J. and Lauritzen, S.L. (1989) Sequential updating of conditional probabilities on directed graphical structures, R 89-10, Institute for Elektroniske Systemer, Aalborg, Denmark.

Induction of Uncertain Rules and the Sociopathicity Property in Dempster-Shafer Theory

Yong Ma and David C. Wilkins

Department of Computer Science
University of Illinois
405 North Mathews Avenue
Urbana, IL 61801, USA
{yongma, wilkins}@cs.uiuc.edu

Abstract

As is well known, Dempster-Shafer theory offers an alternative approach to deal with uncertainty reasoning in expert systems and other fields. In this paper, we present two results that relate to the use of the theory. First, we present and analyze four methods to induce uncertain rules from a training instance set for Dempster-Shafer theory. This is the first attempt to do so, to the best of our knowledge. Second, we show that these "correct" induced rules exhibit the sociopathicity property when they are used in evidential reasoning. The sociopathicity property states that a system's performance can degrade when some individually good pieces of uncertain knowledge (in terms of rules) are added to the knowledge base. The importance of this result is that the performance of evidential reasoning systems based on Dempster-Shafer theory can deteriorate for essentially any size of knowledge base, although all the pieces of knowledge in the knowledge base are "correct".

1 Introduction

Reasoning under uncertainty has been widely and extensively investigated in artificial intelligence and other related fields. Researchers in these fields have developed many methods to represent uncertain knowledge and draw inferences from them. Among these methods are the certainty factor model in MYCIN [Buchanan and Shortliffe, 1984], the Bayesian probability theory (as in PROSPECTOR) [Duda et al., 1976], belief networks [Pearl, 1986b, Pearl, 1986a], Dempster-Shafer's evidence theory [Shafer, 1976, Gordon and Shortliffe, 1985], Zadeh's possibility theory (fuzzy logic) [Zadeh, 1979], and so on. One of the most appealing contenders is the mathematical theory of evidence which was developed by Arthur Dempster, then formulated and extended by Glenn Shafer [Shafer, 1976]. The theory is a generalization of probability theory with its origins in a theory of upper and lower probabilities. Therefore, it reduces to standard Bayesian reasoning when the knowledge is accurate but is more flexible in representing and dealing with ignorance and uncertainty.

In this paper, we present two results that relate to the use of Dempster-Shafer theory. First, we present and analyze four methods to induce uncertain rules from a training instance set for Dempster-Shafer theory. To the best of our knowledge, there is no such attempt in the literature. Second, we show that these "correct" induced rules exhibit the sociopathicity property when they are used in evidential reasoning. The study of the sociopathicity property raises an important concern to all the above mentioned methods for reasoning under uncertainty. As the matter of fact, the sociopathicity property is not unique to Dempster-Shafer theory, as it has been shown that the certainty factor model and Bayesian methods also possess this property [Wilkins and Ma, 1991, Ma and Wilkins, 1990a].

2 Induction of Uncertain Rules

In this section, we propose four methods to compute the strengths of the rules in a rule base when these rules are applied to a training set whose members are classified as positive or negative instances of some hypothesis. To the best of our knowledge, there is no such attempt for Dempster-Shafer theory in the literature.

Assume that there exists a library (training set) of solved cases, and that we wish to construct classification rules that map evidence to hypotheses, let

S denote the training set

R denote a rule in a rule set

$p =$ number of positive instances that R applies

$n =$ number of negative instances that R applies

$P =$ total number of positive instances in S

$N =$ total number of negative instances in S

$m =$ basic probability assignment for R

where a "positive instance" is an instance whose classification is some hypothesis, h, and a "negative instance" is, thus, an instance whose classification is not h. In what follows, we use $\{h, \neg h\}$ to denote the hypothesis space in which rules are induced from the training set.

2.1 Method 1

$$
\begin{aligned}
m(h) &= \frac{p}{p+n} \\
m(\neg h) &= \frac{n}{p+n} \\
m(\Theta) &= 0
\end{aligned}
\tag{1}
$$

This method of assigning weights to rules is that used by standard probability theory. Thus, it does not take advantages of Dempster-Shafer theory that can make use of other quantities such as P, N; and be flexible in using them, as the following methods do.

2.2 Method 2

$$
\begin{aligned}
m(h) &= \frac{p}{P+N} \\
m(\neg h) &= \frac{n}{P+N} \\
m(\Theta) &= 1 - m(h) - m(\neg h)
\end{aligned}
\tag{2}
$$

This is a somewhat improved probability way. But it still has a problem when $p \approx P \approx n \approx N$. In this case, $m(h) \approx 0.5$, $m(\neg h) \approx 0.5$, and $m(\Theta) \approx 0$. Then we are back to the regular probability assignments as in Method 1. However, what we hope to have for this particular case is that $m(h) \approx 0$, $m(\neg h) \approx 0$, and $m(\Theta) \approx 1$, because a rule with $p \approx n$ has virtually no discriminatory power.

2.3 Method 3

$$
\begin{aligned}
m(h) &= \begin{cases} \frac{p-n}{P} & if\ p \geq n \\ 0 & otherwise \end{cases} \\
m(\neg h) &= \begin{cases} \frac{n-p}{N} & if\ n \geq p \\ 0 & otherwise \end{cases} \\
m(\Theta) &= 1 - m(h) - m(\neg h)
\end{aligned}
\tag{3}
$$

The difference $|p - n|$ introduced in this method makes a rule, that covers almost equal number of positive and negative instances, distinct from a rule, that covers unequal number of positive and negative instances. In other words, the discriminatory power of a rule comes mainly from this difference.

2.4 Method 4

In Method 3, there is a strong bias that sets $m(\neg h)$ to 0 if $p > n$. This seems undesirable if n is big. Therefore, to correct this situation and to give some credit to n if $n > 0$, we have the following proposal.

$$m(h) = \begin{cases} \frac{p-n}{P} & \text{if } p \geq n \\ \frac{p}{P}\frac{1}{N(n-p)} & \text{otherwise} \end{cases}$$

$$m(\neg h) = \begin{cases} \frac{n-p}{N} & \text{if } n \geq p \\ \frac{n}{N}\frac{1}{P(p-n)} & \text{otherwise} \end{cases} \tag{4}$$

$$m(\Theta) = 1 - m(h) - m(\neg h)$$

From the definition, we can easily show that

$$\begin{array}{ll} (1). & m(h) + m(\neg h) \leq 1 \\ (2). & m(h) > m(\neg h) \;\; if\; p > n \\ (3). & m(\neg h) > m(h) \;\; if\; n > p \end{array} \tag{5}$$

Now let us see how we corrected the strong bias in Method 3. Without loss of generality, we assume that $p > n$, then $m(h)$ is the same as in Method 3. But $m(\neg h)$ is not 0, instead it is defined to be

$$\frac{n}{N}\frac{1}{P(p - n)} \tag{6}$$

The first fraction takes n into considerations; and $(p-n)$, as the denominator, is to enforce the idea that, the greater the difference between p and n is, the smaller the $m(\neg h)$ should be. Finally, P comes into play to make $m(h) > m(\neg h)$ which is a desirable and derived statement from $p > n$.

2.5 Analysis of the methods

Although the methods are proposed in the order of increasing complexity, each one of them can be used under certain circumstances. Here we present our partial insights of the definitions of basic probability assignments to rules in all the methods.

As one can see, Method 1 is a standard probabilistic method to assign probabilities to each hypothesis for rules. Therefore, if one prefers to allocate all the beliefs among the singleton hypotheses in a hypothesis space, Method 1 is certainly the choice among the methods. But, there is a dangerous situation that should be noticed. That is, if a rule R applies only to either positive or negative instances, then either $m(h) = 1$ or $m(\neg h) = 1$. As is well known, a belief of "1" in Dempster-Shafer theory or a probability of "1" in probability theory is a very strong statement!

Method 2 is a somewhat improved version of Method 1 because it uses the total number of instances in the training set, not just the total number of the instances that a rule applies to. By changing the denominator, we get (1) if $P * N \neq 0$, then $m(h) < 1$ and $m(\neg h) < 1$, thus eliminating the risky possibility of assigning "1" to some hypothesis as in Method 1, and (2) $m(h) + m(\neg h) < 1$ for most of time, thus leaving a portion of the belief to the whole hypothesis set, Θ; i.e., not all the beliefs are allocated among the singleton hypotheses. However, this method is not preferable if $P >> N$ (or $N >> P$), because, in this case, $m(\neg h) \approx 0$, even if $n = N$. Clearly, a rule that applies to (almost) all the negative instances should not get $m(\neg h) \approx 0$ which is true simply because there are many many more positive instances in the training set. Thus, Method 2 is working better for training sets that do not contain greatly unbalanced numbers of positive and negative instances.

Method 3 is proposed to overcome the inability of Method 2 to distinguish rules based on discriminatory power which mainly comes from the difference between p and n. For example, if $p = n$ for a rule R, then R is not a very good rule in terms of ability to discriminate one hypothesis against another. Thus, the assignment of its weight should reflect this point, as shown in Method 3. Method 3 does not suffer from the problem of greatly unbalanced numbers of positive and negative instances in a training set because P and N are separately used for h and $\neg h$ respectively. It also offers simpler assignments for rules because one of $m(h)$ and $m(\neg h)$ is always 0. In summary, Method 3 can be used for most cases, except when $m(h) * m(\neg h) = 0$ is not desirable.

Finally, the proposal of Method 4 is to combine all the advantages of other methods and to overcome a strong bias in Method 3 that sets $m(\neg h)$ to 0 if $p > n$. Obviously, it is the most complicated of all the methods. But it gives the closest matches between the assignments and the past usage of rules, as manifested in equation (5) and the arguments followed.

3   The Sociopathicity Property

In an earlier paper [Wilkins and Ma, 1991], we addressed an unusual property about heuristic uncertain knowledge bases: better individual rules do not necessarily lead to a better overall rule set. We called these knowledge bases *sociopathic knowledge bases*. A very brief summary of the main results from the paper is as follows. Formally, a knowledge base is *sociopathic* if and only if (1) all the rules in the knowledge base individually meet some goodness or correctness criteria; and (2) a subset of the knowledge base gives better performance than the original knowledge base independent of the amount of available computational resources. The process of finding an optimal subset of a sociopathic knowledge base was modeled as a bipartite graph minimization problem and shown to be NP-hard. A heuristic method, the Sociopathic Reduction Algorithm, was developed to find a suboptimal solution for sociopathic knowledge bases. However, the sociopathicity property was studied mainly under the CF model introduced in MYCIN [Buchanan and Shortliffe, 1984] which inspired the study of sociopathic knowledge bases in the first place [Wilkins and Buchanan, 1986].

In this paper, we extend definitions on sociopathicity as follows. An *uncertainty reasoning system* is said to be *sociopathic* (has the *sociopathicity property*) if its knowledge base is sociopathic. Then, an *uncertainty reasoning theory* is said to be subject to the *sociopathicity property* if evidential uncertainty reasoning systems based on it are sociopathic.

Suppose that there is a diagnostic expert system based on Dempster-Shafer theory and that its hypotheses set, or the frame of discernment, is $\Theta = \{a, b, c, ...\}$. A knowledge base of the system is built up either from knowledge engineers with some domain experts or from a machine learning system that learns rules from examples. A rule in the knowledge base is of the form:

R_i: Evidence e_i confirms $A_{i_1}, ..., A_{i_m}$ to the degrees of $s_{i_1}, ..., s_{i_m}$, respectively.

where $A_{i_j} \subseteq \Theta, 1 \leq j \leq m$; and $\sum s_{i_j} \leq 1$. This rule translates to a basic probability assignment m_i as follows:

$$m_i(A_{i_j}) = s_{i_j} \quad 1 \leq j \leq m \tag{7}$$

$$m_i(\Theta) = 1 - \sum_{j=1}^{m} s_{i_j} \tag{8}$$

Note that a piece of disconfirming evidence can also be represented in the above rule format, since the statement "Evidence e_i disconfirms A_{i_j} to the degree of s_{i_j}," is equivalent to "Evidence e_i confirms $\Theta - A_{i_j}$ to the degree of s_{i_j},". We assume there are some instances to be diagnosed. The diagnosis process is, as usual, to gather evidence for each instance, compute the combined impact of evidence, and finally output the decision hypothesis. It is easy to see that the applicability of the rules in the knowledge base varies from instance to instance; some rules may be fired for all the instances while others may be used just once. For simplicity, the following proof is carefully constructed such that the estimates of m, Bel, Pl will all give the same decision for each instance.

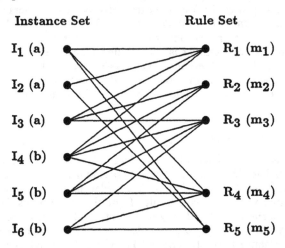

Figure 1: *An example used to illustrate the sociopathicity property in Dempster-Shafer theory. The knowledge base consists of five rules $R_1, ..., R_5$ with basic probability assignments $m_1, ..., m_5$, respectively. The links show which of the training instances $I_1, ..., I_6$ satisfy the preconditions of a rule. The training instances conclude one of two hypotheses: a or b. Note that the links completely determine the values of the basic probability assignments of the rules.*

Theorem 3.1 *An evidential uncertainty reasoning system based on Dempster-Shafer theory has the sociopathicity property.*

Proof: Let $\Theta = \{a, b\}$. Suppose that there are six instances in the training set and that the knowledge base consists of five rules as shown in Fig. 1. The *applicability links* shown in the figure show which of the training instances $I_1, ..., I_6$ satisfy the preconditions of a rule.

The training instances are used in two separate stages. During the first stage, they are used to compute strengths of the rules from the applicability links between instances and rules. Applying Method 3 from the last section, we get

R_1: Evidence e_1 confirms $\{a\}$ to the degree 2/3.
R_2: Evidence e_2 confirms $\{b\}$ to the degree 1/3.
R_3: Evidence e_3 confirms $\{b\}$ to the degree 2/3.
R_4: Evidence e_4 disconfirms $\{a\}$ to the degree 2/3.
R_5: Evidence e_5 disconfirms $\{b\}$ to the degree 1/3.

Their equivalent basic probability assignments are as follows, according to (7) and (8).

$$m_1(\{a\}) = 2/3, \qquad m_1(\Theta) = 1/3 \tag{9}$$
$$m_2(\{b\}) = 1/3, \qquad m_2(\Theta) = 2/3 \tag{10}$$

$$m_3(\{b\}) = 2/3, \qquad m_3(\Theta) = 1/3 \qquad (11)$$

$$m_4(\{b\}) = 2/3, \qquad m_2(\Theta) = 1/3 \qquad (12)$$

$$m_5(\{a\}) = 1/3, \qquad m_5(\Theta) = 2/3 \qquad (13)$$

During the second stage, the training instances are *diagnosed* using the rules that are induced from them. As one would normally expect, every instance would be diagnosed correctly. However, this is not true, as shown below.

Table 1: *The gross combined tableau of m_1 and m_2.*

$m_1 \backslash m_2$	$\{b\}$ (1/3)	Θ (2/3)
$\{a\}$ (2/3)	$\emptyset$ (2/9)	$\{a\}$ (4/9)
Θ (1/3)	$\{b\}$ (1/9)	Θ (2/9)

If all the five rules are used, one can easily verify that I_3 is misdiagnosed, using the Dempster's combination rule. To demonstrate the whole process of computing new basic probability assignments and deciding a final hypothesis, let us work out the detailed calculations for I_3. As shown in Fig. 1, three rules $R_1(m_1), R_2(m_2), R_3(m_3)$ apply to I_3. First, the gross combined effect of m_1 and m_2, i.e., the effect before the normalization step, is shown in Table 1. Then, according to Dempster's combination rule, a new basic probability assignment $m_1 \oplus m_2$ is computed. And the resulting functions and the belief intervals are put together in Table 2 in which only nonzero entries of $m_1 \oplus m_2$ are listed.

Table 2: *The combined effect m_{12} of m_1 and m_2 after the normalization.*

	m_{12}	Bel_{12}	Pl_{12}	$[Bel(A), Pl(A)]$
$\{a\}$	0.571	0.571	0.867	[0.571, 0.867]
$\{b\}$	0.143	0.143	0.429	[0.143, 0.429]
Θ	0.286	1.000	1.000	[1.000, 1.000]

Similarly, the combined impact of $m_1 \oplus m_2$ (denoted by m_{12}) and m_3 are calculated and given in Table 3 and 4, from which one can see that I_3 is misdiagnosed because the final hypothesis is $\{b\}$.

Table 3: *The gross combined tableau of m_{12} and m_3.*

$m_1 \oplus m_2 \backslash m_3$	$\{b\}$ (2/3)	Θ (1/3)
$\{a\}$ (4/7)	$\emptyset$ (8/21)	$\{a\}$ (4/21)
$\{b\}$ (1/7)	$\{b\}$ (2/21)	$\{b\}$ (1/21)
Θ (2/7)	$\{b\}$ (4/21)	Θ (2/21)

By similar computations, all other instances are correctly diagnosed. The error rate is, therefore, $1/6=16.7\%$. However, if rule R_3, and thus m_3, is removed from the knowledge base, then all the instances are correctly diagnosed, and thus the error rate is reduced from 16.7% to 0%. For example, the final hypothesis for I_3 is now $\{a\}$ from Table 2 since only m_1 and m_2 have impacts on it. □

Note that the same result holds if the strengths of the rules are computed using other methods proposed in last section. In particular, we get point probabilities rather than intervals for each hypothesis if Method 1 is used. Note also that the sociopathicity property can occur even when a rule set is as small as the one used in Theorem 3.1.

One may argue that the sociopathicity property exists only because we do not pick the right set of rules. For example, if we started with R_1, R_2, R_4, R_5 in the rule set, then

Table 4: The combined effect m_{123} of m_{12} and m_3 after the normalization.

	m_{123}	Bel_{123}	Pl_{123}	$[Bel(A), Pl(A)]$
$\{a\}$	0.308	0.308	0.462	[0.308, 0.462]
$\{b\}$	0.538	0.538	0.692	[0.538, 0.692]
Θ	0.154	1.000	1.000	[1.000, 1.000]

there were no the sociopathicity problem for the example in Fig. 1. Yes, it is true for this particular example. But, how does one know in advance which set of rules to choose from a large knowledge base, in general? In other words, when a large knowledge base is built up, there is really no way to know beforehand which rules to be included in the knowledge base to avoid this potential sociopathicity problem, because each rule in the knowledge base is individually a good piece of knowledge.

One may also wonder why the small example used in the theorem is sufficient to prove that a general system is sociopathic. As it is known, a knowledge base for a system is built up either from learning programs, or from knowledge engineers with domain experts, or combinations of both. For the knowledge bases built up from learning programs, it is trivially true from the proof for any of the four methods used. How does it also apply to the knowledge bases that are built up from experts? If we imagine that an expert is an induction entity that has seen many many instances during his experience, then (1) the rules he generates are just like the rules in the example; and (2) these rules are then used to reason about old and new instances. Note that it is the second stage when the sociopathicity problem appears. In fact, an expert is indeed a complex learning system. After all, the most important ingredient is that all the rules learned are individually correct, regardless of how they are acquired in the first place.

Corollary 3.1 *Dempster-Shafer theory is subject to the sociopathicity property.*

Proof: It is an immediate result of Theorem 3.1 and the definition of the sociopathicity property.   □

Unlike the Bayesian approach which has many practical implementations in expert system domains, Dempster-Shafer theory, as a new and alternate approach, has fewer implementations to date. Therefore, it is an advantage to have this problem recognized up front before the design of an evidential reasoning system using the theory begins. The designer of such a system should keep in his mind that there is a potential system performance deterioration due to its sociopathic behavior as just shown. One should also try to minimize the bad interactions among the rules as much as possible. The minimization problem is NP-hard, but a heuristic method, called the Sociopathic Reduction Algorithm, can be used to find adequate but suboptimal solutions [Wilkins and Ma, 1991]. On the other hand, for those systems that have been implemented based on Dempster-Shafer theory, we may want to re-evaluate the system performance on the ground of the sociopathicity property, because this problem in most implementations was not identified, and thus ignored at the time when the systems were implemented.

4 Concluding Remarks

In this paper, we first presented and analyzed four methods to compute the basic probability assignments of rules for Dempster-Shafer theory when these rules are induced from a training instance set. The analysis of these methods revealed that each one of them is preferable under different circumstances. Then, after a brief introduction to sociopathic knowledge bases and the sociopathicity property, we showed that Dempster-Shafer theory is subject to the sociopathicity property. Due to the nature of this property, this result sends out a clear signal to evidential reasoning system designers using Dempster-Shafer theory that he may want to control and minimize the bad interactions among good rules in the knowledge base because system performance can deteriorate for essentially any size of knowledge base.

The sociopathicity property is a problem not only for Dempster-Shafer theory [Ma and Wilkins, 1990b], but also for many other uncertainty reasoning systems and methods [Wilkins and Ma, 1991, Ma and Wilkins, 1990a]. As our future research, we are to investigate more potential properties of sociopathic systems and possibly develop a general theory of sociopathicity for reasoning under uncertainty.

References

[Buchanan and Shortliffe, 1984] Buchanan, B. G. and Shortliffe, E. H. (1984). *Rule-Based Expert Systems: The MYCIN Experiments of the Stanford Heuristic Programming Project.* Reading, Mass.: Addison-Wesley.

[Duda et al., 1976] Duda, R. O., Hart, P. E., and Nilsson, N. J. (1976). Subjective Bayesian methods for rule-based inference systems. In *1976 National Computer Conference (AFIPS Conference Proceedings)*, volume 45, pages 1075–1082.

[Gordon and Shortliffe, 1985] Gordon, J. and Shortliffe, E. H. (1985). A method for managing evidential reasoning in a hierarchical hypothesis space. *Artificial Intelligence*, 26(3):323–358.

[Ma and Wilkins, 1990a] Ma, Y. and Wilkins, D. C. (1990a). An analysis of Bayesian evidential reasoning. In *Proceedings of the Pacific Rim International Conference on Artificial Intelligence*, pages 772–777, Nagoya, Japan.

[Ma and Wilkins, 1990b] Ma, Y. and Wilkins, D. C. (1990b). Computation of rule probability assignments for Dempster-Shafer theory and the sociopathicity of the theory. In *Proceedings of the Third International Symposium on Artificial Intelligence*, pages 214–219, Monterrey, N.L. Mexico.

[Pearl, 1986a] Pearl, J. (1986a). Fusion, propagation, and structuring in belief networks. *Artificial Intelligence*, 29(3):241–288.

[Pearl, 1986b] Pearl, J. (1986b). On evidential reasoning in a hierarchy of hypotheses. *Artificial Intelligence*, 28(1):9–15.

[Shafer, 1976] Shafer, G. A. (1976). *Mathematical Theory of Evidence.* Princeton: Princeton University Press.

[Wilkins and Buchanan, 1986] Wilkins, D. C. and Buchanan, B. G. (1986). On debugging rule sets when reasoning under uncertainty. In *Proceedings of the AAAI86*, pages 448–454, Philadelphia, PA.

[Wilkins and Ma, 1991] Wilkins, D. C. and Ma, Y. (1991). Sociopathic knowledge bases: correct knowledge can be harmful even given unlimited computation. *Artificial Intelligence.* (Accepted for publication), Also Technical Report: UIUCDCS-R-89-1538, University of Illinois, August, 1989.

[Zadeh, 1979] Zadeh, L. A. (1979). Approximate reasoning based on fuzzy logic. In *Proceedings of the 1979 IJCAI*, pages 1004–1010, Tokyo, Japan.

HIERARCHICAL DEFAULT LOGIC

Craig MacNish

Department of Engineering, University of Cambridge
Trumpington Street, Cambridge CB2 1PZ, U.K.

Abstract

We present a formal framework for ordered default reasoning which has desirable mathematical properties yet is relatively simple and can be implemented using standard theorem provers. By expressing default logic as a relation from theories to extensions we are able to formalise Brewka's prioritized default logic as a composite relation. We also decompose the extension relation by factoring out deductive closure. The resulting *augmentations* can be computed for decidable cases, and provide an extension membership test for composite extensions. Finally we define the equivalent formalism in autoepistemic logic.

1 Introduction

Symbolic descriptions of real-world problems are rarely (if ever) complete. Uncertainty arises from numerous sources such as the limitations of sensors, storage limitations and changes in information over time. In order to reason from such descriptions using logical inference it is necessary to augment the available knowledge with reasonable assumptions.

In this paper we describe a formal approach for augmenting and reasoning from incomplete logical descriptions. We show that Reiter's default logic [11] can be conveniently expressed as a relation from theories to extensions. This allows us to formalise Brewka's prioritized default logic (PDL) [1] as a composite relation. We show further that deductive closure can be factored out of the extension relation. The resulting augmentations can be computed for decidable cases and provide an extension membership test using a standard theorem prover. The test can be extended to the composite case in a straightforward way. Finally we define the equivalent formalism in autoepistemic logic using Konolige's equivalence relation [5].

The account of the formalism given here is necessarily brief. Proofs of the results are contained in [7]. For a more detailed investigation the reader is referred to [6].

2 Reasoning as Theory Transition

In [6] we show that reasoning formalisms can conveniently be represented by a set of transformations from world descriptions to the beliefs they sanction, or from *object descriptions* to *image descriptions*. The set of all such transformation pairs is simply a *relation* from the object space to the image space, called a *transition relation*. In this paper we use as our descriptive language the set L_S of sentences (or closed formulas) of first-order logic. A description or *theory* is thus a subset of L_S, and the object and image spaces are power sets denoted $\wp(L_S)$. It is often convenient to distinguish a class of transition relations which differ only in some set of parameters. We use the notation R_P to denote a relation R taking parameter set P.

A number of characteristic properties are common among reasoning formalisms. The following are of immediate interest.

- We call a relation R a *total relation* if it specifies at least one image for every object theory, otherwise it is called a *partial relation*. Many reasoning formalisms fail to sanction a belief set for some object theories, and are therefore described by partial transition relations. From a practical point of view total relations are preferable since any theory in the object space can be used as a world description.

- A relation R is said to be *branching* if it specifies more than one image for some object theory and *nonbranching* otherwise. A nonbranching relation is a *function* and permits the functional notation $R(\Phi)$ as shorthand for $\{\Psi \mid \langle \Phi, \Psi \rangle \in R\}$. Branching is a common characteristic of reasoning formalisms which deal with incomplete knowledge since there are generally various ways the knowledge can be completed. For most practical applications, however, we wish to avoid branching since ultimately we require specific results on which to base further actions.

- A transition relation is *consistent* (or more accurately *preserves consistency*) if no consistent theory has an inconsistent image. Consistent transition relations are desirable in order to avoid contradictory results.

A transition relation gives unambiguous results for all consistent object theories if it is total, nonbranching and consistent. We call such relations *deterministic*.

- A transition relation is *logically (deductively) closing* if every image theory specified by the relation is logically (deductively) closed. From a practical point of view closing transition relations are undesirable since they expand finite theories into infinite theories. It is therefore not possible to generate the image sets.

Deductive closure can itself be described by a transition function Th_s from $\wp(L_S)$ to $\wp(L_S)$ defined by $Th_s(\Phi) = \{\psi \mid \Phi \vdash_s \psi\}$. A closing relation can thus be formed from any open relation R on $\wp(L_S)$ by the composite relation $Th_s \circ R$.

3 Default Logic

Default logic is a reasoning formalism proposed by Reiter [11] in which theories are expanded using additional inference rules called *defaults*. A default has the form

$$\frac{\alpha : \beta_1, \ldots, \beta_m}{\gamma}$$

(also written $\alpha : \beta_1, \ldots, \beta_m / \gamma$) where the formulas α, $\beta_1 \ldots \beta_m$ and γ are known respectively as the prerequisite, justifications and consequent. For brevity we restrict our discussion to defaults with single justifications. The results can be extended to include multiple justifications in a straightforward way.

A default is *closed* if it contains only closed formulas and *open* otherwise. We will concentrate chiefly on closed defaults. An open default can be treated as a schema for the set of closed defaults which are its substitution instances [5, 11].

Defaults which can be written in the form $\alpha : \beta \wedge \gamma / \gamma$ are called *seminormal defaults* and those which can be written in the form $\alpha : \gamma / \gamma$ are called *normal defaults*. Normal defaults in which the prerequisite is empty are called *free defaults*. CONSEQUENTS(D) refers to the set $\{\gamma \mid (\alpha : \beta / \gamma) \in D\}$.

An *extension* is a set of beliefs sanctioned by the defaults and the object theory. Extensions can be considered to be the images of theories under a transition relation which takes a set of defaults as parameters. The relation can be defined in terms of Reiter's original characterisation [11, Def 1] as follows.

Definition 3.1 Let D be a set of (closed) defaults and L_S be a closed first-order language. The *extension relation* E_D is a relation on $\wp(L_S)$ such that $\langle \Phi, \Psi \rangle \in E_D$ if and only if

$$\Psi = \Gamma \tag{1a}$$

where Γ is a minimal set satisfying

$$\Phi \subseteq \Gamma \tag{1b}$$

$$Th_s(\Gamma) = \Gamma \tag{1c}$$

$$\text{if } (\alpha : \beta / \gamma) \in D,\ \alpha \in \Gamma \text{ and } \neg\beta \notin \Psi \text{ then } \gamma \in \Gamma \tag{1d}$$

Sets Ψ which satisfy conditions (1a)–(1d) for some theory Φ and default set D are called *fixed points*.

The extension relation preserves consistency [11, Cor 2.2]. However it is neither total nor nonbranching since for some object theories and default sets there are no fixed points satisfying (1a)–(1d) while for others there are many. The former problem is often referred to as *incoherence* and the latter referred to as the *multiple extension problem*. The relation is also deductively closing due to condition (1c).

Total relations can be ensured by restricting the parameter set to normal defaults [11, Thm 3.1]. In [8] we propose a method for converting seminormal defaults to normal defaults by switching to a more descriptive language. The branching problem can often be overcome by providing greater flexibility in the application of defaults. A framework which provides this flexibility is described in Section 5. First we consider the remaining problem of deductive closure.

4 Default Logic Without Deductive Closure

Reiter [11, Thm 2.5] shows that any extension can be written as the deductive closure of a set containing only the object theory and the consequents of some of the defaults. The result can be expressed as follows.

Lemma 4.1 Let E_D be defined according to Definition 3.1. If $\langle \Phi, \Psi \rangle \in E_D$ then $\Psi = Th_s(\Theta)$ where

$$\Theta = \Phi \cup \{\gamma \mid (\alpha : \beta / \gamma) \in D,\ \alpha \in \Psi \text{ and } \neg\beta \notin \Psi\}.$$

Lemma 4.1 shows that for finite default sets and object theories, the extensions are finitely axiomatisable. Furthermore, the proper axioms are a subset of $\Phi \cup$ CONSEQUENTS(D).

A more manageable definition of default logic can be provided by considering sets of proper axioms whose deductive closure is an extension; that is, those for which the converse of Lemma 4.1 holds. These sets, which we call *augmentations* of the object theory, are defined as follows.

Definition 4.2 Let D be a set of (closed) defaults. The *augmentation relation* A_D is a relation on $\wp(L_S)$ such that $\langle \Phi, \Theta \rangle \in A_D$ if and only if

$$\Theta = \Phi \cup \{\gamma \mid (\alpha : \beta / \gamma) \in D, \ \Theta \vdash_s \alpha \text{ and } \Theta \nvdash_s \neg\beta\} \tag{2a}$$

and there is no set $\Theta' \subset \Theta$ such that

$$\Theta' = \Phi \cup \{\gamma \mid (\alpha : \beta / \gamma) \in D, \ \Theta' \vdash_s \alpha \text{ and } \Theta \nvdash_s \neg\beta\}. \tag{2b}$$

The following theorem shows that a set of sentences is an extension if and only if it is the deductive closure of an augmentation.

Theorem 4.3 *Let E_D be defined according to Definition 3.1 and A_D be defined according to Definition 4.2. Then $\langle \Phi, \Psi \rangle \in E_D$ if and only if there exists some Θ such that $\langle \Phi, \Theta \rangle \in A_D$ and $\Psi = Th_s(\Theta)$. That is,*

$$E_D = Th_s \circ A_D. \tag{3}$$

Definition 4.2 provides a test for determining whether a set is an augmentation using a standard theorem prover and simple set manipulation. The test is decidable for instance-finite[1] default sets and decidable first-order subclasses. In this case the following algorithm provides an effective procedure for generating the augmentations of a given theory regardless of the form of the defaults.

Algorithm 4.4 Let D be a set of (closed) defaults and $P = \wp(\text{CONSEQUENTS}(D))$. Let $\Phi \subseteq L_S$ and $A = \{\}$.

Step 1 If P is empty then halt. A contains the augmentations of Φ. Otherwise remove the first element Ω from P.

Step 2 Let $\Theta = \Phi \cup \Omega$. If Θ satisfies (2a) then let $P' = \wp(\Omega) \setminus \Omega$ and go to Step 3, otherwise go to Step 1.

Step 3 If P' is empty then replace A by $A \cup \{\Theta\}$ and go to Step 1. Otherwise, remove the first element Ω' from P'.

Step 4 Let $\Theta' = \Phi \cup \Omega'$. If Θ' satisfies (2b) then go to Step 1, otherwise go to Step 3.

Extension membership can be tested for any formula ϕ by constructing the augmentations and checking the consistency of $\neg\phi$ with each augmentation.

From a technical point of view the procedure is an advance on previous algorithms which which have been shown to be decidable for restricted default classes such as normal defaults [11] and network theories [2], although it is impractical for large numbers of defaults. More efficient procedures are considered for free defaults in [6].

---

[1]We call a default set *instance-finite* if it contains a finite number of closed defaults, or if it contains a finite number of defaults and the underlying language contains a finite number of variables, constant symbols, predicate symbols and no function symbols with arity greater than zero. The latter restriction makes the Herbrand Universe finite, ensuring a finite number of closed instances of open defaults [2].

5 Hierarchical Default Logic

Our approach to the branching problem is to decompose transition relations into a set of independent subrelations of the same type but with different parameter sets. The subrelations are then recursively applied to the object theory.

5.1 Recursive Transition Relations

Definition 5.1 Let R be a relation on $\wp(L_S)$ and $P_1, P_2, \ldots$ be parameter sets for R. A *hierarchical parameter set* is a well-founded linearly ordered set $P = \langle \{P_1, P_2, \ldots\}, \preceq \rangle$. Assume the parameter sets are labelled so that $P_i \preceq P_j$ if and only if $i \leq j$. Then the *recursion of R over P*, denoted R_P, is defined by the composite relation

$$R_P = \ldots \circ R_{P_3} \circ R_{P_2} \circ R_{P_1}. \tag{4}$$

In practice we will deal with finite hierarchical parameter sets $P = \langle \{P_1, \ldots, P_n\}, \preceq \rangle$ in which case the recursion relation is defined by $R_P = R_{P_n} \circ \ldots \circ R_{P_1}$.

The decomposition of transition relations reduces the problem of guaranteeing desirable properties for the overall relation to that of ensuring such properties for each of its components. The following lemma can be verified from the properties of relations and simple set theory.

Lemma 5.2 *Let $P = \langle \{P_1, P_2, \ldots\}, \preceq \rangle$ be a hierarchical parameter set for R. Then*

1. *if each R_{P_i} is consistent then R_P is consistent,*
2. *if each R_{P_i} is total then R_P is total, and*
3. *if each R_{P_i} is nonbranching then R_P is nonbranching.*

In particular the hierarchy obtained by separating and ordering parameter sets can be used to arbitrate between competing parameters without separating those which are compatible. This hierarchical separation appears to be appropriate for many applications. An example is given in Section 5.3.

Note that we have not specified any particular way in which the hierarchy should be chosen, thus allowing previously proposed strategies such as shortest paths or inferential distance [13], specifity [10], causal ordering [12] or any other method which is appropriate to the language and application.

5.2 Hierarchical Augmentations and Extensions

Hierarchical default logic (HDL) is the recursive version of default logic, in which the object theory is expanded by recursion of the augmentation or extension relations over a linearly ordered set of default sets. We denote the recursive augmentation and extension relations by A_D and E_D respectively. For finite hierarchical default sets the recursive extension relation E_D corresponds to Brewka's prioritized default logic extensions [1].

Algorithm 4.4 extends to hierarchical augmentations in a straightforward way. The image theories of each augmentation relation become the object theories of its successor. If the original object theory Φ is finite and the hierarchical default set D is instance finite (that is D is finite and all default sets in D are instance-finite) then all the images will be finite and effectively computable for decidable first-order subclasses. The following theorem shows that this procedure also provides an extension membership test for hierarchical extensions.

Theorem 5.3 *Let* $D = \langle\{D_1, D_2, \ldots\}, \preceq\rangle$ *be a hierarchical default set. Then*

$$E_D = Th_s \circ A_D. \tag{5}$$

Once again we can generate the augmentations, in this case recursive, and use a standard theorem prover to test extension membership. Note that proof procedures which test extension membership directly from a finite object theory cannot be applied recursively in the same way since the images of each extension relation are infinite. Thus the extension membership test relies on the use of augmentations.

The following lemmas extend two of Reiter's results on consistency [11, Cor 2.2] and normal defaults [11, Thm 3.1] to recursive augmentations and extensions.

Lemma 5.4 *All recursive augmentations and extensions preserve consistency.*

Lemma 5.5 *If a hierarchical default set* D *is normal (that is each* D *in* D *contains only normal defaults) then* A_D *and* E_D *are total relations on* L_S.

The final requirement for determinism, that the relations are nonbranching, can be trivially achieved by restricting each set of defaults in D to a single default; in effect imposing a total order on the defaults. In many applications however a hierarchical structure is more appropriate and other methods of preventing branching at each step in the recursion need to be sought.

5.3 Example - The Yale Shooting Problem

As a solution to the frame problem in the situation calculus, McCarthy [9] proposed including frame axioms of the form

$$T(f, s) \wedge \neg AB(f, e, s) \rightarrow T(f, result(e, s))$$

and circumscribing over $\neg AB$, thus minimising "abnormal" changes to facts. Hanks and McDermott [3] show by means of an example, commonly called the *Yale shooting problem*, that this proposal can lead to the occurrence of unintuitive or *anomalous* inferences. The problem is not confined to circumscription but applies generally to branching transition relations. It can be illustrated by the theory

$$
\begin{aligned}
\Phi \ = \ \{ & T(\text{LOADED}), S_1), T(\text{ALIVE}, S_2), \\
& T(\text{LOADED}, S_1) \wedge \neg AB(\text{LOADED}, \text{WAIT}, S_1) \rightarrow T(\text{LOADED}, S_2), \\
& T(\text{ALIVE}, S_2) \wedge \neg AB(\text{ALIVE}, \text{SHOOT}, S_2) \rightarrow T(\text{ALIVE}, S_3), \\
& T(\text{LOADED}, S_2) \rightarrow AB(\text{ALIVE}, \text{SHOOT}, S_2), \\
& T(\text{LOADED}, S_2) \rightarrow T(\text{DEAD}, S_3) \}.
\end{aligned}
$$

To minimise abnormality this theory is augmented using the defaults

$$
\begin{aligned}
D \ = \ \{ & : \neg AB(\text{LOADED}, \text{WAIT}, S_1) \,/\, \neg AB(\text{LOADED}, \text{WAIT}, S_1), \\
& : \neg AB(\text{ALIVE}, \text{SHOOT}, S_2) \,/\, \neg AB(\text{ALIVE}, \text{SHOOT}, S_2) \}.
\end{aligned}
$$

The theory has two augmentations. The intuitively correct augmentation includes $\neg AB(LOADED, WAIT, S_1)$ and entails $T(DEAD, S_3)$; that is, the victim dies as expected. The anomalous augmentation includes $\neg AB(ALIVE, SHOOT, S_2)$ and entails $T(ALIVE, S_3)$; that is, the gun becomes mysteriously unloaded and the victim survives.

This problem can be avoided using HDL by choosing the default hierarchy so that normality assumptions are made in chronological (or causal) order. In other words, we make the sequence of default sets correspond to the sequence of states. In this case the appropriate hierarchy is given by $D = \langle \{D_1, D_2\}, \preceq \rangle$, $D_1 \preceq D_2$ where

$$D_1 = \{ : \neg AB(LOADED, WAIT, S_1) / \neg AB(LOADED, WAIT, S_1) \}, \text{ and}$$
$$D_2 = \{ : \neg AB(ALIVE, SHOOT, S_2) / \neg AB(ALIVE, SHOOT, S_2) \}.$$

It is easily verified that Φ has a single augmentation under A_D which provides the intuitively correct solution.

Of course, this scheme on its own is not sufficient to guarantee a unique solution when there is more than one normality assumption for each state. However it reduces the problem to that of ensuring a unique augmentation based on the assumptions in each state. One way to achieve this is to impose further restrictions on allowable sentences in the style of Shoham's causal theories [12]. This approach is considered further in [6].

6 An Equivalent Autoepistemic Formalism

Konolige [5] has established an equivalence between default theory extensions and strongly grounded autoepistemic (AE) extensions. The equivalence result can be expressed in terms of transition relations as follows.

Definition 6.1 Let D be a set of defaults. Then the *autoepistemic transformation* on $\mathcal{P}(L_S)$, denoted AE_D, is defined by

$$AE_D^{\cdot} : \Phi \mapsto \Phi \cup \{(L\alpha \wedge \neg L\neg\beta) \rightarrow \gamma \mid (\alpha : \beta / \gamma) \in D\}. \tag{6}$$

The *kernel* of an AE theory Φ, denoted $KRN(\Phi)$, is the set of ordinary sentences appearing in Φ.

Theorem 6.2 [5, Thm 5.5] *Let E_{sg} denote the strongly grounded extension relation [6]. Then*

$$E_D = KRN \circ E_{sg} \circ AE_D \tag{7}$$

The AE relation corresponding to the recursive extension relation is therefore defined as follows.

Corollary 6.3 *Let D be a hierarchical default set. Then*

$$E_D = \ldots \circ KRN \circ E_{sg} \circ AE_{D_2} \circ KRN \circ E_{sg} \circ AE_{D_1} \tag{8}$$

The resulting extensions differ markedly from the extensions of Konolige's *hierarchic autoepistemic theories* [4]. In the latter case the problems of partial and branching relations associated with autoepistemic *stable sets* are avoided by applying belief operators only to subtheories lower in the hierarchy. This alters the nature of the operators and sacrifices consistency preservation.

7 Conclusion

Hierarchical default logic provides a viable approach for reasoning from incomplete logical descriptions. The formalism preserves consistency, is total for normal defaults, and provides a framework for overcoming the branching problem which is compatible with many previously proposed solutions. The formalism can be implemented using standard theorem provers and is decidable providing the underlying language is decidable and the default set is instance-finite.

Acknowledgements

This work is supported by the Prince of Wales Studentship from Trinity College, Cambridge. I would also like to thank Frank Fallside, my supervisor, for valuable advice and Raj Goré for interesting discussions.

References

[1] Brewka, G. Preferred Subtheories: An Extended Logical Framework for Default Reasoning. In *Proc. IJCAI-89*, pp. 1043–1048, Detroit, USA, 1989.

[2] Etherington, D. W. Formalizing Nonmonotonic Reasoning Systems. *Artificial Intelligence*, **31** pp. 41–85, 1987.

[3] Hanks, S. and McDermott, D. Default Reasoning, Nonmonotonic Logics, and the Frame Problem. In *Proc. AAAI-86*, pp. 328–333, Philadelphia, USA, 1986.

[4] Konolige, K. Hierarchic Autoepistemic Theories for Nonmonotonic Reasoning. In *Proc. AAAI-88*, pp. 439–443, Saint Paul, USA, 1988.

[5] Konolige, K. On the Relation Between Default Theories and Autoepistemic Logic. *Artificial Intelligence*, **35** pp. 343–382, 1988.

[6] MacNish, C. PhD thesis, Department of Engineering, Cambridge, UK, 1991. In preparation.

[7] MacNish, C. Hierarchical Default Logic (Extended Version). Technical Report CUED/F-INFENG/TR.52, Cambridge University Engineering Department, 1991.

[8] MacNish, C. Well-behaved Reasoning with Seminormal Defaults. In *Proc. 4th International Symposium on AI*, Cancún, Mexico, November 1991. To appear.

[9] McCarthy, J. Applications of Circumscription to Formalising Common-Sense Knowledge. *Artificial Intelligence*, **28** pp. 89–116, 1986.

[10] Poole, D. L. On the Comparison of Theories: Preferring the Most Specific Explanation. In *Proc. IJCAI-85*, pp. 144–147, Los Angeles, CA, 1985.

[11] Reiter, R. A Logic for Default Reasoning. *Artificial Intelligence*, **13** pp. 81–132, 1980.

[12] Shoham, Y. Chronological Ignorance: Experiments in Nonmonotonic Temporal Reasoning. *Artificial Intelligence*, **36** pp. 279–331, 1988.

[13] Touretzky, D. S., Horty, J. F. and Thomason, R. H. A Clash of Intuitions: The Current State of Nonmonotonic Multiple Inheritance Systems. In *Proc. IJCAI-87*, pp. 476–482, Milan, Italy, 1987.

A LOGIC OF IMPRECISE MONADIC PREDICATES AND ITS RELATION TO THE S5-MODAL FUZZY LOGIC

Akira Nakamura
Department of Computer Science, Meiji University
1-1-1, Higashimita, Tama-ku, Kawasaki 214
Japan

1. Introduction

In recent years a variety of formalisms have been developed which address several aspects of handling imperfect knowledge like uncertainty, vagueness, imprecision, incompleteness, and partial inconsistency. For example, see [2],[3],[5]. Along this line, we consider here a logic of imprecise monadic predicates.

In [1], J.P. Cleave proposed the logic of inexact predicates, which is associated to the three-valued logic. The proposed logic in this paper is considered as a generalization of Cleave's inexact predicate logic to the fuzzy case. Also, although Cleave discussed not only monadic predicates but n-ary ones, we treat here the monadic predicates only. And we present a deductive system by making use of the notion of logical consequence used in [1]. Further, we show relations between this logic and the *S5-modal fuzzy logic* presented in our previous paper [3]. This is a similar relation to that between the classical monadic predicate logic and the S5 modal logic.

We shall develop this logic in not only theoretical advances but in practical applications to automated reasoning. That is, we give a formal system from the point of view of tableau method.

2. Imprecise structures

We shall define the formal language L of the logic of imprecise monadic predicates in the usual way. L consists of (i) monadic predicate letters $p_1,p_2,...$, (ii) logical symbols $\lor$, $\land$, $\neg$, (iii) quantifiers $\forall$, $\exists$. Notice that L does not contain the implication $\supset$.

By an *imprecise structure* we mean a structure $S = \langle D, \alpha, v \rangle$ as follows:

(1)   D is a non-empty domain.

(2)   An assignment α is a function for the free individual variables with values in D and for predicate symbols with fuzzy sets in D.

(3.1) Let p_i be a predicate symbol and a_j be a free individual variable, then

$$v(p_i(a_j),\alpha) = \mu_{\alpha(p_i)}(\alpha(a_j)) \in [0,1] .$$

That is, v means a function which gives a membership degree of an individual $\alpha(a_j)$ in a fuzzy set $\alpha(p_i)$.

(3.2) Let A, B be wff's in L,

    (i) $v(A \vee B, \alpha) = max(v(A,\alpha), v(B,\alpha))$,

    (ii) $v(A \wedge B, \alpha) = min(v(A,\alpha), v(B,\alpha))$,

    (iii) $v(\neg A, \alpha) = 1 - v(A, \alpha)$.

(3.3) Let $\forall x A(x)$ and $\exists x A(x)$ be wff's in L,

    (iv) $v(\forall x A(x), \alpha) = \underset{\alpha(x) \in D}{inf} \{v(A(x), \alpha)\}$,

    where $\underset{\alpha(x) \in D}{inf}$ means the infimum of $v(A(x), \alpha)$ when indidiual $\alpha(x)$ runs over

    all of D,

    (v) $v(\exists x A(x), \alpha) = \underset{\alpha(x) \in D}{sup} \{v(A(x), \alpha)\}$,

    where $\underset{\alpha(x) \in D}{sup}$ means the same to that of (iv).

When a structure S is given, a fuzzy value (denoted by S(A)) of a wff A by S is determined. It will be noticed here that the logic of imprecise monadic predicate has no tautologies, namely, wff's which are always true (the fuzzy value 1) in all structures. This, however, is no obstacle to constructing a deductive system by making use of the notion of logical consequence. This notion has been originally introduced in [1]. To this end, we use a meta-symbol $\rightarrow$ between wff's A and B. And we consider an expression $A \rightarrow B$. Then, B is called a *logical consequence* of A iff $S(A) \leq S(B)$ for all structures S. When B is a logical consequence of A, we use the notation $\models A \rightarrow B$.

3. Deductive system

We consider a deductive system **Q** for our logic. We use the notion of logical consequence mentioned in the Section 2 and construct it in a *Gentzen style*.

By a *sequent* we mean an expression of the form $\Gamma \rightarrow \Delta$, where Γ, Δ are sequences of wff's. Usually Γ, Δ are finite but it allows the possibility of being infinite. The sequent $\Gamma \rightarrow \Delta$ is *valid* if for all structure S $min\{S(A): A \in \Gamma\} \leq max\{S(B): B \in \Delta\}$. If $\Gamma = \{A_1,...,A_n\}$ and $\Delta = \{B_1,...,B_m\}$ then $\Gamma \rightarrow \Delta$ is valid iff $B_1 \vee ... \vee B_m$ is a logical consequence of $A_1 \wedge ... \wedge A_n$.

Let p, q are arbitrary predicate symbols and a,b,c are arbitrary free individual variables. Also, let Γ, Δ, and Θ be finite sequences of zero or more wff's. Then, the *axioms* and *rules of inferences* of **Q** are defined as follows:

<u>Definition A</u>   The axioms of **Q** are all finite sequents $\Gamma \rightarrow \Delta$ satisfying either

(A1) there exist atomic formulas p(a), q(b) such that

$$p(a) \in \Gamma, \neg\, p(a) \in \Gamma \quad \text{and} \quad q(b) \in \Delta, \neg\, q(b) \in \Delta,$$

(A2) there exists an atomic formula p(c) such that

$$p(c) \in \Gamma, \; p(c) \in \Delta \quad \text{or} \quad \neg\, p(c) \in \Gamma, \; \neg\, p(c) \in \Delta.$$

<u>Definition R</u>   The rules of inferences of Q are:

(R1)

(∨→)

$$\frac{\Gamma,\, A(a),\, \Delta \rightarrow \Theta; \quad \Gamma,\, B(b),\, \Delta \rightarrow \Theta}{\Gamma,\, A(a) \vee B(b),\, \Delta \rightarrow \Theta}$$

(→∨)

$$\frac{\Theta \rightarrow \Gamma,\, A(a),\, B(b),\, \Delta}{\Theta \rightarrow \Gamma,\, A(a) \vee B(b),\, \Delta}$$

(∧→)

$$\frac{\Gamma,\, A(a),\, B(b),\, \Delta \rightarrow \Theta}{\Gamma,\, A(a) \wedge B(b),\, \Delta \rightarrow \Theta}$$

(→∧)

$$\frac{\Theta \rightarrow \Gamma,\, A(a),\, \Delta \;; \quad \Theta \rightarrow \Gamma,\, B(b),\, \Delta}{\Theta \rightarrow \Gamma,\, A(a) \wedge B(b),\, \Delta}$$

(¬→)

$$\frac{\Gamma,\, A(a),\, \Delta \rightarrow \Theta}{\Gamma,\, \neg\neg A(a),\, \Delta \rightarrow \Theta}$$

(→¬)

$$\frac{\Theta \rightarrow \Gamma,\, A(a),\, \Delta}{\Theta \rightarrow \Gamma,\, \neg\neg A(a),\, \Delta}$$

(∃→)

$$\frac{\Gamma,\, A(a),\, \Delta \rightarrow \Theta}{\rule{0pt}{0pt}}$$

$$\Gamma, \exists x A(x), \Delta \to \Theta$$

, where the free individual variable a does not occur in the conclusion

$$(\to\exists) \qquad \frac{\Theta \to \Gamma, \exists x A(x), \Delta, A(a)}{\Theta \to \Gamma, \exists x A(x), \Delta}$$

$$(\forall\to) \qquad \frac{\Gamma, \forall x A(x), \Delta, A(a) \to \Theta}{\Gamma, \forall x A(x), \Delta \to \Theta}$$

$$(\to\forall) \qquad \frac{\Theta \to \Gamma, A(a), \Delta}{\Theta \to \Gamma, \forall x A(x), \Delta}$$

, where the free individual variable a does not occur in the conclusion.

(R2)

Let Γ and Δ be sequences of wff's. $\neg(A \wedge B)$, $\neg(A \vee B)$, $\neg \forall x A(x)$, $\neg \exists x B(x)$ which appear in Γ or Δ are replaced by $\neg A \vee \neg B$, $\neg A \wedge \neg B$, $\exists x \neg A(x)$, $\forall x \neg B(x)$, respectively and vice versa.

In the above rules, Γ, Δ, Θ were sequences of wff's. But, we stipulate that the order of occurrence of wff's in a sequence is ignored. So, exactly say, they are the sets of wff's which are put in a row. And so, we use the *meta-rules* based on this stipulation such as

$$\frac{\Gamma \to \Delta}{\Gamma, A \to \Delta} \qquad\qquad \frac{\Gamma \to \Delta}{\Gamma \to \Delta, A}$$

$$\frac{\Gamma, A, B, \Delta \to \Theta}{\Gamma, B, A, \Delta \to \Theta} \qquad\qquad \frac{\Theta \to \Gamma, A, B, \Delta}{\Theta \to \Gamma, B, A, \Delta} \quad .$$

When a sequent $A \to B$ is obtained from the axioms by repeated applications of rules in R and the meta-rules, this sequent $A \to B$ is called *provable* and it is denoted by $\vdash A \to B$.

We show that the deductive system Q is sound and complete. That is, for arbitrary wff's A, B $\models A \rightarrow B$ iff $\vdash A \rightarrow B$. It is noticed here that the above inference rules are considered as the *rules of tableau method* if they are used in the reverse direction.

4. Soundness and completeness

In this section, we show the soundness and completeness of Q.

<u>Theorem 4.1</u> (the soundness)   For arbitrary wff's A, B if $\vdash A \rightarrow B$ then $\models A \rightarrow B$.

Proof

(1) We easily know from the definition that the axioms are valid.

(2) Also, it is shown that the validity is preserved in the rules. Here, we prove it for the rule

$(\rightarrow\wedge)$ and $(\exists\rightarrow)$.   For other rules, it is shown similarly.

$(\rightarrow\wedge)$:

Let us assume that both $\Theta \rightarrow \Gamma, A(a), \Delta$ and $\Theta \rightarrow \Gamma, B(b), \Delta$ are valid, Then, for every structure S we have the following inequalities $\min\{S(W): W \in \Theta\} \leq \max\{S(U): U \in \Gamma \cup \{A(a)\} \cup \Delta\}$ and $\min\{S(W): W \in \Theta\} \leq \max\{S(U): U \in \Gamma \cup \{A(b)\} \cup \Delta\}$. Therefore, for every structure S we have $\min\{S(W): W \in \Theta\} \leq \max\{S(U): U \in \Gamma \cup \{A(a)\wedge B(b)\} \cup \Delta\}$.

$(\exists\rightarrow)$:

Let us assume that $\Gamma, \exists x A(x), \Delta \rightarrow \Theta$ is not valid. Then, there is a structure S such that $\min\{S(W): W \in \Gamma \cup \{\exists x A(x)\} \cup \Delta\} > \max\{S(U): U \in \Theta\}$.

Let c be an individual variable which satisfies $v(\exists x A(x),\alpha) = v(A(c), \alpha)$ in this structure S. Then, we have the structure S such that $\min\{S(W): W \in \Gamma \cup \{A(c) \cup \Delta\} > \max\{S(U): U \in \Theta\}$. By making use of this S, we define S' as follows: The free individual variable a does not occur in the conclusion. So, we can construct a structure S' in which every v' and α' are the same to those of S except that $\alpha'(a)=\alpha(c)$. Thus, we get $\min\{S'(W): W \in \Gamma \cup \{A(a)\} \cup \Delta\} > \max\{S'(U): U \in \Theta\}$.

Therefore, we know that $\min\{S(W): W \in \Gamma \cup \{A(a)\} \cup \Delta\} > \max\{S(U): U \in \Theta\}$ follows from $\min\{S(W): W \in \Gamma \cup \{\exists x A(x)\} \cup \Delta\} > \max\{S(U): U \in \Theta\}$.

Thus, we have this case.

From the similar facts on the other rules, we get this theorem.   //

Now, we prove the completeness. The inference rules can be written in the following form:

$$\frac{A}{C} \qquad\qquad \frac{A \;;\; B}{C}$$

Then, we give the following lemma:

Lemma 4.2   Let A, B (possibly A only) be the premise and C be the conclusion of an inference rule, respectively.   For every inference rule, A and B (possibly A only) are valid iff C is valid.

Proof

We have already proved ' only if ' part in Theorem 4.1 .   Hence, we prove ' if ' part.

We prove it for the rule $(\rightarrow\wedge)$ and $(\exists\rightarrow)$.   For other rules, it is shown similarly.

$(\rightarrow\wedge)$:

Assume that $\Theta \rightarrow \Gamma$, $A(a)\wedge B(b)$, Δ is valid.   Then, for every structure S $\min\{S(W): W \in \Theta\} \leq \max\{S(W): W \in \Gamma \cup\{A(a)\wedge B(b)\}\cup\Delta\}$.   Thus, we have: $\min\{S(W): W \in \Theta\} \leq \max\{S(W): W \in \Gamma \cup\{A(a)\}\cup\Delta\}$ and $\min\{S(W): W \in \Theta\} \leq \max\{S(W) : W \in \Gamma \cup\{A(b)\}\cup\Delta\}$.   Therefore, we know that $\Theta \rightarrow \Gamma$, $A(a)$, Δ and $\Theta \rightarrow \Gamma$, $B(b)$, Δ are valid.

$(\exists\rightarrow)$:

Assume that Γ, $\exists x A(x)$, $\Delta \rightarrow \Theta$ is valid.   Generally, $A(a) \rightarrow \exists x A(x)$ is valid from the definition.   Thus, if Γ, $\exists x A(x)$, $\Delta \rightarrow \Theta$ is valid then Γ, $A(a)$, $\Delta \rightarrow \Theta$ is valid.

Therefore, we have the case for $(\exists\rightarrow)$.   And we have this lemma.   //

Theorem 4.3 (the completeness) For arbitrary wff's A, B if $\models A \rightarrow B$ then $\vdash A \rightarrow B$.

Proof

Let us assume that $\models A \rightarrow B$. By (R2), it is sufficient to show for a sequent in which $\neg$ is placed just before atomic formulas. We consider the reverse applications of the Rule (R1), i.e., by starting from $A \rightarrow B$ we go upward by reverse applications of the Rules. Then, we can construct a tree whose *root* is occupied by $A \rightarrow B$. Here, notice that this tree is eventually ended. The reason is as follows: We are considering monadic predicates only, so the number of permutations of the ordering ($\leq$) of their fuzzy values is finite, so it is sufficient to consider (finite) individuals corresponding to their permutations. In this time, every *leaf* of this tree must contain the sequent $\Gamma \rightarrow \Delta$ satisfying (A1) or (A2). If not so, it is known from Lemma 4.2 that $A \rightarrow B$ is not valid. Hence, if $\models A \rightarrow B$ then we can construct a proof tree of $A \rightarrow B$ by starting their leaves.

Therefore, we get this theorem.   //

The procedure in the proof of Theorem 4.3 gives a solution of the decision problem of this logic. It is mentioned here that the technique is strongly related to automated reasoning.

5. Relations to the S5-modal fuzzy logic

The proposed logic in this paper is an extension of the classical monadic predicate logic to the fuzzy case. And it is well-known that the classical monadic predicate logic is strongly related to the S5-modal logic. That is, it is possible to interpret the modal operations M, N as the quantifiers $\exists$, $\forall$, respectively. We have the similar relation between the imprecise monadic predicate logic and the S5-modal fuzzy logic. Here, the S5-modal fuzzy logic is that introduced in [3] and is defined as follows:

Fuzzy sets are defined in the usual way by their membership functions μ. For fuzzy sets S and T, $S \cap T$, $S \cup T$, $\bar{S}$ are also defined in the usual way. Further, a similarity relation R in X is a fuzzy relation in X which satisfies:

(a) reflexive: $\mu_R(x,x)=1$ for all x in dom R,

(b) symmetric: $\mu_R(x,y)=\mu_R(y,x)$, for all x,y in Dom R,

(c) transitive: $\mu_R(x,z) \geq \bigvee_y (\mu_R(x,y) \wedge \mu_R(y,z))$ for all x,y,z in Dom R.

By making use of fuzzy sets and the similarity relation R, we define a function μ° over [0,1] $\times$ X.

$$\mu^\circ_{S \cap T}(\tau, x)=\min(\mu_S(\tau, x), \mu_T(\tau, x)),$$

$$\mu^\circ_{S \cup T}(\tau, x)=\max(\mu_S(\tau, x), \mu_T(\tau, x)),$$

$$\mu^\circ_{\bar{S}}(\tau, x)=1-\mu^\circ_S(\tau, x),$$

$$\mu^\circ_{R^*(S)}(\tau, x)= \sup_{\mu^\circ_R(x,x') \geq \tau} \mu^\circ_S(\tau, x'),$$

$$\mu^\circ_{R_*(S)}(\tau, x)= \inf_{\mu^\circ_R(x,x') \geq \tau} \mu^\circ_S(\tau, x'),$$

, where $\mu^\circ_S(\tau, x)=\mu_S(x)$ if S does not contain R^* or R_* .

Then, the S5-modal fuzzy logic means the following system:

Consider three classes of symbols: propositional variables P,Q,..., propositional operators $\neg$, $\vee$, $\wedge$, and modal operators $\bar{R}$, $\underline{R}$. The set of well-formed formulas is defined in the usual way. Further, semantics of this logic is defined as follows: First, by a model we mean a system M(OB,[0,1],R, μ,v) where OB is a non-empty set of objects, R is the similarity relation on OB, μ is a membership function such that for o$\in$ OB and a fuzzy set A in OB, $\mu_A(o) \in$ [0,1], v is a valuation function such that for propositional variable P, v(P) is a fuzzy set in OB, and

$$v(\neg F)=\overline{v(F)}, \quad v(F \vee G)=v(F) \cup v(G), \quad v(F \wedge G)=v(F) \cap v(G), \quad v(\underline{R}F)=R_* v(F), \quad v(\bar{R}F)=R^*(v(F)).$$

For two wff's F and G , we say $F \leq G$ iff $\overset{\circ}{\mu}v(F)(\tau, x) \leq \overset{\circ}{\mu}v(G)(\tau, x)$ for every model and every τ.

Then, in [3] the following equalities and inequalities were proved:

$$\underline{R}(F \vee G) \geq \underline{R}(F) \vee \underline{R}(G), \qquad \overline{R}(F \vee G) = \overline{R}(F) \vee \overline{R}(G),$$

$$\underline{R}(F \wedge G) = \underline{R}(F) \wedge \underline{R}(G), \qquad \overline{R}(F \wedge G) \leq \overline{R}(F) \wedge \overline{R}(G),$$

$$\underline{R}(F \vee \underline{R}(G)) = \underline{R}(F) \vee \underline{R}(G), \qquad \overline{R}(F \wedge \overline{R}(G)) = \overline{R}(F) \wedge \overline{R}(G),$$

$$\underline{R}(F \vee \overline{R}(G)) = \underline{R}(F) \vee \overline{R}(G), \qquad \overline{R}(F \wedge \underline{R}(G)) = \overline{R}(F) \wedge \underline{R}(G),$$

From the above-mentioned formulas, it is known that the modal operations $\overline{R}$, $\underline{R}$ can be interpreted as the quantifies $\exists$, $\forall$, respectively. Let $A^{\#}$ be a wff of Q which is obtained from a wff of the S5-fuzzy modal logic by the correspondence of $\exists x, \forall x$ to $\overline{R}$, $\underline{R}$, respectively. Then, it is known that $A^{\#} \rightarrow B^{\#}$ is valid in Q iff $A \rightarrow B$ is valid in the S5-fuzzy modal logic. This can be shown by making use of the following facts:

(1) The modal operations of S5-modal fuzzy logic are interpreted as those of the usual S5 modal logic by taking 0 as a level value for fuzzy relations.

(2) The above value 0 does not violate the discussion of deductive system.

6. Remark

From a point of view of automated reasoning, the decision procedure of the proposed imprecise monadic predicate logic seems to be useful in various applications. Thus, it is hoped that practical techniques of the above-mentioned tableau method are developed.

References

[1] J.P. Cleave: The notion of logical consequence in the logic of inexact predicate, *Zeitschr. f. math. Logik und Grundlagen d. Math.*, 20, (1974), 307-324.

[2] L. Farinas del Cerro and H. Prade: Rough sets, twofold fuzzy sets and modal logic. Fuzziness in indiscernibility and partial information, in: A. Di Nola and A.G.S. Ventre (ed.), **The Mathematics of Fuzzy Systems**, Verlag TÜV Rheinland, Köln, (1986), 103-120.

[3] A. Nakamura and J-M. Gao: A logic for fuzzy data analysis, *Fuzzy Sets and Systems*, 39, (1991), 127-132.

[4] A. Nakamura: Topological soft algebra for the S5-modal fuzzy logic, *Proc. of the 21th Intern. Symp. on Multiple-Valued Logic*, (1991), 80-84.

[5] P. Smets, E.H. Mamdani, D. Dubois and H. Prade (ed.): **Non-Standard Logics for Automated Reasoning**, Academic Press, New York, (1988).

EVERY COMPLEX SYSTEM CAN BE DETERMINED BY A CAUSAL PROBABILISTIC NETWORK WITHOUT CYCLES AND EVERY SUCH NETWORK DETERMINES A MARKOV FIELD

Ulrich G. Oppel

Mathematisches Institut der Ludwig-Maximilians-Universität
Theresienstr. 39, D 8000 München 2, Fed. Rep. Germany

Key words: Causal probabilistic network, belief net, directed Markov field, expert system, convergence of causal probabilistic networks, sensitivity analysis of causal probabilistic networks; HUGIN.

Complex technical, biological, economical, and psychological systems consist of a finite (or at most countably infinite) number of components. Such a system V and its components are subject to randomness, uncertainty, imprecision, incompleteness, and vagueness due to the variability between and within its components. The components v of such a system may be characterized by qualitative or quantitative random variables X_v assuming their values in rather general state spaces S_v with σ-algebras $\mathfrak{S}_v$.

From the probabilistic point of view the qualitative and quantitative aspects of the total system are completely determined by the common distribution of the random variables representing its components. Dependent on the time this common distribution may vary continuously or step by step. The system may change by itself or by influences from outside. For example, an expert system may learn by the input of new evidence; the learning may be done by the updating of rules, assumptions or conclusions. At a given time the common distribution is a probability measure $\mathbb{P}: \mathfrak{S} \to [0,1]$ on the product σ-algebra $\mathfrak{S}$ on the product state space S belonging to the family $((S_v, \mathfrak{S}_v): v \in V)$ of state spaces. The system is completely determined by the probability space $(S, \mathfrak{S}, \mathbb{P})$. However, to find $\mathbb{P}$ is often very difficult; usually $\mathbb{P}$ can be determined at most only approximately by theoretical or statistical procedures.

One way of finding $\mathbb{P}$ is to calcuate the empirical distribution from properly collected data. Theorems of the Glivenko-Cantelli type will ensure (weak) convergence of the empirical distributions towards $\mathbb{P}$. Such a procedure may be adequate for multisensor systems which collect lots of data automatically.

Another way of finding $\mathbb{P}$ is to use a causal probabilistic network (CPN); e.g. see Pearl [8] or Lauritzen-Spiegelhalter [5]. Such a CPN is a directed graph $G := (V, E)$ with $E \subset V \times V$ and $(u,v) \notin E$ for $(v,u) \in E$ and a family $\mathcal{P} := (\mathcal{P}_v: v \in V)$ of Markov kernels

$$\mathcal{P}_v: S(Pa(v)) \times \mathfrak{S}_v \to [0,1] \quad \text{with} \quad ((x_u: u \in Pa(v), B) \to \mathcal{P}_v((x_u: u \in Pa(v); B)$$

where $Pa(v) := \{u \in V: (u,v) \in E\}$ is the set of the parents of v in G, $S(U) := \prod_{u \in U} S_u$ for $U \subset V$ is the product of the state spaces of the family $(X_u: u \in U)$ of random variables, and $S(\emptyset) \times \mathfrak{S}_v := \mathfrak{S}_v$. Every node $v \in V$ represents the random variable X_v with the state space $(S_v, \mathfrak{S}_v)$, E describes the dependency of $(X_v: v \in V)$ qualitatively, and $\mathcal{P}$ describes this dependency quantitatively. $\mathcal{P}_v$ is (or is supposed to be) the conditional distribution of X_v given $(X_u: u \in Pa(v))$. Associating a CPN to $\mathbb{P}$ is a localization procedure which reduces the problem of finding the high dimensional distribution $\mathbb{P}$ to finding the family $\mathcal{P}$ of lower dimensional conditional distributions.

First, we shall show that for any CPN without cycles there exists a probability measure $\mathbb{P}$ which is the common distribution of the random variables X_v represented by the nodes $v \in V$, which has the given Markov kernels $\mathcal{P}_v$ as conditional distributions of X_v given the values of the random variables associated to the parent nodes of v, and which is a directed Markov field. This will be done by iterative integration.

Second, we shall show under mild assumptions on the state spaces that there are n! possibly different CPN's without cycles associated with $\mathbb{P}$, if V has n elements. This will be done by iterative desintegration (conditioning).

Hence, the difficult problem of finding the probability measure $\mathbb{P}$ characterizing the total system is mathematically equivalent to the problem of finding such a CPN with the directed graph $G := (V, E)$ without cycles and the Markov kernels $(\mathcal{P}_v: v \in V)$. However, in many applications it seems to be possible (or at least easier) to find and to quantify dependency relations between the components of the system by using theoretical, intuitiv or statistical expert knowledge.

Also the best experts will not know these dependency relations between the components of the system exactly, but only approximately. Therefore it is necessary to examine continuity properties of the above mentioned construction procedures. To achieve this goal properly chosen topological concepts have to be and will be introduced.

To get a feeling about the kind and the speed of the variation of the total system dependent on the variation of the Markov kernels (which represent the expert knowledge about the system), because of the possible complexity of the system it is necessary to observe the variation of the distribution of random variables for selected groups of random variables.

In practice such a sensitivity analysis can be done only with the help of properly designed programs. For a causal probabilistic network constructed using the HUGIN software package such a program will be demonstrated. This program is based on the application program interface of the HUGIN software package and the results are displayed graphically to visualize the sensitivity of the causal probabilistic network towards changes of expert knowledge.

Given any causal probabilistic network $G := (V, E)$ with Markov kernels $(\mathcal{P}_v: v \in V)$

without cycles it is possible to find an enumeration $V := \{v_i: i = 0, \ldots, n\}$ of V such that no descendant is enumerated before any of his ancestors; such an enumeration is a well ordering in the sense of Lauritzen-Dawid-Larsen-Leimer [4]. Let $S^{(i)} :=$ $S(\{v_j: j = 0, \ldots, i\})$ be the product set and $\mathfrak{S}^{(i)} := \overset{i}{\underset{j=0}{\bigotimes}} \mathfrak{S}_{v_j}$ be the product σ-algebra for $0 \leq i \leq n$. Defining Markov kernels

$$P_i: \; S^{(i-1)} \times \mathfrak{S}_{v_i} \to [0,1] \quad \text{for } i = 0, \ldots, n \quad \text{by}$$

$$((x_0, \ldots, x_{i-1}), B) \to P_i(x_0, \ldots, x_{i-1}; B) := \mathcal{P}_{v_i}((x_u: u \in Pa(v_i)); B)$$

we may construct a probability measure $\mathbb{P}: \mathfrak{S} \to [0,1]$ by iterative integration:

$(*)$ $\mathbb{P}(A) := \underset{X_0}{\int} \; \underset{X_1}{\int} \cdots \underset{X_n}{\int} 1_A(x_0, \ldots, x_n) \, P_{n-1}(x_0, \ldots, x_{n-1}; dx_n) \cdots P_1(x_0; dx_1) \, P_0(dx_0)$

for $A \in \mathfrak{S} = \mathfrak{S}^{(n)}$.

$\mathbb{P}$ does not depend on the chosen enumeration of this kind; see Oppel [7]. Also for countably infinite nets such a construction is possible using Ionescu-Tulcea's theorem instead of Fubini's theorem; e.g. see Ash [1] or Neveu [6]. There is no need of transformation (triangulization, forming trees of cliques etc.) of the given causal probabilistic network! In the case of finite and discrete state spaces S_v this probability measure $\mathbb{P}$ is identical to the ones constructed using the procedures proposed by Pearl [8], Lauritzen-Spiegelhalter [5] and Jensen-Lauritzen-Oleson [3] and the procedures implemented in the software package HUGIN for the construction of expert systems based on causal probabilistic networks.

For $0 \leq k \leq i \leq n$ and $\emptyset \neq U \subset V$ let $\pi_i: S \to S^{(i)}$, $\pi_{i,k}: S^{(i)} \to S^{(k)}$, and $\pi_U: S \to S(U)$ be the canonical projections. Let $\mathbb{P}(C \mid \pi_U)$ denote the conditional expectation of the indicator function 1_C of $C \in \mathfrak{S}$ given π_U with respect to the probability measure $\mathbb{P}$. For $\mathbb{P}$ with $(*)$ we get:

$$\mathbb{P}(C \mid \pi_{i-1}) = \underset{S_{v_i}}{\int} \cdots \underset{S_{v_n}}{\int} 1_C \; P_n(\pi_{n-1}(.); dx_n) \cdots P_i(\pi_{i-1}(.); dx_i)$$

For $0 \leq i \leq n$, $A \in \mathfrak{S}_{v_i}$, and $B \in \mathfrak{S}_U$ with $U := \{j: 0 \leq j \leq i-1 \text{ and } v_j \notin Pa(v_i)\}$ we get:

$\mathbb{P}(\pi_U^{-1}(B) \cap \pi_{\{v_i\}}^{-1}(A) \mid \pi_{Pa(v_i)}) = \mathbb{P}(\mathbb{P}(\pi_U^{-1}(B) \cap \pi_{\{v_i\}}^{-1}(A) \mid \pi_{i-1}) \mid \pi_{Pa(v_i)}) =$

$= \mathbb{P}(1_B \circ \pi_U \; \mathbb{P}(\pi_{\{v_i\}}^{-1}(A) \mid \pi_{i-1}) \mid \pi_{Pa(v_i)}) = \mathbb{P}(1_B \circ \pi_U \; P_i(\pi_{i-1}(.); A) \mid \pi_{Pa(v_i)}) =$

$= \mathbb{P}(1_B \circ \pi_U \; \mathcal{P}_{v_i}(\pi_{Pa(v_i)}(.); A) \mid \pi_{Pa(v_i)}) = \mathbb{P}(1_B \circ \pi_U \; \mathbb{P}(1_A \circ \pi_{\{v_i\}} \mid \pi_{Pa(v_i)}) \mid \pi_{Pa(v_i)}) =$

$= \mathbb{P}(1_B \circ \pi_U \mid \pi_{Pa(v_i)}) \; \mathbb{P}(1_A \circ \pi_{\{v_i\}} \mid \pi_{Pa(v_i)}) = \mathbb{P}(\pi_U^{-1}(B) \mid \pi_{Pa(v_i)}) \; \mathbb{P}(\pi_{\{v_i\}}^{-1}(A) \mid \pi_{Pa(v_i)})$

where $\mathbb{P}(f \mid g)$ denotes the conditional expectation with respect to $\mathbb{P}$ of a measurable function $f: (S, \mathfrak{S}) \to \mathbb{R}$ given a measurable mapping $g: (S, \mathfrak{S}) \to (Y, \mathfrak{Y})$. Hence, $\mathbb{P}$ given by $(*)$ is a directed Markov field in the sense of Lauritzen-Dawid-Larsen-Leimer [4].

Vice versa: Let $\mathbb{P}: \mathfrak{S} \to [0,1]$ be any probability measure. By choosing any enumeration $V := \{v_i: i = 0, 1, \ldots, n\}$ and by applying desintegration procedures it is possible to find a probability measure $P_0: \mathfrak{S}_{v_0} \to [0,1]$ and (with respect to $\mathbb{P}$ essentially uniquely determined) Markov kernels

$$P_i : S^{(i-1)} \times \mathfrak{S}_{v_i} \to [0,1] \quad \text{with} \quad ((x_0, \dots, x_{i-1}), B) \to P_i(x_0, \dots, x_{i-1}; B)$$

for $i = 1, \dots, n$ such that $\mathbb{P}$ is uniquely determined by $(P_i : i = 0, \dots, n)$ via the iterative integration (∗).

The Markov kernel P_i is obtained by desintegrating the projection

$$p_i : \mathfrak{S}^{(i)} \to [0,1] \quad \text{with} \quad C \to p_i(C) := \mathbb{P}(\pi_i^{-1}(C))$$

of $\mathbb{P}$ on $S^{(i)}$ with respect to the canonical projection $\pi_{i,i-1}$; desintegrating is equivalent to taking conditional distributions:

$$p_i(C) = \int_{S^{(i-1)}} \int_{S_{v_i}} 1_C(x_0, \dots, x_i) \, P_i(x_0, \dots, x_{i-1}; dx_i) \, p_{i-1}(d(x_0, \dots, x_{i-1}))$$

for all $C \in \mathfrak{S}^{(i)}$

If every $(S_v, \mathfrak{S}_v)$ is a standard Borel space (i.e. there is a topology $\mathfrak{T}_v$ on S_v such that S_v is a polish space and $\mathfrak{S}_v$ is the σ-algebra of the Borel subsets of S_v), then such desintegrating Markov kernels always exist. The Markov kernels P_i may depend not on the full product $S^{(i)}$ but only on $S(\mathrm{Pa}(v_i))$ with some $\mathrm{Pa}(v_i) \subset \{0, 1, \dots, i-1\}$. Hence, P_i defines a Markov kernel

$$\mathcal{P}_{v_i} : S(\mathrm{Pa}(v_i)) \times \mathfrak{S}_{v_i} \to [0,1] \quad \text{with} \quad \mathcal{P}_{v_i}((x_v : v \in \mathrm{Pa}(v_i)); B) := P_i(x_0, \dots, x_{i-1}; B)$$

Let us define $E := \{(v, v_i) : v \in \mathrm{Pa}(v_i) \text{ and } i = 1, \dots, n\}$. Then $G := (V, E)$ is a directed graph. Together with $(\mathcal{P}_{v_i} : i = 0, 1, \dots, n)$ the graph G is a causal probabilistic network without cycles. $\mathcal{P}_{v_i}$ is the conditional distribution of X_{v_i} given $X_v = x_v$ for all the parents v of v_i with respect to $\mathbb{P}$. $\mathbb{P}$ is a directed Markov field with respect to the network G.

Hence, the total system may be represented by a causal probabilistic network. Of course, this causal probabilistic network depends on $\mathbb{P}$ and the enumeration of V. In practical applications, this disadvantage turns out to be an advantage; it allows to choose the dependency structures adopted to needs and possibilities. Indeed, in such a way it is possible to construct every such causal probabilistic network which fits to the given probability measure $\mathbb{P}$.

There are causal probabilistic networks with cycles for which associated Markov fields exist and those for which associated Markov fields (or any probability measures) do not exist.

Updating the system in our context may mean "improving" the common distribution $\mathbb{P}$ or the Markov kernels $\mathcal{P}_v$ or may mean "introducing" new evidence. Introducing new evidence consistently with the old knowledge is essentially desintegrating or, equivalently, conditioning. Introducing new evidence in form of a new finding $X_v = x_v$ is nothing but taking the conditional distribution of $\mathbb{P}$ given $X_v = x_v$. Unfortunately, desintegration is not continuous (for all kinds of reasonable topologies) in general.

Let us take polish spaces S_v with Borel σ-algebras $\mathfrak{S}_v$. It is sensible to consider the weak topology on the spaces of measures; e.g. see Billingsley [2].

For a given measure $\mathbb{P}$ the desintegrating kernel $\mathcal{P}_v$: $S(Pa(v)) \times \mathfrak{S}_v \to [0,1]$ needs not to be continuous in the following sense:
If a sequence $((x_{u,m}: u \in Pa(v)): m \in \mathbb{N})$ converges in $S(Pa(v))$ against $(x_u: u \in Pa(v))$ with respect to the product topology, then the sequence $(\mathcal{P}_v((x_{u,m}: u \in Pa(v)); .): m \in \mathbb{N})$ of probability measures converges weakly against the probability measure $\mathcal{P}_v((x_u: u \in Pa(v)); .)$. Such a kernel is called a Feller kernel.

The desintegration of measures needs not to be continuous in the following sense:
If $(\mathbb{P}_m: m \in \mathbb{N})$ is a sequence of probability measures $\mathbb{P}_m$ on S (with the product topology) with the desintegrating kernels $\mathcal{P}_{v,m}$: $S(Pa(v)) \times \mathfrak{S}_v \to [0,1]$ which converges weakly against $\mathbb{P}$ with the desintegrating kernel $\mathcal{P}_v$: $S(Pa(v)) \times \mathfrak{S}_v \to [0,1]$, then the sequence $(\mathcal{P}_{v,m}((x_u: u \in Pa(v)); .): m \in \mathbb{N})$ of probability measures converges weakly to $\mathcal{P}_v((x_u: u \in Pa(v)); .)$ for every $(x_u: u \in Pa(v)) \in S(Pa(v))$.

Finally, if $(\mathbb{P}_m: m \in \mathbb{N})$ is a sequence of probability measures $\mathbb{P}_m$ on S with the desintegrating kernels $\mathcal{P}_{v,m}$: $S(Pa_m(v)) \times \mathfrak{S}_v \to [0,1]$ and the parent sets $Pa_m(v)$ for $v \in V$ which converges weakly against $\mathbb{P}$ with the desintegrating kernel $\mathcal{P}_v$: $S(Pa(v)) \times \mathfrak{S}_v \to [0,1]$ and the parent set $Pa(v)$ for $v \in V$, then the sets $E_m := \{(u,v): u \in Pa_m(v) \text{ and } v \in V\}$ of edges associated to $\mathbb{P}_m$ may vary rapidly and may not "converge" against the set $E := \{(u,v): u \in Pa(v) \text{ and } v \in V\}$.

However, if for a fixed graph $G := (V,E)$ there is a sequences $(\mathcal{P}_{v,m}: m \in \mathbb{N})$ of Feller kernels $\mathcal{P}_{v,m}$: $S(Pa(v)) \times \mathfrak{S}_v \to [0,1]$ such that for every $v \in V$ and every $(x_u: u \in Pa(v))$ in $S(Pa(v))$ the sequence $(\mathcal{P}_{v,m}((x_u: u \in Pa(v)); .): m \in \mathbb{N})$ of probability measures converges weakly to $\mathcal{P}_v((x_u: u \in Pa(v)); .)$, then the common probability measures $\mathbb{P}_m$ (associated via (*) to $(\mathcal{P}_{v,m}: v \in V)$) converge weakly against the common distribution $\mathbb{P}$ (associated via (*) to the family $(\mathcal{P}_v: v \in V)$ of limiting kernels).

References:

[1] Ash, R.B.: Real Analysis and Probability. Academic Press: New York, 1972.
[2] Billingsley, P.: Convergence of Probability Measures. Wiley: New York, 1968.
[3] Jensen, F.V.; Lauritzen, S.L.; Oleson, K.G.: Bayesian updating in causal probabilistic networks by local computations. Computational Statistics Quaterly 4 (1990), 269-282.
[4] Lauritzen, S.L.; Dawid, A.P.; Larsen, B.N.; Leimer. H.-G.: Independence properties of directed Markov fields. Networks 20 (1990), 491-505.
[5] Lauritzen, S.L.; Spiegelhalter, D.J.: Local computations with probabilities on graphical structures and their applications to expert systems. J. Royal Stat. Soc. B 50 (2) (1988), 157-224.
[6] Neveu, J.: Bases Mathèmatiques du Calcul des Probabilitès. Masson et Cie.: Paris, 1964.
[7] Oppel, U.G.: Kausal-probabilistische Expertensysteme. Vorlesungsskript. Mathematisches Institut der L-M-Universität München, 1991.
[8] Pearl, J.: Probabilistic Reasoning in Intelligent Systems: Networks of Plausible Inference. Morgan Kaufmann: San Mateo, CA, USA; 1988.

Probabilistic Default Reasoning Involving Continuous Variables

Gerhard Paass*
German National Research Center for Computer Science (GMD)
D-5205 Sankt Augustin, Germany

1 Introduction

Let us consider an ecological model of a pond. It describes the equilibrium evolving for a number of chemical and biological quantities. Because of measurement problems only categorical values (high/ normal / low) are available for some variables, while other variables have continuous scale. Obviously the measurement of the values is complicated and in general will be affected by measurement errors. We will discuss methods which allow the evaluation of a probabilistic model for this situation. The model combines discrete and continuous variables and determines its joint probability distribution. Parameters for marginal and conditional distributions may be constrained to known values (probabilities, expectations, variances, quantiles, etc.). Measurement errors can be taken into account and conflicts between different pieces of evidence may be resolved. Finally default values for parameters may be given which are only used as long as there are no conflicting constraints. The structure of the model is arbitrary and may have cycles. Solutions are determined by generating a synthetic sample of the distribution with a Monte Carlo approach. Within the set of feasible distributions maximum entropy solutions may be selected. On the other hand worst case solutions may be determined which give bounds on the parameters in the set of feasible solutions. Vague concepts can be modelled by relating a discrete category of some variable to values of a continuous variable by a conditional distribution.

2 Combination of Evidence

Assume the situation in question can be described by n different variables $x_1, \ldots, x_n$ which may have discrete or continuous values and form a vector x. Let I_d and I_c be the set of indices of discrete and continuous variables respectively. Each discrete variable x_i, $i \in I_d$, can take a finite number $k(i)$ of values from a set $J_i = \{v_1, \ldots, v_{k(i)}\}$, whereas the values of a continuous variable x_l, $l \in I_c$ are in an interval $J_l = [a_l, b_l]$. Then $\mathcal{J} := J_1 \times \cdots \times J_n$ is the set of possible worlds W_τ.

For each discrete x_i, $i \in I_d$, let $\mathcal{F}_i$ be the set of subsets of J_i and for each continuous variable x_l, $l \in I_c$, let $\mathcal{F}_l$ be the Borel field formed from the subintervals of $J_l = [a_l, b_l]$. On the product field $\mathcal{F} := \mathcal{F}_1 \times \cdots \times \mathcal{F}_n$ we may define a probability measure $P : \mathcal{F} \to [0, 1]$ describing the uncertainty about the true possible world. We assume that each $P = P_\phi$ can be characterized by a vector ϕ of parameters. Let $\mathcal{P}$ be a class of probability measures and Φ be the corresponding set of parameters. We assume that there is vector $\theta = \theta(\phi)$ of observable characteristics of marginal distributions: mean values, variances, probabilities, conditional probabilities, etc. Let Θ be the set of all possible parameter values of θ.

*This work was supported by the German Federal Department of Research and Technology, grant ITW8900A7

Let us consider the different types of parameters which may be available for our pond example. First we may have some information on the values of discrete variables, e.g. the probabilities that the number of fish is high: $\theta_1 := P(fish=high) = 0.9$. This value may be subjective probabilities of an expert. Alternatively some 'objective' statistical data from a survey may be used. A related type of evidence concerns conditional probabilities, e.g. $P(water\text{-}flea=high \mid algae=normal) = 0.7$ establishing a probabilistic rule.

The distribution of continuous variables can either be specified completely or described by a few parameters like moments (mean value, variance, skewness,...) or quantiles (median, quartiles, deciles, minimum and maximum value,...). Evidence concerning continuous variables has to be formulated in terms of these parameters. First we may have some information on the mean value of a specific variable, e.g. $\theta_i = E(nitrate) = 0.00021$ g/l. In addition we may have "rules" relating discrete with continuous variables, e.g. the density $p(oxygen \mid algae)$ of oxygen for a given category of algae. If the relation is stochastic we have to specify conditional distributions for each category of the discrete variable. Finally there may be a direct relation between two continuous variables, which may be specified in the form of a conditional distribution or density.

The available information may be evaluated with respect to two criteria: On the one hand we may determine the set of probability measures $\hat{\Phi}$ compatible with the observed values $\tilde{\theta}$. This yields *upper and lower bounds* on arbitrary characteristics (probabilities, moments, quantiles, etc.) of the distribution. On the other hand we may assume that the observations are complete in the sense that there are no stochastic relations between the variables except those covered by the available evidence. Consequently we may assume that all interaction terms not affected by the evidence are zero. This amounts to select a solution $\hat{\hat{\phi}}$ with *maximum entropy* from the set $\hat{\Phi}$ of optimal solutions.

$$\forall_{\phi \in \hat{\phi}} \left(-\int x \log(x) d\hat{\hat{\phi}}(x) \right) \geq \left(-\int x \log(x) d\phi(x) \right) \tag{1}$$

Maximum entropy solutions have a potential representation that automatically implies that higher order interactions between the variables are zero and therefore specific conditional independence conditions hold.

3 Maximum Entropy Solution

The number of parameters of the joint distribution of discrete variables gets prohibitively large even for a moderate number of variables. Most procedures discussed in literature avoid this huge number of parameters by assuming a treelike structure of the inference network [Pearl 88]. For continuous variables such approaches have been discussed in control theory since the early sixties. The Kalman filter [Kalman 60] and related smoothing methods [Jazwinski 70, p.215ff] may be used to propagate the effect of evidences between the variables of a model. The algorithm is exact for joint normal distributions and gives good approximations for symmetric distributions, but is inappropriate for discrete variables. Most approaches proposed in AI literature, e.g. [Pearl 88, p.344], [Xu Pearl 89] , and [Shachter 90], assume normally distributed variables and are variants of this concept.

If normally distributed variables are mixed with discrete variables, the distribution no longer can be described by a single expectation and covariance matrix, but a large number of conditional distributions of the continuous variables given the discrete variables has to be considered. If non-normal distributions have to be taken into account the parametrization gets even more complex. Hence some nonparametric representation is required. [Yeh 90] splits the value space into smaller regions and determines bounds of the densities.

Here we approximate the distribution P by a synthetic random sample $S := \{x(1),\ldots,x(N)\}$ of N elements. The vector $\phi(S)$ of empirical parameters of the sample are automatically consistent, i.e. there exists an underlying distribution with these parameters. By the Law of Large Numbers any distribution can be approximated arbitrary well by a sample if the sample size N is chosen sufficiently large. To measure the deviation between the parameters $\theta(S)$ of the synthetic sample and the known parameters $\tilde{\theta}$ we employ the likelihood function

$$L(\theta(S)) := \prod_{i=1}^{d} P_i(\tilde{\theta}_i \mid \theta(S)) \tag{2}$$

as in [Paass 88]. Here we assume that $P(\tilde{\theta} \mid \theta)$ is an appropriate error distribution (e.g. binomial for probability parameters and normal distribution for expected values). It gets maximal if the parameters of the sample coincide with the known parameter values $\tilde{\theta}$, i.e. for the set $\hat{\Phi}$ of optimal solutions. We now use the simulated annealing algorithm [Aarts Korst 88] to generate a sequence of samples with approximately maximal likelihood. The algorithm starts with an arbitrary sample S. In an iterative fashion the 'current' sample S_{old} is modified to a new sample S_{new} and subsequently it is checked whether the modification can be accepted. A modification usually consist of rather small changes, for instance changing the values of a some variables in a few sample vectors $x(i)$ of S_{old}. If $\theta(S_{old})$ is the empirical parameter corresponding to S_{old} the modification is accepted with probability

$$P_{acc}(S_{old}, S_{new}) := \max\left[1, \frac{L(\theta(S_{new}))^\beta}{L(\theta(S_{old}))^\beta}\right] \tag{3}$$

The simulated annealing algorithm generates a sequence of samples approaching a stationary distribution $\Pr(\theta(S) \mid \tilde{\theta})$ which is proportional to their likelihood (2)

$$\Pr(\theta \mid \tilde{\theta}) \propto \Pr^c(S) L(\theta(S))^\beta \tag{4}$$

The term $\Pr^c(S)$ can be interpreted as a prior distribution which evolves if no constraints are present. As shown in [Paass 91] the algorithm converges to the set $\hat{\theta}$ of maximum likelihood solutions (2) if β is gradually increased.

The remaining parameters of the sample evolve according to the prior distribution $\Pr^c(S)$. This distribution is determined by the way how a modification of the sample is performed. A simple modification scheme is the following: If $S_{old} := \{x(1), \ldots, x(N)\}$ is the current sample of equally weighted vectors, a maximum entropy distribution will evolve if we randomly select an $x(j)$ and randomly select some variables $x_i(j)$. If $x_i(j)$ is discrete we change the value a of $x_j(i)$ to another randomly selected category such that each category has identical probability. If $x_i(j)$ is continuous with value a we select a new value uniformly distributed in $[a - h, a + h]$ for some $h > 0$ (with 'wrap around' at the border of the domain of x_i). For this modification scheme the distribution will fluctuate around the maximum entropy distribution.

This result also applies to continuous distributions. Depending on the given constraints different maximum entropy distributions will evolve: If a mean value α and a variance σ^2 is given then the normal distribution $N(a, \sigma^2)$ is the maximum entropy distribution. If the distribution is confined to an interval $[a, b]$ then the uniform distribution on $[a, b]$ has maximum entropy. If an expected value α is given and the distribution is confined to $[a, \infty]$, then the exponential distribution has maximum entropy. Therefore specific distributions can be generated without explicitly specifying their density. By specifying more moments we can approximate arbitrary continuous distributions.[1]

Assume y_i is a continuous random variable with values in $[0, 1]$. Suppose we modify it using the simulated annealing algorithm with no restriction, i.e. $L(\theta(S)) := const$. Then an uniform distribution distribution over $[0, 1]$ evolves for y_i. Let $F_i(\lambda) := P(x_i \leq \lambda)$ be an arbitrary distribution function of some variable x_i. Then it is well known that the quantity $F_i^{-1}(y_i)$ will have a distribution with distribution function F_i. This mechanism can be used to generate arbitrary univariate prior distributions $\Pr^c$ for specific variables x_i. Instead of x_i the transformed quantity y_i is modified with the simulated annealing procedure. x_i is calculated as $F_i^{-1}(y_i)$ and subsequently the likelihood value

---

[1] Alternatively we may use the bayesian approach and generate complete posterior distributions [Paass 90]. But then we have to specify complex prior distributions which should be 'noninformative'.

can be determined as usual. Note that F_i may depend on the values of other variables x_j and therefore we also can generate conditional distributions $F_{i|x_j}$. This prior distribution only evolves for constant likelihood function. In the case of evidence the prior distribution is adapted to the restrictions and the parameter $\phi(S)$ fluctuates in and around the set $\hat{\Phi}$ of optimal solutions. Within $\hat{\Phi}$ the required distribution of x_i will evolve as long as it does not contradict to the external constraints.

4 Default Reasoning

Usually there are different pieces of evidence collected from different sources: measurement devices, random samples, or expert judgements. The evidence usually will not be exact but unreliable. Then the values $\tilde{\theta}$ are uncertain and may be contradictory to some extent. Like in [Paass 88] we assume that the reliability of the evidence is expressed by a *measurement distribution* $P(\tilde{\theta} \mid \theta)$ reflecting the variation of the evidence $\tilde{\theta}$ around possible parameter values θ. Then maximum likelihood estimate according to (2) selects the parameter $\hat{\theta}$ for which the observed values $\tilde{\theta}$ are most probable. As $\tilde{\theta}$ is disturbed by noise different components $\tilde{\theta}_i$ may be contradictory and there may exist no joint probability measure such that $\tilde{\theta} = \theta(\phi)$. Then the maximum likelihood procedure will find a compromise between the conflicting componentes taking into account the reliability of the different pieces of evidence.

In our toy example the number of fish is determined by the number of water flea and the concentration of oxygen. This 'normal' relation, however no longer holds if a toxic chemical is spilled into the pond. Then we would like to ignore the 'default' relation and conclude that all fish die. We partition the vector θ of measurements into disjoint *default classes* $T_1, \ldots, T_m$. For $i < j$ we assume that the measurements in T_i are only *defaults* with respect to the measurements in T_j. This means that if there is a conflict between some $\tilde{\theta}_r \in T_i$ and $\tilde{\theta}_s \in T_j$ the measurement $\tilde{\theta}_r$ is neglected and only $\tilde{\theta}_s$ is used.

The default classes have an effect only if there is some conflict between a $\theta_r \in T_i$ and a $\theta_s \in T_j$, $i < j$. We reduce this to the case of conflicting evidence by assigning a very high reliability of the observations in T_j in comparison to those in T_i. If this ratio if increased to infinity the evidence in T_i is ignored in case of conlict. On the other hand is shown later that the usual result obtain if there are no conflicts. Again there will be a compromise if there are conflicts between observations of the same default level.

We use a penalty function approach to take into account the default relations. To the different default classes T_i we associate parameters $\gamma(i) > 1$ such that $\gamma(i) > \gamma(j) \Longleftrightarrow i > j$. Instead of maximizing $L(\theta) := \sum_{i=1}^{d} P_i(\tilde{\theta}_i \mid \theta)$ as in (2) we consider the related function

$$L_\beta(\theta) := \sum_{i=1}^{d} P(\tilde{\theta}_i \mid \theta)^{\beta^{\gamma(i)}} \tag{5}$$

Again we use the simulated annealing algorithm to generate a sequence of samples. If $\theta(S_{old})$ is the empirical parameter corresponding to S_{old} the modification is accepted with probability

$$P_{acc}(S_{old}, S_{new}) := \max\left[1, \frac{L_\beta(\theta(S_{new}))}{L_\beta(\theta(S_{old}))}\right] \tag{6}$$

As shown in [Paass 91] the simulated annealing algorithm for $\beta \to \infty$ generates a sample S taking into account the reliability and the default level of the different pieces of evidence $\tilde{\theta}_i$. If $\tilde{\theta}_i$ and $\tilde{\theta}_j$ are contradictory and in different default classes, the evidence with lower default class is neglected. If they are in the same default class a compromise evolves according to their relative reliability. If we replace the term $P_i(\tilde{\theta}_i \mid \theta)^{\beta^{\gamma(i)}}$ by some likelihood term $P_i(\theta_i)$ independent of β a stationary distribution for θ_i will evolve acoording to (4). This is an alternative way to generate arbitrary prior distributions for specific variables.

Upper and lower bounds for arbitrary real-valued features $\psi = \psi(\phi)$ of the distribution may be determined in the following way. We may add a new piece of evidence $\tilde{\psi} = a$ at a default class T_0 with lower priority than any other evidence where a is a lowest possible value of ψ. The simulated annealing procedure will generate a sample S within the set $\tilde{\Phi}$ of optimal solutions where ψ has its smalles possible value. In the same way we may determine an upper bound of ψ.

Let us consider the relation between $Ni=nitrate$ and $Al=algae$ in our example. We assumed that the relation between both quantities is given in the form of a conditional probability $P(Al=hi \mid Ni=\eta)$ and $P(Al=lo \mid Ni=\eta)$ for each possible nitrate concentration η. The relation between both quantities, may however be assessed by some expert in a more qualitative way by $P(Al=hi \mid Ni_q=hi)$, $P(Al=lo \mid Ni_q=hi)$, etc. Then we have to establish a link between the 'vague' categories $high$, $medium$, low of the qualitative variable Ni_q and the exact value of Ni. If another expert has to assess the meaning of these terms he again can provide subjective probabilities $P(Ni_q=hi \mid Ni = \eta)$ for each possible nitrate concentration η. Cheeseman [Cheeseman 88, p.61] interprets such probabilities as the belief that a normal language user will say 'hi' for a nitrate concentration in this context.

The above approach can be utilized to represent these conditional distributions. Vague knowledge is treated as uncertain knowledge about intendend meaning. There is an intensive debate on the adequacy of this approach (cf. the discussion in [Cheeseman 88]). Proponents of the fuzzy set theory claim that probability and vagueness are fundamentally different things. I do not want to take part in that discussion but I only want to show that it is possible to use the concept of 'probabilistic vagueness' in realistic problems. Note that it is difficult to give an semantics fuzzy membership functions. Sometimes it is proposed to derive them from histograms of statistical distributions. Ruspini [Cheeseman 88, p.112] thinks it is possible to define membership functions using probabilistic characterizations, although it is unwise to do so if one wants to develop a reasonable useful scale of conceptual applicability.

References

[Aarts Korst 88] Aarts, E., Korst, J. (1988): *Simulated Annealing and Boltzmann Machines*. Wiley, Chichester

[Cheeseman 88] Cheeseman, P. (1988): An inquiry to computer understanding, *Comp. Intelligence* Vol. 4, p.58-66

[Jazwinski 70] Jazwinski, A.H. (1970) : Stochastic processes and Filtering Theory. Academic press, New York.

[Kalman 60] Kalman, R.E. (1960): A New Approach to Linear Filtering and Prediction Problems. Trans. ASME,Ser. D: Journal of Basic Eng., Vol.82, p.35-45.

[Paass 88] Paass, G. (1988): Probabilistic Logic. In: Smets, P., A. Mamdani, D.Dubois, H.Prade (eds.) *Non-Standard Logics for Automated Reasoning*, Academic press, London, p.213-252

[Paass 91] Paass, G. (1990): Probabilistic Default Reasoning. In Proc. IPMU '90. Springer Verlag. (in print).

[Paass 90] Paass, G. (1990): Second order Probabilities for Uncertain and Conflicting Evidence. *Proc. 6-th Conference on Uncertainty in AI*. Cambridge, Mass. July 1990

[Pearl 88] Pearl, J. (1988): *Probabilistic Reasoning in Intelligent Systems*, Morgan Kaufmann, San Mateo, Cal.

[Shachter 90] Shachter, R.D. (1990): A linear approximation method for probabilistic inference. In R.D. Shachter, T.S. Levitt, L.N. Kanal, J.F. Lemmer (eds.): Uncertainty in AI 4, Elsevier, p.93-103

[Xu Pearl 89] Xu, L., Pearl, J. (1989): Structuring Causal Tree models with Continuous Variables L.N. Kanal, T.S. Levitt, J.F. Lemmer (eds.) : Uncertainty in AI 3. Elsevier, p.209-219

[Yeh 90] Yeh, Alexander (1990): Predicting the likely behaviour of continuous nonlinear systems in equilibrium. In R.D. Shachter, T.S. Levitt, L.N. Kanal, J.F. Lemmer (eds.): Uncertainty in AI 4, Elsevier, p.383-405.

REVISION IN PROPOSITIONAL CALCULUS

Odile Papini

Groupe d'Intelligence Artificielle. Faculté des sciences de Luminy.

163 avenue de Luminy. case 901. 13288 MARSEILLE CEDEX 9

Tel: 91 26 93 12. Fax: 91 26 92 75

ABSTRACT

Knowledge base revision is one of the main problems arising in knowledge representation.
When a new information is added to a knowledge base, inconsistency can result. In this paper,
we describe a revision method for use in propositional calculus. First, some properties of
minimal inconsistent subsets are recalled, then the revision method is described. It involves the
computation of the intersection of minimal inconsistent subsets. Some results are presented
from which an algorithm is deduced. Finally an implementation using Semantic Evaluation as
resolution method, is proposed.

I INTRODUCTION

One of the main problems arising in knowledge representation is that of knowledge base
revision. When a new information is added to a knowledge base, inconsistency can result.
Revision means modifying the knowledge base, in order to maintain consistency, keeping the
new information, and removing the least possible previous information. This problem has been
dealt with by C.Alchourron, P.Gärdenfors and D.Makinson[1]. Their studies consisted of
formulating postulates which express the properties that a knowledge base has to satisfy, after
information has been added. These postulates do not make it possible however to define an
effective revision function which calculates, from the initial knowledge base, the state of the
base after the addition of some information. When a base is revised some of the old information
has to be withdrawn. The main problem is to determine which information should be removed.

Example 1:

*Consider the following knowledge base: $C=\{\neg a \vee d,\ \neg a \vee c,\ \neg c,\ \neg b \vee a,\ \neg d\}$ C is a consistent set
of clauses. If the clause $a \vee b \vee d$ is added to the knowledge base then $C \cup \{a \vee b \vee d\}$ is an
inconsistent set of clauses. If the clause $a \vee b \vee d$ has to remain in the knowledge base, what
clause(s) has to be removed?*

The revision of a finite knowledge base has been studied by B.Nebel[4], but this author's results seem to be sometimes problematical, and no algorithm is proposed, or developed. We propose to define a revision function, which satisfies the first six Gärdenfors postulates, and we present an algorithm, which is able to calculate the state of the knowledge base after the addition of some information. We shall limit ourselves to the case when the items contained by the knowledge base are expressed in propositional calculus. Revision means therefore removing minimal number of clauses, so that the base remains consistent when a new clause is added. The proposed revision function may give several results, in which case, the choice is left to the user.

II REVISION METHOD

When dealing with the revision of a set of clauses C in propositional calculus, two points of view are possible : either consider the maximal consistent subsets of C [2][L.Cholvy] or consider the minimal inconsistent subsets of C. The second approach is chosen here and some properties are now recalled.

II-1 Definitions and properties of minimal inconsistent subsets
Let C' be an inconsistent set of clauses in propositional calculus.

Definition 1 : A finite set of clauses C is minimal inconsistent iff C is inconsistent and each subset C" of C, is consistent.

Definition 2 : Let C be an inconsistent finite set of clauses C. M is a minimal inconsistent subset of C iff M is a subset of C, and M is minimal inconsistent.

In what follows, C denotes a finite consistent set of clauses, and c denotes a clause not belonging to C. Assume that $C'=C \cup \{c\}$ is an inconsistent set of clauses. Obviously C' contains at least one minimal inconsistent subset. Let I be the intersection between all the minimal inconsistent subsets of C'

Property 1 : $c \in I$.

We define removed sets of clauses for the revision. These are the smallest sets of clauses such that if we retract their elements from the base, the base becomes consistent. From now on, M will be used to denote the set of all the minimal inconsistent subsets of C'. Assume that Card(M)=m.

Definition 3 : A subset M' of M is maximal non-trivial iff it complies with the two following properties :

    1- The intersection between the elements of M' is not reduced to $\{c\}$.

    2- $\forall M \in$ M-M', the intersection between the elements of $M' \cup \{M\}$ is reduced to $\{c\}$.

Definition 4 : Let M' be a maximal non-trivial subset of M. R is a removed set iff R is composed of one element of the intersection between the elements of M'(except c), plus one element of each minimal inconsistent subset in M-M'(except c).

Property 2 : For each removed set R , C'-R is consistent.

Remark: If I is not reduced to {c}, then M is the only maximal non-trivial subset of M, hence each removed set is composed of only one element of I-{c}. Therefore, $\forall$ c'$\in$ I-{c} , C'-{c'} is consistent.

II-2 The revision strategy

The revision strategy is as follows, let I be the intersection between minimal inconsistent subsets of C'. Here two cases hold :

1- I is not reduced to {c}

Each removed set is composed of one element of I-{c}, so the revision of the knowledge base consists of removing only one arbitrary clause from I-{c}.

2- I is reduced to {c}

We define M' as the biggest subset of M, such that the intersection of the elements of M' is not reduced to {c}. U denotes this intersection. Assume that the cardinality of M is m, and that the cardinality of M' is m'. Each removed set is composed of one element of U-{c}, plus one element ($\neq$ c) of each minimal inconsistent subset in M-M'. The revision of the knowledge base is carried out by removing i+1 clauses (i$\leq$m-m'), one clause in U-{c}, and i clauses ($\neq$ c), one in each of the m-m' elements of M-M'.

Example 2 :

Consider the set of clauses defined in the previous example. There are 2 minimal inconsistent subsets of C'. M1={ a$\vee$b$\vee$d, $\neg$a$\vee$d, $\neg$d, $\neg$b$\vee$a } and M2={ a$\vee$b$\vee$d, $\neg$a$\vee$c, $\neg$c, $\neg$b$\vee$a, $\neg$d }. M1$\cap$M2={ a$\vee$b$\vee$d, $\neg$d, $\neg$b$\vee$a }. Let M={ M1, M2 } be the only maximal non-trivial subset of M. The set of clauses C' can be revised by removing either $\neg$d, or $\neg$b$\vee$a.

Example 3 :

Consider the following knowledge system: C={$\neg$a$\vee$b, $\neg$a$\vee$d, $\neg$b, $\neg$b$\vee$c , $\neg$d, $\neg$c}. C is a consistent set of clauses. If the clause a is added to the knowledge system then C$\cup${a} is an inconsistent set of clauses. There are 3 minimal inconsistent subsets of C' M={ M1, M2, M3 } M1={ a, $\neg$a$\vee$b, $\neg$b }, M2={ a, $\neg$a$\vee$b, $\neg$b$\vee$c, $\neg$c } and M3={ a, $\neg$a$\vee$d, $\neg$d }. M1$\cap$M2$\cap$M3={a}, and let M'={ M1, M2 } be a maximal non-trivial subset of M, U={ a, $\neg$a$\vee$b}, The set of clauses C' can be revised by removing $\neg$a$\vee$b and either $\neg$a$\vee$d, or $\neg$d.

The efficiency of the method depends on the efficiency of the algorithm which computes the intersection between the minimal inconsistent subsets of C'. Using a resolution method we can obtain all the minimal inconsistent subsets of C', and calculate their intersection, but this is not very efficient. In each possible case of the revision stategy, we propose an algorithm to compute the intersection between the minimal inconsistent subsets of C' without knowing them.

III COMPUTATION OF THE INTERSECTION BETWEEN MINIMAL INCONSISTENT SUBSETS

In the first case of the revision method, an algorithm is proposed which stems from the following properties.

III-1 Inconsistent subset properties

Let J be the intersection between the inconsistent subsets of C', hence obviously I=J .

Property 3 : $\forall$ $c_i \in$ C', $c_i \neq c$.

If C'-$\{c_i\}$ is consistent, then $c_i \in$ I. If C'-$\{c_i\}$ is inconsistent, then $c_i \notin$ I.

This result provides one way of computing I, but this is not at all efficient when the number of clauses in C' is high.

Property 4 : Let E' be an inconsistent subset of C'. Let K be the intersection between the minimal inconsistent subsets of E', then I$\subset$K.

Property 5 : $\forall$ $c_i \in$ E', $c_i \neq c$.

If E'-$\{c_i\}$ is consistent, then $c_i \in$ K. If E'-$\{c_i\}$ is inconsistent, then $c_i \notin$ I.

This property allows us to construct a set K containing I. So the algorithm is as follows :

III-2 Algorithm

1. with a resolution method, determine E' an inconsistent subset of C'
2. construct K with property 5.
3. determine I as follows :

$\forall$ $c_i \in$ K, $c_i \neq c$

If C'-$\{c_i\}$ is consistent, then $c_i \in$ I.

If C'-$\{c_i\}$ is inconsistent, then $c_i \notin$ I.

From property 4 the algorithm is valid, and from property 5 it is complete.

The complexity of the algorithm is estimated in terms of the number of consistency check tests. In order to reduce the complexity, we consider the simplification of the set of clauses C'. Subsumption cannot be taken into account, because it prevents one from finding all the minimal inconsistent subsets of C', and therefore from computing their intersection correctly. We simplify the set of clauses however by removing the clauses that contain litterals the opposites of which do not appear in any clause of C'. The algorithm needs a resolution method, first to find an inconsistent subset of C', and then to check the consistency of some subsets of C'. We use Semantic Evaluation [5][L.Oxusoff & A.Rauzy] which is particularly efficient.

IV CONCLUSION

In conclusion, the proposed algorithm, in the first case of the revision method, computes the intersection between the minimal inconsistent subsets without knowing them. When a suitable inconsistent subset of C', i.e one which is not too big, is found, then the number of consistency check tests is considerably reduced, and the efficiency of the algorithm is improved. In the second case of the revision method, no general properties have been defined so far , but the implementation provides us with an algorithm for computing the removed sets without knowing the minimal inconsistent subsets of C', using a decision tree associated with Semantic Evaluation.

V RELATED WORKS

The revision problem is related to the diagnostic problem dealt with by R. Reiter[6], where the minimal inconsistent subsets are the conflict sets, and the removed sets are the hitting sets.

ACKNOWLEDGEMENTS

I should like to thank C.Schwind, P Siegel and J.L Imbert for helpful discussions and for their support.

REFERENCES

[1] C. Alchourron, P. Gärdenfors, D. Makinson 85: "On the logic of theory change: Partial meet functions for contraction and revision" Journal of Symbolic Logic 50.p 510-530.

[2] L.Cholvy 90: "Querying an inconsistant database" proceeding of AIMSA'90 North Holland.

[3] P.Gärdenfors 88: "Knowledge in flux: modelling the dynamics of epistemic states" MIT Press.

[4] B.Nebel 89: "A knowledge level analysis of belief revision" In R.J. Brachman,H.J. Levesque, and R. Reiter editors. Proceeding of the 1st International Conference on Principles of Knowledge Representation and Reasoning p 301-311. Toronto. Ontario.

[5] L.Oxusoff A.Rauzy 89: "Evaluation sémantique en calcul propositionnel "Thèse de doctorat. GIA Université d'Aix-Marseille II. Luminy.

[6] R.Reiter 87: "A theory of diagnosis from first principles"Artificial Intelligence vol 32 p 57-95.

[7] C.Sabatier 90: private communication GIA Université d'Aix-Marseille II. Luminy.

[8] P.Siegel 87: "représentation et utilisation de la connaissance en calcul propositionnel" Thèse d'état. GIA Université d'Aix-Marseille II. Luminy.

A constraint-based approach to uncertain and imprecise reasoning. Application to expert systems.

T. Pontet

L.I.S.I./E.C.R.I.N.

INSA - Département Informatique - Bât. 502

20 av. Albert Einstein

69621 Villeurbanne cedex

Tel : 72 43 83 83 poste 59 28

1. Introduction.

In order to simulate at best human reasoning (and so to make the same type of expertise), computer must be able to manage uncertain and imprecise knowledge. Deductions will be obtained by applying methods which, from a set of basic chuncks of knowledge, will produce a set of deduced chuncks of knowledge.

Some freedom degrees will be available in these methods and in the their choice. In order to reduce their number, we will have to constrain them.

So, we will first define the form of constraints and will have some thoughts on the satisfaction of one or more constraints. Then, we will present some constraints "useful" in imprecise reasoning. Finally, we will apply some of them on deduction methods expressed as production rules (after having define them).

In this way, we will construct rules like "if X is A then Y is B" (which corresponds to generalized modus ponens), "the more X is A, the more Y is B" (gradual rules), "the more X is A, the more q (is certain)".

2. General remarks on constraints.

2.1. Definition.

A constraint is a pair (set of hypotheses, set of deduced chuncks of knowledge).

2.2. Satisfaction of constraints.

2.2.1. Single constraint.

A constraint is satisfied by a deduction method if this one allows to verify the set of deduced chuncks of knowledge of the constraint whenever the set of hypotheses is verified.

2.2.2. Set of constraints.

If constraints have exclusive sets of hypotheses, each of them will be treated independently.

The other case (non-exclusive sets of hypotheses) is more difficult to handle since many sets of hypotheses can be simultaneously satisfied. So, checking the initial set of constraints means checking all the possible sets of non-exclusive constraints. When the non-exclusive constraints have independent sets of deduced chuncks of knowledge, the final set of deduced chuncks of knowledge to verify is the union of the initial sets. When some deduced chuncks of knowledge affect the same fact, we must define a combination method of deduced chuncks of knowledge, if we want the simultaneous satisfaction of the constraints to have some meaning.

3. "Interesting" constraints.

We will limit ourself to simple constraints : a single hypothesis and a single deduced chunck of knowledge. Here are seven types :

1 : (X is A, Y is B)

2 : $(X \in A_\alpha, Y \in B_\alpha)$ for $\alpha \in]0,1]$

3 : $(X = x, Y \in B_{\mu_A(x)})$ for $x \in S$

4 : $(X \in A_\alpha, N(q) = \alpha)$ for $\alpha \in]0,1]$

5 : $(X \in A_\alpha, B$ is α-certain for Y) for $\alpha \in]0,1]$, where "B is α-certain for Y" means :
$$\forall y \in T, \pi_Y(y) \leq \max(\mu_B(y), 1-\alpha)$$

6 : $(X = x, N(q) = \mu_A(x))$ for $x \in S$

7 : $(X = x, B$ is $\mu_A(x)$-certain for Y) for $x \in S$

4. Application to expert rules.

We suppose that expert rules are expressed under the form : if condition then conclusion.

4.1. Formulation and application of the rules.

From the formula $\Pi(p \wedge q) = \Pi(q \mid p) \otimes \Pi(p)$ linking two facts p and q ($\otimes$ being a triangular norm), we can obtain different uncertain and/or imprecise rules. Here are two of them :

$$\cdot \begin{cases} \Pi(q) = \max(\Pi(q \mid p) \otimes \Pi(p), \Pi(q \mid \neg p) \otimes \Pi(\neg p)) \\ N(q) = \min(N(q \mid p) \oslash N(\neg p), N(q \mid \neg p) \oslash N(p)) \end{cases} \quad \text{(where}$$

$\forall u, v \in [0, 1], u \oslash v = 1 - (1 - u) \otimes (1 - v)$) which can be applied with an imprecise condition using the fuzzy filtering formula of Zadeh (of course, the conclusion can be imprecise too).

$\cdot \quad \forall y \in T, \pi_Y(y) = \underset{x \in S}{\text{Sup}} (\pi_{Y|X}(y, x) \otimes \pi_X(x))$ using both imprecise

condition and imprecise conclusion.

The simultaneous application of many rules needs a combination of the conclusions. In the case of imprecise conclusions on the same variable, the intersection of fuzzy sets will be used (with the chosen "minimum" operator).

4.2. Satisfaction of some constraints.

4.2.1. Generalized modus ponens.

It corresponds to the constraint number 1 and the second formulation of expert rules. Other formulations of rules must be used and will give different results when the hypothesis of the constraint is not satisfied.

4.2.2. Gradual rules.

These are rules like "the more X is A, the more Y is B". Two sets of constraints (the second and third) seem quite to correspond to this type of rule. We will test them by using the second formulation of expert rules.

4.2.2.1. Constraints number 2.

First, we replace each constraint by a type of expert rules satisfying it :

$$\forall (x,y) \in S \times T / \mu_A(x) \geq \alpha, \begin{cases} \mu_B(y) < \alpha \Rightarrow \pi^\alpha_{Y|X}(y,x) = 0 \\ \mu_B(y) \geq \alpha \Rightarrow \pi^\alpha_{Y|X}(y,x) = 1 \end{cases}$$

Then, we find a single type of rules giving the same results (in all cases) that the former set of rules :

$$\forall (x,y) \in S \times T, \begin{cases} \mu_A(x) > \mu_B(y) \Rightarrow \pi_{Y|X}(y,x) = 0 \\ \mu_A(x) = \mu_B(y) = 1 \Rightarrow \pi_{Y|X}(y,x) = 1 \end{cases}$$

But, there is a problem. Indeed, when some hypotheses of constraints are satisfied, the combination of the deduced chuncks of knowledge of these constraints is not necessarily derived. That's because the rules corresponding to the constraints whose hypotheses are not verified will give results which will combine with the other deductions. In order to solve this problem, we must verify that, when hypotheses of constraints are not satisfied, the rules will make no deductions. So, we will add to the initial set of constraints of type (hypothesis, deduced chunck of knowledge) the constraints (hypothesis not verified, no deduced knowledge).

In the present case, new constraints are :

$$\forall \alpha \in]0,1], (X \notin A_\alpha, Y \in T)$$

The hypotheses (modified in order to enable us to conclude) for $\alpha \in]0,1]$ are :

$$\exists x \in S / \begin{cases} \mu_A(x) < \alpha \\ \pi_X(x) = 1 \end{cases}$$

So, we will find :

$$\forall (x,y) \in S \times T, \mu_A(x) < \alpha \Rightarrow \pi^\alpha_{Y|X}(y,x) = 1$$

which gives the total conditions :

$$\forall(x,y)\in S\times T, \begin{cases} \mu_A(x) > \mu_B(y) \Rightarrow \pi_{Y|X}(y,x) = 0 \\ \mu_A(x) \leq \mu_B(y) \Rightarrow \pi_{Y|X}(y,x) = 1 \end{cases}$$

4.2.2.2. Constraints number 3.

The constraints are exclusive, so they will be treated independently. We will find the same type of rules than with the second set of constraints.

4.2.3. Semi-gradual rules.

These are rules like "the more X is A, the more q". They correspond to all the other constraints. We can test them for some formulations of rules. The rules of the first form constrained by the constraints number 4 will give some results (by taking $p = "X \in A_a"$) and will satisfy the constraints number 6 too (taking $p = "X = x"$ gives no result). The rules of the second form constrained by either the constraints number 5 or 7 will give the same results.

5. Conclusion.

The methodology by constraints seems to be very general. It is a way to define deduction methods based on the search of particular results (bottom up method) instead of purely theoretical aspects whose results are subsequently verified (top down).

An application to expert rules has been presented. It is worthnoting that we could do the most exhaustive exploration as possible (by using all the known formulations of rules and all the "interesting" constraints) and, so, make an inventory of the advantages and disadvantages (which depends on their use) of each type of rules for each constraint, and provide, in this way, a guide for the choice of methods.

References.

. Dubois, D. and Prade, H. A typology of fuzzy "if... then..." rules. In : Proceedings of the congress the coming of age of fuzzy logic (3rd IFSA congress). Washington : 1989. p. 782-785
. Dubois, D. and Prade, H. Gradual inference rules in approximate reasoning. In : Advances in approximate reasoning based on fuzzy logic. Toulouse : IRIT, 1990. 54 p. Rapport IRIT/90-6/R

Random Closed Sets: a Unified Approach to the Representation of Imprecision and Uncertainty

Philippe Quinio* and Takashi Matsuyama**

* ATR Auditory and Visual Perception Research Lab., Seika-chō, Kyōto 619-02, Japan
** Information Technology Dep., Okayama Univ., 3-1-1 Tsushima-naka, Okayama 700, Japan

1. Introduction

The representation of uncertain and imprecise information is a crucial issue in Artificial Intelligence. Indeed, knowledge about the world must be acquired and represented into a virtual "knowledge space" before reasoning can take place and this acquisition step in itself introduces both uncertainty (possibility of error) and imprecision (due to the inherently imprecise nature of any physical measurement) into the final representation. A conceptual framework that allows for the explicit representation of both uncertainty and imprecision is therefore needed. The inadequacies of the traditional random point approach have been known for some time ([7]) and alternative formalisms have been proposed, such as the Fuzzy set and Dempster-Shafer theories. In this work, we show how these two formalisms are actually related to probability measure theory through the concept of Random Closed Set, and how this unified topological approach to imprecision and uncertainty solves many of the difficulties inherent to the combination or acquisition of fuzzy sets and Belief functions. All proofs can be found in [1].

2. Random Closed Sets

Imprecision is thought of as a *set-theoretic* concept, of which the so-called "error intervals" in physics are an example. A piece of information, such as a physical measurement, is represented as a subset of a Universe $\mathcal{U}$ and the information is said imprecise with respect to the universe whenever this subset is not reduced to a singleton of $\mathcal{U}$. In contrast, our interpretation of uncertainty is *probabilistic*, i.e. is based on general probability measure theory. This does **not** restrict representation to random <u>point</u> variables, as has been widely implicitly assumed; and indeed, when dealing with problems that involve both imprecision *and* uncertainty, random <u>set</u> variables (i.e. random variables taking value in the power set of $\mathcal{U}$) appear as natural candidates for knowledge representation.

This random set approach is sufficient for finite or at least countable problems. However, many problems are not easily expressed in terms of countable sets: simplifying an uncountable problem into a countable one implies some sort of *sampling* stage, source of artifacts. The major practical advantage of using countable sets comes from the fact that one can access any bounded subset experimentally. In an uncountably infinite set, many bounded subsets are abstract entities that cannot be accessed through experiment; we argue that many of these cannot serve for knowledge representation and should therefore be discarded. One way of doing this is provided by the mathematical notion of Topology, as suggested by Mathematical Morphology (see [6]): one can explicitly state that, for example, the non-closed sets of a given topological space do not provide any additional representation power over their topological closure, and we may as well select the *closed subsets* as the basic entities for representing knowledge. This naturally leads to the Random Closed Set (RACS) theory. We recall here a few definitions and results. Details can be found in [4] and [6].

Starting from a locally compact second-countable Hausdorff topological space $(\mathcal{U}, \mathcal{T})$, we can endow the set $\mathcal{U}' = \mathcal{F}(\mathcal{U})$ of all the **closed** subsets of $(\mathcal{U}, \mathcal{T})$ with a topological structure $\mathcal{T}'$, called the **Hit or Miss topology**: it is the topology generated by $O'_O = \{F \in \mathcal{F}(\mathcal{U}), F \text{ hits } O\} = \{F \in \mathcal{F}(\mathcal{U}), F \cap O \neq \emptyset\}$ for all opens $O \in \mathcal{T}$ and $O'^K = \{F \in \mathcal{F}(\mathcal{U}), F \text{ misses } K\} = \{F \in \mathcal{F}(\mathcal{U}), F \cap K = \emptyset\}$ for all compacts $K \in \mathcal{K}$. A **Random Closed Set** of $(\mathcal{U}, \mathcal{T})$ is a random variable defined on an underlying probability space $(\Omega, \Sigma_\Omega, \mathbf{Prob})$ and taking values in the (compact) measurable topological space $(\mathcal{U}', \Sigma')$, where Σ' is the Borel σ-algebra of $(\mathcal{U}', \mathcal{T}')$. The distribution P' of a RACS X is such that: $\mathbf{Prob}(X \in A') = P'(A')$ for every event A' in Σ', and entirely determines X. A fundamental result, known as Choquet's theorem, shows that X is in fact entirely determined by its *hitting capacity* T_X: $T_X(K) = \mathbf{Prob}(X \text{ hits } K) = \mathbf{Prob}(X \cap K \neq \emptyset)$, $\forall K \in \mathcal{K}$, and that, conversely, a functional T on $\mathcal{K}$ defines a unique RACS X by $\mathbf{Prob}(X \text{ hits } K) = T(K)$ iff it is an alternating Choquet capacity of infinite order verifying $T(\emptyset) = 0$ and $T(K) \leq 1$, $\forall K \in \mathcal{K}$ ([4], pg.30). Another functional often used in practice is the *implying functional* R_X defined on $\mathcal{K}$ by: $R_X(K) = \mathbf{Prob}(K \subset X)$, and if $(\mathcal{U}, \mathcal{T})$ is a **compact** space, the functional P_X defined by: $P_X(K) = \mathbf{Prob}(X \subset K)$, $\forall K \in \mathcal{K}(= \mathcal{F})$ entirely determines X too. P_X is a monotone Choquet capacity of infinite order satisfying $P_X(\mathcal{U}) = 1$ and $P_X \geq 0$, called the *inclusion capacity* of X. In general: $P_X(K) \leq T_X(K) + \mathbf{Prob}(X = \emptyset)$. However, if X is almost surely (a.s.) non-empty, $P_X \leq T_X$ holds and clearly a.s. non-empty RACS play a special role here. This is emphasized by the fact that the compactness of $\mathcal{U}$ makes $\mathcal{K} \setminus \{\emptyset\}$ itself compact, and hence $\{\emptyset\}$ is an isolated point in $\mathcal{K} = \mathcal{F}$.

Finally, note that discrete finite spaces are compact second countable Hausdorff topological spaces; the discrete topology makes **all** subsets open, closed and compact so that $\mathcal{K} = \mathcal{F} = \mathcal{O} = \mathcal{P}(\mathcal{U})$ and RACS can be simply called "Random Sets". In finite spaces, the functionals T_X, P_X and R_X can be written as finite sums of the $2^{|\mathcal{U}|}$ "basic probabilities" $\mathbf{Prob}(X = A)$.

3. Relation to the Dempster-Shafer theory

3.1 Belief and Plausibility functions

Let $\mathcal{U}$ be a *finite* set, equipped with the discrete topology. We proved the following results:

> The Plausibility functions *Pls* defined on a (finite) Frame of Discernment $\mathcal{U}$ are exactly the hitting capacities T_X of the almost surely non-empty Random (Closed) Sets X of the discrete topological space $\mathcal{U}$.

> The Belief functions *Bel* defined on a (finite) Frame of Discernment $\mathcal{U}$ are exactly the inclusion capacities P_X of the almost surely non-empty Random (Closed) Sets X of the discrete topological space $\mathcal{U}$.

The Commonality functions q are the implying functionals R_X of RACS X and the Mass functions m are equivalent to RACS *probability densities* $f = \frac{dP'}{d\nu}$ where ν is the counting measure in the (finite) space $\mathcal{P}(\mathcal{U})$: $\forall A \in \mathcal{P}(\mathcal{U})$, $m(A) = \mathbf{Prob}(X = A)$.

These equivalences provide a canonical framework to extend the DS formalism to general (possibly infinite) compact 2nd countable (i.e. compact metrizable) spaces, by identifying it with the theory of a.s. non-empty Random Closed Sets. See also [5] for a non-topological approach.

3.2 Probabilistic formulation of Dempster's rule

Here we show how a very simple probabilistic formulation of Dempster's rule of combination ([7]) can be derived.

Intersection is the set-theoretic operator traditionally used for pooling imprecise knowledge. However, the Dempster-Shafer formalism deals exclusively with *a.s. non-empty* RACS and since $\mathcal{F}(\mathcal{U}) \setminus \{\emptyset\}$ is not stable for $\cap$, the intersection of two a.s. non-empty RACS need not be a.s. non-empty. If the event $X_1 \cap X_2 \neq \emptyset$ has a non-zero probability, the *conditional RACS $X_1 \cap X_2$ given this event* is a.s. non-empty by construction. A simple calculation gives, for any non-empty compact K: $T_{X_1 \cap X_2 | X_1 \cap X_2 \neq \emptyset}(K) = \mathbf{Prob}(X_1 \cap X_2 \text{ hits } K \mid X_1 \cap X_2 \neq \emptyset) = \frac{T_{X_1 \cap X_2}(K)}{\mathbf{Prob}(X_1 \cap X_2 \neq \emptyset)}$. The quantity $\tau(X_1, X_2) = \mathbf{Prob}(X_1 \cap X_2 = \emptyset)$ is called the *amount of conflict* between X_1 and X_2: it is the probability that the two RACS are disjoint and is thought of as a measure of the "conflict" between the two pieces of evidence represented by X_1 and X_2. In the finite case, we can write:

$$T_{X_1 \oplus X_2}(K) = \frac{\sum\limits_{A \text{ hits } K} \mathbf{Prob}(X_1 \cap X_2 = A)}{\mathbf{Prob}(X_1 \cap X_2 \neq \emptyset)} = \frac{\sum\limits_{A \text{ hits } K} \left(\sum\limits_{B \cap C = A} \mathbf{Prob}(X_1 = B; \, X_2 = C) \right)}{1 - \sum\limits_{A \cap B = \emptyset} \mathbf{Prob}(X_1 = A; \, X_2 = B)} \quad (1)$$

When X_1 and X_2 are *statistically independent*, (1) becomes **Dempster's rule of combination** ([7]). Note however that (1) is more general than Dempster's rule, as no independence assumptions are made. Implying functionals (or their DS counterpart, Commonality functions) provide a more concise formulation when X_1 and X_2 are independent:

$$R_{X_1 \oplus X_2}(K) = \mathbf{Prob}(K \subset X_1 \cap X_2 \mid X_1 \cap X_2 \neq \emptyset) = \frac{R_{X_1 \cap X_2}(K)}{1 - \tau(X_1, X_2)} = \frac{R_{X_1}(K) \cdot R_{X_2}(K)}{1 - \tau(X_1, X_2)} \quad (2)$$

4. Relation to the Fuzzy set theory

4.1 membership functions

Goodman [2] has established that fuzzy sets are nothing but *one-point coverages* of random sets and that all the classical "fuzzy operators" as well as their extensions, have a set-theoretic counterpart in random set theory. We have shown that a similar result holds between Random Closed Sets and *upper semi-continuous* fuzzy sets, i.e. fuzzy sets whose membership functions are upper semi-continuous (u.s.c.) from $\mathcal{U}$ to $[0; 1]$. This is significant since the topological concept of semi-continuity is of considerable importance in any practical application of the theory. The proof of this result can be found in [1]. It is based on Choquet's theorem and on the fact that the *cross-section function* $\nu_S : \xi \longmapsto \nu_S(\xi) = \mu_S^{-1}([\xi; 1])$ of a fuzzy set S with membership function μ_S is *continuous* for the relative topology of $\Re$ in $[0; 1]$ and the Hit or Miss topology on $\mathcal{F}(\mathcal{U})$, and thus *measurable* for the corresponding Borel σ-algebras .

Hence every RACS X defines a unique u.s.c. fuzzy set $\varphi(X)$ which is its point interpretation, and for every u.s.c. fuzzy set S, there exists a (not necessarily unique) RACS of which it is a point interpretation. One such RACS, called canonical and noted $\kappa(S)$, is constructed by uniformly randomizing the cross sections of the membership function of S. Refer to [3] for an interpretation of membership functions in terms of Plausibility in *finite* spaces, in line with our results.

4.2 T-norms/conorms and Fuzzy connectives

Triangular (T-) norms and conorms are fuzzy connectives (binary operators) that verify the basic axioms of commutativity, associativity and monotonicity as well as specific boundary conditions. It is well known that the **Min** operator is the greatest T-norm $\wedge$ whereas the **Max** operator is the smallest T-conorm. Several families of T-norms and conorms have been suggested, including: $\wedge(a, b) = \mathbf{Min}\left(1; (a^p + b^p)^{1/p}\right)$ and the corresponding conorm: $\vee(a, b) = \mathbf{Max}\left(0; 1 - ((1-a)^p + (1-b)^p)^{1/p}\right)$ ($p \in [1; +\infty]$ is a parameter). This family is such that: $\forall (a, b) \in [0; 1]^2$, $\quad \mathbf{Max}(0; a + b - 1) \leq \wedge(a; b) \leq \mathbf{Min}(a; b)$ and $\quad \mathbf{Max}(a; b) \leq \vee(a; b) \leq \mathbf{Min}(1; a + b)$ (3). We proved ([1]) the following results (the corresponding results for T-conorms are obtained by changing $\wedge$ into $\vee$ and $\cap$ into $\cup$):

PROPOSITION 1. *For any T-norm $\wedge$ verifying (3) and any pair (S_1, S_2) of semi-continuous fuzzy subsets of $\mathcal{U}$, there exists a pair (X_1, X_2) of RACS such that S_1 (resp. S_2) is a point interpretation of X_1 (resp. X_2) and $S_1 \wedge S_2$ is a point interpretation of $X_1 \cap X_2$: $S_1 = \varphi(X_1)$, $S_2 = \varphi(X_2)$ and $S_1 \wedge S_2 = \varphi(X_1 \cap X_2)$.*

PROPOSITION 2. *The binary operator $\wedge$ defined on the set of (semi-continuous) fuzzy subsets of $\mathcal{U}$ by: $S_1 \wedge S_2 = \varphi(\kappa(S_1) \cap \kappa(S_2))$ is commutative, associative and verifies the boundary conditions of a T-norm, but is not necessarily monotonic. Several operators can be obtained, some of which are T-norms, depending on the choice of the statistical dependence between $\kappa(S_1)$ and $\kappa(S_2)$.*

The above propositions show that the combination of (u.s.c.) fuzzy sets can always be viewed as the intersection or union of RACS. Different combinations can be obtained by either selecting different (non-canonical) RACS of which they are point representations, or by varying the statistical dependence between the 2 RACS.

Figure 1 summarizes the main results of paragraphs 3 and 4. The main point of this work is that both of two widely used theories that aim at dealing with imprecise and uncertain information can easily be expressed within the purely probabilistic framework of Random Closed Sets. This comparison goes beyond mere rhetoric in that it not only provides useful extensions (Belief/Plausibility functions in infinite spaces, combination of non-independent evidence through Dempster's rule), but it also brings the theories much closer to experimental realities owing to the topological concepts of closedness/semi-continuity. Moreover, our RACS interpretation points out a fundamental inadequacy in the integration schemes of both theories: the widely used combination operators are all equivalent to *set-theoretic* operators (intersection for Dempster's rule, intersection or union for fuzzy connectives). This suggests that they are suitable for combining *imprecise but certain* knowledge, but inherently ill-suited to the pooling of *uncertain* evidence. The latter requires a *probabilistic operator* as is shown below in the context of knowledge acquisition.

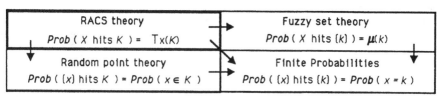

Figure 1: Both the classical random point and the (u.s.c.) fuzzy set theories are particularizations of the RACS formalism, as singletons are particular compact sets in a Hausdorff space.

5. Knowledge Acquisition

5.1 construction of Belief/Plausibility functions from World evidence

One of the weak points of the DS formalism is the absence of any systematic scheme for constructing Belief/Plausibility functions from pieces of evidence. The following theorem particularizes one such construction scheme:

THEOREM 1. *The only order-independent, piecewise and point-compatible combination operator that allows the construction of general Belief/Plausibility functions from (closed) subsets of a Universe is the Mean operator.*

"order-independent" stands for "commutative and associative" and by "general functions", we mean non-trivial (0-1 valued) functions. A *point-compatible combination* is such that the Belief function constructed from subsets of U reduces to an ordinary point probability measure (Bayesian Belief function) whenever all subsets reduce to singletons. This requirement guarantees the compatibility with the point approach, or in other words, insures that our construction scheme is an extension of the point approach. It can also be viewed as an *economy principle*: if all pieces of evidence are points of U, there is no need for a set theory and since ordinary point probabilities are sufficient, they should be used. A *piecewise combination* is such that the combined Belief (or Plausibility) of a proposition A only depends on A, and not on any other proposition $B \neq A$. A non-piecewise combination is said to be *global*.

Note that THEOREM 1 only constrains the construction of Belief/Plausibility functions from *subsets* of U. Indeed, closed subsets of U are the most basic pieces of evidence one can obtain from the World (they are binary in nature), and they are the only ones *directly accessible* through simple *physical* measurements.

Hence, if one wants to use an order-independent and point-compatible operator different from the Mean probabilistic operator, one must drop at least one of the following premises:

1) combination is not piecewise: the combined Belief of a proposition may depend on the Belief of other propositions.
2) the construction of Belief functions does not directly deal with subsets of U: the inputs are other Belief functions. We must assume that "Belief functions can be found in the World" and measured directly without any construction process from subsets of U. As this is obviously

not the case in the *physical World*, it is clear that we are working in a *human World*, where human beings (experts, witnesses, etc) are the sole sources of information.

5.2 construction of Fuzzy sets from World evidence

Fuzzy set theory also suffers from the absence of any systematic scheme for constructing Fuzzy set membership functions from World evidence. In view of the relation between Plausibility/Commonality functions and (u.s.c.) Fuzzy membership functions, we can write:

THEOREM 1′. *The only order-independent, point-compatible and piecewise combination operator that allows the construction of general (u.s.c.) Fuzzy sets from (closed) subsets of a Universe is the Mean operator.*

The strongest argument against one of the premises of the above theorem is the ontological claim that "both the physical and human Worlds are fuzzy" according to which fuzzy membership functions can be measured directly even in the physical World and be used for further combinations. This claim has been discussed at length in [8] and seems difficult to refute for the human World. However, engineers have been increasingly aware of the difficulty of measuring membership functions in the physical World experimentally without using some sort of statistical construction. And indeed, there are some good reasons to think that the simple pieces of information "belongs/does not belong to a set" precede the more complex membership functions, and thus that the latter can be induced from the former.

If we reject the "fuzzy physical World" claim, we may conclude: in systems where the sources of information are not human, or at least *not only* human, the construction of Fuzzy membership functions must be either statistical (Mean operator) or global (non-piecewise). Note that this rejects the classical fuzzy connectives **Min** and **Max**! Indeed they are order-independent and piecewise, but do not enable the construction of general (=non-crisp) u.s.c. Fuzzy sets from subsets of the Universe.

6. Concluding remarks

We have shown how the allegedly "non-probabilistic" Dempster-Shafer and Fuzzy set theories are in fact closely related to probability measure theory, and we investigated these relations in detail within a topological setting. The resulting unified approach emphasized the inadequacies of the traditional operators used for the integration and acquisition of imprecise and uncertain knowledge. It also suggested that, in many practical circumstances, the probabilistic Mean operator is the only reasonable alternative for acquiring such knowledge.

Acknowledgements

The authors would like to thank E. Yodogawa for his help and K. Ueno for fruitful discussions.

References

[1] Ph. Quinio, "Mathematical Connections between the Probability, Fuzzy Set, Possibility and Dempster-Shafer Theories", *ATR technical report*, TR-A-0112, 1991.

[2] I.R. Goodman, "Characterizations of N-ary Fuzzy Set Operations which induce Homomorphic Random Set operations" in *Fuzzy Information and Decision Processes*, North-Holland, 1982.

[3] J. Kampé de Fériet, "Interpretation of Membership functions of Fuzzy Set in terms of Plausibility and Belief" in *Fuzzy Information and Decision Processes*, North-Holland, 1982.

[4] G. Matheron, *Random Sets and Integral Geometry*, Wiley, New York, 1975.

[5] H.T Nguyen, "On Random Sets and Belief Functions" *J. of Math. Anal. and Appl.*, vol. 65, pp.531-542, 1978.

[6] J. Serra, *Image Analysis and Mathematical Morphology*, Academic Press, 1982.

[7] G. Shafer, *A mathematical Theory of Evidence*, Princeton University Press, 1976.

[8] G. Tamburrini and S. Termini, "Some Foundational Problems in the Formalization of Vagueness" in *Fuzzy Information and Decision Processes*, North-Holland, 1982.

Knowledge Extraction in Trivalued Propositional Logic

Antoine Rauzy

LaBRI, Université Bordeaux 1

351, cours de la Libération 33400 Talence FRANCE

56 84 60 83 rauzy@geocub.greco-prog.fr

Abstract : in this paper, we present two methods in order to extract relevant informations from a knowledge represented with a set of trivalued propositional rules. The aim of the introduction of the third value is on the one hand to allow to deal with uncertain informations, and on the other hand to introduce a non-monotonic implication connective. We show how to extend the notion of production fields to this formalism and how the concept of unification can be applied.

Key words : Automatic Deduction, Trivalued Logic, Knowledge Extraction.

Introduction

The aim of this paper is to present two methods in order to extract relevant informations from a knowledge represented with a set of trivalued propositional rules. The main feature of this representation is to allow the user to deal with uncertain informations by introducing a third value : uncertain (in addition to true and false).

Deducing the consequences of a set of rules and responding to a yes/no question is often insufficient for a knowledge based system : the user may want to extract more complex informations (for instance, he may want to produce new rules or a questionnaire). Several methods had been proposed in order to perform this extraction. In this paper, we apply to the trivaluated logic two promising ones : the notion of production fields introduced by P. Siegel [Siegel 87] and the unification in finite algebrae.

The two associated algorithms we present here are both based on the same enumerative method (the construction of a decision tree). A large experience had proved that this method is efficient, i.e. that it allows to deal with quite big problems despite the fact that the knowledge extraction is NP-complete.

I. Trivalued Propositionnal logic.

A trivalued rule (for short a rule) is a formula in the form: $x_1 \wedge x_2 \wedge \ldots \wedge x_m \rightarrow y_1 \vee y_2 \vee \ldots \vee y_n$ where m and n are eventually equal to zero, and where the x_i and the y_j are literals, i.e. either a variable p, either its negation $\neg p$. The truth tables of the connectives are the following :

¬	#t	#f	#u
	#f	#t	#u

∨	#t	#f	#u
#t	#t	#t	#t
#f	#t	#f	#u
#u	#t	#u	#u

∧	#t	#f	#u
#t	#t	#f	#u
#f	#f	#f	#f
#u	#u	#f	#u

→	#t	#f	#u
#t	#t	#f	#f
#f	#t	#t	#t
#u	#t	#t	#t

Note that the non-monotonic implication → introduced in [Delahaye 87] is different from the ones of Kleene [67], Lukasiewicz [63] and Przymusinski [89].

Assume that n variables occur in the set of rules E. E describes a subset of $\{#t, #f, #u\}^n$. The nuples satisfying E are said admissible.

A rule $C : p_1 \wedge \ldots \wedge p_i \wedge \neg q_1 \wedge \ldots \wedge \neg q_j \rightarrow r_1 \vee \ldots \vee r_k \vee \neg s_1 \vee \ldots \vee \neg s_l$ can be interpreted on the power set $\{P(\{#t, #f, #u\}^n), \cup, \cap, -\}$: let us denote respectively T_v, F_v and U_v the subsets of $\{#t, #f, #u\}^n$ in which the variable v has the values true, false and uncertain. C describes the following subset of $\{#t, #f, #u\}^n$:

$$\cup_p (F_p \cup U_p) \cup \cup_q (T_q \cup U_q) \cup \cup_r T_r \cup \cup_s F_s$$

A fundamental operation is to determine, given a set of rules E, its admissible nuples. The most simple (and as the experience has shown, the most efficient) algorithm to do this is to construct a decision tree.

Let us denote $E_{[v \leftarrow c]}$ the set of rules E in which the variable v has been substituted by the constant c. It is easy to realize a procedure deciding, given an assignment A of a subset of the variables occurring in E, whether A satisfies E or A falsifies E or A doesn't assign enough variables to give a value to E.

A decision tree is a ternary tree such that:

    - all the nodes are labelled by an assignment [v ← c, w ← d, …], where v, w, … are variables occurring in E, and c, d,… belong to $\{#t, #f, #u\}$.

    - the root is labelled by the empty assignment [],

If a node is labelled by a assignment A then,

    - if the procedure is able to decide if A satisfy or doesn't satisfy E then it is a leaf,

    - else there exists a variable v occurring in E_A and the node has 3 descendants labelled by $A \cup [v \leftarrow #t]$, $A \cup [v \leftarrow #f]$, $A \cup [v \leftarrow #u]$ (perhaps not in this order).

II. Production fields in trivalued logic.

The notion of production fields had been introduced and explored for the boolean constraints in clausal form by Siegel and als [Siegel 88] [Boï & als 89]. It consists in characterizing by a morphologic property the formula which represent the relevant informations. A production process consists in producing all the formulae belonging to the field and implied by the considered set of constraints.

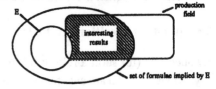

A production field P is defined by a triple $< m, V_1, V_2 >$, where :

1) m is the maximum length of its rules,

2) V_1 is the set of the variables which can occur in its rules both in the right and left members and V_2 is the set of the variables which can occur only in the rigth members.

Property : the production fields defined as above are semantically stable i.e., that every subrule of a rule belonging to field belongs to the field.

Property : the union and the intersection of two production fields are also two production fields.

Algorithm (principle).

The set E can be viewed as a formula in conjunctive normal form. The set $\mathcal{A} = \{A_1, ..., A_k\}$ of the assignments labelling the leaves of a decision tree associated with E and satisfying E can be viewed as a formula in disjunctive normal form, equivalent to E.

The idea of the production algorithm is to compute a decision tree associated with $\mathcal{A}$ in order to come back to a formula in conjunctive normal form

Roughly speaking, the leaves of this tree are labelled by sets of assignements $R = \{v_1 \leftarrow c_1, ..., v_i \leftarrow c_i\}$ such that :

- The number of variables assigned is a most m.

- For each A_j there exists at least one of the $v \leftarrow c$ belonging to A_j.

- Each v belongs to $V1 \cup V2$, R doesn't contain both $v \leftarrow \#t$ and $v \leftarrow \#f$ and if $v \in V2$ then R doesn't contain $v \leftarrow \#u$.

The set of the variables assigned in R can be split up in four subsets : the $p_1,..., p_i$ such that R contains $p \leftarrow \#f$ and $p \leftarrow \#u$, the $q_1,..., q_j$ such that R contains $q \leftarrow \#t$ and $q \leftarrow \#u$, the $r_1,..., r_k$ such that R contains only $p \leftarrow \#t$ and the $s_1,..., s_l$ such that R contains only $p \leftarrow \#f$.

Property : the rule $\bigwedge p \wedge \bigwedge \neg q \to \bigvee r \vee \bigvee \neg s$ belongs to P and is implied by E.

Theorem : the set $\mathcal{R}$ of rules produced by the above algorithm is a precursor of the set of the rules implied by E and belonging to P, i.e., that each rule of this set is either in $\mathcal{R}$ either implied by $\mathcal{R}$.

III. Unification for knowledge extraction.

A critical task for a knowledge extraction mechanism is to express each variable representing an output of the physical system as a function of the variables representing its inputs. This technic has several well-known applications, for instance the computation of the data labels in the ATMS [de Kleer 86a and 86b].

Let $X = \{x_1, x_2, ..., x_n\}$ be the set of the variables representing the inputs and let y be a variable representing an output.

Assume that each A_i (belonging to the $\mathcal{A}$ defined above) assigns a value $c_{i,j}$ to each x_j and the value d_i to y In order to express y as a function of the x_i, we must associate y with a term like:

$$\zeta(x_1,x_2,\ldots,x_n) = \begin{array}{l} \text{if } x_1 = c_{1,1} \text{ and } x_2 = c_{1,2} \text{ and } \ldots x_n = c_{1,n} \text{ then } d_1 \\ \text{or}\ldots\text{or} \\ \text{if } x_1 = c_{k,1} \text{ and } x_2 = c_{k,2} \text{ and } \ldots x_n = c_{k,n} \text{ then } d_k \end{array}$$

where each row corresponds to an A_j.

This term can be constructed in the trivalued logic in the following way :

$$\zeta(x_1,x_2,\ldots,x_n) \leftrightarrow (x_1 \leftrightarrow c_{1,1}) \wedge (x_2 \leftrightarrow c_{1,2}) \wedge \ldots \wedge (x_n \leftrightarrow c_{1,n}) \wedge d_1$$
$$\vee\ldots\vee$$
$$(x_1 \leftrightarrow c_{k,1}) \wedge (x_2 \leftrightarrow c_{k,2}) \wedge \ldots \wedge (x_n \leftrightarrow c_{k,n}) \wedge d_k$$

where the connective $f \leftrightarrow g$ takes the value true if f and g have the same value, the value false otherwise. Note that if d_i is equal to #f, we can simply remove the corresponding line. The problem is to generalized this construction to the case where the decision tree as no particular form. We will see that it is possible to do so by using the concept of unification.

Unification in trivalued logic.

A substitution σ is a unifier of two formulae f and g iff $\sigma(f) = \sigma(g)$, i.e. in trivalued logic iff $\sigma(f \leftrightarrow g) \leftrightarrow \#t$ (since $f \leftrightarrow g$ is itself a formula, it is possible to extend the definition to a single formula.even if it is not in the form $f \leftrightarrow g$). A unifier σ is most general one iff for any other unifier δ there exists a substitution μ such that $\mu \circ \sigma = \delta$.

The interesting property of the most general unifiers is that they can be considered as parametric solutions of the studied formulae, or in other words that they described all the assignments satisfying these formulae.

The idea of the using of the unification concept is to compute a most general unifier σ of the set of rules E, where the variables belonging to X are considered as constants. Therefore, the image $\sigma(y)$ we obtain for each variable representing an output describes the values taken by y for the different values of the variables belonging to X.

Algorithm.

Let us assume now that the decision tree associated with E has no particular form.

As we have done in the previous paragraph, it is possible to associate with each A_i a characteristic conjunction $(x_{i,1} \leftrightarrow c_{i,1}) \wedge (x_{i,2} \leftrightarrow c_{i,2}) \wedge \ldots \wedge (x_{i,n} \leftrightarrow c_{i,n})$, but

- some elements of X may be not assigned in A_i,
- two assignments may have the same associated characteristic conjunction,
- the variable y may be allowed to take several values in A_i,

The first point is not a problem for our purpose. In order to express that the variable is allowed to take several values in A_i (say, for instance, $d_{i,1}$ and $d_{i,2}$) it suffices to create a new variable y' and to add to the characteristic conjunction associated with A_i the term $(((y' \leftrightarrow \#t) \wedge d_{i,1}) \vee ((y' \leftrightarrow \#f) \wedge d_{i,2}) \vee ((y' \leftrightarrow \#u) \wedge d_{i,3}))$. It is easy to verify that this term describes the admissible values of y.

The problem we must solve now is to distinguish several assignments associated with the same characteristic conjunction. Note that if there is only one variable y representing an output, this distinction is not necessary : it suffices to consider the different values of y in the assignments. The problem arises when there are several variables representing outputs and when their values are not independent. In this case, we must distinguish the assignments in order to express this dependency.

Assume that the assignments A_1, A_2, ..., A_g are associated with the same characteristic conjunction. The first step of method consists in creating r new variables z_1, z_2,..., z_r where r is the smallest integer such that $g \leq 3^r$. There are 3^r distinct assignments of the z_i. At each of these assignments corresponds a characteristic conjunction. The second step of the method consists in choosing any surjective mapping from the set of these characteristic conjunction to $\{A_1, A_2, ..., A_g\}$ and to associated with each A_i the disjunction of its inverse images.

It is easy to verify that for any assignments of the z_i, one and only one of the formulae associated with the A_j is true and that the others are false. And now, it is possible to construct the term $\zeta(x_1,x_2,...,x_n)$ in the same way than in the paragraph III.1.

Property : if we compute the terms ζ for all variables which don't belong to X, then we obtain a most general unifier of E, where the x_i are considered as constants.

Conclusion

We have provided two knowledge extraction mechanisms for the trivalued propositional logic. On the one hand this work completes the production fields study, on the other hand it unifies, in an algorithmic point of vue, the two technics. The main question is now to study carefully the efficiency of the algorithms (and the associated heuristics). In particular, it seems very important to study their incrementality. Another question concerns the way in which the technics presented in this paper can be used in practice. The choice of the good production field or of the good constants for the unification is not always easy. We are actually looking for a relevant set of benchmarks.

References

[Boï & als 90] Jean-Marc Boï, Eric Innocente, Antoine Rauzy et Pierre Siegel - Aspect de la démonstration automatique en France. *Actes de Journées Nationales du PRC-IA* 90.

[Delahaye 87] Chaînage avant et calculs de modèles en logique bivaluée et trivaluée *7ièmes Journées Internationales sur le Systèmes Experts* Avignon 87

[de Kleer 86 a & b] An Assumption-Based TMS. *Artificial Intelligence* 28.

[Kleene 67] Introduction to metamathematics North-Holland 67

[Lukasiewicz 63] Elements of Mathematical Logic. Pergamon Press 63.

[Przymusinski 89] Non-monotonic formalisms and logic programing *Proc. 6th ICLP*

[Siegel, 87] Représentation et utilisation de la connaissance en calcul propositionnel, Thèse d'état, Groupe Intelligence Artificielle, Université d'Aix-Marseille II, Juillet 1987

Using Maximum Entropy to Identify Unsafe Assumptions
in Probabilistic Expert Systems

Paul C Rhodes and Gerald R Garside
Department of Computing, University of Bradford
BRADFORD BD7 1DP, UK

Introduction

Expert systems are renowned for being impossible to validate and this is particularly so if they attempt to reason under uncertainty. The problems are twofold, namely (i) the "correct" answer is not known in general and (ii) the errors introduced by simplifying assumptions cannot be quantified. Furthermore these problems are inherent within such systems. However, one should not be deterred from attempting to establish the soundness of a given expert system.

This paper describes a technique for probing the soundness of reasoning mechanisms in probabilistic expert systems by comparing the results they produce with those from a method based on Maximum Entropy (ME). ME based methods are ideal for the purpose [10] but may be computationally too expensive to use for the expert system itself [4].

Probabilistic Expert Systems and Simplifying Assumptions

One class of expert system designed for reasoning under uncertainty is the probabilistic class. Some recent members of this class are now becoming quite refined due to work by Pearl [6], Lauritzen and Spiegelhalter [3] and others. Probabilistic systems face two problems. The first is in obtaining sufficient data to fully specify the system. The second is that probabilistic expert systems are exponentially large. Specifically a probabilistic system having n entities has 3^n probabilities associated with it when all possible joint probabilities and marginals are taken in account. This is, of course, why Pearl, Lauritzen and Spiegelhalter and others propagate information through networks rather than compute the posterior probabilities directly (see [5]).

The purpose of simplifying assumptions is to reduce a problem of $O(2^n)$ down to a problem of $O(n)$ both computationally and in terms of the knowledge required from the expert. Consequently the expert provides $O(n)$ pieces of information and the assumptions must "fill in" the remaining pieces of information which were not given. This is acceptable until the expert has some information which was not part of the reduced set used to build the expert system but is at odds with the results that the expert system is providing. The authors of this paper have examined this phenomenon for the Prospector system [2] and have shown [9] that it is potentially capable of giving entirely the wrong answer.

Granted, this can only occur if the assumptions are violated but expert systems do not, and probably cannot, check that the assumptions have not been violated.

A Test Method Based on Maximum Entropy

One way to avoid making simplifying assumptions is to return to first principles and use the correct method for computing the posterior probabilities, ie from the marginals, by summing the appropriate joint probabilities. Superficially this requires the expert to provide 2^n-1 pieces of information which is clearly impractical. A more practical alternative is to use ME to estimate all the unknown joint probabilities using this information (see [10]). The posterior probabilities can then be computed from these as long as the size of the test scenario is kept within reasonable bounds. Results given in this paper were derived using a method described in [8].

All existing probabilistic expert systems require the expert to give knowledge in a specific form suited to the method being used, eg information associated with the edges of an influence diagram. Consequently, it is not so easy to compare these methods with each other directly. However, methods based on ME can be compared directly with other methods because the form that the expert has used to express the knowledge is immaterial.

A Case Study: HUGIN's Chest Clinic Problem

The method proposed by Lauritzen and Spiegelhalter has been incorporated into a shell called HUGIN [1]. The influence network suggested by Lauritzen and Spiegelhalter and supplied as one of the examples for HUGIN is shown in Figure 1, which also lists the information the expert is deemed to have given.

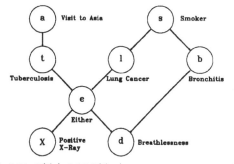

P(a)=0.01 P(t|a)=0.05 P(t|~a)=0.01
P(s)=0.5 P(l|s)=0.10 P(l|~s)=0.01 P(b|s)=0.60 P(b|~s)=0.30
P(e|lt)=1.0 P(e|l~t)=1.0 P(e|~lt)=1.0 P(e|~l~t)=0.0
P(X|e)=0.98 P(X|~e)=0.05
P(d|be)=0.90 P(d|b~e)=0.80 P(d|~be)=0.70 P(d|~b~e)=0.10

Fig 1 : Influence Diagram for Chest Clinic Problem

Table 1 shows what happens when a patient has a positive X-ray but does not have breathlessness symptoms. The difference in the results is significant. Differences occur in all but one of the entities and the discrepancy is approaching 50% in the worst case and more than 30% in 3 of the 6 results.

	a	s	t	l	b	e
ME	0.01	0.52	0.06	0.27	0.18	0.33
HUGIN	0.01	0.50	0.04	0.20	0.25	0.24

Table 1 : Chest Clinic Problem - Results given "X-ray" and not "breathlessness"

At this juncture it is important to stress that we cannot say HUGIN is right and ME is wrong or vice versa. They have both made very different assumptions. If the assumptions of independence used by HUGIN are added to the ME method as extra constraints then the two methods agree.

Although this example is fictitious, it is important to establish what the expert said, since this is where the root of the discrepancy lies. The expert is presumed to have said that "smoking causes lung cancer *and* smoking causes bronchitis". He/she has not said whether or not "lung cancer causes bronchitis *or* bronchitis causes lung cancer". HUGIN's assumption that bronchitis and lung cancer are conditionally independent is not supported by ME and has also been challenged by Pratt [7].

Dependence can be Inferred but Unstated

Figure 2 shows a very small influence diagram and the associated information which is deemed to have been given by the expert. As this example is so small the prior probability for E_3 and all the possible combinations of posterior probabilities can easily be computed and are shown in Table 2.

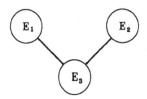

$P(E_1) = 0.3$

$P(E_2) = 0.1$

$P(E_3|E_1 E_2) = 0.99$ $P(E_3|{\sim}E_1 E_2) = 0.20$

$P(E_3|E_1{\sim}E_2) = 0.90$ $P(E_3|{\sim}E_1{\sim}E_2) = 0.70$

Fig 2 : Dependence can be Inferred - an Example

	$P(E_3)$	$P(E_2|E_1)$	$P(E_3|E_1)$	$P(E_1|E_2)$	$P(E_3|E_2)$	$P(E_1|E_3)$	$P(E_2|E_3)$
ME	0.76	0.30	0.93	0.89	0.90	0.36	0.12
HUGIN	0.73	0.10	0.91	0.30	0.44	0.37	0.06

Table 2 : Posterior Probabilities for Figure 2

Closer examination of Table 2 reveals the discrepancy between the two methods precisely. HUGIN's value for $P(E_1 | E_2) = 0.30 = P(E_1)$, ie HUGIN is assuming that E_1 and E_2 are independent. ME, however, does not support this assumption. The values computed using ME are $P(E_1 | E_2) = 0.89$ which is vastly different from 0.30 and so does not support the assumption of independence. In other words a dependence between E_1 and E_2 is implied without specific information to that effect.

The question which must now be asked is "which assumption is the safest". The expert has given the information in Figure 2. For the purposes of this argument we are going to assert that the expert does not know for certain that E_1 and E_2 are independent. The ME analysis concludes that what the expert does know implies that E_1 and E_2 are not independent. ME is a well founded theory for handling minimal information situations. If the ME results are to be overridden this must be on the basis of knowledge about the problem itself. In this respect the HUGIN results are arguably less safe than those derived using ME.

Conclusion

A technique has been proposed which can be used as a benchmark against which other probabilistic inference methods can be compared. One such comparison, between our ME based technique and the HUGIN expert system shell, provided a useful insight into (i) the implied consequences of the available knowledge and (ii) the safety of making simplifying assumptions such as independence.

References

1. Andersen, S.K., Olesen, K.G., Jensen, F.V. and Jensen, F. "HUGIN - a Shell for Building Bayesian Belief Universes for Expert Systems". Readings in Uncertain Reasoning, Eds Shafer, W. and Pearl, J. (1990). Morgan Kaufmann, San Mateo, California.
2. Duda, R.O., Hart, P.E. and Nilsson, N.J. "Subjective Bayesian Methods for Rule-based Inference Systems". National Computer Conference, AFIPS Conf. Proc. Vol.45 (1976) pp.1075-1082.
3. Lauritzen, S.L. and Spiegelhalter, D.J. "Local Computations with Probabilities on Graphical Structures and Their Applications to Expert Systems". J. Royal Statistical Society B., Vol.50, No.2 (1988) pp.157-224.
4. Maung, I. and Paris, J.B. "A Note on the Infeasibility of Some Inference Processes". International Journal of Intelligent Systems, Vol.5, No.5 (1990) pp.595-603.

5. Pearl, J. "Fusion, Propagation, and Structuring in Belief Networks". Artificial Intelligence, Vol.29, No.3 (1986) pp.241-288.

6. Pearl, J. "Probabilistic Reasoning in Intelligent Systems". (1988) Morgan Kaufmann, San Mateo, California.

7. Pratt, I. Comments in "Discussion of the Paper by Lauritzen and Speigelhalter", reference [3] above, p.212.

8. Rhodes, P.C. and Garside, G.R. "Maximum Entropy for Expert Systems: the Horns of a Dilemma". Internal Research Report No. CS-13-91 (1991), Department of Computing, University of Bradford.

9. Rhodes, P.C. and Garside, G.R. "Reappraisal of the Use of Conditional Probability in Early Expert Systems". Knowledge-Based Systems, Vol.4, No.2 (1991) pp.67-74.

10. Wise, B.P. and Henrion, M. "A Framework for Comparing Uncertain Inference Systems to Probability". Uncertainty in Artificial Intelligence, Eds Kanal, L.N. and Lemmer, J.F. (1986). Elsevier Science Publishers B.V. (North Holland).

ON TRUTH AND UTILITY*

Enrique H. Ruspini

Artificial Intelligence Center, SRI International

333 Ravenswood Avenue, Menlo Park, California 94025, U.S.A.

1 Introduction

In this paper we explore abstract structures that permit a conceptual unification of notions from multivalued logic and utility theory. This work is the continuation of previous efforts [9] to develop a unifying framework that simplifies the understanding of approximate reasoning methodologies while facilitating their study and comparison. In particular, this paper further elaborates upon recent results of investigations on the semantic bases of fuzzy logic [8]. These investigations uncovered relations between possibilistic concepts and metric structures defined on a space of possible worlds. In this paper we discuss the relation between the latter structures and utilitarian concepts such as the desirability of certain outcomes or measures of relative preference between different states of affairs.

The results presented herein follow primarily from the application of well-known ideas in fuzzy-set theory ranging from original proposals of Bellman and Zadeh [2] through efforts to introduce decision-theoretic concepts within the framework of fuzzy decision problems [3] to studies on the structure and characteristics of fuzzy relations and operators [10, 11]. Our contribution might be summarized as the incorporation of these ideas within a logical framework with a view toward the integration of logical and operations-research methods. In this regard, we have aimed to develop methods for the synthesis of plans and control policies that lead to decisions that may be explained, i.e., to the production of rational descriptions of the deliberations that led to the selection of such choices. More generally, we were motivated by a desire to produce control and decision-making policies that follow from a rational analysis of an approximate model of reality rather than from poorly explained or understood human introspective processes. Furthermore, we have sought to clarify the relations that exist between individual measures of solution adequacy and global expressions that combine such measures into a single utility function that incorporates information about their relative degrees of importance.

Our approach is close in spirit to the "logics of preference" proposed by Rescher [7] where the truth-value (usually measured in a $[0, 1]$ scale) of a proposition p measures the desirability of p coming about, or, in other words, the degree by which p is a "good thing." Our treatment, however, differs from that of Rescher in a number of substantial regards.

---

*This paper is a slightly revised and expanded version of a previous work presented at the 1991 Conference on Uncertainty in Artificial Intelligence.

In our approach, each of the propositions that define the acceptability of a possible world as a solution is associated with a utility measure that provides a numerical ranking of all potential solutions, from the perspective of that restrictive statement, "all other things being equal." Our measures are, therefore, expressions of the degree of adequacy of solutions from a limited perspective rather than measures of "global" relative desirability, regardless of context. In Rescher's approach, one such global measure is defined as an average of context-specific desirability values, an assumption that leads to the derivation of properties for that function that are similar to those of a probability distribution. This conclusion, however, stems from the arbitrary definition of the combination mechanism, rather than as a necessary burden of clear rational requirements.

We also introduce epistemic modalities, intended to represent degrees of knowledge about the potential utility of certain decisions. In such a way, we enhance the value of multivalued-logic schemes and generalize previous semantic models of fuzzy logic [8] while providing a practical approach to the representation of ignorance about the potential utility of certain choices.

In our formulation, each potential solution of a reasoning problem, or "possible world," is mapped to a set of numbers, each representing the desirability of that alternative from the viewpoint of a different constraint. We do not require that constraints representing operational goals (or "utilities") and constraints that limit expenditures on the acquisition of those goals (or "costs") be represented utilizing different structures. Moreover, every constraint, including behavioral system laws—commonly described as "knowledge" in the artificial intelligence literature—is the source of utility measures expressing the potential costs associated with simplifying assumptions, such as, for example, "the container is filled with a perfect gas."

2   Possible Worlds and Desirabilities

Our formalism is based on the notion of possible world. Informally, a possible world is an assignment of conventional truth-values (i.e, true or false) to the declarative statements, or *propositions*, that describe the possible state, behavior, or characteristics of a real-world system. Introduction of the notion of possible world permits to model the reasoning processes involved in the solution of a problem as the determination of the set of possible worlds that complies with prescribed constraints (i.e., knowledge, evidence). Equivalently, we may also say that the solution of a reasoning problem entails the determination of the acceptability or worthiness of any possible world as an answer to the problem.

In conventional formalisms, restrictive propositions, which may only attain the truth-values "true" or "false," define whether or not a possible world is a solution. More generally, however, we may measure the quality or worthiness of a solution by means of a function that assigns a numerical value between 0 and 1 to every possible world. This measure, which may be thought of as a generalized or *elastic* constraint, gauges the relative adequacy of alternative solutions with respect to a set of ideal solutions that attain or exceed some associated "target value." Such ideal solutions are given a relative measure of adequacy that is equal to 1 while, conversely, a value of 0 indicates that the possible world is not an acceptable answer to the problem.

Each desirability measure may be thought of as a procedure to rank solutions of a problem from the limited perspective of a single specific constraint. These measures must not be confused, therefore, with structures used to represent the relative importance of each constraint or problem-solving goal, called "utilities of satisfaction" by Haddawy and Hanks [4].

2.1 Desirability Measures

Definition: A *desirability measure* is a function $D : \mathcal{U} \mapsto [0,1]$, i.e., a fuzzy set in the universe $\mathcal{U}$ of possible worlds.

The concept of desirability measure is a natural extension of the notion of "hard" or "crisp" constraint. The values $D(w)$ may also be thought of as the truth-values of the proposition "The solution w is acceptable from the viewpoint of D."

If w is a satisfactory solution from the viewpoint of a generalized requirement, which is expressed by means of the desirability measure D, and from the viewpoint of another requirement, expressed by means of another desirability measure D', then it is clear that w should also be acceptable from the joint viewpoint of those two requirements. Well-known arguments [10] show that the desirability of a conjunction of two desirabilities D and D' is expressed by the relation

$$(D \wedge D')(w) = D(w) \circledast D'(w), \quad w \text{ in } \mathcal{U},$$

where $\circledast$ is a *triangular norm*.

Similarly, the desirability of the disjunction of two constraints D and D' can be seen to be given by

$$(D \vee D')(w) = D(w) \oplus D'(w), \quad w \text{ in } \mathcal{U},$$

where $\oplus$ is a *triangular conorm*.

In what follows we will assume that all triangular norms and conorms to be considered are continuous functions of their arguments since it is reasonable to require that the desirability of either the conjunction or the disjunction, respectively, of two arguments does not vary abruptly when there is a slight change of the desirabilities being combined.

Desirability measures that rank possible solutions by the degree by which they do *not* meet some constraint expressed by a desirability D are given by expressions of the form $\sim D$, where $\sim$ is a *negation function*, i.e., a function $\sim$ from $[0,1]$ into $[0,1]$ that reverses the order of its argument, i.e., $\sim b \leq \sim a$ if $a \leq b$, and that, in addition, satisfies the relations $\sim 0 = 1$ and $\sim 1 = 0$.

The pseudoinverse $\oslash$ of a T-norm $\circledast$ is useful to generalize the implication operator $\rightarrow$ of classical logic by means of the expression $(D \rightarrow D')(w) = D'(w) \oslash D(w)$. The importance of pseudoinverses is related to the tautology $(D \circledast (D \rightarrow D')) \rightarrow D'$, which generalizes the classical modus ponens [10].

In closing this section, it is important to remark that, while in many problems, it is sufficient to seek solutions w having adequate values of the conjunction $D_1 \circledast D_2 \circledast \ldots \circledast D_n$, of the constraints $D_1, D_2, \ldots, D_n$ that define a problem— in general, as noted by many authors, it is necessary to consider broader families of connectives [1]. These connectives essentially incorporate the diverse tradeoff, compensation, and differential weight considerations that define the relative importance of the various problem-solving goals.

2.2 Preference Relations

In many problems it is easier to quantify the extent by which one state of affairs is preferrable to another than to provide a measure of absolute desirability. This notion of relative desirability may be formalized by functions of the form $\rho(w|w')$ that map pairs of possible worlds to numbers between 0 and 1 so as to quantify the extent by which a possible world w is preferred to another w', from the viewpoint of a particular constraint. To furnish ρ with the appropriate semantics we shall require that it satisfies the following conditions:

1. No resources should be spent to be in w if we are already in w.

2. If we are willing to spend resources to be in w when we are in w', then we should not spend any resources to be in w' if we were in w

3. The amount that we would be willing to pay to be in w when we are in w'' should be bound by above by a function of the amount that we would be willing to spend to be in w if we were in w' and of the amount that we would be willing to pay to be in w' if we were in w''.

These conditions readily lead to the following
Definition: A function ρ mapping pairs of possible worlds into numbers between 0 and 1 is called a $\oplus$-*preference* relation if and only if

1. $\rho(w|w) = 0$ for all w in $\mathcal{U}$.

2. If $\rho(w|w') > 0$, then $\rho(w'|w) = 0$ for all w and w' in $\mathcal{U}$.

3. For any possible worlds w, w' and w'' it is

$$\rho(w|w'') \leq \rho(w|w') \oplus \rho(w'|w'').$$

It is also easy to see that if ρ has the semantics of a relation representing graded preference, then $\oplus$ should be a conorm.

2.3 Relations between Desirabilities and Preferences

The combination and aggregation of preference relatons is considerably more complex than that of desirability measures as, for example, the negation $\sim \rho$ of a preference relation ρ is not itself a preference relation. In order to develop an aggregation methodology, it is necessary first to study the relations that exist between both types of utilitarian measures.

The derivation of a $\oplus$-preference relation ρ_D from a desirability measure $\mathbf{D}$ is easily achieved by means of the pseudoinverse $\ominus$ of $\oplus$:

$$\rho_D(w|w') = \mathbf{D}(w) \ominus \mathbf{D}(w').$$

The inverse process of derivation of a unique desirability measure from a preference relation is, in general, not possible. One of several representation theorems of Valverde [11] exploiting in this case the identity

$$\rho(w|w') = \sup_{w'' \text{ in } \mathcal{U}} \{\rho(w|w'') \ominus \rho(w'|w'')\},$$

assures, however, that there is always a family $\{\mathbf{D}_\alpha\}$ of desirability measures such that

$$\rho(w|w') = \sup_\alpha \{\mathbf{D}_\alpha(w) \ominus \mathbf{D}_\alpha(w')\}.$$

The above representation has a most natural interpretation as the set of constraints (i.e., desirability measures) that are involved in the generalized order defined by a preference relation, i.e., the criteria that make a solution better than another. As it is often the case with conventional constraints, some of these generalized constraints may never be "active," being, in effect, superseded by more specific restrictions. For this reason, the above decomposition is never unique [6]. We may, however, always define a unique "canonical decomposition," which is suggested by the proofs of Valverde's theorems. We will call the family of desirability measures $\{\mathbf{D}_w\}$ defined by

$$\mathbf{D}_w(w') = \rho(w'|w), \qquad \text{for every } w \text{ in } \mathcal{U},$$

the *Valverde representation* of ρ.

Note that, although this relation essentially defines a mapping from every possible world w into a desirability measure $\mathbf{D}_w$, the collection of generating functions that is so defined may have a cardinality that is considerably smaller than that of $\mathcal{U}$. The question of whether there exists a unique desirability $\mathbf{D}$ measure that generates ρ, i.e., $\rho(w|w') = \mathbf{D}(w) \ominus \mathbf{D}(w')$, is, in view of the above comments, a matter of rather important practical significance which was studied and solved by Jacas [6].

3 Combination of Preference Functions

The ability to express any preference function (i.e., relative adequacy of solutions) in terms of a collection of desirability measures (i.e., criteria for adequacy) also suggests a natural algebraic structure for preference relations.

Definition: Let ρ and ρ' be two preference relations in the universe of discourse $\mathcal{U}$. Furthermore, let $\{\mathbf{D}_w\}$ and $\{\mathbf{D}'_w\}$ be the Valverde representations of ρ and ρ', respectively. Then the conjunction and disjunction of ρ and ρ' are the preference functions, denoted $\rho \circledast \rho'$ and $\rho \oplus \rho'$, associated with the generating families $\{\mathbf{D}_w \circledast \mathbf{D}'_w\}$, and $\{\mathbf{D}_w \oplus \mathbf{D}'_w\}$, respectively. Furthermore, the complement of ρ is the preference relation $\sim \rho$ associated with the generating family $\{\sim \mathbf{D}_w\}$. Finally, the implication preference $\rho \rightarrow \rho'$ is the preference relation generated by the family $\{\mathbf{D}_w \rightarrow \mathbf{D}'_w\}$ of desirability measures.

4 Possibility and Necessity

It is often difficult to assess the adequacy of certain solutions even from the limited perspective of a single problem-solving goal. While steering a mobile robot around an obstacle, for example, it is hard to determine if a particular move is preferrable to another from the viewpoint of a maneuver to be performed later at a remote location.

Modal logics [5], by introduction of notions of possible and necessary truth, permit to represent states of ignorance about the potential truth of the different statements that are being reasoned about. In the formalism presented in this paper, where restrictive propositions have been generalized as relative measures of solution adequacy, the role of the necessity and possibility operators of modal logic is replaced by lower and upper bounds for measures of desirability and preference.

We will say, therefore, that a function N_D mapping possible worlds w into values between 0 and 1 is a *necessary desirability distribution* for a desirability measure D if $N_D(w) \leq D(w)$ for all w in $\mathcal{U}$. Similarly, we will say that Π_D is a *possible desirability distribution* for D if $D(w) \leq \Pi_D(w)$ for all w in $\mathcal{U}$.

The following results permit to manipulate necessary and possible desirabilities along lines that generalize similar derivation procedures for conventional modal logic:

(a) If $N_{\sim D}$ is a necessary desirability for the complement $\sim D$ of D, then $\sim N_{\sim D}$ is a possible desirability for D. Similarly, if $\Pi_{\sim D}$ is a possible desirability for the complement $\sim D$ of D, then $\sim \Pi_{\sim D}$ is a necessary desirability for D. These relations are the generalization of the well-known duality relations $\neg N \neg p \equiv \Pi p$ and $\neg \Pi \neg p \equiv N p$.

(b) If N_D and $N_{D'}$ are necessary desirabilities for D and D', respectively, then $N_D \circledast N_{D'}$ and $N_D \oplus N_{D'}$ are necessary desirabilities for $D \circledast D'$ and $D \oplus D'$, respectively. A similar statement holds for possible desirabilities.

(c) If N_D is a necessary desirability for D and if $\Pi_{D'}$ is a possible desirability for D', then $N_D \ominus \Pi_{D'}$ is a necessary desirability for $D' \rightarrow D$. A dual statement also holds for possible desirabilities.

Bounds, called *necessary* and *possible preference functions*, may also be introduced to represent ignorance about relative preference between solutions. Rules for their manipulation, however, are considerably more complex than those for their desirability counterparts. A rather straightforward consequence, nonetheless, of the definition of preference functions is that if if N_D and Π_D are necessary and possibility desirability distributions for a desirability measure D, then the functions defined by the expressions

$$N_\rho(w|w') = N_D(w) \ominus \Pi_D(w'), \quad \text{and} \quad \Pi_\rho(w|w') = \Pi_D(w) \ominus N_D(w'),$$

are necessary and possible preferences for $\rho_D(w|w') = D(w) \ominus D(w')$.

It should be also clear that necessary and possible preference functions can always be chosen to satisfy the first two properties (generalized nonreflexivity and antisymmetry) of the definition of preference function. Less obvious is the fact that a possible preference function may always be selected to satisfy the third (or transitive) property. Since then such possible preference relation will be itself a preference relation, it may be represented by a family $\hat{D}_w$ of desirability measures that is related to the Valverde representation D_w of ρ by the inequality $D_w \leq \hat{D}_w$.

5   Preference, Similarity, and Fuzzy Logic

A recent semantic model of the author [8] presented a rationale for the interpretation of the possibilistic structures of fuzzy logic and for its major rule of derivation on the basis of similarity relations between possible worlds. Similarity relations S assign a value $S(w, w')$ between 0 and 1 to every pair of possible worlds w and w' in such a way that

1. $S(w, w) = 1$ for all possible worlds w,

2. $S(w, w') = S(w', w)$ for all possible worlds w and w', and

3. $S(w, w') \leq S(w, w'') \circledast S(w'', w')$ for all possible worlds w, w' and w'', where $\circledast$ is a T-norm.

Two possible worlds w and w' may be considered similar if, from the perspective of all constraints defining a problem, the solutions that they represent have close desirability values. This statement, reflected by the well known relation

$$S(w, w') = \min(\sim \rho(w|w'), \sim \rho(w'|w)),$$

permits derivation of a similarity relation from a preference relation. Extensions of the notion of similarity to allow definition of bounds for the resemblance between subsets of possible worlds, called *degree of implication* and *degree of consistence*, play an essential role in the interpretation of the possibility distributions of fuzzy logic.

Acknowledgements

This work was supported in part by the United States Army Research Office under Contract No. DAAL03-89-K-0156 and in part by a contract with the Laboratory for International Fuzzy Engineering Research. The views, opinions and/or conclusions contained in this note are those of the author and should not be interpreted as representative of the official positions, decisions, or policies, either express or implied, of his sponsors.

The author wants to thank F. Esteva, L. Godo, N. Helft, D. Israel, J. Jacas, J. Lowrance, R. Perrault, E. Trillas, L. Valverde, and L. Zadeh for many useful insights and exchanges.

References

[1] N. Piera and J. Aguilar Martin. *Mixed Connectives of Lineal Compensation*. Report LAAS 88031, Laboratoire d'Automatique et d'Analyse des Systemes, Toulouse, France, September 1988.

[2] R.E. Bellman and L.A. Zadeh. Decision-making in a fuzzy environment. *Management Science*, 17:B141–B164, 1980.

[3] D. Dubois and H. Prade. Criteria aggregation and ranking of alternatives in the framework of fuzzy set theory. In H.J. Zimmerman, L.A. Zadeh, and B.R. Gaines, editors, *Fuzzy Sets and Decision Analysis*, pp. 209–240, North Holland, Amsterdam, 1984.

[4] P. Hadawy and S. Hanks. Issues in Decision-Theoretic Planning: Symbolic Goals and Numeric Utilities. In K.P. Sycara, editor, *Proceedings of a Workshop on Innovative Approaches to Planning, Scheduling, and Control*, pp. 48–58. San Diego, California, 1990.

[5] Hughes, G.E. and M.E. Creswell, *An Introduction to Modal Logic*, Methuen, London, 1968.

[6] J. Jacas Moral. Contribució a l'estudi de les relacions d' indistingibilitat i a les seves aplicacions als processos de clasificació. Ph. D. Thesis. Polytechnic University of Barcelona, 1987.

[7] N. Rescher. Semantic Foundations for the Logic of Preference. In N. Rescher, editor, *The Logic of Decision and Action*, Pittsburgh, 1967.

[8] E.H. Ruspini. On the Semantics of Fuzzy Logic. *Int.J. Approximate Reasoning*, 5, 45–88, 1991.

[9] E.H. Ruspini. Approximate Reasoning: Past, Present, Future. *Information Sciences*, forthcoming, 1991. Also published as Technical Note No. 492, Artificial Intelligence Center, SRI International, Menlo Park, California, 1990.

[10] E. Trillas and L. Valverde. On mode and implication in approximate reasoning. In M.M. Gupta, A. Kandel, W. Bandler, J.B. Kiszka, editors, *Approximate Reasoning and Expert Systems*, North Holland, Amsterdam, 157–166, 1985.

[11] L. Valverde. On the structure of F-indistinguishability operators. *Fuzzy Sets and Systems*, 17: 313–328, 1985.

On Commitment and Cumulativity in Default Logics*

Torsten Schaub
FG Intellektik, TH Darmstadt
Alexanderstraße 10, D–6100 Darmstadt
e-mail: xiistsch@ddathd21.bitnet

Extended Abstract

This paper examines Poole's notion of "commitment to assumptions" as well as Makinson's demand for cumulativity in the context of default logic. It provides a semantical characterization of Brewka's approach which can be regarded as a realization of both notions. Moreover, another variant of default logic is introduced that shares the nice properties of Brewka's variant but avoids some of its problems.

1   Introduction

Non–commitment to assumptions and non–cumulativity have been two problems of default logic [9] that have been recently discussed in the literature [8, 5]. These phenomena led to several unintuitive results. In [1], a variant of default logic was given that remedied both defects. But a little beauty spot was the introduction of so–called *assertions*, ie. formulas labeled with their underlying assumptions. Keeping track of the assumptions was necessary to ensure that adding a nonmonotonic theorem to the premises does not alter the nonmonotonic theory. Otherwise, the underlying assumptions would get lost.

In [10], a semantics for *assertional default theories* was given that shed some light on the two notions. One of the insights was that it is not really necessary to extent the first order language towards assertions. Moreover, from a semantical viewpoint, it was enough to establish a focus on those models satisfying all assumptions made. So, semantically a kind of awareness was modeled wrt the nonmonotonic theory whereas syntactically (ie. using assertions) the same has been done locally to the nonmonotonic theorems.

Back to the logic, we suggest a similar approach, viewing assumptions as constraints on a given theory. But instead of constraining the nonmonotonic theorems, we provide the notion of a *constrained extension*. Hence, our logic can be seen as directly induced by the semantics presented in [10].

In what follows, we expect the reader to be familiar with default logic [9] as well as its semantics [3]. In Section 2, we briefly resume the basics of cumulative default logic [1] and illustrate by example how the two problems are remedied. In Section 3, we provide its semantical characterization [10] and introduce our notion of *constrained default theories* and show how they cope with commitment and cumulativity.

---

*This research was supported by the Federal Ministry for Research and Technology within the project TASSO under grant no. ITW 8900 A7.

2   Towards Assertional Default Theories

Default logic deals with many commonsense examples very well, but it has the already mentioned problems: *non–commitment* and *non–cumulativity*. These are sketched by the following examples.

Example 2.1 *The default theory* $(\{\frac{:B}{C}, \frac{:\neg B}{D}\}, \emptyset)$ *has only one extension*, $Th(\{C, D\})$. *Both default rules have been fired, although they have contradicting justifications.*

Example 2.2 *The default theory* $(\{\frac{:A}{A}, \frac{A\vee B\, :\, \neg A}{\neg A}\}, \emptyset)$ *has one extension*, $Th(\{A\})$. *This extension inevitably contains* $A\vee B$. *Adding the theorem to the premises yields the default theory* $(\{\frac{:A}{A}, \frac{A\vee B\, :\, \neg A}{\neg A}\}, \{A \vee B\})$ *that has two extensions* $Th(\{A\})$ *and* $Th(\{\neg A, B\})$.

Brewka [1] solved the two problems by strengthening the applicability condition for default rules and making the reasons for believing something explicit. In order to keep track of the assumptions syntactically, he introduced so–called *assertions*, ie. formulas marked with the set of justifications and consequents of the default rules that have been used during their derivation.

An assertional default theory becomes a pair $\Lambda = (D, \mathcal{W})$, where D is a set of default rules and $\mathcal{W}$ is a set of assertions. Due to the previously mentioned changes, assertional default theories are able to cope with the problems already mentioned.

Example 2.3 *The assertional default theory* $(\{\frac{:B}{C}, \frac{:\neg B}{D}\}, \emptyset)$ *has now two extensions,* $\widehat{Th}(\{\langle C, \{B, C\}\rangle\})$ *and* $\widehat{Th}(\{\langle D, \{\neg B, D\}\rangle\})$.

Example 2.4 *The assertional default theory* $(\{\frac{:A}{A}, \frac{A\vee B\, :\, \neg A}{\neg A}\}, \emptyset)$ *has still one extension,* $\widehat{Th}(\{\langle A, \{A\}\rangle\})$. *It contains* $\langle A \vee B, \{A\}\rangle$. *Adding this to the premises yields the theory* $(\{\frac{:A}{A}, \frac{A\vee B\, :\, \neg A}{\neg A}\}, \{\langle A \vee B, \{A\}\rangle\})$ *that has still the same extension and no other.*

We see how easily we obtain the desired effects if we keep track of the justifications and the formulas derived using default rules. But how can this "syntactic sugar" be realized semantically?

3   A Semantics and its induced logic

In order to characterize assertional default theories and their behaviour, a similar preference relation can now be defined by considering pairs like $(\Pi, \breve{\Pi})$, where Π and $\breve{\Pi}$ are sets of models. The intuition behind such a semantical structure is as follows. Viewing the justifications more as a kind of *working assumptions*, we need to *focus* on those models that satisfy our assumptions. But since we cannot prove their validity, there have to exist models that falsify them and "overlap" our focused models concerning our working assumptions. So, we just impose more structure on the sets of models under consideration, viewing the second component $\breve{\Pi}$ — that is just a subset of Π — as our focused set of models. Formally, we can achieve this by defining an appropriate order relating the consistency of the justifications with their validity in the focused models.

Definition 3.1 *Let* $\delta = \frac{\alpha \, : \, \beta}{\omega}$, Π *a set of models and* $\Pi_1, \Pi_2, \check{\Pi}_1, \check{\Pi}_2 \in 2^\Pi$. $(\Pi_1, \check{\Pi}_1) \succeq_\delta$ $(\Pi_2, \check{\Pi}_2)$ *holds iff*

1. $\forall \pi \in \Pi_2.\pi \models \alpha$,

2. $\exists \pi \in \check{\Pi}_2.\pi \models \{\beta\} \cup \{\omega\}$,

3. $\Pi_1 = \Pi_2 \setminus \{\pi \mid \pi \models \neg\omega\}$,

4. $\check{\Pi}_1 = \check{\Pi}_2 \setminus \{\pi \mid \pi \models \neg\beta \text{ or } \pi \models \neg\omega\}$.

The induced ordering $\succeq_D$ is defined as the transitive closure of $\succeq_\delta$ wrt to all $\delta \in D$. In [10] it has been shown that the $\succeq_D$–maximal elements form a semantical characterization of assertional extensions.

Due to this characterization, we see why in Example 2.3 none of the other default rules is applicable any longer: The focus does not fulfill their justifications. Applying one of the default rules does not just add the consequents. It also makes us aware of the underlying assumptions. Adding C under the assumption that B is consistent prohibits us from assuming $\neg B$ to be consistent also, or vice versa. Similarly, we see why the second default rule in Example 2.4 is blocked, even though we have added the assertion $\langle A \vee B, \{A\} \rangle$ to the premises: Asserting $A \vee B$ by focusing those models satisfying A does not allow $\neg A$ to be consistently assumed. Once again, we have been aware of the underlying assumptions.

But there is a difference between modeling awareness using focussed models or labeled formulas. Concerning the logic, the semantics obviously suggests to drop the extension of formulas towards assertions. Our approach can be regarded as directly induced by the semantics: An extension is formed by all formulas that are valid in all models of a model structure whereas the focused models reflect themselves as constraints surrounding the theory. Together, they form a so-called *constrained extension*. Thereby the constraints can be regarded as an *intended theory*, ie. the theory that contains the premises, the nonmonotonic theorems as well as all underlying consistency assumptions.

Since we do not alter the language nor the default rules the notion of a default theory stays the same. But we have to define how constrained extensions are built and how they look like. Therefore, a two–placed fixed point operator[1] has to be introduced that captures our demands.

Definition 3.2 *Let* (D, W) *be a closed default theory. For any pair of sets of sentences* (S, T) *such that* $S \subseteq T$ *let* S', T' *be the smallest sets of sentences such that*

1. $W \subseteq S' \subseteq T'$,

2. $S' = Th(S')$ *and* $T' = Th(T')$,

3. *For any* $\frac{\alpha \, : \, \beta}{\omega} \in D$, *if* $\alpha \in S'$ *and* $T \cup \{\beta\} \cup \{\omega\} \not\vdash \bot$ *then* $\omega \in S'$ *and* $\beta, \omega \in T'$.

This pair is denoted by $\Upsilon(S, T)$. *A pair* (E, C) *is a constrained extension of* (D, W) *iff* (E, C) *is a fixed point of* Υ.

When computing an extension we have to preserve its consistency with all of the constraints. This means we are establishing the previously mentioned context containing all our beliefs as well as their underlying assumptions.

As assertional extensions [1] do, constrained extensions commit to their assumptions.

---

[1] Observe, that a one–placed fixed point operator on the constraints would work as well.

Example 3.1 *The default theory* $\left(\left\{\frac{:B}{C}, \frac{:\neg B}{D}\right\}, \emptyset\right)$ *has two constrained extensions,* $(Th(\{C\}), Th(\{C, B\}))$ *and* $(Th(\{D\}), Th(\{D, \neg B\}))$.

Clearly, we inherit all properties from the semantics: the *existence of extensions* is guaranteed, they are *semimonotonic* and all extensions of a given assertional default theory are *weakly orthogonal* to each other.

Due to the closeness to our semantics, we are also very close to Brewka's cumulative default logic. In [11] it shown that (E, C) is a constrained extension iff $\mathcal{E}$ is an assertional extension such that $E = Form(\mathcal{E})$ and $C = Th(Form(\mathcal{E}) \cup Supp(\mathcal{E}))$. But since we stick to normal formulas we are far enough that we do not run into the "floating conclusions problem" (see [6]).

Now, imagine a system using cumulative default logic [1] for diagnosis. As desired the system draws conclusions in the absence of information. Let $\langle \ell, Supp(\ell) \rangle$ be such a conclusion. Due to some reasons (eg. the user or computational aspects) it has been decided to make the assertion explicit and, hence, to add it as an assertional lemma to the set of premises. Because of cumulativity the reasoning process continues without any substantial changes.

After a while the system gets new and perhaps more specific information, say $\langle \alpha, Supp(\alpha) \rangle$ that contradicts our previously added nonmonotonic lemma, ie. $\{\ell\} \cup Supp(\ell) \cup \{\alpha\} \cup Supp(\alpha) \vdash \bot$. We obtain a "hard" contradiction. Since the smooth default properties of the lemma have been lost. Ie. if our lemma would still be a nonmonotonic theorem it would be either retractable (since a default rule's justification is not consistent anymore) or we would obtain a second extension.

How to abandon this dilemma? The answer is quite simple. Viewing nonmonotonic lemmata as abbreviations for the corresponding default inferences it is natural to add them as nonmonotonic inference rules.

Definition 3.3 *Let* Δ *be a closed default theory and* (E, C) *a constrained extension of* Δ. *Let* $\ell \in E$ *and* D_ℓ *a minimal set of default rules such that* $W \cup \{Conseq(\delta) \mid \delta \in D_\ell\} \vdash \ell$. *We define a lemma default rule wrt to* ℓ *as follows.*

$$\delta_\ell = \frac{: \bigwedge_{\delta \in D_\ell} Justif(\delta) \wedge \bigwedge_{\delta \in D_\ell} Conseq(\delta)}{\ell}.$$

Using this construction we are able to provide an appropriate cumulativity result (see [11]): (E, C) is a constrained extension of Δ iff (E, C) is a constrained extension of $(D \cup \{\delta_\ell\}, W)$. How things work is illustrated in the next example.

Example 3.2 *The default theory* $\left(\left\{\frac{:A}{A}, \frac{A \vee B : \neg A}{\neg A}\right\}, \emptyset\right)$ *has one constrained extension,* $(Th(A), Th(A))$. *It contains the disjunction* $A \vee B$. *But this proposition is a nonmonotonic theorem, ie. default rules,* $\left\{\frac{:A}{A}\right\}$, *have been used to derive it. Adding* $A \vee B$ *as a nonmonotonic lemma makes it necessary to add the corresponding lemma default rule,* $\frac{:A}{A \vee B}$, *and we obtain the extended default theory* $\left(\left\{\frac{:A}{A}, \frac{A \vee B : \neg A}{\neg A}, \frac{:A}{A \vee B}\right\}, \emptyset\right)$ *that has still the same extension and no other.*

4 Conclusions

The advantages of this formulation are obvious. We obtain a clear correspondance of the logic to the semantics. We do not have to extend the language (as [1]). Hence, we can use conventional theorem provers and, moreover, do not run into the "floating conclusions problem". Having a large set of constraints, it becomes easier to check their consistency. We do not have to propagate unnecessary supports. Using lemma default rules we can do so by need. Furthermore, this makes nonmonotonic lemmata automatically retractable and, therefore, later inconsistencies are avoided. Last but not least, we are able to separate the notions of commitment and cumulativity.

The idea of constraining nonmonotonic theories is quite similar to Poole's [7] approach to default reasoning. Although Poole's constraints are specified by the user — often to block contraposition or to introduce priorities between defaults — they share the notion of "cutting off unwarranted theories". They direct the inferences but are not a part of them. The technical issues of constrained default theories are closely related to that of Lukaszewicz' [4] variant of default logic and of Delgrande and Jackson's J–default logic [2]. Similar to our approach, they take a closer look at the underlying consistency assumptions to achieve their desired effects. Moreover, we get even closer to Reiter's [9] proof theory, since we enforce cumulativity by looking at the default rules that have been used in a given derivation. But this is not surprising since default logic as such is a proof theoretic approach.

Acknowledgements

Thanks are due to Wolfgang Bibel, Uwe Egly and especially Gerd Brewka for fruitful discussions on the topic.

References

[1] G. Brewka. Cumulative default logic: In defense of nonmonotonic inference rules. To appear in *AIJ*, 1991.

[2] J. P. Delgrande and W. K. Jackson. Default logic revisited. In *KR'91*, 118–127, 1991.

[3] D. W. Etherington. *Reasoning with Incomplete Information*. Pitman, 1988.

[4] W. Lukaszewicz. Considerations on default logic - an alternative approach. *CI*, 4:1–16, 1988.

[5] D. Makinson. General theory of cumulative inference. In *2nd Workshop on NMR*, 1–18, 1988.

[6] D. Makinson and G. Brewka. A cumulative inference relation for JTMS and lp. In *NIL'90*, LNAI, 1991.

[7] D. L. Poole. A logical framework for default reasoning. *AIJ*, 36:27–47, 1988.

[8] D. L. Poole. What the lottery paradox tells us about default reasoning. In *KR'89*, 333–340, 1989.

[9] R. Reiter. A logic for default reasoning. *AIJ*, 13:81–132, 1980.

[10] T. Schaub. Assertional default theories: A semantical view. In *KR'91*, 496–506, 1991.

[11] T. Schaub. On constrained default theories. Technical report, THD, 1991. In preparation.

A TABLEAU-BASED CHARACTERISATION FOR DEFAULT LOGIC

Camilla B. Schwind, Vincent Risch

Faculté des Sciences de Luminy,
Groupe d'Intelligence Artificielle, CNRS
163 Avenue de Luminy, Case 901
13288 Marseille, Cedex 9, FRANCE
Phone : ++3391269195, E-mail : Schwind @ frmrs11.bitnet

ABSTRACT

This paper has two objectives :

- We first give a necessary and sufficient criterion for the existence of extension of default theories in the general case.

- Second, we present a new, efficient and clear method for computing extensions and deriving formulae of default theory in the general case. It is based on the semantic tableaux method [Smullyan 1968] and works for default theories with a finite set of defaults that are formulated over a decidable subset of first-order logic. We prove that all extensions (if any) of a default theory can be produced by constructing the semantic tableau of <u>one</u> formula built from the general laws and the default consequences.

I. INTRODUCTION

Since default theories were first defined by [Reiter 1980], many papers have been written about this obviously very appealing theory, whose formulation is so simple. However, it is very difficult to understand how default proofs can be obtained. As far as we know, up to now, a general theorem prover has never been proposed for non-normal default theories (including those which have <u>no</u> extension, i.e. a theorem prover which provides extensions if there are any, and can decide if there are none). Furthermore, a criterion for the existence of extensions has never been proposed. [Etherington 1987] provides a necessary but not sufficient criterion for the existence of extensions for semi-normal default theories. Nothing can be asserted if the criterion does not hold. Only a few theorem provers have been conceived for default logic. Most of them are based on resolution and work only for normal defaults without free variables[1] [Reiter 1980, Besnard and al. 1983, Schwind 1990] or variants of the original theory of Reiter [Lukaszewicz 1987, Gueirreiro and al 1990]. Brown has proposed a deduction system for nonmonotonic logics including default logic which is based on a modal logic [Brown 1986]. However, he does not prove that his theory covers default logic.

---

[1] The term used by Reiter is "closed default theory". Since "closed" is a term used to design contradictory tableaux (see chapter III), we use the term "default theory without free variables" in order to omit confusion.

In this paper, we present a new proof method for default logic which, in addition, characterizes extensions. This method was originally developped for normal theories [Schwind 1990] and is now extended to the general case.

II. DEFAULT LOGIC

We first introduce default logic as defined by Reiter (1980).

Definition 1 :

A default is an expression having the form $\dfrac{\alpha(x):\beta1(x)\beta2(x)...\beta n(x)}{\omega(x)}$, where $\alpha(x)$, $\beta_i(x)$ and $\omega(x)$ are all formulae of first order logic. $\alpha(x)$ is called the *prerequisite*, $\beta_i(x)$ the *justifications* and $\omega(x)$ the *consequent* of the default. A default theory is a pair (W, D) where W is a set of first-order formulae and D a set of defaults.

A default is called *without free variables* when α, β and $\omega(x)$ are closed formulae.

A default theory is called *without free variables* when all its defaults are without free variables.

Given a set Γ of formulae, we denote by $Th(\Gamma)$ the theory over Γ, i.e. $Th(\Gamma) = \{F : \Gamma \vdash F\}$.

Definition 2 :

An *extension* of a default theory (W, D) without free variables is defined in the following way :

Let S be a set of formulae without free variables. Let $\Gamma(S)$ be the smallest set satisfying

(D1) $W \subseteq \Gamma(S)$

(D2) $Th(\Gamma(S)) = \Gamma(S)$

(D3) If $\dfrac{\alpha:\beta_1\beta_2...\beta_n}{\omega}$ $\in D$ and $\alpha \in \Gamma(S)$ and $\neg\beta_i \notin S$, for all i with $1 \le i \le n$ then $\omega(x) \in \Gamma(S)$.

A set of formulae without free variables E is an extension for (W, D) iff $\Gamma(E) = E$.

Definition 3 :

The set of *generating defaults* of an extension, E, of a default theory without free variables $\Delta = (W, D)$ is defined by

$$GD(E, D) = \{d : d \in D, d = \dfrac{\alpha:\beta_1\beta_2...\beta_n}{\omega} \text{ and } \alpha \in E \text{ and } \neg\beta_i \notin E\}$$

The set of *consequents* of a set D of defaults is defined by

$$CONS(D) = \{\omega : \dfrac{\alpha:\beta_1\beta_2...\beta_n}{\omega} \in D\}$$

The set of *prerequisites* of a set D of defaults is defined by

$$PREREQ(D) = \{\alpha : \dfrac{\alpha:\beta_1\beta_2...\beta_n}{\omega} \in D\}$$

Example 1 :

$\Delta1 = (W1, D1)$ where $D1 = \{\dfrac{A:B}{C}, \dfrac{:D}{D}, \dfrac{C:E}{F}\}$

$W1 = \{A, D \rightarrow \neg B \wedge \neg E, C \rightarrow \neg D\}$

$\Delta1$ has two extensions : $E_1 = Th(W1 \cup \{D\})$, $E_2 = Th(W1 \cup \{C, F\})$

In [Reiter 1980] we find the following theorem, which characterizes extensions in terms of theories over W and consequences of defaults.

Theorem 1 (Theorem 2.5. from Reiter)

Suppose that E is an extension for a default theory without free variables $\Delta = (W, D)$. Then

$$E = Th(W \cup CONS(GD(E, \Delta))).$$

III. THE THEOREM PROVER

The theorem prover we have used is based on the analytic tableaux method [Smullyan 1968] and is described in [Schwind 1985], where the classical part contains only predefinite variable clauses. Within the scope of this paper, we will consider only its propositional part (for classical logic). This is sufficient because the idea of our algorithm is the same whether the logic has quantifiers or not. TP proves a formula F by trying to derive a contradiction from assuming $\neg F$. TP builds for $\neg F$ a set of sets of formulae (called semantic tableaux) by applying a number of operations to $\neg F$ yielding this set. The tableau for a formula corresponds to its disjunctive normal form, i. e. each set represents the conjunction of its elements and the tableau represents the disjunct of its elements.

Definition 4 :

A set of literals is *closed* if it contains two opposite literals (i.e. L and $\neg L$). A set of sets of literals is closed if each of its elements is closed.

The fundamental property of TP for theorem proving is the following completeness theorem :

Theorem 3 :

F is a theorem iff $TP(\{\neg F\})$ is closed. (Proof in [Smullyan 1968]).

Corollary 1 :

Let be Γ a finite set of formulae and F a formula. $F \in Th(\Gamma)$ iff $TP(\Gamma) \otimes TP(\{\neg F\})$ is closed.

Proof : Consider G the conjunction of the formulae of Γ. $F \in Th(\Gamma)$ iff $\Gamma \vdash F$ iff $\vdash G \rightarrow F$ (deduction theorem) iff $TP(\{\neg(G \rightarrow F)\})$ is closed (completeness theorem) iff $TP(G \wedge \neg F) = TP(\Gamma) \otimes TP(\{\neg F\})$ is closed.

We consider TP not only as a theorem prover (or consistency checker) for first-order formulae but also as an application which has useful properties for formulae and formula sets. We will frequently use the following notations :

$\Gamma \otimes \Gamma = \{X \cup Y : X \in \Gamma \text{ and } Y \in \Gamma\}$,

$T + L = \{Y : Y = X \backslash L \text{ for } X \in T\}$.

IV. EXISTENCE OF EXTENSIONS

By theorem 1, an extension is the set of theorems over W and a set of default consequences. But theorem 1 does not assert anything for default theories which have no extension. Here we will give a necessary **and sufficient** existence criterion for extensions. In theorem 4 we will show that a default theory has an extension **iff** there is a set of defaults, for which the defaults which belong to the set have a property (i), and the defaults which do not belong to the set have another property (ii).

Définition 5 :

A set D of defaults without free variables is *grounded* in W iff for all $d \in D$ there is a finite sequence $d_0, d_1,$ ...d_n of elements of D, $d_i = \dfrac{\alpha_i : \beta^i{}_1...\beta^i{}_{n_i}}{\omega_i}$ such that $\alpha_0 \in Th(W)$,

$\alpha_{i+1} \in Th(W \cup CONS(\{d_0, d_1, ... d_i\}))$ for $0 \le i \le n-1$ and $d_n = d$.

Lemma 2 :

The set of generating defaults $GD(E, \Delta)$ of an extension E of a default theory $\Delta = (W, D)$ is grounded in W.

proof : consequence of theorem 1.

The following theorem, which is the main result presented in this paper, shows that all extensions of a closed default theory are obtained in this way.

Theorem 4 :

A default theory without free variables $\Delta = (W,D)$ has an extension, E, iff there exists $D' \subseteq D$, D' grounded in W and $E = Th(W \cup CONS(D'))$, and $\forall d \in D, d = \dfrac{\alpha:\beta_1\beta_2...\beta_n}{\omega}$ (i) and (ii) hold :

   (i) if $d \in D'$ then $\alpha \in E$ and $\neg\beta_i \notin E$, for all $1 \le i \le n$.

   (ii) if $d \notin D'$ then $\alpha \notin E$ or $\neg\beta_i \in E$, for some i, such that $1 \le i \le n$.

Proof :

The theorem clearly holds for inconsistent W by theorem 2. Let now be W consistent.

"$\Rightarrow$" (immediately by theorem 2)

Let E be an extension of Δ. By setting $D' = GD(E, \Delta)$:

- $E = Th(W \cup CONS(GD(E, \Delta))$ (theorem 2),

- $GD(E, \Delta)$ is grounded (lemma 2),

- Let be $d \in D, d = \dfrac{\alpha:\beta_1\beta_2...\beta_n}{\omega}$,

$d \in GD(E, \Delta)$ iff $\alpha \in E$ and $\neg\beta_i \notin E$, so (i) and (ii) are true.

"$\Leftarrow$"

On the other hand, consider $D' \subseteq D$, D' grounded in W, and $E = Th(W \cup CONS(D'))$ consistent, for which (i) and (ii) holds. E is an extension iff $\Gamma(E) = E$. We first show that D1, D2, D3 from definition 2 hold for E, where :

(D1) $W \subseteq E$

(D2) $Th(E) = E$

(D3) if $\dfrac{\alpha:\beta_1\beta_2...\beta_n}{\omega} \in D, \alpha \in E$ and $\neg\beta_i \notin E$ then $\omega \in E$.

(D1) and (D2) are trivialy true by the definition of Th(W ∪ CONS(D')).

(D3) : Suppose for the contrary $\dfrac{\alpha:\beta_1\beta_2...\beta_n}{\omega} \in D$, $\alpha \in E$, $\neg\beta_i \notin E$ for $1{\le}i{\le}n$ and $\omega \notin E$, i.e.

$\omega \notin Th(W \cup CONS(D'))$ and consequently $\dfrac{\alpha:\beta_1\beta_2...\beta_n}{\omega} \notin D'$, hence $\alpha \notin E$ or $\neg\beta \in E$ by (ii) :

contradiction!

E verifies (D1), (D2), (D3) hence, by minimality of the operator Γ, we have $\Gamma(E) \subseteq E$.

In order to show $E \subseteq \Gamma(E)$, consider the default $\dfrac{\alpha:\beta_1\beta_2...\beta_n}{\omega} \in D'$. We have to show that $\omega \in \Gamma(E)$:

D' is grounded, therefore there exists a finite sequence $d_0, d_1, ..., d_n$ of elements of D', $\dfrac{\alpha_i : \beta^i_1...\beta^i_{m_i}}{\omega_i}$

, such that $\alpha_0 \in Th(W)$ and $\alpha_{i+1} \in Th(W \cup CONS\{d_0, d_1, ..., d_n\})$ for $0{\le}i{\le}n1$ and $d_n = d$. We show by induction that for all i, $1{\le}i{\le}n$, $\alpha_i \in \Gamma(E)$ and $\omega_i \in \Gamma(E)$. We begin by observing that $\neg\beta^0_j \notin E$ for $1 \le j \le m_0$, (condition (i)). Moreover, $\alpha_0 \in Th(W) \subseteq \Gamma(E)$, hence $\omega_0 \in \Gamma(E)$ by (D3). Let be $\alpha_i \in \Gamma(E)$ and $\omega_i \in \Gamma(E)$. D' is grounded therefore $\alpha_{i+1} \in Th(W \cup CONS\{d_0, d_1, ..., d_n\}) = Th(W \cup \{\omega_0, \omega_1, ..., \omega_i\}) \subseteq \Gamma(E)$ since $\omega_k \in \Gamma(E)$ for all $k \le i$ by induction hypothesis. Hence, since $\neg\beta^{i+1}_j \notin E$, for $1{\le}j{\le}m_{i+1}$, $\omega_{i+1} \in \Gamma(E)$ by (D3). Therefore, $\omega \in \Gamma(E)$. Q.E.D.

Remark 1 :

By the corollary 1 :

- Condition (i) is equivalent to TP(W) ⊗ TP(CONS(D')) ⊗ TP($\{\neg\alpha\}$) closed, and
  TP(W) ⊗ TP(CONS(D')) ⊗ TP($\{\beta\}$) open;
- Condition (ii) is equivalent to TP(W) ⊗ TP(CONS(D')) ⊗ TP($\{\neg\alpha\}$) open, or
  TP(W) ⊗ TP(CONS(D')) ⊗ TP($\{\beta\}$) closed.
- Conditions (i) and (ii) are equivalent to say :

  $(\forall \, d \in D, d = \dfrac{\alpha : \beta}{\gamma}, : d \in D'$ iff $\alpha \in E$ and $\neg\beta \notin E)$.

V. COMPUTING EXTENSIONS

The idea of our proposed method is very simple : An extension E for a default theory $\Delta = (W,D)$ is roughly speaking the set of theorems over the union of W and a set of default consequences (see Theorem 1). This set of exists whenever the conditions (i) and (ii) hold (see theorem 4). It is a maximal set of this kind in the sense that the addition of any other default consequence is not possible because the prerequisite or the condition justification does not hold or this would make E inconsistent (and then falsify the second part of condition (i)). Therefore, we have to find all subsets D' of D, corresponding to extensions : if it is not possible to find such a subset (anyway, this will be caused by the fact that the justification condition can never be satisfied), the theory has no extension. Now the idea of our algorithm is as follows. We consider the set $W \cup CONS(D)$. There are two possible cases :

- $W \cup CONS(D)$ is consistent. Then D' is the greatest subset of D such that every default verifies the prerequisite and justification condition of (i). So every default for which such conditions are not verified has to be dropped out of D and hence, has now to verify the condition (ii). But if there exists a default for which neither (i) nor (ii) holds, the theory cannot have this extension and if there is such a default for every subset of D, the theory cannot have any extension.

- in the other case, $W \cup CONS(D)$ is not consistent. Then the tableau T constructed for $W \cup CONS(D)$ is closed, i.e. each set in T is closed. But it is possible to "open" T by removing within T literals "responsible" for the contradiction. Note that T is open whenever at least one of its sets is open. Every time we open each of the sets of T in this way, we generate two subsets D' and D" of D for which (i) and (ii) have to be verified, like preceedingly. In this way, every extension can be obtained on the condition that there is no particular default for which neither (i) nor (ii) holds. Indeed, note that for any D' grounded, the prerequisite condition of (i') is verified.

Example 1 (continued) :

$\Delta 1 = (W1, D1)$ where $D1 = \{\frac{A:B}{C}, \frac{:D}{D}, \frac{C:E}{F}\}$ and $W1 = \{A, D \rightarrow \neg B \wedge \neg E, C \rightarrow \neg D\}$.

The extensions are obtained as follows :

TS(W1) = {{A, ¬D}, {A, ¬B, ¬E, ¬C}}

TS(CONS(D1)) = {{C, D, F}}

Γ = TS(W1) ⊗ TS(CONS(D1)) = {{A, ¬D, C, D, F }, { A, ¬B, ¬E, ¬C, C, D, F}}

is closed. There are two ways of opening it by removing literals coming from default consequences : we can remove D responsible for the contradiction in its first element; or we can remove C, responsible for the contradiction in the second element. The corresponding opened tableaux are :

$\Gamma_1 = \Gamma + \{D\}$, $\Gamma_2 = \Gamma + \{C\}$.

Consider then : $D1_1 = D1 \setminus \{\frac{:D}{D}\}$, $D1_2 = D1 \setminus \{\frac{A:B}{C}\}$.

We then still have to verify conditions (i) and (ii) for those sets.

- For $D1_1$: Γ_1 ⊗ TP({¬A}) is closed and Γ_1 ⊗ TP({B}) is open. Therefore condition (i) is true for the default $\frac{A:B}{C}$. Similarly, Γ_1 ⊗ TP({¬C}) is closed and Γ_1 ⊗ TP({E}) is open. Condition (i) holds for the default $\frac{C:E}{F}$ too. On the other hand, condition (ii) holds for $\frac{:D}{D}$, not in $D1_1$: Γ_1 ⊗ TP({D}) is open.

- For $D1_2$: Prerequisite condition (i) trivially holds for the normal default $\frac{:D}{D}$. On the other hand, Γ_2 ⊗ TP({¬C}) is open. This contradicts condition (i), therefore the default $\frac{C:E}{F}$ has to be retracted from $D1_2$. Let be $D1'_2 = \{\frac{:D}{D}\}$, and $\Gamma'_2 = \Gamma + \{C, F\}$. Justification condition (i) obviously holds for the remainder normal default $\frac{:D}{D}$ in $D1'_2$. Indeed, condition (ii) holds for $\frac{A:B}{C}$ and $\frac{C:E}{F}$: Γ'_2 ⊗ TP({B}) is closed, and Γ'_2 ⊗ TP({E}) is closed.

It is easy to verify that $D1_1$ and $D1'_2$ are grounded. Therefore, they yield the two following extensions for $\Delta 1$: $E_1 = Th(W1 \cup \{C,F\})$, $E_2 = Th(W1 \cup \{D\})$.

Example 2 :

$\Delta 2 = (W2, D2)$ where $D2 = \{\frac{Q:\neg R}{P}\}$, $W2 = \{\neg P \wedge Q\}$.

$TS(W2) = \{\{\neg P, Q\}\}$,

$TS(D2) = \{\{P\}\}$,

$TS(W2) \otimes TS(CONS(D2)) = \{\{\neg P, Q, P\}\}$.

Because this tableau is closed, we should have to remove the litteral P obtained from D2. But then, the

default $\frac{Q:\neg R}{P}$ should verify condition (ii). However, this is not the case since $TS(W2) \otimes TS(CONS(D2 \setminus \{$

$\frac{Q:\neg R}{P}\}))$ $\otimes$ $TS(\{\neg Q\}) = \{\{\neg P, Q, \neg Q\}\}$, which is not open. The default $\frac{Q:\neg R}{P}$ neither verifies (i) nor

(ii), hence the theory has no extension.

Example 3 :

$\Delta 3 = (\varnothing, D3)$ where $D3 = \{ \frac{:\neg A}{A} \}$.

$TS(\varnothing) = \{\varnothing\}$, $TS(CONS(D3)) = \{\{A\}\}$, and $\Gamma = TS(\varnothing) \otimes TS(CONS(D3)) = \{\{A\}\}$ (consistent). But
(i) : $\Gamma \otimes TS(\{\neg A\})$ is closed whereas it should be open and (ii) : $\Gamma \otimes TS(\{A\})$ is open whereas it
should be closed. Hence $\Delta 3$ has no extension.

Example 4 :

$\Delta 4 = (\varnothing, D4)$ where $D4 = \{ \frac{:A}{\neg B}, \frac{:B}{\neg C}, \frac{:C}{\neg A} \}$. $\Gamma = TS(\varnothing) \otimes TS(CONS(D4)) = \{\{\neg B, \neg C, \neg A\}\}$

consistent. However, since $\Gamma \otimes TS(\{A\})$ is closed instead of being open (i), there is no extension for

which the three defaults can be kept together. Consider then $D6'= \{ \frac{:A}{\neg B}, \frac{:B}{\neg C} \}$ and the corresponding

$\Gamma' = \{\{\neg B, \neg C\}\}$. But, $\Gamma' \otimes TS(\{B\})$ is closed whereas it should be open, according to (i). It is easy

to verify that the two other subsets $\{ \frac{:B}{\neg C}, \frac{:C}{\neg A} \}$ and $\{ \frac{:A}{\neg B}, \frac{:C}{\neg A} \}$ yield analogous situations.

Let $D4'' = \{ \frac{:A}{\neg B} \}$ and $\Gamma'' = \{\{\neg B\}\}$. Because the third default does not belong to D4', it has to verify

(ii). But $\Gamma' \otimes TS(\{C\})$ is open whereas it should be closed. Again, the two other subsets $\{ \frac{:B}{\neg C} \}$ and

$\{ \frac{:C}{\neg A} \}$ yield analogous situations.

Finally, let be $D4' = \varnothing$. It is obvious that condition (ii) does not hold.

Therefore, there is no extension for $\Delta 4$.

Example 5 :

$\Delta 5 = (\varnothing, D5)$ where $D5 = \{ \frac{A:B}{B}, \frac{B:A}{A} \}$. $TS(\varnothing) \otimes TS(CONS(D7)) = \{\{B, A\}\}$ (consistent). However,

D5 is not grounded, neither is $\{ \frac{A:B}{B} \}$ or $\{ \frac{B:A}{A} \}$. On the other hand, condition (ii) holds for both $\frac{A:B}{B}$,

and $\frac{B:A}{A}$. Hence $\Delta 5$ has one extension $E = \varnothing$.

Remark 2 :

It is also straightforward to deduce formulae from the default theory. A formula F is deducible if it is in an
extension $Th(\Gamma)$, i.e. if $TP(\Gamma) \otimes TP(\{\neg F\})$ is closed (by Corollary 1). Since, with our algorithm, all
extensions are constructively produced and then available in the form $TP(...)$, it is sufficient to construct
$TP(\{\neg F\})$ and to check whether $TP(\Gamma) \otimes TP(\{\neg F\})$ is closed using lemma 1.

VI. CONCLUSION

We presented a very simple and powerful method for computing all the extensions of a default theory without free variables. The algorithm presented here seems to be more efficient than all other algorithms presented up to now, because it computes extensions by producing the semantic tableau for one formula (the conjunction of the general laws and the consequences of the defaults) only once. Moreover, the method applies very naturally to defaults with free variables. All other proof methods for default theories given so far could only apply to normal defaults without free variables.

The concept underlying our method has already been applied for producing the states resulting from the performance of an action [Lafon and Schwind 1988]. Roughly speaking, it is simply a matter of obtaining a precise method for finding a maximal consistent subset of an inconsistent set of formulae (naturally, subject to additional conditions). Hence our method also appears very promising for application to other nonmonotonic logics such as autoepistemic logic or supposition-based logic [Besnard and Siegel 1988] as well as to theory revision.

REFERENCES

[1] Besnard P., Quiniou R., Quinton P. 1983. A Theorem-Prover for a decidable subset of default logic. Proceedings of the AAAI - 83 : 27 - 30.

[2] Besnard P, Siegel P. 1988. Supposition-based logic for automated nonmonotonic reasoning. Proc. 9th Conf. on Automated Deduction, Argonne, I1.

[3] Bossu G., Siegel P. 1985. Saturation, Nonmonotonic reasoning and the Closed-World Assumption. Artificial Intelligence 25, 1 : 13 - 63.

[4] Brown F. M. 1986. A commonsense theory of nonmonotonic reasoning. Proc. 8th Conf. on Automated Deduction, Oxford. Lecture Notes in Computer Science, Vol. 230, Springer Verlag : 209-228.

[5] Etherington D. W. 1987. Formalizing Nonmonotonic Reasoning Systems. Artificial Intelligence, 31, 1 : 81 - 132.

[6] Gueirreiro R. A., Casanova M. A., Hermely A. S. 1990. Contributions to a Proof Theory for Generic Defaults. Proceedings of the 9th European Conference on Artificial Intelligence, ECAI - 90 : 213 - 218.

[7] Lafon E., Schwind C. 1988. A Theorem Prover for Action Performance. Proceedings of the 8th European Conference on Artificial Intelligence, ECAI - 88 : 541 - 546.

[8] Lukaszewicz W. 1988. Considerations on Default Logic - An Alternative Approach. Computational Intelligence 4 : 1 - 16.

[9] Schwind C. 1985. Un démonstrateur de théorèmes pour des logiques modales et temporelles en PROLOG. 5ème Congrès AFCET Reconnaissance des formes et Intelligence Artificielle, Grenoble, France : 897-913.

[10] Schwind C. 1990. A tableau-based theorem prover for a decidable subset of default logic. Proceedings of the 10th International Conference on Automated Deduction, CADE 10, Springer Verlag : 541 - 546.

[11] Reiter R. 1980. A logic for default reasoning. Artificial Intelligence, 13, 1 : 81 - 132.

[12] Smullyan R. 1968. First-Order Logic. Springer Verlag.

RESTRAINING THE PROLIFERATION OF WORLDS IN PROBABILISTIC LOGIC ENTAILMENTS

Paul Snow
Department of Computer Science, Plymouth State College
P.O. Box 6134 Concord, New Hampshire 03303-6134 USA
paulsnow@oz.plymouth.edu

ABSTRACT: Probabilistic logic leads to intractable linear programs when there are too many 'possible worlds'. Practical inference problems, however, often have structural regularity which can trim linear constraint systems. This paper emphasizes <u>modus ponens</u> with consequents of unknown probability. Contingency tables provide linear constraints for the priors and motivate useful revision assumptions.

INTRODUCTION

Nilsson's (1986) probabilistic logic seeks to unify propositional logic and the probabilistic representation of belief. The method uses the known (or bounded) prior probabilities of a collection of **source** sentences to infer bounds on a **target** sentence's unknown prior. The analyst enumerates the **possible worlds**, an exclusive and exhaustive set of conjunctions of source and target sentences or their negations. This enumeration provides the foundation for simultaneous linear constraints which describe all the possible probability distributions over these worlds that are consistent with the source priors. Two linear programs are then used to find bounds on the target prior.

The number of worlds can be enormous, even with a few sentences. Boolean compaction techniques familiar to digital circuit designers can, with suitable adaptations, contain the number of worlds in some cases of practical interest (Snow, 1991b).

Nilsson also considers the problem of Bayesian revision of the prior estimates. Not surprisingly, assumptions about conditional independence play an important role in revision.

This paper explores some simple ways to exploit the structural regularities of a common family of inference patterns. Both prior and posterior inference are considered. Throughout the paper, we shall speak of known priors, but what we have to say generalizes readily to the case of bounded priors.

PRIOR CONSTRAINTS FROM CONTINGENCY TABLES

Suppose an inference problem involves a target sentence **B**, for which we have no prior. We seek an interval estimate of the prior of **B**. There are n sentences a_i, i = 1..n, whose priors are known. The sentences a_i are not necessarily atomic, but none contain any terms in the target sentence **B**. There is also some Boolean function of the premises, **A**, whose prior is unknown in the interesting case. Finally, we have the sentence **A implies B**, and a known prior for this sentence.

What we know can be summed up in an ordinary, albeit underdetermined, 2x2 contingency table, each entry being the joint probability of its row and column headings:

	A true	A false
B true	q	s
B false	r	t

Although we don't have all the values in the table, we do know some things about the numbers. The value r is the <u>complement</u> of the prior of **A implies B** (its cell being the only one where the implication would be false). The worlds contributing to s and t differ only in their truth assignment for **B**, and so while the sum s + t is constrained, how much comes from s and how much from t is unconstrained (except by non-negativity). This freedom is assured by the assumption that no sentence a_i has any terms in **B**.

This yields an easy upper bound on the prior of **B**: the prior of **A implies B**, or 1 minus r, which arises from the possibility that t = 0. This bound is as tight as what would be derived from linear programming, since the freedom to 'shift mass' between s and t corresponds to the freedom to shift mass among corresponding worlds.

A lower bound of **B** = q would arise when s = 0, although we need more information since we have no prior for q. Given that we know r, bounding q is equivalent to bounding P(**A**), which equals q + r. The sources for a lower bound on P(**A**) higher than r depend on the details of the problem. If we can't do better than r, then the bound on q and hence on **B** is just 0 and we are done. If we can do better then r, then the lower bound on **B** is just the difference between P_{low}(**A**) and r.

The tightness of the lower bound depends, of course, on the tightness of the P_{low}(**A**) bound. If the linear 'possible worlds' system is intractably large, settling for a true but loose lower bound may be an attractive alternative to an unattainable tight one.

One possible source of a bound is the relationship between **A** and the premise a_i's. For instance, if **A** is a simple disjunction, we know its prior is at least **max** (P(a_i)). Alternatively, perhaps we have been given a lower bound on the conditional P(**B** / **A**) in addition to values for selected priors. If so, a floor on P(A) can be found from

$$r = (1 - P_{low}(B \ / \ A)) * P(A)$$

This expression follows directly from r being the joint probability that it is.

AND IF PROGRAM WE MUST...

If the system is tractable, then we can seek our lower bound on P(A) using a linear program on the system implied by the worlds. The contingency table analysis would still pay dividends in that case: we need only one linear program instead of two, since we need no upper bound on P(A). Note that this single linear program fulfills any need for consistency checking, if we have doubts on that score.

Further, the possible worlds we need would involve truth assignments among only the source sentences. The target need not be considered since without a prior, P(B) provides no constraint on P(A). Thus, the number of worlds would typically be smaller than in Nilsson entailment. (Each world is a variable in the linear program, and so affects the cost.) This last savings is of the same magnitude and kind as that achieved by Kane (1989), and doesn't require the user to make any additional conditional assessments to bound the target prior.

Another savings of worlds can be made by rewriting the constraint involving A **implies** B. Since we are looking for a lower bound on P(A), all that matters is that the sum of the worlds where A is false be less than or equal to P(A **implies** B). The row vector that expresses this new constraint will have zeroes for worlds where A is true, and ones where A is false.

This maneuver saves worlds because for every truth assignment for the a_i in which A is true, the implication can be either true or false. With the rewritten constraint, there is only one world per premise assignment to contend with, not two. The maneuver is sound because we are unconcerned about how mass would be shifted among the worlds where A is true to satisfy an equation constraint. That shifting doesn't change P(A). We are only concerned that the mass is non-negative.

Finally, the a_i assignments may be candidates for Boolean compaction in the manner of Snow (1991b). Although there are collections of worlds that cannot be profitably compacted, the potential savings in worlds is large.

Revision is more difficult, but ideas based on the contingency table structure can serve once again.

ASSUMPTIONS FOR REVISION

Our problem seems a natural place to apply the approach to inference called Jeffrey's rule (Jeffrey, 1983). When evidence comes, we assume it will bear on the sentences a_i and hence indirectly on **A**, but not on our opinion about the conditional probability of **B** given **A**. Our current estimate of **P(B)** will depend on our current **P(A)** according to:

$$P(B) = P(B / A) * P(A) + P(B / \text{not } A) * P(\text{not } A)$$

The approach comports well with the contingency table introduced in the last section. If we learned **A** to be false, we would remain ignorant about **B**, i.e. **P(B / not A)** would be vacuous. Mass would remain free to switch between **s** and **t**. If on the other hand we learned **A** to be true, our interval estimate of **P(B)** would just be our interval estimate of **P(B / A)**. With intermediate knowledge, Jeffrey's rule amounts to assessing a "weighted average" of the estimate given **A** and the estimate given **not A**. The intervals work out to

$$P_{high}(B) = P_{high}(B / A) * P_{low}(A) + (1 - P_{low}(A)) \tag{1a}$$

$$P_{low}(B) = P_{low}(B / A) * P_{low}(A) \tag{1b}$$

Note that it is the <u>lower</u> current estimate of **P(A)** that counts, even when finding an upper bound on **P(B)**.

Because our estimates of the conditional will be unchanged by evidence, we can bound the conditional by using the prior interval of **P(B)** and the prior lower bound for **P(A)**. The required values are found by solving the simple equations (1 a,b). When evidence is viewed, we use it to revise the lower bound on **P(A)**, and then use that new value with the assumed-to-be unchanged conditionals to derive our new bounds on the target, again from the simple (1 a,b).

Our assumption is that evidence will arrive about an individual a_i sentence, not directly about **A**. More assumptions (or knowledge) are therefore needed to use conditionals for some a_i to revise **A**. One convenient assumption imputes the conditionals for evidence **E** to the worlds. That is, for each world **w** and one sentence **a**:

$$P(E / w) = P(E / a) \quad \text{if a is true in w} \tag{2a}$$
$$= P(E / \text{not } a) \quad \text{otherwise} \tag{2b}$$

Under (2 a,b), we have one conditional distribution over the possible worlds. If the prior system (based on source sentences and with the new **P(A implies B)** constraint explained earlier) is tractable, it can be revised simply and exactly using these conditionals (Snow, 1991a). Only one linear program is required.

Note that the need to make assumptions like (2 a,b) isn't a cost of shifting the emphasis in inference to **P(A)**. These, or something similar, would arise in practice anyway, for multiple updates.

THE NEW ASSUMPTIONS COMPARED TO NILSSON'S

Nilsson also made a "Jeffrey's rule" assumption, although he arranged it to hold between the target and any one sentence about which evidence happens to be observed. Assuming it to hold between the antecedent and the target, as in the last section, may be easier to motivate and has the advantage of limiting the amount of revision work to one linear program.

The second assumption which imputes premise conditionals to the worlds allows successive revision when several pieces of conditionally independent (given each world) evidence are viewed. It is easy to show that Jeffrey's rule can't generally hold between the target and <u>all</u> the source sentences if there are more than one. Generally, the price of a constant conditional between the target and the first revised sentence will be change in the conditionals between the target and the other sentences. (Just work out what happens in the trivial system where the source is two atomic premises a_1 and a_2 and the target is their conjunction, and a_1 is revealed to be true.)

CONCLUSIONS

We have discussed a practical and frequently encountered case of probabilistic logic entailment, and shown that attention to some structural regularities can greatly reduce the work needed to infer a target prior bound. In particular, organizing inference around the truth or falsehood of the <u>modus ponens</u> antecedent, a "hidden variable" in ordinary Nilsson entailment, saves effort and reduces the number of needed worlds. Revision in the face of evidence can similarly benefit, although more assumptions are needed.

LITERATURE CITED

Jeffrey, R., **The Logic of Decisions**, Chicago: U. Chicago, 1983.
Kane, T., Maximum entropy in Nilsson's probabilistic logic, **Proc. IJCAI**, 452-457, 1989.
Nilsson, N.J., Probabilistic logic, **Artif. Intell. 28**, 71-87, 1986.
Snow, P., Improved posterior probability estimates from prior and conditional linear constraint systems, **IEEE Trans. Syst. Man & Cybern. 21**, 464-469, 1991a.
_, Compressed constraints in probabilistic logic and their revision, in B.D. D'Ambrosio, P. Smets, and P.P. Bonissone (eds.), **Uncertainty in Artificial Intelligence**, San Mateo, CA: Morgan Kaufmann, 1991b.

Managing Uncertainty in Environmental Analysis:
An Application to Measurement Data Interpretation

Marcus Spies

IBM Germany   F A W
Institute for Knowledge-based Systems   University of Ulm
Wilckensstr1a   Helmholtzstr. 16
D - 6900 Heidelberg   D - 7900 Ulm

1. Introduction

Environmental analysis is concerned with improving environment quality. This goal is achieved by providing suitably precise and fine measurements of pollutants in the air, in water, and in organisms. Often, measurement methods provide ambiguous results which need being interpreted by experts. For instance, the most widely used methods for substance identification are chromatographic analyses. However, these analyses are based on mere separation methods, which only provide hints as to substance identification. Therefore, measurement data interpretation is an important concern in environmental analysis. In the present application, only water analysis with chromatographic methods is considered (see Fresenius, Quentin, Schneider, 1988).

A gas chromatogram is produced as follows. First, a sample is taken. Sample taking methods differ systematically in eliminating or keeping particular substances.Thus, sample taking constitutes a first substance selection step. Second, relevant substances are extracted from the water sample using an adsorbent and an elution solvent. In this process certain substances may be lost, either because they are not withheld by the adsorbent or because they are not washed out by the elution solvent. Thus, extraction is a second substance selection step. In gas chromatography, the extract is injected into a heated capillary. The elution solvent is heated up and works as a carrier gas which transports the eluted substances through a thin capillary. On the inner side of this capillary, a further substance ("coating") holds back the sample substances due to chemophysical interactions. Due to the different times these interactions take with different substances, the substances leave the capillary at different times. A detector is used to record the appearance of some substances when they come out of the capillary. The detector signal plotted against time constitutes the chromatogram. The chromatogram shows a peak at each point in time where a substance leaves the capillary and passes the detector. The choice of selective detectors constitutes a third substance selection step. Only substances that were not excluded by any of the three selection steps--sampling, extraction, detection---can produce a peak in the resulting chromatogram.

Thus, in gas chromatography, each substance can at most produce ONE peak (=detector signal); however, under one peak, there can be SEVERAL substances (due to insufficient capillary separation). Moreover, the process of sample taking, extraction and separation is in itself a selection process where some of the substances to be identified may become lost. The chromatograph works as a mere separation device, which provides no direct support to substance identification. It is presently a task of highly skilled experts to interpret chromatograms, i.e. to assign substances to peaks and to take into account the various selection processes explained before.

2. An Expert System for Interpretation of Chromatographic Data from Water Samples

The prototype WANDA (WAter ANalysis Data Advisor) is a knowledge-based system designed to support measurement data interpretation in the realm of water analysis by chromatographic methods (see Scheuer, Spies, Verpoorten, 1990). It should be noted that, generally, in environmental analysis, no stable patterns of substances from different samples can be expected. Stable patterns with some distortions occur in other applications of chromatography, in medicine, for instance. Therefore, in WANDA, a pattern oriented analysis technique is not suitable.

All presently available software for supporting measurement data interpretation in chromatography is primarily based on matching incoming measurement data from a chromatograph with reference measurements from known substances. However, the quality of these identification proposals is doubtful, because no knowledge about specific environmental and measurement conditions is taken into account.

The WANDA system embodies these traditional facilities. But, additionally, it integrates three kinds of inference procedures for modeling background knowledge:

First, *environmental data* trigger inference processes which lead to so-called substance candidate lists. These lists correspond to check lists in a chemical expert´s knowledge when a sample is to be analysed w.r.t. harmful substances.

Second, properties of the *measurement method* employed are used to infer which substances will probably NOT be in the chromatogram. For instance, an elution solvent might fail to elute particular substance classes from the adsorbing material. Furthermore, specific sensitivity ranges of detectors can be used in these inference processes. Finally, selection properties of different detectors are taken into account. Thus, all threee substance selection steps that were mentioned in the introduction are modelled and integrated into measurement data interpretation in WANDA.

Third, several measurements taken with different methods from the same sample can be combined to yield a more plausible list of substance identifications. Taking several measurements enhances discriminability of peak identification proposals.

3. Uncertainty Management in Measurement Data Interpretation

All inferences in the process of interpreting results from chromatography are tangled with uncertainty. Environmental data only allow for rough conclusions about substances being present in a water sample. Measurement methods usually do not exclude substances safely from detection in a chromatogram. Thus, it is a crucial requirement to a knowledge-based support of measurement data interpretation to provide a tool for managing uncertainty.

The specific demands of the present application have led to the conclusion that a "non standard" calculus is to be used: First, chemists can neither assess precise probabilities of the different environmental effects nor can they provide the knowledge engineer with precise numbers on the frequencies with which the measurement configuration fails to detect common substances. Second, there is a clear distinction between the "degree of uncertainty" that a substance is present in the chromatogram and the "degree of uncertainty" that a substance could have been eliminated during the various processes of sample taking, extraction and detection. This distinction is vital to the thinking of a professional environmental analyst.

The principal requirement to be met by an expert system in this area is, therefore, a good model for expressing and handling the distinction between detectability of substances in a specific measurement method on the one hand and apriori beliefs in substance occurences due to environmental influences on the other hand. This distinction readily suggests adopting the Dempster/Shafer theory for managing uncertainty in WANDA and in similar expert systems (see Shafer, 1976; Baldwin, 1986). Detectability corresponds to degrees of plausibility in Dempster/Shafer theory, while positive support of candidate substances corresponds to a degree of belief. We then have a belief function for each single substance. The frame of discernment underlying the belief function consists of the following elements:

1. Substance x is candidate (and, hence, detectable).

2. Substance x is detectable, but not candidate.

3. Substance x is undetectable.

Thus, we assume that a substance can be candidate only if it is detectable. In this situation, it is sufficient to work with dichotomous belief functions (like in Baldwin´s support logic, see Baldwin, 1986), whose focal elements are:

1. Substance x is candidate. (C)

2. Substance x is undetectable. (D)

We denote the basic probability mass of a hypothesis H as m(H), the degree of belief in the hypothesis by Bel(H), and the degree of plausibility as Pl(H) (for definitions and properties, see Shafer, 1976). In the special case of WANDA, we have

(1) $m(C) = Bel\ (C)$,

(2) $Pl(C) = 1 - Bel(D)$,

(3) $m(D) = Bel(D)$.

Eq. 1 indicates that the mass on the event that a substance is candidate sufficiently describes the degree of belief attributed to the substance's "candidateness". Eq. 2 says that a substance can be candidate at most with the probability with which it is detectable (measured by $1 - Bel(D)$). Eq. 3 is similar to eq. 1. Finally,

Pl(C) - Bel(C)

measures the difference between probabilities of detectability and "candidateness". At the outset of each run of WANDA, this difference is initialized to 1, i.e., Bel(D) = 0, Bel (C) = 0, which amounts to a vacuous belief function representing total ingnorance. This representation of ignorance is of vital importance to WANDA, since we may not assume anything (even no uniform distribution of detectability) before any information comes in. Like in Baldwin's support logic, we write (and store) dichotomous belief functions as intervals in [0, 1] (see Baldwin, 1986; Spies, 1989).

There are belief intervals for substances associated with conclusions of rules. This indicates that, if the rule fires, the substances in the conclusion are supported by new evidence to the degrees specified in the belief interval. There are three principal classes of rules:

- Rules referring to measurement procedures. Typically, these rules will not assign mass to the event that a substance is candidate, but only to its detectability under specified conditions of sample taking, extraction, and so on.

- Rules referring to knowledge about environmental facts. These rules will affect degrees of belief in the event that substances are candidates, i.e. that, to some degree, one expects them to be in the sample.

- Rules identifying peak area relationships for multiple chromatography (i.e., several chromatograms taken from one sample with different selection devices). These rules are used to match an empirical peak area relationship for two measurements against a reference relationship from identified substances. Thus they provide another hint as to changing the supports of substances within peaks.

All incoming information from different firings of rules relating to substance properties is used to derive *detectable substance lists*. These lists are all separately stored in an object representation of the whole sample taking and analysis procedure. On user´s demand, the different detectable substance lists can be combined using Dempster´s rule for each substance and its associated support intervals. This combination of evidence corresponds to assessing the joint effect of a set of measurement procedures on a sample. The resulting list will be referred to as *global detectable substance list*.

On the other hand, once a chromatogram is entered, WANDA establishes and maintains a *candidate list for each peak in the chromatogram*, using the conventional technique of reference matching based on retention times. The resulting list (of lists) will be referred to as *within peak candidate list*.

The decisive step in peak identification, then, consists of combining the two lists, namely the global detectable substance list and the within peak candidate list with Dempster´s rule. The result is another within peak substance list, however, each support interval is now corrected for the effects of detectability given measurement procedures from sample taking to detector choices. Thus, one obtains a *consolidated within peak candidate list*.

This resulting consolidated within peak candidate list usually provides a substantial help as to identifying the substances "behind" the peaks in a chromatogram. Whereas a typical within peak candidate list on the basis of reference measurements usually contains from 5 to 10 substance proposals, the consolidated list will typically reduce beliefs and/or plausiblities for about 2 to 5 of these substance proposals by sizeable amounts. As a result, the number of remaining plausible substance identifications is greatly reduced.

The use of multiple chromatography leads to deducing *several* consolidated within peak candidate lists. Using the third class of rules mentioned above, these lists are combined as well. The result is an even better discriminative information concerning substance proposals for each peak.

In WANDA, the combination process of different lists of detectable / candidate substances is severely controlled such as to avoid the famous "double counting" of evidence (see Lauritzen & Spiegelhalter, 1988; Pearl, 1988). For instance, if multiple chromatography is used on a given extracted sample, evidences stemming from sample preparation and extraction remain unchanged. As a consequence, they will not be used to update support intervals more than once.

4. Acknowledgement

WANDA is a joint project commissioned by IBM Germany, Hewlett Packard Germany, and The State of Baden-Württemberg. The project is situated at the Institute for Applied Knowledge-Processing at the University of Ulm (FAW), in a department dedicated to AI applications in environmental research. I am indebted to my colleagues S. Dmochewitz, K. Scheuer, and U. Verpoorten for many discussions on the practically adequate use of support intervals in this project. Our chemical advisors comprise Prof. Ballschmiter, University of Ulm, and Dr. Lepper from the Landesamt für Umweltschutz in Karlsruhe.

References

Baldwin, J. (1986): Support Logic Programming. In: A. Jones, A. Kaufmann, H.-J. Zimmermann (eds.): Fuzzy Sets Theory and Applications. NATO ASI Series, D. Reidel, Dordrecht, pp. 137-170.

Fresenius, W., Quentin, K., Schneider, W. (1988): Water Analysis. Springer, Heidelberg.

Lauritzen, S., Spiegelhalter, J. (1988): Local Computations with Probabilities in Graphical Structures and their Application to Expert Systems. J. Roy. Stat. Soc., B, vol. 50(2), pp. 157-224.

Pearl, J. (1988): Probabilistic Reasoning in Intelligent Systems. Networks of plausible Inference. Morgan Kaufmann, San Mateo, CA.

Scheuer, K., Spies, M., Verpoorten, U. (1990): Das FAW Projekt WANDA. University of Ulm, FAW-TR 90002.

Shafer, G. (1976): A mathematical Theory of Evidence. Princeton University Press.

Spies, M. (1989): Syllogistic Inference under Uncertainty. Psychologie Verlags Union, München.

HANDLING UNCERTAINTY IN KNOWLEDGE-BASED COMPUTER VISION

L. Enrique Sucar, Duncan F. Gillies
Department of Computing, Imperial College
180 Queen's Gate, London SW7 2BZ, ENGLAND

Donald A. Gillies
Centre for Logic and Probability in Information Technology, King's College
Manresa Road, London SW3 6LX, ENGLAND

1. INTRODUCTION

Recognition in computer vision consists in matching the internal representations of the objects in the world with the data obtained from the images. We can classify vision systems into two main categories: *model-based* and *knowledge-based*, according to their representation and recognition mechanisms In model-based systems the internal representation is based on a geometric model and the process of recognition consists in matching this model with a description obtained from the image. The representation in knowledge-based systems is symbolic, including assertions about the objects and their relationships. The visual recognition processes within a knowledge-based framework consists of inferring the identity of the objects in the image from firstly the visual data in the form of a symbolic image, and secondly previous knowledge about the world stored in the knowledge-base (KB). The main problem is that the image data underdetermines the structure of the observed scene. The transformation of a real-world scene into an image represented in the computer also involves uncertainty, introducing noise and distortions. Further processing, such as edge detection and segmentation, generally involves the loss of some useful information. So the process of recognition is based on *evidential information* [8] that is uncertain, imprecise and inaccurate.

In this paper we review the different techniques of knowledge representation and reasoning that have been proposed for handling uncertainty in high-level vision. Then we present our approach based on objective probability theory and a practical application in an expert system for endoscopy.

2. HANDLING UNCERTAINTY IN VISION SYSTEMS

Previous work in knowledge-based vision uses representations based on predicate logic, production systems, semantic networks, and frames [8]. These systems have logic as their underlying principle, and reasoning based on logical inference. Thus, handling uncertainty has been done by enhancing the basic representation and reasoning mechanisms, using non-numerical methods, certainty factors, Dempster-Shafer theory or fuzzy-logic, or *ad-hoc* methods developed for specific applications. Provan [7] proposed a *truth maintenance system* for object recognition. Perkins [6] uses a certainty factors approach in an expert system for region classification of aerial photographs. Wesley [86] uses Dempster-Shafer theory for recognizing objects in natural scenes. Ohta [4] combines fuzzy logic and probability in a production system for natural scene interpretation. Other systems, such as *SPAM* [3] for the interpretation of airport aerial images, define *ad-hoc* factors and formulas for combining uncertain evidence.

Non-numerical methods could be useful to represent certain types of uncertainties as exceptions in some domains such as legal reasoning, but for computer vision a numerical technique seems necessary due to the stochastic nature of the relationships between propositions. Previous knowledge-based vision systems use non-probabilistic numerical techniques, but most base their degrees of belief on statistical data. Only probability provides a clear semantic interpretation, either as a statistical frequency (objective), or as a subjective estimate used traditionally in expert systems. It satisfies the adequacy criteria for visual knowledge representation [2], and provides a preference ordering for competing hypotheses. Thus, probability theory is an adequate framework for handling uncertainty in high-level vision.

3. PROBABILISTIC REASONING IN COMPUTER VISION

Our representation starts from a *probabilistic network* model whose structure corresponds to the qualitative visual knowledge in the domain. A probabilistic or Bayesian network represents the probability distribution of a set of variables and makes explicit the dependency information between them. For a visual knowledge-base, we can think of the network as divided into a series of layers, in which the nodes of the lower layer correspond to the feature variables and those of the upper layer to the object variables. The intermediate layers have nodes for other visual entities, such as parts of an object or image regions, or represent relations between features and objects. The links point from nodes in the upper layers toward nodes in the lower layers, express a causal relationship. The structure of a probabilistic network for visual recognition is shown in figure 1.

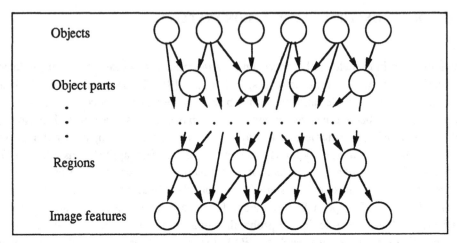

Figure 1. Hierarchical Probabilistic Network for Visual Recognition.

Reasoning in a probabilistic network is done through *probability propagation* from the evidence nodes to the hypotheses nodes. In a general network it is computationally expensive [1], so in practice it is necessary to restrict our representation to certain types of networks. The hierarchical visual network can be thought of as a series of trees, with each tree having its root at one object, connected to other nodes in the intermediate layers, and with the leaves of the tree as the feature nodes. It is generally the case that we can represent the intermediate objects and features as separate nodes for each object hypothesis, with common nodes only for features and relations. Certain nodes have no parent (objects), other nodes have one parent (intermediate objects/features), and some nodes have multiple parents (features and relations). We will restrict the multiple parent nodes to the leaves, and called this type of network a *multitree*.

Pearl [5] has developed efficient methods for probability propagation in singly connected networks: *trees* and *polytrees*. But a multitree is not singly connected; that is, there can be multiple paths between nodes. By *conditioning* [5] we block the pathways that go through an instantiated node, partitioning the network along this node, and connecting a copy of it to each one of its parents. Thus, if all the leaf nodes are instantiated, we can separate a multitree into a series of independent trees, and obtain the posterior probability of the different objects (root) by the following algorithm:

1. Decompose the network into N trees by partitioning it in every leaf node.
2. Instantiate all leaf nodes by using the measured features.
3. For all instantiated nodes B, set $\lambda(B_i)=1$ for the instantiated value, 0 otherwise.
4. For every tree, repeat until the root is reached:
   4.1. From each leaf node B send a message to its parent node A calculated as:
   $$\lambda_B(A_i) = \sum_j P(B_j|A_i) \, \lambda(B_j) \tag{1}$$
   4.2. For each node A update its $\lambda(A_i)$ with the messages received from its children:
   $$\lambda(A_i) = \prod_k \lambda_k(B_i) \tag{2}$$

5. Obtain the posterior probability of each root node C_j by:

$$P(C_j|V) = \alpha \, \pi(C_j) \, \lambda(C_j) \tag{3}$$

where $\lambda(B_i)=P(V_B|B_i)$, $\pi(B_j)=P(B_j)$ and α is a normalizing constant, and V represents the evidence variables (using the same notation as Pearl [5]).

4. LEARNING STRUCTURE FROM DATA

Given a KB represented as a probabilistic network, the process of knowledge acquisition is divided naturally into two parts: *structure learning* and *parameter learning*. Parameter learning consists of finding the required prior and conditional probability distributions. By using an objective interpretation of probability, we obtain the probabilities statistically from images of the intended application domain. This permits the system to learn and improve its performance as more images are processed.

Structure learning has to do with obtaining the topology of the network, that is the dependency relationships between the variables. We start from a qualitative structure derived from heuristics or subjective rules about the problem, representing the relevant variables and their dependency relations. The structure of the network determines the features and relations which are considered relevant for recognizing an object. It is also important to check the implicit dependencies and independences we are assuming in the network. For this we have developed a methodology to verify the independence assumptions with statistical tests (correlation) and modify the structure of the network accordingly, eliminating redundant information [10]. We also test the discriminatory capability (probabilistic distance) of each feature for distinguishing similar objects, selecting the features variables for maximum performance.

5. IMAGE UNDERSTANDING FOR ENDOSCOPY

Endoscopy is one of the tools for diagnosis and treatment of gastrointestinal diseases. The endoscope is a flexible tube with viewing capability. It has a manoeuvrable tip whose orientation is controlled by pull wires that bend it in four orthogonal directions. The navigation of the endoscope is a difficult task, especially in the colon. We are developing a computer assistant for aiding a physician with the navigation of the endoscope inside the colon [9]. For this the system must recognize the important features for navigation in colon images. We have constructed a knowledge-base with the help of expert endoscopists and it has been implemented as a probabilistic network. The initial structure was then improved with statistical tests and the required probabilities were estimated from real colonoscopy sessions stored in video tapes.

We have tested our system using real colon images with encouraging results. The initial performance has improved by dropping correlated variables and variables with low discriminatory capability, and at the same time it became more efficient. We can recognize the centre part of the colon (lumen) and differentiate it from pockets in the walls (diverticula) that sometimes confuse the doctors.

6. CONCLUSIONS

Probability theory provides a sound theoretical foundation for handling uncertainty in computer vision. Its objective interpretation allows us to use data for improving the quantitative and qualitative structure of our KB. An important challenge in vision is to find which are the important features to recognize the different objects in the world, and a probabilistic approach provides a useful tool for advancing in this direction.

7. REFERENCES

[1] Cooper, G.F. (1990), "The Computational Complexity of Probabilistic Inference Using Bayesian Networks", *Artificial Intelligence*, Vol. 42, pp. 393-405.

[2] Mackworth, A. (1988) "Adequacy Criteria for Visual Knowledge Representation", in Z. Pylyshyn (ed.), *Computational Processes in Human Vision: An Interdisciplinary Prespective*, Ablex, Norwood, NJ, pp. 464-476.

[3] McKeown, D.M., Harvey, W.A. and McDermott, J. (1985), "Rule-Based Interpretation of Aerial Imagery", *IEEE PAMI*, Vol. 7, No. 5, pp. 570-585.

[4] Ohta, Y. (1985), *Knowledge-based Interpretation of Outdoor Natural Colour Scenes*, Pitman, Boston, Mass., USA.

[5] Pearl, J. (1988), *Probabilstic Reasoning in Intelligent Systems*, Morgan-Kaufmann, San Mateo, Calif., USA.

[6] Perkins, W.A. (1986), "Rule-based Interpreting of Aerial Photographs using the Lockheed Expert System", *Optical Engineering*, Vol. 25, No. 3, pp. 356-362.

[7] Provan, G.M (1987), "The Visual Constraint Recognition System (VICTORS): Exploring the Role of Reasoning in High-Level Vision", *Proc. IEEE Workshop on Computer Vision*, pp. 170-175.

[8] Rao, A.R. and Jain, R. (1988), "Knowledge Representation and Control in Computer Vision Systems", *IEEE Expert*, Vol. 3, No. 1, pp. 64-79.

[9] Sucar, L.E. and Gillies, D.F. (1990), "Knowledge-Based Assistant for Colonoscopy" in *Proc. Third International Conference on Industrial and Engineering Applications of Artificial Intelligence and Expert Systems*, Vol. II, ACM, pp. 665-672.

[10] Sucar, L.E., Gillies, D.F., and Gillies, D.A. (1991), "Handling Uncertainty in Knowledge-Based Systems Using Objective Probability" in *Proc. World Congress on Expert Systems*, Orlando, Fl., Dec. 16-19 (to be published).

[11] Wesley, L.P. (1986), "Evidential Knowledge-based Computer Vision", *Optical Engineering*, Vol. 25, No. 3, pp. 363-379.

Probabilistic Reasoning
With Facts And Rules
In Deductive Databases

H. Thöne[1]   U. Güntzer[1]   W. Kießling[2]

[1]Wilhelm-Schickard-Institut, Universität Tübingen, Sand 13, D-7400 Tübingen 1
[2]Institut für Informatik, Techn. Universität München, Orleansstr. 34, D-8000 München 80

Abstract

In this paper we present a new method for probabilistic reasoning with true
facts and uncertain rules within a deductive database. Besides a *cautious*
approach to inferences on uncertain rules, we show a *default* approach for
uncertainty reasoning including factual knowledge, based on the ideas of maximal context and detachment. Integrated into a database these approaches
support many important applications with probabilistic value dependencies.
One sample application will be provided: Lead qualification within a marketing database.

1. Introduction

In the near future, significant commercial applications, such as the identification of features from digital satellite images and the technical risk assessment in nuclear power
plants, will require efficient reasoning under uncertainty on massive amounts of data.
To tackle the underlying tasks of this requirement a confluence of uncertainty reasoning
techniques coming from artificial intelligence (see e.g. [Pea 88] and [KSH 91]), operations
research ([AnHo 90]) and database technology ([BMP 90]) seems to be necessary. [1]
A novel approach for reasoning under uncertainty with full database support was presented in [GKT 91]. Founded on probabilistic grounds it offers a sound rule-based uncertainty reasoning mechanism which operates like a deduction system in logic. There,
an uncertain rule of the form $A \xrightarrow{x_1, x_2} B$ is interpreted with lower and upper bounds for
the conditional probability of B given A, i.e. $0 \leq x_1 \leq P(B|A) \leq x_2 \leq 1$. Logical deduc-
tions on such uncertain rules are performed by means of powerful inference rules being
implemented on top of a deductive database system.

---

[1]Quoting Hooker ([Hoo 88]) "... the inference problems are hard enough to justify several angles of
attack".

The rest of this paper is organized as follows: Section 2 describes the method for uncertainty reasoning with facts and uncertain rules. We introduce an inference rule called detachment within a maximal context to draw plausible conclusions from a database. In section 3, a real application dealing with a decision scenario demonstrates the need for numerical uncertainty reasoning with full database support.

2. Reasoning with Facts and Uncertain Rules

Let us start with a well-known example adjusted from default logic (see e.g. [Rei 80]).

Facts: $bird(Ted)$,

$bird(Tweety)$, $penguin(Tweety)$,

$bird(Sam)$, $\overline{penguin}(Sam)$

Uncertain rules: $penguin \xrightarrow{1.0} bird$

$bird \xrightarrow{0.8, 0.9} fly$

$bird \xrightarrow{0.01, 0.02} penguin$

$penguin \xrightarrow{0.0} fly$

We might ask whether individual Ted, Tweety or Sam can fly?

Because of the non-monotonic nature of probabilistic reasoning we can not jump to any conclusions about an individual unless we know the maximal context for that individual. The **maximal context** of an individual t, written $C[t]$, is defined to be the conjunction of all the predicates in the database which are true when applied to t, i.e. $C[t]$ accumulates everything known in the database concerning t. For instance,

$$C[Ted] = bird, \quad C[Tweety] = bird \wedge penguin, \quad C[Sam] = bird \wedge \overline{penguin}.$$

In our considerations, we always presume a type of *closed world assumption*, which means that the database contains all relevant information of a given problem domain. Whenever we learn some additional knowledge we have to reevaluate the maximal context.

Although probability theory provides a clean mathematical foundation for probabilistic reasoning, it does not possess a method for combining facts and rules. Therefore we define a logical inference rule called **detachment** as follows: For a given individual the maximal context can be detached from a corresponding uncertain rule, which has a premise equal to the maximal context.[2] This inference rule is quite reasonable, because we typically assume that - in a given maximal context - the concluded events hold also for the individual itself. The detachment rule will be shown in the sequel.

A prerequisite to apply detachment is the existence of suitable uncertain rules. Since there are no rules at hand with a premise equal to $C[Tweety]$ or $C[Sam]$, we have to trigger a goal-directed deduction with the calculus, described in [GKT 91], to compute the bounds for the needed uncertain rules. The calculus does neither rely on any hidden assumption not already expressed by the given uncertain rules nor on the availability of complete information. Conditional independence information[3] can be entered in addition explicitly,

---

[2] The straightforward generalization of modus ponens $\{A(t), A \xrightarrow{x_1, x_2} B\} \vdash \xrightarrow{x_1, x_2} B(t)$ is not sound. A counter-example is: $\{bird(Tweety), bird \xrightarrow{0.8, 0.9} fly\} \nvdash \xrightarrow{0.8, 0.9} fly(Tweety)$.

[3] A is independent of C under condition B, denoted $I(A, B, C)$, iff $P(A|BC) = P(A|B)$.

if justified by the problem domain. This is a **cautious** approach to uncertain inferences in the tradition of INFERNO ([Qui 83]). The reader is referred to [KTG 91] for a comparison of our approach to other proposals. In the example[4], we get:

$$\{ penguin \xrightarrow{1.0} bird, penguin \xrightarrow{0.0} fly \} \;\; \overline{\underset{WCL}{\vdash}} \;\; bird \wedge penguin \xrightarrow{0.0} fly$$

$$\{ bird \xrightarrow{0.01, 0.02} penguin \} \;\; \overline{\underset{N}{\vdash}} \;\; bird \xrightarrow{0.98, 0.99} \overline{penguin}$$

$$\{ bird \xrightarrow{0.01, 0.02} penguin, penguin \xrightarrow{0.0} fly \} \;\; \overline{\underset{WCR}{\vdash}} \;\; bird \xrightarrow{0.0} penguin \wedge fly$$

$$\{ bird \xrightarrow{0.8, 0.9} fly, bird \xrightarrow{0.0} penguin \wedge fly \} \;\; \overline{\underset{CRN}{\vdash}} \;\; bird \xrightarrow{0.8, 0.9} \overline{penguin} \wedge fly$$

$$\{ bird \xrightarrow{0.98, 0.99} \overline{penguin}, bird \xrightarrow{0.8, 0.9} \overline{penguin} \wedge fly \} \;\; \overline{\underset{CL}{\vdash}} \;\; bird \wedge penguin \xrightarrow{0.81, 0.92} fly$$

Now, we can employ the detachment, denoted by " $\underset{D}{\vdash}$ ", using the first and last derived uncertain rule above. At this point, we switch from the cautious approach to the **default** approach of uncertainty reasoning.

$$\{ C[Ted] \xrightarrow{0.8, 0.9} fly \} \;\; \underset{D}{\vdash} \;\; \xrightarrow{0.8, 0.9} fly(Ted)$$

$$\{ C[Tweety] \xrightarrow{0.0} fly \} \;\; \underset{D}{\vdash} \;\; \xrightarrow{0.0} fly(Tweety)$$

$$\{ C[Sam] \xrightarrow{0.81, 0.92} fly \} \;\; \underset{D}{\vdash} \;\; \xrightarrow{0.81, 0.92} fly(Sam)$$

The detachment rule provides features that extend the usual framework known from reasoning with defaults ([GePe 90]). On the one hand large fact and rule bases can be utilized and on the other hand conclusions can be quantified numerically. For instance, we conclude that Ted can fly with a probability between 80 and 90 percent - but we have to believe that Sam is a little bit more likely to fly, i. e. we attach a probability between 81 and 92 percent to his flying ability, because we know that he is not a penguin being unable to fly. This feature can be exploited, e. g. for a detailed what-if analysis in uncertain and incomplete knowledge domains, as presented in the following section.

3. Sample Application: Lead Qualification

Suppose, you are a marketing manager with the task to identify prospects for yachts by searching for names in a given leads database. You are concerned with the problem of guessing the buyer behavior under incomplete knowledge. A small portion of available data is represented in the following relation *LEADS* with the attribute NAME as key:

NAME	HOME	EDUCATION	CAR
Cathy Austen	luxurious	NULL	expensive
Fred Jones	luxurious	very good	NULL
Jack Gordon	expensive	excellent	NULL
Maggie O'Hara	expensive	NULL	middle
Pam Quincey	NULL	good	expensive
Gill Fowler	normal	NULL	NULL

---

[4]The extended calculus, as presented in [KTG 91], consists of 16 inference rules. The inference rules applied in this section are listed in the appendix. The bounds are represented with a scale of two digits, but really they are computed with type rational.

You decide to investigate the buyer behavior in a what-if scenario by making some probabilistic assertions. For instance, you estimate that *"almost all people who live in a luxurious house have an expensive car, but only few of those who have an expensive car live also in a luxurious home"*. In order to describe the probabilistic dependencies and independencies we use the following abbreviations here, where σ denotes the usual selection operator in relational databases and all attributes are ordered in the intended sense (e.g. expensive < luxurious):

$$H_{lux} = \sigma_{HOME=luxurious}(LEADS) \qquad H_{exp} = \sigma_{HOME=expensive}(LEADS)$$
$$C_{exp} = \sigma_{CAR=expensive}(LEADS) \qquad H_{\geq exp} = \sigma_{HOME\geq expensive}(LEADS)$$
$$E_{\geq good} = \sigma_{EDUCATION\geq good}(LEADS) \qquad P = Prospect$$

Then you assume:

$$H_{lux} \xrightarrow{0.9,1.0} C_{exp}, \quad C_{exp} \xrightarrow{0.05,0.1} H_{lux}, \quad H_{exp} \xrightarrow{0.7,0.9} C_{exp},$$
$$H_{lux} \xrightarrow{0.4,0.5} P, \quad H_{exp} \xrightarrow{0.1,0.3} P, \quad I(P, H_{\geq exp}, E_{\geq good}).$$

The derived uncertain facts are:

$$\xrightarrow{0.33,0.56} P(Cathy\ Austen), \quad \xrightarrow{0.4,0.5} P(Fred\ Jones), \quad \xrightarrow{0.1,0.3} P(Jack\ Gordon).$$

Now suppose that you get some more insight into your knowledge domain.[5] Additionally, you assume:

$$\overline{H_{\geq exp}} \xrightarrow{0.0,0.01} P, \quad H_{lux}C_{exp} \xrightarrow{0.5,0.55} P, \quad H_{exp}\overline{C_{exp}} \xrightarrow{0.0,0.05} P,$$
$$I(P, C_{exp}, E_{\geq good}), \quad I(P, H_{lux}C_{exp}, E_{\geq good}), \quad I(P, H_{exp}\overline{C_{exp}}, E_{\geq good}).$$

Then the derived uncertain facts are:

$$\xrightarrow{0.50,0.55} P(Cathy\ Austen), \quad \xrightarrow{0.45,0.50} P(Fred\ Jones), \quad \xrightarrow{0.1,0.3} P(Jack\ Gordon),$$
$$\xrightarrow{0.0,0.05} P(Maggie\ O'Hara), \quad \xrightarrow{0.025,0.978} P(Pam\ Quincey), \quad \xrightarrow{0.0,0.01} P(Gill\ Fowler).$$

Summarizing, detachment within a maximal context is a reliable and extremely useful way to infer uncertain facts about individuals in problematic domains. Maximal context computation and query optimization are currently under investigation.

Appendix: Some Inference Rules

Note that A, B and C denote conjunctive events, whereas F denotes a basic event.

(1) Conjunction left (CL):

$$\{A \xrightarrow{x_1,x_2} B, x_1 > 0, A \xrightarrow{y_1,y_2} BC\} \vdash AB \xrightarrow{z_1,z_2} C, z_1 = \frac{y_1}{x_2}, z_2 = \min(1, \frac{y_2}{x_1})$$

(2) Weak conjunction left (WCL):

$$\{B \xrightarrow{x_1,x_2} A, x_1 > 0, B \xrightarrow{y_1,y_2} C\} \vdash AB \xrightarrow{z_1,z_2} C, z_1 = \max(0, \frac{x_1+y_1-1}{x_1}), z_2 = \min(1, \frac{y_2}{x_1})$$

---

[5]Note that the consistency of the knowledge base is maintained during run-time.

(3) Weak conjunction right (WCR):

$$\{ A \xrightarrow{x_1, x_2} B, B \xrightarrow{y} C, A \neq C \} \vdash A \xrightarrow{x_1, x_2} BC,$$

$$z_1 = \begin{cases} 0 & \text{if } y = 0 \\ x_1 & \text{if } y = 1 \end{cases} \qquad z_2 = \begin{cases} 0 & \text{if } y = 0 \\ x_2 & \text{if } y = 1 \end{cases}$$

(4) Negation (N):

$$\{ A \xrightarrow{x_1, x_2} F \} \vdash A \xrightarrow{z_1, z_2} \overline{F}, z_1 = 1 - x_2, z_2 = 1 - x_1$$

(5) Conjunction right with negation (CRN):

$$\{ A \xrightarrow{x_1, x_2} C, A \xrightarrow{y_1, y_2} FC \} \vdash A \xrightarrow{z_1, z_2} \overline{F}C, z_1 = \max(0, x_1 - y_2), z_2 = \max(0, x_2 - y_1)$$

References

[AnHo 90] K.A. Anderson and J.N. Hooker: Bayesian Logic. Workshop "Uncertainty in Knowledge-Based Systems", Forschungsinstitut für angewandte Wissensverarbeitung, Ulm, 1990, pp. 1-54.

[BMP 90] D. Barbara, H. Garcia-Molina and D. Porter: The Management of Probabilistic Data. *Proc. EDBT*, Venice, 1990, pp. 60-74.

[GePe 90] H. Geffner and J. Pearl: A Framework for Reasoning with Defaults. *Knowledge Representation and Defeasible Reasoning*, H. Kyburg, R. Loui and G. Carlson (eds.), Kluer Academic Publishers, 1990, pp. 69-87.

[GKT 91] U. Güntzer, W. Kießling and H. Thöne: New Directions for Uncertainty Reasoning in Deductive Databases. *Proc. ACM SIGMOD Int. Conf. on Management of Data*, Denver, 1991, pp. 178-187.

[Hoo 88] J.N. Hooker: A Quantitative Approach to Logical Inference. *Decision Support Systems 4*, 1988, pp. 45-69.

[KSH 91] R. Kruse, E. Schwecke and J. Heinsohn: Uncertainty and Vagueness in Knowledge Based Systems: Numerical methods. *Springer Verlag*, 1991.

[KTG 91] W. Kießling, H. Thöne and U. Güntzer: Database Support for Problematic Knowledge. *Technical Report TUM-I9109*, Institut für Informatik, Technische Universität München, June 1991.

[Qui 83] J.R. Quinlan: INFERNO: A cautious approach to uncertain inference. *The Computer Journal* 26. 1983, pp. 255-269.

[Pea 88] J. Pearl: Probabilistic Reasoning in Intelligent Systems. *Morgan Kaufmann*, San Mateo, 1988.

[Rei 80] R. Reiter: A logic for default reasoning. *Artificial Intelligence* 13, 1980, pp. 81-132.

AN ENTITY-RELATIONSHIP APPROACH TO
THE MODELLING OF VAGUENESS IN DATABASES

R.M. Vandenberghe and R.M. de Caluwe
Computer Science Laboratory, State University of Ghent
Grotesteenweg-Noord 2, B-9052 Zwijnaarde, Belgium

Almost all intelligent systems rely on an underlying separate or integrated database component where the data and/or knowledge for use is kept. Appropriate database design taking into account the possible vagueness of information is needed. In this paper we try to contribute to this by proposing an adapted Entity-Relationship model, including the most important advanced "semantic" concepts found in literature (cfr. [1], [2], [3], [4], [5]), and moreover able to incorporate the fuzziness (i.e. uncertainty, impreciseness, incompleteness) which is inherent to the natural way of describing the Universe of Discourse (UoD).

Similar work has been carried out by Zvieli and Chen [6] and by Ruspini [7]. However, our approach to the problem is substantially different from theirs.

Basic definitions and notations

In our model, the fuzzification of concepts is, in essence, based on the notion of the *fuzzy truth value* of a fuzzy proposition, as introduced by A. Van Schooten in [8], [9] :

Let $I = \{true, false\}$, let $\Im(I)$ the set of all fuzzy sets defined in I, and let P be the set of all fuzzy or non-fuzzy propositions and propositional forms.

Then the *fuzzy truth value* $\widetilde{t}(p)$ of a proposition $p \in P$ is determined by :

$$\widetilde{t} : P \to \Im(I) : p \to \widetilde{t}(p), \text{ where } \begin{cases} (\widetilde{t}(p))(true) = \text{Possibility (p is true)} \\ (\widetilde{t}(p))(false) = \text{Possibility (p is false)}. \end{cases}$$

Based on the notion of fuzzy truth value, a *fuzzy propositional logic* has been built. To this end, the rules of the classical propositional logic, for obtaining the truth value of compound propositions, have been extended using Zadeh's extension principle.

We list only the results for the basic operators $\neg$, $\wedge$ and $\vee$:

$$. \ \widetilde{t}(\neg p) = \widetilde{\neg}(\widetilde{t}(p)) \qquad \forall p \in P$$
$$. \ \widetilde{t}(p \wedge q) = \widetilde{t}(p) \ \widetilde{\wedge} \ \widetilde{t}(q) \qquad \forall p, q \in P$$
$$. \ \widetilde{t}(p \vee q) = \widetilde{t}(p) \ \widetilde{\vee} \ \widetilde{t}(q) \qquad \forall p, q \in P$$

where $\tilde{\neg}$, $\tilde{\wedge}$ and $\tilde{\vee}$ are the extended logical operators, defined on $\Im(\{true, false\})$, by applying Zadeh's extension principle on the corresponding classical operators, e.g. :

$$\tilde{\wedge} : \Im(I) \times \Im(I) \to \Im(I) : (a, b) \to a \tilde{\wedge} b$$

where $(a \tilde{\wedge} b)(true) = \min (a(true), b(true))$
and $(a \tilde{\wedge} b)(false) = \max (a(false), b(false))$

Furthermore, we define: $\forall a, b \in \Im(I) : a \tilde{\leq} b \Leftrightarrow a(true) \leq b(true) \wedge a(false) \geq b(false)$

Based on the notion of fuzzy truth value, we now extend the definition of fuzzy set. A *generalized fuzzy set* A in the universal set X is defined as

$$A : X \to \Im(\{true, false\}) : x \to \tilde{t}(x \in A)$$

where $\tilde{t}(x \in A) = \{p/true, n/false\}$, with $\begin{cases} p = \text{Possibility } (x \in A), \\ n = \text{Possibility } (x \notin A). \end{cases}$

A generalized fuzzy set A is called *normalized* if $\tilde{t}(x \in A)$ is normalized for all $x \in X$.

The proposed model

Fundamentally, the proposed extended ER model, uses extended definitions for entity-sets and for relationship-sets. Both are conceived as generalized fuzzy sets, in which a fuzzy truth value is associated with each entity or relationship instance respectively.

Entity-sets
The reason for the extended definition of entity-sets is, that in a real world situation, the occurrence of an entity in an entity-set can be "fuzzy".
This can, on the one hand be due to the fact that the entity is ill-described (manifesting itself in the fuzziness of some of its attribute values) or ill-located among the members of the set, on the other hand be due to the inherent fuzziness of the entity set itself, or be due to both.
Hence, for each entity-set E, and with each entity e of the universal set corresponding to the UoD, a fuzzy truth value will be associated, i.e.

$$\tilde{t}(e \in E) = \{p/true, n/false\}, \text{ where}$$

$p = \text{Possibility } (e \in E)$: possibility that entity e belongs to the entity-set E
$n = \text{Possibility } (e \notin E)$: possibility that entity e does not belong to the entity-set E

Relationship-sets

Relationships are used to model associations between entities in the real world.
Conventionally, a relationship-set between entity-sets E_1, E_2, ..., E_n, is formally defined as a set of n-tuples $(e_1, e_2, ..., e_n)$, with $e_i \in E_i$, $i=1, ..., n$, called relationship instances. In our model, just as the occurrence of an entity in an entity-set, the occurrence of a relationship instance between specific entities, in the relationship-set concerned, will be allowed to be fuzzy (corresponding to a real world situation).

Indeed, on the one hand, for relationships that are crisp by nature, the existence of the association in question between some particular entities of the entity sets involved, can be uncertain. On the other hand, the relationship itself can be inherently fuzzy. Think of a recursive relationship "is friendly with" between persons.

Hence, each relationship-set R will be represented as a generalized fuzzy set as well, in which a fuzzy truth value is associated with each n-tuple $(e_1, e_2, ..., e_n)$ of entities of the sets involved, i.e.

$$\tilde{\tau}((e_1, e_2, ..., e_n) \in R) = \{p/true, n/false\}, \quad \text{where}$$

  p : possibility that there is an association between the entities e_1, e_2, ..., e_n.
  n : possibility that the association does not exist between the entities e_1, e_2, ..., e_n.

Attributes

Of course, the values of attributes, used to describe entity or relationship types, can also be fuzzy, i.e. imprecise, incomplete or cursed with uncertainty.

Hence, we allow in our model, besides the usual simple/composite and single-valued/multivalued characteristics, an additional characteristic to be specified for each attribute (and attribute component), namely crisp/fuzzy.

These characteristics, together with the domain associated with the attribute (if it is simple), or with each of its simple components (if it is composite), determine the value set of the attribute (i.e. the set of all possible values it can take).

Composite attributes take their values from the cartesian product of the domains involved, multivalued attributes take subsets of the appropriate domain as values, and fuzzy attribute values are modelled by means of fuzzy sets on the domain involved.

The characteristics of attributes can be nested in an arbitrary way, should it be useful.

In our model, we also extended the definitions of the most widespread, more advanced "semantic" modelling concepts, namely the concepts of subclass and superclass, the related concept of specialization, and the concept of category. Both user- and predicate-defined variants have been considered.

The extensions were made by expressing the constraints involved - between members of the superclass(es) and members of the subclass(es) - in terms of the fuzzy truth values associated with the entities of the sets concerned, and by applying the rules of the fuzzy propositional logic introduced above.

In the same way, additional constraints applying to specializations (disjointness, completeness) and to categories (total/partial), have been reinterpreted or extended.

Sub- and superclasses, specializations

Let E and F be entity sets represented by generalized fuzzy sets. Then we define :

E is a *subclass* of F iff $\widetilde{t}(e \in E) \lesssim \widetilde{t}(e \in F)$ for all entities e of the UoD.

Now, let E_i be a so-called *attribute-defined subclass* of entity set E, i.e. a subclass defined by means of a condition on some attribute A of E, which can be expressed as "A is F", F being a fuzzy set defined on an appropriate set U, depending on the characteristics of A. Then the entities constituting subclass E_i are the entities from superclass E, which satisfy the specified condition, i.e.

$$\widetilde{t}(e \in E_i) = \widetilde{t}(e \in E \wedge A(e) \text{ is } F) = \widetilde{t}(e \in E) \; \widetilde{\wedge} \; \widetilde{t}(A(e) \text{ is } F)$$

The fuzzy truth value of the proposition " A(e) is F ", can be calculated as follows (e.g. calculating the possibility measure Π and the necessity measure N according to the definitions given by Zadeh [10] and Dubois & Prade [11] respectively) :

$$t = \widetilde{t}(A(e) \text{ is } F) \text{ (true)} = \text{Possibility } (A(e) \text{ is } F) = \Pi (X \text{ is } F \mid X \text{ is } A(e))$$
$$f = \widetilde{t}(A(e) \text{ is } F) \text{ (false)} = \text{Possibility } (A(e) \text{ is not } F) = 1 - N (X \text{ is } F \mid X \text{ is } A(e))$$

Now, let's consider a *specialization* of entity type E that is *attribute-defined* on some (possibly fuzzy-valued) attribute A of E, i.e. a set of subclasses of E, $\{E_i, i=1, ..., n\}$, each defined by means of a formal condition " A is F_i ", $i=1, ..., n$, on the same attribute A. Then the above formula's can be used to obtain for each entity from the superclass, the fuzzy truth value of the entity belonging to each of the subclasses.

Notice that, since we have rules to obtain the fuzzy truth value of a compound proposition, nothing prevents us from defining more general, *condition defined subclasses and specializations* by means of composite conditions.

A specialization is said to be *total* if the superclass is equal to the union of the defining subclasses. In terms of fuzzy truth values, this means :

$$\widetilde{t}(e \in E) = \widetilde{t}(e \in E_1 \vee ... \vee e \in E_n) = \widetilde{t}(e \in E_1) \; \widetilde{\vee} \; ... \; \widetilde{\vee} \; \widetilde{t}(e \in E_n)$$

Shared subclasses

Let E_1, E_2, ..., E_n be entity-sets represented by generalized fuzzy sets. Then a *shared subclass* E of the superclasses E_1, E_2, ..., E_n, consists of entities e satisfying :

$$\tilde{\tau}(e \in E) \precsim \tilde{\tau}(e \in E_1 \cap E_2 \cap ... \cap E_n) = \tilde{\tau}(e \in E_1) \tilde{\wedge} \tilde{\tau}(e \in E_2) \tilde{\wedge} ... \tilde{\wedge} \tilde{\tau}(e \in E_n)$$

Now, consider a *predicate-defined shared subclass* E defined by resp. predicates P_i on entity sets E_i, $i=1$, ..., n. The entities constituting the shared subclass E are the entities which belong to E_i and satisfy the condition P_i, for all $i \in \{1, ..., n\}$.
In terms of fuzzy truth values, this means :

$$\tilde{\tau}(e \in E) = \tilde{\tau}(e \in E_1) \tilde{\wedge} ... \tilde{\wedge} \tilde{\tau}(e \in E_n) \tilde{\wedge} \tilde{\tau}(P_1(e)) \tilde{\wedge} ... \tilde{\wedge} \tilde{\tau}(P_n(e)).$$

Categories

Let E_1, E_2, ..., E_n be entity-sets represented by generalized fuzzy sets. Then a category E with defining superclasses E_1, E_2, ..., E_n, consists of entities e satisfying :

$$\tilde{\tau}(e \in E) \precsim \tilde{\tau}(e \in E_1 \cup E_2 \cup ... \cup E_n) = \tilde{\tau}(e \in E_1) \tilde{\vee} \tilde{\tau}(e \in E_2) \tilde{\vee} ... \tilde{\vee} \tilde{\tau}(e \in E_n)$$

It can be seen that "shared subclass" and "category" are in fact dual concepts.

A category is called *total* if it is equal to the union of its defining superclasses, otherwise, it's said to be *partial*. For a total category, the above inequality becomes an equality.

A *predicate-defined category* E is a category using a predicate P_i - possibly fuzzy - for each defining superclass E_i, $i=1$, ..., n, to specify which members of E_i are members of E. The formula's can be obtained from those for predicate-defined shared subclasses by duality.

Finally, adapted diagrammatic conventions have been developed to display a "Fuzzy Extended Entity Relationship" (FEER) schema, incorporating all of the fuzzified modelling concepts introduced above.

Work in progress

A complete set of operators for a Fuzzy ER algebra is under construction. Some basic operators, namely those for selection, projection, cartesian product and relationship join, have already been studied in depth. A fundamental requirement is, that the result of any operation on entity- or relationship-sets is again an entity- or relationship-set (and that each resulting entity inherits all the relationships in which the operand entities participate), so that this result can be used as an operand in subsequent operations.

References

[1] Chen, P. P., The Entity-Relationship Model - Toward an Unified View of Data. ACM ToDS, Vol. 1, No. 1, March 1976, pp. 9-36.

[2] Smith J. and Smith D., Database Abstractions : Aggregation and Generalization. ACM ToDS, Vol. 2, No. 2, June 1977, pp. 105-133.

[3] Hammer M. and McLeod D., Database Description with SDM : A Semantic Data Model. ACM ToDS, Vol. 6, No. 3, September 1980, pp. 351-386.

[4] Elmasri R. et al., The Category Concept: An Extension to the Entity-Relationship Model. International Journal on Data and Knowledge Engineering, Vol. 1, No. 1, May 1985.

[5] Tucherman L. et al., A Proposal for Formalizing and Extending the Generalization and Subset Abstrations in the Entity-Relationship Model. Entity-Relationship Approach to Database Design and Querying, Lochovsky (ed.), Noth-Holland, Amsterdam, 1990.

[6] Zvieli A., Chen P. P., Entity-Relationship Modeling and Fuzzy Databases. Proceedings of the 2nd International Conference on Data Engineering (Los Angeles, Feb. 1986), IEEE, New York, 1986, pp. 320-327.

[7] Ruspini E.H., Imprecision and Uncertainty in the Entity-Relationship Model. Fuzzy Logic in Knowledge Engineering, Prade H. & Negoita C.V. (eds.), Verlag TÜV Rheinland GmbH, Köln, 1986, pp. 18-28.

[8] Van Schooten A., Ontwerp en Implementatie van een Model voor de Representatie en Manipulatie van Onzekerheid en Imprecisie in Databanken en Expert Systemen (Design and Implementation of a Model for the Representation and Manipulation of Uncertainty and Imprecision in Data Bases and Expert Systems). Ph. D., State University of Ghent, 1988 (unpublished).

[9] Van Schooten A., De Caluwe R., Kerre E., Approximate Reasoning Based on Possibility Theory. Cybernetics and Systems '88, Trappl R. (ed.), Kluwer Academic Publishers, Dordrecht, 1988, pp. 643-650.

[10] Zadeh L. A., Fuzzy Sets as a Basis for a Theory of Possibility. Fuzzy Sets and Systems 1, 1978, pp. 3-28.

[11] Dubois D. & Prade H., Théorie des Possibilités. Applications à la Représentation des Connaissances en Informatique. Masson, Paris, 1985.

A PREFERENTIAL MODEL SEMANTICS FOR DEFAULT LOGIC*

Frans Voorbraak
Department of Philosophy, University of Utrecht
P.O. Box 80.126, 3508 TC Utrecht

1. Introduction

In Shoham (1987,1988) a uniform approach to systems for nonmonotonic logic is proposed. This approach consists in considering preference logics, i.e., standard logics together with a preference relation on the interpretations. Γ is said to *preferentially entail* φ if any preferred model of Γ is a model of φ, where M is called a *preferred model* of Γ if M is model of Γ and there is no model M' of Γ which is preferred to M. McCarthy's circumscription (McCarthy (1980)) can easily seen to be a special case of this preference logic framework, since the minimal models of circumscription can be viewed as preferred models. However, capturing Reiter's default logic (Reiter (1980)) in the preferential model approach turned out to be more difficult (cf. Shoham (1987)), and is even thought to be impossible by some researchers of nonmonotonic reasoning.

In this paper a preferential model semantics for default logic is given, by defining a preference relation on partial models called hypervaluations. An alternative preferential model semantics can be obtained by considering a closely related preference relation on Kripke models for **K45**. In fact, we only slightly amend the semantics given in Etherington (1988), which interprets a default as an expression of a preference between *sets* of models. A set of models can be considered to be a partial world description, and hypervaluations are precisely this kind of partial models.

In section 2 some elementary properties of the consequence relation $\vDash_h$ induced by hypervaluations are mentioned and it is pointed out that $\vDash_h$ and the consequence relations for the modal logics **K(D)45** and **S5** are closely related. This latter fact might justify an epistemic reading of $\Gamma \vDash_h \Delta$: if every formula of Γ is believed/known, then some formula of Δ is believed/known. The preferential model semantics for default logic is given in section 3. We end the paper with a short discussion of the results.

---

* The Investigations were supported by the Foundation for Philosophical Research (SWON), which is subsidized by the Netherlands Organization for Scientific Research (NWO).

2 Hypervaluations

L_{PL} is a propositional language built on a set of propositional letters PL and the logical connectives $\neg$ for negation and $\vee$ for disjunction. $\wedge, \supset, \equiv$ are assumed to be defined in the usual way.

DEFINITION 2.1
(i)   An *hyperinterpretation* I is a set of 2-valued interpretations J : PL $\rightarrow$ {T,F}.
(ii)   For any 2-valued interpretation J, V_J : L_{PL} $\rightarrow$ {T,F} denotes the usual 2-valued valuation induced by J. $V_J(\varphi) = T$ and $V_J(\varphi) = F$ will sometimes be written as $\models_{2,J} \varphi$ and $\dashv_{2,J} \varphi$, respectively.
(iii) The *hypervaluation* V_I : L_{PL} $\rightarrow$ {T,F,U} induced by the hyperinterpretation I is given by
$$V_I(\varphi) = \quad T \text{ iff } \forall J \in I \, V_J(\varphi) = T$$
$$F \text{ iff } \forall J \in I \, V_J(\varphi) = F$$
$$U \text{ otherwise.}$$
$V_I(\varphi) = T$ and $V_I(\varphi) = F$ will sometimes be written as $\models_{h,I} \varphi$ and $\dashv_{h,I} \varphi$, respectively.

The definition of hypervaluations is strongly reminiscent of the definition of van Fraassen's supervaluations. In fact, a supervaluation corresponds with a hypervaluation whose elements are the complete extensions of some 3-valued interpretation. The *consequence relation* $\models_x$ induced by $\models_{x,I}$ is defined by $\Gamma \models_x \Delta$ iff $\forall I$ ($\forall \psi \in \Gamma \models_{x,I} \psi \Rightarrow \exists \varphi \in \Delta \models_{x,I} \varphi$). We do *not* require that $\forall I$ ($\forall \varphi \in \Delta \dashv_{x,I} \varphi \Rightarrow \exists \psi \in \Gamma \dashv_{x,I} \psi$), as some authors do (cf. Blamey (1986)). This stronger definition would for example render the inference from {p $\vee$ q,$\neg$q} to p invalid. (A counterexample would be I = {J,J'}, where J(p) = J'(p) = F, J(q) = T, and J'(q) = F.)
It is well-known that the supervaluation consequence relation $\models_s$ is strictly weaker than the ordinary consequence relation. (See e.g. Langholm (1988).) The hypervaluation consequence relation $\models_h$ is weaker still:

PROPOSITION 2.2 $\models_h \subset \models_s \subset \models_2$.

Proof. $\models_h \subseteq \models_s \subseteq \models_2$ is trivial. $\models_s \not\subseteq \models_h$ follows from the fact that {p $\vee$ q} $\models_s$ {p,q}, whereas {p $\vee$ q} $\not\models_h$ {p,q}. $\models_2 \not\subseteq \models_s$ follows from the fact that $\models_2$ {p,$\neg$p}, whereas $\not\models_s$ {p,$\neg$p}.

It is easy to see that $\models_h$, $\models_s$, and $\models_2$ coincide in case the consequence set Δ is $\varnothing$ or a singleton. It is also clear that $\Gamma \models_h \Delta$ iff for every *non-empty* hyperinterpretation I ($\forall \psi \in \Gamma \models_{h,I} \psi \Rightarrow \exists \varphi \in \Delta \models_{h,I} \varphi$). Further, $\models_h$ is closely related to the consequence relations of the modal logics **K45, KD45,** and **S5**:

PROPOSITION 2.3   Let $\Gamma, \Delta \subseteq L_{PL}$, let for any $\Omega \subseteq L_{PL}$ $\square\Omega$ denote the set {$\square\varphi \mid \varphi \in \Omega$}, and let S $\in$ {**K45, KD45,S5**}. Then $\Gamma \models_h \Delta \Leftrightarrow \square\Gamma \models_S \square\Delta$.

Proof. It is easy to see that there exists a 1-1 correspondence μ between non-empty hyperinterpretations and distinguishable connected S5 models such that $V_I(\varphi) = T$ iff $\mu(I) \models \Box\varphi$. The equivalence of $\models_{S5}$, $\models_{KD45}$, and $\models_{K45}$ restricted to boxed formulas is well-known.

The above proposition justifies to some extent the epistemic reading of the hypervaluation consequence relation which was mentioned in the introduction, since **K(D)45** is widely regarded to be a good candidate for the logic of the beliefs of a rational agent, whereas S5 is often mentioned as a suitable logic of knowledge. Below we mention some properties of $\models_h$.

PROPOSITION 2.4   Suppose $\Gamma \models_h \Delta$ and $\Delta \neq \varnothing$. Then $\exists\varphi \in \Delta$ s.t. $\Gamma \models_h \varphi$.

COROLLARY 2.5   Suppose $\Delta \neq \varnothing$. Then $\Gamma \models_h \Delta$ iff $\exists\varphi \in \Delta$ s.t. $\Gamma \models_2 \varphi$.

COROLLARY 2.6   (Compactness) If $\Gamma \models_h \Delta$, then there exists finite sets Γ', Δ' such that $\Gamma' \subseteq \Gamma, \Delta' \subseteq \Delta$, and $\Gamma' \models_h \Delta'$.

COROLLARY 2.7 $\Gamma \models_h \Delta$ is decidable for finite Γ and Δ.

Hypervaluations are generalized to first-order languages in the obvious way: First-order hyperinterpretations are just sets of ordinary first-order interpretations, and the first-order hypervaluation induced by a first-order hyperinterpretation I is defined as in the propositional case. Propositions 2.2 and 2.4 remain valid in the first-order case, and so do corollaries 2.5 and 2.6. For corollary 2.7 the decidability of propositional $\models_2$ is of course essential. The first-order analogue of proposition 2.3 will only be valid for a suitable first-order generalization of the propositional Kripke models. Such a generalization is given in Voorbraak (forthcoming).

3. Default logic and preferential model semantics

For convenience, we repeat some basic definitions of default logic. For a proper introduction, see e.g. Reiter (1980), Etherington (1988), or Lukaszewicz (1990). Our presentation of the preferential model semantics relies heavily on Makinson (1989).

Let L be some (standard) first-order language and let Th : $\wp L \rightarrow \wp L$ be given by Th$(\Sigma) = \{\varphi \mid \Sigma \models_2 \varphi\}$. $\alpha, \beta, \ldots$ denote formulas of L.

DEFINITION 3.1   A *default rule* (or simply a *default*) is an expression of the form $\alpha : \beta_1, \ldots, \beta_n / \omega$ $(n \geq 1)$. α is called the *prerequisite*, $\beta_1, \ldots, \beta_n$ the *justifications*, and ω the *consequent* of the rule. A default rule $\alpha : \beta_1, \ldots, \beta_n / \omega$ is called *closed* iff the set of its free variables FV$\{\alpha, \beta_1, \ldots, \beta_n, \omega\} = \varnothing$.

DEFINITION 3.2   A *default theory* is a pair $\langle D,W \rangle$, where D is a set of defaults and W is a set of closed formulas of L. A default theory is called *closed* iff every default in D is closed.

DEFINITION 3.3   E is an extension of a closed default theory $\langle D,W \rangle$ iff $E = \cup_{i \geq 0} E_i$, where

- $E_0 = W$
- $E_{i+1} = Th(E_i) \cup \{ \omega \mid \alpha : \beta_1,...,\beta_n / \omega \in D, \alpha \in E_i \text{ and } \forall j \in \{1,..,n\} \ \neg \beta_j \notin E \}$.

An extension of a default theory $\langle D,W \rangle$ is intended to represent a reasonable state of belief based on the defaults in D and on the propositions in W. As extensions of a default theory $\langle D,W \rangle$ which is not closed one simply takes the extensions of the closed default theory $\langle D',W \rangle$, where, roughly speaking, D' is obtained from D by taking all closed instances of D. (Since the defaults of D' may contain Skolem constants, the extensions of $\langle D',W \rangle$ have to be restricted to L. Details can be found in e.g. Lukaszewicz (1990).)

DEFINITION 3.4   Let $\delta = \alpha : \beta_1,..,\beta_n / \omega$ be a closed default and let Γ be a set of first-order models. The *preference relation corresponding to* δ, $\geq_\delta$, over $\wp \Gamma$ is defined as follows:

$$\Gamma_1 \geq_\delta \Gamma_2 \text{ iff } \forall M \in \Gamma_2 \ M \models_2 \alpha,$$
$$\forall i \in \{1,..,n\} \ \exists M_i \in \Gamma_2 \ M_i \models_2 \beta_i,$$
$$\text{and } \Gamma_1 = \Gamma_2 - \{M \mid M \not\models_2 \omega\}.$$

Intuitively, $\Gamma_1 \geq_\delta \Gamma_2$ means that on account of δ the (partial) world-description Γ_1 is preferred to the (partial) world-description Γ_2. The preference relation $\geq_D$ corresponding to a set of defaults D is simply the transitive closure of the union of the preference relations corresponding to the elements of D. Notice that, in spite of the suggestive notation, $\geq_\delta$ and $\geq_D$ are not necessarily partial orderings, since in general neither of them is reflexive. Using the reflexive closures of $\geq_\delta$ and $\geq_D$ instead of the relations themselves would have worked as well, but we stick to the definition given in Etherington (1988).

Let MOD(W) be the set of first-order models of W. The extensions of a closed default theory $\langle D,W \rangle$ correspond with the $\geq_D$-maximal elements of $\wp (MOD(W))$ which have some additional property called stability:

DEFINITION 3.5   Let $\Delta = \langle D,W \rangle$ be a closed default theory and let $\Gamma \subseteq MOD(W)$. Γ is called *stable for* Δ iff $\exists D' \subseteq D$ such that $\Gamma \geq_{D'} MOD(W)$ and for every justification β of a default of D' $\exists M \in \Gamma \ M \models_2 \beta$.

PROPOSITION 3.6 (Etherington (1988))   Let $\Delta = \langle D,W \rangle$ be a closed default theory.
(i)   If E is an extension of Δ, then $\{M \mid M \models_2 E\}$ is stable for Δ and a $\geq_D$-maximal element of $\wp (MOD(W))$.
(ii)   If Γ is stable for Δ and a $\geq_D$-maximal element of $\wp (MOD(W))$, then $\{\varphi \mid \forall M \in \Gamma \ M \models_2 \varphi\}$ is an extension of Δ.

In the above proposition, $\geq_D$ can be replaced by $\geq_\Delta$, defined by $\Gamma_1 \geq_\Delta \Gamma_2$ iff $\Gamma_1 \geq_D \Gamma_2 \geq_D$ MOD(W) or $\Gamma_1 \geq_D \Gamma_2 = $ MOD(W).

DEFINITION 3.7   A *preferential model structure* (p.m.s.) for L is a tuple pr $= \langle \mathcal{M}, \models, \sqsubset \rangle$, where $\mathcal{M}$ is a set of models, $\models \subseteq \mathcal{M} \times L$ is a satisfaction relation, and $\sqsubset \subseteq \mathcal{M} \times \mathcal{M}$. We often write $M \models \varphi$ for $\langle M, \varphi \rangle \in \models$.

For technical reasons, Makinson (1989) imposes no constraints on $\models$ and $\sqsubset$. However, Shoham (1987,1988) seems to allow only partial orderings $\sqsubset$ and models of standard logics. He does not make precise what he understands by 'standard' and just assumes standard logics to be propositional or predicate (modal) logics, but a reasonable interpretation of his intentions is to require that $\models$ induces a (standard) consequence relation satisfying inclusion, idempotency, and monotony. The preferential model structures proposed below are also preferential model structures in this stricter sense.

DEFINITION 3.8   Let pr $= \langle \mathcal{M}, \models, \sqsubset \rangle$ be a p.m.s. for L.

(i) $M \in \mathcal{M}$ *preferentially satisfies* $\Gamma \subseteq L$, notation $M \models_{pr} \Gamma$, iff $M \models \Gamma$ (i.e., $\forall \varphi \in \Gamma\, M \models \varphi$) and $\neg \exists\, M' \sqsupset M\ M' \models \Gamma$. The set of *preferred models* $\mathcal{M}_{pr} = \{M \in \mathcal{M} \mid \exists \Gamma \subseteq L\ M \models_{pr} \Gamma\}$. We will usually write $M \models_{pr} \varphi$ instead of $M \models_{pr} \{\varphi\}$.

(ii)   The operation $\mathrm{Th}_{pr} : \wp L \to \wp L$ of *preferential entailment* is given by $\varphi \in \mathrm{Th}_{pr}(\Gamma)$ iff $\forall M\, (M \models_{pr} \Gamma \Rightarrow M \models \varphi)$.

(iii) Γ is called *preferentially satisfiable* iff $\exists M\, M \models_{pr} \Gamma$.

(iv) Γ is called *preferentially valid* iff $\Gamma \subseteq \mathrm{Th}_{pr}(\emptyset)$.

Notice that φ is preferentially valid iff φ is true in every preferred model of $\emptyset$, or, in other words, iff for every $\sqsubset$-maximal model M $M \models \varphi$. Shoham gives a slightly different, and in our opinion less intuitive, definition of preferential validity, namely φ is preferentially valid iff $\neg \varphi$ is not preferentially satisfiable. In general, both definitions are *not* equivalent.

DEFINITION 3.9   Let $\Delta = \langle D, W \rangle$ be a closed default theory.

(i)   m is called Δ-*bounded* iff $\exists m' \geq_\Delta m$ such that m' is $\geq_\Delta$-maximal and stable for Δ.

(ii)   The *p.m.s. associated with* Δ is the p.m.s. $\mathrm{pr}(\Delta) = \langle \mathcal{M}, \models, \sqsubset \rangle$, where $\mathcal{M} = \wp\,(\mathrm{MOD}(W))$, $\models = \{\langle m, \varphi \rangle \mid m \in \mathcal{M},\ \varphi \in L,\ \text{and} \models_{h,m} \varphi\}$, and $\sqsubset$ is defined as follows:

$\qquad m \sqsupset m'$ iff   m is Δ-bounded and m' is not Δ-bounded,

$\qquad\qquad\qquad\qquad$ or m and m' are not Δ-bounded and m' $\neq$ m $= \emptyset$,

$\qquad\qquad\qquad\qquad$ or m and m' are Δ-bounded, m $\neq$ m', and m $\geq_\Delta$ m'.

Th_Δ, $\models_\Delta$ and $\mathcal{M}_\Delta$ abbreviate $\mathrm{Th}_{\mathrm{pr}(\Delta)}$, $\models_{\mathrm{pr}(\Delta)}$, and $\mathcal{M}_{\mathrm{pr}(\Delta)}$, respectively, and $\sqsubset_\Delta$ denotes the preference relation of $\mathrm{pr}(\Delta)$. $\sqsubset_\Delta$ is a strict p.o. and $\mathcal{M}_\Delta = \{\emptyset\} \cup \{m \in \mathcal{M} \mid \neg \exists m' \sqsupset_\Delta m\}$. Hence the only preferred model which is not necessarily $\sqsubset_\Delta$-maximal is the trivial model $\emptyset$.

PROPOSITION 3.10   Let $\Delta = \langle D, W \rangle$ be a closed default theory and $pr(\Delta) = \langle \mathcal{M}, \models, \sqsubset \rangle$ its associated p.m.s.

(i)   If E is an extension of Δ, then $\{M \mid M \models_2 E\} \models_\Delta E$.

(ii)   If $m \in \mathcal{M}_\Delta$ and $m \neq \varnothing$, then $\{\varphi \mid m \models \varphi\}$ is a consistent extension of Δ.

(iii)   If $\mathcal{M}_\Delta = \{\varnothing\}$, then Δ has no consistent extension.

(iv) $Th_\Delta(\Gamma) = \cap\{E \mid E \text{ is an extension of } \Delta \text{ such that } \Gamma \subseteq E\}$.

Proof. (i) If E is an extension of Δ, then, by proposition 3.6, $m = \{M \mid M \models_2 E\}$ is $\geq_D$-maximal and stable for Δ. Hence $\neg \exists m' \sqsupset m$. Since $m \models E$, we have $m \models_\Delta E$.

(ii) If $m \in \mathcal{M}_\Delta$ and $m \neq \varnothing$, then m is $\geq_D$-maximal and stable for Δ. Hence, by proposition 3.6, $\{\varphi \mid m \models \varphi\}$ is an extension of Δ. Since $m \neq \varnothing$, this extension is consistent.

(iii) If $\mathcal{M}_\Delta = \{\varnothing\}$, then either there are no Δ-bounded models, and therefore no extensions for Δ, or $\varnothing$ is Δ-bounded, and thus $\{\varphi \mid \varnothing \models \varphi\}$ is the unique, inconsistent extension of Δ.

(iv) Assume $\varphi \in Th_\Delta(\Gamma)$ and let E be an extension of Δ such that $\Gamma \subseteq E$. Then, as in (i), $\neg \exists m' \sqsupset m = \{M \mid M \models_2 E\}$. Since $m \models \Gamma$, we have $m \models_\Delta \Gamma$. Hence $m \models \varphi$, and thus $\varphi \in E$.
On the other hand, assume $\varphi \notin Th_\Delta(\Gamma)$. Then $\exists m$ such that $m \models_\Delta \Gamma$ and $m \not\models \varphi$. By (ii), $E = \{\psi \mid m \models \psi\}$ is an extension of Δ and clearly $\Gamma \subseteq E$. Since $\varphi \notin E$, $\varphi \notin \cap\{E \mid E \text{ is an extension of } \Delta \text{ such that } \Gamma \subseteq E\}$.

Notice that $\varnothing$ being the only preferred model corresponds to Δ having an inconsistent extension or having no extension at all. It is possible to give an alternative definition of $\sqsubset_\Delta$ such that $\varnothing \in \mathcal{M}_\Delta$ iff Δ has an inconsistent extension and $\mathcal{M}_\Delta = \varnothing$ iff Δ has no extension. However, this alternative $\sqsubset_\Delta$ will in general not be a strict partial ordering, since for any $pr = \langle \mathcal{M}, \models, \sqsubset \rangle$ with finite $\mathcal{M}$ and s.p.o. $\sqsubset$ we have $\mathcal{M}_{pr} \neq \varnothing$. The collapsing of the cases that Δ has an inconsistent extension and that Δ has no extension can be defended by pointing out that both are boundary cases added for technical convenience, rather than representations of belief states of truly rational agents. (In both cases a rational agent would have to revise his belief state.)

An immediate corollary of proposition 3.10(iv) is the monotony of Th_Δ. Hence as long as you keep the default theory constant, the reasoning is monotonic. Default consequence is nonmonotonic because default theories are updated in the light of new information. To capture this in terms of preferential model semantics, we propose a strengthening of the notion of preferential consequence and we define a preferential model semantics for a class of default theories with the same defaults. The strong notion of preferential consequence is equivalent to the usual notion in case the models are two-valued. Applied to hypervaluations, the strong notion takes account of the intuition that default extensions—the preferred models of default theory—have to be grounded on the facts. The definition of a p.m.s. associated with a class of defaults is a global version of the corresponding definition for a single default theory.

DEFINITION 3.11   Let $pr = \langle \mathcal{M}, \models, \sqsubset \rangle$ be a p.m.s. $M \in \mathcal{M}$ *strongly preferentially satisfies* Γ, notation $M \models_{pr*} \Gamma$, iff $M \models_{pr} \Gamma$ and $\forall M' (\Gamma \subseteq \{\varphi \mid M' \models \varphi\} \subset \{\varphi \mid M \models \varphi\} \Rightarrow M' \sqsubset M)$. $\varphi \in Th_{pr*}(\Gamma)$ iff $\forall M(M \models_{pr*} \Gamma \Rightarrow M \models \varphi)$

DEFINITION 3.12   Let D be a set of closed defaults. The *p.m.s. associated with D* is the p.m.s. pr(D) = $\langle \mathcal{M}, \models, \sqsubset \rangle$, where $\mathcal{M} = \wp(\text{MOD}(\varnothing))$, $\models = \{\langle m, \varphi \rangle \mid m \in \mathcal{M}, \varphi \in L, \text{ and } \models_{h,m}\varphi\}$, and $\sqsubset$ is defined as follows: $m \sqsupset m'$ iff $m \sqsupset_\Delta m'$, where $\Delta = \langle D, \{\varphi \mid m' \models \varphi\} \rangle$.

We write $\sqsubset_D$ for the preference relation of pr(D) and we use obvious abbreviations, such as Th_{D*} and $\models_{D*}$ for $\text{Th}_{\text{pr}(D)*}$ and $\models_{\text{pr}(D)*}$, respectively. Th_{D*} corresponds with C_D of Makinson (1989), since $\text{Th}_{D*}(\Gamma)$ is the intersection of all extensions of $\langle D, \Gamma \rangle$.

PROPOSITION 3.13 $\text{Th}_{D*}(\Gamma) = \cap\{E \mid E \text{ is an extension of } \langle D, \Gamma \rangle\}$.

Proof. Assume $m \models_{D*} \Gamma$. Then $m \models_D \Gamma$ and $m \sqsupset_D \text{MOD}(\Gamma)$, and thus $\neg\exists m' \sqsupset_{\langle D, \{\varphi \mid m \models \varphi\}\rangle} m$ $m' \models \Gamma$, and $m \sqsupset_{\langle D, \Gamma\rangle} \text{MOD}(\Gamma)$. But then also $\neg\exists m' \sqsupset_{\langle D, \Gamma\rangle} m$ $m' \models \Gamma$. Hence $\{\varphi \mid m \models \varphi\}$ is an extension of $\langle D, \Gamma \rangle$. On the other hand, assume that $\{\varphi \mid m \models \varphi\}$ is an extension of $\langle D, \Gamma \rangle$. Then $m \models \Gamma$ and $\neg\exists m' \sqsupset_D m$ $m' \models \Gamma$. Thus $m \models_D \Gamma$. Let m' be such that $\Gamma \subseteq \{\varphi \mid m' \models \varphi\} \subset \{\varphi \mid m \models \varphi\} \Rightarrow$ Then $m \sqsupset_D m'$, since each default that is applied to get from $\text{MOD}(\Gamma)$ to m can be applied to get from m' to m. Hence $m \models_{D*} \Gamma$. We can conclude that $m \models_{D*} \Gamma$ iff $\{\varphi \mid m \models \varphi\}$ is an extension of $\langle D, \Gamma \rangle$, and the proposition follows immediately.

In view of proposition 2.4 it is no surprise that one can also obtain a modal preferential model semantics for default logic. There is a quite obvious reformulation of the above results in terms of K45 models instead of hypervaluations. The use of KD45 or S5 is less straightforward since these logics lack models matching inconsistent extensions. If one assumes extensions to be consistent, then, from a technical point of view, default rules can be interpreted as well in terms of (KD45-)belief as in terms of (S5-)knowledge. See Voorbraak (forthcoming).

4. Discussion

We have given a preferential model semantics for default consequence understood in the 'meet' or 'sceptical' sense. (φ is a sceptical default consequence of Δ iff φ is true in every extension of Δ.) Makinson (1989) has shown that credulous default consequence (φ is a credulous default consequence of Δ iff φ is true in some (arbitrarily chosen) extension of Δ) does not satisfy cumulative transitivity ($\Gamma \subseteq \Delta \subseteq \text{Cn}(\Gamma) \Rightarrow \text{Cn}(\Delta) \subseteq \text{Cn}(\Gamma)$) and can therefore not be captured in a p.m.s. (Makinson's result that Th_{pr} satisfies cumulative transitivity also holds for $\text{Th}_{\text{pr}*}$.) Sceptical default consequence does satisfy cumulative transitivity, although it is still not a cumulative consequence operation, since it does not satisfy cumulative monotony ($\Gamma \subseteq \Delta \subseteq \text{Cn}(\Gamma) \Rightarrow \text{Cn}(\Gamma) \subseteq \text{Cn}(\Delta)$).

A failure of cumulative monotony implies that (implicitly) facts and derived formulas have a different status. But nonmonotonic formalisms which distinguish facts from derived formulas may very well be cumulative. The failure of cumulative monotony in default logic seems to be a corollary of the requirement that extensions have to be grounded on the facts. Learning new facts, even previously derivable ones, can result in more grounded (partial) world descriptions. This might be defended by taking the difference between facts and derived formulas serious. Alternatively, one could argue that one should not require that the *logic* is cumulative, but rather that the state of belief of an ideally rational agent should not contain a set of defaults D such that Th_{D*} fails cumulative monotony.

In a forthcoming paper (Voorbraak (forthcoming)) we argue that both default and superstrongly autoepistemic extensions can be obtained by applying essentially only two different filters, which can roughly be described as taking justification-minimal models and taking grounded models, respectively. A model is called justification-minimal iff the set of false justifications is minimal. Justification minimization is implemented in default logic by requiring the $\geq_D$-maximal elements to be stable, it is implemented in autoepistemic logic by strengthening minimal AE extensions to superstrongly grounded AE extensions, and it is closely related to the minimization in circumscription.

The groundedness filter requires the extensions of a default theory $\langle D,W \rangle$ to be $\geq_D$ MOD(W) and AE extensions to be minimal. This groundedness filter is not applied in circumscription. This more or less explains why we need a stronger version of preferential consequence for default logic than for circumscription.

Acknowledgments

I would like to thank Albert Visser for commenting on preliminary versions of this paper and the members of the (Dutch) National Working Group on Non-Monotonc Reasoning for enduring a presentation of one of those versions.

References

BLAMEY, S., 'Partial Logic', *Handbook of Philosophical Logic Vol III*, D. Gabbay and F. Guenthner (eds.), D. Reidel, Dordrecht, (1986) 1-70.

ETHERINGTON, D., *Reasoning with Incomplete Information*, Research Notes in Artificial Intelligence, Pitman, London (1988).

LANGHOLM, T., *Partiality, Truth and Persistence*, CSLI Lecture Notes 15, CSLI, Stanford (1986).

LUKASZEWICZ, L., *Non-monotonic Reasoning: Formalization of Commonsense Reasoning*, Ellis Horwood, Chichester (1990).

MAKINSON, D., 'General Theory of Cumulative Inference', *Non-Monotonic Reasoning (Proceedings 2nd Internatonal Workshop, Grassau, FRG, June 1988)*, M. Reinfrank, J. de Kleer, M. Ginsberg, E. Sandewall (eds.), Springer, Berlin (1989) 1-18.

MCCARTHY, J., 'Circumscription - a Form of Nonmonotonic Reasoning', *Artificial Intelligence* 13 (1980) 27-39.

REITER, R., 'A Logic for Default Reasoning', *Artificial Intelligence* 13 (1980) 81-132.

SHOHAM, Y., 'A Semantical Approach to Nonmonotonic Logics', *Readings in Nonmonotonic Reasoning*, M. Ginsberg (ed.), Morgan Kaufmann, Los Altos CA. (1987) 227-250.

SHOHAM, Y., *Reasoning about Change*, MIT Press, Cambridge MA, (1988).

VOORBRAAK, F., 'Epistemic Logic and Nonmonotonic Reasoning', forthcoming.

Elementary Hyperentailment
Nonmonotonic reasoning about defaults

Emil Weydert
emil@adler.philosophie.uni-stuttgart.de
IMS, University of Stuttgart
Keplerstr. 17, 7000 Stuttgart 1
Germany

1 Background

Nonmonotonic reasoning, the art of jumping to plausible, but defeasible conclusions from incomplete knowledge, is best thought of as being strongly linked to some form of generalized or qualitative probabilistic reasoning. Thus, conditional approaches like probabilistic [Adams 75, Pearl 88] or ranked entailment [Lehmann / Magidor 90], overcoming several drawbacks of the classical proposals (no specificity rule or very low expressiveness) by implementing directly or indirectly some aspects of this idea, have become increasingly popular. However, to deal adequately with irrelevant strengthenings of the antecedent, nonmonotonic closing-up procedures (like rational closure [Lehmann / Magidor 90]) are needed, which reflect to a certain extent nonmonotonic reasoning about defaults. Unfortunately, most of the existing accounts aren't really satisfying, especially when it comes to natural language processing. For instance, they don't allow an integrated treatment of facts, defaults and meta-defaults, i.e., no defaults embedded in propositional or other default expressions (lack of generality and uniformity), nor a correct handling of reasonable defeasible inference patterns involving implicit independence assumptions (intuitive inadequacy). In particular, their semantic/syntactic backgrounds are too restricted for realizing necessary further generalizations. In this paper, we propose therefore a new, more general semantic framework for nonmonotonic reasoning with and about defaults, which also reflects qualitative probabilistic considerations, and exemplify it by its simplest instance, elementary hyperentailment.

Our approach is directly based on what one might call qualitative magnitude reasoning. This means that, in accordance with everyday experience, expressions like "if A, then by default B" or "if A, then normally B" are interpreted as telling us that the class of states supporting A and not B is qualitatively (i.e., not bothering with finite unions, no explicit numerical values) of less weight than the class of those supporting A and B. Note that this view should be compatible as well with a statistically inspired or realist view as with a normative or conventionalist conception. Everything depends on how you choose your abstract model, in particular your reference class of states. Especially in the case of natural language applications, this becomes an important issue. In what follows, we shall give a partial formal implementation of this concept using a two-placed comparative modality "<" (the QM-modality).

Let L be a classical language (i.e., closed under the usual propositional connectives). Then, the smallest classical language containing L and with A and B also A<B is denoted by L(<). "P<Q" should be read as "P is qualitatively smaller / has a lower qualitative magnitude than Q" resp. "P is less normal than Q". We think that working

with such an order-modality is intuitively more appealing than starting with a more complex conditional notion. Anyway, interpreting normality as relative qualitative magnitude, which is our philosophy, we get "normally", our default-conditional, as a derived concept.

Def 1.1 $P \Rightarrow Q := P\&\neg Q < P\&Q$ for all P, Q in L(<) ("P normally implies Q")

2 Expectation-realization semantics

We begin by looking for an adequate generalized monotonic semantics for the flat fragment (no nested modalities) of our language. Ranked model structures however, the semantic counterpart of Lehmann's rational consequence relations, aren't suitable for our purposes, even if we modify them in some obvious way. Shortcomings are the isolated treatment of objective and modal statements, artificial ordering constraints (smoothness), the cognitively probably inappropriate ranking of single models, an unavoidable lottery paradox even in the infinitary case, and the absence of explicit ranking scales or structures required for better comparisons and differentiations.

Therefore, we shall adopt another model concept, which in its most unconstrained form can be characterized by its integration of the factual and modal aspects, its explicit qualitative reference orderings and its ranking of model- or world-sets. That is, we implement what might be called the *qualitative ranking measure paradigm*.

In the following, we shall assume an arbitrary classical language L and a classical (i.e., usual interpretation of the propositional connectives) satisfaction relation |= for L-structures as given. Let's start with the most general notion.

Def 2.1 $\underline{M} = (M, lM, lP, O, R)$ is called a *general expectation-realization model* w.r.t. (L, |=) iff

GER 1 $M \in lM$ (M is the *actual, factual* or *realization model*)

GER 2   lM is a set of L-structures   (lM is the *universe*)

GER 3 $\emptyset, lM \in lP \subseteq P(lM)$ and lP is closed under finite unions
                                        (lP is the *domain algebra*)

GER 4 $O = (S, \ll)$, with $\ll$ a strict linear ordering on S having a maximal and a minimal element, called 0 and $-\infty$. ($\ll$ is the *reference ordering*)

GER 5 $R : lP \to S$ with for all P, P' $\in$ lP, (R is the *ranking measure*)
           $R(P \cup P') = \max_{\ll}\{R(P), R(P')\}$, $R(\emptyset) = -\infty$ and $R(lM) = 0$

GER 6 $M \notin \cup\{P \mid R(P) = -\infty\}$ (*coherence postulate*)

A GER-model $\underline{M}$ can be seen as modeling a possible correspondence between an actual state of affairs, represented by the corresponding realization model M, and a highly idealized epistemic state, represented by the so-called expectation part (lM, lP, R, O) and characterized by some full-commitment (i.e., linear) qualitative normality measure evaluating a set of model-classes (or propositions) on an abstract scale (for more about qualitative magnitude and GER-models, consult [Weydert 91]).

For the applications we have in mind, e.g., formulating a suitable semantics for nested default conditionals, we have to extend this basic notion in several ways.

1. We are primarily interested in evaluating relative normality for sentences from the background language L.

2. We would like to grasp at least finite sets (i.e., intersections) of propositions.

3. The original postulates allow arbitrary linear orderings with endpoints as reference structures. However, this might not be what we are looking for. For instance, in a given context we might want to lower or raise the ranking value of propositions without changing the local relative ranking structure of their subsets in lP. The order in which such shifts are effected also shouldn't matter. But then, we have to insure that there are commuting canonical isomorphisms between the nontrivial initial segments of the reference ordering.

4. When we have to compare (sets of) expectation-realization models in the higher order case, they should preferably share a unique domain algebra and reference structure. Therefore, the latter have to be sufficiently universal (e.g., realize any possible reference structure of cardinality $\leq$ l lP l as a substructure).

4.' We think that structurally indiscernible ranking values agree rather well with our intuitions for qualitative ranking measures, which might lead us to look for maximally homogeneous reference structures.

All this seems to justify the following model concept.

Def 2.2 $\underline{M} = (M, lM, lP, O, R)$ is called a *standard expectation-realization model* wrt. $(L, \models)$ iff $\underline{M}$ is a GER-model and we have

> SER 1 $\underline{M}$ is *L-complete*, i.e., for all $A \in L$, $\{M \in lM \mid M \models A\} \in lP$
>
> SER 2 lP is a lattice, i.e., it is closed under finitary intersections
>
> SER 3 $O = (S, \#, \ll)$ represents the negative half of an ordered divisible abelian group structure extended by a minimal, absorptive element $-\infty$, s.t. for all $x \in S$, $-\infty \ll x$ and $-\infty \# x = x \# -\infty = -\infty$
>
> SER 4 $O = (S, \#, \ll)$ is l lP l - saturated

> $\underline{M}$ is called *finitary* iff $\{N \in lP \mid R(N) \neq 0\}$ is finite.

Observe, that SER 1 doesn't mean that $\{M \in lM \mid M \models A\} \neq \emptyset$ for $\models$-consistent $A \in L$. The additive structure introduced in SER 3 can be seen as a qualitative equivalent to the multiplicative structure in the quantitative probabilistic reasoning case.

Starting right from the beginning with an order-modality and set-rankings, our definitions of satisfaction and (Tarskian) monotonic consequence for GER- or SER-models (w.r.t. $(L, \models)$) over $L_0(<)$ (the flat part of $L(<)$) are rather easy to formulate.

Def 2.3 For all GER-models $\underline{M} = (M, lM, lP, O, R)$ w.r.t. $(L, \models)$ and $A, A' \in L$,

> $\underline{M} \models_{GER} A$ iff $M \models A$
>
> $\underline{M} \models_{GER} A<A'$ iff $R(\{M \in lM \mid M \models A\}) \ll R(\{M \in lM \mid M \models A'\})$
>
> or $R(\{M \in lM \mid M \models A\}) = -\infty$
>
> .... (as usual for the propositional connectives w.r.t. $\underline{M}$)

Def 2.4 Let $\Sigma \cup \{B\} \subseteq L_0(<)$. $\Sigma \vdash_{S/GER} B$ iff for all S/GER-models $\underline{M} / (L, \models)$,

> if for all $A \in \Sigma$, $\underline{M} \models_{S/GER} A$, then $\underline{M} \models_{S/GER} B$

In fact it can be shown that $\vdash_{GER} = \vdash_{SER}$ for a given classical $(L, \models)$. Looking at our conceptual background, the following result doesn't come as a surprise.

Fact 2.1 Lehmann's rationality postulates are GER-valid for the QM-conditional $\Rightarrow$.

3 Hypersemantics

In the first part, we have presented a very general monotonic framework for expressing and interpreting boolean combinations of factual assertions and flat, propositional defaults. Now, the time has come to think about appropriate meta-level notions of nonmonotonic reasoning, telling us not only how and when to jump to conclusions if default expressions are involved, but also insuring a correct interpretation of the latter. In particular, defeasible modus ponens (e.g., "If Garfield is hungry and if Garfield is hungry normally implies Garfield is dangerous, then we can conclude by default that Garfield is dangerous") will be a conditio sine qua non. On the other hand, the formalization of natural language semantics and pragmatics as well as more sophisticated forms of causal reasoning seem to require a theory handling nested defaults already at the object-level. One way to achieve all this within a uniform, flexible, transparent and well-motivated framework is to consider instances of what we call *hyperentailment* (-relations). For lack of space and didactic purposes, we shall restrict ourselves to one of its simplest, but perhaps most relevant and practical forms, involving only two levels of defaults and finitary sets of premises. This will be enough to deal with facts, flat defaults and their defeasible relationships. Without any convincing inherently three-level principles, the higher levels will anyway only reflect what happens below.

Now, what will be the ingredients of our proposal ? What has been right for the object-level, should be correct at the meta-level. Opting for uniformity, we shall follow our favourite semantic paradigm and look for appropriate 2nd order SER-models, whose universes should consist of sufficiently representative classes of old-fashioned first order SER-models, whose domain algebras and reference structures should extend those of their SER-worlds, and whose qualitative ranking measures should reflect our intuitions about the (relative) normality of different SER-model-characteristics (e.g., satisfaction of given flat $L(<)$-sentences) as well as about any systematic interactions occuring between object- and meta-level. Anchored in maximally normal actual SER-models, they will be called *hypermodels*. We shall illustrate this concept by the family of *elementary hypermodels*.

Def 3.1 $\underline{H} = (\underline{M}^\circ, lM^*, lP^*, O^*, R^*)$ is called an *elementary hypermodel* ($\in lH0$) iff

1. $(L, \models)$ is a propositional logic with countably many variables A_i

2. $\underline{H}$ is an SER-model w.r.t. $(L_0(<), \models_{GER})$

3. $\underline{M}^\circ = (M, lM, lP, O, R^\circ)$ is a *canonically normal* (i.e., $R^\circ(P) = 0$ for all $\emptyset \neq P \in lP$) SER-model w.r.t. $(L, \models)$

4. $lM = \{v \mid v : \{A_i \mid i \in lN\} \rightarrow \{T, F\}\}$

5. $\text{IP} = \{\{v \mid v \models A\} \mid A \in L\}$

6. $O = (S, \#, \ll)$ is the usual ordered additive structure of negative (with 0) rational numbers extended by a minimal and absorptive element $-\infty$

7. $\text{IM}^* = \{\underline{N} \mid \underline{N} = (N, \text{IM}, \text{IP}, O, R)$ is a finitary SER-model w.r.t. $(L, \models)\}$

8. $\text{IP}^* = \{\{\underline{N} \in \text{IM}^* \mid \underline{N} \models_{\text{GER}} A\} \mid A \in L_0(<)\}$

9. $O^* = O$

10. $R^*(\{(N, \text{IM}, \text{IP}, O, R) \in \text{IM}^* \mid N \in P\}) = 0$ for all $\emptyset \neq P \in \text{IP}$

11. R^* is an *elementary hyperranking-measure*

These clauses seem to describe in fact the "minimal" non-trivial 2nd order SER-structures as far as the non-hyperranking-measure-part is concerned. The tenth condition is important to avoid a clash between the GER-satisfaction rules for the formulas in the background and those in the extended language. The last one, which is in fact the heart of the whole notion, will be explained and developed in the next section.

A basic idea of hyperentailment is now to provide candidates for higher order (in our case flat and finitary) nonmonotonic entailment relations by interpreting the QM-default-conditional w.r.t. such hyperstructures. In particular, we have

Def 3.2 For every finite subset $\{A, \dots, A^{(n)}\}$ of $L_0(<)$,

$$\{A', \dots, A^{(n)}\} \models_{\text{IH0}} A \text{ iff for all } \underline{H} \in \text{IH0}, \ \underline{H} \models_{\text{GER}} A' \& \dots \& A^{(n)} \Rightarrow A$$

$\models_{\text{IH}}$ is called the *elementary hyperentailment relation*

In general, different conceptions (e.g., scepticality, speculativity, ...) or fragments (e.g., use of special logics, languages, ...) of nonmonotonic consequence could be realized by differently tailored hypermodels. Note that hyperentailment relations are always preferential, but, like elementary hyperentailment, not necessarily rational.

4 Hyperranking measures

When constructing hypermodels, the most difficult and interesting task consists in defining appropriate qualitative ranking measures for comparing classes of SER-models contained in the universe. We have based our account on the so-called *transformation principle* or *shifting paradigm*. In the following, we shall discuss the corresponding philosophy for the finitary case, which will be enough to illustrate the basic ideas.

In our context, shifting simply means lowering the ranking values of some propositions such that subsets inherit shifting requests from their supersets. More precisely, let $\underline{M}^\circ = (M, \text{IM}, \text{IP}, O, R^\circ)$ with $O = (S, \#, \ll)$ be a canonically normal SER-model. A *shift* w.r.t. $\underline{M}^\circ$ is then simply a finite partial function $r : \text{IP} \to S$. The *shifting by* r w.r.t. $\underline{M}^\circ$ will be the function transforming a finitary SER-model $\underline{N} = (N, \text{IM}, \text{IP}, O, R)$ into an $\underline{N}' = (N, \text{IM}, \text{IP}, O, R')$ by "adding" r to R and looking for the (pointwise) $\ll$ - maximal ranking measure R' compatible with the result, that is:

$R' = \sup_{\ll}\{\underline{R} \mid \underline{R} \text{ rkg. measure, for all } P, \underline{R}(P) \ll \Sigma_{\#}\{r(P') \mid P \subseteq P' \in \text{dom } r\} \# R(P)\}.$

We start from the fact that every finitary SER-model $\underline{N} = (N, 1M, 1P, O, R)$ can be reached by shifting the corresponding canonically normal model $\underline{N}^\circ = (N, 1M, 1P, O, R^\circ)$ (normal shifts). Let's associate with every proposition P the set $Sh(P) \neq \emptyset$ of all the normal shifts constructing one of its elements. Now, we can try to classify these construction sets $Sh(P)$ according to those features of their elements which bear some relationship to the degree of normality exhibited by the constructed SER-models. In fact, we have some intuitions concerning the realization "costs" of different shifts, summarized by the idea that SER-models requiring involved, complex constructions could or should lead to lower ranking measure values for the sets they build up than SER-models which are easier to reach. Consequently, we will try to find precise natural criteria for evaluating shifting costs.

First, observe that the effective shifting lengths $r(P)$ for single propositions are only relevant within a given SER-model. Because normality and therefore costs shouldn't be affected by (the numerous) automorphisms of the (|1P|-saturated) reference structures, they don't have a real significance. What really matters for our external comparisons are the structural aspects. For instance, it seems plausible to assume that shifting fewer or smaller (i.e., sub-) propositions is usually less expensive than shifting more or bigger ones. Furthermore, we can try to split up shifts in sequences of maximally uniform (hence presumably less costly) subshifts, evaluate them separately and put the results together following for instance some lexicographic procedure. Seeing shifting as a kind of abstract sampling process opens the way for illuminating qualitative probabilistic and statistic considerations, which motivate additional evaluation strategies. In fact, there is a whole hierarchy of interesting partial "cost" orderings on shifts. They induce in a straightforward way partial orders on construction sets (of shifts), which can then be used to constrain possible hyperranking measures.

However, this is not the whole story. We also have to take care of the actual models. Following an important principle of meta-default reasoning, which says : *Give priority to the higher levels*, they will be considered only if the ranking measures are indistinguishable w.r.t. transformation costs. The obvious comparison criterion will be the relative structural position of the minimal propositions they belong to, encoding the actual world's degree of normality.

The corresponding hyperranking measures should then reflect these differences. Now, let's illustrate all this by looking at elementary hyperranking measures (cf. 3.1).

For a given $\underline{N} = (N, 1M, 1P, O, R) \in 1M^*$, let a_i be the i+1th-largest element of Im R, $P_i = \cup\{P \mid R(P) \underset{\ll}{\ll} a_i\}$ for $i < |$ Im R $|$ and $P_i = P_j$ for $i,j \geq |$ Im R $| - 1$. Then R can be seen as resulting from a sequence of atomic subshifts r_i, s.t. $r_i(P_{i+1}) = a_{i+1} - a_i$. Because to construct R, we have to push down (possibly incrementally) the P_{i+1} by $a_{i+1} - a_i$ anyway, the *elementary canonical shift* $r = \cup\{r_i \mid i < |$ Im R $| - 1\}$ might represent the most uniform and intuitively least expensive way to achieve this. It is plausible to assume that the transformation costs are larger for those canonical subshifts having to move a bigger part of 1M. Therefore, when comparing two SER-models $\underline{N}$ and $\underline{N}'$ in $1M^*$, if at the first i with $P_i \neq P_i'$, P_i is strictly included in P_i', we might already conclude that $\underline{N}$ as a whole is easier to reach than $\underline{N}'$. The remaining r_j with $j > i$ being fundamentally less costly anyway, they will be unable to influence the overall judgement. If on the other hand $P_i = P_i'$ for all i (i.e., $\underline{N}$ and $\underline{N}'$ are equivalent up to an automorphism of $(S, «)$ and possibly differing actual parts), we look at the structural position of their actual models, determined by the index act = i of the smallest P_i they belong to. Of course, $\underline{N}$ will be in a less normal situation than $\underline{N}'$, if the characterizing index for N is higher than that for N'. Putting things together, we can then define a strict partial ordering $<<$ on lM^*, s.t. for all $\underline{N} = (N, lM, lP, O, R)$, $\underline{N}'$ $= (N, lM, lP, O, R') \in lM^*$, if $<_{lex}$ is the lexicographic ordering based in the last component on the classical larger-than- and in the previous ones on the strict set theoretic including-relation, then $\underline{N} << \underline{N}'$ iff $((P_i)_{i \in lN}, act) <_{lex} ((P_i')_{i \in lN}, act')$.

This relation can now be extended in a straightforward way to a partial ordering on lP^*. For all P, P' $\in lP^*$, $P <<' P'$ iff for all $\underline{N} \in P$, there is an $\underline{N}' \in P'$, s.t. $\underline{N} \underline{\underline{<}} \underline{N}'$ and

$$\text{there is } \underline{N}' \in P', \text{ s.t. for no } \underline{N} \in P, \underline{N}' \underline{\underline{<}} \underline{N}$$

Def 4.1 R^* is called an *elementary hyperranking measure* (cf. 3.1) iff
for all P, P' $\in lP^*$, $P <<' P'$ implies $R^*(P) «^* R^*(P')$

The best way to become acquainted with the strength of this formalism will be to apply it to some popular defeasible reasoning patterns which are difficult to realize or even to express for lots of existing proposals.

Let P, Q, R, S $\in$ L be propositional variables and set $\models$: = $\models_{lH0}$.

√ **Defeasible transitivity:**

$P \Rightarrow Q, Q \Rightarrow R \models P \Rightarrow R$ $P \Rightarrow \neg R$; $P \Rightarrow Q, Q \Rightarrow R \not\models P \Rightarrow R$

√ **Defeasible modus ponens:** P, $P \Rightarrow Q \models Q$; $P, \neg Q, P \Rightarrow Q \not\models Q$

√ **Defeasible monotony:** $P \Rightarrow Q \models P\&R \Rightarrow Q$; $P \Rightarrow Q, R \Rightarrow \neg Q \not\models P\&R \Rightarrow Q$

√ **Defeasible contraposition:** $P \Rightarrow Q \models \neg Q \Rightarrow \neg P$; $T \Rightarrow P, P \Rightarrow Q \not\models \neg Q \Rightarrow \neg P$

√ **Specificity (weak penguin principle):** P, $P \Rightarrow \neg R, P \Rightarrow Q, Q \Rightarrow R \models \neg R$

√ **Global homogeneity:** $T \models \neg (P \Rightarrow Q)$

√ **Lexicography:**

$(T \Rightarrow P \& T \Rightarrow Q) \vee (T \Rightarrow P \& \neg P\&\neg Q \Rightarrow F) \models T \Rightarrow P \& \neg P\&\neg Q \Rightarrow F$

¬ **Defeasible exceptional monotony:** $T \Rightarrow P, T \Rightarrow Q \not\models \neg P \Rightarrow Q$

¬ **Robustness:** $T \Rightarrow \neg P, T \Rightarrow \neg Q, R \vee P \Rightarrow \neg R \models R \vee Q \Rightarrow \neg R$

5 Discussion

All these results clearly document the strength of our approach. Nevertheless, we should be aware of some problems of the particular form of hyperentailment presented here, e.g., its rather speculative character, grasping every opportunity for defeasible inference, even in cases where most real-world cognitive agents would probably refrain from expressing a definite opinion (lacking robustness). Another important point to note is that we don't get defeasible exceptional monotony, i.e., inheritance for exceptional subclasses. Fortunately, there are more sophisticated versions of hyper-entailment, however, which get rid of these problems. Parts of the machinery intro-duced in this paper, in particular the additive structure, will make real sense only for these more complex cases. In fact, there are several possible formal implementations of our principles, differing with regard to complexity, transparency, intuitive correctness, reliability and expressiveness. So, we think that hyperentailment is a flexible, very powerful approach, whose basic philosophy (qualitative ranking measure and shifting paradigm) is intuitively appealing and which surely deserves further research. Elementary hyperentailment is especially interesting insofar as it provides a relatively efficient procedure (cf. lexicographic strategy) to determine what a finite knowledge base containing boolean combinations of facts and defaults should defeasibly entail, if we restrict ourselves to its structural characteristics.

There are several competing frameworks in the recent literature which allow nonmonotonic reasoning about defaults. Lehmann's rational closure for conditional knowledge bases [Lehmann / Magidor 90] is a syntactically inspired procedure, whose semantic counterpart is in the finite case very close to what we are doing. The idea to make things as normal as possible is present in both approaches. For finite sets of conditionals, the only difference is that we handle local impossibilities (ranking -∞) in a somewhat more coherent way (cf. lexicography). However, the language of rational logic is much weaker, allowing neither embedded conditionals nor mixed knowledge bases containing contingent and modal information. Furthermore, the straightforward extension of rational closure to embedded conditionals, based on Lehmann's ordering of rational consequence relations, will still be weaker and less efficient than elementary hyperentailment. The maximum entropy approach [Goldszmidt / Morris / Pearl 90] is concerned with maximizing property independence based on an entropy measure. It handles defeasible exceptional monotony correctly, but it depends strongly on the syntactic form, violating in particular right conjunction. Conditional entailment [Geffner 89] is formulated as an assumption-based default theory and supports at least some simple instances of defeasible exceptional monotony. Its main drawbacks are the heterogeneous framework, the weak language comparable to Lehmann's, the missing rational monotony at the object-level and the strong, uncontrolled influence of syntax. Commonsense entailment [Asher / Morreau 91] is a very expressive formal framework primarily designed to deal with the complexities of generics. They get most of the important patterns right. Some of the major disadvantages of this approach are however the huge machinery necessary to verify even the simplest default rules, the current absence of a (complete) proof theoretic perspective, the lacking of rational monotony and cumulativity at the object-level, the violation of defeasible contraposition and the altogether very weak nonmonotonic consequence relation.

[Adams 75] The Logic of Conditionals. Dordrecht, Netherlands. D. Reidel.
[Asher / Morreau 91] Commonsense entailment: a modal theory of nonmonotonic reasoning. *Proc. of the First European Conference on Logic in AI, Amsterdam 1990.* Springer.
[Geffner 89] *Default reasoning : causal and conditional theories.* Technical report R-137, UCLA Cognitive Systems Laboratory. PhD thesis.
[Goldszmidt / Morris / Pearl 90] A maximum entropy approach to nonmonotonic reasoning. *Proc. of AAAI-90.*
[Lehmann / Magidor 90] *What does a conditional knowledge base entail ?* Technical report, Dept of Computer Science, Hebrew University, Jerusalem 91904, Israel (submitted).
[Pearl 88] *Probabilistic Reasoning in Intelligent Systems: Networks of Plausible Reasoning.* San Mateo, Morgan Kaufmann Publishers.
[Weydert 91] Qualitative magnitude reasoning. *Proceedings of NIL 90, Karlsruhe.* Springer.

Author Index

A

S. Acid   99
S. Amarger   33

B

J.F. Baldwin   107
P. Besnard   38
E. Binaghi   115
G. Brewka   120, 211

C

R.M. de Caluwe   338
L.M. de Campos   99
J. Cano   42
L. Cardona   125
P. Chatalic   70
A. Chateauneuf   130
P. Chung   141
M. Clarke   48
G. Coletti   135
F.S. Corrêa da Silva   141
J. Cussens   146

D

M. Delgado   42
A. Di Nola   161
E. Diday   153
M. Dohnal   63
D. Driankov   166
D. Dubois   33, 53

E

O. Etzion   171

F

L. Fariñas del Cerro   58
J. Fox   63
Ch. Froidevaux   70

G

D.M. Gabbay   3
L. Gâcogne   176
A. Gammermann   232
P. Gärdenfors   12
G.R. Garside   292
J. Gebhardt   81
A. Gilio   135
D.F. Gillies   328
L. Godo   76
A. Gonzáles   99
S.D. Goodwin   182
E. Grégoire   190
U. Güntzer   333

H

J. Heinsohn   198
H. Hellendoorn   166, 206
A. Herzig   58
Y-T Hsia   91
A. Hunter   146

J

U. Junker   211

K

R. Kast   130
R. Kennes   91
W. Kießling   333
F. Klawonn   81
J. Kohlas   125
P. Krause   63
R. Kruse   81

L

J. Lang   53
A. Lapied   130
F. Lévy   219
G. Lohmann   227

R. Lopez de Mantaras	76		T. Schaub	305
Z. Luo	232		C.B. Schwind	310
			R. Scozzafava	135
M			S. Sessa	161
			P. Smets	91
Y. Ma	238		P. Snow	318
C. MacNish	246		M. Spies	323
T. Matsuyama	282		L.E. Sucar	328
J. Mengin	70			
R. Molina	99		**T**	
P.A. Monney	125			
S. Moral	42		H. Thöne	333
			A. Trudel	182
N				
			U	
A. Nakamura	254			
E. Neufeld	182		E. Umkehrer	91
O			**V**	
U.G. Oppel	262		R.M. Vandenberghe	338
			F. Voorbraak	344
P				
			W	
G. Paass	267			
O. Papini	272		E. Weydert	352
S. Parsons	86		D.C. Wilkins	238
W. Pedrycz	161		N. Wilson	48
T. Pontet	277			
H. Prade	33, 53		**X**	
Q			H. Xu	91
P. Quinio	282			
R				
A. Rauzy	287			
M. Reinfrank	206			
P.C. Rhodes	292			
V. Risch	310			
D. Robertson	141			
E.H. Ruspini	297			
S				
A. Saffiotti	91			

Lecture Notes in Computer Science

For information about Vols. 1–454
please contact your bookseller or Springer-Verlag

Vol. 455: C.A. Floudas, P.M. Pardalos, A Collection of Test Problems for Constrained Global Optimization Algorithms. XIV, 180 pages. 1990.

Vol. 456: P. Deransart, J. Maluszyński (Eds.), Programming Language Implementation and Logic Programming. Proceedings, 1990. VIII, 401 pages. 1990.

Vol. 457: H. Burkhart (Ed.), CONPAR '90 – VAPP IV. Proceedings, 1990. XIV, 900 pages. 1990.

Vol. 458: J.C.M. Baeten, J.W. Klop (Eds.), CONCUR '90. Proceedings, 1990. VII, 537 pages. 1990.

Vol. 459: R. Studer (Ed.), Natural Language and Logic. Proceedings, 1989. VII, 252 pages. 1990. (Subseries LNAI).

Vol. 460: J. Uhl, H.A. Schmid, A Systematic Catalogue of Reusable Abstract Data Types. XII, 344 pages. 1990.

Vol. 461: P. Deransart, M. Jourdan (Eds.), Attribute Grammars and their Applications. Proceedings, 1990. VIII, 358 pages. 1990.

Vol. 462: G. Gottlob, W. Nejdl (Eds.), Expert Systems in Engineering. Proceedings, 1990. IX, 260 pages. 1990. (Subseries LNAI).

Vol. 463: H. Kirchner, W. Wechler (Eds.), Algebraic and Logic Programming. Proceedings, 1990. VII, 386 pages. 1990.

Vol. 464: J. Dassow, J. Kelemen (Eds.), Aspects and Prospects of Theoretical Computer Science. Proceedings, 1990. VI, 298 pages. 1990.

Vol. 465: A. Fuhrmann, M. Morreau (Eds.), The Logic of Theory Change. Proceedings, 1989. X, 334 pages. 1991. (Subseries LNAI).

Vol. 466: A. Blaser (Ed.), Database Systems of the 90s. Proceedings, 1990. VIII, 334 pages. 1990.

Vol. 467: F. Long (Ed.), Software Engineering Environments. Proceedings, 1989. VI, 313 pages. 1990.

Vol. 468: S.G. Akl, F. Fiala, W.W. Koczkodaj (Eds.), Advances in Computing and Information – ICCI '90. Proceedings, 1990. VII, 529 pages. 1990.

Vol. 469: I. Guessarian (Ed.), Semantics of Systems of Concurrent Processes. Proceedings, 1990. V, 456 pages. 1990.

Vol. 470: S. Abiteboul, P.C. Kanellakis (Eds.), ICDT '90. Proceedings, 1990. VII, 528 pages. 1990.

Vol. 471: B.C. Ooi, Efficient Query Processing in Geographic Information Systems. VIII, 208 pages. 1990.

Vol. 472: K.V. Nori, C.E. Veni Madhavan (Eds.), Foundations of Software Technology and Theoretical Computer Science. Proceedings, 1990. X, 420 pages. 1990.

Vol. 473: I.B. Damgård (Ed.), Advances in Cryptology – EUROCRYPT '90. Proceedings, 1990. VIII, 500 pages. 1991.

Vol. 474: D. Karagiannis (Ed.), Information Systems and Artificial Intelligence: Integration Aspects. Proceedings, 1990. X, 293 pages. 1991. (Subseries LNAI).

Vol. 475: P. Schroeder-Heister (Ed.), Extensions of Logic Programming. Proceedings, 1989. VIII, 364 pages. 1991. (Subseries LNAI).

Vol. 476: M. Filgueiras, L. Damas, N. Moreira, A.P. Tomás (Eds.), Natural Language Processing. Proceedings, 1990. VII, 253 pages. 1991. (Subseries LNAI).

Vol. 477: D. Hammer (Ed.), Compiler Compilers. Proceedings, 1990. VI, 227 pages. 1991.

Vol. 478: J. van Eijck (Ed.), Logics in AI. Proceedings, 1990. IX, 562 pages. 1991. (Subseries in LNAI).

Vol. 479: H. Schmidt, Meta-Level Control for Deductive Database Systems. VI, 155 pages. 1991.

Vol. 480: C. Choffrut, M. Jantzen (Eds.), STACS 91. Proceedings, 1991. X, 549 pages. 1991.

Vol. 481: E. Lang, K.-U. Carstensen, G. Simmons, Modelling Spatial Knowledge on a Linguistic Basis. IX, 138 pages. 1991. (Subseries LNAI).

Vol. 482: Y. Kodratoff (Ed.), Machine Learning – EWSL-91. Proceedings, 1991. XI, 537 pages. 1991. (Subseries LNAI).

Vol. 483: G. Rozenberg (Ed.), Advances in Petri Nets 1990. VI, 515 pages. 1991.

Vol. 484: R. H. Möhring (Ed.), Graph-Theoretic Concepts in Computer Science. Proceedings, 1990. IX, 360 pages. 1991.

Vol. 485: K. Furukawa, H. Tanaka, T. Fuijsaki (Eds.), Logic Programming '89. Proceedings, 1989. IX, 183 pages. 1991. (Subseries LNAI).

Vol. 486: J. van Leeuwen, N. Santoro (Eds.), Distributed Algorithms. Proceedings, 1990. VI, 433 pages. 1991.

Vol. 487: A. Bode (Ed.), Distributed Memory Computing. Proceedings, 1991. XI, 506 pages. 1991.

Vol. 488: R. V. Book (Ed.), Rewriting Techniques and Applications. Proceedings, 1991. VII, 458 pages. 1991.

Vol. 489: J. W. de Bakker, W. P. de Roever, G. Rozenberg (Eds.), Foundations of Object-Oriented Languages. Proceedings, 1990. VIII, 442 pages. 1991.

Vol. 490: J. A. Bergstra, L. M. G. Feijs (Eds.), Algebraic Methods II: Theory, Tools and Applications. VI, 434 pages. 1991.

Vol. 491: A. Yonezawa, T. Ito (Eds.), Concurrency: Theory, Language, and Architecture. Proceedings, 1989. VIII, 339 pages. 1991.

Vol. 492: D. Sriram, R. Logcher, S. Fukuda (Eds.), Computer-Aided Cooperative Product Development. Proceedings, 1989 VII. 630 pages. 1991.

Vol. 493: S. Abramsky, T. S. E. Maibaum (Eds.), TAPSOFT '91. Volume 1. Proceedings, 1991. VIII, 455 pages. 1991.

Vol. 494: S. Abramsky, T. S. E. Maibaum (Eds.), TAPSOFT '91. Volume 2. Proceedings, 1991. VIII, 482 pages. 1991.

Vol. 495: 9. Thalheim, J. Demetrovics, H.-D. Gerhardt (Eds.), MFDBS '91. Proceedings, 1991. VI, 395 pages. 1991.

Vol. 496: H.-P. Schwefel, R. Männer (Eds.), Parallel Problem Solving from Nature. Proceedings, 1990. XI. 485 pages. 1991.

Vol. 497: F. Dehne, F. Fiala. W.W. Koczkodaj (Eds.), Advances in Computing and Information - ICCI '91. Proceedings, 1991. VIII. 745 pages. 1991.

Vol. 498: R. Andersen, J. A. Bubenko jr., A. Sølvberg (Eds.), Advanced Information Systems Engineering. Proceedings, 1991. VI, 579 pages. 1991.

Vol. 499: D. Christodoulakis (Ed.), Ada: The Choice for '92. Proceedings, 1991. VI, 411 pages. 1991.

Vol. 500: M. Held, On the Computational Geometry of Pocket Machining. XII, 179 pages. 1991.

Vol. 501: M. Bidoit, H.-J. Kreowski, P. Lescanne, F. Orejas, D. Sannella (Eds.), Algebraic System Specification and Development. VIII, 98 pages. 1991.

Vol. 502: J. Bārzdiņš, D. Bjørner (Eds.), Baltic Computer Science. X, 619 pages. 1991.

Vol. 503: P. America (Ed.), Parallel Database Systems. Proceedings, 1990. VIII, 433 pages. 1991.

Vol. 504: J. W. Schmidt, A. A. Stogny (Eds.), Next Generation Information System Technology. Proceedings, 1990. IX, 450 pages. 1991.

Vol. 505: E. H. L. Aarts, J. van Leeuwen, M. Rem (Eds.), PARLE '91. Parallel Architectures and Languages Europe, Volume I. Proceedings, 1991. XV, 423 pages. 1991.

Vol. 506: E. H. L. Aarts, J. van Leeuwen, M. Rem (Eds.), PARLE '91. Parallel Architectures and Languages Europe, Volume II. Proceedings, 1991. XV, 489 pages. 1991.

Vol. 507: N. A. Sherwani, E. de Doncker, J. A. Kapenga (Eds.), Computing in the 90's. Proceedings, 1989. XIII, 441 pages. 1991.

Vol. 508: S. Sakata (Ed.), Applied Algebra, Algebraic Algorithms and Error-Correcting Codes. Proceedings, 1990. IX, 390 pages. 1991.

Vol. 509: A. Endres, H. Weber (Eds.), Software Development Environments and CASE Technology. Proceedings, 1991. VIII, 286 pages. 1991.

Vol. 510: J. Leach Albert, B. Monien, M. Rodríguez (Eds.), Automata, Languages and Programming. Proceedings, 1991. XII, 763 pages. 1991.

Vol. 511: A. C. F. Colchester, D.J. Hawkes (Eds.), Information Processing in Medical Imaging. Proceedings, 1991. XI, 512 pages. 1991.

Vol. 512: P. America (Ed.), ECOOP '91. European Conference on Object-Oriented Programming. Proceedings, 1991. X, 396 pages. 1991.

Vol. 513: N. M. Mattos, An Approach to Knowledge Base Management. IX, 247 pages. 1991. (Subseries LNAI).

Vol. 514: G. Cohen, P. Charpin (Eds.), EUROCODE '90. Proceedings, 1990. XI, 392 pages. 1991.

Vol. 515: J. P. Martins, M. Reinfrank (Eds.), Truth Maintenance Systems. Proceedings, 1990. VII, 177 pages. 1991. (Subseries LNAI).

Vol. 516: S. Kaplan, M. Okada (Eds.), Conditional and Typed Rewriting Systems. Proceedings, 1990. IX, 461 pages. 1991.

Vol. 517: K. Nökel, Temporally Distributed Symptoms in Technical Diagnosis. IX, 164 pages. 1991. (Subseries LNAI).

Vol. 518: J. G. Williams, Instantiation Theory. VIII, 133 pages. 1991. (Subseries LNAI).

Vol. 519: F. Dehne, J.-R. Sack, N. Santoro (Eds.), Algorithms and Data Structures. Proceedings, 1991. X, 496 pages. 1991.

Vol. 520: A. Tarlecki (Ed.), Mathematical Foundations of Computer Science 1991. Proceedings, 1991. XI, 435 pages. 1991.

Vol. 521: B. Bouchon-Meunier, R. R. Yager, L. A. Zadek (Eds.), Uncertainty in Knowledge-Bases. Proceedings, 1990. X, 609 pages. 1991.

Vol. 522: J. Hertzberg (Ed.), European Workshop on Planning. Proceedings, 1991. VII, 121 pages. 1991. (Subseries LNAI).

Vol. 523: J. Hughes (Ed.), Functional Programming Languages and Computer Architecture. Proceedings, 1991. VIII, 666 pages. 1991.

Vol. 524: G. Rozenberg (Ed.), Advances in Petri Nets 1991. VIII, 572 pages. 1991.

Vol. 525: O. Günther, H.-J. Schek (Eds.), Advances in Spatial Databases. Proceedings, 1991. XI, 471 pages. 1991.

Vol. 526: T. Ito, A. R. Meyer (Eds.), Theoretical Aspects of Computer Software. Proceedings, 1991. X, 772 pages. 1991.

Vol. 527: J.C.M. Baeten, J. F. Groote (Eds.), CONCUR '91. Proceedings, 1991. VIII, 541 pages. 1991.

Vol. 528: J. Maluszynski, M. Wirsing (Eds.), Programming Language Implementation and Logic Programming. Proceedings, 1991. XI, 433 pages. 1991.

Vol. 529: L. Budach (Ed.), Fundamentals of Computation Theory. Proceedings, 1991. XII, 426 pages. 1991.

Vol. 530: D. H. Pitt, P.-L. Curien, S. Abramsky, A. M. Pitts, A. Poigné, D. E. Rydeheard (Eds.), Category Theory and Computer Science. Proceedings, 1991. VII, 301 pages. 1991.

Vol. 531: E. M. Clarke, R. P. Kurshan (Eds.), Computer-Aided Verification. Proceedings, 1990. XIII. 372 pages. 1991.

Vol. 532: H. Ehrig, H.-J. Kreowski, G. Rozenberg (Eds.), Graph Grammars and Their Application to Computer Science. Proceedings, 1990. X, 703 pages. 1991.

Vol. 533: E. Börger, H. Kleine Büning, M. M. Richter, W. Schönfeld (Eds.), Computer Science Logic. Proceedings, 1990. VIII, 399 pages. 1991.

Vol. 534: H. Ehrig, K. P. Jantke, F. Orejas, H. Reichel (Eds.), Recent Trends in Data Type Specification. Proceedings, 1990. VIII, 379 pages. 1991.

Vol. 535: P. Jorrand, J. Kelemen (Eds.), Fundamentals of Artificial Intelligence Research. Proceedings, 1991. VIII, 255 pages. 1991. (Subseries LNAI).

Vol. 536: J. E. Tomayko, Software Engineering Education. Proceedings, 1991. VIII, 296 pages. 1991.

Vol. 537: A. J. Menezes, S. A. Vanstone (Eds.), Advances in Cryptology – CRYPTO '90. Proceedings, XIII. 644 pages. 1991.

Vol. 538: M. Kojima, N. Megiddo, T. Noma, A. Yoshise, A Unified Approach to Interior Point Algorithms for Linear Complementarity Problems. VIII, 108 pages. 1991.

Vol. 539: H. F. Mattson, T. Mora, T. R. N. Rao (Eds.), Applied Algebra, Algebraic Algorithms and Error-Correcting Codes. Proceedings, 1991. XI, 489 pages. 1991.

Vol. 540: A. Prieto (Ed.), Artificial Neural Networks. Proceedings, 1991. XIII, 476 pages. 1991.

Vol. 541: P. Barahona, L. Moniz Pereira, A. Porto (Eds.), EPIA '91. Proceedings, 1991. VIII, 292 pages. 1991. (Subseries LNAI).

Vol. 543: J. Dix, K. P. Jantke, P. H. Schmitt (Eds.), Nonmonotonic and Inductive Logic. Proceedings, 1990. X, 243 pages. 1991. (Subseries LNAI).

Vol. 545: H. Alblas, B. Melichar (Eds.), Attribute Grammars, Applications and Systems. Proceedings, 1991. IX, 513 pages. 1991.

Vol. 548: R. Kruse, P. Siegel (Eds.), Symbolic and Quantitative Approaches to Uncertainty. Proceedings, 1991. XI, 362 pages. 1991.